FIGHTING DIRTY

also by Peter Harclerode

Go To It! The History of the 6th Airborne Division

Unholy Babylon - The Secret History of Saddam's War
(with Adel Darwish)

PARA! Fifty Years of The Parachute Regiment

Arnhem - A Tragedy of Errors

The Lost Masters - The Looting of Europe's Treasurehouses
(with Brendan Pittaway)

Equinox: Warfare

Secret Soldiers - Special Forces in the War against Terrorism

FIGHTING DIRTY

**The inside story of covert operations from
Ho Chi Minh to Osama Bin Laden**

PETER HARCLERODE

CASSELL&CO

Cassell & Co
Wellington House, 125 Strand, London WC2R 0BB

First published 2001

British Library Cataloguing-in-Publication Data
A catalogue record for this book is available from the British Library

ISBN 0-304-35382-5

Distributed in the United States by
Sterling Publishing Co. Inc, 387 Park Avenue South
New York NY 10016-8810

Printed and bound in Great Britain by
Creative Print & Design Ltd
Ebbw Vale, Wales

For Edwina and Zoë

CONTENTS

PREFACE

The end of the Second World War did not bring peace. The Soviet Union and China, former allies of the West against the Axis powers, turned to pursue their own ambitions which, along with those of emerging nationalist movements, posed new global threats during the late 1940s and early 1950s by supporting revolution, insurrection and ultimately war in Eastern Europe, the Baltic, the Balkans, Indochina, Malaya and Korea.

Having disbanded much of their wartime armed forces, including their special forces and much of their intelligence apparatus, the United States and Britain found themselves ill-equipped to counter the revolutionary groups opposing them. Only France possessed special forces, which were soon heavily committed in Indochina.

Meanwhile, in Eastern Europe, the Baltic states and the Balkans, it was Britain's Secret Intelligence Service (SIS) and the United States' fledgling Central Intelligence Agency (CIA) which led the attempts to counter the spreading influence of the Soviet Union.

The start of the Malayan Emergency in 1948 and the Korean War in 1952 saw the creation of ad hoc specialist units, but it was not until the early 1950s that the British Army re-formed the Special Air Service (SAS) for operations against communist terrorists in Malaya and the US Army raised its 10th Special Forces Group (Airborne), elements of which first appeared in Korea towards the end of the conflict there.

During the war in Algeria, France once again made extensive use of its special forces, principally the 11ème Bataillon Parachutiste de Choc, while also forming additional specialist units for covert operations against the guerrillas of the National Liberation Army (ALN).

At the end of the 1950s, Britain deployed forces to the Sultanate of Oman to counter a rebellion by dissident tribes supported by Saudi Arabia; among them were two squadrons of 22nd SAS Regiment (22 SAS) which took part in the gruelling campaign to dislodge the rebels from their base on the Djebel Akhdar.

Thousands of miles away on the roof of the world, the CIA was meanwhile supporting Tibetan guerrillas in a long-running war against China and the occupying forces of the People's Liberation Army.

The 1960s saw unconventional warfare playing a major role in the war in Vietnam, with the CIA and elements of the US Army Special Forces also deployed secretly in Cambodia and Laos. Responsibility for such operations was ultimately invested in the most highly classified of all such units, the Military Assistance Command Vietnam – Studies and Observations Group (MAC-V-SOG).

During this period, British, Australian and New Zealand SAS squadrons were taking part in operations against Indonesian forces during the Borneo Confrontation of 1963–6.

The 1970s found 22 SAS back in the Sultanate of Oman in a six-year-long campaign against communist-backed guerrillas in the southern Omani region of Dhofar. As in Malaya, Borneo and the earlier Djebel Akhdar campaign, the regiment played a key role in winning the war.

In December 1979, the Soviet Union occupied and sparked off a conflict which lasted just over nine years. In a secret operation throughout that period, the CIA provided financial and military aid for the guerrillas of the mujahidin through Pakistan's Directorate of Inter Services Intelligence (ISI) which channelled the majority of it to fundamentalist factions. The conflict ended with the withdrawal of Soviet forces in February 1989, being followed by almost seven years of civil war that culminated in the coming to power of the Taliban. While the CIA operation ended in 1992, it left a deadly legacy in the form of an international army of mujahidin under the control of a man whose name is now notorious throughout the world: Osama bin Laden.

I AM HEAVILY INDEBTED TO many people who provided me with a considerable amount of assistance and thus contributed significantly to this book: Louise Arnold-Friend and Colonel Don Boose of the US Army Military History Institute; Anne Aldis of the Conflict Studies Centre at the Royal Military Academy Sandhurst; military historian Bob Bragg, who possesses an encyclopaedic knowledge of unconventional warfare; Barry Harrison, who spent many hours translating French documents; military historian Danny O'Hara, who specialises in the First Indochina War; journalist and Middle East specialist Adel Darwish;

writer and Soviet specialist James G. Shortt who twice spent several weeks with the mujahidin of the late General Ahmed Shah Massoud during the war in Afghanistan; well-known photographer and journalist John Gunston, who entered Afghanistan on many occasions, producing extensive and impressive coverage of the conflict; journalist Alastair McQueen; Colonel Robin Letts, who served with 22 SAS during the Borneo Confrontation and with the Australian SAS Regiment in Vietnam; Colonel Anthony Swallow, Secretary of the Royal Leicestershire Regimental Association; weapons experts Ian Hogg and Christopher Foss; Major Charles Fuglesang, a troop commander during the Borneo Confrontation; Brigadier Christopher Bullock, curator of the Gurkha Museum and a company commander during the same campaign; Mrs Amanda Moren, curator of the Royal Irish Fusiliers Museum; Mr Puntsok Wangyal of the Tibetan Foundation in London; Jim Keck, chief navigator for Civil Air Transport/Air America and Roland H. Andersen, a parachute despatch officer, both of whom took part in CIA airdrop operations supporting the resistance in Tibet; and George Patterson, who witnessed many of the events which took place during the war in Tibet and the author of *Tibet in Revolt* and several other books.

In addition, a number of fellow authors were very generous in providing me with help, allowing me to draw on information in books previously written by them and in some cases supplying photographs from their collections for use as illustrations: Stephen Dorril, author of *MI6 – Fifty Years of Special Operations*; Colonel David Smiley, author of *Albanian Assignment* and *Arabian Assignment*, who was responsible for the training of Albanian guerrillas in Malta and subsequently served as Commander of the Sultan's Armed Forces in Oman; Eric Deroo and Commandant Raymond Muelle, authors of *Services Speciaux: GCMA – Indochine 1950–54*, the latter a former officer of the 11ème Bataillon de Choc in Indochina and Algeria; Colonel Michael E. Haas, author of *In The Devil's Shadow – UN Special Operations During The Korean War*, who served with special operations forces in the US Army and US Air Force; Ed Evanhoe, author of *Dark Moon – Eighth Army Special Operations in The Korean War*, a veteran of special operations in Korea and thereafter an intelligence officer in South East Asia; Roger E. McCarthy, author of *Tears of the Lotus – Accounts of Tibetan Resistance to the Chinese Invasion, 1950–1962*, and the CIA operations officer leading the operation in support of the Tibetan resistance; John Kenneth Knaus, author of *Orphans of The Cold War – America and The Tibetan Struggle*, who also served as the CIA officer in charge of the Tibetan operation; Professor William M. Leary of the History Department at the University of Georgia and author of *Perilous Missions: Civil Air Transport and CIA Covert Operations in Asia*; Sheila Brannum, Judy Smith and Diane Tedeshing of the Smithsonian Institute's *Air & Space Magazine*; Tenzing Sonam and Ritu Sarin, producers of the television documentary *Shadow Circus – The CIA in Tibet*; Major General Tony Jeapes, author of *SAS – Secret War*, who commanded D Squadron 22 SAS on operations in the Dhofar region of Oman, later commanding the regiment itself during the latter part of the campaign; General Sir John Akehurst, author of *We Won a War* and commander of the Dhofar Brigade of the Sultan's Armed Forces during 1974–6; Major John Plaster, author of *SOG – The Secret Wars of America's Commandos in Vietnam*, who served three tours of operations with the MACV Studies & Observation Group; Kenneth Conboy, a specialist in Asian military affairs and author with James Morrison of *Shadow War – The CIA's Secret War in Laos;* and Mark Adkin and Brigadier Mohammad Yousaf, authors of *The Bear Trap – Afghanistan's Untold Story*, the latter the head of the Afghan Bureau of Pakistan's Directorate of Inter-Service Intelligence during the war in Afghanistan.

The following were also kind enough to allow me to use their photographs: Lord Patrick Beresford, Major Charles Fuglesang, Major L. M. 'Phil' Phillips, Frank Greco, Conrad 'Ben' Baker, Billy Waugh, Mecky Schuler and Eugene McCarley.

Furthermore, there were a number of individuals who also provided me with a considerable amount of assistance but who wish to remain anonymous.

To all the above I express my sincerest thanks.

Peter Harclerode
OCTOBER 2001

CHAPTER ONE

EASTERN EUROPE AND THE BALTIC 1949–1956

At 3.30 p.m. on 20 September 1945, President Harry S. Truman signed an executive order abolishing the United States's wartime intelligence and unconventional warfare organisation, the Office of Strategic Services (OSS). Like its British counterpart, the Special Operations Executive (SOE), OSS had conducted covert operations in enemy-occupied territories throughout Europe, Scandinavia, the Balkans, the Mediterranean, North Africa, South Asia and South-east Asia. There it had joined forces with local resistance movements, conducted offensive operations and gathered intelligence.

In June 1944, OSS agents took part in JEDBURGH operations during which they were dropped into Normandy in three-man teams, each comprising an SOE or OSS officer, an officer of French nationality and a radio operator who was either British or American. Their tasks were to liaise with the French resistance, arm and train maquis units and, wherever possible, coordinate resistance activity. In South Asia a 300-strong OSS unit, designated Detachment 101, operated from India into Burma, where it formed a force of over 10,000 Kachin tribesmen for intelligence-gathering and guerrilla operations against the Japanese. During 1945, up to the Japanese surrender in August, OSS was also active in Siam and Indochina, supporting elements of Thai and Viet Minh resistance movements. By the end of the war, it numbered some 12,000 personnel – and had accumulated vast experience and expertise in the arts of clandestine intelligence gathering and covert operations.

Immediately following the disbandment of OSS, its secret intelligence (SI) branch was transferred to the State Department, while its unconventional warfare element was taken over by the War Department and designated the Strategic Services Unit (SSU). In January 1946 a presidential directive established a successor organisation called the Central Intelligence Group (CIG). During that year, the SSU was transferred from the War Department to the CIG, where it was redesignated the Office of Special Operations (OSO) and expanded to a strength of some 800. In early 1947 the National Security Act was passed by Congress, followed by the establishment of the National Security Council (NSC) tasked with advising the president on defence and foreign affairs.

On 8 September 1947, the CIG was renamed the Central Intelligence Agency (CIA). Its responsibility would be to advise the NSC and make recommendations on matters of intelligence; provide reports and estimates; provide 'additional services of common concern' for US government departments; and carry out 'such other functions and duties related to intelligence affecting the national security as the National Security Council may from time to time direct'. The phrase 'such other functions' provided vague authority for a further role – the conduct of unconventional warfare and paramilitary operations. These were to be carried out by a unit called the Special Procedures Group (SPG), formed at the end of 1947.

In June 1948 a further directive, designated NSC-10/2, was signed by President Truman. This specifically authorised the CIA to conduct psychological warfare and paramilitary operations. It stipulated: 'Such operations shall include any covert activities related to: propaganda, economic warfare; preventive direct action, including sabotage, anti-sabotage, demolition and evacuation measures; subversion against hostile states, including assistance to underground resistance movements, guerrillas and refugee liberation groups, and support of indigenous anti-communist elements in threatened countries of the free world.' Following the issuing of the directive, SPG was renamed the Office of Special Projects, and shortly afterwards its name was changed yet again to the Office of Policy Coordination (OPC).

Initially, the US Department of Defense indicated a reluctance to have any involvement with OPC and refused to permit military personnel to be assigned to it. In August 1948, however, there was a change of heart, and the Joint Chiefs of Staff expressed their support, indicating that unconventional warfare should remain the sole preserve of OPC. While the armed forces would not form their own special operations units, assignment to OPC of military personnel – primarily former members of the OSS – would be permitted after all.

Meanwhile, in Britain, virtually all special forces, including the two Special Air Service (SAS) regiments and other units formed during the war, were disbanded in 1945. The end of the following year found the

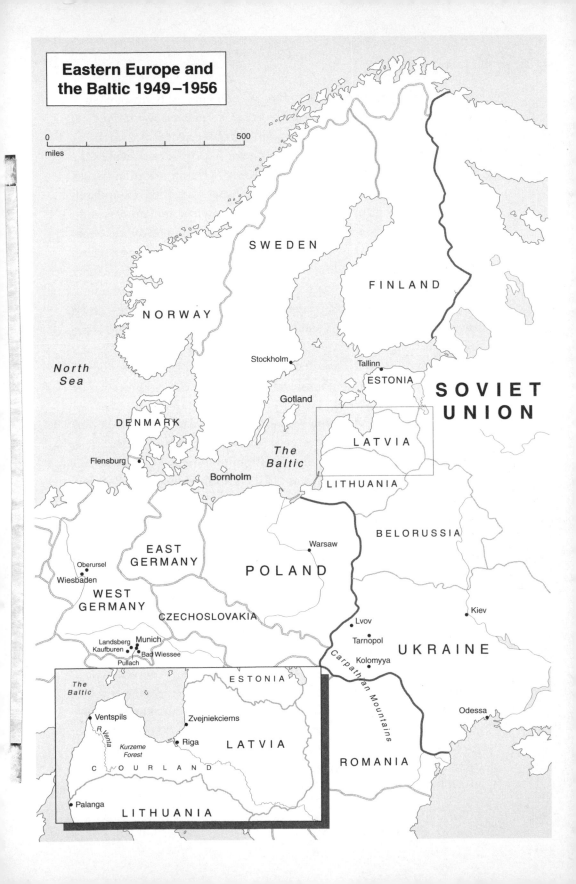

Eastern Europe and the Baltic 1949–1956

```
0                    500
miles
```

North Sea

SWEDEN

FINLAND

NORWAY

Stockholm

Tallinn

ESTONIA

SOVIET
UNION

Gotland

DENMARK

The Baltic

LATVIA

Flensburg

Bornholm

LITHUANIA

BELORUSSIA

Warsaw

EAST
GERMANY

POLAND

Oberursel

Wiesbaden

WEST
GERMANY

CZECHOSLOVAKIA

Kiev

Landsberg   Munich
Kaufburen   Bad Wiessee
Pullach

Lvov

Tarnopol

Kolomyya

UKRAINE

Carpathian Mountains

Odessa

ROMANIA

The Baltic

ESTONIA

Ventspils

Zvejniekciems

R. Venta

Kurzeme Forest

Riga

LATVIA

COURLAND

Palanga

LITHUANIA

armed forces possessing little in the way of an unconventional warfare capability, this comprising merely a unit of 60 swimmer/canoeists grouped together in the Royal Marines Boom Patrol Detachment (RMBPD). On 1 January 1947, however, that deficiency was partly remedied by the reformation of the SAS as a Territorial Army (TA) unit – the 21st Special Air Service Regiment (Artists) TA. Later that year, RMBPD merged with the School of Combined Operations Beach and Boat Section (SCOBBS) to form the Combined Operations Beach and Boats Section (COBBS). Compared with their wartime strength and infrastructure, however, Britain's special forces towards the end of the 1940s were very thin on the ground.

SOE had suffered a similar fate to OSS, being officially dissolved on 15 January 1946, but with much of its assets being absorbed into the Secret Intelligence Service (SIS), popularly known as MI6. SIS was undergoing a considerable reduction from its wartime strength but, according to author Stephen Dorril in his book *MI6 – Fifty Years of Special Operations*, a report on future requirements had recommended that it should possess a limited capability to carry out clandestine operations along the lines of those conducted by SOE during the war. This proposal was accepted: a number of former SOE personnel and certain assets were transferred to SIS, where they formed the Special Operations Branch.

Meanwhile, the end of the war against Nazi Germany in 1945 found Russia in occupation of most of Eastern Europe. During the conflict, relations between Stalin and his two fellow Allied leaders, Franklin D. Roosevelt and Winston Churchill, had at best been cordial but beset by mutual suspicion. During the immediate post-war period, by which time Harry S. Truman and Clement Attlee had replaced Roosevelt and Churchill, relations deteriorated sharply as it became plain that the Soviet Union was tightening its grip throughout the occupied countries of Eastern Europe and was actively supporting communist movements in the West. The Truman administration responded by adopting a policy of containment designed to limit Soviet expansionism. This included the Truman Doctrine, which in 1947 provided $400,000,000 of aid to Greece and Turkey, to prevent them falling into communist hands, and the Marshall Plan (aka the European Recovery Program) which over the following five years would provide $13,000,000,000 of aid for the reconstruction of European economies and thus eliminate the conditions in which communism could otherwise flourish.

Under the Marshall Plan, aid was also offered to the countries of Eastern Europe. But Stalin, not surprisingly, viewed this as an effort by the United States to loosen his grip on Soviet-occupied countries. He vetoed it. Czechoslovakia, however, which was not under Soviet control at the time, was eager to take advantage of the proffered aid. In February 1948 this resulted in Stalin moving swiftly to bring the country within the Soviet fold, non-communist elements of the government being forced out and replaced by Czech communists. This inevitably resulted in a further heightening of tension between the Western allies and the Soviets. At the end of March, the latter imposed restrictions on road and rail access to the western zones of Berlin occupied by the United States, Britain and France. By July there was a full-scale blockade. The Allies resorted to supplying their zones by air, a process the Soviets attempted to impede. During the twelve months of the airlift there were a total of 733 incidents in which Soviet aircraft tried to prevent Allied supply missions from reaching Berlin. Not until July 1949 was the blockade lifted.

Meanwhile, Britain and the United States were actively seeking to foster anti-Soviet resistance within the Soviet Union and Eastern Europe. For SIS, which had been conducting operations against the Bolsheviks since 1918, it was a case of reverting to fight the old enemy. In 1945, contact was re-established with SIS by Stephan Bandera, the leader of the Organisation of Ukrainian Nationalists (OUN) which had been formed by Ukrainian émigrés in Paris in the early 1920s. SIS had previously been in contact with Bandera and his organisation since the mid-1930s, financing operations by OUN agents infiltrated into the Soviet Union via Finland. In March 1941, the organisation split into two factions – OUNB and OUNM – led respectively by Bandera and another nationalist, Andrei Melnyk. Germany, meanwhile, had also been supporting OUN in order to bolster Ukrainian nationalism as part of its efforts to undermine the Soviet Union in the region. Following the split, it concentrated its support on OUNB, which shortly afterwards formed two units under the aegis of the Abwehr, the Wehrmacht's military intelligence service. These took part in operations in Poland and, following the German invasion of the Soviet Union, in the Ukraine. In September 1941, however, after the outbreak of fighting between OUNB and

OUNM, the Germans turned on the Ukrainian nationalist movements and imprisoned large numbers.

In the wake of the German invasion of the Soviet Union in 1941 and the latter's switch to the Allied side, SIS was forced to cease anti-Soviet operations, including those in support of the Ukrainian nationalists, on the orders of Churchill himself. In early 1943 elements of OUNB formed the Ukrainian Insurgent Army (UPA), whose ranks were swelled by deserters from the German and Russian armies, among them Georgians, Belorussians and other Soviet nationals. In mid-1943, the Germans began to withdraw from the Ukraine, and by October 1944 the country had been completely reoccupied by the Soviets. Following the Soviet reoccupation, the UPA, which by then numbered between 30,000 and 40,000, initiated a campaign of resistance primarily in the western half of the Ukraine. During the winter of 1945–6, however, it suffered heavy losses as a result of counter-guerrilla operations conducted by Soviet Ministry of Interior (MVD) forces.

Stephan Bandera and large elements of OUNB, meanwhile, had fled to Slovakia, hiding in the mountains before making their way to the British occupation zone in western Germany. On his arrival, Bandera re-established contact with SIS and began to organise resistance activities in the Ukraine. It was not long, however, before his presence was detected by the Soviets, who demanded that he and other leading nationalists be extradited to the Soviet Union for war crimes. Warned by SIS of Soviet attempts to track him down, Bandera made his way to the American zone and the city of Munich, where he established a new headquarters. This was shortly afterwards renamed OUN Revolution (OUNR). Further Soviet attempts to locate him were thwarted by US denials of his presence – despite the fact that the US Army's Counter Intelligence Corps (CIC) had evidence pointing to his possible involvement in war crimes.

Soon after his arrival in Munich, Bandera approached the United States for support. He offered in return to provide manpower from among the large numbers of Ukrainians who had fled to western Germany to escape communist rule in the Ukraine. According to author Stephen Dorril, a senior member of OUNB initially made contact with US Secretary of Defense James Forrestal in August 1948. The matter was then taken up by the State Department, whose Policy and Planning

Staff deliberated during the latter part of 1948 on the question of using dissident organisations to combat communism. They agreed to proceed. Responsibility for doing so was then handed to the CIA, which delegated the task to its intelligence-gathering Office of Special Operations (OSO) and OPC, which was responsible for paramilitary operations.

OPC subsequently established a number of training centres in West Germany, located at Bad Wiessee, Landsberg, Kaufbeuren and Oberursel, to which Ukrainians, Russians and other émigrés from the Soviet Union were sent for training. Those members of OUNR selected by Bandera to work for SIS were despatched to Britain, where they underwent training in London and at Fort Monckton, a former training facility outside Gosport, on the coast of Hampshire, and one of the assets taken over by SIS from SOE on the latter's disbandment. Parachute training was carried out at the RAF's No. 1 Parachute Training School at Abingdon, near Oxford.

From the beginning, however, relations between the Americans and OUNR failed to prosper. Bandera and his hierarchy displayed a deep distrust of the Americans, while the latter found the Ukrainians' conditions for total collaboration impossible to meet. Relations between the two sides deteriorated following the discovery by the Americans of firm evidence that large numbers of OUNR had collaborated with the Germans. Indeed, many had been employed by the SS and Gestapo. The Americans also looked unfavourably on the bitter internal strife between the various Ukrainian factions fighting for control of the Ukrainian population in the displaced persons camps in Germany, Austria and Italy, where OUNR conducted a campaign of terror.

In the Ukraine, meanwhile, resistance continued against Soviet rule. Stalin's determination to stamp it out had been illustrated by the arrival in the Ukraine in July 1946 of Marshal Georgi Zhukov, former commander of the Red Army forces that had invaded Germany in January 1945. Thereafter, anti-guerrilla operations had been stepped up considerably, and there were reports of major losses being inflicted once again on the UPA. On 28 March 1947, following the killing of neighbouring Poland's vice-minister of defence by UPA guerrillas, further operations were mounted by the Soviets, in conjunction with Polish and Czech forces, in the western border areas of the Ukraine and south-east Poland in an effort to eliminate UPA completely. By July, serious losses had been inflicted on the guerrillas, the Poles claiming that they had killed or captured approximately 2,000 men.

In September 1947, following a decision by UPA commander Roman Shukheyevich to disband his forces and convert them to an underground organisation, a large number of guerrillas made their way out of the Ukraine, subsequently fighting their way 1,500 miles through Czechoslovakia over the mountains to the American occupation zone in Austria. The remaining UPA elements, located mainly in the Carpathian Mountains in the far west of the Ukraine, continued their campaign of resistance against the Soviets, conducting it primarily through acts of terrorism, raiding isolated military posts, gathering intelligence and disseminating nationalist propaganda.

In 1949, OPC and SIS began a joint operation codenamed INTEGRAL. It was run by the latter's Northern Division, while the SIS control element was headed by Colonel Harold Gibson, a long-serving SIS officer who had been born in Russia. The aim of INTEGRAL was to infiltrate agents into western Ukraine to link up with the remaining UPA resistance organisation. In July the first group, comprising three men, was dropped in the area of Kiev. Although all three were seen to have landed safely, nothing was heard from them thereafter, and eventually it was assumed they had been captured.

OPC carried out its first infiltration on 5 September 1949 when two agents were dropped near Lvov, in western Ukraine, from an unmarked C-47 flown by a two-man Czech crew who had served with the RAF during the war. Trained during the previous ten months as radio operators and in intelligence gathering, they were the first of a planned 2,000 agents whom OPC intended to position at strategic locations throughout the Soviet Union. Their mission was twofold: first, to report any Soviet preparations for an attack on western Europe, and second, to support resistance groups in operations to hinder any Soviet advance towards the west. A few days later, four more agents were dropped in the Carpathian Mountains, but within a few days they had been arrested and were subsequently executed.

The following year saw a Soviet amnesty for members of UPA resulting in the surrender of some 8,000 of its members, thus reducing further the scale of resistance and the organisation's capability to cause serious trouble for the Soviets. Apparently unaware of this major setback, SIS continued to drop more agents into western Ukraine and eastern Poland where the UPA was reported as still being active.

In early 1950 the head of SIS's Northern Division, Harry Carr, travelled to Washington to discuss operations being conducted in the Ukraine and elsewhere in the Soviet bloc. Also in attendance at meetings with OPC and OSO representatives was the SIS representative in Washington, Kim Philby, who had taken over the post on 8 October of the previous year. Based at the British Embassy with the diplomatic cover of a first secretary, Philby's duties included acting as SIS's link with the CIA, OSO and OPC.

As the world now knows, Philby was a Soviet agent. Having become a Marxist during his university days at Cambridge in the early 1930s, he subsequently lived for a year in Vienna, where he married his first wife, Alice 'Litzi' Kohlmann, a communist closely involved with the pre-war socialist underground movement in Austria. Taking up freelance journalism, from early 1937 onwards he covered the Spanish Civil War and was appointed *The Times*'s special correspondent attached to the Nationalist forces of General Francisco Franco. Late 1939 found him in France as a war correspondent for *The Times*, covering the operations of the British Expeditionary Force. He returned to Britain after the fall of Paris in June 1940. Shortly afterwards, however, he was recruited by SIS into Section D, the branch responsible for subversion, sabotage and paramilitary operations. Thus began his career in intelligence. Thereafter, he served briefly with SOE before returning to SIS where he joined Section V, the counter-espionage department, taking over command of its Iberian sub-section.

Early in 1944, Philby moved to a new post, that of head of R5, SIS's newly formed Soviet department – thus providing the Soviet intelligence service, the NKGB, with a presence deep in the heart of the British intelligence apparatus. Three years later, at the beginning of 1947, he handed it over to take up the post of head of the SIS station in Istanbul, his first overseas posting. In mid-1949, however, he was offered the post of SIS representative in Washington and returned to London at the end of August for briefings prior to taking up his new post during the second week of October.

During Henry Carr's visit to Washington, the Americans made clear their disapproval of Stephan Bandera, whom they declared to be anti-American, and of OUNR/UPA, regarded as nationalist extremists whose support within the Ukraine was reportedly declining and who were incapable of playing any serious role in paramilitary operations. Moreover, they maintained that continuing support for Bandera would only result in a split among the remaining elements of Ukrainian resistance to which they were providing support. As a result of their increasing dissatisfaction with Bandera and the OUNR, the Americans had in 1949 broken off all contact with him and his organisation. Meanwhile, unlike SIS, OSO had succeeded in maintaining radio contact, albeit irregularly, with the first two agents it had dropped near Lvov. From these, and from information brought out by couriers, it had learned of the declining scale of resistance in the Ukraine. These reports contradicted those of the OUNR which maintained that its groups were continuing to conduct an effective campaign against the Soviets. Despite American pressure, however, Carr refused to terminate support for Bandera and his organisation, and this resulted in a certain amount of acrimony between him and his American counterparts.

Both OSO and OPC were directing their support to a number of other bodies, including Andrei Melnyk's organisation, which had changed its name to OUN Solidarity (OUNS) and a nationalist political organisation called the Ukrainian Supreme Liberation Council (UHVR). The latter had been created by OUNB in July 1944 to unite all nationalist factions, providing a broad foundation for resistance movements in the Ukraine and to act as a political body for the UPA pending the achievement of independence for the Ukraine and the formation of a national government. Others included the Russian Narodnyi Trudovoy Soyuz (National Labour Council) headed by Vladimir Poremski. Better known by its acronym of NTS, it had been formed in the late 1920s by a faction of Socialists and Mensheviks who had taken part in the revolution of October 1917 but thereafter, having incurred the wrath of the Bolsheviks, had been forced to flee into exile in the West.

NTS and the other anti-Soviet organisations supported by OSO and OPC were recruited by a group known as the Gehlen Org. Its head was General Reinhard Gehlen, the former head of Fremde Heere Ost (FHO), the military intelligence section of the wartime German High Command, Oberkommando Wehrmacht (OKW), responsible for operations against the Soviet Union. Gehlen had foreseen the defeat of

Hitler's Nazi regime and in October 1944 had begun making plans to offer his services to the Western Allies, who he knew would soon be confronting the Soviet Union as the new enemy. During the weeks prior to the unconditional surrender of Germany on 7 May 1945, he had hidden FHO's files and archives in 52 steel containers concealed in three caches in the mountains of Bavaria. He and his entire staff had then ignored one of Hitler's directives, ordering all military staffs and officers to assemble at the newly relocated OKW headquarters at Flensburg in northern Germany, and had taken refuge in Bavaria. There they surrendered to the Americans during the latter half of May 1945.

In August, Gehlen and three of his officers were flown to the United States. During the following weeks he negotiated a deal with the Americans whereby he would be permitted to establish an autonomous organisation, independent of the US post-war intelligence apparatus, pending the establishment of a government in western Germany, which would thereafter absorb it as a national intelligence agency.

During 1946 the Gehlen Organisation, as it was called, was formed. In December 1947 it moved to Pullach, eight miles from Munich, where it took over a large compound formerly occupied by a housing estate built for SS officers and their families. It began operating under the guise of a scientific research and development corporation, and in 1948, initially financed with an annual budget of $600,000 supplied by the United States, set about operations in eastern Europe and the Soviet Union. One of its initial tasks was to trawl the displaced persons camps and refugee organisations for eastern Europeans suitable for recruitment as agents. Among those it approached for personnel to carry out missions into the Ukraine were NTS and OUNS.

During 1950, the Americans dropped a number of agents into the Ukraine in groups of between four and six men, two of these disappearing without making any subsequent contact. That year also saw the death of the UPA commander, Roman Shukheyevich, who by then had been targeted by the Special Bureau No. 1 of the MGB (successor to the NKGB), commanded by General Pavel Anatolevich Sudoplatov, himself a Ukrainian, and responsible for the conduct of operations against nationalists in his home country. After months of searching fruitlessly for Shukheyevich in the area of Lvov, the MGB had persuaded a prominent member of OUNR, a lawyer named Gorbavoy, to reveal his whereabouts. It did so by obtaining the release of Gorbavoy's niece, who was being held in a prison camp in Russia on the grounds that she was a relative of a prominent nationalist. Shukheyevich was subsequently tracked down to a general store in a village near Lvov, which was surrounded by a detachment of troops led personally by General Sudoplatov. Demands for Shukheyevich and two female companions, both armed and members of UPA, to surrender were met by a hail of automatic fire and two grenades. In the ensuing battle, all three attempted to break out but were killed.

Shukheyevich was replaced by an experienced guerrilla leader, Vasel Koval, but after several months nothing had been heard from him. Accordingly, Bandera despatched a group led by the head of OUNR's internal security service, Mynon Matviyeko, to investigate the situation and put the UPA on a firm footing once more. General Sudoplatov, however, had by this time succeeded in penetrating OUNR, planting an agent in a group which made its way out of the Ukraine to Germany via Czechoslovakia from where it was flown by SIS to Britain for training. During the ensuing months there was no communication between the agent and his MGB controller except for a single postcard, mailed to an address in Germany just prior to the group's departure from Britain; on it was written a coded message giving the details of the planned method and route by which Matviyeko's group would return to the Ukraine.

By this time, all SIS flights into the Ukraine were being staged from British bases on the islands of Cyprus and Malta. Matviyeko's aircraft took off from the latter and the drop was carried out successfully – courtesy of the Soviets, who had ordered their fighter interceptors and air defence units not to attack the unmarked C-47. Following the drop, Matviyeko reported that he had made contact with Vasel Koval's network and would be meeting him shortly. He subsequently came on the air twice thereafter, saying that he had still not met Koval as there had been a delay for reasons of security. After that, his radio fell silent.

It later transpired that Matviyeko's group had been under constant surveillance since their landing. According to Pavel Anatolevich Sudoplatov in his book *Special Tasks: The Memoirs of an Unwanted Witness – A Soviet Spymaster*, in May 1951 Matviyeko and his companions were lured to an apartment that was ostensibly a UPA safe house but was in fact staffed by Soviet agents. Falling asleep after a heavy meal, which had been drugged, they awoke to find themselves in the hands of the MGB. During the ensuing sessions of interrogation, Matviyeko's interrogators demonstrated that not only the OUNR but also virtually all the Ukrainian émigré organisations had been heavily penetrated. In its efforts to convert him to their cause, the MGB handled him gently and housed him in one of its villas in Lvov. From there he escaped shortly afterwards and, while in hiding, attempted to make contact with OUNR sympathisers and locate safe houses whose details he had not revealed to his interrogators. To his dismay, he found that the contacts did not exist and the addresses were incorrect. It later transpired that this had been due to exaggerated claims of local support made by OUNR in the Ukraine to its headquarters in London and Munich. Realising that any genuine contacts or safe houses would be under surveillance, Matviyeko decided to surrender himself to the MGB. Thereafter, he decided to cooperate and subsequently appeared at a press conference at which he denounced OUNR and appealed for national reconciliation among all Ukrainians.

At about the same time, an unmarked RAF aircraft operating from Cyprus delivered three six-man groups into the Ukraine. The first was dropped at a location between Lvov and Tarnopol, the second near Kolomyya, not far from the source of the River Prut, and the third just inside the Polish border near the headwaters of the River San. Once again, however, all three missions had been compromised. Details of the three groups and the locations of their respective drop zones had been given by Kim Philby to another Soviet agent – Guy Burgess, an alcoholic and flamboyant homosexual serving as a first secretary in the British embassy in Washington. Burgess passed the information on via yet another British traitor, Anthony Blunt, an eminent art historian who held the appointments of Surveyor of the King's (later Queen's) Paintings and Director of the Courtauld Institute. A former wartime Security Service officer, Blunt in turn relayed it to an MGB Officer, Yuri Modin, based at the Russian Embassy in London. Nothing was heard from any of the three groups following their landings.

During 1952 and 1953, OPC operations continued with further drops being carried out into the Ukraine. A four-man NTS team was dropped on the night of 25/26 April 1953. Well trained and equipped with miniature radio beacons to guide in aircraft dropping agents or carrying out reconnaissance missions, their destinations were Kiev and the Black Sea port of Odessa. Nothing was heard from them after the drop, but on 27 May an announcement was made in the Soviet newspaper *Pravda* that four men had been caught soon after landing and, following their trial in Kiev at which they had made full confessions, they had been executed by firing squad on 20 May. A further twelve of those agents dropped by OPC into the Ukraine were arrested, and it can only be assumed that SIS and OSO missions during the same period also suffered similar casualties.

In 1954, a large OUNR group infiltrating overland was ambushed and wiped out in the Carpathian Mountains by Soviet forces who had been forewarned of its arrival. This was the final straw for Stephan Bandera, who by then had become increasingly disillusioned with SIS and decided to break away from the existing OUNR network to regroup and reform. This he proceeded to do, building an entirely new, smaller organisation. Inevitably, however, this made him a prime target for the KGB, which had succeeded the MGB in 1954. On 15 October 1959, as he unlocked the front door of his apartment in Munich, he was assassinated by a man armed with a special pistol containing a firing device and an ampoule of prussic acid. When such a weapon was discharged at close range into a victim's face, a spring initiated a small charge crushing the ampoule so that the acid was emitted from the the pistol barrel in the form of a spray. The acid, when inhaled, swiftly induced death through contraction of the blood vessels in exactly the same way as a fatal heart attack. Bandera's assassin was later identified as Bogdan Stashinsky, a member of Department 13, the unit within the KGB's First Chief Directorate responsible for assassinations – or 'wet affairs' as they were known within the Soviet intelligence apparatus. Two years earlier in Munich, on 12 October 1957, Stashinsky had murdered another leading Ukrainian émigré leader, Lev Rebet, in the same fashion.

The SIS/OPC operation to foster subversion in the Ukraine thus failed dismally. The primary reason was that from 1940 onward the NKVD had penetrated OUN at high level, its post-war successors (NKGB, MGB and KGB) following suit with virtually all the other anti-communist organisations. Added to this was the treachery of Kim Philby who undoubtedly played a principal role in compromising the SIS-supported OUNR/UPA element of the operation, and possibly that of the

OPC-sponsored OUNS and NTS as well. Another major factor was the limited support provided by SIS and OPC – it paled into insignificance beside the political, military and logistical support provided to resistance organisations during the war. It would have taken support on a wartime scale for the Ukrainian resistance movements to have had any realistic chance of ousting the Soviets, who would in any case have retaliated massively. But, having only recently undergone almost six years of global conflict at vast economic and human cost, neither Britain nor the United States were prepared to commit themselves to such an extent and thereby risk a major confrontation with the Soviet Union.

Meanwhile, SIS and OPC were also actively attempting to foster resistance against communist rule in Poland. Prior to the war, SOE's chief, Major General Colin Gubbins, had served as GSO 1 and chief of staff of a British military mission, led by General Sir Adrian Carton de Wiart VC, which was deployed to Poland during the summer of 1939 with the task of monitoring the impending invasion by Germany. Gubbins was at that time serving with Military Intelligence (Research) (MI(R)), a small section of the War Office tasked with planning and providing covert support for Eastern European countries overrun by the Germans. Accompanied by a small group of MI(R) officers forming part of the mission, he had witnessed the invasion of the western two-thirds of Poland by Germany and the occupation of the remainder of the country by the Soviet Union. Following the German invasion of the Soviet Union in 1941, however, the whole of Poland had come under Nazi rule.

Throughout the war, support for the Polish resistance movement, the Home Army, known by its acronym AK (Armia Krajowa), was provided by the Polish section of SOE which dropped supplies of arms and equipment. In August 1944, AK staged an uprising in Warsaw in an attempt to oust the occupying German forces and seize control of the city. It was anxious to do so as advancing Soviet forces had already gained control of eastern Poland and had established a communist body, the Polish Committee of National Liberation, to administer Soviet-occupied Polish territory.

During the first two years of the war, SOE had encouraged the AK to plan for an uprising to take place when the time was ripe. Thereafter, however, such action had been seen by the British and the Polish government-in-exile, headed by General Wladislaw Sikorski, as impracticable, and had been abandoned. In Poland, however, the AK regarded the liberation of Warsaw as its ultimate aim, being recompense for the five or so dangerous years spent in waiting and preparation. As the Soviet forces continued their advance westward, the AK sought orders from the government-in-exile in London but to little avail. At that time, the Polish prime minister, Stanislaw Mikolajczyk, who had succeeded Sikorski on the latter's death in an air crash on Gibraltar in early July 1943, and the commander-in-chief of the Free Polish forces, General Kazimierz Sosnkowski, were both absent. Mikolajczyk was in Moscow, seeking some form of political accommodation with Stalin, while Sosnkowski was in Italy visiting Polish I Corps in an effort to provide reassurance following the news of the occupation of eastern Poland by Soviet forces. From there the latter sent a number of contradictory signals to the AK, some of which were perceived to give approval for limited action.

Meanwhile, however, the Soviets were actively encouraging the AK uprising and on 1 August 50,000 Polish guerrillas, under General Tadeusz Komorowski, launched attacks on the relatively weak German forces, gaining control of the city within three days. Support was provided by SOE, which during August and September carried out 192 drops delivering personnel, arms and equipment. But the cost was heavy, 41 aircraft being lost during this period. The Germans retaliated by sending in massive reinforcements. They proceeded to shell and bomb the AK's positions for the following nine weeks. Meanwhile, Soviet forces had halted along a line to the east of the River Vistula from which they watched as the Germans decimated the Poles. On 2 October, the AK was forced to surrender – by now, 200,000 civilians and 10,000 guerrillas had been killed. Once Komorowski and his remaining guerrillas had been taken prisoner, Warsaw's population was rounded up and deported, while the Germans systematically razed much of the city to the ground. The left-bank suburbs, which was the area under their control, were emptied of their remaining population and all buildings either set ablaze or demolished with explosives. In putting down the uprising, the Germans had inflicted massive damage on the AK. Scattered elements outside Warsaw had survived the onslaught and remained in contact with London, but Komorowski's capture had severely dislocated the AK network.

On 26 December 1944 an SOE mission, codenamed FRESTON, was despatched to Poland, despite Soviet objections, to assess how much of the resistance had survived. Comprising three British officers, Colonel D. T. 'Marko' Hudson, Major Peter Kemp and Major Peter Solly-Flood, and two Poles, Anton Popieszalski and Roman Rudkowski, it discovered that most of the SOE agents dropped during the war had perished either at the hands of the Gestapo or the NKVD, whose detachments accompanied the leading elements of the Red Army. In mid-January 1945, Hudson and his companions made their way to the nearest Soviet headquarters where they were promptly placed under house arrest and kept on a diet of bread and water, being interrogated by the Soviets but refusing to divulge any information. On 12 February they were despatched to Moscow, from where they were subsequently released and returned to Britain.

Once hostilities had ended, however, the Soviets turned on the AK, arresting and deporting its members or conscripting them into a Soviet-sponsored Polish Army formation, the Kosciuszko Division, commanded by Major General Zygmunt Berling. The AK was officially disbanded by the Polish government-in-exile in January 1945, but its surviving members reverted to the underground role, becoming an anti-communist resistance movement and forming a political organisation called Niepodleglosc (Nie). The Soviets retaliated with a massive crackdown, the NKGB arresting some 50,000 members of the former AK and Nie and transporting them to Siberia. Despite such drastic losses, however, the Polish underground continued to survive and turned to Britain and the United States for assistance.

SOE had meanwhile retained its radio communications networks in Poland, a fact that came to the notice of the Soviets, who lodged a formal protest with the British government. When the Foreign Office, which was by then primarily concerned with maintaining good relations with Stalin, demanded that they be closed down forthwith, the networks were handed over to SIS, which had established a covert operations network shortly after the country had been liberated from German occupation.

May 1946 saw the formation of a new resistance organisation in Poland, the Delegatura Sil Zbrojnych (DSZ) (Delegation of Armed Forces), recruited from the remnants of the AK. Its existence, however, was short-lived, and it was disbanded in August. During the following month, a new organisation called Wolnosc i Niepodlegtnosc (WiN) (Freedom and Independence) was formed under Colonel Jan Rzepecki; but in November he was arrested and subsequently called for all armed resistance to cease, a call that was ignored by the majority of WiN. Two other active resistance organisations were the Narodowy Zwiazek Wojskowy (NZW) (National Military Union), an extreme right-wing nationalist group, and the Ukrainian UPA, which operated in the south-east of the country.

Resistance activity increased during 1946 with operations against government security forces being stepped up until October when the leader of WiN, Franciszek Niepokolczycki, and seventeen members of the organisation's supreme command were arrested by the Polish internal security service, the Urzad Bezpiecznstwa (UB). In January 1947, their replacements were also arrested and a number of the organisation's networks and elements of its command structure destroyed. Moreover, an amnesty declared by the government during the following month persuaded more than 50,000 members of the underground to leave its ranks.

January 1947 also saw a coalition of left-wing socialists and communists win a landslide victory in an election held under conditions little short of a reign of terror, with threats of imprisonment, and worse, being issued against other political parties, while strict censorship of the press was imposed. The communists were in the majority and, backed by the Soviet Union, exercised control of key government organs such as the Ministry of Public Security. During the previous September, they had come to an accord with Stalin and his foreign minister, Vyacheslav Molotov, on the composition of Poland's new government.

The new regime managed to persuade a number of Poles living in exile in Britain to return home. SIS recruited some of them as agents, a few subsequently supplying information of value and providing contact with the remnants of WiN. In June 1947, SIS dropped a number of agents and equipment into Poland as part of an intelligence-gathering operation, but the government responded with a further crackdown by the UB, and it became apparent that WiN had almost been destroyed.

Two years later, however, the organisation appeared to have resurrected itself when contact was established with General Wladislaw Anders, the wartime commander of the Free Polish forces, based in London. According to Steven Dorril, this enabled SIS, in mid-1950, to re-establish a link with WiN, which set up a base in London under Anders, and subsequently launched an operation conducted by its Northern Division. Codenamed BROADWAY, its aim was to expand WiN into a paramilitary organisation capable of delaying a Soviet military advance westward into Europe. At the same time, WiN was also tasked with gathering intelligence on the Soviet order of battle in Eastern Europe. During the following months agents, weapons, equipment and money were dropped to WiN, but by November the increasing scale and cost of the operation was such that SIS turned to its friends in OPC and proposed a joint operation. After due consideration, the latter agreed, providing two of its officers as members of the operation's control staff.

Throughout the following year, BROADWAY appeared to be making good progress, with WiN steadily expanding as planned and apparently providing information on the Soviet forces in Eastern Europe. The organisation, however, was making increasing demands, which eventually caused unease within the CIA. Indeed, the head of OSO's counter-intelligence division, James Angleton, voiced his disquiet to the CIA's head, the Director of Central Intelligence, General Walter Bedell Smith, and the Agency's Deputy Director of Plans, Allen Dulles, that WiN was a Soviet deception operation. These suspicions were dismissed by the head of OPC, Frank Wisner, who maintained that WiN was a genuine resistance organisation.

Bedell Smith, however, did recognise that WiN would inevitably be a target for a Soviet counter-intelligence operation, and in April 1951 he despatched a retired senior US Army officer, General Lucian Truscott, to West Germany with the task carrying out an assessment of BROADWAY and other OSO and OPC covert operations being conducted in Russia and Eastern Europe. Truscott was not impressed by what he unearthed, nor by the OSO and OPC controllers he met. After inspecting the OPC training centre at Kaufbeuren, he reported in disparaging terms on the poor quaility of intelligence supplied by WiN. Moreover, he expressed his belief that the agents he had watched undergoing training had no chance of survival – they would undoubtedly be known among the émigré groups, which by this time were almost certainly penetrated.

Truscott's report was rejected by both SIS and OPC, which continued with their joint operation. Eighteen months later, however, they received a rude shock. During the last few days of 1952, Radio Warsaw revealed that WiN had been under communist control since early 1948. During 1946–7, the UB had evidently succeeded in penetrating and destroying parts of the organisation's network before arresting one of its leaders, Stefan Sienko, who subsequently agreed to become a double agent. As a result, the communists had experienced little difficulty in penetrating the remainder of the organisation. All agents, equipment and funds dropped thereafter to WiN ended up in the possession of the UB, which also acquired full details of BROADWAY. In return, SIS and the OPC received information fabricated by the UB and, no doubt, the KGB.

Once again, SIS and OPC had fallen victim to a Soviet deception operation, and once more the finger of blame was pointed at Kim Philby, who undoubtedly played a part in supplying information on BROADWAY to the Soviets. But the principal factors mitigating against the success of the operation were poor security within WiN, the efficiency of the Soviets in penetrating such organisations and mounting deception operations, and the tight control exerted on Poland by its communist regime.

Despite this catastrophe, however, Poland and BROADWAY would not be the last occasion on which Britain and the United States would fall prey to the Soviets.

IN 1940, THE INDEPENDENT Baltic states of Lithuania, Latvia and Estonia were forcibly occupied and incorporated into the Soviet Union, which in 1939 had signed a secret agreement with Germany, recognising Soviet hegemony over them. Following the German invasion of the Soviet Union in June 1941, all three states were formed, along with Belorussia, into a province called Ostland. In Latvia and Estonia, the Germans recruited formations of SS, such as the Latvian Legion and the 15th and 19th Latvian and 290th Estonian Waffen SS Divisions, as well as paramilitary and police units, which took part in ethnic cleansing operations against Jews. In Latvia, one such paramilitary unit was the Arajs Kommando which in August 1941 slaughtered 15,000 Jews and between September and December deported 29,000 more for execution.

During the three-year period of Nazi occupation, a number of nationalist organisations were formed in the Baltic states. In Latvia, the Latvian

Central Council (LCC), was set up during 1943, while in Estonia the Republic National Committee (RNC) was established in 1944. In Lithuania, the Lithuanian Freedom Army (LFA) was created in 1941, followed two years later in October 1943 by the Supreme Committee for the Liberation of Lithuania (SCLL). All these bodies sought national independence for their respective states, hoping that the end of the war would see both Germany and the Soviet Union weakened and therefore incapable of reasserting their former holds on the Baltic region. Some looked to the West for support and by 1944 had established contacts with SIS, OSS and the Swedish military intelligence service, SMT.

In late 1944, however, the Soviet Union invaded the Baltic states. While thousands fled before the advancing Red Army formations, seeking sanctuary wherever they could, large groups of nationalists took to the forests to form anti-Soviet resistance groups. In Lithuania one such group, the Forest Brotherhood, numbered some 30,000 men. In Latvia another group, comprising 14,000 fully armed and equipped guerrillas who had previously served in SS and Wehrmacht units, was based in Courland, a huge, densely forested area stretching along the Baltic coast. A further 10,000 guerrillas were meanwhile active in Estonia. During this period, elements of the Latvian and Estonian SS formations fled to the West, making their way to Germany, where they arrived in the British and American zones to be interned in prisoner-of-war camps.

By the beginning of 1945, SIS was already gathering intelligence on the Soviet presence in the Baltic. The first attempt to infiltrate a small group of four agents, including a radio operator named Arturs Arnitis, who had been a member of one of the wartime resistance networks, was carried out by SIS on 15 October. But the operation, mounted in conjunction with the Swedish SMT, had to be aborted after the boat carrying the group and a consignment of American weapons and equipment capsized in heavy seas off the Courland coast. Abandoning attempts to salvage their weapons and equipment, the four agents headed for the nearby forest and made good their escape from the area. Discovery of items of equipment on the beach at dawn the following day, however, prompted the Soviets to carry out a huge hunt for the four men. Two days later, two of them were captured. Under interrogation, they revealed the existence of Arnitis, who was arrested three weeks later in possession of his radio and codebooks. Unfortunately, he had by then been in contact with the operation's base in Stockholm and had reported his safe arrival.

When Arnitis either would not, or was unable to cooperate with his captors, who had used physical torture on him and his three companions, the Soviets immediately resorted to their favourite ploy: the deception operation. The officer in charge, Major Janis Lukasevics of the Latvian MGB's Second Chief Directorate, which was responsible for counter-intelligence, located a trained radio operator from among members of a resistance group captured and imprisoned earlier in the year. The individual concerned, Augusts Bergmanis, was persuaded to cooperate and in early 1946 began to operate Arnitis's radio under MGB control. Initially there was no answer as he transmitted his call-sign, but after some three months a response was at last elicited from the SIS base in Stockholm. Initially suspicious, SIS was eventually convinced by Bergmanis's explanation that he had taken over Arnitis's set after being advised of its whereabouts by members of his group who had previously been in contact with the latter prior to his capture.

On the night of 6 August 1946 two more agents, Rihards Zande and Eriks Tomson, were landed in Latvia at the port of Zvejniekciems. Zande's mission was to discover the fate of Arnitis and establish a new radio communications link. During the following month, however, Zande's radio developed a fault that corrupted his transmissions, and in November he was instructed to attend a rendezvous with Bergmanis. Despite initial misgivings, Zande was reassured by Bergmanis and agreed that the latter should transmit his messages to Stockholm. Thus, with one stroke, the MGB had penetrated a second SIS mission in Latvia.

December 1946 saw the mounting of another mission into Latvia when SIS despatched a boat, the *Hagbard*, from Stockholm. Travelling on board were three guerrillas, including another radio operator. They were carrying a small consignment of weapons and equipment including replacement crystals for Zande's radio. The vessel sailed for the Swedish island of Gotland from where, on the night of 19 December, it headed for the Latvian coast and the Bay of Skulte. As the ship entered Latvian waters, however, the leader of the group, Elmars Skobe, fearing dawn would break while the landing was taking place, ordered the crew to head back to Gotland. As it neared the island, the *Hagbard* was stopped by a Swedish police launch. A search of the vessel uncovered the weapons and equipment on board. Skobe and his companions were arrested and taken to the nearby port of Tjelders on the island.

Skobe found it easy to resist the questioning of the local police, who subsequently transferred him to Stockholm, where the investigation was handed over to the Forsvarsftaben Operativ Enhat (FOE), the Swedish civilian intelligence service. Under intensive interrogation during the first week of January 1947, he eventually confessed and provided details of his planned mission in Latvia. The involvement of SIS in the operation, however, had been carefully camouflaged. Skobe insisted that the man who had handed the weapons and equipment to him was an American, but on being shown photographs of officials from the US Embassy in Stockholm, he could not pick out the face of the individual concerned. Persistent investigation by the FOE paid off, however, and eventually the finger of suspicion was pointed at SIS. Shortly afterwards, Elmars Skobe was expelled from Sweden. Meanwhile the SIS officer running the operation, McLachlan Silverwood-Cope, who was based at the British Embassy under diplomatic cover as a third secretary, had already returned to Britain temporarily to avoid a similar fate.

In Latvia, meanwhile, Rihards Zande and Emil Tomsons had been making plans to return to Sweden, accompanied by a group of thirty guerrillas from the area of the capital of Riga. Through Bergmanis, Zande had been advised that a boat would collect his group on the night of 5 January; but no suitable vessel could be found in time to replace the *Hagbard*, so the pick-up was postponed. Tomsons then devoted himself to finding another boat while Zande continued to gather intelligence for transmission to Stockhom. All the while, however, both men were under surveillance by the MGB. By March, Tomsons had found a suitable craft and the Soviets apprehended them before they could leave. News of their arrest was transmitted to SIS in a suitably agitated fashion by Bergmanis, who reported that he had successfully evaded capture.

SIS decided to send another agent, Feliks Rumnieks, into Latvia to discover the fate of the earlier groups. But Rumnieks, a former member of the SS Latvian Legion, from which he had deserted in January 1945, was arrested by the MGB shortly after his arrival. After admitting under interrogation to working for SIS, he was tried and sentenced to a lengthy term of imprisonment.

Meanwhile, plans were being laid for covert operations in Lithuania.

During early 1946 a number of meetings were held in West Germany by the SIS officer responsible for operations in the Baltic, Alexander 'Sandy' McKibbin. Among those who attended were Stasys Zymantas and Walter Zilinskas, two Lithuanian nationalists who had worked for SIS in Sweden since 1945. At the first meeting, which took place in Hamburg, the decision was taken to despatch agent/radio operators at the earliest opportunity to enable SIS to establish radio contact with the resistance in Lithuania.

A subsequent meeting was held in Lübeck to hear the report of Jonas Deksnys, leader of the LFA, who had just returned from Lithuania. He had travelled there with another nationalist, Klemensas Brunius, to assess the degree of active resistance being conducted by the guerrillas against the Soviets, but had returned without Brunius, who had apparently been arrested. Deksnys now reported that some 30,000 or so guerrillas were active in Lithuania despite the repressive countermeasures being carried out by the Soviets. He announced, furthermore, that the guerrillas distrusted the SCLL as it had collaborated with the Nazis during the war, and recommended that an alternative organisation be formed to coordinate partisan operations in Lithuania.

The source of this adverse report on the SCLL, and the recommendation to form a new organisation, was Dr Juozas-Albinas Markulis, a nationalist who purported to be a prominent figure in the guerrilla movement inside Lithuania. Deksnys had met him during his trip and had eventually been sufficiently impressed by him to hand over radio codes and transmission/reception schedules for communication with SIS in Stockholm. Markulis had in turn provided Deksnys with safe house accommodation and a forged passport to enable him to leave Lithuania again.

McKinnon and Stasys Zymantas apparently accepted Deksnys's report and recommendations without reservations, deciding that the new organisation would receive full financial and logistical support from SIS. In June 1946 the United Democratic Resistance Movement (UDRM) was formed to unite all the various resistance groups in Lithuania, and by the end of the year it had apparently succeeded in doing so. During 1947, however, internal dissent plagued the organisation. The guerrillas were unwilling to abandon active resistance in favour of the UDRM's proposed policy of passive resistance; nor were they willing to become a

'Home Army' on the lines of that which had existed in Poland without having any say in the future of their country once independence had been achieved.

IN LITHUANIA, meanwhile, the suspicions of the leader of the Forest Brotherhood, Juozas Luksa, had been aroused by the apparent ease with which Markulis was able to supply money, forged papers and safe houses. When, in January 1947, he and other senior guerrilla leaders received an invitation from Markulis to attend a meeting, Luksa warned as many as he could contact in time to ignore it and stay away, meanwhile placing the rendezvous area under surveillance from a distance. His suspicions were confirmed when KGB personnel were observed surrounding the building in which the meeting was to be held. Those guerrillas inside the building who had not received Luksa's warning in time were arrested.

Possessing no lines of communication, Luksa was unable to warn SIS of the trap that had been set and into which it was now falling. In mid-1947, he set off for the West accompanied by fifteen of his men, arriving in West Germany early in 1948 after a journey that had seen three of his group killed in clashes with Soviet forces. There he not only revealed the details of Markulis's treachery but also cast suspicion on Jonas Deksnys. This inevitably caused dissent within the UDRM, serving to heighten suspicions that the organisation had already been penetrated by the Soviets. Such suspicion was well founded – Markulis was in fact a KGB officer tasked with penetrating the resistance in Lithuania. By denouncing the SCLL group and successfully proposing the formation of the UDRM, he had laid the foundations for a split in the movement. Subsequently, following an unsuccessful attempt on his life by four men, the KGB removed Markulis from Lithuania and despatched him to the safety of Leningrad.

During 1947, guerrilla activity in Lithuania reached a plateau. Training courses were carried out during the summer at secret forest sites which were shifted frequently for maximum security. In February 1948, the guerrillas carried out their largest operation when a force of 120 from two groups attacked a Soviet garrison of 250 troops. In September, however, the Soviets struck back when they located and surrounded a training camp in the forest. A day-long battle ensued as the guerrillas fought their way out.

By the end of 1948, resistance in Lithuania had declined significantly, the guerrillas having suffered some 20,000 casualties.

The beginning of 1949 saw the transfer of control of SIS's Baltic operations from Sweden to Hamburg, in the British occupation zone of West Germany. At the same time, groups of Baltic émigrés were moved to Britain, where they underwent training in London and at Fort Monckton. Trainee agents were also instructed in the arts of escape, evasion and survival over the rugged terrain of Dartmoor and areas of Scotland.

SIS continued to favour infiltrating its teams by sea rather than dropping them by parachute. In early 1949, the Royal Navy's Director of Naval Intelligence (DNI) procured two former wartime E-boats which, stripped of their armament and other equipment and with certain other modifications, attained a top speed of almost 50 knots, thus outpacing any other vessels then in service, while also being capable of approaching a shoreline virtually unheard. Crewed by former wartime Kriegsmarine personnel, one of them, *S208*, was commanded by a former E-boat captain, Hans Helmut Klose, who had extensive experience of dropping German agents behind Soviet lines during the closing year of the war.

Flying the white ensign and operating under the auspices of the Fishery Protection Service of the British Control Commission Germany (BCCG), the boats came under the overall command of Commander Anthony Courtney, head of the DNI's Russian Section. From their base at Kiel they were to sail for the Danish island of Bornholm. There they would wait for a signal from the SIS base in Hamburg before proceeding with their respective missions. The entire operation was financed by OPC, which paid for the refitting of the boats, as well as paying the crews and the agents.

The operation, codenamed JUNGLE, began in the early hours of 5 May 1949 when the first group of six agents was landed by Klose's *S208* at Palanga on the Lithuanian coast and made its way into the nearby forests. One of their number, however, was an MGB double agent, a Latvian named Vidvuds Sveics, who separated himself from the group and contacted the local Soviet security forces. Three of his five companions were ambushed shortly afterwards, all being killed. The remaining pair, Jonas Deksnys and Kazimieras Piplys, had already left the area and avoided capture.

Having made his way to Riga, Sveics subsequently reported to SIS, under the supervision of his MGB controller, Major Janis Lukasevics, that the group had been ambushed while landing and that he had managed to escape with his radio set intact. Prior to embarking on the operation, he had been given a list of sympathisers whom he and the other members of the group could contact: among them were a priest named Father Valdis Amols and the sole radio operator still operational in Latvia, Augusts Bergmanis. Sveics had contacted Father Amols, subsequently reporting to SIS that all the safe houses were still secure. He had then received a letter from Deksnys, who described his somewhat hazardous journey to Riga after the landing and asked him to transmit a request to SIS for another radio operator. Deksnys had since disappeared, and there was no indication of what had befallen him. During June, Piplys despatched a message to Stockholm asking for news of him. By then Deksnys had been arrested by the MGB. Faced with execution or (at best) a lengthy term of imprisonment, he had reportedly agreed to cooperate.

At the end of October, following one unsuccessful attempt, aborted because of bad weather, two agents, Vitolds Berkis and Andrei Galdins, were landed by *S208* on the Latvian coast, on a remote beach west of the port of Ventspils. The landing was completed without incident and the two men, equipped with two suitcases containing a radio set and weapons, made their way to the house of Father Amols, with whom they stayed that night. The following day, having seen them on their way to Riga, where they were to contact the radio operator Augusts Bergmanis, Amols informed Vidvud Sveics of their arrival.

Berkis and Galdins reached Riga on 5 November and made their way to Bergmanis's apartment, arriving unannounced. On the next day, Bergmanis informed Major Lukavesics about the two agents, and the decision was taken to accommodate them in a safe house while a major deception operation was hastily put into action under another MGB officer, Major Alberts Bundulis. Codenamed LURSEN-S, it was controlled by MGB General Janis Vevers from the MGB headquarters in Riga. In the course of the winter, with the two agents cooped up in the safe house (during which time they met Sveics), the MGB created a group of bogus guerrillas living in the forests to dupe the agents into believing they were in contact with the resistance. The planning and preparation were meticulous, each 'guerrilla' being carefully grounded and rigorously tested in his new identity and carefully crafted life history. As the winter neared its end and the weather improved, a pseudo-guerrilla camp was constructed in the Kurzeme forests.

In mid-May, Berkis and Galdins were taken to the forest, and spent the following months with the band of pseudo-guerrillas led by an MGB agent named Arvits Gailitis and subsequently allocated the codename of MAXIS. During that time, Berkis trained one of the 'guerrillas', Kazimirs Kipurs, as a radio operator – unknown to him, the latter was already a highly skilled MGB communications specialist.

The Americans, meanwhile, had also begun operations in the Baltic with the CIA establishing a field station in Stockholm, its chief being a former member of OSS, William Colby. In early 1949 SCLL threw in its lot with the United States following a visit to Washington in January by its leader, Mykolas Krupavicius, during which the Americans promised full political and logistical support for anti-Soviet resistance operations. The MGB's scheme to cause a split among the different Baltic resistance factions had by then, however, proved highly successful, relations between SCLL and UDRM, led by Zymantas and Deksnys, having further deteriorated following the latter's return to Latvia. During the previous eighteen months, SCLL had been receiving support from France and its military intelligence service, the Deuxième Bureau, which had trained six Lithuanians. Three had been despatched from Sweden but had been arrested shortly after their arrival. Suspicions of treachery had been directed at the remaining three: Forest Brotherhood leader Juozas Luksa, Klemensas Sirvys and Benediktas Trumpys. These doubts were, in fact, unfounded and resulted in Luksa and his two companions offering their services to the Americans, who accepted with alacrity. At the time, Luksa expressed to his new CIA controllers his strong conviction that the UDRM movement was heavily penetrated by the Soviets, a belief apparently rejected by SIS.

On the night of 3 October 1950, the first CIA operation in the Baltic area was launched by OSO when an unmarked C-47 transport aircraft, flown by a Czech crew, took off from the US Air Force base at Wiesbaden in West Germany. On board were Luksa, Sirvys and Trumpys, who were to be dropped by parachute and to link up with their comrades in the Forest Brotherhood. Flying at an altitude of 200 feet to avoid detection by radar and fighter interceptors, the aircraft crossed into Soviet airspace and headed north-east for Lithuania. During the final approach to the predetermined drop zone it climbed to 500 feet, remaining there long enough for the three parachutists and their equipment containers to be despatched before diving to 200 feet and heading back to West Germany. While his two companions landed safely, Luksa was injured and one container was found to have gone astray. To make matters worse, next morning the three men discovered they had been dropped 100 miles from their intended DZ. So it was a week before they succeeded in linking up with the Forest Brotherhood. Shortly afterwards Sirvys transmitted a message to Stockhom confirming their safe arrival.

On 19 April 1951 two more agents, Julijonas Butenas and Jonas Kukauskus, the latter a radio operator, were dropped into Lithuania and, having buried their equipment, also made contact with the Forest Brotherhood. Butenas set off in search of Luksa, who was away visiting other Brotherhood groups, while Kukauskus remained at base as Sirvys and a group of guerrillas set off to retrieve the equipment containers dropped with the new arrivals. During their absence, however, Soviet troops attacked the base, capturing Kukauskus who soon agreed to collaborate with the MGB. Two weeks later, in early May, Butenas was surrounded while hiding in the forest and committed suicide rather than be captured. In October, the MGB succeeded in luring Luksa into a trap, using Kukauskus as bait, and shot him dead.

Meanwhile, in April, despite the singular lack of success it had enjoyed so far, SIS despatched another four agents into Latvia. One of them, however, Janis Erglis, was a communist agent. Landed by the MGB on the coast of Gotland in 1950, he had convinced the Swedes that he was a refugee. Having been granted political asylum, he had made his way to West Germany and a displaced persons camp, where he had eventually been recruited by SIS. After a year's training in Britain, he had been despatched to the SIS base in Hamburg together with three other Lithuanians: a radio operator named Janis Berzins; a Latvian called Lodis Upans; and an Estonian known only by the alias of Gustav. Two weeks later, the four men embarked aboard S208, which landed them at the estuary of the River Venta, near Ventspils.

The group split into two pairs immediately after landing. While Upans and Gustav made off in another direction, Erglis and Berzins headed for a railway station but were stopped by two militiamen who, dissatisfied with the two agents' identity papers, started to escort them to a nearby village. It is not clear whether the incident had been contrived by the MGB – Erglis had informed his MGB controller, Major Janis Lukavesics, of the impending arrival – but apparently Erglis managed to bribe the militiamen, who fired over the agents' heads as they broke free and sprinted into the nearby forest. Eventually, they reached Riga, where Erglis took Berzins to an apartment.

Lodis Upans, accompanied by Gustav, had meanwhile met up with the MAXIS group – the MGB pseudo-guerrillas led by Arvits Gailitis. Upans's mission was to investigate it for any indications of Soviet penetration before making his way to the area of Stende where he was to check on another group codenamed ROBERTS. After a few days, having satisfied himself that MAXIS was genuine, Upans departed on the next stage of his journey accompanied by Gustav. On 24 April, the two men separated and the latter departed on his journey to Estonia. At some point, Gustav was apprehended by the MGB, but, using the cyanide pill with which all agents were issued, he succeeded in committing suicide. To allay any suspicion on the part of Upans, his death was made out to be the result of a chance encounter with border guards.

Upans had brought with him instructions from SIS for Andrei Galdins and Vitolds Berkis to return to Germany. In the event, it was Arvits Gailitis who was picked up with Berkis, whose health had suffered badly during almost two years in the forests, by *S208* on the night of 28/29 September. Once again, the MGB had succeeded in insinuating one of its agents into the very heart of SIS's Baltic operation. As Berkis and Gailitis boarded the *S208*, three agents were making their way from the beach through the forest to the MAXIS group's camp. One was a radio operator, a Latvian named Bolislav Pitans, while the other two were Estonians, Leo Audova and Mark Pedak, who were to proceed to their home country and establish contact with the resistance there. A few days later, they set off and four weeks later reached the capital of Tallinn, where they sought out their contact, a local resistance leader. However, the long arm of the MGB ensured that well before their arrival the contact had been arrested and replaced by one of its agents – with predictable consequences.

Another OPC operation in the spring of 1952 saw a pair of agents,

Janis Plos and Zigurd Krumins, being landed on the Estonian coast with the task of making contact with local partisan groups before making their way to the Latvian capital of Riga. Unlike other agents, whose orders had been to operate with resistance groups and to organise the supply of weapons and equipment, they were to establish a network to monitor the movements of Soviet warships in the Baltic. During the following month, the two men reported that they had made contact with a resistance group. Eighteen months later, however, Krumins was captured by troops searching a farm; in due course, he was tried and imprisoned. Nothing was learned of the fate of Plos.

April saw the return of Arvits Gailitis after almost seven months in Britain, the MGB having expedited it by arresting and executing Andrei Galdins and engineering the death of Janis Berzins. SIS had complied with the MAXIS group's subsequent request for Gailitis to be returned as soon as possible, despatching three more agents with him. The four men were landed on 20 April near Ventspil by *S208*. The boat also collected Lodis Upans, who had suffered a nervous breakdown.

The CIA, meanwhile, was also continuing to send in more agents. On 30 August 1952 three Latvians, Nikolai Balodis, Alfreds Riekstins and Edvins Osolins, parachuted into the Courland area close to the border with Lithuania. Having escaped after being spotted by a patrol, Riekstins and Osolins were cornered a few days later during a sweep of the area by the MGB. Riekstins committed suicide, using his suicide pill, but Osolins was captured. Meanwhile Balodis, a radio operator, who had landed some distance away from his companions, made good his escape. This caused alarm within the MGB where those controlling LURSEN-S feared that he could uncover the entire deception operation. In the event, however, their concern was needless. Having disposed of his equipment, Balodis absconded with the considerable sum of money given to him by his CIA controllers and proceeded to indulge in high living. His eventual downfall came when his forged passport failed to pass scrutiny when checked during a journey. He soon found himself in the hands of the MGB, whose interrogators quickly satisfied themselves that he had not transmitted any information since his arrival. In any case, having heard nothing from the three agents since they were dropped, the CIA had already assumed that they had been arrested and had therefore written them off.

At the end of September 1952, SIS sent in four agents, two of whom were Lithuanians, Zigmas Kudirka and a shadowy individual known solely as 'Edmundes'. In fact, he was an MGB officer who had been planted among the pseudo-guerrillas and, on 20 April, despatched as a senior representative to Germany via *S208*, accompanying Lodis Upans on his journey home. He had subsequently been flown to Britain where he had spent almost five months, during which he had been involved in discussions with SIS on future strategy for resistance operations in Lithuania. The two others who were landed were both Latvians, one of them a pseudo-guerrilla who had lived six months in Britain, and the other a radio operator. As *S208* slid away from the Lithuanian coast into the darkness, another MGB infiltrator, Janis Klimkans, was on board. Not long afterwards, he arrived in London, where he began several months of training.

Despite the paucity of success achieved so far, operations in the Baltic continued into 1953. In May, OSO dropped a single agent, Leonids Zarins, into Latvia with the mission of gathering intelligence on the Soviet military presence in the country. In addition, he was to make contact with Edvins Osolins who, as far as his OSO controllers were concerned, was still free and operational. A week later Zarins made a rendezvous in Riga with Osolins and was immediately arrested. Osolins subsequently transmitted a series of messages to the CIA saying that Zarins had failed to meet him and asking his whereabouts.

By this time there was mounting concern within the CIA about OSO and OPC operations in the Baltic. On 6 May 1953, a Latvian agent named Leonids Bromberg, who had been an instructor at one of the CIA training camps in West Germany, was dropped into Latvia to discover the fate of the agents sent in previously. Travelling by train to Riga, he met briefly with Osolins, whom he knew from his days as an instructor in West Germany. A further rendezvous was arranged. The result was inevitable, and Bromberg was arrested by the MGB. After several weeks of interrogation, he agreed to cooperate and during July began transmitting to his base in West Germany.

Each individual radio operator using morse communications has his own unique style or 'fist', which is recognisable to a trained operator at a receiving station. Such transmissions were recorded for comparison purposes in the event that there was any doubt over the identity of an operator. Bromberg's MGB controllers were well aware of the system of minute variations in 'fist' used by operators to warn that they were transmitting under control and warned him against attempting to use them. Nevertheless, by the end of the year he had succeeded in introducing the variations to warn that he was operating under duress. It appears, however, that his warnings went undetected or were ignored as he continued to receive transmissions from his base.

Suspicions had been aroused, however, by transmissions from Jonas Kukauskus, who had been dropped with Julijonas Butenas in April 1951. Since his capture shortly afterwards, he had been collaborating with the MGB in sending reports by radio. At this juncture, the CIA and SIS carried out a comparison in London of the reports received from their respective agents. The lack of hard intelligence, together with the almost identical material supplied by Bromberg and other agents based with guerrilla groups, made it immediately apparent to the CIA that it had been the victim of a Soviet deception operation. Shortly afterwards, the Agency terminated its Baltic operations.

Despite this, SIS still believed that its networks in Latvia and Lithuania remained free of Soviet control. In the meantime, however, it decided to check on its single network in Estonia and transmitted a message ordering one of the guerrilla leaders to be despatched for training in Britain. At the beginning of November 1954, *S208* duly picked up Walter Luks who arrived in London a few days later. He was subjected to questioning, but after a week his interrogators found nothing to alarm them and he proceeded with his training.

Luks spent four months in Britain, returning to Estonia at the end of March 1955 when he was landed by *S208* on the Estonian coast. On the same day, in a gesture designed to allay any further vestiges of suspicion on the part of SIS, the KGB in Estonia despatched an agent named Heino Karkman who arrived in London during April. Karkman, a radio operator who had been landed in Estonia in the autumn of 1953, had been operating as part of guerrilla group but had become suspicious in the weeks following his arrival. He had sensibly kept his doubts to himself and had eventually convinced his 'comrades' to allow him to return to Britain to obtain further support.

No sooner had he arrived in London than Karkman revealed the awful, stark reality to SIS that all its networks throughout the Baltic were being operated by the Soviets. During the following weeks, SIS began to cut itself off from its surviving eleven agents, all of whom were under KGB control. Requests for further equipment and funds were met with the response that seaborne landings were no longer possible. Meanwhile, in an effort to re-establish SIS confidence, the MGB's MAXIS group requested that one of its senior members, Janis Klimkans, who had previously spent about a year in London during 1952–3, should come to Britain. SIS, seeing the opportunity of interrogating him and obtaining further proof of Soviet penetration, agreed but refused to send S208 to collect him for fear it would sail into a trap.

In September 1956, having travelled via Sweden, where he had been held for two months, Klimkans arrived in London. Here he was incarcerated in an SIS safe house and interrogated for four weeks – at which point he broke. During the following two months he provided full details of the KGB deception operation. Meanwhile, SIS was finally closing down all contact with its agents throughout the Baltic. In November, Klimkans was returned to Sweden. In the meantime, SIS's remaining agents were rounded up by the KGB, who now had no use for them.

Operations in Eastern Europe and the Baltic therefore ended ignominiously for SIS and the CIA, both of which had derived little or no benefit in exchange for the considerable amount of resources devoted to them. For the agents who had returned to their respective homelands in the hope that they would be furthering the cause for freedom and independence, there was the brutal reality of capture and ultimately the awful prospect of lengthy imprisonment in Siberia or death.

CHAPTER TWO

ALBANIA 1949–1954

While embroiled in the Baltic and Eastern Europe, the Secret Intelligence Service (SIS) and Office of Policy Coordination (OPC) were also heavily involved in another major clandestine undertaking. In 1947, SIS had begun to plan an operation in the Balkan republic of Albania. Codenamed VALUABLE and forming part of a scheme to limit Soviet dominance in the Balkans and Adriatic, it was designed to disrupt the activities of communist guerrillas in Greece, whose safe havens were in Albania. It was also aimed at instigating an uprising to topple the regime of Enver Hoxha, the dictator and secretary-general of the Albanian Communist Party (CPA) who had headed the communist resistance movement, the Levizje Nacional Çlirimtare (Movement of National Liberation – LNÇ), during the war. The intention was to wrest the country from the Soviet bloc and assist in the establishment of a democratic pro-Western government.

Located on the western Adriatic coast of the Balkan peninsula, Albania is bordered on the north and north-east by Yugoslavia, and by Macedonia and Greece respectively to the east and south-east. Previously part of the Turkish Ottoman Empire for five centuries, it became an independent state in 1912 but, following the outbreak of the First World War in September 1914, was invaded by the armies of Austria-Hungary, France, Italy, Greece, Montenegro and Serbia. At the end of the war, the country would have disappeared but for a veto by the United States of a plan by Britain, France and Italy for it to be divided up among its neighbours.

The mid-1920s saw further internal upheaval following the ousting in June 1924 of a liberal government led by Fan Noli, an American-educated bishop who sought to establish a Western-style democracy. He was replaced by a clan chieftain from the the north of the country, Ahmed Bey Zogu, who ruled the country as president until 1928, when he was crowned King Zog I. His power base was a coalition of private landowners or beys, who dominated the southern half of Albania known as Toskeria, and clan chieftains, called bajraktars, who ruled their respective areas in Ghegeria, the north of the country.

In April 1939, Albania was invaded and occupied by Italy, which saw it as a bridgehead for military expansion into the Balkans. Albanian forces, led by a local police chief named Major Abas Kupi, made a stand at Durazzo, on the coast to the west of the capital of Tirana, where they held up vastly superior Italian forces long enough for King Zog to escape to Greece. From there he made his way to France, subsequently travelling to Britain after the French surrender in the summer of 1940. Thereafter, resistance against the Italians was somewhat half-hearted, being limited to sporadic attacks by bands of guerrillas on police and officials in the more remote, mountainous areas.

The British nevertheless sought to capitalise on anti-Italian sentiment in the country. During 1940, Section D, the department of SIS responsible for subversion, sabotage and other aspects of unconventional warfare (operating under the cover name of the Statistical Research Department of the War Office), mounted an operation via Yugoslavia to foment unrest and foster resistance in Albania. It recruited exiled Albanians in Greece and Turkey while establishing arms dumps at locations on the Greek–Albanian border.

On 6 April 1941, Germany attacked Yugoslavia. On the following day, as Yugoslav forces battled to hold the invaders, Colonel Dayrell Oakley-Hill, who had served as an adviser to the Albanian gendarmerie prior to the war and subsequently had been sent by SOE to Belgrade as a liaison officer with an Albanian organisation called the United Front, was dispatched to establish a resistance force in northern Albania. Crossing into the country from Kosovo, he was accompanied by Abas Kupi and three other Gheg leaders, Gani Kryeziu and his brothers Hasan and Said, leading a force of 300 men of the United Front. Oakley-Hill and his companions reached Scutari where they were welcomed by the tribes in that area.

Meanwhile, however, Yugoslavia had capitulated to the Germans after a week of fighting: the government had fled to the Middle East and the army had surrendered. With no logistical support, Oakley-Hill's expedition collapsed and he was forced to return to Yugoslavia where he was taken prisoner. Abas Kupi, nevertheless, remained in Albania and succeeded in rallying the pro-monarchist or Zogist tribes of which he thereafter became the acknowledged leader. November 1941 saw the formation of the CPA in Toskeria, followed in September 1942 by that of

Albania 1949–1954

0   100
miles

GOZO

MALTA

0   10
miles

Fort Benjimma
Medina
Rabat
Valetta

YUGOSLAVIA

MONTENEGRO

KOSOVO

BULGARIA

Adriatic Sea

MACEDONIA

Bari

ALBANIA

Kastoria

Salonika

GREECE

CORFU

Jakova
Kukës
Prizren
Scutari
DIBRA

Bulqizë
Tirana
MARTENESH
Durazzo
Kavaja
Elbasan
ALBANIA
Berat
Korçe
Saseno
Is.
Valona
KURVELESH
Karaburun
Peninsula
Tragjas
Nivica
Gjirokaster
Corfu
Channel
NORTHERN
EPIRUS

Kalanissia
Islands

Athens

Ionian Sea

the LNÇ, a body which initially also contained a number of nationalists and Zogists, the latter led by Abas Kupi who was a member of the organisation's Central Council. The creation of these two organisations resulted in the first effective organised resistance in the south of the country against the Italians.

In April 1943, SOE despatched a four-man mission codenamed CONCENSUS (sic.) to Albania. Led by Lieutenant Colonel Neil 'Billy' McLean and Captain (later Major) David Smiley, it was dropped into Greece, in the mountains of northern Epirus, where it was met by an SOE mission operating in that area. From there it made its way into Albania where on 1 May it established contact with the LNÇ, subsequently sending back a series of reports accompanied by requests for arms and equipment, the first drop taking place during the last week of June. During the following weeks the mission trained, armed and equipped many partisans who were subsequently formed into the 1st Partisan Brigade. Soon, however, McLean and his companions realised that the partisans appeared to have little interest in attacking the Italians, and there were occasions when they were reluctant to take part in operations.

In July, meanwhile, events had taken a dramatic turn when, following the fall of Benito Mussolini, Italy switched to the Allied side under Marshal Pietro Badoglio. A few weeks later, the Germans, for whom Albania was of strategic importance as a major source of chrome, responded by despatching an airborne division which seized Tirana. A large proportion of Italian forces in Albania threw in their lot with the Germans, who within a few days had gained control of the country; others escaped to the mountains where they joined forces with the communist or nationalist resistance groups. The Germans now formed a puppet government, at the same time annexing Kosovo and Çamëria from Yugoslavia and setting up governing bodies from local leaders in both regions.

Meanwhile, a faction of predominantly anti-royalist nationalists led by Midhat Frasheri, one of the architects of Albanian independence in 1912, split from the LNÇ and formed their own movement in the south: the National Front (Balli Kombëtar – BK). Despite this split, the two movements came to an agreement and on 2 August established the Committee for the Salvation of Albania to fight against the occupying forces of Italy and Germany. The communist-dominated Central Council of the LNÇ strongly opposed the new body and condemned it. In November Abas Kupi also broke away from the LNÇ and formed a Zogist faction in the north called Legaliteti. On 9 September, the LNÇ issued a circular to all its forces, ordering them to prevent the nationalists from exercising any influence on the population, to assert themselves wherever possible, and to present themselves through the LNÇ as the only 'power of the Albanian people'. It was in fact conserving its forces in preparation for civil war against the BK and Zogists.

During the ensuing weeks a number of other SOE missions dropped into Albania, including some to the Zogists in the north, and in due course SOE decided to send in a mission comprising a senior officer and staff to take over the command and control of them from Maclean. Codenamed SLENDER, it was led by Brigadier E. F. 'Trotsky' Davies, who was accompanied by his GSO1, Lieutenant Colonel Arthur Nicholls of the Coldstream Guards, and a small staff of officers and NCOs. Shortly afterwards McLean and Smiley were withdrawn, making their way overland to the coast where, during November 1943, they were picked up by a Royal Navy motor torpedo boat. Transported across the Adriatic, they eventually reached the SOE base at Bari, in southern Italy, from where they were flown to the organisation's headquarters in Cairo.

On arrival in Cairo, McLean and Smiley were debriefed, the former submitting a report which in essence stated that the LNÇ was the principal body with any capability of fighting the Germans, even though it was more obviously interested in waging civil war on the nationalists. The latter meanwhile had shown no enthusiasm for fighting the Germans with whom some elements were reported to be collaborating in order to protect themselves from the LNÇ. McLean recommended not only that the LNÇ should continue to receive military aid but also that contact with the nationalists and Zogists should be maintained in order to prevent a civil war; moreover, efforts should be made to persuade the more anti-German factions among them to cooperate with the communists in fighting the common foe.

McLean's conclusions and recommendations were supported in December when Brigadier 'Trotsky' Davies reported on 17 December 1943 that elements of the BK were collaborating actively with the Germans and recommended that recognition and support be given solely to the LNÇ. There was evidence supporting Davies's allegations, notably that the Germans had been able to recruit four battalions of troops from among members of the BK who were then grouped to form the SS Division Skanderberg, named after an Albanian national hero. These subsequently took part in operations against the LNÇ and in Yugoslavia where they fought against the communist partisans. Further evidence of nationalist collaboration came three weeks after Davies sent his report when he and his group were ambushed by a pro-Nazi BK group; in the ensuing action, he was wounded and captured, but the rest of his group escaped under Colonel Arthur Nicholls who later died while leading his men to safety.

In April 1944 McLean and Smiley, accompanied by another SOE officer, Captain Julian Amery, parachuted back into Albania in an operation codenamed CONCENSUS II, their mission being threefold: to reorganise the SOE missions in the north and centre of the country and coordinate resistance; to raise the Gheg people in general, and the Zogist forces in particular, against the Germans; and to try to achieve some form of cooperation between the Zogists and the LNÇ. Shortly afterwards, while en route to the headquarters of Abas Kupi, they met Captain Alan Hare, Brigadier Davies's staff captain, and the remnants of the SLENDER mission.

McLean managed to persuade Abas Kupi to mobilise his forces, in return for which the latter requested supplies of arms from SOE. He was told, however, that these would be forthcoming once he had commenced operations against the Germans and his men had shown their worth. When news of this reached them, LNÇ forces attacked Abas Kupi's headquarters and several strongholds belonging to the clan chiefs in the Gheg region of Mati. Shortly afterwards, they also attacked and overran the base of the SLENDER mission, kidnapping Hare and his radio operator. They then set out to seize McLean's group but the latter succeeded in avoiding capture. Meanwhile, proposals by the British for an armistice between the LNÇ and Abas Kupi's forces met with a flat refusal from Enver Hoxha.

McLean's mission thereafter concentrated on persuading the various nationalist factions to rally under Abas Kupi and bring about a rising against the Germans throughout northern Albania. No sooner had this been achieved than the LNÇ launched further attacks. At the same time, Enver Hoxha demanded the withdrawal of all military missions in Albania or he would take them prisoner and subject them to courts martial. This ultimatum was rejected, although it worried the British who were anxious not to compromise the negotiations they were currently conducting with Hoxha.

During the following weeks Abas Kupi's forces and those of other nationalist leaders carried out a series of operations against the Germans in order to prove their readiness to fight and thus justify supplies of arms. Only a fraction of the weapons promised by SOE were dropped, however, and sensing this declining lack of support, some elements lost heart and began to desert the nationalist cause.

One faction, nevertheless, led by Gani Kryeziu who in 1941 had established the United Front, continued to operate against the Germans. While engaged in attacking the enemy-held city of Jakova, however, it was attacked by LNÇ forces who overran Kryeziu's headquarters, capturing his SOE liaison officer Major Tony Simcox and Sergeant Bill 'Gunner' Collins, a radio operator. Both were abducted together with an Albanian named Lazar Fundo who was Kyeziu's political adviser and who also acted as interpreter for the SOE mission. Simcox and Collins were later taken to Berat where they were handed over to a British military mission which evacuated them to Bari. Fundo, who had resigned from the Communist Party in 1938, was not so fortunate; having been recognised, he was executed soon afterwards.

Abas Kupi, in the meantime, agreed to fight on without further arms supplies, merely requesting a letter from King Zog ordering him to do so. This was not forthcoming, however, due to Foreign Office fears of an adverse reaction from the United States which was already critical of the support being given by Britain to the king of Greece. Nothing daunted, McLean used a direct channel of communication to the Foreign Secretary, Anthony Eden, requesting a letter from King Zog for Abas Kupi. Shortly afterwards, fighting broke out anew when the 1st Partisan Brigade attacked Zogist forces. SOE despatched an officer from its forward headquarters at Bari with a proposal for an armistice between the two sides but this was rejected out of hand by Enver Hoxha who set out to capture McLean and his group to prevent any further liaison between them and Abas Kupi. On 25 August, McLean received a signal from Bari stating that Hoxha had alleged that he and his group were working against the LNÇ with collaborationist elements and warning that he had given an ultimatum that they must leave Albania, or hand themselves over within five days to partisans; failing that, they would be captured and submitted to trial by courts martial. Confronted, however, by a firm response from the British to the effect that all military aid would cease immediately and British liaison officers would be withdrawn, Hoxha withdrew his threat.

McLean and his companions, for their part, had no intention of handing themselves over to the communists and continued with their operations alongside Abas Kupi's forces against the Germans. But on 4 September they received a further signal from Bari ordering McLean and Smiley to return to Bari while Amery was to remain with Abas Kupi as an observer only. The signal added that no further arms would be dropped to the Zogists. During the rest of September and through into October, however, McLean's group continued its activities, ignoring orders from Bari to give themselves up to partisan forces for subsequent evacuation. Unlike their superiors, he and his companions had few illusions as to the treatment they might suffer at the hands of the partisans. They were well aware, too, that despite the withdrawal of Hoxha's threat, they had already been tried in absentia by a 'People's Court' and condemned to death as 'enemies of the people'.

Around the end of October, McLean's mission was evacuated. Prior to his leaving Albania, he had received a signal stating that only British personnel were to be evacuated and that their companions, who by then included Abas Kupi and a number of others who had fought alongside the mission, were to be left behind. On arrival at Bari, they discovered that McLean's signal sent to Foreign Secretary Anthony Eden, requesting Abas Kupi's evacuation, had been intercepted by SOE and destroyed. It later transpired that certain SOE officers on the staff at Bari were known communists and one of them was subsequently identified as being responsible for the interception of the said signal. Nothing daunted, McLean sent another message to Eden who responded immediately, confirming that Abas Kupi and his party should be evacuated. Further opposition was voiced by the SOE staff at Bari, and therefore McLean and Smiley took the matter higher, approaching General Sir Henry Maitland Wilson, the Supreme Allied Commander Mediterranean, who promptly gave orders for Abas Kupi's evacuation. By that time, however, Kupi and his companions had managed to escape on a boat from Albania, subsequently being picked up by the Royal Navy in the middle of the Adriatic.

During November, German forces withdrew from Albania and wholesale civil war broke out between the LNÇ and BK. By the end of 1944, the communists had gained control of the country and Enver Hoxha became its new leader. Two years later, by which time he had secured the country in an iron grip, he proclaimed the People's Republic of Albania. Meanwhile, his relations with Britain and the United States deteriorated rapidly, with diplomatic representatives being restricted to the capital of Tirana and subjected to much harassment.

On 15 May 1946 two Royal Navy cruisers, HMS *Orion* and *Superb*, were fired on by Albanian shore batteries while passing through the Corfu Channel. Albania then added insult to injury by imposing a three-mile exclusion zone off her coastline, thereby closing the channel to all foreign shipping. On 22 October 1946 the British decided to ignore this and despatched two destroyers, HMS *Saumurez* and *Volage*, through the channel. Unfortunately, it had since been sown with mines which damaged both vessels and killed 44 men. Britain retaliated by confiscating ten million pounds-worth of Albanian gold deposited in the Bank of England for safekeeping during the war, and shortly afterwards diplomatic relations between Britain and Albania were broken off.

FOLLOWING ITS ELECTION to power in July 1945, the post-war Labour government of Clement Attlee from the very start had adopted a hostile attitude towards the Soviet Union. Much of this was due to Britain's new Foreign Secretary, the forthright Ernest Bevin, who showed an implacable loathing for Stalin and his regime. This antipathy stemmed from an extensive knowledge of the Soviet system gained from Bevin's lengthy service as a trade union official, during which he had fought many a bitter struggle against communist infiltration. Supported by Attlee, he was determined to oppose the Soviet dictator whenever possible.

The first opportunity to do so arose in the Balkans where by 1945 the governments of Albania, Bulgaria and Yugoslavia were reported to be providing logistical support and safe havens for communist guerrillas in Greece. During the war, German and Italian occupying forces had been

opposed by communist partisans of ELAS (Ethnikós Laïkós Apeleft-
herotikós – National Popular Liberation Army), the military wing of
EAM (Ethnikón Apeleftherotikón Métopon – National Liberation
Front), and guerrillas of EDES (Ellínikos Dímokratikos Ethnikós Strátos
– Greek Democratic National Army). Both factions separately fought
the common enemy, receiving support from SOE which supplied liaison
officers who provided training and arms. In early 1944, EAM established a 'political committee' in the mountains of northern Greece while
disowning the Greek royalist government-in-exile in Cairo. This was the
start of civil war between EAM and EDES while in Egypt there were
mutinies among units of the Greek army and navy based there.

In October 1944, after the withdrawal of German forces from Greece,
the communists and nationalists were brought together by the British
to form a coalition government. This proved short-lived, however, and on
3 December civil war broke out, being suppressed by British forces with
some difficulty as by then EAM controlled almost two-thirds of Greece.
The communists nevertheless admitted defeat and on 12 February 1945
a peace treaty was signed under which the ELAS forces were disbanded
and their arms surrendered in return for the KKE (Kommunistikon
Komma Ellados – Greek Communist party) being permitted to exist as
a constitutional political party.

At the general election held on 31 March 1946 under international
supervision, the royalists won a large majority, largely due to the communists claiming that it was unfair and refusing to take part. This was
followed in September by a plebiscite which restored the Greek monarch,
King George II, to his throne. In northern Greece, however, the communists rebelled once again and recommenced their campaign of guerrilla war by carrying out a series of attacks on towns and villages. Their
forces, fighting under the name of the Democratic Army, was headed
by 'General Markos', the alias of Markos Vafiades, a former trade union
official who had fought as a partisan against the Italians and Germans.

By this time Britain, under whose care Greece had been placed by
the Allies at the end of the Second World War, was heavily committed
elsewhere and was no longer willing, nor could afford, to shoulder alone
the task of maintaining Greek security. She therefore turned to the
United States and in March 1947 President Harry Truman declared that
the United States would provide $400,000,000 of military and economic

aid to Greece, which was under threat from communist insurrection, and Turkey, which was facing pressure from Soviet expansion in the Mediterranean area.

During 1947 there were reports that the Democratic Army was receiving support from Albania, Bulgaria and Yugoslavia. Greece appealed to the United Nations (UN) for assistance and in October the UN General Assembly established a committee to investigate the allegations. Eight months later, in mid-1948, it reported that it had found evidence that all three countries were providing safe havens and logistical support for Vaphiades's guerrillas, naming Albania as the principal culprit.

In 1948, Yugoslavia broke with the Soviet Union which had been attempting to subjugate it in the same way that it had Bulgaria as part of a plan to turn the Balkans into a bridgehead threatening British and American communications in the eastern Mediterranean. Stalin had for some time harboured suspicions that the Yugoslav leader, Tito, intended to form his own communist bloc independently of the Soviet Union within south-eastern Europe and thus intended to prevent any such ambition by enfolding Yugoslavia within the USSR. Tito managed to thwart Stalin's plans and in June the split between the two leaders resulted in the expulsion of Yugoslavia from the Communist Information Bureau (Cominform) – the organisation established in 1947 to consolidate and expand communist rule in Europe. Shortly afterwards, Tito turned to the United States and through the CIA requested military aid to forestall any attempt by Stalin to take Yugoslavia by force. At the same time, he halted support for Markos Vaphiades and the Democratic Army.

During this period, relations between Yugoslavia and Albania also deteriorated rapidly. Belgrade and Tirana had hitherto enjoyed close relations, the Yugoslavs providing much in the way of economic and other support. Within the Albanian government a pro-Yugoslav faction, led by the Minister of Interior Koci Xoxe, worked closely with its counterparts in Belgrade. Hoxha, however, feared that Tito intended to absorb Albania into a federation headed by Yugoslavia, and his suspicions hardened when Xoxe attempted to force some of Hoxha's supporters from positions of influence in the CPA and the government. In 1947, Hoxha began to turn towards Moscow and develop his relationship with Stalin, who had hitherto ignored Albania, considering it to be under Tito's wing. This move, combined with Yugoslavia's expulsion from the Cominform, enabled the Albanian leader to thwart Xoxe's plans to remove him from power. The latter was subsequently arrested, tried for treason and executed on 11 June 1949.

It is interesting to note that Stalin insisted that his replacement as Interior Minister should be Mehmet Shehu, a graduate of the Voroshilov military academy in Moscow. Xoxe's trial was followed by a highly publicised series of others in which the defendants were accused of spying for the British and Americans, or involvement in plots to topple Hoxha and his government. These were accompanied by a purge among those elements of the population suspected of being pro-Tito.

During the summer of 1948, former SOE officer Julian Amery travelled to Greece where he saw for himself how serious a threat the communists were posing to Greece. He considered that the only way of defeating the Democratic Army would be to strike at its safe havens, either by mounting direct attacks from Greece or by forming a guerrilla movement to carry out operations inside those countries providing sanctuary for Vaphiades's guerrillas. Furthermore, he was convinced that the time had come to take action to counter the Soviet attempts at expansion in Eastern Europe; in his view, an operation against Albania would provide a response to both threats. On his return from Greece, Amery proceeded to lobby his contacts within circles of influence, including members of the British government among whom his ideas fell on fertile ground.

In April 1946, a body called the Russia Committee, including representatives of the War Office, Air Ministry, Admiralty and SIS, was established by the Foreign Office to analyse Soviet strategy and produce recommendations for British policy in response. As described by Stephen Dorril in his book *MI6 – Fifty Years of Special Operations*, it formed in turn the Cold War Sub-Committee, better known as the Jebb Committee as it was chaired by Gladwyn Jebb, Assistant Under Secretary of State at the Foreign Office, who during the war had been Chief Executive Officer of SOE during the early stage of its existence. The Jebb Committee's role was the conduct of political and economic warfare, and to exercise oversight of SIS covert and paramilitary operations against the Soviet Union.

At a meeting of the committee on 25 November 1948, the subject of Albania was raised and the idea of instigating a civil war considered. The committee came to no specific conclusions but decided that the aim of any action against Soviet satellites should be to liberate countries within the Soviet sphere of influence 'by any means short of war'. The problem, though, was that Britain could not afford to finance any such operation and therefore would have to seek assistance in funding it. The United States, being the only nation to have profited from the war, was the obvious choice and thus the Russia Committee decided on 16 December that 'there could be no question of taking any action without coordination with the United States government'.

On 13 February 1949, the committee was informed that sanction had been received for action to be taken against the Hoxha regime. The decision had been taken by Ernest Bevin, with Prime Minister Clement Attlee's verbal support, to mount a small-scale operation, knowledge of which was confined to only a very few senior members of the government and the Cabinet Secretary. A month later, a British delegation headed by a senior SIS officer, William Hayter, flew to Washington for a conference with its counterparts from the State Department and the CIA, the latter including the OPC chief Frank Wisner. Hayter was accompanied by Foreign Office Assistant Under-Secretary of State and Russia Committee member Gladwyn Jebb; another member of the Foreign Office, the Earl of Jellicoe, who had commanded the Special Boat Squadron in the Aegean and Greece during the war; and Peter Dwyer, SIS's representative in Washington. The three days of the conference were devoted to the subject of cooperation between Britain and the United States in countering the threat from the Soviet Union.

The British proposals for action against Albania met with a favourable response from the Americans, particularly so from Wisner who was anxious for the OPC to be involved in any such venture. During the first half of April, the Policy and Planning Staff of the US State Department recommended that support be given to the operation and the formal decision to do so was taken shortly afterwards. A joint committee to oversee the operation was established, the British representatives of which included the SIS officer based at the embassy in Washington. The Americans were represented by members of the State Department and OPC, the latter including the deputy chief, Frank Lindsay.

In London, the task of overseeing the organisation and conduct of the British element of the operation, codenamed VALUABLE, was given to

SIS which established a special committee under the service's Assistant Chief, Air Commodore Jack Easton. Direct command was given to Colonel Harold Perkins who had headed SOE's Polish, Czech and Hungarian sections during the war and had joined SIS in 1946, being appointed head of the newly formed Special Operations Branch. In 1947, he had conducted an operation to interdict supplies of arms and Jewish refugees being smuggled to Palestine. This had been achieved by attaching limpet mines to some twelve ships being used for transporting refugees

The plan for VALUABLE called for the infiltration of trained personnel into Albania where they were to establish an active resistance movement for subsequent operations against the Hoxha regime. It was determined from the start there was no question of sending in British or American personnel because of the potential political embarrassment which would have been caused in the event of their capture. Albanians would have to carry out the task and fortunately there was no shortage of potential recruits among the nationalists and royalists living in refugee camps throughout Europe, many having fought as guerrillas during the war.

Such men, however, would have to be properly trained for the task in hand, and once again Perkins turned to Major David Smiley who was by then in Germany serving with his regiment, the Royal Horse Guards. After the end of his second tour in Albania, Smiley had been posted to Force 136, the Far Eastern arm of SOE, and at the end of May 1945 he was dropped into north-east Thailand where he led a mission code-named CANDLE. Returning to Britain at the beginning of 1946, he attended a six-month course at the British Army's Staff College before being posted to Warsaw as assistant military attaché at the British Embassy. His tour of duty, however, was cut short after he was declared *persona non grata* and expelled by the Polish authorities. Back in London, he was seconded for a year to SIS where he worked in Section I of the War Planning Department, collaborating closely with Colonel Brian Franks over proposals for the role of SOE to be taken over in any future conflict by the Special Air Service, which was reformed in January 1947, having been disbanded during the previous year. He then returned to his regiment as second-in-command, a post for which he had little enthusiasm. On being approached by Perkins, he happily accepted the latter's offer of a return to special duties.

Smiley's task was to conduct the training of the Albanian guerrillas at a base to be established for the purpose. OPC chief Frank Wisner had offered facilities at the large US Wheelus airbase in Libya but the British had deemed it unsuitable for political reasons and had looked elsewhere, eventually selecting Fort Benjimma on the island of Malta. A disused castle built during the Napoleonic era, it was in an isolated location and featured facilities ideal for the accommodation of trainee guerrillas and a small staff of instructors. For security purposes, Smiley was posted to Malta as Deputy Chief of Staff at the headquarters of the island's garrison located in the capital of Valetta, this providing a cover for his presence on the island.

In order to obtain the necessary recruits, SIS meanwhile approached the leaders of the various Albanian factions in exile. The royalists were still led by Abas Kupi while the various elements of the republican BK included those headed by Midhat Frasheri, Said Kryeziv and Abas Ermanji. Both factions were sworn enemies of a third organisation called Independenza which comprised Catholic independent nationalists principally from the north-west of Albania. All the senior royalists and republicans had left Albania following the communist take-over and were living in different countries: Abas Kupi and Said Kryeziv in Italy, Midhat Frasheri in Turkey and Abas Ermanji in Greece. Julian Amery and his wartime brother-in-arms Neil 'Billy' McLean had maintained contact with all of them and were asked by SIS to assist in establishing the necessary political organisation or government-in-exile on behalf of which the operation would be carried out.

They set off in April to visit the various leaders with the aim of persuading them all to unite under a single banner. This was no easy task as the three main groups were constantly at loggerheads with one another. Two common factors, nevertheless, would unite them. The first was their hatred of communism, the second their deep suspicion of Yugoslavia, which they knew had coveted their homeland in the past and sought to annexe it, and of the Greeks, who maintained a long-standing territorial claim to southern Albania, an area that had previously formed the region of northern Epirus in north-western Greece.

With this latter factor in mind, McLean and Amery travelled in May to Greece in an attempt to persuade prominent Greek figures to drop this claim – a major obstacle to gaining the cooperation of the Albanian exile groups. At the same time, they had to enlist Greek support for the operation and obtain certain facilities, including agreement for the positioning of a radio monitoring station on the island of Corfu. Through an intermediary, Amery managed to obtain the consent of the commander-in-chief of the Greek Army, Field Marshal Alexander Papagos. Accompanied by their former SOE comrade Alan Hare, who had joined SIS after the war and was also on the team planning the operation, McLean and Amery also visited Abas Ermanji, the commander of the BK's military wing, who was living in the port of Piraeus. It had been decided that the first phase of the operation would take place in southern Albania, and therefore the initial group to be landed would have to be recruited from members of the BK.

By raising the possibility of Albania being annexed by Yugoslavia and posing the idea of its liberation from communist rule, they had little problem in enlisting Ermanji's support. He insisted, however, that Midhat Frasheri should also give his consent. This was agreed and shortly afterwards the BK leader travelled from his home in Turkey to Rome where he was joined by Amery, Hare and Ermanji, the last having been provided with a false passport enabling him to enter Italy. On 20 May, McLean, together with Colonel Harold Perkins, also arrived and a series of meetings took place at which the two BK leaders were asked to produce a small force of 30 men. This posed no problem as the refugee camps in the area of Naples held large numbers of young Albanian men only too keen to return to their homeland to fight the communists. Within a matter of days Ermanji had selected those whom he considered most suitable.

Five days later, McLean and Amery returned to London to report to SIS on their progress. There they met Robert Low, an OPC officer assigned to the operation; in addition to reporting to Washington, his role was to provide evidence to the Albanians and Greeks of American participation. On 24 June the SIS team, accompanied by Low and another OPC officer, Robert Minor, returned to Rome where the leaders of the three Albanian groups had assembled for the concluding negotiations over the establishment of the political committee, these to commence on the 25th. Problems were initially caused by Abas Ermanji who objected to the involvement of the Zogists and Independenza in the operation. Aware that his intransigence threatened to affect the negotiations, SIS decided to remove him from the proceedings and spir-ited him away from Rome on the grounds that he had entered the country illegally using a false passport and that there was a possibility that members of Independenza would report him to the Italian author-ities. He was taken to Trieste where he was kept under the watchful eye of an SIS officer, Archie Lyall.

On 7 July, after twelve days of lengthy discussions and negotiations, agreement was reached. A covert military committee was formed for control of the operation, being chaired by the Zogist leader Abas Kupi, with republicans Abas Ermanji and Said Kryeziu appointed as his deputies. Another Zogist, Gaqi Gogo, was made the committee's secre-tary. A separate body, the Albanian National Committee, was also estab-lished as the overt political wing of the organisation under the chairmanship of Midhat Frasheri.

Although there were Zogist elements within the new organisation, there could be no question of any participation in it by the king. He, nevertheless, was aware of the proposed operation, having already been visited in May by the two OPC officers, Low and Minor. He would have to be informed of the creation of the committee and on 14 July McLean, Amery and Low attended a meeting with the king at his villa. Zog's reac-tion to the establishment of the committee, which was in effect an Alban-ian government-in-exile, without his consent was one of anger and his visitors were dismissed forthwith. Later that day, however, they were permitted to return and it was Amery, the consummate diplomat and politician, who poured oil on very troubled waters and eventually per-suaded the king to give his support. Three days later, another meeting with King Zog took place in Alexandria at which he gave his final approval; and on 18 July McLean and his two companions returned to Rome, their task completed.

David Smiley, meanwhile, promoted to lieutenant colonel for his new assignment and accompanied by his family, had arrived in Malta in June and had established his training base at Fort Benjimma. Located on an isolated hill in rough terrain in the centre of the island, on the far side of Medina from the capital of Valetta, the fort was only accessible via a single unmetalled track. It was surrounded on its southern and eastern approaches by a moat and featured a drawbridge which gave access to the keep which would provide accommodation for the Albanians and their instructors. Nearby were beaches providing good facilities for training in the use of small craft.

In addition to Smiley, who taught mine-laying and basic demolitions, the training team comprised five officers and a number of NCOs. Among them were Major (QM) Alfred Howard of the Scots Guards who would teach map reading and navigation; Captain Alastair Grant, responsible for weapon training; Captain Robert 'Doc' Zaehner, a former member of SOE who had served in Persia, who would serve as interpreter for the Albanian trainees who spoke no English; two Albanians (temporarily commissioned as officers), Abdyl Sino and Jani Dilo, who would also act as interpreters, the latter additionally providing instruction in basic field intelligence training and unarmed combat; Sergeant George Odey, who was in charge of the armoury; two former Royal Marine sergeants, Terence 'Lofty' Cooling and 'Derby' Allen, who had served with the Special Boat Squadron during the war and who would provide physical fitness training and instruction in small boat handling; and Sergeant Bill 'Gunner' Collins, who had served in Albania with SOE and had been Smiley's signaller during the CANDLE mission in Thailand in 1945. In addition to training the Albanians in radio procedures, he would be responsible for maintaining communications between the fort and SIS in London. Smiley's wife, who had served as a cipher officer during the war and had undergone refresher training before leaving for Malta, was employed in a similar capacity with two sergeant cipher clerks to assist her.

On 14 July, while McLean, Amery and Low were in audience with King Zog, the first two of the 30 men recruited by Abas Ermanji were flown by the RAF from Rome to Malta where they were met by an SIS officer, Rollo Young, and Captain Alastair Grant. From there they were taken to the fort which would be their home until such time as they returned to their homeland as trained guerrillas. Shortly afterwards, they were joined by the rest of their number.

Training of the 30 BK guerrillas, referred to by SIS as the 'pixies', was conducted throughout the summer. In addition to weapon training with pistols, machine pistols and grenades, which took place in the fort's moat, they were trained in basic demolitions and mine-laying. Much emphasis was also laid on improving their standard of physical fitness, this including long runs with trainees and instructors wearing full packs and carrying weapons. Swimming and operations in small boats also formed part of the curriculum, as did map-reading and navigation. Communications would be a vital factor in the operation and the 'pixies' were trained in the use of the B2 radio set which had seen service during the war with SOE. Lack of time, however, meant that they could not be trained to use morse code and therefore they were limited to voice communication only, using a very basic code based on a book containing key words, each of which was allocated a unique number. Another limitation was that the use of batteries and charging engines would not be possible as they were too heavy to be carried; each group would thus need to carry a cumbersome and somewhat fragile pedal-propelled generator to provide power. Apart from their B2 radios, all other weapons and equipment to be used by the 'pixies' were of foreign manufacture and clean of any serial numbers or markings which would otherwise identify their sources of origin. They were provided by Frank Quinn, a member of SIS's quartermaster's department, who was responsible for providing logistical support for the operation.

When off-duty, the 'pixies' were allowed to visit the towns of Medina, Rabat and Lima, which lay only a few miles away. Wearing British Army uniform with Royal Pioneer Corps insignia, it was not long before they came to the attention of the military police who, on apprehending them for some minor misdemeanour such as being incorrectly dressed, became suspicious when they discovered that they spoke no English. Any arrest was followed swiftly by an order to release the individuals concerned. Eventually, the local representative of the Security Service on the island was compelled to provide some form of explanation to the military police and subsequently there were no further problems.

SIS, from the start, had decided that the simplest method of infiltration would be landings from the sea. Frank Quinn located a suitable diesel-powered craft in Malta and SIS had recruited an elderly but experienced sailor to captain it. Having been flown to Malta, however, he promptly fell ill and had to be evacuated to London where he subsequently died. Meanwhile the head of the SIS Athens station, Commander Patrick Whinney, who had commanded the African Coastal Flotilla, one of the clandestine naval units operating in the Mediterranean in support of SOE, OSS and other Allied special forces during the war, had engaged the services of two ex-naval officers, John Leatham and Sam

Barclay. During the first half of 1948, he had employed them and their ketch, *Bessie*, to run arms and supplies from Athens to Salonika for Greek government forces during the civil war. In August, *Bessie* had been sold off and next month Leatham and Barclay had ordered a new craft, a Greek caique (schooner), to be built for them. The expense soon exceeded their budget but fortunately, towards the end of the year, Whinney learned of their plight and offered to cover the cost of completion and the installation of a powerful engine. In return, Leatham and Barclay agreed to join the operation.

The new boat, christened *Stormie Seas*, was launched on 15 December and minus her engine, which was to be fitted in Malta, sailed from Piraeus on 18 February 1949, subsequently being towed through the Corinth Canal to Patras from where she embarked across the Mediterranean. After suffering damage caused by a violent storm, she arrived in Malta on 31 March. Shortly afterwards, Leatham and Barclay flew to London for a briefing by SIS while repairs were carried out on their boat and the engine was installed. By the middle of September, she was ready to play her part in Operation VALUABLE.

The 'pixies', meanwhile, were completing their training and on 28 September nine of them embarked from a cove near Fort Benjimma and boarded a Royal Navy motor fishing vessel (MFV) in which they sailed for the port of Otranto, on the tip of the heel of Italy. On the following day, *Stormie Seas* left Malta and also headed for Otranto; in addition to Leatham and Barclay, and their Greek boatman Dino Mavros, there were five other people aboard: Barclay's wife, Eileen, whose presence was designed to give the impression that it was a family aboard the vessel; 'Lofty' Cooling and 'Derby' Allen; a radio operator named Geoffrey Kelly and SIS officer Rollo Young.

Three days later, on 2 October, the MFV sailed from the Italian port, followed an hour or so later by the caique. Once over the horizon from Otranto, the two vessels sailed for a rendezvous location twenty miles east of the port. There the nine 'pixies', together with their arms and equipment, were transferred to *Stormie Seas* which then headed across the Strait of Otranto for the coast of Albania. That night, however, a violent electric storm rose and the boat was struck by lightning which damaged the radio, putting it out of action. A landing in such conditions was impossible and so Leatham and Barclay put into a cove on the small

Greek island of Othoni where the vessel spent out the rest of the night at anchor.

The following morning saw the unwelcome sight of a Greek customs launch approaching. Fortunately, however, its crew did not board the caique, and after a friendly exchange of conversation and a cigarette, it went on its way to the vast relief of all aboard. During the late afternoon, with the radio repaired, Leatham and Barclay weighed anchor and headed for the Albanian coast. The landing point, which was the exact spot from which Smiley and McLean had been evacuated at the end of their CONCENSUS mission in November 1943, was in a small cove located south of Valona on the Karaburun peninsula. Prior to the start of the operation, Smiley had inspected recent air photographs taken of the area, verifying there were no new buildings or tracks since he had last been there, before selecting it once again. A goat track led up from the cove through the cliffs and up a mountainside covered in thick scrub which provided good cover, avoiding any villages or houses until it reached the road linking Valona and Himara.

Arriving off the cove at about 9.00 p.m. that night, Leatham and Barclay hove to approximately half a mile offshore. 'Lofty' Cooling and five of the 'pixies' transferred into a surf boat towed behind *Stormie Seas* and headed for the shore, followed by 'Derby' Allen in the caique's dinghy bringing the weapons and equipment. It was a moonless night as they rowed the two boats toward the shore, the only illumination being provided by distant lightning. It took an hour or so before the remaining four 'pixies' and their equipment had been landed and *Stormie Seas* could leave the area and head back for Malta.

The only detailed account of the events that followed the landing appears in Nicholas Bethell's book *Betrayed*. According to this, the nine Albanians climbed the track out of the cove and up the mountainside above, making their way along the ridge of the peninsula. Avoiding well-used tracks and sources of water, such as streams, which they well knew could be locations for ambushes, they travelled under cover of darkness and lay up by day, hiding in caves. Forty-eight hours later they reached Mount Tragjas, some ten miles to the east of their landing place. There they split into two groups: five men, led by Bido Kuka, headed for their home region of Kurvelesh, near the border with Greece, while the remaining four turned north towards Valona.

Within a few hours, however, the latter group was ambushed by Albanian troops lying in wait for them. Three men were killed but the fourth succeeded in escaping. Meanwhile, as Kuka's group approached the village of Gjorm, it was warned of the presence of government security forces in the area and took refuge in nearby caves. Kuka and his companions also learned of their comrades' fate and were told that the Albanian army had deployed units throughout the coastal region.

The SIS radio monitoring station, meanwhile, based in a large villa on the north-east coast of Corfu, listened for the 'pixies' to come up on the air. Together with Alan Hare and his team of radio operators were two of the instructors from Malta, Jani Dilo and Abdyl Sino, acting as interpreters. It was not until 12 October, nine days after the landing, that the first message was received from Kuka's group hiding near Gjorm, telling of the ambush and the deaths of three of the 'pixies'. Maintenance of communications was proving difficult for the surviving group. In order to use its radio, it was forced to leave its hiding place in the caves near the village and move to a suitable location on high ground from which transmission could be made. The pedal-propelled generator itself caused a major problem: bulky and highly susceptible to damage, it made a loud whining noise when operated by a man sitting on its unfolded frame and pedalling to create sufficient power.

After leaving Gjorm, Kuka and his companions made their way to their home town of Nivica, in the area of Kurvelesh. There they rested while carrying out the initial phase of their mission, approaching those whom they trusted and broaching the subject of opposition to the Hoxha regime. But their proposals for the formation of resistance groups, financed and supported by Britain and the United States which would drop arms and equipment, met with a mixed response. While some were enthusiastic, others questioned why only five men had been sent and why agents and weapons had not been dropped as they had been during the war. Only when they saw real commitment by the British and the Americans would they take the idea seriously.

In late October, Kuka and the rest of his group decided to split up and make their way to Greece to report their findings. The journey would be arduous and dangerous, across mountains patrolled by government troops. Bido Kuka and two others, Hysen Isufi and Ramis Matuka, set off along one route while his cousin, Ahmet Kuka, and the fifth member of the group, Turhan Aliko, took another. The latter pair had an uneventful journey, reaching Greece without incident, but the other three were not so fortunate and encountered government patrols more than once. One such encounter took place at night while they were making their way through a ravine; they were challenged by police and opened fire but in the ensuing firefight Ramis Matuka was killed. Bido Kuka and Hysen Isufi, however, managed to escape and eventually reached the border.

On 10 October, meanwhile, another group of eleven 'pixies' had been landed north of Valona. Although the landing itself was completed successfully, *Stormie Seas* was unable to clear the area by dawn due to a strong headwind blowing up while the landing was taking place. As the winds increased to storm force, Leatham and Barclay, out of reach of either the Greek or Italian coasts and having sailed only a few miles southward, were forced to seek shelter and entered the Gulf of Valona, well aware that there was a Russian submarine base on Saseno Island to their starboard.

On the following morning, any hopes that they might escape detection were dashed when troops were observed taking up positions on the beach only some 100 yards away. Shouted demands for the caique's crew to come ashore were ignored and when the crew spotted a light machine gun being set up on the beach, John Leatham severed the anchor rope. *Stormie Seas* departed at speed, pursued by a hail of machine-gun fire which fortunately passed harmlessly overhead. Despite the strong gale still blowing, the vessel succeeded in struggling into harbour on Corfu on the morning of 13 October.

The eleven 'pixies', meanwhile, had split into two groups, five men heading for Korçe and the remainder for Gjirokaster. The leader of the Korçe group, Sefer Muço, was welcomed by villagers but he and his companions hid in a cave high on a mountainside to minimise the risk of betrayal. By the end of October, however, winter had arrived and heavy snow which revealed their tracks was making life difficult for the five guerrillas. Meanwhile, travelling by night and lying up in woods or caves by day, the six-man Gjirokaster group had followed a carefully planned route with the aid of air photographs which proved to be of more use than the maps with which they had been issued. Eventually reaching Gjirokaster, they made contact with their families and friends but soon met the same lukewarm reaction encountered earlier by Bido Kuka and the other members of the first group landed on 3 October. They succeeded in establishing radio contact with the SIS radio station on Corfu but reception was difficult because of the mountainous terrain. A further problem developed when the generator became inoperable and so, leaving their radio with the cousin of Haki Gaba, one of their number, the group made its way to the Greek border, only some thirteen miles away, in the hope that it could obtain a replacement and return.

In the meantime, due to the problems caused by the snow, the Korçe group had moved to a new hiding place further down the mountainside below the snow line, although this increased the risk of discovery. Unlike the Gjirokaster group, it experienced little difficulty in maintaining contact with Corfu and it was with relief that it received a signal one evening, ordering it to return to Greece.

Having obtained a replacement generator, two members of the Gjirokaster group, Bardhyl Gerveshi and Haki Gaba, made their way back into Albania. On contacting Gaba's brother Betas, however, they learned that his cousin, with whom they had left the radio, had been arrested. The latter had apparently attempted to recruit a friend for anti-communist operations but had been betrayed to the authorities and arrested. Realising that any further efforts in the area were futile, the two men withdrew and, taking Betas Gaba with them, returned to Greece.

The first two VALUABLE missions thus ended in failure. Part of the blame for this has been laid at the door of Kim Philby who had arrived in Washington on 8 October to take over from Peter Dwyer as SIS's representative. As such, he was a member of the Special Policy Committee (SPC), the joint SIS/OPC body established to oversee the operation in Albania, the US element of which was codenamed FIEND. Prior to taking up his post, he had been given a series of detailed briefings in London which, according to Nicholas Bethell in *Betrayed*, included information about VALUABLE. He would therefore have been privy to details of the two landings to be carried out in October and, in Bethell's opinion, passed them to his KGB controller in London before his departure for the United States towards the end of September.

In addition to SIS and OPC, the State Department and the Foreign

Office also had seats on the SPC, the Foreign Office being represented by the Earl of Jellicoe who was based at the British embassy as a first secretary responsible for Balkan affairs. As Nicholas Bethell states in his book, Jellicoe later recalled frequent meetings with Philby at which they read SIS and Foreign Office telegrams giving details of VALUABLE's progress. According to Jellicoe, Philby was responsible for making operational decisions jointly with his OPC counterpart, James McCargar.

Following the first two landings and the subsequent debriefings of the surviving sixteen 'pixies', it was plain that the Albanian government had received prior warnings of the landings. Although much of the blame for this would later be attributed to Philby, it was also subsequently acknowledged that security within the Albanian émigré organisations was poor and that they had been heavily penetrated by the Soviet KGB. Indeed, the latter would ultimately boast that it had penetrated virtually every anti-communist organisation throughout the free world.

There is no doubt that the efforts of Amery, McLean and Hare in drawing together the three principal Albanian factions would soon have attracted the attention of the Hoxha regime, as well as that of the Soviets, which would surely have devoted some of its own intelligence assets among the émigré communities in Italy and Greece to discovering what was afoot. The Italian intelligence service had obviously been forewarned by its agents within the Independenza group; on the morning of 2 October it had officers positioned on top of the lighthouse at Otranto from where they were able observe the transfer of the 'pixies' from the Royal Navy MFV to *Stormie Seas*.

It is possible that the Soviets may have struck back at the Albanian émigré factions at precisely the time that the first landing took place. On 26 August, the formation of the Albanian National Committee was announced at a press conference given in Paris. Thereafter, five members of the committee, including Abas Kupi and Midhat Frasheri, travelled to London where they were met by another former member of SOE, Peter Kemp, who had served in Albania alongside McLean, Smiley and Amery. During September they flew to New York and then to Washington where they were hosted by the Committee for Free Europe, a newly formed organisation later revealed as being financed by the CIA. As in London, however, Midhat and his delegation received a lukewarm reception and a request to meet President Truman was refused, the US government being anxious to distance itself from the Albanian National Committee in order to ensure that Operation FIEND remained deniable.

The delegation then returned to New York where Frasheri and Nuçi Kota remained to establish an office while the rest flew back to Rome. In the early hours of 3 October, as the first group of 'pixies' were landing on the Albanian coast from *Stormie Seas*, the police were called to the hotel where Frasheri and Kota were staying in Manhattan. There they found the former lying dead on his bed, having apparently died of a heart attack. A post-mortem stated that this was the cause of death and there was no evidence to dispute the verdict. While there is no proof that Frasheri was murdered by the MGB, there is sufficient reason to believe this may have been the case. It was not until after the murder in 1959 of the Ukrainian OUNB leader Stephan Bandera, and the subsequent revelations concerning the special pistol used by Bogdan Stashinsky (as described in Chapter 1), that further credibility could be given to claims that Frasheri had been the victim of an MGB assassin.

The OPC, meanwhile, was preparing to launch the first of its FIEND operations. During the first half of 1950, through the Albanian National Council, it began to recruit a force of 250 Albanians who would be enlisted into a labour unit of the US Army in West Germany. Commanded by an American officer and designated Company 4000, it would be based near the Bavarian state capital of Munich and comprise three platoons under Albanian officers and NCOs. At the same time, a guerrilla training school was established in a large house situated in secluded grounds near Heidelberg, in Baden-Württemberg in the south-west of the country. The first batch of recruits arrived at the unit's barracks at Karlsfeld, some fifteen miles from Munich, on the morning of 7 June. Six days later, they began their initial training to prepare them for the duties required by their cover role, that of guarding a large arms dump.

As the members of Company 4000 began their training, SIS was preparing to despatch a third group into Albania. In April Lieutenant Colonel David Smiley left Malta, his place being taken by Anthony Northrop who had also served in Albania with SOE, and moved to Greece where he took up the cover post of GSO 1 (Operations and Intelligence) with the British Military Mission in Athens. It had been decided that groups would henceforth infiltrate over the Greek border into Albania, and in July, accompanied by Captains 'Doc' Zaehner and Abdyl

Sino as conducting officers, a six-man group of 'pixies' was flown from Malta to Athens where it stayed at an SIS safe house in Kifissia before flying to a military airfield at Yanina in northern Greece. The mission had to aborted, however, following the group's arrival at Yanina and a disagreement with Greek intelligence officers which led to the 'pixies' being detained in a cell. On the following day, Zaehner and Sino returned to Kifissia with their charges.

David Smiley set to work using his contacts within the Greek intelligence service to ensure there was no repeat of the Yanina fiasco. Two months later, the six 'pixies' were taken north by road in a convoy of cars; on this occasion their conducting officers were Colonel Dayrell Oakley-Hill, recruited back into SIS service for the operation, Abdyl Sino, and two Greek officers who accompanied the group during the final approach to the border.

After crossing the border, the 'pixies', led by Sefer Muço, set off for the area of Korçe. Once again, however, misfortune struck when an OPC aircraft, carrying out a leaflet drop as part of the propaganda war against the Hoxha regime, dropped its load around Korçe instead of Gjirokaster. As a result, the area was infested by Albanian security forces sent in to gather up the leaflets, causing Muço and his companions considerable anxiety as they hid in a cave. The group was due to rendezvous with another three 'pixies' but they never appeared. It transpired that careless talk by the mother of one of them had resulted in his arrest when next visiting his village. His two companions had immediately returned to Greece. They were followed by Muço's group which by then had spent almost two months in Albania and had decided that it was too risky to remain in the Korçe area any longer.

Other groups had also been infiltrated into Albania by way of the Greek border, and during November a further two were landed by sea. Leatham and Barclay had earlier been paid off, along with *Stormie Seas*, the latter's place being taken by *Henrietta*, a converted Luftwaffe high speed air-sea rescue launch captained by James Blackburn, a former RAF officer. Both groups were captured almost immediately after landing and thus achieved nothing.

By the end of 1950 it had become apparent to Anthony Northrop and his team in Malta that VALUABLE was making little headway. Morale among the 'pixies' was low and Northrop himself began to harbour doubts about the feasibility of continuing the operation in view of the tight control being maintained throughout most of Albania by Enver Hoxha's security forces. The population was mostly cowed by fear and reluctant either to provide support or become involved in anti-communist activities. Such conditions made it virtually impossible for the 'pixies' to carry out their allotted missions. The total lack of success led senior elements within SIS to become highly critical of the 'pixies', blaming them and putting pressure on Northrop to produce results. Their concern, however, was wholly selfish, as VALUABLE was the principal British effort to counter Stalin's activities in Eastern Europe and its failure would harm the interests of those ultimately responsible for it. They spared little thought for those who risked lengthy imprisonment or death at the hands of Hoxha's brutal regime.

During 1950 there were further signs of the lack of security surrounding the operation. On 27 March, *The New York Times* published an article by its Mediterranean correspondent, Cyrus Sulzberger, stating that two groups had been landed in Albania with the mission of establishing contact with anti-communist elements. When taken to task by OPC FIEND chief James McCargar, Sulzberger retorted that he had obtained his information from a variety of sources among whom the operation was common knowledge. Thus it would appear that poor security, as well as Kim Philby's treachery, played a key role in compromising VALUABLE.

BY THIS TIME Albania had withdrawn its support for the Greek communist guerrillas of the Democratic Army and hence one of the aims of VALUABLE had been achieved. On 25 June 1950, however, North Korea invaded its southern neighbour without warning and the United States was sucked into the ensuing conflict. Inevitably, Moscow's hand was seen behind this latest communist incursion into the free world, lending added impetus to VALUABLE and putting pressure on OPC to launch its own groups into the field.

October 1950 saw OPC's first group of sixteen Albanians from Company 4000, a mixture of Zogist and republicans, undergoing guerrilla training at the school near Heidelberg. Unlike their SIS-trained counterparts, they would be parachuted into Albania but were given only the most basic ground training, merely being taught the rudiments of landing. Their instruction lasted less than a month and during the second week of November they were flown to Athens where they were accommodated in an OPC safe house prior to being dropped into northern Albania. At this juncture, however, eight of them refused to continue with the mission and only the remainder, plus a last-minute volunteer, Iliaz Toptani, who had previously served with the French Foreign Legion, took off on the evening of 10 November in an unmarked DC-3 flown by Polish aircrew who had served in the RAF during the war.

One group of five, led by Adem Gjura, was to be dropped on a drop zone (DZ) on the Martenesh Plain (used on a number of occasions by SOE during the war), the other near Kukës in the north-eastern region of Lüme. Poor visibility, however, prevented the aircraft from finding the first DZ and so the flight was aborted. Nine days later, the mission was launched again and once again the DZ could not be located. Nevertheless, on this occasion the first group decided to jump blind. Gjura and three of his companions, Sali Daliu, Seli Daci and Xhetan Daci, all landed in woods near Bulqizë, 25 miles north-east of Tirana. Iliaz Toptani was missing; it later transpired that he had been betrayed and captured after seeking shelter from local inhabitants. Of the group's equipment containers there was also no sign.

The aircraft meanwhile continued its flight north-eastward towards the area of Kukës. Once again, however, the pilot was unable to locate the DZ in the area of Degë and the second group similarly jumped blind. Its containers were released shortly afterwards but landed in the village of Zarrisht which was some six hours march away.

Unsure of their location, Adem Gjura and his three companions spent the night in the woods near where they had landed. They were still there on the following day when, during the afternoon, they were surrounded by Albanian security forces. Breaking out of their hide in two pairs, the four guerrillas made a bid for freedom but Xhetan Daci was shot dead and Selim Daci captured. Gjura and Daliu, however, managed to escape although the latter was wounded in the leg. Having shaken off their pursuers, they headed for Gjura's village, but progress was painfully slow because of Daliu's wound and they were forced to travel by night and lie up by day. Meanwhile, they learned from sympathetic villagers that their arrival had been expected and that Albanian troops had moved into the area two days before the drop; not only had the latter known that the guerrillas would be dropped by parachute but they were also aware that Adem Gjura would be among them. It was only the inaccuracy of the drop that had saved them from being captured immediately after landing.

After travelling south to Elbasan, where they were sheltered for two weeks, Gjura and Daliu decided to resume their attempt to escape from Albania by making for Yugoslavia. Heading east, they eventually reached the border and with the help of a guide, crossed into Yugoslavia where they were imprisoned for several months. When the Albanian security forces learned of Gjura's escape, they took reprisals by arresting and imprisoning his entire family, subsequently shooting two of them.

The second group had also avoided capture because of the inaccuracy of their drop. The landing of its containers in the middle of Zarrisht had, however, alerted police and it was not long before the entire area was teeming with troops. The four guerrillas, nevertheless, avoided capture and, after lying up for five days, headed east towards the border region of Lumë and the village of one member of the group, Halil Nerguti. The weather was deteriorating, with heavy snowfalls, and after some four weeks they changed their plans and in mid-December 1950 crossed into Yugoslavia, making their way to the town of Prizren. There they recruited a number of Albanian volunteers to return home and accomplish their mission. Meanwhile, having received no communication from either group, OPC despatched the Polish aircrew in its DC-3 over both areas in a series of fruitless attempts to establish radio contact.

Early 1951 saw further disasters for OPC. In January, the latter dropped 43 guerrillas in northern Albania; but these were soon intercepted by Albanian security forces who killed 29 and captured the rest. Despite this major setback, another group was dropped in February and managed to reach its intended area of operations where it enjoyed some success in organising anti-communist resistance. This, however, was short-lived and in early May, after some members of the group had been caught, the survivors made their way to Yugoslavia where they were arrested and imprisoned.

In London and Washington, meanwhile, long-harboured suspicions of a highly placed mole in SIS had centred on Kim Philby following the disappearance and flight to the Soviet Union in late May 1951 of Guy

Burgess and another member of the Foreign Office, Donald Maclean. Both men, like Philby, were long-serving Soviet agents, having been recruited while at Cambridge University during the early 1930s. Maclean was now head of the American Department at the Foreign Office and Philby had warned Burgess that Maclean was under suspicion. Shortly afterwards, Burgess, who was given to outrageous behaviour, was recalled to London for disciplinary reasons. Fearing arrest, he and Maclean fled to Moscow on 25 May.

A few days later Philby was also recalled to London where he was questioned by a leading barrister and wartime Security Service officer, Helenus 'Buster' Milmo, who failed to obtain any evidence of Philby's treachery. Even so, there was by this time sufficient cause at senior levels within the Security Service and SIS to believe that Philby had been working for the Soviets, fuelled not least by the disastrous results of VALUABLE and FIEND which he had been jointly controlling from Washington with Jim McCargar until the latter was replaced by another OPC officer, Gratian Yatsevich. This, coupled with a threat from the Director of Central Intelligence, General Walter Bedell Smith, to sever all connections between SIS and the CIA, was sufficient for SIS to retire Philby forthwith.

Yet despite the setbacks suffered earlier in the year, OPC continued to expand its operations in Albania and by June 1951 there were a further 40 members of Company 4000 undergoing training. In April, SIS landed two four-man groups of 'pixies', with two more being inserted in June. During the latter part of July, sixteen members of Company 4000 arrived in Athens for OPC's next operation. Three days later, three groups of four were dropped respectively in the areas of Gjirokaster in the south, Kavaja on the coast in the centre of the country, and Scutaria (aka Shkodër) in the north. Once again, the Albanian security forces appeared to have been forewarned. Two of the Gjirokaster group were killed and the other two captured, while all four members of the group dropped at Kavaja were trapped in a house and killed after government forces set it alight. The Shkodër group, meanwhile, were surrounded and killed immediately after they landed.

In October, the two surviving members of the Gjirokaster group, Kasem Shehu and Muhamet Hoxha, were put on trial along with twelve others who included Selim Daci and Iliaz Toptani, captured after being dropped with Adem Gjura's group in November. All four OPC-trained guerrillas were found guilty and jailed: Toptani and Daci were given life imprisonment while Shehu and Hoxha received twenty years each. It became apparent during the trial, details of which were broadcast world-wide, that the four had revealed, under interrogation and torture, every-thing about their recruitment, training and missions as well as identities of other members of Company 4000.

Undeterred by the fact that FIEND was compromised, OPC pressed on and dropped five more guerrillas on the night of 15 October into the eastern region of Dibra, the group's leader, Hysen Salku, sustaining a broken leg on landing. At dawn on the following day, as the group came under attack from Albanian troops, Salku and another man, Hysen Bajrami, were killed. The remaining three, Ramazan Dalipi, Hajrulla Terpeza and Hakik Abdullah, escaped and headed for the border with Yugoslavia which they reached four days later. Since all were Albanians with homes in Yugoslavia, they made their way to Dalipi's home town of Krcova where they spent several days before resuming their journey back to Greece where they arrived on 31 October.

Despite the total lack of success achieved by either VALUABLE or FIEND, SIS continued its participation. In early 1952, a number of Albanians underwent training in Britain, after which they were returned to Fort Benjimma in Malta. During that summer, four landings were carried out from *Henrietta* but the 'pixies', well aware of the losses suffered and the lack of success achieved by VALUABLE, were becoming increasingly disillusioned; so, too, were many in SIS. Moreover, the death of Ernest Bevin on 14 March 1951 saw the removal of one of the prime movers behind the operation. At the end of 1952, SIS wound up VALUABLE and within a few months Fort Benjimma was closed down with the staff and remaining 'pixies' paid off and dispersed.

OPC meanwhile persisted with FIEND. A special eight-man team was recruited early in 1952 to carry out seaborne landings on the Albanian coast. Unlike other OPC groups, their training lasted several months; in addition to the normal range of guerrilla skills, they received instruction in radio communications and the use of ciphers. They were inserted by high-speed craft operating from Panaghia, one of the three Kalanissia islands sit-uated north of Corinth, which was also a base for CIA operations being conducted in Bulgaria and elsewhere, including the Soviet Union.

Early in 1952, OPC also assembled a small group of royalists for a particular mission. This followed a visit in the summer of 1951 to the United States by King Zog who was concerned at the lack of success achieved by FIEND. While meeting with OPC officers, including FIEND controller Gatian Yatsevich, he suggested that members of his Royal Guard, which had accompanied him into exile in 1939, should be recruited for an operation to determine the reasons for FIEND's failures. Gratian Yatsevich subsequently travelled to Egypt and, with the assistance of the commander of the Royal Guard, Colonel Hysen Selmani, selected three individuals: Zenel Shehu, Halil Branica and Haxhi Gjyle. Early in March 1952, the three men travelled by ship from Alexandria to Marseilles, and then by train to Paris. There they were met by OPC officers with whom they travelled by car to Germany and an OPC safe house near Munich. A week later they continued their journey to Greece where they arrived on 26 March.

During the following four weeks, they underwent instruction which comprised mainly map-reading, navigation and weapon training, and were introduced to Hamit Matjani and two others, Xhelo Tresova and Tahir Prenci. On 27 April all six were flown from Athens to Kastoria from where, on the following day, they were escorted by Greek intelligence officers fifteen miles to the border. Shortly after crossing it, however, Halil Branica fell ill and was forced to return to Greece while the others pressed on to Matjani's home area of Mati. Having reached it, Matjani, Tresova and Gjyle returned to Greece leaving Shehu and Prenci, a radio operator, with a group of anti-communist sympathisers recruited by Matjani the previous year. During the following months OPC regularly received messages from Prenci who informed his base that he and Shehu had recruited more sympathisers, including three members of Enver Hoxha's much-feared secret police, the Sigurimi. On 4 August Halil Branica, fully recovered from his illness, was dropped into Albania to join Shehu and Prenci.

While Gratian Yatsevich and others in OPC responsible for FIEND began to believe that the tide had finally turned in their favour, one matter was cause for concern. As described in Chapter 1, every radio operator using morse code has his own style, known as a 'fist', which becomes easily recognisable to a trained base operator. Prenci's 'fist', like all others, had been recorded and studied by those listening for it.

Shortly after his transmissions commenced, they showed noticeable signs of change, but Prenci explained this by saying that he had broken his right arm and was therefore transmitting with his left hand.

As the months went by, Shehu and Prenci reported that their network was expanding and now included a number of police and army officers disenchanted with Enver Hoxha's regime. They requested that Matjani rejoin them in order to escort some of the officers back into Greece for discussions on mounting a *coup d'état*. OPC was, however, still anxious about Prenci's 'fist' and the possibility that he had been captured and replaced by another operator, or was transmitting under duress. As recounted in Chapter 1, the MGB and security forces in the Baltic states had carried out such deception operations which had proved totally successful in snaring agents and destroying British and US networks. Prior to that, during the war, the German Abwehr (military intelligence service) in the Netherlands had conducted a long-running radio deception operation codenamed NORTH POLE which had resulted in the penetration and destruction of all SOE networks in the country.

The proper procedure was for further security checks to be carried out by asking Prenci a series of questions to which only he would have known the correct answers. According to Nicholas Bethell in *Betrayed*, one such query related to the fact that Prenci had left his valuables in the care of King Zog's wife, Queen Geraldine, something known only to him. The question requesting details of their whereabouts met with an irritated response from Prenci, telling OPC not to waste his time. Instead of treating this as cause for further concern, however, OPC disregarded the matter and agreed that Matjani should be dropped back into Albania.

On 1 May 1953 Matjani and two companions, Naum Sula and Gani Malushi, were dropped into the Mati area and during the following weeks a series of messages continued to assure OPC that all was well. After a while, however, it became apparent that little was happening and once again doubts began to resurface about the authenticity of the transmissions. On 31 December, all was revealed when the Albanian government announced over national radio that Matjani, Shehu, Branica, Sula and Malushi were all in prison awaiting trial. Shehu and Prenci had apparently been captured shortly after Matjani had left them in Mati and returned to Greece. Of Prenci there was no mention and his fate remained unknown, although it was suspected by some that he had been a communist agent.

Matjani and his companions were brought to trial at the beginning of April 1954, the proceedings being broadcast for all the world to hear. Under interrogation by the Sigurimi, they had not only revealed the details of their mission but also much information relating to FIEND over the previous five years. Moreover, it transpired that the Sigurimi, with Soviet assistance, had been conducting a radio deception operation for eighteen months which resulted in the complete destruction of the FIEND networks in Albania. On 12 April, Matjani was sentenced to death by hanging; his four companions were to be executed by firing squad.

After the trial, a systematic campaign of terror was launched by the Hoxha regime which conducted a witch-hunt for anti-communists throughout the country, executing those it deemed guilty; according to Bethell, some 400 people from the Mati area alone were executed. Elsewhere, large numbers were arrested and imprisoned, the total throughout the whole of Albania reportedly reaching several thousand.

During the ensuing weeks, FIEND was wound up by OPC, which in August 1952 had been absorbed into the CIA's Directorate of Plans, formed during that year as its new covert operations arm. Company 4000 was disbanded while the training school near Heidelberg and the base on Panaghia were dismantled. The SIS 'pixies' and their OPC counterparts were meanwhile dispersed to new homes in Britain, the United States and elsewhere. According to Stephen Dorril, by the time the operation was finally terminated approximately 200 of their number had been lost to the communists.

In hindsight it can be seen that the principal aim of VALUABLE/FIEND, the toppling of the Hoxha regime, had been in no way feasible and that the operation itself was built on foundations of sand, particularly in view of the limited resources allocated to it by the OPC and SIS. By the time it was launched, Albania had been under communist rule for six years during which Enver Hoxha had maintained an iron grip. In 1945 he began a programme of ruthless social re-engineering with agrarian reform which broke up the large estates of the powerful beys, whose power was destroyed as their lands were distributed to peasants. Shortly afterwards, however, all agriculture was collectivised and the peasants lost title to their newly acquired properties. Meanwhile, all industry, commercial organisations and banks were nationalised.

Hoxha also turned his attention to the former predominantly royalist areas of northern Albania and their clans whose semi-feudal institutions and patriarchal structures were dismantled by the new socialist order, which destroyed the power of the bajraktars. Domination of the country was maintained by the Sigurimi, which penetrated all areas of the population and established a wide network of informers who picked up even the slightest whisper of dissent which was swiftly crushed.

In the light of these facts, it would appear that those who proposed Albania as fertile ground for an anti-communist insurrection were misinformed about, and thus badly misjudged, the situation in the country, doubtless misled by those keen to see Britain and the United States topple the Hoxha regime on their behalf. If Abas Kupi, Midhat Frasheri and the other émigré leaders were expecting Anglo-American support to the tune of that supplied during the war, they were soon disabused of that notion. The fact that no large quantities of arms and equipment were dropped following the insertions of SIS and OPC agents was without doubt a major factor in the failure of the latter to persuade the local population to join them in organising a rebellion against the Hoxha regime. As mentioned earlier in this chapter, poor security also appears to have a played a major role in enabling the communists to counter VALUABLE/FIEND so effectively. Moreover, the Sigurimi reportedly planted numbers of agents among Albanian émigré organisations abroad among whom security was so poor that the police would quickly have picked up details of the operation.

Ever since VALUABLE/FIEND ended, there has been no satisfactory answer to the question of why SIS and the OPC continued with the operation long after it became all too apparent that it was making no headway and a considerable number of casualties had been incurred. Furthermore, long-concealed suspicion of Kim Philby, who had played a controlling role and whose treachery was undoubtedly largely responsible for the failure of the operation, surfaced in June 1951 following the defection to Moscow of Guy Burgess and Donald Maclean. Yet VALUABLE was not terminated until the end of 1952 and FIEND not until mid-1954. It is difficult to believe that the possibility of the operation having been compromised by Philby did not occur in some minds when SIS, presumably, carried out a damage assessment after dismissing him from its ranks at the end of July 1951. It can only be assumed that there were those in SIS and OPC who were reluctant to admit failure for their own ends, particularly in the light of the effort and resources that had been channelled into the operation.

The final word in this sorry saga belongs to a CIA officer who summed up the operation with the following words:

> The Albanian operation was the first and only attempt by Washington to unseat a Communist regime within the Soviet orbit by paramilitary means. It taught a clear lesson to the war planners. Even a weak regime could not be overthrown by covert paramilitary means alone.

CHAPTER THREE

INDOCHINA 1950–1954

During the years that Britain and the United States were engaged in their attempt to limit Soviet expansionism in Eastern Europe and the Balkans, on the other side of the globe France was heavily involved in efforts to stem the communist takeover of her empire in Indochina: this region comprised the countries of Vietnam (consisting of Tonkin, Annam and Cochin China), Laos and Cambodia.

The invasion and conquest of Asia by the Japanese during 1941–2 had overrun parts of the colonial empires of Britain, France and the Netherlands. The populations in those regions saw their former colonial masters as no longer invincible and this inevitably strengthened demands for independence and self-determination. This was certainly the case in Indochina where the defeat of France by Germany in June 1940, followed by the occupation of the region by Japan, served to encourage the establishment of an indigenous resistance movement whose ultimate aim was freedom from French rule.

September 1940 saw the first outbreak of hostilities in Indo-China after the French stalled a request by Japan to allow its forces to march through northern Vietnam to attack the Chinese nationalist forces of General Chiang Kai Shek in the southern Chinese province of Yunnan, cutting them off from supplies from the United States being shipped into the country via the port of Haiphong. The French Vichy government of Marshal Philippe Pétain, which on 19 June had signed an armistice with Germany, was in the process of negotiating with Japan when on 22 September the latter's forces crossed into northern Vietnam at Lang Son and Dong Gang and attacked a number of French forts over a front of some 30 miles. The fighting lasted two days until ammunition supplies were exhausted, by which time the French had suffered 800 killed.

On 24 September, Japanese aircraft bombed Haiphong which that evening was the scene of landings by troops who proceeded to march on Hanoi, the capital of Tonkin. The Vichy regime, to which the French administration in Indochina had remained loyal following the fall of

France, capitulated without further ado and signed an agreement permitting Japanese forces to be based in the region.

At the beginning of 1941 war broke out between French Indo-China and Thailand. Hostilities ceased on 28 January after the intervention of Japan which negotiated a ceasefire, followed by an agreement which was signed on 11 March whereby the French ceded to Thailand two provinces in Laos and three in Cambodia.

January meanwhile saw the arrival in Indochina of a man named Nguyen Ai Quoc, who would subsequently gain international renown under his pseudonym of Ho Chi Minh. A communist since 1920 and one of the founders of the Indochinese Communist Party (ICP) formed in 1930, he was swift to exploit the recently exposed weakness of the French colonial authorities following the occupation of the country by Japan. Crossing from China into Tonkin, Ho Chi Minh made his way to Pac Bao, in Cao Bang Province, where he established his headquarters. Two months later, after a meeting of the central committee of the ICP, a national resistance movement was formed with the title of Viet Nam Doc Lap Dong Minh Hoi (League for the Revolution and Independence of Viet Nam) – or, for convenience, Viet Minh. Command of its military wing went to an individual who would subsequently become equally renowned in the annals of guerrilla warfare, Vo Nguyen Giap. A former schoolmaster, he had become a communist in 1930 and fled to China in 1939 following a crackdown on communists by the French authorities.

The Viet Minh began its initial operations in the Bac Son region of northern Vietnam where the Tho tribes had already been engaged in an insurrection against the French. From there, it began to extend its influence throughout the other northern provinces. Short of arms, it concentrated its attacks on easy targets such as isolated border posts manned by small units of border guards known as Gardes Indochinoises.

By the beginning of 1945, the Japanese were concerned that the French in Indochina might turn against them in the event of Allied landings. They were aware that the Free French of General Charles de Gaulle had infiltrated a number of personnel into the region and established a clandestine radio communications network. This had been carried out by the Direction Générale des Etudes et Recherches (DGER), the French foreign intelligence service formed in November

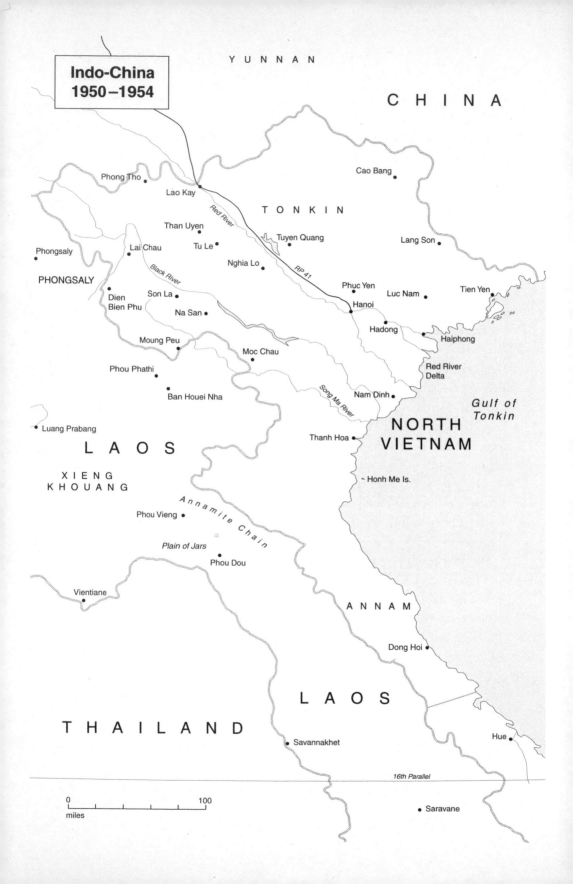

**Indo-China
1950–1954**

Y U N N A N

C H I N A

Phong Tho

Lao Kay

Cao Bang

T O N K I N

Than Uyen

Tuyen Quang

Lang Son

Phongsaly

Lai Chau

Tu Le

Red River

Nghia Lo

RP 41

Phuc Yen

Luc Nam

Tien Yen

PHONGSALY

Black River

Dien
Bien Phu

Son La

Na San

Hanoi

Hadong

Haiphong

Moung Peu

Moc Chau

Nam Dinh

Red River
Delta

Phou Phathi

Song Ma River

Ban Houei Nha

Thanh Hoa

Gulf of
Tonkin

Luang Prabang

L A O S

NORTH
VIETNAM

X I E N G
K H O U A N G

Honh Me Is.

A
n
n
a
m
i
t
e
C
h
a
i
n

Phou Vieng

Plain of Jars

Phou Dou

Vientiane

A N N A M

Dong Hoi

L A O S

T H A I L A N D

Savannakhet

Hue

16th Parallel

0   100
miles

Saravane

**Indo-China
1950–1954**

Savannakhet

Hue

Da Nang

L A O S

A N N A M

THAILAND

Saravane

Cu Lao Re Is.

Bolovens Plateau

Quang Ngai

Pakse

Paksong

Attapu

Kon Plong

Kon Tum

S O U T H
V I E T N A M

C A M B O D I A

R. Mekong

Hon Quan

Tay Ninh

Saigon

C O C H I N

Cape St. Jacques
(Vung Tau)

Bentre

*South China
Sea*

Can Tho

*Plain of
Reeds*

Phung Hiep

*Gulf of
Thailand*

1944 from the Direction Générale des Services Spéciaux (DGSS) which during the previous year had replaced the Bureau Central des Renseignements et d'Action (BCRA). Shortly afterwards, the DGER established a unit called the Section de Liaison Française en Extrême Orient (SLFEO) (Far East French Liaison Section) which was based in Calcutta, in southern India, under the command of Commandant (Major) Boucher de Crèvecoeur, and included the French Indochina Section (FIS), a special operations unit. Based in Kandy, on the island of Ceylon, the latter was employed by Force 136, the Asian and Far East arm of the Special Operations Executive (SOE) which provided equipment and the use of its special training centres in India and Ceylon. The FIS numbered 40 officers and 108 other ranks, the latter including 27 Indochinese.

In early 1944 de Gaulle had decided that the French in Indochina should recognise his Comité de Libération Nationale and decreed that a resistance organisation should be formed along similar lines to those established in France. The concept, however, was unsound as there was little enthusiasm for the return of French rule among the local populations. Furthermore, the French decided that there should be no indigenous involvement in such a resistance movement and thus its recruits could only come from the French population in Indochina, which numbered some 30,000, and the 14,500 French troops remaining in the region.

Many of these troops, however, were supporters of the Vichy regime and thus had no liking for de Gaulle and the Free French. Among them were General Eugène Mordant, commander of French forces in Indochina, who showed little enthusiasm when selected by de Gaulle to lead the resistance movement. During the first week of July, François de Langlade, head of the Indochina section of SLFEO, was dropped near Lang Son in northern Vietnam to bolster Mordant's resolve. No sooner had de Langlade left Vietnam and returned to India, however, than dissent broke out between Mordant and Admiral Jean Decoux, the governor-general of Indochina, who objected strongly when told that Mordant was the supreme authority in the region.

From December 1944 onwards, the FIS carried out an operation in which 24 agents were dropped along with large quantities of arms and explosives. Their mission was to establish a resistance movement and

conduct guerrilla operations against the Japanese in anticipation of landings by 15,000 troops of the Forces Expéditionnaires Françaises d'Extrême Orient (FEFEO) based in Ceylon. On 22 December alone, a total
of seven FIS personnel, codenamed GAUR, after a wild ox indigenous to
the region, were dropped into Laos: five on to the area known as the
Plain of Jars and two near a French base in the Laotian 'Panhandle' in the
south of the country. During the following two months, seven further
drops were carried out over Laos, the GAUR mission being to enlist groups
of partisans, known as 'maquis', prior to the arrival of a 1,200 man Free
French force being raised in North Africa.

A clandestine communications network, comprising eleven radio stations, was meanwhile established. The French, however, committed a
number of major errors, later blamed on lack of experience in unconventional warfare among those responsible for the planning and
execution of the operation. Evidently they made little effort to conceal
their plans from the Japanese, who were in any case well informed: parachute drops were made in broad daylight and almost all the dropped
arms, equipment and explosives were stored in the barracks of French
garrisons.

The Japanese decided to forestall any uprising on the part of the
French and on 9 March carried out a pre-emptive strike, attacking all
the French garrisons. In Tonkin, the latter fought to the last man; at
Lang Son, the Japanese beheaded the French commander, General
Lemonnier and the senior civil administrator, Governor Auphelle, after
the garrison refused to surrender. A small force under General Marcel
Alessandri fought its way out through northern Tonkin and over the
Chinese border into Yunnan where they were promptly imprisoned by
Chiang Kai Shek's forces. Throughout the rest of Vietnam, French forces
were disarmed and confined; all military officers, including Mordant
and Decoux, and civil administrators were arrested and imprisoned. The
Japanese, who had been informed of locations beforehand, also took
the opportunity of seizing the arms, equipment and explosives stock-
piled for the doomed resistance movement.

Apart from the main cities and towns, the Japanese made little effort
to maintain a tight grip on the rest of Vietnam. This, combined with the
absence of French forces, enabled the Viet Minh to expand its influence and operations elsewhere, establishing people's committees as the

basis for a new post-war administration. Without the French it was the only, albeit seemingly, pro-Allied organisation in Indochina and as such from May 1945 onwards began to receive support from the United States which dropped arms and a number of OSS personnel; within a short space of time it possessed a well-armed and equipped force of approximately 5,000 troops.

When Japan surrendered unconditionally on 14 August 1945, the Viet Minh established itself as the sole authority in the country. On 2 September, it proclaimed the Democratic Republic of Vietnam with Ho Chi Minh as president. Vietnam's ruler, Emperor Bao Dai, recognised the new government and abdicated in its favour. Meanwhile, thirty personnel were dropped by the DGER into Indochina in a bid to re-establish French authority wherever possible: twenty-one into Tonkin and Annam, nine into Cambodia and nine into Cochin China in southern Vietnam.

The Viet Minh's period of rule, nevertheless, was short-lived. A few days later, Chinese nationalist forces arrived in Hanoi and occupied the entire north of Vietnam down to the 16th Parallel. Moreover, in early October, British forces entered Saigon and released the French still languishing in prison. French troops, now rearmed, lost little time in ejecting the Viet Minh from Saigon and in October further forces arrived from France. After a period of hard fighting, the French regained control of the principal cities and towns in southern Vietnam up to the 16th Parallel. During this period, the communists increased the size of their forces in the north, acquiring large quantities of weapons from Japanese troops who had not been disarmed by the Chinese, and smuggling in further quantities from China.

The French then entered into negotiations with the Chinese nationalists and the Viet Minh. On 6 March 1946, they signed an agreement which recognised the Democratic Republic of Vietnam, albeit within the French Union and thus stopping short of granting full independence, and permitted French entry into Haiphong. Immediately after this, a French force of just under two divisions entered Tonkin.

Negotiations continued during the rest of that year which saw the withdrawal of the Chinese nationalists and the remaining Japanese forces. It was a period of uneasy peace, however, and there was considerable opposition within the French administration in Indochina, which rejected out of hand any suggestion of independence for Vietnam. This had an adverse effect on negotiations and led to an increasing number of clashes. On 20 November, an incident involving a French attempt to intercept a vessel believed to be carrying arms for the Viet Minh rapidly escalated into an engagement between forces of both sides, and subsequent fierce fighting resulted in the communists being expelled from Haiphong.

During the first half of December 1946, Giap surrounded Hanoi with 30,000 troops and on the 19th launched an attack to dislodge the French and drive them out of the capital. After a day of very heavy fighting, however, during which several hundred civilians were killed, the French managed to eject the Viet Minh from the city. Thereafter, Giap and his forces withdrew to regroup in the mountains of Viet Bac in the extreme north of the country. The first of two major wars in Indochina, which would see the region ravaged by unceasing conflict for the next 27 years, had begun.

OVER THE NEXT THREE years Giap conducted a campaign of guerrilla warfare against the French, using part-time guerrilla units while keeping the bulk of his forces in reserve in the Viet Minh's mountain strongholds in the far north. At the same time, the communists continued to extend their influence throughout the country, in many instances using terror tactics, such as the elimination of tribal chiefs and village elders who resisted their approaches, to drive a wedge between the local population and French civil administrators.

The French, under their commander-in-chief General Jacques Leclerc, meanwhile attempted to use conventional tactics against the Viet Minh but soon found that these were ill-suited to dealing with a guerrilla enemy. A large percentage of their forces was dispersed in small garrisons spread throughout the jungles and mountains of northern Vietnam, with over-extended lines of communication constantly under attack. Some were besieged by the Viet Minh for prolonged periods, the garrison at Nam Dinh only being relieved after four months. The principal assets of the French were massed firepower and air transport and on a number of occasions these saved isolated garrisons from being overrun.

With the French unable to dislodge the Viet Minh from their mountain strongholds and with the latter unsuccessful in their attempts to oust the French from the area of the Red River delta and the key cities of Hanoi, Haiphong, Lao Kay, Cao Bang and Lang Son, there was a period of stalemate during which Giap reorganised his main forces as a conventional army broken down into divisions and regiments.

In October 1950, the communists launched a major assault on the line of French forts located along northern Vietnam's border with China and connected by a highway, designated RC4, which stretched between Cao Bang and Tien Yen. By 17 October all these, including the key fort at Lang Son, had been lost. The French had suffered heavy casualties, losing 6,000 troops and large quantities of arms and equipment later estimated as being sufficient to equip a Viet Minh division of 10,000 men.

During the period from mid-January to mid-June 1951, Giap launched three more attacks in northern Vietnam, at Vinh Yen, Mao Khé and on the Day River, in a further attempt to drive the French out of the Red River delta. On each occasion he was defeated by a combination of mobile French reinforcements, massive artillery firepower and air support, with heavy losses that forced the Viet Minh to withdraw once again to their mountain fastnesses.

The French, meantime, had developed an alternative strategy of counter-insurgency. In June 1949 a special training centre, the Centre de Perfectionnement Commando, had been established by the Etat-Major – Opération des Troupes Aéroportées (EMO–TAP) (General Staff – Airborne Troops) at Cap St. Jacques (now Vung Tau), in southern Vietnam. Its role was to train hill tribesmen, including those of the Hmong, Moïs and Nung, as intelligence agents, saboteurs and radio operators for deployment in areas controlled by the Viet Minh. At the end of the year, the task of providing staff for the centre was delegated to a small group drawn from the Demi-Brigade Coloniale de Commandos Parachutistes, formerly the 1er Demi-Brigade d' Parachutistes SAS.

During this period, a small group of twenty officers under Lieutenant Colonel Edmond Grall, a paratroop officer who had previously com-manded the 5ème Bataillon de Parachutistes d' Infanterie Coloniale (5e BPIC), were assigned to work with the hill tribes and other indigenous groups. Among them was an individual who would play a leading role in the development of French unconventional warfare strategy and tactics in Indochina: Major (later Colonel) Roger Trinquier. It was he who conceived the idea of creating a number of maquis along the lines of some of the larger wartime French resistance groups formed at home, and had established bases in the more remote areas of the country. During 1950, in the mountains of northern Vietnam, the first EMO–TAP maquis of Hmong tribesmen was set by Lieutenant Pierre Cavasse in the area of Pha Long.

Other groups persuaded to join the French cause were religious minorities and criminal elements, including Nung pirates in the Gulf of Tonkin, and the Binh Xuyen, a large organisation of gangsters and river pirates operating in and around the southern Vietnam capital of Saigon. The key figure in dealing with the Binh Xuyen, whose activities were coordinated by the Deuxième Bureau (the French military intelligence service), was Captain Antoine Savani, a Corsican who, like Trinquier, emerged as a leading figure in unconventional warfare in Indochina.

At the start of 1950 Colonel Pierre Fourcaud,the Technical Director of the Service de Documentation Extérieure et du Contre-Espionage (SDECE) – as the DGER had been renamed in January 1946 – visited Hanoi to study the feasibility of establishing a unit to conduct guerrilla operations against the Viet Minh. The wartime BCRA had possessed a branch called the Action Service whose role was the conduct of special operations, but it had been disbanded when the war ended. The SDECE establishment in Hanoi had six vacant posts and it was decided to fill them by forming a small Action Service branch.

Based in Saigon and operating under the cover name of the Fifth Section of the Etat-Major Inter-Armées Terrestres (EMIAT) (General Staff of Joint Land Forces), the SDECE in Indochina was commanded by an Air Force officer, Colonel Maurice Belleux, who had served with the BCRA during the war. In addition to the Action Service, it comprised three other branches responsible for intelligence, counter-intelligence and interception of communications/deciphering respectively. Along with the Indochina branch of the Deuxième Bureau and two other intelligence organisations, the Service de Renseignement Opérationnel (SRO) and the Bureau Technique de Liaison et de Coordination (BTLC), it was subordinate to the Direction Générale de Documentation (DGD). Commanded by Colonel Gracieux, who was replaced by Colonel Maurice Labadie in May 1950, the DGD was responsible for oversight of all French intelligence organisations in Indochina.

The United States, meanwhile, was continuing to take an interest in the problems facing the French in Indochina. During early 1950, an approach was made by the Central Intelligence Agency's (CIA) OPC with a suggestion that it should also establish an organisation similar to the Action Service in Saigon. This proposal was reportedly made in person to High Commissioner Pignon by Lieutenant Colonel Edward Lansdale, a US Air Force (USAF) officer who had served with the OSS during the Second World War, later being seconded from the USAF to the newly formed OPC in November 1949. At the time, Lansdale was based in the Philippines where he was playing a leading role in the suppression of a revolt by communist rebels of the Hukbong Magpapalaya ng Bayan (People's Liberation Army), popularly known as Huks, which had plagued the country since 1946. It was largely due the efforts of Lansdale and of the OPC that President Ramón Magsaysay was eventually elected in 1953, duly ending the rebellion.

The OPC's approach was seen by the French as an attempt by the United States to take over the leading role in countering the communists in Indochina. At a secret conference, Colonel Maurice Belleux listened at length to the American proposal before turning it down. The OPC was not prepared to give up so easily, however, and during the latter part of 1950 suggested that the training school at Cap St. Jacques should be transferred to United States control and be staffed by American instructors under an operation codenamed SAINT-PHALLE. This proposal found favour with Belleux but in December 1950 Marshal Jean de Lattre de Tassigny arrived as the new commander-in-chief of French forces. He strongly supported the concept of an Action Service operated and led by French officers and thus was opposed to the idea of SAINT-PHALLE, vetoing all direct involvement by the United States. Indeed, he was sufficiently suspicious of OPC's motives to ban Lansdale from entering Indochina again.

Shortly afterwards, however, such differences were resolved when the US Director of Central Intelligence, Allen Dulles, and the SDECE station chief in Washington, Thyraud de Vosjoli, reached agreement with regard to Franco-American liaison over special missions and the supply by the United States of financial and logistical support. With de Lattre's agreement, a US special liaison mission was set up in Saigon, located close to the headquarters of the SDECE. Its chief was Colonel

Helwin Hall who proceeded to establish a good rapport with Colonel Maurice Belleux by presenting him with two C-47 Dakota transports for use by the Action Service in Indochina, although the aircraft were subsequently appropriated by the SDECE in Paris.

In April 1951, de Lattre put the Action Service programme on a firmer footing when he authorised its expansion into a formation for the conduct of unconventional warfare operations against the Viet Minh. During the following month, the Action Service assumed the cover name of Groupes de Commandos Mixte Aéroportés (GCMA) (Composite Airborne Commando Groups). Commanded by Lieutenant Colonel Edmund Grall, it was subordinate to the SDECE but reported directly to the high command of the French forces in Indochina which was responsible for tasking it. With its headquarters in Saigon and its administrative and training centre, the Centre d'Instruction et de Formation (CIF) at Cap St. Jacques, the GCMA was divided into four operational regions: Tonkin in the north; central Vietnam (which comprised the plains and coastal region of Annam as well as the mountains and plateaux bordering the frontiers with Laos and Cambodia); southern Vietnam; and Laos. Each was under the direction of a body called the Représentation Régionale. A number of GCMA outposts, each commanded by an officer, were set up in each of these regions.

The role of the GCMA was to establish a series of large groups or maquis, each comprising up to 3,000 trained partisans, which would dominate their own respective areas by seeking out and eliminating the Viet Minh. Small detachments of GCMA personnel were deployed to different areas throughout each of the four operational regions where, with the assistance of partisans trained at Cap St. Jacques, they trained further tribesmen, arming them with weapons comprising primarily small arms, grenade launchers and mortars and forming them into 100-strong units known as 'centaines'. Individual GCMA officers, NCOs and ordinary soldiers, each accompanied by a group of partisans, were assigned to live with hill-tribe communities whose men would also be trained in the rudiments of guerrilla warfare for operations against the Viet Minh.

Volunteers for service with the GCMA were recruited from French forces throughout Indochina. Initially, the majority came from parachute and commando units but after a while it became necessary to look for volunteers from elsewhere, particularly those who already had a knowledge of hill-tribe dialects. Notable among those who served in the GCMA were elements of the 11ème Bataillon Parachutiste de Choc (11e Choc), a unit formed from former members of the two wartime Free French SAS units, SOE/OSS Jedburgh teams and the BCRA's Action Service. Established on 1 September 1946, the 11e Choc was a politico-military special forces unit whose role was the conduct of clandestine operations and unconventional warfare. In 1947, for example, during strikes by miners which were widespread throughout France, some of its members, dressed in the uniforms of the paramilitary Gardes Mobiles, had been deployed in an operation to combat suspected communist subversion.

Life in the GCMA was extremely hazardous. Individuals would find themselves deployed hundreds of miles inside Viet Minh-controlled areas, living among hill tribes whose customs and taboos they had to learn in order to avoid giving offence. Some proved highly amenable to such an existence, being adopted by their respective tribes and even marrying the daughters of chieftains in order to cement the bonds formed with them. The strains of such a lone existence, however, were considerable, with illness and disease a constant hazard. One example of this was the case of a warrant officer commanding a GCMA team 60 miles to the south of Lai Chau, in the north of Tonkin. Suffering from a severe case of malaria combined with physical and mental debilitation caused by a long tour of duty, he shot dead a member of his team while under the delusion that the latter was a member of the Viet Minh. On recovering his senses and demented with grief and remorse, he made his way to Lai Chau where he presented himself, pleading to be court-martialled. Added to such hardships suffered by GCMA personnel was the constant risk of betrayal by a disaffected partisan in the pay of the Viet Minh which had formed a special unit, the 421st Intelligence Battalion, to counter the GCMA.

By the end of 1951, the GCMA had not reached its full strength of French personnel, possessing 32 officers and 176 other ranks rather than the established figures of 47 and 228 respectively. Recruitment of indigenous personnel for service with the GCMA also proved to be a problem, since the requirement for maximum possible security inevitably hampered the search for suitable, highly motivated men. Moreover, the level of finance allocated to the GCMA was such that it only partially covered the cost of recruiting local personnel. Officers therefore had to resort to various measures to overcome this difficulty, including the recruiting of a number of men who officially remained on the strength of their original units.

There were also problems with specialist equipment which, supplied from France, took a long time to arrive. Moreover, certain items, notably radio transmitter/receivers, proved unsuitable for the harsh conditions in the field. Similarly, weapons supplied for use by the maquis frequently turned out to be of poor quality and of different calibres, later causing problems with the supply of ammunition. Small arms consisted of a mixture of British and German weapons of wartime vintage, including Sten 9mm submachine-guns, Lee Enfield .303 rifles and Mauser 98K 7.92 mm rifles.

Radio communications between the maquis and Hanoi were initially maintained by use of low-powered SCR 536 AM transmitter/receivers communicating with French aircraft flying overhead. Direct rear link communications with Hanoi were subsequently established through the use of high-powered SCR 694 sets operated by trained indigenous operators parachuted into maquis bases. These also afforded more security, allowing the use of codes and ciphers.

The GCMA's central area of operations was in the region comprising the coastal plain of Annam, bordered in the north by Tonkin, and in the south by southern Vietnam, including Cochin China. A Représentation Régionale (RR) was established in July 1951 under the command of Captain Françisque Richonnet who proceeded to form the first centaine, later setting up outposts at Fai Fo, Dong Hoi and Hué.

From 1945 onward, the communists had found fertile ground for subversion among the Annamites and so succeeded in establishing control over a large part of the region which provided important sanctuaries for their forces. Such was the strength of the Viet Minh's control over its zone of influence and the local population that the GCMA rapidly concluded that it would be impossible to establish maquis groups within it. The Viet Minh encountered opposition, however, among the important Catholic communities which were strongly opposed to communist ideology and it was among these that the GCMA sought to recruit agents. By the end of July 1951, several had been trained at the Ty Wan training centre and, equipped with a radio set, were ready to be parachuted into the Viet Minh zone with the mission of forming an intelligence network. In the event, however, lack of aircraft resulted in their having to infiltrate overland from Hué. Given the high degree of security and surveillance exercised by the Viet Minh, this was a hazardous undertaking and the team experienced major problems in surviving the journey.

It was in Annam that the first major GCMA operation was conducted, on the island of Cu Lao Rê which lies off Quang Ngai, south of the Annamite port of Da Nang. On 30 August 1951, in a combined operation codenamed PIRATE, a company of the 6th Colonial Parachute Battalion and a GCMA commando force under the command of an officer of the 11e Choc, Captain Jean Prévot, seized the island. Prévot installed himself and his centaine there, constructing an airstrip and a base which was one of a number subsequently established for maritime operations along the coast of Annam. From Cu Lao Rê, he carried out raids in the region of Lien Khu, while from the island of Honh Mê another unit, commanded by Captain René Bichelot, conducted similar operations in the area of Thanh Hoa. A further two centaines, and later a third, were formed on an islet, known as the Observatory, in the Bay of Tourane.

During 1952, GCMA island- or coastal-based centaines also took part in a number of combined operations, some being controlled by the headquarters in Saigon and involving French warships, airborne units, ground troops and air support. Smaller commando-type operations were carried out in conjunction with naval units or the GCMA's own maritime assets which comprised converted junks or pinnaces. The latter were also used for the infiltration or extraction of agents or small teams, as well as for mounting a large number of sabotage attacks or raids on enemy installations and lines of communications in coastal areas.

September saw the reported death in action of Captain Richonnet who was replaced by Captain Frédéric 'Freddy' Bauer. By then the GCMA forces in central Annam comprised the RR command element and a centaine at Tourane; a centaine on the Observatory islet under Lieutenant Roger Flamand; Captain Prévot's centaine on Cu Lao Rê; and the three outposts at Fai Fo, Dong Hoi and Hué.

The following year saw little progress in attempts to establish maquis groups in enemy-held areas and eventually these were discontinued. In the coastal areas, however, the centaines at Tourane and Cu Lao Rê were continuing to achieve success in their raiding operations and in maintaining surveillance on, or intercepting, coastal maritime traffic. On Cu Lao Rê, where Captain Prévot was relieved by Captain Paul-Alain Léger, the centaine took part in operations mounted by the GCMA in other regions: fighting alongside airborne troops in parachute assaults launched by the GCMA in Kontum, or participating in raids organised by the Tonkin GCMA on the coast of Than Hoa or by the South Vietnam GCMA in southern Annam and Cochin China.

To the west of Annam's coastal plain lie the heavily forested and jungle-clad plateaux of the Annamite Chain of mountains bordering the frontiers with Laos and Cambodia. Known by the Vietnamese as the Truong Son (Long Mountains), they are inhabited by tribes known collectively by the French term of Montagnards but who refer to themselves as 'Degar' – translated as 'Sons of the Mountains'. Numbering some half a million at the time of the First Indochina War, they comprise over 40 tribes who speak a number of dialects of Malayo/Polynesian and Mon/Khmer origins. Among them are the Bahnar, Bong, Bru, Cham, Chil, Cru, Cua, Drung, Halang, Hré, Jarai, Jeh, Katu, Kayong, Koho, Lat, Maa, Mien, Monom, Muong, Nongao, Nop, Pacoh, Ragulai, Rai, Rhade, Roglai, Rongao, Sedang, Srè, Stieng and Tuong.

The Montagnards settled along the coasts and valleys of south-eastern Indochina 2,000 years ago. They were followed by other ethnic groups including the Cham, whose kingdom gradually expanded along the coastal lowlands and the Mekong Valley, and the Chinese forebears of the Vietnamese, who migrated southwards along the coasts of the South China Sea. This caused the Montagnards to move farther inland and up into the mountains and plateaux, retaining their culture and experiencing little contact with the outside world until the arrival of French missionaries in the mid-nineteenth century. While the hill tribes benefited in some ways from such contact, the missionaries establishing schools and hospitals, they also found themselves being exploited and abused by the French and the Annamites. Furthermore, the encroachment on hill-tribe areas by the latter and other outsiders, and attempts to inflict their culture and policies on the tribes, inevitably provoked resentment among the Montagnards and caused a further deterioration in their relations with the lowland population. After the turn of the century there were several uprisings which were put down by the French, who subsequently established an improved system of hill-tribe administration. In 1946, in an attempt to improve relations with the Montagnards, the French granted the tribes an extensive degree of autonomy with the establishment of five Montagnard provinces as an entity separate from Vietnam, albeit still within the French colonies comprising Indochina.

During 1945–6, the Viet Minh took advantage of the truce with the French to deploy their forces and bring under their influence the provinces of Binh Dinh, Quang Ngai and Quang Nam. From there they spread west into the foothills and plateaux, temporarily setting aside the long-standing hatred between the hill tribesmen and the Annamites, who referred to them as 'Moïs', a derogatory term meaning savage or barbarian. In 1946, Ho Chi Minh included in his political assembly two members of the Hré, the tribe inhabiting the area north of the city of Kontum, between the mountains and Quang Ngai, who supposedly were to act as representatives for all the hill tribes. Throughout the northern Hré territory the communists resorted to terror in order to force local chiefs into submission, establishing a centre of administration and local government at Batö. Meanwhile, young tribesmen were conscripted into the Viet Minh, those who resisted being forced to work as coolies in the salt marshes. Having removed the major part of the male population, the Viet Minh introduced Annamite communities into each Hré village. In 1949, however, the tribesmen rebelled. Led by their chief Dinh Loye, they were followed by the entire northern Hré who turned on the Annamites living among them. Some 5,000 men, women and children were massacred by the tribesmen, their bodies being thrown into the rivers or burned along with their houses.

Fearing Viet Minh reprisals, the Hré turned to the French with whom they made contact at four outposts located at Dakto, Vimouk, Mambuk and Kon Plong, all of which, prior to the formation of the GCMA, were manned by teams of officers and NCOs of the Bataillon de Marche d'Extrême Orient (BMEO), a Franco-Cambodian unit operating in Cochin China and southern Annam. Meanwhile, the Viet Minh reacted swiftly, despatching a regiment to reoccupy the northern Hré country and carry out reprisals from which the tribesmen fled from their valleys to the mountains.

The French lost little time in providing support for the tribes whose maquis operations thereafter were controlled by the BMEO teams at

Dakto, Vimouk and Mambuk. At the same time, a Hré independence movement, the Doc Lap Hré, was created and fostered by the team at Kon Plong whose primary task was the training of tribesmen as regular troops for conducting operations against the Viet Minh. The French, meantime, turned their attention to establishing contact with the southern Hré tribes and winning them over. As their region had not been occupied by the Viet Minh, they had not taken part in the rebellion, maintaining a position of neutrality.

In addition to the BMEO team, the outpost at Kon Plong was manned by the 1st Company of the 4th Hill Battalion of the BMEO and some 200 Hré partisans, the entire force being under the BMEO team commander, Captain Pierre. The outpost itself consisted of a series of heavily fortified strongpoints, including a network of trenches and barbed wire defences, and featured an airstrip usable by Morane light aircraft in the dry season. It occupied a strategic location in the foothills of the Annamite Chain, being situated at the intersection of the Kontum valleys and a pass that provided access to the Son Ha and Batö plains which led to the coast.

Prior to the Second World War, Kon Plong had been an outpost for a militia unit. In 1946, it had been reoccupied by French forces and during the following two years had been fortified. The Viet Minh had attempted on several occasions to overrun and seize the post as it had proved to be an obstacle to their operations in the valleys and plains. From 1948 onward, the garrison had switched from defence of the outpost to conducting raids into Viet Minh-held areas along the Hré River. At the same time, reconnaissance patrols made contact with hill-tribe communities, many of which rallied to the French side. Captain Pierre and his team did much for the local populations, constructing a road to Batö and establishing a market at which tribes could trade their produce for commodities such as salt, dried fish, cloth and other items. This led to an improved flow of information and soon Pierre's intelligence officer, 2nd Lieutenant Duret, was able to pinpoint the locations of Viet Minh units up to three days' march from Kon Plong.

Pierre's BMEO team comprised two other officers, three warrant officers and twelve NCOs. One of the latter was Corporal (later Sergeant) René Riesen who had been serving with the 5th Colonial Infantry Regiment when selected for service with the BMEO. The experiences of the team, later recounted in his book *Jungle Commando*, which provides one of the very few eyewitness accounts of French unconventional warfare operations in Indochina published in English, were typical of those of French military personnel deployed on their own to live among the Montagnards. Reisen outlined his early experiences following his first operation at Kon Plong which was an ambush to capture prisoners:

After this battle, Captain Pierre frequently sent me out alone with Hré partisans into the Monome country, as far as the Dadzas. Their dialect had become familiar to me. The crude phonetic scrawls which I had made in June had turned into a vocabulary which was daily increased with a new word. Nobody smiled any longer when they heard a French soldier speaking in Hré or Monome. To settle a difference, gain information, or issue hurried orders, every NCO now found it quicker to consult the outpost's interpreter.

Slowly too I had changed my name. As I liked and sympathised with the Moïs and was exceptional, to the dark hillmen, in having fair hair, I became Ba tchiac gaho tabouac or the father with white hair – then Ba Tamoï, father of the Moïs.

The partisans had adopted me as one of their own people, as the captain had hoped. I lived in their own style, adapting myself to their customs, learning their law, eating their own dishes, and studying their way of life. Captain Pierre made me take a first-aid course, so that I could be a doctor to them in their jungle villages.

Wherever I went I took with me a stock of counters which could be exchanged for a fixed amount of rice, dried fish, salt, or cloth at the outpost, so that on my way I would be able to pay for fresh meat, fruit and vegetables for the partisans – or better still get a welcome from a village chief, information from a messenger, or win over one who had been hesitating. The prestige of a white man, going out alone with the hillmen, sometimes several days' march from his base, was not slow in spreading to the most distant huts.

As I distributed quinine, aspirin, and other medicines, doing what I could for any sickness I came across, paying attention to the old men, the women and children, and in matters of policy guarding against mistakes in interpreting, which might sometimes have serious consequences and make an enemy of one who had come over to our side, so

I gradually extended the area of activity around our outpost.

In November, the Hrés wanted to do me the honour of offering me a wife from their tribe. Dumbfounded, I refused this proposal with a smile. But the captain did not approve of my attitude. He knew how sensitive the hillmen were, and he was also aware, from his own experience with the T'aïs in Tonkin, that an Asiatic may regard a refusal as an insult and view a show of aloofness as quite unforgivable, having a social and moral code different from our own.

So the proposal had to be considered. To marry a Moï girl, according to tribal law, of course, might make a difficult job a little easier, so long as one made a real ally of her. In the course of my lonely expeditions across their country, such a union might be regarded by the natives as a whole, and in particular by the chiefs, as an important guarantee – a decisive stake in considering what position to adopt in the struggle between the Viet Minh and the French. For never, never under any circumstances could a Moï so much as consider a girl of his own race becoming the wife of their traditional enemies, the Yoanes [Annamites – author].

Custom, which also meant the law, only allowed marriage with a for-eigner in order to achieve an alliance which was in the interests of all, or, inside the clan, as a very exceptional mark of honour or respect. Looked at from this psychological angle, my refusal was something of an insult. So, pleading that it was only modesty which had led me to think it over, I had made good my mistake. On a second occasion I accepted, with some confusion, the young girl who was destined for me.

Her name was Ilouhi, and she came from the village of Vikli on the Song Hré [the Hré River is known as the Diac Hré in the mountains and foothills – in the plains it is called the Song Hré, becoming the Song Tra Cuk when it approaches its estuary – author]. During the 1949 revolt against the Viets, some of her family had been massacred by the Yoanes and their possessions burnt or confiscated. When the tribe came over to our side at Kon Plong, she too came with her mother to follow her uncles and cousins who were serving in our ranks, to free their country and await the moment when they could exact their revenge. That was a first and essential safeguard – Ilouhi would never betray me for the sake of her family's assassins and the invaders of her country.

THE FORMATION OF the GCMA in May 1951 saw the establishment of the Réprésentation Régionale Plateaux Montagnards (RRPM) at Kontum under the command of Captain Pierre Hentic. A Breton and originally a member of the French army's famous mountain troops, the Chasseurs Alpins, with whom he had seen action in Norway in 1940, Hentic had subsequently served with the BCRA's Action Service throughout the rest of the Second World War. Thereafter, he had served with the 11e Choc as an intelligence officer, being the main instigator of the northern Hré revolt against the Viet Minh in 1949.

At the beginning of August 1951, however, the communists managed to achieve their long-standing aim of destroying the outpost at Kon Plong in an attack which wiped out the garrison. The French responded by dropping airborne troops while three Hré centaines infiltrated into the enemy rear, where they carried out harassing operations with some success. Later in the year, three Hré centaines took part in operations designed to tie down two Viet Minh units, the 108th and 803rd Regiments.

On 2 May 1952, the French mounted a major operation to regain the area dominating the province of Quang Ngai. A force of 300 Hré partisans, commanded by Captain Hentic and accompanied by four other French officers and a number of warrant officers, reached Ba To which was located some 20 kilometres from the Viet Minh-controlled zone. Three days later, however, largely due to lack of adequate support from a regular Montagnard unit, the force suffered heavy casualties at the hands of the enemy, two French officers and 40 partisans being killed.

Late 1952 saw a force of almost 1,500 Hré partisans on operations throughout the Plateaux Montagnards. On the orders of the French high command, however, it was subsequently deployed in the coastal province of Binh Dinh where the partisans carried out a campaign of guerrilla warfare, conducting ambushes, mining roads and attacking Viet Minh bases. This was followed by a long-range operation carried out by a partisan centaine and a Vietnamese commando unit under the command of Captain Hentic, both specially selected for the task. Setting off, the force headed for Quang Ngai which it reached after 40 days' march over heavily forested mountains. Having reached their objective, a Viet Minh supply base, Hentic and his men attacked and destroyed it before embarking on another march, this time into Laos where their destination was the town of Attapu which was reached after 20 days. En route, they came across evidence of the Viet Minh's secret principal supply route, later to become famous as the 'Ho Chi Minh Trail': heavily camouflaged stretches of road, usable by vehicles and equipped with staging posts and rest areas. In addition, Hentic's force intercepted and captured a Viet Minh mission returning from Thailand, this providing intelligence of considerable value.

On arrival at Attapu, Hentic's force was transferred to the area of Ankhé where it carried out harassing operations against the Viet Minh. These proved very effective but Hentic was faced with the problem that his Hré partisans were unhappy at being deployed outside their own territory. But he received scant sympathy from the French high command, who showed little concern, and ultimately the morale and effectiveness of the partisans suffered considerably.

In July 1953, by then suffering from ill health, Hentic was relieved as the commander of the RRPM by Captain Vincent. The latter had different ideas to those of his predecessor and ceased all large-scale operations which he considered should be the responsibility of regular Montagnard units recruited from other tribes, namely Rhades, Sedangs and Djarais. Instead, he concentrated on parachute and infiltration operations carried out by small teams of partisans in the coastal zone held by the Viet Minh. These achieved varying degrees of success as the Hré proved not altogether suitable for this type of action.

The end of November of that year brought further changes which resulted in the disbandment of the RR Plateaux Montagnards and the transfer of its units to the RR Central Annam at Tourane.

To the south of Annam lay southern Vietnam, including Cochin China, where the Catholic minorities, while less powerful than those in the northern region of Tonkin, nevertheless possessed considerable political influence in certain areas throughout the region. With the exception of the area of Bentre, which was controlled by a French colonel named Leroy, who had set himself up as a local potentate and waged war with a degree of success against the Viet Minh, the Catholic communities in southern Vietnam tended to adopt either an anti-French attitude or a pragmatic policy of wait-and-see.

Other religious minorities in the region included the Cao Dai, who inhabited the region of Tay Ninh, and the Hoa Hao, who were located between the Bassac and Mekong rivers. In 1946, members of the Demi-Brigade Parachutiste SAS, the predecessor to the Demi-Brigade Coloniale de Commandos Parachutistes, had established contact with the Cao Dai; but efforts to use them as irregular troops proved unsuccessful after casualties incurred during training, including a number of deaths while parachuting. Thereafter, the Cao Dai established their own forces which operated in their own areas with French logistical support. Meanwhile, the area of Cholon and the capital of Saigon were occupied by the Binh Xuyen. As mentioned earlier, the latter were a well-armed clan of criminals and river pirates enjoying close contact with the Deuxième Bureau through Captain Antoine Savani, who also had dealings with the Cao Dai and the Hoa Hao. Early on in the conflict, Savani succeeded in rallying all three of these factions and thus secured their respective areas of influence against the Viet Minh.

During 1946, the GCMA had established a Représentation Régionale Vietnam Sud (RRVS) in Saigon under the command of Captain Chaume. It soon found, however, that a severe shortage of trained personnel, coupled with the political and military situation in southern Vietnam, required it to adopt methods different to those employed by the GCMA in other regions. An outpost was established at Hon Quan, to the north of Saigon and close to the areas held by the Cao Dai and the Viet Minh. In addition to the formation of a centaine, a small training centre was set up where partisans and maquis cadres underwent training. The centaine became operational in October 1951 and shortly afterwards undertook a series of actions against the Viet Minh, infiltrating into enemy-held areas where it conducted ambushes and attacks on enemy bases. By the end of that year, a second centaine was in the process of being recruited.

In the west of the region, an outpost was established at the end of 1952 at Can Tho by Captain Jean-Henri Loustau, who succeeded in raising and training three centaines. These operated initially from Binh Tuy and subsequently from Phung Hiep, to the west of the Bassac River. They performed tasks similar to those of the centaines in the northern zone and at the same time provided support for the forces of the Hoa Hao and Cao Dai. In addition, they conducted a number of airborne assaults alongside regular airborne units, and also took part in combined operations, carrying out landings on the coasts of southern Annam and Cochin China.

The northernmost region of Vietnam was Tonkin which was divided into three areas of operations: the High Region, inhabited by the T'ai hill tribes; the Central Region, from the northern edge of the Red River delta to the border with China, and including the area inhabited by the Muong south of the delta as far as Thanh Hoa and Laos; and the coastal area of northern Annam, from the estuary of the Day River to Thanh Hoa, inhabited by Catholic minorities.

Recruiting for the maquis in Tonkin was carried out by Major Roger Trinquier who took command of the RR Vietnam Nord (RRVN) at the beginning of 1952. Trinquier had previously served in Indochina during the 1930s as a second lieutenant in the colonial infantry, at one point commanding a detachment in a remote location at Chi-Ma on the Sino-Tonkinese border while conducting operations against pirates and opium smugglers. During that time he had become familiar with some of the northern hill tribes, learning their various dialects. In 1946, he had served as a platoon commander in the Commando Ponchardier, before being posted in February 1947 as a captain to the newly formed training centre for airborne troops. In November of that year, he returned to Indochina as second-in-command of the 1er Bataillon de Parachutistes Coloniaux (1er BPC). In September 1948 he assumed command of the battalion, following the death of its commanding officer in action, and led it on operations against Viet Minh guerrillas in the Plain of Reeds in the Mekong River delta. Following a tour of duty in France as head of a commando training centre at Fréjus and the Colonial Paratroop School, Trinquier returned to Indochina again in December 1951 and was assigned to the GCMA.

It was as a result of his service with commando and parachute units, together with his knowledge of the northern hill tribes, that Trinquier had been selected for this appointment. His recruitment technique initially consisted of officers flying over hill-tribe villages in small Morane liaison aircraft to test the reaction of the villagers; if they responded in a friendly fashion or waved the French flag, it was assumed that the area was possibly suitable for the establishment of a GCMA force. A small group of GCMA troops would then be dropped into the area with the mission of recruiting the nucleus of a maquis. Once a chief had been persuaded to join the French cause, a cadre of 50 tribesmen would be flown to the Ty Wan training centre at Cap St. Jacques where they would undergo a ten-week course in parachuting, counter-guerrilla tactics, weapon training, demolitions, radio communications and basic field intelligence techniques. Approximately half of the men in a cadre would be trained for combat, the other half being divided between radio communications specialists and intelligence operatives. On completion of its training, each cadre returned to its respective village, to be supplied by airdrop with weapons and equipment with which to form irregular units of 300–400 men, ultimately leading to the formation of a maquis of some 1,000 in strength. Meanwhile, the local administration previously established by the Viet Minh would be dismantled and replaced by the maquis which would thereafter control its area.

Despite vigorous intervention from Chinese forces since the spring of 1951, Nung and Hmong partisans in the highlands of Tonkin had remained active and by the beginning of 1952 a centaine had been established at Laï Chau, later to become a principal GCMA base. In the north-west, two teams of GCMA personnel and partisans had been parachuted into the rear area of the Viet Minh's 308th Division after the latter's failure to capture the city of Nghia Lo in September 1951. Meanwhile, two centaines were set up in the coastal region at Tien Yen and Pho Ba Che respectively, with a third being located at Haiphong with the role of carrying out marine operations in the area stretching from the mouth of the Day River to the north of Annam.

In June 1952, the GCMA achieved some success in the High Region to the east of the Red River when Hmong and Nung maquis, totalling some 2,500 partisans and led by a chief named Chau Quang Lo, took part in an operation against the Viet Minh's 148th Regiment at Lao Kay. Codenamed CHOCOLAT, the operation was controlled by the GCMA officer responsible for the north-west region, Lieutenant Pierre Hautier, and was commanded on the ground by a Hmong chieftain named Chau Quang Lo. Chief of the Hmong in the region of Pha Long, the latter had formed the first maquis in 1950 with the help of Lieutenant Pierre Cavasse of the EMO-TAP and at the beginning of 1952 had joined forces with the GCMA.

Finding themselves losing the battle, the Viet Minh appealed for help to the Chinese communists who had occupied southern China in 1949 following the defeat of Chiang Kai Shek's nationalists. The Chinese 302nd Division was despatched to reinforce the Viet Minh but soon was suffering heavy casualties from maquis attacks and ambushes supported by French air strikes. Meanwhile, the GCMA had made contact with Hmong tribes in the region of Ha Giang to the east of the CHOCOLAT area of activities. In July, a GCMA cadre was parachuted in to assist in the formation of another maquis operation codenamed PAVOT.

To the west of the Red River, centaines had meanwhile been established at Nghia Lo and Than Uyen with support being provided by a GCMA cadre based at Nghia Lo. Previously, although the local people were favourably inclined towards the French, they had lacked the necessary organisation and infrastructure to form an effective resistance against the Viet Minh. In order to overcome this problem and to unite the different ethnic factions, Lieutenant Emile Hanns, the officer in command of the GCMA outpost at Nghia Lo, set up local administrative organisations, self-defence and strike forces, and cells for provision of intelligence and propaganda. The results were highly successful and Viet Minh influence in the area soon waned as Hanns's centaine extended the area under its control.

The situation in the High Region was eventually such that Trinquier planned to extend the areas under GCMA/partisan control so that CHOCOLAT and PAVOT could be combined, being reinforced with a further centaine inserted at Than Uyen under the command of Lieutenant Castagnoni. Success, however, was short-lived, and by August Chinese forces had succeeded in virtually annihilating CHOCOLAT. During September the remaining elements of Chau Quang Lo's maquis were dispersed through enemy action and he himself was killed shortly afterwards.

Mid-October 1952 saw a similar fate befall a maquis of T'ai and Nung guerrillas when three Viet Minh divisions, the 308th, 312th and 316th, launched a major offensive from Laos on the line of French posts in the area between the Red and Black Rivers. Less than six days after crossing the Red River, the 308th Division had penetrated through 40 miles of jungle and appeared in the area of Nghia Lo. On 17 October, the Viet Minh launched their assault on the city and such was the weight of the communist onslaught that the French were forced to pull back to Na San, their withdrawal being covered by the maquis. The centaine at Nghia Lo was annihilated and its commander, Lieutenant Hanns, captured and later executed following a mock trial. The centaine at Than

Uyen was evacuated at the last minute, while a third, led by a chieftain named Ly Seo Nung, managed to escape and make its way to Son La without loss. GCMA personnel attached to the maquis were hunted down and killed or captured.

Meanwhile, the decision had been taken to drop a parachute battalion as a rearguard to cover the withdrawal of French units to the Black River. On 16 October, the 6ème Bataillon de Parachutistes Coloniaux (6e BPC), commanded by Commandant (Major) Marcel Bigeard, was dropped at Tu Le, 20 miles to the north-west of Nghia Lo. On the morning of the following day, a patrol from the battalion encountered leading elements of the 312th Division some five miles from Tu Le. On the evening of the 18th, Viet Minh troops reached the high ground to the south and east of the town.

On the night of 19 October, Bigeard received orders to withdraw his unit to the Black River but delayed doing so until the following morning to give French troops retreating from Gia Hoi more time to reach safety. By the early hours of the 20th, however, Tu Le was being subjected to a heavy barrage of mortar fire. As dawn broke, the battalion began its withdrawal towards the Black River but soon fell into a trap laid by the Viet Miinh between the Tu Le Pass and the first line of hills. Two companies acted as a rearguard, holding off the Viet Minh as the remainder of the battalion made good its escape. That evening, Bigeard and his men reached Muong Chen, a hilltop post held by 80 T'ai partisans of the 248ème Compagnie Suppletif led by a GCMA team of four NCOs commanded by Master Sergeant Peyrol. Overlooking the path which led to the Black River, it comprised a small fortified barracks equipped with bunkers.

Bigeard made it clear to Peyrol that he needed three hours for the 6e BPC to reach the Black River. Peyrol therefore prepared his small force of partisans to block the passage of an entire Viet Minh division. He did not have long to wait. At approximately 7.00 p.m., less than an hour after the last of Bigeard's men had disappeared from view, the post came under mortar fire which was followed by an attack on one of the bunkers whose construction had not been completed. Sappers first blew gaps in the post's barbed wire defences, enabling troops armed with grenades to attack the bunker which was taken after heavy losses had been inflicted on the attackers. Nevertheless, Peyrol and his men hung on grimly, determined to give the 6e BPC the three hours it needed to reach the Black River.

By 10.00 p.m. it became apparent that it would be futile to attempt to hold up the Viet Minh any longer. Ammunition stocks were low and approximately half the T'ai partisans and one French NCO had been killed. Under the cover of darkness, having laid booby traps in the remaining bunkers, Peyrol and the rest of his force succeeded in escaping along a path which they had cut through the jungle only a few days beforehand. Shooting their way out of their positions, they disappeared into the darkness.

The Viet Minh were determined to hunt down the small force whose gallant action had cost them so dear and despatched two companies in hot pursuit. The chase was on as Peyrol and his men hacked their way through thick jungle, crossed rivers and climbed mountains up to 8,000 feet in height. Their rations were exhausted by the third day and thereafter they had to rely on the partisans' ability to live off the land. Fortunately, the group was equipped with an SCR-300 radio set on which Peyrol attempted to contact French forces. One such transmission resulted in the receipt of instructions to march to a drop zone (DZ) north of their line of march. Peyrol, however, was suspicious and much to the chagrin of his companions decided to ignore the order. It was fortunate he did so as it later transpired that it had been a Viet Minh trap.

Peyrol and his men continued their march towards the Black River, narrowly avoiding contact with a platoon of Viet Minh encamped along the path they were following at the time. On 5 November, however, they climbed the last ridge-line from which they could observe the river in the distance. By that afternoon, they had descended to the valley below and were heading for the river when they met a T'ai tribesman who warned them of the presence of Viet Minh patrols. Accepting his advice and his offer to guide them to the river after dark, Peyrol and his men moved into a lying-up position (LUP). The T'ai was as good as his word and returned, bringing with him rice for the by now starving group.

Because it was impossible to cross that night because of the presence of Viet Minh troops in the area, Peyrol and his men were forced to remain in their LUP. On the following day, 6 November, a Morane light reconnaissance aircraft flew overhead and the group attracted the attention of the pilot who dropped a message, advising them to stay under cover and promising to warn the French forces on the other side of the river of their presence.

Under cover of darkness, Peyrol and his men crossed the river on rafts provided by the T'ai tribesman. On reaching the far bank they were met by French troops from the nearby post of Muong Bu. By then, on the verge of physical and mental collapse, Peyrol's force of forty-three had been reduced to sixteen men. Its dramatic escape had lasted twelve days during which it had covered over 200 kilometres.

During this period, GCMA forces were also active in the delta and coastal region. The centaine based at Tien Yen was engaged in raiding and other operations in an area abandoned by French forces in the autumn of 1950. Although the local population was friendly, it refused to become involved in establishing a maquis. The Haiphong centaine meanwhile took part with French commando units in raids against Viet Minh lines of supply and communication. Further success was achieved by centaines based at Luc Nam and Phat Diem, the latter an area inhabited by Catholic minorities. A centaine based at Phuc Yen, under the command of Lieutenant Borcard, conducted a number of successful raiding operations while at the same time inserting a surveillance team equipped with a radio to observe the main route between Tuyen Quang and Thai Nguyen. In addition, an airborne operation was carried out by a nine-man GCMA team, led by Lieutenant Léonce Barrière, which destroyed a Viet Minh ammunition depot at Phu Nho Quan.

Despite the setbacks suffered during the latter part of the previous year, at the beginning of 1953 the French High Command in Saigon decided to increase the scope of GCMA operations and allocated additional resources to it. In February Major Roger Trinquier was appointed deputy commander of the GCMA, subsequently replacing Lieutenant Colonel Edmund Grall as commander. He was replaced as commander of the RRVN in Tonkin by Major Roger Fournier.

In the High Region of Tonkin, several units of T'ai partisans had been formed and trained by a centaine based at Laï Chau. The capital of the T'ai Federation, headed by a chieftain called Déo Van Long, it was also the French airhead behind communist lines, playing a prominent role in the resupply of GCMA groups. This had subsequently led to further units being set up at Tsinh Ho and Phong Tho near the border with

China. In January 1953, an operation was mounted from Laï Chau against Viet Minh units at Dien Bien Phu where a force of GCMA centaines, reinforced by companies of T'ai partisans, threatened the town. The operation lasted several weeks until 20 March when a force of 56 partisans, led by a GCMA NCO, was parachuted into the town; it encountered strong opposition and was almost annihilated. By that time, the Tai companies had become demoralised after spending too long outside their own territory and withdrew.

In February, meanwhile, a GCMA officer, Captain René Hébert, formed a maquis on the Long He massif. An initial approach to the Hmong, T'ai and Man tribes by two GCMA NCOs, accompanied by a T'ai interpreter, had fallen on fertile ground and the tribesmen proceeded to expel the Viet Minh from their respective areas while happily accepting the arms parachuted to them by the GCMA. By August Hébert had 3,000 well-armed men organised into three maquis designated AIGLON, CALAMAR and COLIBRI. Between 4 and 8 August, this force covered the withdrawal of the garrison from Na San by seizing Son La to distract the Viet Minh and by interdicting the Route Provinciale 41 and the area between the Song Ma and the Black River. In so doing, it delayed the advance of the enemy's 312th Division while the garrison was evacuated by air. During the following month, the three maquis repulsed several heavy attacks by the Viet Minh.

In October, a diversionary operation, codenamed CHAU QUAN TIN, took place as part of a plan for a further extension of maquis into the region of Baxat, Binhlu, Chapa and Than Uyen. The intention was to draw away enemy forces, compelling the Viet Minh to commit themselves heavily against a major attack. On 3 October, the village of Coc Leu Laokay, an important Viet Minh supply centre, was attacked by a maquis of 600 Hmong and T'ai partisans led by Lieutenant Long, and a 47-man GCMA para-commando unit. French B-26 Invader light bombers provided air support during the operation which was successful, with the GCMA force entering and seizing the village. Having destroyed the Viet Minh supply base, the partisans and para-commandos withdrew into the hills. Viet Minh casualties were estimated at 150 killed and wounded.

October, however, saw the reappearance of the Viet Minh's 316th Division which inflicted severe losses on the maquis in a series of fierce actions.

Requests for support from the 8ème Groupe de Commandos Coloniaux de Parachutiste, a unit previously allocated for reinforcement of the GCMA, were turned down while problems arose over resupply by parachute of ammunition, due to the different types and calibres of weapons in service with the maquis. Meanwhile, evacuation of the wounded by air soon ceased. By the end of November, the three maquis had been overrun and COLIBRI wiped out during a major offensive by the Viet Minh; a few survivors were able to make their way to Dien Bien Phu, which had been seized and occupied by the French on 20 November.

IN NEIGHBOURING Laos, meanwhile, the GCMA was achieving greater success. As described by authors Kenneth Conboy and James Morrison in *Shadow War – The CIA's Secret War in Laos*, a nationalist movement called the Lao Issara (Free Lao) had been formed during the Japanese occupation under two of the sons of the Lao monarch, King Sisavong Vatthana: the princes Phetsarath and Souvanna Phouma. Comprising members of the Lao elite, this organisation had declared independence and, after the surrender of the Japanese, received support from the United States. Along with the Viet Minh, the Americans were keen to see Indochina wrested away from French domination, and OSS personnel were accordingly deployed to Laos in an effort to achieve that aim. The Free French, however, enjoyed support not only from King Sisavong Vatthana but also among the local population in the rural areas. Britain backed France and supplied Force 136 personnel who provided support for the FIS GAUR teams.

During the autumn of 1945, with Chinese forces crossing into Indochina, the GAUR force, by then headed by Lieutenant Colonel Boucher de Crèvecoeur, made two attempts to take control of the country. These proved unsuccessful and thus the French turned their efforts to raising locally recruited forces: by November they had formed four light infantry battalions known as Bataillons de Chasseurs Laotiens (BCL). In January of the following year these units took part in a successful operation on the Bolovens Plateau, in the south of the country, against guerrilla forces of the Lao Issara. During the following weeks, further operations in southern Laos resulted in the capture on 13 March of the town of Savannakhet, situated in the central southern Laotian 'panhandle' on the left bank of the Mekong River, and ultimately the Lao Issara's main base farther north at Thakhek.

On 24 April, French paratroops dropped on the Laotian capital of Vientiane and two weeks later a similar operation was carried out at Luang Prabang. Laos was again under French rule and three months later re-emerged as a principal component of French Indochina. The French, however, were eager for Laos to be granted independence. In May 1947, the country became a constitutional monarchy and two years later was permitted to form its own army, the Armée National Laotienne (ANL). By the end of October 1951, with French assistance, the ANL had formed four light infantry battalions and a parachute battalion. In December, the United States began to supply military aid to Laos via France.

The French had been laying plans for GCMA operations in Laos for some time and had identified four areas as suitable: Xieng Khouang Province in the northern central region of the country, in particular the Tranninh Plateau which had been a reception area for GAUR parachutists in 1944; the north-eastern province of Sam Neua; the Bolovens Plateau; and the far north-west region of Laos in the area of Moung Sing and Ban Houei Sai near the borders with Burma and China. The provinces of Xieng Khouang and Sam Neua were inhabited by Hmong hill tribesmen whose chieftain, Touby Lyfoung, had assisted a GAUR team commanded by Captain Desfarges who had been one of those dropped into Laos in December 1944. The latter had established a good relationship with the Hmong chief, a factor that would pay dividends later.

During 1952, GCMA efforts in Laos were hampered by the priority given to operations in neighbouring Tonkin as well as lack of materiel resources and trained personnel to provide instructors and advisers. Efforts were therefore concentrated on recruitment of indigenous personnel and the formation of centaines, and the establishment of a small training centre in Xieng Khouang. Despite such difficulties, however, there was some progress. One centaine, based at Muong Soi in Sam Neua Province, extended its area of operations to the east and north-east and managed to win over the local population in the country of the Red T'ai tribes, compelling the local Viet Minh forces to relocate their bases elsewhere. To the south, a centaine at Pak Song operated in the area of Tha Teng, carrying out reconnaissance tasks and psychological warfare operations among the local population. During this period, several Viet Minh arms caches were uncovered and considerable quantities of weapons, including 300 rifles, were captured.

The Viet Minh offensive in Tonkin at the end of 1952, which resulted in the communists taking Nghia Lo, Moc Chau and Dien Bien Phu, brought an immediate demand from the French high command for the GCMA to establish maquis in northern Laos. At the end of November Desfarges re-established contact with Touby Lyfoung with a request that the Hmong provide recruits for maquis groups. Touby agreed on condition that the partisans would only be required to operate within their own territories. At the end of December, the Regional Representation of the GCMA in Laos was established in Vientiane under the command of Desfarges. January of the following year saw the allocation of further resources in the form of additional French personnel (an officer and four NCOs), ten indigenous radio operators trained at the GCMA's Ty Wan training centre, weapons and radio sets.

By February 1953 the nuclei of two centaines, each commanded by a Hmong chief, had been established: the first at Phou Dou, on the eastern edge of the Plain of Jars, and the second 35 miles north of the plain in the area of Phou Vieng. Each under the supervision of a French NCO, these formed a maquis codenamed MALO. Meanwhile, preparations for the formation of a second maquis, codenamed SERVAN, were being undertaken in Sam Neua Province. These had to be put on hold when, on 10 April 1953, a Viet Minh force of ten battalions thrust across the border and overran the province, virtually wiping out a force of 1,700 French and Laotian troops attempting to reach the fortified base on the Plain of Jars from Sam Neua. It was largely due to actions on the part of a SERVAN centaine from Sam Neua, and a MALO centaine from Nong Het in Xieng Khouang Province, that 83 French and 109 Laotian troops reached the base. At the same time, a combined force of Viet Minh troops and Pathet Lao communist guerrillas crossed the border and headed south for Luang Prabang. Having overrun a Lao parachute unit dropped as a blocking force, the Viet Minh force advanced to within 30 kilometres of the city, which by then had been reinforced with French troops, before they were halted on 12 May by the onset of the annual monsoon rains and forced to withdraw. The French subsequently reoccupied Xieng Khouang, Ban Ban and Muong Soi.

A third Viet Minh thrust meanwhile crossed into Laos at the border town of Nong Het and headed westward for the Plain of Jars. The French responded by flying in troops which by the end of April comprised two battalions of Foreign Legion infantry, three Laotian light infantry battalions, five companies of the Garde Nationale, a battery of 4.2 inch mortars and a 105mm howitzer battery. At this juncture, the United States stepped in with the supply of six C-119 transports complete with aircrew provided by Civil Air Transport, an airline owned by the CIA. The aircraft arrived during the first week in May and began carrying out supply drops to French forces in north-east Laos. On 13 May they dropped two French and one Vietnamese parachute battalions on to the plain. By the end of the month, the Viet Minh had been pushed back to the border.

In early June a five-man GCMA team, commanded by Lieutenant Brehier, was parachuted into Sam Neua Province to resume the reconnaissance and planning tasks for the establishment of the SERVAN maquis. Subsequently, 50 Hmong tribesmen accompanied Brehier to Hanoi and thence to the Ty Wan training centre at Cap St. Jacques where they underwent training in guerrilla warfare and qualified as parachutists. On 19 October, Brehier and his new partisans were dropped back into their home area at Moung Yut, just south of Brehier's command post location at Phou Phathi, some 20 miles west of the town of Sam Neua. A further three groups were subsequently formed for SERVAN: one centaine was co-located with Brehier's headquarters team at Phou Phathi for operations in the valleys to the immediate west, north-west and south-west. The second group of four centaines, accompanied by 22 French personnel, was based at Ban Houei Nha, 12 kilometres south-east of Phou Phathi, while the third, comprising five centaines and seventeen French GCMA advisors, was located at Nong Khang, 24 kilometres north of the town of Sam Neua.

Meanwhile MALO, under the command of Lieutenant Max Mesnier, was extending its area of operations in Xieng Khouang province and throughout the rest of 1953 raised a further six centaines. Mesnier divided his area of operations into six sub-sectors, each occupied by a force of up to three or four centaines accompanied by a GCMA team under the command of a senior NCO. According to Kenneth Conboy and James Morrison, these were organised as follows: Subsector E comprised the area occupied by Mesnier's headquarters and the hills to the north beyond Phou Dou on the eastern rim of the Plain of Jars; Sub-sector A covered to the north-east around the area of the village of Moung Hiem; Sub-sector U stretched east of the plain around the border town of Nong Het; Sub-sector L, located 30 kilometres to the south-west of Nong Het, incorporated the village of Moung Ngan; and Sub-sector C covered the area of the hills to the south of the plain.

By this time, Captain Desfarges had been relieved in Vientiane by Captain Marson. Meanwhile, both the SERVAN and MALO maquis, which comprised the GCMA forces in north-eastern Laos, were under the overall command of Captain de Bezon de Bazin. In October, however, he was replaced by Captain Jacques Sassi. That same month SERVAN, which by then numbered 1,000 partisans, was reinforced by a group consisting of one French officer and two NCOs, a radio operator and 35 Hmong para-commandos trained at Ty Wan. This considerably increased the offensive capability of the maquis and allowed Lieutenant Brehier to establish detachments in the Red T'ai country as nuclei for two more groups.

In December Captain Sassi conducted the first of a series of training courses at Khang Khay on the Plain of Jars. Two centaines from the Nong Het area were the first to undergo them, subsequently being deployed for operations in the area of Sub-sector Y. One of these was commanded by Lieutenant Vang Pao of the Laotian Army who would subsequently become a principal figure in the continuing secret war against communism in Laos.

During 1953 the GCMA was equally active elsewhere in northern Laos. In the north-east, in Phongsaly Province, two more GCMA networks had been established. The first, codenamed CARDAMONE and under the control of the RRVN in Hanoi, comprised five maquis deployed in an area extending from the north and east of Phongsaly into north-western Tonkin. The second, established in the autumn and under the control of the GCMA Laos in Vientiane, consisted of two maquis covering the area from Moung Sai to the town of Phongsaly, the capital of the province, cutting across Viet Minh lines of communications and supply. Meanwhile, Captain Paul Mourier assumed command of the Muong Sing area, linking up with a centaine at Muong Khua over the border in Tonkin.

Within a year of commencing its operations in Laos, the GCMA had succeeded in extending its control throughout almost the entire north of the country. In Sam Neua Province, the SERVAN maquis totalled almost 1,000 in strength and such was the effectiveness of the GCMA's grip that the communist Pathet Lao was forced to move its headquarters from Sam Neua town to the village of Vieng Sai some 28 kilometres to the south-east. In Phongsaly Province, the MALO maquis controlled the area from the Plain of Jars westward to the border with Tonkin, while in the far north-west another maquis was being formed in the area of Moung Sing.

The beginning of the following year, 1954, saw another maquis, code-named SANGSUE, established in the Red T'ai country under the command of Lieutenant Marc Geronimi. Controlled by the RRVN in Hanoi, its area of operations was vast, encompassing Muong Sai, Sam Teu and Hua Xieng in Laos and stretching over the border into Tonkin where it extended to Hoi Xuan and Cu Rao. This was part of Lieutenant Colonel Roger Trinquier's plan to increase the strength of partisan forces to some 50,000 and to recover the entire area of the T'ai country from the Viet Minh.

The latter part of 1953 had also seen the GCMA establishing two further networks of maquis in the southern 'panhandle' of Laos. The first comprised three groups: one in the area of Khamkeut, a village in the upper area of the region; a second near an airbase at Seno; and a third close to the border town of Lao Bao. The second network was located farther to the south in the area of Pakse with two areas of operations based respectively on Saravane and Paksong, the latter on the Bolovens Plateau. From the bases on the plateau at Tha Teng and Houei Kong, the centaines commanded by Captain Jestin carried out harassing raids and attacks against the Viet Minh in addition to conducting intelligence gathering and psychological warfare operations.

In December 1953, the GCMA was redesignated the Groupe Mixte d'Intervention (GMI) but with no change to its role and operational activities. During the previous month in Tonkin the French commander-in-chief, General Henri Navarre, who had replaced General Raoul Salan in May, had ordered the establishment of a fortified base in the valley of Dien Bien Phu astride the Route Provinciale 41 highway which linked it with Laï Chau to the north and Son La, Na San, Hadong and Hanoi to the east. This was ostensibly a measure to block an expected thrust into Laos by the Viet Minh, and Navarre declared it as such while also stating that he intended to lure Giap's forces into killing grounds where they would be destroyed. While Dien Bien Phu was undoubtedly of strategic importance as the so-called 'gateway' into Laos, Navarre's decision to deploy 15,000 troops to an isolated base over 200 miles from their principal area of operations in the delta was nevertheless not based solely on concern for the defence of Laos.

Throughout the conflict, the principal problem encountered by the Deuxième Bureau and the GCMA was the lack of funds to finance their operations; in the case of the latter, the establishment and maintenance of its maquis groups. The war in Indochina was not a popular cause in France, which had reduced its military expenditure in the region to the minimum. As the French high command had no extra funds to allocate to the GCMA, the latter was forced to look elsewhere for additional financial resources for its operations.

The solution was found in opium, the staple cash crop of the Hmong hill tribes in Laos and Tonkin. In 1952, the Viet Minh had confiscated almost the entire crop, causing great anger and resentment among the T'ai and Hmong, and had sold it on the open market in the Thai capital of Bangkok to finance the purchase of more arms from China. In 1953, sensing their opportunity, the Deuxième Bureau and Lieutenant Colonel Trinquier approached the hill tribes and offered to purchase the next crop at a competitive price. The results of this move were threefold: good relations were restored between the GCMA and the tribes, having suffered since the reverses in the autumn of 1952; the Viet Minh's advance into Laos was aborted as the seizure of the opium crop had been its sole objective; and the opium could be sold to raise funds, part of which were handed over to the GCMA to finance the maquis.

This resulted in the creation of an operation, codenamed merely 'x', under the auspices of which opium was purchased from the tribes at market prices negotiated by GCMA officers and loaded aboard French DC-3 aircraft at Tan Son Nhut, ostensibly being flown to the Plain of Jars. In fact, the aircraft flew a great deal farther, to the airstrip close to the GCMA's Ty Wan training centre at Cap St. Jacques in Southern Vietnam. It was then transported in trucks 90 kilometres to Saigon where it was handed over to the Deuxième Bureau's gangster protégés, the

Binh Xuyen, for refining. There was little possibility of any interference from the authorities as the head of the Binh Xuyen's military wing was the city's chief of police.

The opium was refined at two boiling plants, one located in the Cholon quarter of the city and the other close to the National Assembly building. Once refined, part of the opium was distributed to dens and shops throughout Saigon, many of which were owned by the Binh Xuyen. The remainder was sold off to Chinese merchants, who exported it to Hong Kong, and the Union Corse, the Corsican mafia which was well represented in Indochina. The latter exported it to France, shipping it to Marseilles where drugs trafficking was controlled by four families whose members included individuals employed by the SDECE. The Binh Xuyen split the profits from such sales with the Deuxième Bureau and the GCMA, the latter using part of its share to finance its maquis operations.

Some of the consignments of opium exported from Indochina eventually reached the United States, which launched an investigation. In June 1953, Lieutenant Colonel Edward Lansdale reappeared in Saigon as a member of a US military mission headed by Brigadier General John 'Iron Mike' O'Daniel which visited Indochina for the purpose of providing advice to General Navarre. Lansdale was asked by the French commander-in-chief for his recommendations on unconventional warfare operations and was thus permitted to journey freely throughout Tonkin, Annam and Vietnam, visiting Freench and Vietnamese garrisons. It was as a result of his movements around the country that he subsequently pinpointed the source of the opium as being the GCMA. Colonel Maurice Belleux conducted an investigation and ordered that the stocks stored secretly at Cap St. Jacques should be seized. As recounted by Roger Faligot and Pascal Krop in their book *La Piscine – The French Secret Service Since 1944*, Belleux later explained the situation facing him:

> The GCMA was under Colonel Grall, who knew Indochina well. He was aided by Commandants (Majors) Trinquier and Rozen. During his enquiry Colonel Bertin, of Military Security, uncovered hundreds of kilos of opium in GCMA buildings. General Salan blamed us for it; in theory we should have passed on the opium.

But this opium, from Touby Lyfoung, had to be bought by someone. If it had not been for SDECE, the Viets would have gained the allegiance of the Meos. The opium was to have been sent in part to the 'Golden Triangle' in Burma, with the help of the Chinese connection. If a slip-up occurred, the CIA and the SDECE would have been involved. The Americans were being hoodwinked. Moreover, another part of the cargo was to have been despatched by Bai Vien to the Roger Bellon pharmaceutical laboratories, on board Jacquier's planes. It was envisaged that Trinquier's operation would be covered by Salan. Yet in the end Colonel Grall was sentenced to 45 days' close arrest, which enabled his deputy, Trinquier, to replace him.

Two of the individuals named by Belleux, Roger Bellon and General Paul Jacquier, were both members of the SDECE. Head of a pharmaceutical organisation, Bellon was also a reservist in the SDECE Action Service while Jacquier, a career intelligence officer, would be appointed the service's director in 1962.

Dien Bien Phu, hitherto held by the Viet Minh, was recaptured by the French without difficulty in an airborne operation codenamed CASTOR which took place on 20 November 1953. French forces there were subsequently built up to a garrison initially comprising twelve battalions. A month later, however, Viet Minh forces, comprising the 316th Division and 148th Regiment, struck at Laï Chau. Such was the ferocity of the assault that the T'ai force of 2,100 irregulars, together with their French GCMA advisers, were forced to abandon the city and withdraw towards Dien Bien Phu; by the time they reached it, they numbered only 175 men. This was a major blow to the French because, as already mentioned, in addition to being the capital of the T'ai Federation, Lai Chau was the principal GMI airhead and logistical support centre for its operations in Tonkin. Furthermore, it played a key role in the control of opium in the region. These factors were recognised by the Viet Minh's commander, Giap, who, consequently, was determined not only to capture the city but also to lure the French into deploying major forces from their principal area of operations in the Tonkin delta. Such was the importance of Laï Chau and opium to the French that they took the bait and occupied Dien Bien Phu. In so doing, however, they sowed the seeds for their ultimate defeat and withdrawal from Indochina.

Until this time, Giap had avoided large set-piece confrontations with the French since the premature offensive of 1951 which had ended in disaster for the Viet Minh. He now approached Dien Bien Phu cautiously and concentrated on building up his forces which possessed a large quantity of artillery, including anti-aircraft guns. Massive logistical preparations were put in place, including a network of depots linked by roads which threaded their way through the jungle from base supply depots in Viet Minh-held areas. When the monsoon rains made roads impassable to vehicles, the Viet Minh switched to using thousands of porters who carried supplies to forward supply dumps.

French intelligence was meanwhile well aware of the communist advance towards Dien Bien Phu. In November, the Deuxième Bureau had given a remarkably accurate estimate of Giap's infantry strength as comprising 29 battalions – in fact the actual number was 28. On 27 December 1953, French air photographic intelligence estimated the total communist strength to be some 49,000 men, of whom some 33,000 were combatant personnel.

Meanwhile, GMI partisans and French paratroops, notably reconnaissance elements of the 8ème Bataillon Parachutiste d'Assaut, commanded by Captain Tourret, were carrying out two operations, codenamed REGATTA and POLLUX, to track the Viet Minh formations as they advanced towards Dien Bien Phu, and to observe and interdict their lines of communication. Information on the communist advance was relayed to Diem Bien Phu and its commander, Brigadier General Christian de Castries.

Numbering some 5,000 in total, the forces deployed on these two operations succeeded in tying down some 15,000 Viet Minh troops but, even with French air support, failed in their primary task of cutting the communist supply routes in Tonkin. The principal problem facing them was the sheer size of the Viet Minh logistic network which consisted of roads and tracks extending from inside China to Lang Son and 800 kilometres beyond to Dien Bien Phu. Along these routes thousands of porters, some using bicycles, delivered hundreds of tons of supplies daily.

The siege of Dien Bien Phu dragged on through March and April.

During the battle, the garrison was reinforced by five parachute battalions, one Vietnamese, one Foreign Legion and three French units, and three airborne surgical detachments. A further 1,530 troops, including 800 Vietnamese, jumped in as replacements for specialist casualties such as artillerymen and signallers; of these, some 680 had never previously parachuted.

At the end of April, the GMI took part in Operation D, a relief exercise launched from Laos. It was carried out by two separate elements. The first, comprising one Foreign Legion and three Laotian battalions under the overall command of Colonel Yves Godard, the commanding officer of the 11e Choc, headed north-east from Moung Sai towards Dien Bien Phu. The second, under the overall command of Captain Jacques Sassi and consisting of 800 partisans of the SERVAN maquis under Lieutenant Brehier, 200 partisans of MALO's Sub-Sector A under Lieutenant Max Mesnier, and a 100-man Laotian Hmong commando unit under Lieutenant Vang Pao, struck out north-westward on 30 April to create a diversion in the area of Muong Peu, a village on the Lao–Tonkinese border some 85 kilometers to the south-east of Dien Bien Phu. They would be reinforced by the 1er Bataillon de Parachutistes Coloniaux (1er BPC) under Captain de Bezon de Bazin. In addition, a French unit, the 610ème Commando de Reconnaissance, was assigned to the operation with the task of carrying out an intelligence-gathering mission for the French high command.

Colonel Godard's force initially made good progress, reaching a point over halfway to Dien Bien Phu. At that juncture, however, it encountered the Viet Minh's 148th Regiment which blocked its way. The SERVAN and MALO contingents meanwhile were advancing separately towards Moung Peu, Lieutenant Brehier's force marching in from the east while Mesnier approached from the south. Bringing up Mesnier's rear were Lieutenant Vang Pao and his commandos. Brehier and Mesnier were supposed to rendezvous at the village of Moung Son, 30 kilometres south of Moung Peu. Brehier arrived on 1 May but Mesnier did not arrive until six days later, having had to cover a greater distance. By that time, however, Dien Bien Phu had fallen and four days later Brehier and Mesnier were ordered to withdraw their forces.

Two further GMI operations had in the meantime been under way to relieve the pressure on the beleaguered garrison at Dien Bien Phu.

CONDOR was mounted in the centre and south of Laos's Phongsaly Province while VULTURE covered the northern and eastern areas of the province. CONDOR suffered heavy casualties when the Viet Minh launched an attack on the province's capital, decimating two maquis. VULTURE enjoyed more success, establishing a partisan force and securing a DZ where it was due to link up with Captain de Bazin's 1er BPC. In the event, the latter was dropped at Dien Bien Phu instead and the partisans withdrew on 2 May, subsequently forming a screen which managed to rescue 78 paratroops and Foreign Legionnaires who had fought their way out of Dien Bien Phu and avoided capture.

On 21 July 1954, in Geneva, the French signed a ceasefire agreement with the communists. Shortly afterwards, the GMI received instructions to withdraw its teams and immediately ordered them to abandon their maquis and withdraw to Hanoi. In Laos, Captain Jacques Sassi was ordered to disarm his partisans, but refused. He did so not only as a matter of honour but also because such a task would have been impossible, given the mood of the Hmong population at the time. Lieutenant Marc Geronimi marched his SANGSUE maquis across the border into Laos and headed for Moung Soi where he established a base. Part of the maquis was subsequently formed into three Laotian units designated Commandos 34, 35 and 36, and commanded by their own Hmong officers, who had received scant training in leadership. Other elements of the SANGSUE maquis were organised into self-defence partisan groups. On 7 August the GMI's RR Laos was withdrawn although some 1,500 French officers, warrant officers and NCOs remained in the country. On the following day, the three commando units were attacked by Viet Minh regular forces and put up little resistance, retreating and losing a number of radio sets and some 2,000 weapons in the process. The self-defence groups meanwhile avoided all contact and vanished into the Muong Lan region with their weapons. By September, the SANGSUE maquis had ceased to exist.

Other GMI teams also refused to comply with the order to withdraw, choosing instead to remain with their maquis. Under the Geneva agreement, the French were barred from resupplying the partisans. Lieutenant Colonel Roger Trinquier turned to the United States for assistance but his request was refused. He himself was in trouble with his superiors in the SDECE as he had, without their authority, set up a body called the Liberation Committee for the Upper Red River with the aim of continuing operations against the Viet Minh. He was subsequently apprehended and served ten days under close arrest.

Some of the tribes in Tonkin and Annam, notably the Nung and Muong, made their way to the non-communist south of Vietnam where they settled in the hills near Dalat. The Tonkinese hill tribes, including the Hmong and T'ai, were forced to continue their battle against the Viet Minh or flee over the border into Laos. The communists, evidently determined to stamp out any opposition in the north, committed considerable forces, comprising 31 battalions, including the Viet Minh's 421st Intelligence Battalion counter-partisan unit and 17 regional force companies to hunting down the remaining GMI elements. In September 1957, the communist weekly publication *Quan-Doi Nhan-Dan* reported that during the period from July 1954 to April 1956 183 partisans had been killed and 300 captured, while 4,336 tribesmen had surrendered.

The last French troops left Indochina in April 1956 but resistance continued. During the latter part of that year, radio operators in South Vietnam picked up a radio transmission in French, frantically appealing for help: 'You sons of bitches, help us! Parachute us at least some ammunition so we can die like fighting men, not slaughtered like animals!'

The aftermath of the demise of the GMI resulted in unfortunate revelations concerning the desertion of some GCMA/GMI officers to the Viet Minh. As described by Roger Faligot and Pascal Krop in *La Piscine*, one such defector was Captain Banhiot who had served during the Second World War as a lieutenant colonel in the Francs-Tireurs et Partisans (FTP), the communist resistance organisation. In 1952, Banhiot was summoned to appear before an inquiry in Saigon which had been convened to examine his wartime activities in the FTP. But instead of showing up, he fled to to the town of Luc Nam, in north-eastern Tonkin, where he surrendered himself to the Viet Minh.

Another who defected to the communist cause was Captain Françisque Richonnet, who had been a GAUR commando in Laos in 1946 and subsequently served in the GCMA in central Annam, being reported as killed in action in September 1952. Like Banhiot, he had served as a lieutenant colonel in the FTP. Apparently the pro-communist sympathies of certain GCMA officers were known to their superiors and, according to Faligot and Krop, the decision had been taken to execute them. In the case of Richonnet, a GCMA warrant officer was detailed with the task of shooting him and attempted to do so. Richonnet, however, was quicker off the mark and fired first, wounding his assailant and making good his escape, later making contact with the Viet Minh to whom he handed himself over.

A particularly interesting case was that of an unidentified GCMA officer who, according to a former chief of the Deuxième Bureau, Colonel Henri Jacquin, in an account given to Roger Faligot and Pascal Krop, defected on 15 January 1954. He was a particularly valuable prize for the communists as he had been responsible for counter-espionage and was familiar with material gleaned from intercepts of Viet Minh communications. After the end of the First Indochina War he remained in North Vietnam where he was later interviewed by an American journalist. During the conversation he revealed that, following his defection, he had advised the Viet Minh that the French forces at Dien Bien Phu had been warned of an impending attack. On being taken to General Giap's headquarters, he had handed over details of French plans for an offensive which resulted in the Viet Minh commander postponing his own assault.

Opinions vary as to the results achieved by the GCMA/GMI during the three years of its brief existence. Undoubtedly, the GCMA teams themselves carried out their task of organising, training and leading the hill-tribe maquis with great dedication but with limited resources. Not least of the considerable problems they encountered were the difficulties of keeping their tribesmen armed and supplied, particularly with sufficient food for them and their families, without which the maquis would have disintegrated, the tribes returning to their homes to plant crops and grow opium. Furthermore, the motivation of certain tribal chiefs was open to question, in some cases personal profit prevailing over a desire to engage in operations against the Viet Minh.

As Douglas Porch points out in his book *The French Secret Services*, a good example of this was Deo Van Long, the minority White T'ai leader of the T'ai Federation in Tonkin which included some 100,000 Black T'ai and approximately 50,000 Hmong in its population. His maquis saw little action against the Viet Minh, being used instead to quell any opposition among the Black T'ai who inhabited the region in which Dien

Bien Phu was situated. The ruthless and brutal fashion in which it did so aroused strong opposition against the T'ai leader and the French who trained and armed his private army. The Hmong were similarly ill-disposed towards Van Long who forced them to sell their opium to him at less than the market price. The disaffection of both groups towards the French cause manifested itself during the siege of Dien Bien Phu when they willingly provided the Viet Minh with guides and porters.

The effectiveness of the maquis in operations against the Viet Minh was restricted by their unwillingness to operate outside their home areas, as was shown by the Hré partisan element of Captain Pierre Hentic's force during the long-range operation carried out in Laos during the second half of 1952. Moreover, the ability of the maquis to gather detailed and precise intelligence was limited by the fact that nearly all the tribesmen were illiterate. Critics have pointed to the failure of the GCMA and its maquis to disrupt effectively the Viet Minh lines of communication and supply which stretched for 800 kilometres between Lang Son and Dien Bien Phu. It should be borne in mind, however, that Giap devoted considerable resources to protecting these and that the maquis were organised and trained for guerrilla warfare, not for major confrontations with large bodies of well-equipped enemy troops. Moreover, on several occasions maquis succeeded in carrying out operations in communist rear areas where they created conditions of instability and kept the Viet Minh off-balance. In so doing, they diverted and tied down considerable numbers of enemy units which would otherwise have been committed against regular French forces.

CHAPTER FOUR

MALAYA 1948–1958

While France was heavily engaged in fighting the forces of Ho Chi Minh and Vo Nguyen Giap in Indochina, Britain was also facing a threat to one of the jewels in its colonial crown.

Bordered on the north by Thailand, to which it is linked by the Kra Isthmus, the Malayan Peninsula extends some 500 miles south to the island of Singapore. To its north and east are the Gulf of Thailand and the South China Sea, and to the south and west, Singapore, the Straits of Malacca and Indonesia. To the south-east lies the island of Borneo with the states of Sabah, Sarawak, Brunei and Indonesian Kalimantan.

The peninsula is largely mountainous, comprising several mountain ranges aligned north–south which are dominated by a 300-mile-long main range rising to over 7,000 feet above sea level. Bordering these are areas of coastal lowlands which are heavily populated in the west, with narrow areas of swamp and dense jungle in the east. Some three-fifths of the peninsula is covered in dense jungle, the major part of which is evergreen rain forest. The climate is hot and humid, being strongly affected by monsoons blowing from the south-west from June to October, and from the north-east from November to March.

The British made their first appearance in Malaya following their establishment in 1819 of a settlement on Singapore. By 1867 they had founded the Straits Settlements of Malacca, Singapore and Penang, and by 1896 each of the nine Malay states was ruled by its own sultan and had its own British political adviser. These comprised Johore, the federation of Pahang, Negri Sembilan, Selangor and Perak, Kedah, Perlis, Kelantan and Trengganu. From the 1890s onward the British invested heavily in Malaya, promoting the planting of rubber and mining of tin, which became the country's prime exports, as well as encouraging the production of pepper, gambier, tobacco and palm oil. They also devoted considerable effort to developing Malaya's infrastructure, establishing a network of roads and railways to link plantations and mines to towns and port facilities which were improved to handle the country's rapidly increasing export trade. By the early twentieth century, Malaya had become the world's leading exporter of natural rubber and tin.

By 1911 the country's population was a mixture of races, 60 per cent being Malay and the remainder principally Chinese and Tamil, the latter having been recruited from southern India as the workforce for the country's numerous rubber plantations. The Chinese, who by 1940 numbered several million, prospered and eventually controlled much of the merchant and retail businesses throughout the country. In addition, living within the jungles that covered the major part of the country, were some 50,000 aborigines who comprised essentially three groups. In the north and north-east were the Negritos, small, dark-skinned and woolly-pated, with a nomadic way of life, living in lean-to shelters and surviving on roots and game trapped or killed with their blowpipes. In central Malaya were the Senoi, divided into two sub-groupings or tribes named the Semai and Temiar, who lived respectively in the southern and northern parts of the region. Of fairer skin with wavy hair, they lived in permanent huts or dwellings, growing crops while also hunting for game and fish. In the south of the country were a people referred to by anthropologists as Proto-Malays, with lank hair and similar in appearance to Malays, but speaking an obscure dialect of their language.

In December 1941, Malaya was invaded by Japan whose forces swept swiftly southward through the entire peninsula, overrunning the British, Indian and Australian forces which faced them. At sea, on 10 December, the Royal Navy suffered the humiliating loss of the battleships HMS *Repulse* and *Prince of Wales* as a result of attacks by Japanese torpedo bombers. On 15 February 1942, the garrison on Singapore surrendered and the myth of British invincibility had been shattered for ever.

Resistance to the Japanese occupation forces in Malaya came predominantly from the adherents of communism, which had been introduced into Malaya in the early 1920s by the Chinese Communist Party. In 1928 the Nanyang (South Seas) Communist Party was formed but made little headway in a country prospering under British colonial rule. It was dissolved and replaced two years later by the Malaysian Communist Party (MCP). During the worldwide economic depression of the 1930s, which affected even Malaya, the party made some progress in establishing communism in the country and by 1939 its membership totalled some 39,000, half of it in Singapore.

On the outbreak of war in 1939, and using the excuse that Russia was

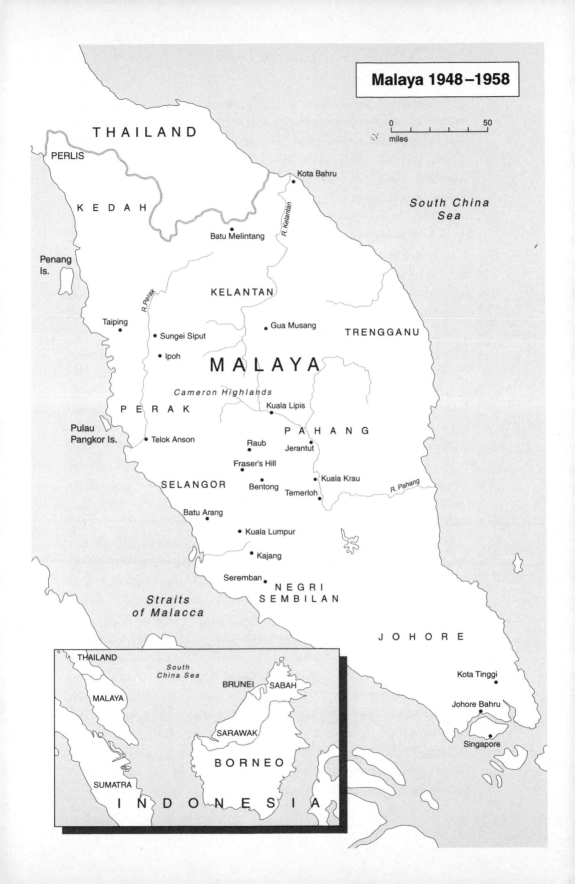

on the same side as Germany, the MCP mounted an anti-British campaign; but in June 1941 it was forced to adopt a very different tune following the German invasion of Russia. On orders from Moscow and
Peking, the party, headed by its secretary general Loi Tak, offered to
cooperate with the federal government which in turn agreed to free all
communists being held in prison. Fifteen individuals were selected and
despatched to Singapore where they underwent training at Special Training School 101, an establishment run by the Oriental Mission, a Singa-
pore-based detachment of the Special Operations Executive (SOE).
They subsequently returned to Malaya and disappeared into the jungle
together with a number of British personnel who had also undergone
rudimentary training in guerrilla warfare. A few of the latter survived,
among them Major Freddie Spencer Chapman who later would become
renowned for his exploits. In the initial period of chaos after the Japanese invasion, contact was lost between the guerrillas in the jungle and
the MCP headquarters in Singapore. During the following months,
however, it was re-established and the guerrillas formed into a cohesive
force. Called the Malayan Peoples Anti-Japanese Army (MPAJA), it was
organised into eight regiments totalling some 7,000 guerrillas based
throughout Malaya. It was supported by the Malayan People's Anti-
Japanese Union (MPAJU), a highly secret civilian organisation which
provided support in the form of supplies, recruits and funds, as well as
gathering intelligence and distributing propaganda.

In 1943, communication with the MPAJA was established by SOE's
Asian and Far Eastern arm, Force 136, whose headquarters was at
Colombo, on the island of Ceylon. On 4 August, Major John Davis, an
officer in Force 136 who knew Malaya well as he had served as a police
officer there before the war, was landed from a submarine at Tanjong
Hantu, on the west coast, at the northernmost end of the Dindings
Channel between the mainland and the island of Pulau Pangkor. Setting
up camp in the jungle at Segari, he proceeded to make contact with the
guerrillas and in particular with a senior representative of the MPAJA
headquarters in Perak, Ong Boon Hua. Better known by his alias of Chin
Peng, he was a committed communist who had joined the MCP in 1940
at the age of eighteen and had then been appointed a member of its
Perak state committee, later becoming state secretary. His performance
as one of the leaders of the communist movement against the Japanese

would subsequently earn him the gratitude of the British and the award of a decoration, albeit he would never receive it.

Davis was eventually joined by other British personnel and thereafter Force 136 supplied the MPAJA with arms, equipment and training, the latter being provided by experts in guerrilla warfare who were parachuted into the jungle or landed by submarine. By 1945 the guerrillas were a highly trained and well-armed force. Towards the end of the year, after the surrender of Japan and the return of British forces to Malaya, the MPAJA was officially demobilised and disbanded, handing over its weapons to the authorities.

The return of British rule to Malaya was followed in due course by a proposal to transform the country into a single Malayan Union, incorporating all the Malayan states with the exception of Singapore. This encountered very strong objections and resistance from the Malay population who recognised that such a move would result in the diminution of individual state autonomy and the granting of citizenship and political rights to non-Malays within the country. The outcome was the formation in 1946 of the United Malays National Organisation (UMNO). Faced with strikes, demonstrations and boycotts, the British climbed down and entered into negotiations with UMNO, these leading in 1948 to the establishment of the Federation of Malaya which united the states, guaranteed the rights of Malays and secured the positions of the sultans.

These developments caused considerable alarm among the Chinese element of the population and in particular the MCP which decided to pursue its aims through armed insurrection. It mobilised its military wing, initially renamed the Malayan People's Anti-British Army (MPABA), and subsequently changed to the Malayan Races Liberation Army (MRLA). Comprising by mid-1948 some 4,000 to 5,000 experienced guerrillas, the MRLA was organised in eight regiments ranging in strength from 200 to 700 and was based in a number of camps, some of which had been constructed during the war. The largest of these could accommodate up to 600 guerillas while others were able to house around 300. Each included barracks, classrooms, administrative offices, kitchens, latrines and washing areas, with well-hidden sentry posts sited up to 400 yards away on all approaches. In the event of an attack, it was a firm policy that a camp would be abandoned and therefore pre-reconnoitred escape routes were also established. Two regiments were based in Johore and two in Pahang, while the remaining four were located in Selangor, Negri Sembilan, Perak and Kedah, the largest being the Perak regiment which numbered 700 guerrillas. In addition to the regiments which remained static within their respective states, there were a number of independent sub-units which had a roving brief, being free to roam throughout their allocated areas of operations.

The MRLA was well equipped with quantities of weapons acquired during the war and hidden in well-concealed caches. During the disbandment of the MPAJA in 1945, each guerrilla had received a gratuity of Malay $350 in return for his weapons. As would later be revealed, however, the MPAJA had concealed large quantities of arms dropped by Force 136 while reporting them as having not been received due to airdrops having gone astray. In addition, it had removed weapons from Japanese armouries following the surrender.

The MRLA's first attacks took place near Sungei Siput, a tin-mining town eighteen miles north of Ipoh, the capital of the state of Perak. At 8.30 p.m. on 16 June 1948, three young Chinese men arrived on bicycles at the offices of the Elphil Estate, a rubber plantation situated some twenty miles east of the town. Walking into the office of the manager, Arthur Walker, they shot him dead. Half an hour later and ten miles away, twelve armed Chinese surrounded the offices of the Sungei Siput Estate and shot dead the manager, John Allison, and his assistant, Ian Christian. A third attack, at Kamuning near Sungei Siput, failed because the jeep belonging to the intended victim, estate manager Donald Wise, had broken down and thus delayed his arrival at his office. Waiting for him were three guerrillas, or Communist Terrorists (CT) as they soon became known. Growing nervous at his failure to appear, they abandoned their mission and disappeared.

During the following day, reports of other attacks flooded into the federal capital of Kuala Lumpur. In Johore, on the Voules Estate, a group of five CT wearing jungle-green uniforms and armed with Sten 9mm submachine-guns had appeared at the house of the Chinese head labourer and ordered him to exact a 'subscription' of 50 cents per week from each member of the estate's labour force. When he refused, he was tied to a tree and, with his wife and young daughter forced to watch, had both arms hacked off with a parang. Such was the terrorists' confidence that the leader of the group identified himself to the distraught wife as Goh Peng Tun. During the next eight years, he would become one of the most notorious CT leaders.

Meanwhile, on the Senai Estate near the town of Johore Bahru, another Chinese head labourer had been shot dead by ten men lying in wait for him as part of another attempt to terrorise the labour forces of the rubber plantations and tin mines. At the same time, attacks were launched on the isolated homes of the rubber planters themselves.

The reaction of the authorities to these and other attacks which took place on 16 June was slow, particularly in view of the fact that there had been a number of warnings of trouble from the Malayan Security Service. During the previous year, rubber plantations and tin mines throughout Malaya had been plagued by over 300 communist-organised strikes, and in January 1948 police had been forced to open fire on a group of rioters armed with spears and stones, killing seven. Tension had been growing ever since and with increasing signs of unrest around them, planters had expressed their concern to the federal government and the High Commissioner, Sir Edward Gent. The latter, however, had accused them of being alarmist and had refused requests for protection. Even a three-page report from a highly experienced senior military intelligence officer, Colonel John Dalley, providing accurate estimates of the strengths of the MRLA and warning of an imminent armed insurrection, failed to spur the High Commissioner into action. Despite such warnings and the events of the previous day, on 17 June he insisted on declaring a state of emergency only in certain areas of Perak and Johore. Such was the outcry from the press and the public, however, that on 23 June he was forced to extend it throughout Malaya. Emergency measures were introduced immediately, including curfews and special powers of search, arrest and detention.

The decision to carry out the 16 June attacks had been taken some weeks beforehand at a secret conference of the MCP's politburo held in Pahang. Some 50 senior members of the party had gathered at a large camp deep in the jungle between the towns of Bentong and Raub. Among those present were MCP deputy secretary general Yeung Kwo; Ah 'Shorty' Kuk; senior commander in southern Malaya Hor Lung; Lau Fatt; propaganda expert and district committee secretary Osman China; Pahang rear base commander and state committee member Hor Leong; Ha Yong; Willie Kwok; regional committee leader Yap Lian; and chairman of the MCP's military committee Lau Yew, all of whom had served in the MPAJA during the war against the Japanese. Presiding over the conference was Chin Peng, who had been appointed to the MCP's central committee after the end of the Second World War and by this time was secretary general of the party. Over the next four days he outlined his strategy for the communist takeover of Malaya, based on that followed by Mao Tse Tung during his conquest of China.

It was divided into three stages. The first would comprise attacks on rubber estates and tin mines, as well as members of the police and government officials in towns and villages. The aim of this stage was to force the federal government to evacuate the countryside which would be secured by the MRLA as 'liberated areas'. The second stage would consist of bases being established where additional recruits, attracted by the successes in the first stage, would be trained and the guerrillas' strength increased in preparation for the third and final phase. This would see MRLA forces breaking out from the 'liberated areas' to attack towns and other major targets, such as railway installations, before ultimately seeking to engage British forces, with the support of China.

Chin Peng foresaw that the campaign would be a long one, predicting that it could take up to ten years for the MCP to achieve its aims. This was reflected in a directive issued during 1948 which maintained that the MRLA's objective was to conserve and expand its strength and warned against any 'impetuous' and 'adventurous' operations. It continued by stating:

> We want to strike hard to score victory in every encounter and to ensure that the enemy is eliminated and his arms seized. Thus we will train our forces, expand them and raise their quality until ultimately the position of superiority in strength of the enemy and our position of inferiority and weakness is reversed. For this reason, our army is adopting the policy of a protracted war ... We are not afraid of a protracted war; on the contrary, subjectively we seek the strategy of a protracted war.

The MCP central committee clearly expected to receive assistance from China, particularly in the final stage, but in this it was mistaken. Mao Tse Tung was heavily committed to crushing the nationalists of Chiang Kai Shek and could not afford to send any material support to the MCP which thus had to conduct the struggle on its own. It could, however, count on considerable support from another source, the extensive secret organisation of the wartime MPAJU, since renamed the Min Yuen (People's Movement), whose members were to be found at all levels of Chinese society within Malaya, ranging from wealthy merchants and members of the professional classes to taxi drivers, domestic servants and barbers. The size of the organisation has never been established. A Malayan government report hazarded a guess of some 500,000, but Colonel John Dalley estimated it as about half that number.

In addition to the Min Yuen, the MCP and MRLA set up a courier system which criss-crossed the entire length and breadth of Malaya. Given the absence of available transmitter/receivers (after a ban on radio sales by the federal government) and the nature of the terrain, which hampered radio signals, this was the only effective alternative. Couriers moved along jungle tracks, delivering and collecting messages to and from a series of carefully camouflaged letter boxes, each knowing only the locations of those on his particular route. Schedules were such that couriers never met one another when making deliveries or collections. While it was a relatively secure means of communication, the system was very slow, with messages taking months to arrive at their intended destination.

According to one of those who attended the conference in Pahang, propaganda expert Osman China, who later divulged its details to a senior Special Branch officer, members of the central committee were so confident that the possibility of failure apparently never entered their minds. In reality, however, resorting to armed insurrection was a last desperate measure to save the MCP from disintegration. All political activities to achieve communist political domination of Malaya had hitherto failed, and other more direct measures, such as intimidation and disruption of labour, had also proved fruitless. Moreover, during 1947, the MCP had been dealt a major body blow by its former secretary general, Loi Tak, who had disappeared with the party's funds. His successor, Chin Peng, had subsequently used him as a scapegoat for the failure of communism to take sufficient root in Malaya and had published a manifesto giving full details.

Unknown to Chin Peng at the time, however, was the fact that Loi Tak had been a long-term agent in the employ of the British. An

Annamite by nationality, he had previously worked for the French Sureté in Indochina until he had been 'blown', being spirited away to Hong Kong and then Singapore where he had been employed by the Straits Settlements Police Special Branch. Thereafter, he had infiltrated the MCP and quickly worked his way up through its ranks to the central committee, ultimately being appointed secretary general. Throughout the war, he appeared to lead a charmed life, experiencing little difficulty in avoiding arrest by the Japanese security forces. On one occasion he was absent from an MCP meeting when it was raided by the Kempei Tai, the Japanese secret police, who massacred a large number of party members. After the surrender of the Japanese and the return of the British to Singapore and Malaya, Loi Tak continued to hold the position of secretary general and thus the British were able to control the activities of the MCP, ensuring that they continued to be unsuccessful.

In early 1947, however, a member of the central committee who had collaborated with the Japanese raised suspicions that Loi Tak had also been an enemy agent. Although he survived this allegation, he was accused of 'adopting a right-wing policy' by hard-line members of the central committee who advocated armed insurrection. A meeting of the committee was scheduled for 6 March but, fearing that he was about to be 'blown' once again, his Special Branch controllers removed him immediately from the scene. When the Central Committee convened, Loi Tak was absent. By that time, in possession of the MCP's funds and a further sum supplied by the Special Branch, he was aboard a ship sailing for Hong Kong where he subsequently disappeared. It was later reported that he had been tracked down in Thailand and executed, although this was never confirmed.

British forces in mainland Malaya in 1948 comprised six Gurkha battalions and three of the Malay Regiment. All were understrength, numbering in total only some 4,000 men: but there were an additional two Gurkha battalions available, in Singapore and Hong Kong, and three British units, two in Singapore and one on the island of Penang. Those Gurkha units in Malaya, however, had only been in their respective locations since March, having arrived from India after the trauma of Partition which had seen the Indian Army divided between India and the newly established state of Pakistan. Of its ten Gurkha regiments, six remained in India while the other four, the 2nd, 6th, 7th and 10th Gurkha Rifles, were transferred to the British Army. In February 1948, they had sailed for Malaya where they would all be based henceforth, with the exception of the 2nd Gurkha Rifles whose regimental home would be in Singapore.

Prior to their departure from India, however, all Gurkha ranks in these four regiments had been given the choice of remaining in India, by transferring to another unit, or of staying with their regiment and joining the British Army. A number had opted to remain in India and these had been replaced with untrained recruits. One unit, the 2nd Battalion 2nd Gurkha Rifles (2/2GR), had three training companies comprising 400 men under its command. Furthermore, a high proportion of the men of all eight battalions in Malaya, Singapore and Hong Kong were absent in Nepal on their long leave periods to which they were entitled every three years.

The police force in Malaya totalled some 10,200 officers and other ranks spread throughout all nine states and the settlements of Penang and Malacca. Understrength and suffering from poor morale, its divisions covered the whole of Malaya with stations in each district and town. Following the outbreak of violence on 16 June, it rapidly became apparent that the force lacked the numbers, arms and equipment to counter the CT effectively. As the terrorists continued their strategy of attacking the rubber estates, tin mines and isolated police stations, as well as ambushing traffic on remote roads, it became increasingly clear that there was an urgent need for extra manpower to provide sufficient protection.

The response was the formation of the Special Constabulary, recruited almost entirely from Malays. Armed with rifles, its constables took over static guard duties on the estates, mines and vital installations, while also providing bodyguards for British estate and mine managers. A few weeks after its formation, it was reinforced by a force of several hundred British NCOs demobilised from the Palestine Police following Britain's withdrawal from Palestine at the end of June 1948. Within six months of its formation, the Special Constabulary numbered 30,000 and was playing a vital role in the war against the terrorists.

The CT attacks, meanwhile, continued. On 28 June, a force of 40 to 50 CT appeared in the town of Kuala Krau in central Pahang and, having cut the telephone wires, attacked the police station. The three constables inside fought back bravely and inflicted casualties on the terrorists who withdrew 30 minutes later, leaving blood-trails behind them. The only casualty inside the station was a policeman's wife who had been killed. On the following day, a group of CT attacked the town of Jerantut, some 20 miles north of Kuala Krau, burning down the police station and abducting a number of Malays and Chinese before returning to the jungle. That same day saw another attack on a police station at Sedenak in the southern state of Johore; it was driven off after a fierce gun battle which resulted in one of the terrorists being shot dead.

On 12 July, a large force of CT led by a terrorist named Siu Mah launched an attack on a coal mine at Batu Arang in Selangor. They stormed the police station, murdered five people and destroyed much plant and machinery before making good their escape. A few days later, CT units in Kelantan attacked the town of Gua Musang and the neighbouring village of Pulai, occupying them for four days until the arrival of a strong force police and troops. The scale of these two terrorist operations illustrated clearly the scale of the resources which the MRLA had at its disposal.

Four days later, however, the communists suffered their first major setback. Following a tip-off from an informer, a force of fourteen police detectives led by Superintendent Bill 'Two Gun' Stafford, a legendary figure in Malaya who rejoiced in the Chinese nickname of 'Tin Sau-pah' (Iron Broom), surrounded three huts in the centre of a small valley near the town of Kajang, south of Kuala Lumpur. Inside one of the huts was Lau Yew, chairman of the MCP's military committee and commander of the MRLA, and two other CT. In the other two huts were five women; a sixth was outside, tending a fire, and it was she who spotted the approaching police and raised the alarm. The three male terrorists attempted to shoot their way out, but were gunned down. Lau Yew and one other were killed, the third being badly wounded and taken prisoner. All six women, one of them Lau Yew's wife, were captured along with a haul of rifles, shotguns, pistols, ammunition and maps of Kajang and Klang, the latter a town on the coast of Selangor.

No sooner had Stafford's force set fire to the huts and begun withdrawing from the area, however, than it was attacked by a force of some 40 CT armed with Bren light machine-guns. A major battle developed as the police fought back, the terrorists withdrawing as Stafford led his men in a counter-attack. During the mêlée, Lau Yew's wife escaped and the five women prisoners were killed in the crossfire. As Stafford and his men regrouped, they were attacked again and during the brief ensuing engagement a further three CT were killed before the terrorists finally retired. It later transpired that Lau Yew and his two companions, both of whom were senior members of the MCP's military committee, had been putting the final touches to a plan for a major operation to capture Kajang. His death was a severe blow for the MCP, from which it never recovered, as he was a very able guerrilla commander and the only senior CT sufficiently competent to command the MRLA.

A few days later came not only evidence of the resources which the terrorists had at their disposal but also confirmation that the MPAJA had withheld large quantities of British-supplied arms when disbanded in 1945. Another of Superintendent Bill Stafford's informants provided details of a large arms cache located not far from the spot where Lau Yew had been killed. Accompanied by the informant and four detectives, Stafford made his way at night into the jungle six miles outside Kajang. Digging up a clump of young trees indicated by the informant, he and his men uncovered twelve caches lined with timber. Each contained a number of sealed steel containers of the type which had been parachuted to the MPAJA by Force 136. Inside them were a large quantity of Bren .303 light machine-guns, Sten 9mm submachine-guns, 237 Lee Enfield .303 rifles and 10,000 rounds of ammunition.

In the meantime, there had been changes at the highest levels of the federal government. On 29 June 1948, Sir Edward Gent was relieved as High Commissioner. His demise had ultimately been brought about by a copy of Colonel John Dalley's report which had been sent to Malcolm MacDonald, the Commissioner-General for South-East Asia, whose residence was in Johore. Impressed by its content, MacDonald had forwarded it to London before travelling to Kuala Lumpur for a meeting with Gent. The latter had refused to change his view that the terrorists were little more than a disorganised rabble and did not pose a serious threat. Dalley's report caused the Colonial Office in London to think otherwise and, acting upon Macdonald's recommendations that Gent should be replaced, recalled him. Tragically, he was killed a few days later in an air crash over London.

The new High Commissioner did not arrive until September. During the interim period it had been mooted that Gent's successor should be a

senior military officer but this idea had been firmly rejected by Mac-
Donald. In the event Sir Henry Gurney, who had previously been Chief
Secretary in Palestine, was appointed.

Until this time the Army in Malaya, under the General Officer Commanding (GOC) Malaya District, Major General Charles Boucher, had
taken the lead in the war against the CT. Gurney, however, recognised
that the conflict was of a political nature, communism versus democracy, and thus the solution to be sought was a political one supported
by armed force. He was supported in this view by a key member of the
Government Secretariat, Robert Thompson, who had previously been
serving as a Chinese Affairs Officer in the town of Ipoh, in Perak.

A special unit, meanwhile, had been formed from British, Gurkha
and Malay troops led by former officers of Force 136 and the Chindits.
Designated Ferret Force and commanded by Lieutenant Colonel John
Davis, the police officer and former member of Force 136 who had met
Chin Peng during the war, it consisted of a headquarters and six groups,
each comprising four sections. Guided by trackers, in the form of Iban
tribesmen imported from the state of Sarawak on the island of Borneo,
Ferret Force took the war to the enemy by going into the jungle in search
of the CT and proved very successful, locating camps and arms caches,
unearthing information about the terrorists and accounting for a number
of them. For example, No. 3 Group, three of whose sections comprised
Gurkhas of 2/2GR, between July and October killed ten terrorists in
Pahang and Kelantan, in the areas of Kerdan, Gua Musang and Temer-
loh. Unfortunately, however, Ferret Force fell prey to the bickering and
disagreements between the police and army over matters of policy,
administration and methods of operation, and was disbanded in December 1948 after only a brief existence.

In April 1950, Lieutenant General Sir Harold Briggs was appointed
Director of Operations with responsibility for planning, coordination
and direction of the counter-terrorist campaign. Aged 55, he had retired
from the Army in 1948 after a successful career, during the latter part
of which he had commanded the 5th Indian Division in Burma. Within
two weeks of his arrival in Malaya, he produced a policy which would
play a key role in defeating the communists there.

Known as the 'Briggs Plan', its objective was to isolate the terrorists
from all sources of logistical and intelligence support. It had four aims:

to dominate the populated areas and build up a feeling of security which would ultimately result in an increasing flow of information to the security forces; to break up the communist organisation within populated areas; to isolate the terrorists from their supplies of food and information; and to destroy the terrorists by forcing them to attack the security forces on the latter's own ground. Briggs also planned to bring under administrative control the large communities of Chinese 'squatters' living in ramshackle huts on the edges of the jungle, eking out a living by growing crops and raising pigs and poultry on land that did not belong to them. They were particularly vulnerable to coercion and extortion by the terrorists, and therefore were likely to accede to demands for food, money and information.

As part of his measures to improve coordination of planning and of operations, Briggs established a series of executive bodies. At national level was the Federal War Council comprising himself, the Chief Secretary to the government, the Commissioner of Police and the commanders of the ground and air forces in Malaya. A State War Executive Committee was formed in each state, consisting of the Prime Minister, the chief police officer and the commander of the brigade stationed in the state. Next were the District War Executive Committees which comprised the District Officer, the senior police officer and the commanding officers of the battalions deployed in each district.

Briggs was well aware that intelligence would be the most vital factor in winning the war against the communists. He directed that the Special Branch should be the sole intelligence organisation. With its headquarters in Kuala Lumpur, where it formed part of the Malayan Police Criminal Investigation Department, the Special Branch had been formed in November 1948, replacing the Malayan Security Service, which had been created in 1946, and covered both Singapore and Malaya.

Meticulously planned with great secrecy, and carried out in each district with no warning whatsoever, the relocation of the 600,000 squatters throughout Malay took place with entire communities being transported in Army trucks to newly built fortified villages. Relocations were carried out with the utmost care and consideration on the part of the troops; in Perak, members of one community asked permission to name their village Kampong Coldstream in honour of the guardsmen who had helped move them to their new home. Every family was given a new house with electricity and a plot of 800 square metres, with a further two acres for cultivation outside the perimeter, while each village was equipped with its own clinic and a police post. Security was tight, the gates being manned day and night by armed guards, and only those with identity cards issued to the community were permitted entry. Perimeters of all villages were surrounded by seven-foot-high double chain-link fences fitted with lights.

The strength of British forces in Malaya had meanwhile been increasing steadily. Among the initial reinforcements in 1948 were the 2nd Guards Brigade from Britain and the 1st Battalion Royal Inniskilling Fusiliers from Hong Kong. Other units and formations had followed during the next two years, among them 3 Commando Brigade RM which arrived in May 1950. Personnel from all these units underwent training at the Far East Training Centre's Jungle Warfare Wing at Johore Bahru which had been formed in October 1948 by Lieutenant Colonel Walter Walker of the 6th Gurkha Rifles. In due course, this became an establishment in its own right as the Jungle Warfare School.

Under the command of Headquarters Malaya in Kuala Lumpur, the country was divided into sub-districts for North and South Malaya with their respective headquarters at Kamunting in Perak, and Seremban in Negri Sembilan. By mid-1950 the Army's order of battle comprised the following. In North Malaya were 3 Commando Brigade RM at Ipoh, in Perak; 1 Malay Brigade at Kota Bahru in northern Kelantan; and the 1st Battalion The King's Own Yorkshire Light Infantry which was stationed on the island of Penang. In the south were 18 Infantry Brigade, based in Kuala Lumpur; 26 Gurkha Infantry Brigade at Johore Bahru; and 63 Gurkha Infantry Brigade at Seremban. An additional formation, 48 Gurkha Infantry Brigade, was based at Kuala Lipis, in Pahang, under direct command of Headquarters Malaya. Further troops were also available from Hong Kong where 28 Infantry Brigade and a further two infantry battalions, together with artillery, armour and engineer units, were stationed.

The success of Ferret Force during its brief existence had emphasised the requirement for small sub-units capable of operating deep inside the jungle for extended periods of time. It was not until May 1950, however, that wheels were put in motion to raise a unit to carry out such a role. The initiative came from none other than the Chief of the Imperial General Staff (CIGS), General Sir William Slim, a former Gurkha and wartime commander of the Fourteenth Army in Burma. Slim was aware that the security forces in Malaya were not winning the war against the terrorists and suggested to the Commander-in-Chief Far East Land Forces, General Sir John Harding, that he should consider appointing a well-qualified officer to carry out a study of the problem and produce recommendations for a solution. The CIGS went further by suggesting an officer eminently qualified for the task – Major Michael Calvert, a Royal Engineers officer who during the war had been a leading figure in the Chindits and had subsequently commanded the Special Air Service Brigade from late 1944 until its disbandment in 1945. Like many others who had stayed in the army following the end of the war, Calvert had been reduced to his substantive rank and was a staff officer in Hong Kong, an appointment little to his liking.

Harding took up Slim's suggestion and summoned Calvert from Hong Kong. During his briefing, the Commander-in-Chief explained the problems caused by the lack of cooperation between the police and the army, the poor relations between the Malay and Chinese, the intransigence of the sultans who believed in their absolute right to rule, the lack of action on the part of the civil authorities, and the commercial interests of the rubber plantations and tin-mining companies. He also summarised the activities of Ferret Force and the problems that had led to its demise. He ended by giving Calvert a totally free hand to travel where he wished throughout Malay and to interview anyone, investigate all problems and report back to him personally.

Calvert took Harding at his word and during the following six months travelled the length and breadth of Malaya. Some of his time was spent with British infantry units, accompanying them on operations and observing their methods of operation. Just under seven months after his first meeting with the Commander-in-Chief, he submitted his report. In it, he recommended the formation of a special counter-insurgency unit for long-range deep penetration operations conducted over protracted periods with the aim not only of engaging the CT but also of winning over the trust and confidence of the aborigine population. Shortly afterwards, he was summoned to the War Office in London for discussions concerning his recommendations. It was agreed that Calvert himself should raise the proposed unit.

Based at Kota Tinggi in Johore, Calvert's new unit was designated A Squadron Malayan Scouts (SAS). Much has already been written elsewhere about the story of its formation and thus will not be repeated here. Suffice it to say that it initially comprised a squadron of some 100 all ranks recruited from British units throughout Far East Land Forces. Its first deployment took place in August 1950 when it undertook a training operation in Perak. In October, it mounted its first operation, in which patrols set off deep into the jungle in search of the terrorists.

In January 1951, Calvert was authorised to form a second squadron which was raised from members of M Independent Squadron, a unit formed for service in Korea from reservists of 21st Special Air Service Regiment (TA), many of whom had served in the SAS during the Second World War. The conflict in Korea had ended before the squadron could be despatched from Britain but approximately half of its members had volunteered to be sent to Malaya instead. At the end of March, the Malayan Scouts received a third squadron. While carrying out his study for the Commander-in-Chief, Calvert had learned that Rhodesia was raising a 100-man contingent for service in Malaya. He had travelled there and, having interviewed members of the unit, had proposed that it be incorporated into his force. This idea had been accepted and on 29 March C (Rhodesian) Squadron joined A and B Squadrons. Shortly afterwards, D Squadron, raised from volunteers in Britain, also arrived in Malaya. Like the other squadrons, the newcomers underwent a short period of initial instruction before being committed to operations during which they continued their training through learning by experience. During the period from April to July, two operations, PROSAIC and SUNSET, were carried out by the unit.

In July, however, Calvert was invalided home due to exhaustion and ill health. His replacement was Lieutenant Colonel John 'Tod' Sloane of the Argyll and Sutherland Highlanders. Although he had no previous experience of special operations or jungle warfare, Sloane had seen action with his regiment during the Second World War and in Korea, and was a highly experienced and capable officer who proceeded to remedy some major shortcomings within his new command, notably the lack of properly constituted administrative and logistical support elements. One of his first moves, too, was to withdraw all four squadrons to Singapore for six weeks' rest and training.

Three months later, an event occurred which was to have far-reaching consequences in the war against the communists in Malaya. During the first week of October, a 50-strong force of CT, comprising men of Nos 24 and 30 Companies of the MRLA's 6th Regiment, under the command of a leading terrorist named Siu Mah, moved into the area of Fraser's Hill, a popular hill resort in Pahang. On the 4th, it set up an ambush on the narrow winding road leading up to the resort, siting it over a front of 200 yards around a sharp bend. Siu Mah's men were positioned on a bank 20 feet above the road, hidden behind screens of palm leaves and atap (a thatch woven from the leaves of the nipa palm), and were heavily armed, being equipped with rifles, Sten guns and three Bren LMGs. The three machine-gun positions were linked by tracks, and a withdrawal route had been reconnoitred and cleared.

During the next two days, a number of vehicles passed up and down the road but Siu Mah held his fire as he was waiting for a military convoy which a member of the Min Yuen had advised would shortly be passing along the road. The purpose of the operation was to capture sorely needed weapons and ammunition once the troops in the convoy had been wiped out.

At midday on the third day, Siu Mah was about to withdraw his force when two vehicles appeared on the bend: the first was a Land Rover carrying six policemen, and the second a black Rolls Royce in which was travelling the High Commissioner, Sir Henry Gurney, together with his wife and his private secretary, Mr D. J. Staples. Siu Mah gave the order to open fire, the terrorists raking both vehicles. Five of the police were wounded but the sixth escaped injury and proceeded to return the terrorists' fire. A few seconds later, however, the High Commissioner himself opened his door and stepped out, calmly walking towards the terrorists who responded by cutting him down in another hail of bullets. No sooner had they done so than Siu Mah gave the order to withdraw and he and his men disappeared swiftly into the jungle. Lady Gurney and Mr Staples survived unscathed and it was later concluded by those investigating the killing that Sir Henry had exposed himself in order to draw the terrorists' fire away from his wife.

The security forces' response was swift. In an operation codenamed PURSUIT, a force comprising the 1st Battalion Royal West Kent Regiment, 2/2GR, 1st Battalion The Worcestershire Regiment, 12th Royal

Lancers and 93 Field Battery RA, with RAF aircraft in support, was deployed to locate and intercept the terrorists. The operation lasted almost two months during which 2/2GR accounted for eight of Siu Mah's force.

During his three years as High Commissioner, Gurney had left his mark on Malaya, initiating a number of measures that had proved highly effective in the war against the terrorists. Foremost among these was the introduction of compulsory national registration whereby every man, woman and child was required to possess an identity card showing a photograph and the holder's details, including a thumbprint. Members of the MRLA and Min Yuen would not register themselves in order to conceal their identities, and thus the absence of identity cards would inevitably restrict their freedom of movement. The communists reacted furiously and tried to dissuade people from registering, claiming that the British planned to conscript men for military service or forced labour. At the same time, photographers were killed and registration teams attacked, but this failed to stop people turning up at the registration centres. The CT then attempted to forge identity cards but these were crude and easily detected.

Another important measure introduced by Gurney just prior to his death was the announcement of rewards for information leading to the capture or killing of terrorists. The idea was to encourage CTs to surrender and then subsequently to 'sell out' their former comrades. Prominent terrorist leaders had prices placed on their heads, Chin Peng being worth M$80,000. In addition, rewards were offered to anyone who arranged the surrender of a known terrorist. There was an immediate response to the announcement: in Perak, the deputy commander of the MRLA's 5th Regiment and his wife surrendered to police at Sungei Rotan and subsequently persuaded eleven of his men to follow his example, thereafter collecting a reward of $12,875.

FOLLOWING THE MURDER of Gurney, an important event took place in October when the MCP held a conference of its Politburo attended by officers of the Chinese People's Liberation Army (PLA). By this time, despite successes achieved against the security forces, the communists had failed to win the hearts and minds of the population

and hence support in its attempts to eject the British from Malaya. Chin Peng declared that terror tactics had alienated the people and that these were to cease forthwith, with attacks being carried out only on members of the security forces. This and other aspects of the new policy were contained in a document published under the title of the 'October 1951 Directive' which was to have a major effect on the course of the war, apparently containing a tacit admission of partial defeat.

During 1951, casualties on both sides had escalated with 504 members of the security forces and 1,079 CT killed, and 322 terrorists captured or having surrendered. The previous year had seen 294 police and troops killed and a total of 942 terrorist losses. Civilian deaths had decreased, with 533 being killed in 1951, compared to 646 the previous year. The end of 1951 saw the retirement of Sir Harold Briggs as Director of Operations. He left Malaya tired and disillusioned after a year during which he had been plagued by serious problems – limitations on his own powers and authority as Director of Operations, deep internal divisions within the police, insufficient coordination of intelligence between the civil and military authorities, and a general lack of urgency on the part of the civil service which continued to operate at a peacetime pace.

His departure coincided with the election of a Conservative government in Britain and the return of Winston Churchill as Prime Minister. The latter was well aware that the situation in Malaya was deteriorating and despatched his Secretary of State for the Colonies, Oliver Lyttleton, on a fact-finding visit. The latter was appalled by what he found and during his visit dismissed the Commissioner of Police, Colonel Nicol Gray. On his return he recommended six measures to be taken immediately: the post of High Commissioner and Director of Operations to be held by a single individual; reorganisation of the police; a compulsory programme of education 'as a means of winning the war of ideas'; formation of a Home Guard organisation incorporating large numbers of Chinese; and a shake-up of the civil service with high-quality personnel being recruited in Britain and Malaya.

At the beginning of January 1952, it was announced that the new High Commissioner and Director of Operations would be General Sir Gerald Templer, at that time serving in Britain as GOC Eastern Command. During the Second World War he had been a brigade, divisional and corps commander, and from November 1944 had served on the staff of SOE before being appointed Director of Civil Affairs and Military Government at Headquarters 21st Army Group in March of the following year. After the war he had been Director of Military Government in the British Sector of West Germany and Vice Chief of the Imperial General Staff before being appointed Director of Military Intelligence at the War Office.

January also saw the Malayan Scouts (SAS) redesignated as 22nd Special Air Service Regiment (22 SAS) and moving to a new base at Sungei Besi near Kuala Lumpur. During February, B, C and D Squadrons were deployed on Operation HELSBY as part of a combined force comprising units of the Police Field Force (PFF), Royal Marine Commandos and Gurkhas, tasked with locating and destroying a CT base in the Belum Valley in northern Malaya near the border with Thailand. The information concerning the base had been supplied by four CT who had surrendered to the security forces. They had indicated that it was occupied by some 100 terrorists who had achieved complete domination of the valley and the two villages, Kampong Belum and Kampong Sepor, situated respectively at its western and eastern ends. The CT had been reported as ruling the area by fear, forbidding the villagers on pain of death to leave the valley.

The plan was that C Squadron under Major Peter Walls, and D Squadron, commanded by Major John Woodhouse, the overall SAS force commander, would deploy on foot from the town of Batu Melintam, situated to the south-east, marching over the mountains to the eastern end of the valley where they would set up ambushes and cut-off groups. A week later B Squadron, commanded by Major Alistair MacGregor, would parachute into the western end of the valley area, its DZ being paddy fields bordered by the Sungei Belum (Belum River) on one side and jungle on the other. It would then advance eastward through the valley and both villages, flushing out any CT who would, it was hoped, be caught by C and D Squadrons' ambushes.

The operation began with C and D Squadrons deploying by air on 1 February to the town of Khota Bahru in the north-east corner of Kelantan, some fifteen miles from the border with Thailand. B Squadron would make its drop on 8 February. From there C and D Squadrons departed in transport for Batu Melintang. After a few miles, however, the road became impassable due to floods caused by heavy rain the day

before. Forced to debus, the two squadrons continued on foot to Batu Melintang from where they set off on 4 February for the Belum Valley, marching over the mountains that dominated the area to reach their objective.

As described by Alan Hoe and Eric Morris in their book *Re-enter the SAS – The Special Air Service and the Malayan Emergency*, the approach march was long and extremely arduous, over difficult terrain comprising steep ridge-lines and valleys through which ran the Belum River. The squadrons marched all day, halting just before dusk and resuming the march at dawn. Navigation was difficult, not helped by maps that showed little more than large expanses of green intersected only by river-lines. Furthermore, the local guide heading the column proved unreliable. After six days, the squadrons had only covered half the distance and Major John Woodhouse decided to split his force, despatching C Squadron down the Sungei Belum to the eastern end of the Belum Valley while he took his own squadron over the mountains to Kampong Sepor at the western end.

B Squadron's drop by this time had been postponed 24 hours to 9 February. By dawn on the 9th, D Squadron had reached a point to the east of Kampong Sepor but found itself confronted by a major obstacle in the form of the Sungei Belum which was in spate as a result of the previous days' heavy rain. Nothing daunted, Woodhouse and his men proceeded to cross it: one man bravely swam across first, taking the end of a rope which was fastened securely on the far bank, and the rest of the squadron was then ferried across on two rafts made from bamboo.

B Squadron was dropped at approximately 9.15 a.m. from three Royal Australian Air Force (RAAF) Dakota transports. The weather was difficult, with low cloud covering the area and clearing only briefly for the actual drop. Each aircraft carried out a preliminary run, releasing a parachute weighted with a man-size dummy to determine the strength and direction of the wind before dropping its stick of parachutists. This proved hazardous, only four out of the squadron's total strength of 54 landing on the DZ, the remainder being blown into the primary jungle at the end of the DZ where they landed among small trees and undergrowth. One man found himself hooked up on a small tree but used his tree-escape line to slide safely to the ground.

C Squadron, meanwhile, had encountered some terrorists, coming under fire as it advanced westward through the valley towards Kampong Sepor. Once the three squadrons had regrouped, patrols were sent out and a number of contacts took place, one terrorist being wounded and captured but subsequently dying of his wounds. Immediately after the operation, the populations of Kampongs Belum and Sepor were evacuated and resettled elsewhere, both villages and their cultivated areas being destroyed to prevent them being of any benefit to the CT. Whether this achieved the required result is open to doubt, as it was later discovered that the terrorists had returned to the Belum Valley within a few weeks of the operation.

Earlier in the month, on 7 February 1952, General Sir Gerald Templer had arrived in Malay to take up his new combined post. The task facing him was a major one. As High Commissioner he would have to deal with a host of difficult political problems while at the same time continuing the social and economic programmes begun by his predecessor. He was, above all, aware that his primary role was to prepare Malaya for independence, this having been emphasised prior to his departure from Britain by Winston Churchill, who had stated, 'The policy of the British government is that Malaya should in due course become a self-governing nation.'

Templer believed firmly that independence could only be achieved if the entire nation was united. Within a month of his arrival, municipal elections were held in Kuala Lumpur which did much to create a racial alliance between the Malays and Chinese. The United Malays National Organisation (UMNO), headed by Tunku Abdul Rahman, and the Malayan Chinese Association (MCA) led by Tan Cheng-Lok agreed not to stand against each other and formed the Alliance Party which won nine of the eleven seats on the council.

As Director of Operations Templer had to initiate a major campaign against the CT, regaining the initiative from them. Shortly after taking office, he announced considerable increases in the rewards payable for the capture or killing of terrorists. The amount payable for Chin Peng was trebled to M$250,000 (£30,000) while members of the Politburo were rated at M$150,000; and members of state or regional committees henceforth commanded a reward of M$120,000. A low-ranking terrorist would fetch M$2,500 alive or M$2,000 dead. Announcement of these new rewards was made through large numbers of leaflets dropped by aircraft over known terrorist-occupied areas.

Templer was a dynamic individual and his influence was soon felt at all levels in the security forces throughout the country. He was ruthless in dealing with inefficiency and made it clear to the war executive committees, which had until then been plagued with constant disagreements between their civilian, police and army elements, that he would not tolerate any such discord, sacking those who continued to be obstructive. He quickly turned his attention to the police, by then under its new Commissioner, Colonel Arthur Young. The latter had requested large quantities of much-needed arms and equipment to bolster his force, including 600 armoured personnel carriers, 120 armoured cars, 250 scout cars and large quantities of small arms. Templer not only gave his blessing to the supply of these items but also seconded a number of army technical experts to the police. During the following twelve months, a total of £30 million was spent on re-equipping Young's force.

As a former Director of Military Intelligence, Templer was well aware that the foremost weapon against the communists was that of intelligence, commenting to a journalist shortly after his arrival, 'The Emergency will be won by our intelligence system – our Special Branch.' Recognising that it required reorganisation and expansion as a matter of urgency, he brought in an expert from Britain: Jack Morton, Deputy Director General of the Security Service in Britain. Given priority for funding and recruiting, Morton set about his task. At the same time, Guy Madoc, a serving police officer, was appointed as the new Head of Special Branch with two responsibilities: first, provision to the federal government of political, security and counter-espionage intelligence relating to current and long-term threats; second, supply of intelligence to the security forces for operations against the MRLA.

The Army in Malaya had seen a considerable increase in its strength as there were by now over 40,000 troops in Malaya: 10,000 Gurkhas, incorporated in 17 Gurkha Infantry Division comprising 16 and 99 Gurkha Infantry Brigades in Johore, 48 Gurkha Infantry Brigade in Pahang and 63rd Gurkha Infantry Brigade in Negri Sembilan; 25,000 British troops (including RAF and Royal Navy personnel); five battalions of the Malay Regiment; two battalions of the King's African Rifles; and a battalion of the Fiji Infantry Regiment. In addition, the RAAF provided bomber and transport squadrons. In later years, other units from Australia, New Zealand, Rhodesia and Singapore would also see service in Malaya.

From September to October 1952, 22 SAS was involved in a major operation, codenamed HIVE, in the area near the town of Seremban in Negri Sembilan. Also taking part were two Gurkha battalions and a company of the 1st Battalion Fiji Infantry Regiment. The purpose was to flood the area with a large number of troops and police, the latter establishing roadblocks and carrying out searches and checks within villages. This forced the CT, whose strength was estimated as some 100, to remain in the jungle consuming their reserves of food, while harassed by troops laying ambushes and carrying out patrols to flush them out of the jungle where, it was hoped, they would be caught by stop-groups. Sixteen terrorists were killed in a series of ambushes in the course of the operation which covered an area of some 600 square miles.

During 1953, Lieutenant Colonel Oliver Brooke took over command of 22 SAS from Lieutenant Colonel Tod Sloane and towards the end of the year C Squadron finished its tour of operations and returned to Rhodesia where it was disbanded. The emphasis now was on the construction of a series of jungle forts which were an important component of General Templer's 'hearts and minds' campaign. These were established by the police, being sited on high ground providing good defensive positions. Manned by 30-man PFF jungle squads, they comprised a barracks for the police detachment and up to one squadron of SAS, with fortified bunkers and an LZ within the perimeter. The first fort was set up at Kuala Medang, a location on the Sungei Pahang twelve miles from the state capital of Kuala Lipis. While acting as advanced posts to which the aborigines would come, once their confidence had been won, these forts also enabled squadrons to remain in the jungle for extended periods. A good illustration was that of D Squadron, commanded by Major John Cooper, which in October 1953 stationed itself at Fort Brooke, on the Sungei Brok in Pahang, and was not relieved until 7 February 1954. During its tour of 122 days, it had lost half of its original strength through disease.

Towards the end of 1953, in Perak, a three-man reconnaissance patrol of 22 SAS, comprising Lieutenant Angus Cherrington and two Iban trackers, Lance Corporal Nyulin and Private Jackik, came across a trail left by a large body of men – 100 or so, in the trackers' opinion. After following it for 200 yards the Ibans spotted another track, left by one man only minutes beforehand, leading off to the right. Here the patrol came across a tunnel and as they cautiously crawled through, Lance Corporal Nyulin heard the sound of a match being struck. On scrambling out, he was confronted by a CT sitting on a log smoking a pipe. The terrorist, mistaking him for an aborigine in the MRLA, asked Nyulin if he was an Asal, only to realise his mistake when the latter replied that he was an Iban. The terrorist dived for his submachine-gun but was shot and wounded by Nyulin who opened fire first. At that point, Lieutenant Cherrington and Private Jackik appeared from the tunnel and shot the terrorist dead. With the probability of a large number of CT in the vicinity, Cherrington quickly searched the body, removing some documents and the dead man's weapon, before disappearing swiftly into the jungle.

When the patrol returned to base, study of the documents identified the dead CT as the bodyguard of Lau Lee, the MRLA's chief of propaganda. A major operation was mounted with five battalions of troops being deployed and the RAF carrying out bombing raids. Although this resulted in a number of contacts and a large number of camps being located, there was no sign of Lau Lee's group and the operation was terminated six weeks later.

Cherrington had been correct in assuming that a large group of terrorists were near by. Totalling 75 in strength and headed by Lau Lee, it was en route to southern Thailand where it would wait for another 45-strong group headed by Chin Peng himself. Some eighteen months earlier, in April 1952, the MCP leader had presided over what was to prove the last conference of the party's Central Committee in Malaya. Three members of the committee, Deputy Secretary General Yeung Kwo, Perak State Secretary Ah Hoi and Pahang State Secretary Foo Thin, sent messages saying they were unable to attend due to the military situations in their areas. A fourth member, Ah 'Shorty' Kuk, did not appear; unknown to Chin Peng, he had been murdered by his two bodyguards who took his head to a police station where they surrendered, claiming the reward of $200,000.

During the conference, Chin Peng announced that he had decided to move his headquarters from Pahang to southern Thailand due to the growing threat from the security forces who were working their way steadily into the depths of the jungle in their search for him. Immediately after the conference, two senior CT commanders, Siu Mah, who had commanded the terrorist force which had killed Sir Henry Gurney in October 1951, and Siu Chong, commander of the MRLA's 6th Regiment, departed on the long trek to Thailand to reconnoitre the route and arrange for guides and supplies of food. Three months later the main party, travelling in the two groups headed by Chin Peng and Lau Lee, set off. Chin Peng travelled by way of a camp in the area of Raub, to the north-east of Fraser's Hill, where he waited in the hope of sighting Ah Kuk. Shortly after his arrival there, however, the camp was attacked by RAF bombers and strafed by fighters as a result of information provided to the security forces by a member of the Min Yuen. Chin Peng and his companions fled the area immediately and moved to another camp seven miles away, subsequently making their way to another on the Sungei Jelai. Not long afterwards, however, a PFF patrol under a British inspector came across the outer perimeter of the camp. Realising from its size that a large number of terrorists were in the area, it attempted to withdraw but came under fire. A heavy firefight ensued before the patrol succeeded in escaping back to its base where its commander reported his discovery by radio.

On receiving the report, Special Branch was convinced that it was Chin Peng, having already received news that he was leaving Pahang. Moreover, a copy of the minutes of the Central Committee's conference was already in its possession. The RAF was instructed to mount a bombing operation on the camp whose exact location had been provided by the PFF inspector. The bombers were preceded by an Auster light aircraft tasked with dropping a smoke marker on the centre of the camp. Unfortunately, the bombers overtook the Auster and, unable to drop their bombs as it was directly below them, were forced to fly and circle before starting their second approach. This gave Chin Peng and his group time to make their escape, fleeing to Perak from which three months later they and Lau Lee's group set off for Thailand. It was during this last stage of their journey that the incident with Lieutenant Cherrington's patrol took place.

By the latter part of 1953, it had become apparent to General Templer that the CT were receiving considerable support from the aborigine tribes. During the Second World War, contact between the MPAJA's guerrillas and the aborigines had been facilitated by a British anthropologist, Pat Noone, well known for his earlier discovery in 1931 of the Temiar, whose existence had hitherto only been rumoured.

On the outbreak of war in Malaya, Noone, together with his younger brother Richard, also an anthropologist, had been serving in a locally raised unit, the Frontier Patrol, whose role was intelligence-gathering along the Thai border and reconnaissance of the routes crossing it. Led by the country's chief game warden, it comprised four sections commanded by British officers. Each was allocated a sector of operations and was responsible for recruiting his own men: Pat Noone enlisted Temiar while his brother recruited Malays. In December 1941, however, the Frontier Patrol was disbanded. Richard Noone, after a series of adventures, escaped to Sumatra, where he joined SOE with whom he spent the rest of the war training guerrillas for operations in the Far East. Pat Noone remained in the jungle with the Temiar and during 1942 joined forces with the communist guerrillas. Unfortunately, he not only introduced them to the aborigines but also, in a series of lectures, afforded them an insight into aborigine psychology and social behaviour, including their philosophy of shared liability in which one individual's adverse behaviour reflected on his entire family or community. The communists would make good use of this information in due course.

In July 1943, a disenchanted Noone split from the communists. By then, however, the damage had been done as the MPAJA had set up a department for aboriginal affairs under a guerrilla named Low Mah who established a network of agents, these being used to make contact with the tribal groups living deep within the jungle. In November 1943, Noone, who had married a Temiar woman, was murdered by a rival for his wife's affections, so there was no one to combat the growing influence of the communists among the aborigines.

In 1948, with its MRLA bases deep in the jungle and therefore too remote to be supported by the Min Yuen in towns and villages, the MCP decided that the 'Asal' (the Malay word meaning 'original inhabitant') should be mobilised to cultivate crops to provide food for them. A directive was published, explaining the role of the aborigines and its relevance to the revolutionary effort, and stressing the importance of a gentle approach when dealing with the tribesmen. This is illustrated by a document captured by the security forces which stipulated:

All comrades engaged in the work of the Asal must take full responsibility in investigating and studying the habits of living, customs, tradi-
tions, rituals and other racial characteristics of the Asal ... Information
on the foregoing should be compiled for reference. This will help us
improve our methods of work ... We should try to identify ourselves
with them by adopting their way of living.

A special Asal organisation was established by the MRLA, consisting
of guerrillas who had previous experience in dealing with aborigines as
traders or tappers of jelutong, the sap of a tree used in the production
of a number of items including chewing gum, and who spoke the different aboriginal dialects. The communists moved slowly at first, gradually
re-establishing contacts made with the tribes deep in the jungles of
Perak, Kelantan and Pahang during the wartime years and introducing
their own personnel with care. These came equipped with small pres-
ents of the types much valued by the tribesmen: long jungle knives called
'parangs', axeheads, tobacco, seeds, salt, medicines and bolts of cloth.
They were careful to refer to the aborigines by the correct term of 'Asal'
and not 'Sakai', a derogatory word meaning 'slave', used frequently by
the European population in Malaya. Some of them, having wormed their
way into the tribes' confidence, married aborigine women and thus
became members of communities.

The communists were swift to take advantage of the federal government's disastrous attempts to resettle the aborigine tribes living in the
outer jungle areas and easily accessible riverside communities. This was
an extension of the Briggs Plan and its measures to deny the CT food
and support. Communities were uprooted by troops and police who
transported them to camps where they were confined behind barbed
wire. To a people used to roaming freely through the jungle, this was
anathema. Moreover, within a very short time, health problems became
endemic. Reliant on the cool climate of the jungle highlands, the aborigines suffered greatly from the humidity and heat of the lowland areas
where the resettlement camps were located. Accustomed, too, to a staple
diet of cassava roots, fresh meat, vegetables and wild fruit, their systems
could not adjust to one of rice and salt fish. Large numbers died from
physical causes, others succumbed after losing the will to live. Those
determined to return to their home areas escaped from the camps and

fled back to the jungle. Thousands more, hearing of the horrors of the resettlement camps, fled deeper into the jungle and sought sanctuary with the CT.

The second phase of the communist subversion of the aborigines began with the arrival of teams which toured the jungle communities, holding meetings at which the tribesmen were subjected to communist propaganda. Although the CT were always careful to maintain a friendly attitude, they also made it clear as to what would befall those who failed to commit themselves fully to the struggle. Taking into account the aborigines' philosophy of shared liability, as explained to them by Pat Noone, they emphasised that failure on the part of any individual would result in punishment of the whole of his or her family. The terrorists also made many promises, undertaking to look after the aborigines and provide them with everything they needed once the British had been driven out of Malaya. One group was promised the sole rights for tapping jelutong throughout Pahang, while another was told that under a communist regime it would be permitted to enter any shop and appropriate anything without payment.

Not surprisingly, the majority of aborigine groups accepted communist domination as the line of least resistance. Indeed, some tribesmen espoused the cause to the extent that they were recruited into a body known as the Asal Protection Corps, whose role was the maintenance of high levels of food production by communities, using force whenever necessary. By late 1953, the communists had penetrated all the major tribal groups, totalling some 30,000 out of the total aborigine population of approximately 50,000, from Negri Sembilan and southern Pahang northward to the Thai border.

In October 1953, however, it had become apparent to Templer that the aborigines held the key to the terrorists' capability to operate deep in the jungle, supplying them with food and providing them with intelligence on the movements of the security forces. He was well aware that in order to terminate such support, it would be necessary to win back the support of the tribes with a well-organised, full-scale propaganda and welfare campaign. He began by appointing Richard Noone, who had returned to Malaya when the Second World War ended, as head of the Federal Department of Aborigines. At the time of his appointment, he was secretary to the Federation Intelligence Committee and well aware of the situation concerning the aborigines and the communists.

As he later described in his book *In Search of the Dream People*, Noone began by classifying the 30,000 aborigines known to be under communist domination into three categories. The first consisted largely of the most hostile, hard-line members of the Asal Protection Corps who lived side-by-side with the CT and, in addition to maintaining food supplies, provided guides and also porters as sentries for terrorist bases, and fed the terrorists with intelligence on the movements of security force units inside the jungle. The second category comprised those aborigines living near CT bases, providing food and intelligence, while the third was formed of those living some distance from the terrorists but still being required to supply food.

Shortly after Richard Noone assumed his new appointment, a patrol of B Squadron 22 SAS operating east of the Cameron Highlands in north-west Pahang shot dead a terrorist and discovered a track leading towards a hill believed to be the location of a major CT camp. There were grounds to suspect it might be the base of the MCP's Politburo and thus an operation, codenamed VALIANT, was launched with four infantry battalions being guided into the area by SAS patrols. On the orders of the GOC Malaya, Lieutenant General Sir Hugh Stockwell, Noone was flown in on the following day to join the headquarters of B Squadron, commanded by Major John Salmond, which was located at Kuala Misong, a spot at the northern end of the Telom Valley where the Sungei Misong was joined by the Jelai. His task was to persuade the local aborigines to assist the SAS to locate the terrorist base as by then heavy rain had obliterated the signs of the patrol's tracks from the previous day and its Iban tracker had since fallen ill.

As VALIANT continued, with four battalions of infantry and two SAS squadrons combing the Telom Valley, Noone established his headquarters close to B Squadron's. From then on there was a stream of aborigine visitors to whom he distributed parangs, tobacco, cloth and other welcome gifts. Gentle, unhurried questioning of them eventually elicited the information that a large CT camp was located farther to the southwest, over the Perak mountain divide, in Semai territory. As a result, VALIANT was switched to the area of Batang Padang, in the Perak jungle north-east of the town of Bidor. Led by Semai guides, the troops encircled the location of the suspected terrorist base and began a search of the area. After two weeks nothing had been found. Then Noone received information that an individual named Bah Pelankin, a Semai headman and the local leader of the CT Asal organisation, was in the Batang Padang area. Notorious for his brutality, having tortured and murdered a number of aborigines who had failed to cooperate fully with the CT, he was apparently touring the area warning on pain of death against any cooperation with the British.

Shortly afterwards, during November, VALIANT was terminated, the terrorists in Perak and Pahang having successfully avoided contact with a force of some 5,000 troops. That they were able to do so was entirely due to intelligence and guides supplied by the aborigines. The failure of the operation, however, reinforced General Templer's view that the aborigines had to be won over in order to deny the communists their support.

In the meantime, Richard Noone had met with his informant, a Semai headman who told him that Bah Pelankin was in the habit of visiting a house on the edge of the jungle to collect rice. Noone persuaded the headman that the Asal leader should be killed and the Semai agreed that he and two of his relatives would undertake the task. Soon afterwards, he received a message telling him that Bah Pelankin and his bodyguard had been shot dead while crossing a log bridge across a river.

Noone's next step was to establish field teams, each comprising a small welfare unit that contained a Malay field assistant and a number of aborigine staff. These were located at the jungle forts established by the PFF and 22 SAS, and at other outposts where clinics, schools and shops were set up. The teams were also responsible for explaining to the aborigines that the CT were criminals who had committed atrocities and would be punished by the government whose forces were winning the war. Furthermore, there would be handsome rewards for anyone whose assistance resulted in the arrest of terrorists. Noone also set out to counter propaganda distributed by the CT who had explained that the presence of British troops in the jungle was because they were hiding from the Chinese who had defeated them in Korea and were now hounding them throughout Malaya. He did so by arranging for 100 aborigine headmen to be flown to Kuala Lumpur where they watched a parade of a large number of military and police units staged for their benefit, followed by a firepower demonstration by Royal Artillery batteries. Thereafter they were taken on tours around Kuala Lumpur and to the coast, being treated as VIPs before being returned to the jungle.

It took a few weeks for Noone's strategy to take effect. The first indication of success came when a large group of 54 Semai from the Upper Rening area, ten of them armed, appeared at a fort at Telanok near the Cameron Highlands and presented themselves to the SAS squadron based there. Classed in the 'hostile' category, they now wished to defect from the communist cause. Having abandoned their home area or 'ladang', they were seeking protection. Noone arranged for an immediate airdrop of food, tobacco and other items, and for the headman to be flown to Kuala Lumpur for questioning.

Over the following weeks and months, other aborigine groups began to appear at the jungle forts, requesting assistance. Medical treatment in particular proved to be a powerful factor in persuading the tribesmen to come forward and Noone responded by despatching his medical assistants with patrols into the jungle. The aborigines were encouraged to give information on CT locations and movements, some of it resulting in a number of terrorists being killed. Very soon entire communities began to leave their homes, making their way to the nearest forts for protection. Some even turned on the CT, with one group in Perak, on the Sungei Lanweng, claiming the most victims. Two Semai known to Noone lay in wait for four months on a known MRLA courier route, high in the mountains close to the Pahang border, and shot dead two couriers. A search of their bodies revealed documents addressed to the MCP Politburo and telling of low morale among the terrorists.

Another casualty was a particularly notorious character, a Semai headman named Chawog, from the area of the Sungei Betau in Pahang, who had behaved with great brutality towards his own people. He was shot dead a week after Noone had asked for volunteers to deal with him. An announcement of Chawog's demise was broadcast over the Betau Valley from an aircraft equipped with loudspeakers and shortly afterwards the entire community of 750 aborigines came over to the government side. By the end of 1954, a total of 6,100 aborigines of all three of Noone's categories had deserted the communist cause.

The MCP, however, did not take take these reverses lying down and responded by ordering the MRLA to reduce its demands on the aborigines. CT units were instructed to purchase food from them, provided only that they had produced it themselves, on a scale laid down by the MRLA. The terrorists encouraged those aborigines still under their domination to produce crops for sale and the latter, no longer feeling themselves under coercion, responded by doing so.

The end of May 1954 saw the departure from Malaya of General Sir Gerald Templer after just over two years as High Commissioner and Director of Operations; he was replaced in those appointments by Sir Donald McGillivray and Lieutenant General Sir Geoffrey Bourne respectively. During his tenure, the number of terrorist incidents had fallen from 500 to below 100 a month. In addition, he had witnessed the establishment of considerable political unity in the country, the Alliance Party by this time including the Malayan Indian Congress (MIC). Yet he was fully aware that the battle for the hearts and minds of the population had still not been won. Food and medicines were still being obtained in sufficient quantities by the Min Yuen to enable it to supply the MRLA units, and labourers were still being forced to hand over $1.50 each month, with shopkeepers and others being required to pay out larger amounts of between $25 and $100. Moreover, despite their increased strength, the security forces, which by this time comprised 23 infantry battalions plus supporting arms and the police, found themselves fully extended in countering the terrorists whose strength Special Branch estimated to be approximately 4,000. Before his departure on 30 May, Templer warned that there were hard, tough days ahead and ended by adding, 'In fact, I'll shoot the bastard who says this Emergency is over.'

22 SAS WAS AMONG those units which continued to be heavily committed on operations against the CT. In July, three of the regiment's squadrons and several infantry battalions took part in Operation TERMITE, the purpose of which was to take control of Malaysia's central mountain region. The operation commenced with heavy bombing by RAF Lincoln bombers, followed by a parachute insertion of the SAS force. Several forts were put in place and contact was established subsequently with aborigine groups. Although only fifteen CT had been killed by the time the operation ended four months later in November, the main benefit of TERMITE was the considerable number of aborigines who came over to the government side.

The regiment at this time comprised only three sabre squadrons, A, B and D, following the return of C Squadron to Rhodesia. In the spring of 1955, however, reinforcements appeared in the form of the Independent Parachute Squadron, commanded by Major Dudley Coventry and formed from volunteers from all three regular battalions of The Parachute Regiment. Following its arrival, the squadron underwent six weeks of training at the Jungle Warfare School at Kota Tinggi before joining 22 SAS which by then was commanded by Lieutenant Colonel George Lea; he had relieved Lieutenant Colonel Oliver Brooke, the latter having suffered a severe leg injury during a parachute descent. It was organised in the same way as the regiment's other three squadrons: a small headquarters and four troops. During the latter part of its tour, a fifth troop was formed from additional personnel.

The squadron's first operation took place in the Iskander Swamp, an area in southern Malaya, and lasted three months. The terrain was difficult, comprising large areas of secondary jungle interlaced with small rivers and streams. Moreover, the area had not been mapped accurately, making navigation problematic. During the operation, the squadrons set up ambushes in the area of a number of cultivated areas discovered by its patrols but without success.

January 1955 found the squadron operating in southern Selangor, under the command of an infantry brigade, where it was deployed in an area of swamp called Tasek Bera. It was detailed to collect intelligence on terrorist activity before taking part in an operation to destroy the CT organisation in the area. Its patrols discovered signs of activity in the area of the Sungei Palong, and had several encounters with terrorists. During one of them, a member of a patrol was wounded and had to be evacuated by helicopter.

Throughout the rest of the year, the squadron was deployed in the area between Ipoh and the Cameron Highlands to its east. It spent much time patrolling the mountainous, jungle-covered terrain but encountered only a few CT. One of these was a woman who was shot dead by a patrol who then discovered she was carrying a six-month-old baby. The squadron also mounted a highly successful ambush which resulted in the capture of a leading terrorist on the road leading to the town of Tapah.

In December 1955, 22 SAS was further reinforced with the arrival of the 1st New Zealand SAS Squadron. Formed from volunteers from throughout the New Zealand Army, it was commanded by Major Frank Rennie. On its arrival, the squadron underwent parachute training at RAF Changi in Singapore before joining the regiment and commencing its jungle warfare training. The first operation in which it was involved took place in the area of Bukit Tapah and was targeted on the MRLA's 31 Independent Platoon. The squadron was tasked with locating the terrorists but during several weeks of patrolling did not produce any contacts. It did result, however, in the discovery of CT maps, documents, letters and other information which led the Special Branch to believe that 31 Independent Platoon was no longer active in that area.

The squadron then moved 50 miles north to Fort Brooke from where it would carry out an operation in Perak and Kelantan. Its tasks were to provide support for the possible resettling of an aborigine group to a protected village and to hunt down and destroy a twelve-man CT Asal section led by an individual named Ah Mingh. A few days beforehand, 3 Troop was inserted by helicopter, its task being to establish contact with a small group of ten aborigines who, unknown to the terrorists, had come over to the government side. The promise of the gift of a shotgun for each man had persuaded them to work for the security forces and thereafter, led by their headman, the group proved invaluable in leading the squadron's patrols in their hunt for the terrorists. Within a few days, the troop had located the Asal section's camp and mounted a dawn attack during which the troop commander, Lieutenant Ian Burrows, killed two CT, one of them subsequently being identified as Ah Mingh. Further successes came as the squadron followed up after the other ten members of the Asal section, with one contact resulting in the death of Ah Mingh's second-in-command, Kam Chen. Unfortunately, the success of the three-month-long operation was marred by the death of a squadron member, Trooper Thomas, during an unexpected contact with some CT.

After a period of rest and recuperation out of the jungle, the NZSAS Squadron returned to Fort Brooke to relieve A Squadron which had been experiencing problems of gradually deteriorating relations with the aborigines. The New Zealanders found that the Maori members of the squadron were able to establish a rapport with the tribesmen and harmony was soon restored. This, together with the realisation that the terrorists' influence was diminishing rapidly, resulted in the aborigines cooperating fully with the squadron and ultimately led to their providing information about a group of CT in the area. An operation to track it down was subsequently mounted by two of the squadron's troops, commanded by Lieutenants John Mace and Earle Yandall respectively, with the latter leading a combined patrol.

Seven days later, Yandall and his men came across a cultivated area where crops had been harvested recently and discovered tracks leading away from the site. They followed up throughout the rest of the day until dusk. On the morning of the eighth day, the patrol continued to follow the tracks until they heard the sound of wood being chopped. Advancing to a point where he could observe a number of terrorists, Yandall deployed his men, his support group moving to a flank position from which it could give covering fire. As the assault group silently edged its way closer, however, one of the terrorists spotted it and opened fire. Yandall and his men immediately returned it, killing four CT and wounding a fifth who succeeded in escaping. Shortly afterwards, a patrol led by Lieutenant Ian Burrows accounted for two more terrorists whom the aborigines identified as being the last remaining members of the Asal section formerly commanded by Ah Mingh.

Other squadrons, too, were enjoying success. In May, B Squadron, commanded by Major Johnny Cooper, was deployed on an operation on the frontier of northern Perak and Kelantan following receipt of information about a large group of some 30 CT located in the area of the Sungei Klub to the south of the Thai border. The information had come from a terrorist who had surrendered to the security forces; under questioning, he had not only revealed the existence of the group but also the location of a clandestine radio transmitter in an area known as the Valley of No Return.

B Squadron moved to Kota Bahru from where it travelled by boat up the Sungei Kelantan to a point where it disembarked and began an arduous trek over the Akik Ring mountains. Eight days later, it reached a point from which its four troops deployed into the valley below. Not long afterwards, there was a contact in which three CT were killed and one was wounded. A few weeks later, two aborigine headmen, both leaders of hostile groups, were tracked down by B Squadron patrols and agreed to desert the communist cause.

During the first week of July, a patrol came across evidence of the reported clandestine radio transmitter. Having located a deserted camp in a jungle clearing, it found in a nearby stream a waterwheel designed to provide electrical power for a dynamo. A search of the area uncovered further items comprising radio components and batteries; it was subsequently learned from CT who surrendered later that the transmitter had never worked satisfactorily and had been dumped together with its generator. This discovery led to an expansion of the operation, with A and D Squadrons being deployed in ambush positions around the edge of the area while B Squadron was joined by elements of Headquarters Squadron who were parachuted into the area. Unfortunately, one man was seriously injured during the drop, necessitating his evacuation by helicopter.

As the operation continued during the following weeks, there were a number of contacts, some of which resulted in terrorists being killed. As described by Alan Hoe and Eric Morris in *Re-enter the SAS*, one of these occurred on 4 September when a D Squadron patrol, commanded by Sergeant Bob Turnbull, renowned for his expertise in tracking, was following tracks which led through an overgrown area of cultivation. As Turnbull and his men slowly continued forwards, they spotted a small movement in the jungle ahead; guessing it was a sentry, they took cover and settled down to wait for dusk. Two hours later, the sentry, for some unknown reason, left his position. The patrol moved up swiftly, deployed into line and put in an immediate assault, killing three terrorists and wounding a fourth who later died of his wounds. A search of the camp revealed weapons, documents and radio components, indicating that the four had been senior CT.

November 1956 found the NZSAS Squadron deployed on operations in Negri Sembilan in support of 26 Gurkha Infantry Brigade, attempting to track down a group of 20 terrorists led by an individual named Tan Fut Lun, who inevitably had been nicknamed 'Ten Foot Long' by the security forces. In the event, however, he was located by Special Branch who managed to insert a radio homing device into a receiver belonging to him. This guided in RAF bombers which pounded the area, killing Ta Fut Lun and sixteen other members of his group, the survivors of which surrendered a few days later.

Next month the squadron was deployed farther north in Negri Sembilan, hunting another 20-strong group of CT. Led by a terrorist named

Li Hak Chi, it had recently gained notoriety by ambushing a military vehicle. All five occupants had been killed, the CT taking their weapons and throwing their bodies back into the vehicle before setting it ablaze. The squadron deployed its patrols into the area, each reconnoitring a sector and setting up ambushes along routes most likely to be used by the terrorists. The first contact occurred ten days later when two terrorists were caught, one being killed and subsequently identified as a courier. Three days later, another was also shot dead after walking into an ambush.

At the start of 1957, another prominent terrorist found himself being hunted by 22 SAS. A member of the CT Asal named Ah Tuk, he was responsible for providing aboriginal support for a number of CT independent units, including the remaining elements of 31 Independent Platoon. During January, he appeared in an area east of Taiping in Perak where D Squadron was operating at the time. Once again, it was Sergeant Bob Turnbull's patrol which picked up Ah Tuk's trail. While moving through an area of jungle, Turnbull himself sighted the head of a terrorist and immediately opened fire with the semi-automatic shotgun with which he was always armed. Identification of the dead CT revealed him to be Ah Tuk who was carrying documents which provided a considerable amount of valuable intelligence.

The NZSAS Squadron, meanwhile, was continuing its hunt for Li Hak Chi in Negri Sembilan. By mid-March it had completed thirteen weeks in the jungle and was extracted for two weeks of rest and recuperation before being inserted again in early April. During the next four months, it patrolled and searched without success, achieving very few contacts with the CT, none of which resulted in any kills. Of Li Hak Chi's group there was no sign. On 12 August, the squadron was about to be extracted from the jungle when Special Branch reported that Li Hak Chi and four other CT had reappeared, collected supplies from a food cache and were heading back to their base whose location was unknown.

An operation was mounted immediately to intercept the five CT, with the squadron setting up ambushes on two alternative routes which it was expected that Li Hak Chi would use. A patrol commanded by Lieutenant Noel O'Dwyer took up position on the first route which, although more risky for the terrorists due to the lack of cover, followed a track over a ridge and offered easy going. The second and longer route, via lower-lying dense jungle, was covered by a patrol under Lieutenant Ian Burrows. A third patrol, led by the squadron's expert tracker, Corporal Huia Woods, was followed up behind the CT.

The operation commenced 24 hours after the terrorists had left the food cache from where Corporal Woods's patrol began its pursuit. By late afternoon of the fourth day, it was apparent that the CT had chosen the lower route and were heading for Lieutenant Burrows's position. By that time, Corporal Woods's patrol had caught up to a point where it was ten minutes behind Li Hak Chi and his four companions. Just before dusk, two terrorists entered Burrows's ambush area and the patrol opened fire, killing both of them. The remaining three, who were a short distance back down the track, escaped into the jungle. On the following morning, the two bodies were identified as those of Li Hak Chi and his bodyguard, Ah Song.

The operation to hunt down the remainder of Li Hak Chi's group continued until the end of October when its remaining members surrendered. The NZSAS Squadron's persistence had paid off and it had got its man. The following month, however, saw the end of the squadron's tour of operations in Malaya and its return to New Zealand where it was disbanded.

In May 1957, meantime, a major operation codenamed CHIEFTAIN had been launched in south Perak, with 22 SAS being tasked to hunt down a notorious CT named Choy Foong, who was eventually accounted for by a patrol from an infantry battalion. Shortly afterwards B Squadron was presented with the chance of eliminating another leading terrorist, Ng Pak Thong, who had been directly involved in several murders of civilians, ambushes on the security forces and extortion of money from timber-loggers. The opportunity arose when a CT named Chow Chek Kong, a member of an MRLA district committee, surrendered and offered his services to the security forces. He managed to do so without alerting anyone outside his own camp and thus his defection was never publicised in the hope that he could be used to approach other terrorists and induce them to surrender as well.

Chow was despatched to 22 SAS in the company of a Special Branch officer, also Chinese, who was his bodyguard. Attached to B Squadron, he led patrols to routes used by CT units carrying supplies, enabling the squadron to establish ambushes with successful results. He also lured his erstwhile comrades to prearranged rendezvous locations where they were shot dead. Accompanied by his Special Branch bodyguard, Chow entered villages at night and left messages for members of the branch committee, saying that he had just returned to the area and asking them to meet him. Those who did so were arrested and persuaded to surrender. Three weeks later, he received a letter from a terrorist named Ng Pak Thong, a fellow member of his district committee, saying that he had heard of Chow's return and wished to meet him. The two men arranged to do so at a location in the jungle some five miles away in an area that was being logged for timber.

On the day of the rendezvous, Chow, accompanied by Joe Goh, a Chinese civil liaison officer attached to B Squadron who would be his bodyguard on this operation, left the squadron base at 3.00 a.m, with an eight-man patrol led by Captain Peter Raven, one of the troop commanders. The rendezvous location was on a small track close to a railway line used by logging wagons for transporting timber through the jungle. Trees had been felled to one side of the path and these provided ideal cover for Raven and his men. The patrol prepared an ambush just before dawn, Raven having given Chow clear instructions to meet Ng Pak Thong on the track and lead him along it. He was to take off his cap and drop to the ground as he reached the point opposite the position of the last member of the patrol, this being the signal for Raven to initiate the ambush.

Shortly after the patrol took up its positions, a party of loggers appeared on the railway line with their wagons and were greeted by Chow and Joe Goh who by then were dressed in CT uniforms. After a brief conversation, during which they promised to tell Ng Pak Thong that Chow was at the rendezvous, the loggers departed. At 11.00 a.m., as Chow and Goh waited at the edge of the clearing, voices were heard and two men in uniform, Ng Pak Thong and a bodyguard, a young Indian, appeared and joined them. As Chow and Ng talked, Goh accompanied the Indian in patrolling the area.

After some minutes of conversation, Chow and Ng moved into the ambush area. At this point, Chow lost his nerve and began to run, then suddenly dropped to the ground but forgetting to take off his cap. Alarmed, Ng turned and began to run but was shot dead by the patrol. Joe Goh meanwhile opened fire with his shotgun at Ng's bodyguard but by that time the latter was out of range and succeeded in escaping into the jungle.

Chow continued to work for 22 SAS, one of his last missions being to lead B Squadron to a major CT arms cache whose location had only been known to him and the late Choy Foong. It contained a large quantity of items including lathes, grinders, blowlamps and other tools for manufacturing and repairing weapons. As an officer subsequently commented:

> The ingenuity they used for repairing weapons or making new ones was incredible. Their patterns for magazines were accurate in measurements and in size. They were also putting bits of one weapon on to another. For instance, half of one automatic was a Mark V rifle, the breech was American, the barrel British – and the barrel was held to the main body with wire.

ON 31 AUGUST 1957, the Federation of Malaya achieved independence under an Alliance government headed by Tunku Abdul Rahman as prime minister. Singapore, with its predominantly Chinese population, remained outside the federation as a British crown colony. The arrangement tended to favour the Malays politically, with UMNO leaders holding most federal and state offices and the position of king as monarch rotating in turn between the sultans. The Chinese, however, were granted full rights of citizenship and were permitted to maintain their strong economic base within the country.

In February 1958 a major operation, codenamed THRUST, was mounted by 22 SAS in response to information concerning a group of CT known to be hiding in the area of swamp at Telok Anson, a vast area of jungle in Lower Perak. The terrorists were led by a notorious individual named Ah Hoi. Leader of the MCP's Perak State Committee, Ah Hoi had been nicknamed 'Baby Killer' after his murder of the pregnant wife of a man suspected as being an informer for the security forces.

As described by General Peter de la Billière in his autobiography *Looking for Trouble – SAS to Gulf Command*, B Squadron was selected to carry out the operation. Its commander, Major Harry Thompson, opted for a parachute insertion and the squadron was dropped at dawn into the area of the swamp from RAF Beverley transports. Unfortunately, one man, Trooper Jerry Mulcahy, was injured when his parachute canopy failed to snag in a tree and he crashed to the ground below, breaking his back. An emergency evacuation by helicopter had to be arranged immediately, an LZ being cut to enable the aircraft to hover sufficiently low for Mulcahy to be loaded aboard.

Despite losing the element of surprise, the squadron pressed on with the operation and began patrolling through the swamp in its search for Ah Hoi's group. Captain Peter de la Billière's 6 Troop was given the task of searching along the Sungei Tengi. Although it did not encounter the CT, it found evidence of their presence in the form of several abandoned campsites. This information enabled the squadron commander to redeploy his other three troops to intercept the terrorists who appeared to be heading inland towards the centre of the swamp, following the course of the river. It was more than likely that they had been alerted by the helicopter 'casevac' and were trying to make good their escape.

A troop under Sergeant Sandilands headed for the centre of the swamp, moving under cover of darkness and the incessant croaking of bullfrogs and other nocturnal jungle noises, constantly alert for the smell of cooking fires and sounds of voices. In the late afternoon on the eighth day of its patrol, the troop was preparing to cross a wide stretch of water before dusk when the leading members observed two CT sitting on some mangrove roots approximately 70 yards away. Entering the water unseen and hiding behind a floating log, Sergeant Sandilands and another member of the troop succeeded in closing to within 50 yards of the two terrorists before opening fire. One was killed while the other escaped.

On the following day, Sandilands's troop followed the terrorists' tracks for four miles until it came upon a recently abandoned camp. Meanwhile, Major Harry Thompson redeployed the rest of the squadron to a point farther up the Sungei Tengi, where it received a resupply by helicopter, while the entire area was cordoned off by military and police units. Two days later, a female terrorist appeared and surrendered herself to the security forces. Under questioning, she identified herself as Ah Niet and stated that she had been sent by Ah Hoi with a message demanding payment of a sum of money for himself and the other members of his group, and an amnesty for all CT being held in prison.

Needless to say, these demands were refused and Ah Niet was sent back to Ah Hoi with a warning that unless he surrendered within 24 hours, he would be hunted down and killed by the troops surrounding the area. If they failed, then the area would be bombed by the RAF. Ah Hoi obviously realised this was no idle threat as he surrendered a few hours later. A troop of B squadron, led by Major Thompson and guided by Ah Niet, then went in search of the other members of Ah Hoi's group. It failed to find them, but 48 hours later they gave themselves up.

During the previous year, the head of the Federal Aborigine Department, Richard Noone, had concluded that the aborigines should play a more active role in combating the terrorists. This would ensure that they were no longer regarded as 'Sakai', mere second-class citizens, and that they should have an element of their own which would command their respect and admiration. After much lobbying at high level, Noone was given permission to raise a 180-strong force called the Senoi Pra'ak (Fighting Senoi), comprising Temiar and Semai who had previously been members of hostile groups. Commanded by him, the unit was equipped and trained by 22 SAS under whose direction it operated in the reconnaissance and scout role. It soon proved its worth, the aborigines impressing the SAS with their ability to move swiftly and silently through the jungle, remaining there for prolonged periods of time without resupply. Moreover, they enjoyed the greatest advantages of all: operating in their own home environment with the support of aborigine groups.

In 1958, during a period when contacts between the security force and the CT were becoming increasingly rare, the Senoi Pra'ak, at Noone's request, were permitted to conduct a mission on their own. An operation was mounted in central Perak which resulted in a group of eight CT being killed and over 200 Semoq Beri aborigines being persuaded to come over to the government side. Thereafter, the unit was authorised to operate on its own and over the next two years achieved the highest number of terrorists killed. After the end of the Emergency in 1960, the Senoi Praak became a permanent component of the Police Field Force of the Royal Malaysian Police, becoming part of the PFF brigade of four battalions based at Ipoh, in Perak. Its role was one of patrolling the Malay–Thai border, its detachments operating in cooperation with Special Branch and another specialist unit, 69 Police Commando popularly known by its nickname of VAT 69.

Towards the end of 1958, by which time Lieutenant Colonel Anthony Deane-Drummond had assumed command of 22 SAS, some 6,500 CT had been killed while another 3,000 had either surrendered or had been captured. At the end of October, D Squadron, which had been on operations in the Belum Valley, was suddenly withdrawn and on 18 November left Malaya for the Persian Gulf and the Sultanate of Oman, with which Britain had long-standing treaties. Here it was deployed on operations against dissidents seeking to overthrow the regime of Sultan Sa'id bin Taymur. Two months later, A Squadron also left Malaya for Oman where it joined D Squadron. In mid-1959, the remainder of the regiment left Malaya and returned to Britain.

For 22 SAS, the Malayan Emergency was over. During the campaign, the CT casualties totalled 6,398 killed and 1,245 captured, while 1,938 surrendered themselves to the security forces. Of those killed, 108 died at the hands of 22 SAS. While this may seem a very small proportion of the total, especially in comparison to those British, Gurkha and Commonwealth units which achieved particularly good results, a large proportion of those making up that figure were leading terrorists, and their deaths were thus severe blows to the MRLA. Furthermore, the emphasis during a large part of the regiment's operations was on intelligence gathering, and on the crucial task of winning the hearts and minds of the aborigines, rather than on seeking direct confrontations with the terrorists. Finally, on a number of occasions, it was intelligence from 22 SAS that led to successful engagements of terrorist groups by other security force units.

CHAPTER FIVE

KOREA 1950–1953

Some 3,000 miles to the north-east of Indochina and Malaya, where France and Britain respectively were actively occupied in combating the communist threats, another conflict was raging between South Korea, supported by the United Nations (UN), and communist North Korea, backed by China and the Soviet Union.

Approximately 600 miles in length and variably 125–200 miles in width, the Korean Peninsula extends southward from the north-eastern Chinese region of Manchuria and Russian Siberia, dividing the Yellow Sea to the west from the Sea of Japan to the east. To the south, the 30-mile-wide Korea Strait separates its southernmost tip from the Japanese island of Tsushima. For centuries, Korea's geographical location made it a natural approach route for Chinese or Russian armies intent on invading Japan, which in turn regarded it as a buffer zone against foreign aggression, particularly after the outbreak of the Russo-Japanese War in February 1904. At the end of hostilities in 1905, Korea became a Japanese protectorate and remained so until 1945 and Japan's defeat at the hands of the Allies.

Any celebration by Korea over freedom from foreign domination, however, proved short-lived. On 8 August 1945, two days after the dropping by the United States of an atomic bomb on the city of Hiroshima and on the day prior to a second being dropped on Nagasaki, the Soviet Union declared war on Japan. Its armies advanced almost unopposed through Manchuria, hitherto occupied by the Japanese, and continued southward into Korea. The United States, meanwhile, hastily produced a proposal for joint US–Soviet stewardship of Korea under which the country would be divided into two regions demarcated by the 38th Parallel. There were no US forces in Korea at the time and thus it was fortunate that the Soviets agreed to the American proposal. In September, troops of the US Army's XXIV Corps arrived in South Korea from Okinawa.

In August 1948, following democratic elections which saw the rise to power of President Syngman Rhee, South Korea became the Republic of Korea (ROK). Three weeks later, the Soviet-occupied north was proclaimed the People's Democratic Republic of Korea under its leader, Kim Il Sung. For the sake of convenience, they will be referred to respectively as South and North Korea throughout this chapter.

On 1 January 1949, the Soviets announced that they had withdrawn all their forces from the country; in fact, between 3,000 and 5,000 advisers and technical personnel remained as part of an on-going programme to train and equip North Korea's newly created armed forces. The nucleus of the latter had been formed by Koreans who had served during the war in the Chinese armies and were released to return home. In February 1948, they established the North Korean People's Army (NKPA). Initially numbering approximately 135,000, this force was organised into ten infantry divisions supported by some 150 T-34 tanks, 1,650 artillery pieces and 200 aircraft comprising Yak-9 fighters and Il-120 medium bombers.

In the United States, meanwhile, the post-war administration of President Harry S. Truman was primarily concerned with balancing the country's economy and thus paid little attention to the growing threat in North Korea. Moreover, the armed forces had been cut drastically following the end of the Second World War, the US Army being reduced in manpower from a wartime strength of 6 million to just 530,000. According to Colonel Michael Haas in his book *In the Devil's Shadow – UN Special Operations During the Korean War*, the combat readiness in the US Army at that time was described by its Chief of Staff, General Omar Bradley, as being in a 'shockingly deplorable state'. In Bradley's view, only one formation, the 82nd Airborne Division, could remotely be considered as combat-ready. The US Air Force (USAF) and US Navy were in equally parlous states, the latter having suffered over a 90 per cent cut in the number of its warships, reduced from 6,768 in 1945 to 634 by mid-1950.

On 30 June 1949, the last elements of US forces withdrew from South Korea, leaving behind a 473-man unit, the Korean Military Advisory Group (KMAG), with the task of training and advising the newly formed ROK armed forces. These initially comprised little more than a 95,000-strong paramilitary constabulary force geared primarily to the maintenance of internal security. Lulled into a false sense of security by the withdrawal of Soviet forces from North Korea, the Americans had turned

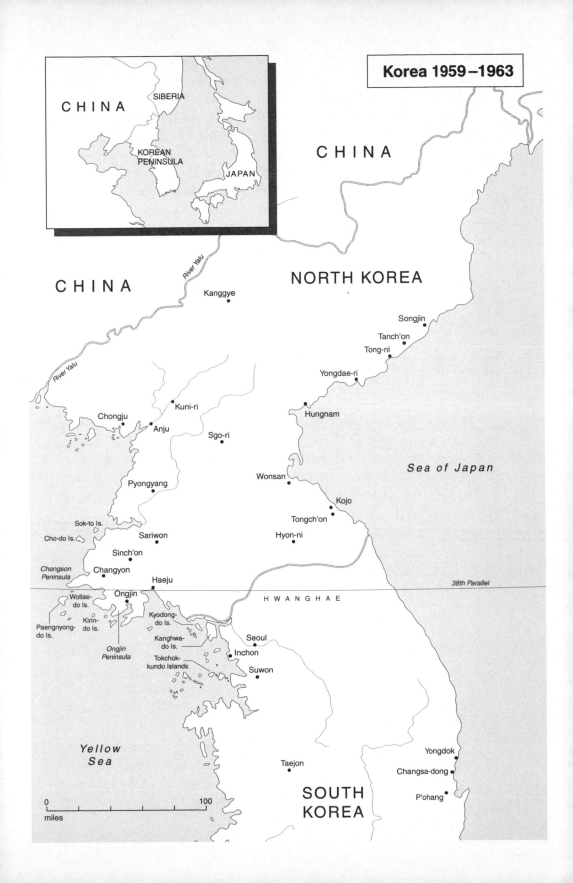

Korea 1959–1963

CHINA

SIBERIA

KOREAN
PENINSULA

JAPAN

CHINA

River Yalu

CHINA

NORTH KOREA

Kanggye

Songjin

Tanch'on

Tong-ni

River Yalu

Yongdae-ri

Kuni-ri

Chongju

Hungnam

Anju

Sgo-ri

Sea of Japan

Wonsan

Pyongyang

Kojo

Sok-to Is.

Tongch'on

Cho-do Is.

Sariwon

Hyon-ni

Sinch'on

Changson
Peninsula

Changyon

Haeju

38th Parallel

Wollae-
do Is.

Ongjin

H W A N G H A E

Paengnyong-
do Is.

Kirin-
do Is.

Kyodong-
do Is.

Kanghwa-
do Is.

Seoul

Ongjin
Peninsula

Tokchok-
kundo Islands

Inchon

Suwon

Yellow
Sea

Yongdok

Taejon

Changsa-dong

P'ohang

SOUTH
KOREA

0   100

miles

down President Syngman Rhee's demands for arms and equipment which included P-51 Mustang fighters, B-25 Mitchell bombers, destroyers, submarines and minesweepers. Instead, fearing that the South Korean president would sooner or later use these to launch an assault on his hated northern neighbour, the United States limited supplies merely to small arms, light weapons and a quantity of transport which had already seen extensive service and was already well worn.

Tensions between South and North Korea meanwhile increased markedly and the number of incidents along the 38th Parallel demarcation line rose as attacks were carried out by both sides. Despite the apparent indifference of the Truman administration, the US State Department recognised the growing communist threat, notably that the Soviet Union would attempt to bring about the fall of Syngman Rhee's government at the earliest opportunity.

After the withdrawal of US troops, responsibility for the security of Korea had been transferred from the Pentagon's US Far East Command (FECOM), based in Japan and headed by General Douglas MacArthur, to the State Department. MacArthur, however, had taken the precaution of directing his chief of intelligence, Major General Charles Willoughby, to establish a secret organisation in South Korea with the role of monitoring communist activities. Based in the capital of Seoul and designated the Korean Liaison Office (KLO), it comprised a small group of FECOM intelligence officers. One of its first discoveries was that the North Koreans had infiltrated several thousand guerrillas into the south, some two-thirds of whom were South Koreans opposed to the regime of Syngman Rhee.

By the beginning of 1950, the situation along the 38th Parallel had become extremely serious, with increasingly frequent outbreaks of fighting. At the same time, North Korean guerrillas carried out some 30 attacks inside South Korea. Shortly afterwards, Kim Il Sung paid two visits to Moscow, where he met both the Soviet leader Josef Stalin and his Chinese counterpart Mao Tse Tung, convincing them of his ability to invade South Korea and thus reunify the entire country. He returned to Pyongyang with their endorsements for his plan.

During the following week, North Korean forces massed unseen in their assault positions just north of the 38th Parallel. At 4.00 a.m. on the morning of 25 June 1950, the darkness of the stormy night sky was rent

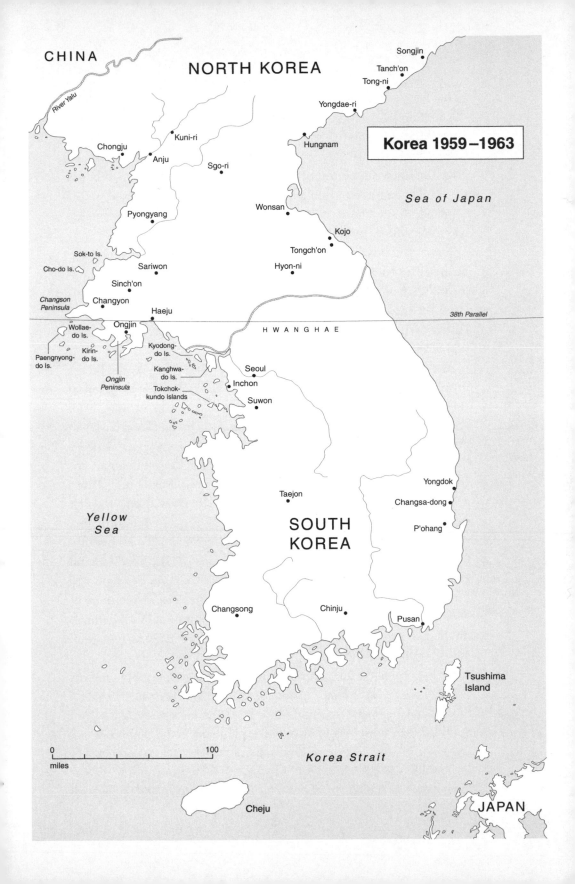

CHINA

NORTH KOREA

River Yalu

Songjin

Tanch'on

Tong-ni

Yongdae-ri

Chongju

Kuni-ri

Anju

Sgo-ri

Hungnam

Korea 1959–1963

Pyongyang

Wonsan

Sea of Japan

Kojo

Tongch'on

Sok-to Is.

Cho-do Is.

Sariwon

Hyon-ni

Changson Peninsula

Sinch'on

Changyon

Haeju

38th Parallel

Wollae-do Is.

Ongjin

H W A N G H A E

Kyodong-do Is.

Paengnyong-do Is.

Kirin-do Is.

Kanghwa-do Is.

Seoul

Ongjin Peninsula

Tokchok-kundo Islands

Inchon

Suwon

Yellow Sea

Yongdok

Taejon

Changsa-dong

P'ohang

SOUTH KOREA

Changsong

Chinju

Pusan

Tsushima Island

0   100

miles

Korea Strait

Cheju

JAPAN

by the muzzle flashes of over 1,500 artillery pieces as they opened fire on the positions of the three ROK divisions manning the demarcation line. Understrength and with some 30 per cent of their number at home helping with the rice harvest, the ROK forces were swiftly overrun by NKPA infantry supported by armour and artillery. Within two hours they had been routed, fleeing before the enemy which pressed south-ward in four spearheads towards the South Korean capital of Seoul situated some 30 miles away.

News of the North Korean invasion simultaneously reached the headquarters of the US FECOM in Tokyo and the State Department in Washington. At 2.00 p.m. local time in New York, the United Nations (UN) Security Council convened an emergency meeting and two hours later issued a unanimous resolution calling on North Korea to withdraw immediately.

The United States had been caught totally off-guard by Kim Il Sung's invasion and inevitably the finger of blame was pointed at the Central Intelligence Agency (CIA). In fact, the Agency had given warning of an attack less than three weeks prior to the attack. This had been based on information received from agents infiltrated into North Korea in 1948 by the US Army Liaison Group, the cover name for an American intelli-gence unit attached to Chinese nationalist forces in Manchuria. These agents had remained in place undetected since then and during the first six months of 1950 had sent back a considerable amount of information which indicated North Korean preparations for an attack on the south. On 20 June the Director of Central Intelligence (DCI), Rear Admiral Roscoe Hillenkoetter, had delivered copies of the Agency's report to President Truman, Secretary of State Dean Acheson and Secretary of Defence Louis Johnson. Such was the lack of concern in Washington at the time, however, that the reports were either ignored or remained unread until it was too late.

On the evening of 26 June, following a meeting with senior members of his Cabinet and the Joint Chiefs of Staff, President Truman decided on three initial measures: the evacuation of 2,000 Americans civilians from South Korea; the supply of arms and equipment to the South Korean armed forces; and the extension of General Douglas MacArthur's area of responsibility to include Taiwan. In addition, the US Seventh Fleet was immediately to position itself between Taiwan and mainland China with the task of forestalling any attempt by the communists to attack the nationalist-held island in an attempt to escalate the Korean conflict.

On 27 June, the UN Security Council passed a further resolution calling on member nations to provide military assistance to South Korea in order to restore peace and security to the region. The evening of the same day saw the departure from Japan of a group of fifteen staff officers from FECOM who flew to an airfield at Suwon, some 25 miles south of Seoul which by then was in the hands of the North Koreans. Next day they were briefed on the situation by the US ambassador, John Muccio. On the day after, General MacArthur himself arrived in his personal aircraft, a C-121 Constellation christened *Bataan*, escorted by a flight of four P-51 Mustang fighters; as the *Bataan* was commencing its approach to Suwon, these intercepted and shot down a Yak-9 fighter which made a sudden appearance. Accompanied by a small band of staff officers and press, MacArthur carried out a tour of the South Korean rear areas where he watched the hordes of refugees and elements of shattered ROK forces heading south; in the distance he was able to observe the enemy-held capital of Seoul.

MacArthur returned to Tokyo that same day and submitted a report to the Pentagon in which he stated that the situation could only be rectified by swift and decisive commitment of US forces, and requested authority as well to engage elements of the US occupation forces in Japan. This request was approved by President Truman who also gave his consent for a naval blockade of the entire Korean Peninsula and the commitment of the USAF to operations against military targets north of the 38th Parallel. Within hours, troops of the 24th US Infantry Division were boarding aircraft in Japan en route to South Korea.

The North Koreans had halted their advance to regroup after their capture of Seoul and resumed it on 5 July, by which time the 24th US Infantry Division had landed at Pusan and deployed northward. Their first clash with American troops occurred on the same day north of Osan, a town on the highway linking Seoul and the city of Taejon, when they encountered the 1st Battalion 21st Infantry Regiment. The latter, lacking armour or artillery support, was unable to check the NKPA advance which swept on to confront the 1st Battalion 34th Infantry Regiment defending a river-line. Once again, the North Korean forces experienced little difficulty in overrunning the ill-equipped American troops who were soon routed and retreating southward, abandoning vehicles and equipment in the process.

These scenes were repeated elsewhere as elements of the 24th US Infantry Division found themselves outflanked and encircled, being forced to fight their way out and suffering heavy losses. Eventually, they were driven back to Taejon where they attempted to stand. On 19 July, however, the North Korean armour smashed its way through and the remnants of the division resumed their retreat southward, having suffered over 2,400 casualties.

In the meantime, on 10 July, General MacArthur had been appointed commander-in-chief of all UN forces in South Korea. Operational responsibility and command were delegated by him to the commander of the Eighth US Army, Lieutenant General Walton H. 'Johnnie' Walker, who arrived with his headquarters on 13 July. He was followed by two more American formations, the 25th US Infantry and 1st US Cavalry Divisions. On 20 July, the 25th received its baptism of fire at Yechon where one of its three regiments, the 24th Infantry, broke and ran under the North Korean onslaught. The division succeeded, however, in holding its positions until 30 July when it was forced to withdraw. On the previous day, the 1st US Cavalry Division had been compelled to pull back from its positions in the area of Yongdong to avoid encirclement. By the end of July, the Eighth US Army had been forced into an enclave, the front line of which stretched from the southern town of Chinju northward to Kwan-ni, then north-east to Yechon and ultimately to Yongdok on the east coast.

No sooner had the Pusan Perimeter, as the enclave came to be dubbed, been stabilised than MacArthur began to plan a major counter-attack in the form of a landing by the X US Corps on the west coast, to take place simultaneously with a break-out from Pusan by Eighth Army. Codenamed Operation CHROMITE, it would take place at the port of Inchon with the aim of attacking the North Koreans in the rear.

The only deep-water approach to Inchon is the twisting 45- mile-long Flying Fish Channel which opens some 30 miles to the south-west of the port in the area of the Tokchok-kundo Islands. While it will comfortably accommodate large vessels at high tide, this is not the case at the low-water mark when its depth can be only a few feet at the most. This caused considerable anxiety to planners on FECOM's staff who were also concerned at the proximity of the channel to some of the islands around which it meanders towards Inchon. At one point it passes between three of the larger – Taebu-do and Yonghung-do to the south and Taemuui-do to the north, the width of the channel between them being approximately five miles. All three islands were held by the North Koreans who thus controlled the single approach to Inchon. In order for the operation to proceed, the islands would have to be taken and secured beforehand.

The task of doing so was given to an officer on the FECOM staff, Lieutenant Eugene Clark USN, who had earlier suggested the formation of an irregular partisan force on the islands, recruited from refugees and local people, especially fishermen. A veteran of wartime maritime operations with the Office of Strategic Services (OSS), he had been attached to the ROK Navy on intelligence duties prior to being assigned to FECOM and had discovered that the three islands were held by two understrength platoons of NKPA troops. Initially turned down, his plan had been resurrected after further reflection by those responsible for planning the landing operation.

On 26 August, Clark was advised that his idea had been accepted and on the following day flew to Pusan where he collected two Korean interpreters before returning to Japan. There he recruited the rest of the group who would accompany him – three Korean communications specialists and ten civilians. At the same time, he enlisted the support of the Royal Navy in the form of the cruiser HMS *Jamaica* and the destroyer HMS *Charity* which, in addition to transporting his group to the Tokchok-kundo Islands, would provide naval gunfire and other support during the operations to seize the three islands.

Clark and his group embarked on *Jamaica* and the two warships sailed for the islands, arriving off Tokchok-do on the morning of 31 August. Ashore he met the commander of a South Korean National Police paramilitary unit who confirmed that Yonghung-do, Taebu-do and Taemuui-do were still held by weak NKPA forces of less than platoon strength. He provided a platoon of his own unit to reinforce Clark's group.

In the early hours of the following day Clark's force, together with the National Police platoon and *Jamaica's* own detachment of Royal Marine commandos, landed on Yonhung-do. As dawn broke, an alert enemy sentry opened fire on the cruiser's boats as they appeared offshore, but any further resistance was discouraged by a single 8-inch shell from *Jamaica*. The island was swiftly taken before Clark's force moved on to secure Taebu-do which was captured just after 4.00 p.m., its small garrison surrendering without firing a shot.

Clark set to establishing his partisan force whose ranks were quickly swelled by local civilians and South Korean soldiers who, separated from their units, had been evading capture by the communists. Some were despatched as scouts to discover the situation on Taemuui-do, duly reporting that the enemy were in platoon strength and in the process of constructing defensive positions on the southern slopes of a small hill that rejoiced in the somewhat grandiose name of Tiger Mountain, at the southern end of the island.

At 4.30 a.m. on the morning of 8 September, Clark's force landed at the northern end of Taemuui-do from a ROK Navy LST (Landing Ship Tank) and advanced to within some 400 yards of Tiger Mountain where it halted. Shortly afterwards, HMS *Jamaica* opened fire on the enemy's positions with her 8-inch guns, laying down a heavy barrage. When Clark and his men resumed their advance and stormed the mountain, they found little in the way of resistance and by 6.30 the island had been taken. Later that day, Yongu-do was also captured.

The following days and nights were spent reconnoitring the surrounding islands and the area of Inchon itself, with a stream of information on enemy dispositions being transmitted to Pusan. One reconnaissance mission was carried out by Clark himself and one of his two interpreters, a ROK Navy lieutenant, to gauge the depth of the water at high and low tides at Inchon. This vital information was required by FECOM to determine whether there would be a minimum depth of 25 feet required to navigate the Flying Fish Channel and Inchon Harbour, with 29 feet being necessary for landing ship tanks (LST) carrying MacArthur's forces. The information in the US Navy's tide tables differed from that given on old Japanese tide charts and thus Clark needed to assess which were accurate. He and his companion succeeded in determining the depth of the water and measuring the height of the seawall; they also discovered that the mudflats at low tide were too soft to accommodate the weight of their naked bodies, let alone that of a fully equipped marine or soldier. Clark's mission proved that the Japanese tide charts were accurate and the landing plans were altered accordingly.

By 13 September the majority of islands in the area had been secured. The notable exceptions were Wolmi-do and Yongchong-do, both of which were heavily defended, and the small island of Palmi-do, which featured a lighthouse whose beacon had been extinguished by the North Koreans. On the night of 14 September, the latter launched a counter-attack against Clark's force on Yonghung-do but were observed before they landed. Taking to their boats, Clark and his men made good their escape and sailed to Palmi-do where, in the early hours of 15 September, he reignited the lighthouse beacon in time to guide in the advance element of the landing force tasked with capturing the island of Wolmi-do prior to the main landings at Inchon, which subsequently proved successful.

A further operation involving partisans was under way meanwhile on Korea's eastern coast. This took place at the same time as a break-out from the Pusan Perimeter and comprised a landing behind North Korean lines by the Miryang Guerrilla Battalion, a unit of partisans led by a single American adviser, Lieutenant William S. Harrison, who had served with the 17th US Airborne Division during the Second World War. On the morning of 15 September, the battalion, which had embarked in a ROK Navy LST, arrived off its designated landing point, a beach at Changsa-dong, a small fishing village south of Yongdok. Adverse weather conditions delayed the landing, which had been scheduled to take place before dawn, and led to the LST being swept on to rocks at the southern end of the beach. The battalion nevertheless succeeded in making its way ashore and clearing the enemy from Changsa-dong and the surrounding area. Four hours later it was subjected to a heavy counter-attack by a North Korean regiment which had been concentrated in the area for rest and recuperation after previous heavy fighting.

Driven back to the beach, the battalion fought a desperate battle to prevent the North Koreans from overrunning it. Naval gunfire support was provided by a frigate, USS *Endicott*, joined late that evening by a US Navy task force which also brought its guns to bear and managed to keep the enemy at bay until the afternoon of 17 September when the battalion was evacuated under fire.

By this time, FECOM's Intelligence Directorate had established an organisation called the Far East Command Liaison Group (FEC-LG). Based in Tokyo, its role was the collection of tactical and strategic intelligence. This had come about as the result of General MacArthur's determination that any agencies not under his command, such as the CIA, be prohibited from operating in Korea. During the Second World War he had exercised a similar policy, successfully preventing the OSS from operating in the Pacific theatre. While its initial activities were concentrated almost solely on intelligence acquisition, the FEC-LG formed the nucleus from which other unconventional warfare units would subsequently be spawned during the three years of conflict in Korea.

Within the Eighth US Army, tactical intelligence-gathering was undertaken up to a depth of 20 miles behind North Korean lines by an organisation called the Tactical Liaison Office (TLO) which had sections attached to various US corps headquarters. TLO teams, each comprising an American officer/handler, two NCOs and up to 25 Korean agents, were assigned to each division. Agents infiltrated on foot into the north disguised as refugees or, once the war assumed a more static nature, as NKPA troops. They were not equipped with radios and therefore had to return with their intelligence, time being of the essence as divisions in forward areas needed up-to-date information on North Korean positions and deployments. On their return, they underwent thorough debriefing by US Army Counter Intelligence Corps (CIC) personnel at divisional headquarters.

Strategic intelligence tasks were meanwhile carried out by the KLO whose agents were inserted by parachute or, in the case of those whose targets were in coastal areas, landed from the sea.

After MacArthur's successful landing at Inchon, North Korean forces were in full retreat northward and FECOM was in dire need of intelligence with regard to enemy dispositions and withdrawal routes. The task of providing it was given to the FEC-LG which delegated it to its airborne operations section, codenamed AVIARY, which had been formed in August. The parachute training given to KLO agents was somewhat rudimentary, comprising synthetic training only: aircraft exit drill and position, control of the parachute, landing position, drills for landing in trees and water, and subsequent disposal of the parachute. In those early days, agents were not afforded the luxury of training descents prior to being despatched on operations.

The first AVIARY mission took place on the night of 26 September 1950 when nine KLO agents were dropped on to two drop zones (DZ) from two USAF C-47 transports, five on one and four on the other. Both groups established surveillance on seven of the major withdrawal routes being used by the North Koreans and a few days later eight of the nine agents exfiltrated through UN lines to make their reports. By the time they were debriefed by their controllers, however, their information was out of date. In order to overcome this problem, subsequent missions were equipped with SCR-694 transmitter/receivers which enabled them to talk to US aircraft, fitted with radios linked to tape recorders, flying within sight of the agents on the ground. These sets were cumbersome and heavy and were later replaced by lightweight SCR-300 sets. The latter, however, were in very short supply and other methods of communication had to be developed, among them the use of coloured smoke grenades which were activated by agents as US aircraft flew overhead, their respective colours indicating pre-designated signals that gave information on enemy dispositions and strengths.

Seaborne insertions of KLO agents being deployed into coastal areas were carried out under the auspices of Operation SALAMANDER. High-speed patrol craft or USAF crash rescue boats, along with junks or fishing boats, some powered by diesel engines, were used for landings along Korea's extensive coastlines. Missions were launched from forward bases on UN-controlled islands which could call on naval forces for protection in the event of enemy attack. Like their AVIARY counterparts, SALA-MANDER teams produced useful intelligence during the first six months of the conflict; in many instances their courage and determination were the principal factors in achieving success in their missions.

Early December 1950 saw China come to the aid of the hard-pressed North Koreans. UN forces, which had not long before been pursuing the NKPA north of the 38th Parallel, retreated south under the onslaught of the 13th Army Group of the Chinese People's Liberation Army (PLA) until, at the end of the first week in January 1951, they managed to establish a defensive line south of the 38th Parallel.

Indications of Chinese intervention had been given as early as mid-October by KLO agents dropped by AVIARY along North Korea's border with China. Later that month, details of up to 60,000 Chinese troops crossing into North Korea reached FECOM and the headquarters of US Eighth Army. As Colonel Michael Haas states in his book, on 31

October FECOM's Chief of Intelligence, Major General Charles Willoughby, debriefed a leading KLO agent who had previously been deployed in the Kangge–Mampojin area. The latter provided Willoughby with extensive details of the Chinese formations which had crossed over the Mampojin Bridge into North Korea during that month.

Slow passage of intelligence was a major problem for FECOM and in November 1950 steps were taken to rectify the situation with the formation of the FECOM Intelligence Committee, comprising senior representatives from the three service intelligence branches and the CIA, its role being to eliminate duplication and expedite the flow of intelligence.

During the second week of January 1951, Headquarters Eighth US Army formed a department tasked with the conduct of unconventional warfare operations in Korea. Designated the Attrition Section, it was an element of the headquarters' G-3 Miscellaneous Division. Its formation came about as a result of the large numbers of anti-communist refugees who had fled to Korea's western coastal areas and the islands lying off them. Colonel John McGee, an officer who had seen service with guerrilla forces in the Philippines during the Second World War, had earlier submitted a plan for the creation of a joint service organisation to form the refugees into partisan units. This had been turned down by FECOM but on 15 January authorisation was given to establish the Attrition Section. Although it was under the operational command of the Operations Division of Headquarters US Eighth Army, its activities would be guided by FECOM's Intelligence Directorate.

The Attrition Section's first task was to establish Task Force William Able, a partisan command based on the island of Paengnyong-do. Situated off the south-west peninsula of Korea's Hwanghae Province just below the 38th Parallel, the island offered several advantages including a rock-free beach which at low tide could be used as an airstrip and at high tide enabled landing craft to unload men and stores.

Led by Major William Burke, the task force's first mission was to form, equip and train a number of partisan units, subsequently establishing a series of bases on islands off the western coast of Korea. These were centred on existing groups of anti-communist elements already in place on some of the islands. Initially, the leaders of five such groups, each accompanied by 20 of their men, were brought to Paengnyong-do for training in tactics, demolitions, radio communications, navigation, combat survival and first aid. Selected members of each group were trained as advanced demolitions specialists, combat medics or radio operators. The last were instructed in the use of HF radio communications using morse code as well as enciphering and deciphering of messages.

On completion of their training on Paengnyong-do, the five leaders and their men returned to their respective groups who by that time had been given the codename DONKEY followed by a number – for example DONKEY 1. At the same time, Task Force William Able was redesignated Operation LEOPARD. A further unit was formed on Paengnyong-do to carry out sabotage, raiding and intelligence gathering operations. This was Task Force Redwing, a ROK Marine Corps company commanded by Americans.

Operations by LEOPARD began with a landing on the Changson Peninsula by the 38-strong DONKEY 1 which had earlier been deployed to the smaller island of Wollae-do for further training prior to its mission. In an operation codenamed SHINING MOON, the unit, under its commander Chang Chae Hwa, landed on the peninsula on the night of 3/4 March and made its way inland to the mountains south of Sinch'on which it reached three days later, installing itself in a base on Pukt'a Mountain. Shortly afterwards, a major problem occurred with the unit's AN/GRC-9 HF radio set which began to fail but not before the mission controller, based on Paengnyong-do, had undertaken to send a replacement with DONKEY 2 which would land on 15 March. The controller was Lieutenant William S. Harrison who had previously been adviser to the Miryang Guerrilla Battalion, accompanying it on its landing on the east coast at Changsa-dong in September of the previous year.

DONKEY 2 failed to rendezvous (RV) with DONKEY 1 and thus the latter, lacking an operable radio, remained out of contact with its base. Nevertheless, it proceeded to carry out assaults on a number of targets. On the evening of 21 March, it attacked a police station at the small town of Buchong-ni where communist officials were conducting a meeting, killing 27, including seven policemen. Nine light vehicles and trucks belonging to the police and officials were destroyed, while a number of weapons, several cases of ammunition and a large quantity of food were captured. The next target, shortly afterwards, was an NKPA staging post at Sinch'on, where trucks and buses were destroyed.

On the night of 18 April, DONKEY 1 attacked four large warehouses in Sinch'on where some 1,700 prisoners, former members of a UN security police organisation, known anti-communists and relatives of partisans, had been incarcerated by the North Koreans. Only some 400 of those liberated, however, were capable of walking and being evacuated by Chang's partisans who led them away to the mountains south of Sinch'on. The remainder were left behind and were later massacred by Chinese troops who subjected the warehouses to a fierce bombardment of mortar and artillery fire. The Chinese lost little time in intercepting DONKEY 1 as it headed for the mountains and a major engagement took place in which the partisans suffered 50 casualties. Splitting up into four groups, the rest made good their escape and scattered in four different directions to shake off the pursuing enemy.

Chang and his headquarters element made their way to an area some 40 miles south-east of Sinch'on where they established a new base and began to rebuild DONKEY 1. By early May the unit had returned to the mountains south of Sinch'on and was back in action, carrying out small-scale raids, ambushes, blowing up a bridge and assassinating prominent communist officials. On 11 May, DONKEY 1 attacked a minerals mine eight miles south-west of Sinch'on, freeing the 800-strong slave labour force and destroying a number of warehouses containing a large quantity of food. This raid stung the enemy into action once again and shortly afterwards two divisions of Chinese PLA troops conducted a sweep of the mountains around Sinch'on. DONKEY 1 moved west to avoid them but, on encountering an NKPA division, was forced to split up into small groups, each heading for a prearranged RV north of Changyon. But only fifteen men reached it and at the beginning of July Chang decided to withdraw and return to Paengnyong-do.

On the night of 23 July, he and his remaining twenty men of DONKEY 1 left the mainland at Kumsu-ri and made for the island of Yuk-do which was held by another LEOPARD unit, DONKEY 4. During the four and half months of SHINING MOON, DONKEY 1 had killed several hundred NKPA and PLA troops and police, inflicting casualties on many more, had assassinated nearly nearly 300 communist officials, attacked warehouses and blown up bridges. In addition, it had forced the North Koreans and Chinese to divert troops, sorely needed at the front line, to carry out anti-partisan operations in their rear areas. By the end of July, the number of enemy troops in DONKEY 1's area of operations had risen from 2,000 to over 30,000.

The Attrition Section, meanwhile, had formed a partisan organisation on the east coast of Korea, albeit considerably smaller than LEOPARD and with more limited objectives. Designated Charlie Section, it was made up of 200 partisans selected from the Miryang Guerrilla Battalion, the unit which had landed on the east coast of Korea at Changsa-dong in September 1950. Lieutenant William S. Harrison, who had been the unit's adviser during that operation, was selected by Colonel John McGee to command it.

Most of the larger islands situated off the east coast of Korea had been occupied by ROK Marine, USAF radar and US Army signals intelligence (sigint) units, their populations having been sent to the South Korean mainland. In addition, as described later in this chapter, the CIA was in evidence under the cover name of Joint Advisory Commission Korea (JACK), conducting operations on the mainland in the area north of the port of Wonsan. When the CIA became aware of the Attrition Section's plans for Charlie Section, it objected on the grounds that these would probably compromise JACK activities. As a result, Charlie Section's area of operations was restricted to an area stretching southward from Wonsan to the UN front lines.

The offshore base selected for Charlie Section was the island of Nam-do, lying some ten miles off the Korean east coast on the 39th Parallel. About 600 yards in length and 300 in width, it featured a ridge-line rising to a height of approximately 300 feet which permitted good radio communications with units on the mainland. In addition, it possessed a spring providing an excellent supply of fresh water. A small bay on the western side of the island was the only place where landings could be carried out but large rocks presented a serious hazard even in calm conditions.

In April 1951, Charlie Section was redesignated Task Force Kirkland and during the latter part of May occupied Nam-do. It also set up a rear headquarters and logistical base at the small fishing port of Chumunjin, seven miles south of the 38th Parallel. On 16 June, Lieutenant Harrison deployed an observation post (OP) on Song-do, a small four-acre island situated some twelve miles south-west of Nam-do and 800 yards off the North Korean coast. The NKPA, however, soon detected the presence of the partisans on Song-do, and in the next two weeks twice attempted to land troops. They were repulsed by naval gunfire support called down by the partisans from UN warships in the area.

Kirkland's first operation, codenamed LASSO, took place four days later on the night of 30 June. A raiding force of 60 partisans landed from two US Navy landing craft on a beach at the small fishing village of Kojo which was garrisoned by a small force of 30 men comprising NKPA railway engineers and military police. The nearest NKPA unit was the railway engineer battalion based near Tongch'on six miles to the south. Under cover of rain and mist, the partisans got ashore unseen and immediately attacked the village, killing 18 North Koreans before the rest broke and fled. A search of the village revealed a number of weapons and much documentation, including maps giving details of NKPA units in the neighbouring foothills. By dawn on the following day, the raiders had returned to Nam-do.

In late June, Lieutenant Harrison had departed for the United States, being replaced as commander on Nam-do by Lieutenant Ulatoski who had joined the Attrition Section from the 5th Ranger Infantry Company (Airborne). In early July, Major A. J. Coccumelli took over command of Task Force Kirkland. Later in the month, there were rumours that the North Koreans were preparing for another assault on Song-do which by then was occupied by a force of 50 partisans. Lieutenant Ulatoski arranged for naval gunfire support and trawlers to be on stand-by to evacuate the garrison if so required. Shortly after midnight on 6/7 August, a force of NKPA troops launched a fleet of some 20 small boats from the mainland coast just to the south of Song-do. As they reached a point midway across the channel, two 60mm light mortars on the island fired parachute flares, illuminating the boats which came under heavy fire. From the mainland, however, came supporting fire from NKPA heavy mortars which brought down a barrage. Thirty minutes later, the North Koreans had succeeded in landing.

Dawn on 7 August found Song-do in the possession of the NKPA force but under attack from US Navy aircraft and a destroyer. Heavy bombing and napalm reduced the island to a mass of flame which forced the enemy to withdraw, but not before they had mined and booby trapped the entire area. Four days later, however, a Kirkland observation team was deployed once again on Song-do.

In early September 1951, Kirkland deployed a 50-strong force, codenamed BIG BOY, on the mainland. Inserted by the amphibious landing ship USS *Begor*, it was landed in two groups over two nights; but due to the second group missing the prearranged RV, they did not meet up until they had infiltrated into the mountains. BIG BOY achieved limited success, partly because the partisans were not from the area and were therefore unfamiliar with it. Moreover, they received little support from the local people and had to rely on airdrops for resupply. By the end of the month, the force had been reduced to a strength of sixteen. Despite this, FECOM insisted on its remaining in the field to act as a reception committee for agents who would be dropped during the coming winter. This was a fatal mistake as, unknown to FECOM or Kirkland, the entire force either defected or was captured and forced to collaborate. Agents and supplies were subsequently dropped into the hands of the North Koreans who extended their deception operation by maintaining regular radio contact, transmitting reports to Nam-do which relayed them to Kirkland's rear headquarters, which in turn passed them to FECOM.

Meanwhile, in early 1951, the Attrition Section had also formed a unit to carry out airborne operations. Designated Baker Section and based at Kijang, a fishing village situated a short distance north-east of Pusan, its role was to train partisans as parachutists and to provide instruction in the necessary skills required for clandestine operations. In addition to its facility at Kijang, it possessed a detachment, based at an airbase just outside Pusan, whose role was the airborne dispatch of teams of Attrition Section personnel into North Korea and the subsequent support of them during operations. Another facility, also located on the outskirts of Pusan, provided training in demolitions and sabotage.

Immediately after its formation, Baker Section began preparing for its first operation, codenamed VIRGINIA I, which was to be led by the section's commander, Captain Eugene Perry. Its mission was to sabotage a railway tunnel 30 miles inland of the east coast, approximately three-quarters of a mile south-west of the town of Hyon-ni, situated on the banks of a tributary of the River Bukhan. Explosives would be planted inside the tunnel, being initiated by pressure switches on the line itself. A group comprising 40 ROK Army officer cadets was assembled for the task, the latter undergoing four weeks of sabotage training at the training facility at Pusan. They were to have undergone full parachute training but in the first practice descent eleven of the first batch of twenty cadets suffered broken limbs. It was therefore decided that the remaining twenty should be given only one day of ground training and four weeks of sabotage instruction instead.

Four members of the 4th Ranger Infantry Company (Airborne), Corporals Martin Watson, Edward Pucel and William Miles, and Private First Class (Pfc) Raymond Baker (recently demoted from sergeant for striking an officer), were meanwhile selected from ten volunteers to take part in the mission. All were qualified parachutists and had undergone basic demolitions training, while Corporal Pucel had served with the OSS in Yugoslavia during the Second World War.

According to Ed Evanhoe, author of *Dark Moon – Eighth Army Special Operations in the Korean War*, who served in Korea as a member of the Eighth US Army's G-3's Miscellaneous Group, planning and briefings for the mission were somewhat haphazard, and the Rangers' proposal that a group should be dropped in advance of the main body to secure and mark the DZ was turned down on the grounds that the operation might be compromised. Furthermore, the time-scale was unrealistic, the group being given only 72 hours to make the drop at night, move to its objective, carry out its task and exfiltrate 30 miles through an area held by two NKPA divisions to a pick-up point on the coast. To make matters worse, the climate during March (late winter in Korea) was highly unpredictable with temperatures well below freezing and violent storms from the north bringing heavy snowfalls.

On 13 March, the ROK cadets joined the four Rangers at Pusan. Two days later, a few hours before the group's scheduled departure, it was announced that Captain Perry was being withdrawn from the mission due to his extensive knowledge of Attrition Section operations and the risk of it being revealed to the enemy in the event of his capture. Somewhat surprisingly, no one was nominated to replace him as commander. At 8.00 p.m. hours that evening, the group took off from K-3 airbase in a C-47 flown by a crew of USAF reservists who had only just arrived in Korea. Heading north, the aircraft carried out a series of leaflet drops as part of a deception plan before heading for the mountains which overlooked the DZ in the Hyon-ni Valley.

Weather conditions had deteriorated by the time the drop took place at 11 p.m. On landing, the group found itself eight miles to the south of the DZ and scattered over a large area: Corporal Miles and a group of the ROK officer cadets had landed on the slopes of a mountain, with Corporal Pucel and five more in a valley below. Pfc Baker and another five had meanwhile landed on the other side of the mountain while Corporal Watson and four more cadets ended up in the centre of the small village of Uchon-ni, on the banks of the Bukhan River. Fortunately, no injuries were incurred and all equipment was retrieved; but the onset of a severe snowstorm prevented the group from joining up until the morning of the following day.

Once orientated, and led by Corporal Watson who had assumed command, the Rangers and cadets set off for their target area. Despite deep snow and the handicap of being without skis or snowshoes, they arrived at their intended DZ rally point on the morning of the 18th. Attempts were made to contact UN aircraft to arrange a resupply of rations but the group's radio was virtually useless due to its batteries being weakened by the sub-freezing temperatures. On the morning of the 19th, a reconnaissance of the objective revealed the presence of a Chinese railway repair unit and heavily fortified defensive positions at both ends of the tunnel. Watson and his men wisely decided to abort the mission and head for the coast.

The group made initially for Samdae-ri, in the hope that another tunnel could be attacked and blown up en route. It, too, was discovered to be heavily guarded. Without further ado, Watson and his men cached their explosives and booby trapped them before continuing their march. On 28 March, they reached the final mountain pass beyond which lay the coast. There they took refuge from the driving winds and heavy snow which lasted until the morning of the 29th.

Next day, having partly resuscitated his radio batteries by exposing them to warm sunlight, Corporal Miles managed to make contact with an airborne forward air controller of the 7th US Infantry Division who communicated the group's position to Headquarters Eighth US Army. Four hours later, a C-47 dropped supplies to the group but the latter's radio transmissions had been picked up by the NKPA and by that evening enemy units were closing in on VIRGINIA I's position.

Fortunately, the seriousness of the group's plight had been fully realised and a contingency rescue operation put into effect immediately. At dawn on 30 March, three small US Navy Sikorsky HO5S helicopters took off from the US Navy LST 799 and flew to the coast, escorted by a flight of A-7 Corsair fighters from the aircraft carrier USS *Coral Sea* which would provide air and ground support if necessary. Meanwhile, a C-47 was circling above the group's position, which by then was under heavy attack, guiding in the approaching aircraft. The first helicopter made its approach but was shot down hovering above the group as the pilot, Lieutenant John Thornton, attempted to winch up the first man. Fortunately, Thornton survived the crash and managed to reach the Rangers' position. The second helicopter, under cover of an air strike by the Corsairs, winched up Corporals Pucel and Miles, the latter being wounded in the face from ground fire. The third aircraft picked up Pfc Baker but the winch jammed and the plane had to leave with him suspended underneath.

Close air support continued but failed to prevent the enemy outflanking Corporal Watson and the remainder of the group. Eventually, under cover of an air strike, the survivors broke out from the position, charged through the surrounding enemy and headed for the mountains to the south. Only seven got away: Watson, five cadets and the helicopter pilot, Lieutenant Thornton. That night, however, the two Americans became separated from their Korean companions. They remained at liberty until 8 April when Thornton, by then suffering from frostbitten feet following the disintegration of his flying boots, surrendered to the North Koreans at Imbong-ni. Watson was absent at the time, foraging for food, but was captured on the following day south-east of Yanggu by a patrol searching for him. Both men remained in North Korean captivity for the rest of the war. Of the five ROK officer cadets, only two returned through the lines to South Korea. Under interrogation, however, they revealed that they had been captured and their lives spared after agreeing to spy for the North Koreans. Both were subsequently executed by the ROK Army.

Thus VIRGINIA I ended in disaster. Abysmal planning and preparation, combined with poor intelligence concerning the target, terrain and local weather conditions, were all factors contributing to its abject failure.

ON 5 MAY 1951, the Attrition Section was disbanded and re-formed on the same day as the Miscellaneous Group, 8086th Army Unit (AU

8086). This established it as an official unit formally authorised to employ US personnel and equipment for the purpose of training and supporting partisans which by that time numbered some 7,000.

Another airborne operation, codenamed SPITFIRE, was mounted in June for setting up a permanent partisan base deep inside North Korean territory, linking up with three small groups of anti-communist partisans operating in the mountains south-west of Wonsan. The team selected to carry out the mission was a mixture of American, British and Korean personnel commanded by a British officer, Captain Ellery Anderson, who reportedly had served with the Special Air Service during the war. Since January 1951, he had been commanding the Attrition Section's sabotage training facility at Pusan. Others included another British officer, Lieutenant Leo Adams-Acton, Corporal William Miles, who had taken part in the VIRGINIA I operation, and Sergeant Charles Garrett, a radio operator. The rest of the seventeen-strong group were Koreans.

The plan was for Captain Anderson, Sergeant Garrett, Corporal Miles and two Koreans to be dropped as a pathfinding team, followed approximately a week later by the first main group, codenamed LIGHTNING and comprising Lieutenant Adams-Acton, a radio operator named Fusilier George Mills, and eleven Koreans. A second main group, codenamed STORM and consisting of a further 20 Koreans, would be dropped seven to ten days after that. This would be led by Lieutenant David Hearn who, as a sergeant, had served as a member of a JEDBURGH team in Normandy during the Second World War. A third, codenamed NORTHWIND, would be dropped a week later.

The DZ selected for the initial drop was a bowl in the mountains some five miles south-east of the town of Karyoju-ri. Located in a remote and thinly populated area and easily recognisable from the air, it was five miles long and thus suitable for dropping personnel and stores. Uninhabited, its floor was covered with plantations of small pine trees.

The southern and northern ends of the bowl were marked respectively by Yangam Mountain and Sat'ae Mountain. The eastern rim was formed by a ridge-line linking the two mountains, while on the western side was a plateau. At the southern end, between the plateau and Yangam Mountain, lay a narrow canyon through which a stream flowed westward out of the bowl.

On the night of 18 June, Anderson's advance team was dropped successfully but he himself suffered a severe back injury as he landed. On the following day, the team moved to a base camp on a plateau on the western face of Sat'ae Mountain. From here Corporal Miles and one of the two Koreans, Lieutenant Ho, reconnoitred the area between the plateau and Karyoju-ri which lay six miles to the west. On the evening of 20 June, Miles reported by radio to Anderson that he had discovered a Chinese PLA division moving towards the North Korean front lines 70 miles to the south. The Chinese had established a series of heavily camouflaged way stations at which their troops lay up during the day, to avoid detection by UN reconnaissance aircraft, resuming their advance under cover of darkness. This information was relayed by Anderson to the operation's base and an air strike requested. On the morning of 21 June, aircraft bombed the areas indicated by Miles and killed many PLA troops. A further strike took place at dawn on 23 June, once again causing heavy casualties.

On the morning of the following day, Anderson and one of the Koreans, who had fallen ill, were evacuated by helicopter. Two days later, in the early hours of 26 June, Lieutenant Adams-Acton's LIGHTNING group was inserted. Unfortunately, although the DZ was clearly marked, the drop was inaccurate and the group landed approximately half a mile away on the eastern face of Sat'ae Montain. The terrain was covered in trees and rocks and it was fortunate that there was only one casualty, Adams-Acton himself, who suffered a gashed leg on landing. Unable to walk, he had to be carried to the base camp on the plateau while Miles and Ho cached the group's supplies.

On the night of 5/6 July an aircraft attempted to carry out a resupply drop but was unable to locate the DZ. Instead of waiting until the following night to try again, the pilot returned before dawn and circled the area, despite being ordered by Corporal Miles via radio to leave. To make matters worse, the aircraft then proceeded to drop the supplies on the base camp, thus revealing its position. The SPITFIRE team had no alternative but to abandon the camp immediately and head east into the mountains. At dawn on the 6th its scouts, Corporal Miles and Lieutenant Ho, encountered an enemy ambush and fought a delaying action while the main group, under Adams-Acton, made good its escape and headed for a predetermined RV at a series of caves north of the plateau. In the event, neither Miles nor Ho appeared. Judging by signs found by Adams-

Acton and two of his Koreans who returned to the ambush area at dawn next day, they had either been killed or captured. A search of the plateau and the bowl revealed that the enemy had discovered the team's caches of supplies and the AN/GRC-9 HF radio which provided rear link communications with the operation's base.

By 9 July it had become apparent that misfortune had befallen SPIT-FIRE and that night, in accordance with a prearranged contingency plan, an aircraft with Lieutenant David Hearn aboard was despatched to search for the team. Adams-Acton managed to make contact with it via his remaining PRC-10 radio but then the batteries failed. Realising that there was no alternative but to exfiltrate on foot, he and his men set off to the south, heading for the UN front lines. On the night of 13/14 July, Lieutenant Hearn and a Korean parachuted on to the eastern face of Sat'ae Mountain and found notes for Corporal Miles and Lieutenant Ho left earlier at two emergency RVs by Adams-Acton. Of the SPITFIRE team, however, there was no sign and the two men were extracted by helicopter at dawn on 20 July.

Just before dawn on 23 July, Adams-Acton and his men reached a point from where they could observe Allied artillery fire impacting to the south. Soon after taking shelter in an abandoned bunker complex, they sighted a small squad of NKPA troops approaching their position. Adams-Acton, whose leg injury was by then making it difficult to walk, ordered Sergeant Garrett to lead the rest of the group away while he engaged the enemy. At a range of no more than a few yards, he opened fire with his pistol, downing four of them before running out of ammunition. As he staggered forward in an attempt to bludgeon the remaining three with his empty weapon, Sergeant Garrett and one of the Koreans reappeared and swiftly despatched them. Withdrawing under heavy fire from NKPA positions to the south, the SPITFIRE team made good its escape and by dawn on 25 July was in sight of positions held by American troops of the 35th Infantry Regiment. Next night Adams-Acton and his team crossed successfully over No Man's Land and by the afternoon of the following day were at Headquarters Eighth US Army.

In the aftermath of SPITFIRE, accusing fingers were justifiably pointed at the pilot of the resupply aircraft who had been responsible for compromising the operation. The USAF moved swiftly to remedy the situation and a specialist unit was formed by the Fifth Air Force trained to carry out covert air drops of personnel and supplies. Located at Atsugi air base outside Tokyo, with crews and aircraft deployed to Korea where they were based at K-16 airbase outside Seoul, it was equipped with C-46 Commandos and C-47 Skytrains. In addition, a Fifth Air Force special missions liaison detachment was formed and attached to FEC-LG.

In July, Colonel John McGee handed over command of the Attrition Section, AU 8086 to Lieutenant Colonel Samuel Koster. Responsibility for partisan operations was given to another new arrival, Lieutenant Colonel Jay Vanderpool, who had previously served on secondment with the CIA. That same month saw the formation in Korea of the Far East Command Liaison Detachment, Korea (FEC-LD(K)) as a sub-unit of FEC-LG in a further effort to improve coordination of intelligence-gathering activities and the flow of information between FEC and Head-quarters Eighth US Army.

In August, the Attrition Section mounted another operation, code-named MUSTANG II, whose mission was the rescue from North Korea of Major General William Dean, commander of the 24th US Infantry Division, who had disappeared on 21 July 1950 during his division's with-drawal from Taejon. Nothing had been heard of Dean's whereabouts until the following year when interrogation of a prisoner-of-war (PoW) revealed that the general was still alive and in captivity. In late June 1951 a North Korea police officer, recruited by JACK as an agent, reported that Dean was being held at a PoW camp at Ha-ri, a village two miles east of Kangdong and 39 miles from the west coast. A few weeks later he produced a photograph of Dean and informed his handlers that the commander of the camp was prepared to engineer the general's escape in exchange for US citizenship and $50,000.

It was decided to infiltrate two teams of Mustang Raiders, Baker Section's partisan parachute unit, into the Ha-ri area. One would take up positions around the PoW camp while the other secured and marked two DZs for two more teams which would be dropped just before dawn on the following day. These would then take attack the camp, releasing Dean and other PoWs, and withdraw to an LZ from which the entire force and freed prisoners would be extracted by US Marine Corps H-19 Chikasaw helicopters.

On 17 September, an air reconnaissance of the two DZs and LZ was carried out by a B-26 Invader light bomber. On board were the MUSTANG

II commander, Captain David Hearn, and his second-in-command, Lieutenant William Lewis. On reaching the area, the aircraft was making a low-level pass over Ha-ri when it came under anti-aircraft fire from the ground and from hills on either side. Taking a number of hits, the aircraft was losing power as Lieutenant Lewis and a member of the crew, Lieutenant Frederick Pelser, bailed out. Captain Hearn and the two other crew members, the pilot Captain E. O. Evans and Sergeant Frank Stafas, followed them but were too low when they did so, hitting the ground before their parachutes could deploy. Lieutenants Lewis and Pelser were subsequently captured and remained in captivity for the rest of the war, as did Major General Dean.

Next month saw further operations mounted by LEOPARD. On 8 October, a group of partisans of DONKEY 15 landed on the island of T'an-do, one of a pair lying five miles off the west coast and twelve miles north of Taehwa-do. It was defended by a small force of North Korean paramilitary troops who, despite suffering eleven of their number killed and twelve captured, defended their positions stoutly, killing three partisans and wounding twelve.

This was followed six days later by an attempt to capture the island of Sinmi-do which was lightly garrisoned by 28 North Korean paramilitary troops deployed at two locations at its northern and southern ends respectively. In addition, the NKPA had established an OP manned by a small squad of six men and every two weeks deployed a company of troops to carry out a sweep of the island to check for any signs of infiltration by partisans. The operation, which was to be carried out by a 100-man force of DONKEY 13 and DONKEY 15, was scheduled to take place in the early hours of 14 October, but earlier, at midnight, several hundred Chinese PLA troops arrived by boat on Sinmi-do and took up positions around the partisans' planned landing area. When the latter appeared offshore in a number of junks, the Chinese opened fire, killing eight and wounding 32 before the partisans could withdraw into the darkness.

On 6 November DONKEY 14 was evicted from its base on the island of Ae-do by Chinese troops as part of an operation to clear the partisans from the islands lying north-west of the mainland. A week later, DONKEY 13, too, was compelled by a large force of PLA to abandon T'an-do and neighbouring Tan-do, withdrawing to Sohwa-do and Taehwa-do. Sohwa-do was subsequently abandoned, with DONKEY 13, 14 and 15 all concentrating on Taehwa-do. The adviser to the three partisan units was Lieutenant Leo Adams-Acton, the British officer who had taken part in Operation SPITFIRE and had then been transferred to LEOPARD, arriving on Taehwa-do on 1 October with a radio operator, Sergeant Charles Brock. With a Chinese attack impending, he now arranged for naval gunfire support from a Royal Navy task force, but this was limited to a 'window' of only a few hours each night as the warships were required to withdraw before daylight to the south, within range of UN air cover.

On 20 November, the Chinese began their attack on Taewha-do, carrying out air strikes daily. Ten days later, on the night of 30 November, they opened fire with a battery of artillery which had been moved on to Sohwa-do following its abandonment by the partisans. Thirty minutes later an assault force appeared off the beach on Taehwa-do's northern side. Lieutenant Adams-Acton immediately radioed the American commander of a Korean-manned patrol boat, on loan to LEOPARD from the CIA, which had been stationed off the island each night ready to evacuate him, his signaller and two Royal Navy NGFO personnel, in the event of a landing by the Chinese. Adams-Acton requested that the craft, which was armed with .50 heavy machine-guns and a recoilless rifle, move round the island to engage the Chinese fleet of junks and fishing boats. Its commander, a US Army lieutenant, agreed and shortly afterwards the vessel weighed anchor and sped off into the night to do battle with the Chinese; in fact it disappeared from the area and was not seen again. It later transpired that its commander had avoided all contact with the enemy although he had reported to the contrary and had been decorated for his part in the action. After the war he was court-martialled.

An hour and a half later, Chinese troops had landed and were advancing south towards the partisans' headquarters on the island. At Adams-Acton's request, a Royal Navy destroyer was meanwhile bringing down gunfire support on the northern half of the island, but this failed to stem the advance of the Chinese. By 2.00 a.m. they had surrounded the bunker in which Adams-Acton, his signaller and the two Royal Navy men were sheltering. Aware that the enemy were about to attack his position, Adams-Acton called down gunfire on his location; unfortunately, however, one round scored a direct hit on the bunker, knocking out both its radios. He and his three companions survived unscathed but were taken prisoner. The remaining 28 partisans, including their commander and 33 women and children, escaped to a rocky islet to the south-west of Taehwa-do where they were spotted by a UN reconnaissance aircraft, being rescued next night by a Royal Navy destroyer.

The four Britons were taken to the mainland and an interrogation centre at Changsong. Unfortunately, the names of Adams-Acton and Sergeant Brock were on lists of those known to be involved in UN intelligence and partisan operations. Both underwent interrogation and torture, Brock being sent to a PoW compound known as Camp Two where he was held in a special section reserved for known staunch anti-communists and intelligence/special operations personnel. He survived captivity and was repatriated after the war. Adams-Acton was subjected to five months' solitary confinement before being sent in August 1952 to Camp Two. He succeeded in escaping en route and reached the west coast where he was recaptured while attempting to steal a boat. After a further three months in solitary confinement, he was transferred in November to Camp Two from which, together with an American PoW, he attempted to escape in July 1953. Recaptured within a few minutes, however, he was murdered by Chinese guards who shot him through the head at point-blank range.

Late in the year, the Attrition Section formed another unit, designated WOLFPACK, to take over LEOPARD operations along the coast to the east and south of the Onjin Peninsula. LEOPARD continued to be responsible for the area west of the peninsula and northward to the Yalu River. On 10 December 1951, there was a further rationalisation of the command structure of UN unconventional warfare forces in Korea. The Attrition Section itself was absorbed by the FEC-LD(K), Army Unit 8240 which thereafter came under direct control of the FEC-LG in Tokyo rather than Headquarters Eighth US Army.

IN A FURTHER ATTEMPT to prevent any duplication of, or inadvertent interference between, missions and agencies, another unit was formed on 10 December with the role of coordinating all covert operations and related activities in Korea. Called the Combined Command Reconnaissance Activities Korea (CCRAK), Army Unit 8240 (AU 8240) and based in Seoul, it was headed by a US Army officer, Colonel Washington M. Ives. From December onwards, CCRAK and FEC-LD(K) came under direct control of FEC-LG which in turn was under the operational control of the Assistant Chief of Staff G2 at FECOM.

By this time, the amount of activity behind North Korean lines had increased considerably and those responsible for partisan activities had begun to encounter those of other US forces and agencies, among them JACK.

Nine months earlier, in March, General Douglas MacArthur had been dismissed by President Truman as commander of UN forces and commander-in-chief of US forces in the Far East. This had been the result of growing disagreement between the two men over US policy towards the Chinese and their role in the war. MacArthur had demanded that he be given authority to blockade China's coastline and bomb its bases in Manchuria. Truman had refused, fearing that such a course of action would bring the Soviet Union into the war. MacArthur had responded by going over the President's head and appealing directly to the American people for their support. This move proved unsuccessful and on 11 April 1951 Truman sacked MacArthur, replacing him with General Matthew B. Ridgway who during the Second World War had distinguished himself while commanding the 82nd US Airborne Division in Normandy and, subsequently, the XVIII US Airborne Corps.

Until his demise, MacArthur had persisted in his determination to prevent the CIA from operating in Japan and Korea, and the formation of the Attrition Section had been evidence of such. But following sustained pressure from the Joint Chiefs of Staff, he had been forced to allow the Agency's intelligence-gathering division, the Office of Special Operations (OSO), to establish a small presence, comprising three officers, in Tokyo a month before hostilities broke out in Korea. After the North Korean invasion, OSO personnel had been deployed to the US Embassy in Seoul and to Suwon where they were joined by CIA communications specialists. Following the withdrawal to the Pusan perimeter, they set to work recruiting and training agents for infiltration through North Korean lines while also attempting to contact previously established networks left behind after the evacuation from Seoul.

Some four weeks after the outbreak of war, Hans Tofte, a member of the CIA's unconventional warfare arm, the Office of Policy Coordination (OPC), had been assigned to Tokyo. A former member of the OSS, with which he had served in Italy, France and the Adriatic, his first task was to establish a base for operations in Korea, including facilities for the training of Korean agents. He soon found suitable locations at Chigasaki, on the outskirts of Tokyo, and Atsugi Air Base, located some 45 miles south of the capital.

In addition to his headquarters in Japan, Tofte set up a forward base in Korea. This was done by one of his subordinates, Lieutenant Colonel Vincent 'Dutch' Kramer USMC, who established it on the island of Cheju, in the Tsushima Straits. Shortly after the landing at Inchon, however, the base was moved to the island of Yong-do, off Korea's southern coast, 90 miles south-west of Pusan, and a force of several hundred partisans was subsequently recruited from the thousands of refugees in camps around Pusan. Those selected were transported to Yong-do where they were put through a crash course in guerrilla warfare skills such as weapon training, demolitions and small boat handling. Instruction was provided by US military personnel, including marines and US Navy Underwater Demolitions Team (UDT) personnel on assignment to the OPC.

Partisans were duly despatched into North Korea to carry out reconnaissance and intelligence-gathering tasks. At the same time, the OPC launched Operation BLOSSOM under which small groups were infiltrated into North Korea to establish a resistance network. During 1951, BLOSSOM teams were inserted by air and sea into the central and north-east regions of North Korea. While some of these were captured or killed shortly after arrival, others succeeded in avoiding detection and began to transmit back information, including data on potential targets for air strikes and naval gunfire.

At the beginning of 1951, North Korea had been divided into two operational areas for intelligence purposes: the larger western part was allocated to Eighth US Army while the eastern was given to the OPC, seeing that the latter was already active in there and had formed a partisan group in the far north-east. This arrangement, however, was soon broken when Eighth US Army's Attrition Section began to expand its operations to islands off the east coast with the establishment of Task Force Kirkland. The OPC objected strongly to this and consequently, as described earlier, Kirkland's operations were restricted to an area south of Wonsan, within a 50-mile radius of the port.

Occasionally lines became crossed within the sphere of OSO and OPC operations, and in a move to avert any further duplication, and to reduce the confusion resulting from the number of intelligence organisations active in the Korean theatre, the CIA amalgamated its OSO and OPC operations into one organisation under its cover name of JACK.

The US Navy, meanwhile, had also formed a group for special operations. Designated Task Force 90, it was one of four naval task forces created as the naval element of FECOM for operations in Korea. The others were Task Force 77, a carrier force; Task Force 95, given blockading and escort duties; and Task Force 96, comprising US naval forces in Japan. Immediately after the United States entered the war, an ad hoc force of Underwater Demolitions Team (UDT) combat swimmers and elements of the 1st Marine Division Reconnaissance Company had been flown from Coronado Naval Base in southern California to Japan. On 5 August, it carried out its first mission when two members of UDT made a beach reconnaissance behind North Korean lines, having been deployed offshore from the high-speed transport USS *Diachenko*..

On the following day, twenty members of Underwater Demolitions Team No. 1 (UDT 1) and sixteen more marines arrived at Yokosuka aboard a sister vessel, USS *Horace A. Bass*. Like *Diachenko* and her two other sister vessels of the same class, USS *Begor* and *Wantuck*, *Bass* had been specially constructed for the amphibious raiding role during the Second World War. Carrying four landing craft, it was capable of accommodating a force of 160 troops in addition to a UDT and a marine reconnaissance platoon. All four vessels made up a sub-unit of Task Force 90 called Transport Division 111.

On 6 August, elements of the 1st Marine Reconnaissance Company and UDT 1 were formed into a small force called the Special Operations Group (SOG) which three days later sailed from Japan aboard *Bass* for the east coast of Korea. Between 12 and 15 August, it carried out three missions 200 miles behind North Korean lines, attacking and cutting the railway running along the coast. Further raids were conducted throughout the rest of the month, comprising further attacks on the railway and enemy lines of communication. Late August saw the arrival in Japan of UDT 3, some of whose members were among those forming the SOG. At the end of August, after less than a month in existence, the SOG was disbanded and its personnel sent back to their respective units, the marines returning to their reconnaissance company and the 1st Marine Division to prepare for the landing at Inchon.

Their place in Task Force 90 was taken by a unit of their British counterparts, 41 Independent Commando Royal Marines, which had been formed in Britain from selected volunteers for service in Korea. Commanded by Lieutenant Colonel Douglas Drysdale and numbering approximately 150 in strength, it included swimmer/canoeists and specialists in demolitions and heavy weapons in its ranks. On its arrival in Japan, it was joined by another 150 volunteers who had originally been destined to join 3 Commando Brigade on operations against communist terrorists in Malaya. The commando immediately began a period of intensive training with the four high-speed transports of Transport Division 111 and another vessel which had joined it, the submarine USS *Perch*.

Built during the Second World War, *Perch* had been extensively modified in 1948 for amphibious raiding operations, the removal of two of its four engines and all of its torpedo tubes providing accommodation for a force of up to 110 fully equipped troops. In addition, it had been fitted with a 36-foot-long cylindrical watertight hangar, mounted on its rear casing, which had been designed originally to accommodate an amphibious tracked vehicle. Other modifications included the installation of a snorkel system which enabled the vessel to be propelled by its diesel engines, instead of its electric motors, when submerged.

The first operation by 41 Independent Commando began on the night of 25 September 1950 when *Perch* left Yokosuka and headed for Korea. It was carrying 67 commandos whose target was a stretch of the coastal railway 150 miles behind North Korean lines. Five nights later, it surfaced four miles off the east coast of North Korea. The plan called for seven inflatable assault boats to be towed inshore by a 24-foot wooden motorboat carried in the submarine's hangar. Unfortunately, the boat's engine proved inoperable and the distance to the shore was too far for the commandos to paddle themselves ashore. At that juncture, however, a North Korean vessel was detected by *Perch's* radar and lights were observed in the area of the proposed landing area. There was no choice but for the mission to be aborted and the submarine to withdraw from the area.

On the evening of 1 October, having travelled farther south, *Perch* surfaced again and the raiding force disembarked without any further problems. Its target was once again the railway, on this occasion a tunnel and culvert. Having been towed by the motorboat to within 500 yards of the shore, the commandos paddled the remaining distance and landed on the beach. As they moved to secure the area, however, they encountered enemy troops and a firefight erupted as the demolitions teams headed for their objectives and began placing their charges which subsequently exploded, destroying both targets. Its task completed, the entire force carried out a fighting withdrawal, re-embarking in its inflatables and paddling out to sea where it rendezvoused with *Perch's* motorboat, which towed them back to the submarine. The operation had been successful although not without cost, one member of the raiding force having been killed during the battle.

Subsequent operations by 41 Independent Commando, UDTs and CIA-trained Korean partisans were carried out in conjunction with Transport Division 111's high-speed transports. Commando raiding groups were landed by the LCPs carried by each vessel, while guerrillas were embarked in inflatable boats towed by an LCP to a point from which they could paddle ashore. Prior to a landing, the raiding force waited offshore as UDT swimmers reconnoitred the beach to ensure it was clear before signalling the LCPs or boats to continue their approach.

Landings were high-risk operations and on occasions the amphibious raiding forces of Task Force 90 were surprised by the enemy. On the night of 23 September 1950, members of UDT 3 encountered heavy enemy fire as they made their approach in five inflatable boats towed by an LCP from *Bass*. Twelve swimmers were thrown into the water and in the darkness considerable difficulty was experienced in recovering them all, two of their number eventually being located 4,000 yards offshore. Fortunately, all survived unharmed.

Beach reconnaissance missions in particular were highly perilous but such was the skill of the UDTs that throughout the war only two swimmers were killed during such tasks. On 19 January 1951, four members of UDT 1 were spotted by enemy troops who opened fire. As the swimmers returned to the sea and withdrew, towing their inflatable behind them, one was shot and killed. Efforts to keep hold of his body failed and the other three continued to swim towards the LCP waiting for them offshore. They were still under fire, however, as they were hoisted aboard the landing craft and in the process another swimmer was killed and two more wounded, along with two members of the LCP's crew.

The period from December 1950 to the end of March 1951 had seen a temporary halt to raiding following the transfer of 41 Independent Commando to the Chosin area of North Korea where it fought under American command. After its return to Japan, the commando resumed operations with a further attack on the east coast railway in conjunction with a UDT. In July, its B and C Troops established bases on two islands off Wonsan from which they carried out raids and reconnaissance missions. In December 1951, the commando finished its tour of operations and returned to Britain, its place being taken by a 50-strong CIA unit designated the Special Missions Group (SMG). Formed in July 1951, it consisted of Koreans trained by UDT personnel to conduct reconnaissance and raiding operations which it began in August.

Of all the US elements conducting special operations in Korea, the first to do so, somewhat surprisingly, was the USAF which had established an intelligence organisation throughout the country during the late 1940s and by the end of the conflict was conducting unconventional warfare and intelligence-gathering missions on land and sea as well as in the air. This initially came about as a result of the activities of a senior NCO in the Counter-Intelligence Corps (CIC), Master Sergeant Donald Nicholls, of Sub-Detachment K, 607th CIC Company based at Kimpo Airfield situated to the west of Seoul.

According to Colonel Michael Haas in his book, Nicholls had arrived in 1946 and had then successfully set up a network of agents throughout the Korean peninsula. By 1950, his organisation was proving to be extremely effective, having penetrated the political establishments of both the north and south of the country at all levels. An indication of its success was the defection of a North Korean pilot with his Soviet-manufactured IL-10 ground-attack fighter. Having subsequently dismantled the aircraft, Nicholls was thwarted in his plan to ship it to the United States by the North Korean invasion of the south. He was forced to depart hastily, having been delayed while he destroyed aircraft and vital equipment at Kimpo Airfield, but he soon returned to the fray, his first task being to secure one of the Russian-built T-34 tanks, in service with the NKPA, which was proving remarkably resistant to attacks by US aircraft. Having located one tank abandoned in a front-line sector, he loaded it on to a transporter while under fire and removed it for subsequent inspection. His next assignment was to deal with the problem of North Korean guerrillas threatening the air base at Taegu. Leading a team of 20 ROK troops in an operation conducted at night, Nicholls carried out an attack on the guerrillas which markedly curtailed their activities.

Nicholls's organisation, whose missions by the end of 1950 had included dropping 48 agents into North Korea on thirteen separate intelligence-gathering missions, was operating on a somewhat ad hoc basis. In early 1951, however, it was formally established by Headquarters Far East Air Force as the Special Activities Unit No.1 (SAU 1). A month later, it was redesignated the 6004th Air Intelligence Service Squadron (6004th AISS) and in March was given a very wide-ranging brief of its role which included intelligence gathering, destruction of targets through demolitions, sabotage and/or guerrilla operations, provision of escape and evasion facilities for downed UN aircrew, and coordination with other UN intelligence agencies. The inclusion of guerrilla operations inevitably sparked a protest from Eighth US Army's Attrition Section and JACK, and therefore the Fifth Air Force was forced to remove this from the 6004th AISS's official role, albeit Nicholls tended to disregard this limitation.

The squadron would ultimately comprise three detachments, each with specific responsibilities: Detachment 1 (DET 1) was tasked with acquisition of air technical intelligence and PoW interrogations; Detachment 2 (DET 2) was responsible for collection and dissemination of air intelligence; and Detachment 3 (DET 3) was to plan, coordinate and support escape and evasion for downed UN aircrew.

On 17 April 1951, Nicholls and a five-man team from DET 1 deployed on an operation inside North Korea. Flying in an unarmed helicopter from the island of Cho-do, situated off the west coast 100 miles behind enemy lines, they landed at the site of a crashed MiG-15, a Soviet-built fighter which was at that time the most advanced aircraft in service with the North Koreans and thus a potent threat. Nicholls and his team photographed the wreckage, removing essential parts. Their helicopter, however, had received several hits from enemy fire and suffered damage to one of its rotor blades. Nevertheless, the pilot managed to take off and fly back to Cho-do where he carried out an emergency landing.

Early June saw DET 1 carry out a mission which was apparently beyond its specified responsibilities. A small force of fifteen members of the ROK Air Force was dropped into North Korea to destroy two railway bridges. The mission failed as the entire group was captured by Chinese forces. DET 1's activities thereafter remained within its brief.

On 25 July, DET 2 was formed and Nicholls assumed command. Its vaguely worded responsibilities gave it a great deal of leeway and he was quick to take advantage of this. He was authorised to conduct operations behind enemy lines and to plan and direct special missions in support of Fifth Air Force intelligence operations. Most of these missions would require the insertion of DET 2 personnel to conduct direct surveillance and reconnaissance of targets. Nicholls was well aware that American personnel had little chance of survival within operational areas and thus the composition of DET 2 was predominantly Korean; by the end of 1951, Americans numbered only 38 out of a total strength of 665 men.

Special operations continued throughout Korea into 1952 but on the west coast the North Koreans persisted in their efforts to clear partisan units from the islands, including those situated below the 38th Parallel and off the southern coast of the Ongjin Peninsula. On 1 January 1952, NKPA troops landed in strength on Yongh-do, forcing the withdrawal of DONKEY 1 which evacuated the island under covering fire from war-ships and aircraft of a UN naval task force, losing 32 killed and 40 wounded. The partisans sailed to Ohwa-do but two days later, along with their comrades of DONKEY 11, had to flee to Changlin-do when the North Koreans launched a further attack. On the night of 9/10 January, the latter continued their remorseless advance by attacking the island. Yet again, the partisans were forced to withdraw, DONKEY 1 and 11 making their way to Kirin-do where they consolidated and established a new base.

The North Koreans were also countering CCRAK operations else-where. In January 1952, they mounted a deception operation on the east coast using BIG BOY, the Task Force Kirkland group which, as mentioned earlier, had been captured and turned during September of the previous year. A US Navy pilot, Lieutenant Harry Ettinger, who had been shot down on 13 December and was used as bait, being moved from an interrogation centre to the Kirkland area of operations south of Wonsan. Here he was handed over to a group of pseudo partisans, who told him that his release had been effected by a North Korean senior officer in their pay. On 2 February, BIG BOY informed Kirkland that it had received a shot-down pilot from another partisan group and requested instructions. This was confirmed in a voice radio transmission by the duped Ettinger and an operation was mounted to extract him. In the early hours of 5 February, a helicopter took off from a US naval task force lying off Wonsan, but when hit by ground fire while crossing the coastline had to abort the mission and return to its parent vessel. On the morning of the following day, a second aircraft, carrying Kirkland's Executive Officer, Lieutenant Albert Naylor-Foote, who had served with the OSS in China during the Second World War, flew inland escorted by US Navy fighters. Having successfully located the predetermined LZ where Lieutenant Ettinger was observed standing alone, the aircraft landed, coming under fire as he was pulled aboard. On attempting to take off, however, the helicopter crashed and all three of its occupants were taken prisoner.

BIG BOY remained out of radio contact for the next four days. When it eventually came up on air, it offered the unconvincing explanation that NKPA activity had forced it to leave the area and maintained that it had no knowledge of the three Americans. Suspicions about the group increased and CCRAK sent agents into the Diamond Mountain area to investigate the matter. A few weeks later, these returned and reported that BIG BOY had indeed defected to the communists. This had a major impact on Kirkland as it was naturally assumed that all agents previously despatched to BIG BOY and supposedly still active had been turned. Kirkland was effectively closed down immediately and remained moribund until reformed six months later as Task Force Scannon.

Next month AVIARY fell victim to communist penetration of Baker Section operations. In the early hours of 19 February, a C-46 transport took off from K-16 Air Base and headed north. In addition to its five-man crew, it carried two members of AVIARY, Master Sergeant David Harrison and Corporal George Tatarakis; two USAF officers assigned to CCRAK as flying instructors, Lieutenant John Dick and Captain Lawrence Burger; Pfc Dean Crabb of FEC-LD(K)'s Intelligence Operations Section; and six Korean agents. The aircraft was due to carry out three drops that night, landing the six agents in three pairs in the areas of Wonsan and Hungnam. But as the first pair were being despatched over their DZ, located west of Wonsan, one of them tossed a fragmentation grenade back into the aircraft, killing Pfc Crabb and the other four agents, and wounding a member of the aircrew. Master Sergeant Harrison was the first to bail out, followed by all those who had survived the blast with the exception of Captain Burger who was flying the aircraft and remained at the controls. The C-46 subsequently crashed, approximately two miles away, Burger dying in the impact. Harrison and the others meanwhile landed safely but were captured shortly afterwards.

On the west coast, late April saw the commencement of operations by LEOPARD to retake the islands captured by the North Koreans in December and January. DONKEY 1 and 11 mounted an attack on Changlin-do which they took after heavy fighting. During the following days, they recaptured Ohwa-do, Sunui-do and Yongho-do. DONKEY 15, with Captain Robert Keslinger and Lieutenant James Mapp as advisers, followed suit and towards the end of May occupied the small island of Unmu-do, situated 20 miles east of Taehwa-do. In the first week of June, Mapp and a patrol landed on Taehwa-do in search of a pilot who had been observed bailing out of an F-51 Mustang. The island was found to be deserted, having been abandoned by the Chinese almost immediately after capturing it. Shortly afterwards, it was occupied by DONKEY 15 which set up outposts on two other islands, Uri-do and Chamchae-do, six miles to the east. In early July, however, the Chinese launched a series of counterattacks which forced DONKEY 15 to abandon its three islands and withdraw to Nap-som which lay ten miles to the south, and subsequently to Cho-do.

The rest of 1952 saw a series of raids on the Korean mainland by subunits of LEOPARD. In late September, DONKEY 1 mounted a raid on Chiggal, a small fishing village a few miles north of the 38th Parallel. Led by their adviser, Master Sergeant Roy Meeks, who had previously served with the 1st Ranger Company (Airborne), the partisans engaged and routed a large enemy force. At the end of October, over 200 members of the unit were in action again when they conducted a large raid on the town of Pongyong, west of Ongjin. The landing took place just after midnight on the 29th and at approximately 6.00 a.m. the raiding force encountered a company of NKPA troops who were put to flight after fierce fighting. Heavy mist prevented naval gunfire and air support from being brought to bear and once it became clear that further NKPA and Chinese troops were approaching the area, the partisans began a fighting withdrawal to the landing beach. By this time the mist had lifted and air strikes and naval gunfire were able to engage the enemy, covering the withdrawal of DONKEY 1 which suffered ten killed, seventeen wounded and twenty-two missing, the last returning to their unit during the next two weeks. Enemy casualties were estimated as being considerable, mostly as a result of air strikes and naval gunfire.

In May 1952 WOLFPACK became operational. Formed initially from DONKEY 5 and 8, it was then expanded to eight sub-units designated WOLFPACK 1 to 8, the largest being WOLFPACK 2 which numbered 1,250 partisans and one American adviser. On 1 June, WOLFPACK 5 carried out a successful reconnaissance mission on the Ongjin Peninsula, locating several hitherto undetected concentrations of Chinese troops which were engaged on the following day with air strikes. A second operation conducted on 15 June produced similar results.

Towards the end of September, WOLFPACK mounted a reconnaissance-in-force operation. A large force of 475 partisans of WOLFPACK 1 and 2 landed on the mainland at a point opposite the latter's base on Kyodong-do. The size of the force proved a disadvantage, however, hampering rapid deployment and resulting in withdrawal on 30 September, by which time the partisans had incurred heavy casualties, including an American adviser killed.

Adverse weather conditions had plagued WOLFPACK activities during the summer and a number of its vessels had been damaged or sunk during two typhoons which had struck at the middle and end of July. A third at the beginning of September sank another ten junks and three freighters. With the onset of winter at the beginning of October, LEOPARD and WOLFPACK ceased all further operations on the mainland for the remainder of the year.

Further airborne operations were carried out by Baker Section, again using teams from its Mustang Raiders. According to Ed Evanhoe in his book *Dark Moon*, the first took place on the night of 21/22 January when a 19-man team, codenamed MUSTANG III, was dropped into North Korea with the mission of blowing up a bridge situated between the towns of Yuhyon and Yyomt'am-ri and spanning the river feeding the Aadak reservoir. The mission was a failure as the team was killed or captured immediately after landing. MUSTANG IV, a 16-man team, was dropped into the north-west of North Korea on the night of 17/18 March with the primary mission of cutting a main supply route and railway between Chongju on the Yellow Sea and Ch'ongsongjin on the Yalu River. Its secondary task was to collect information on prisoners being held in Camp Two, the PoW compound situated south-west of Ch'ongsongjin. MUSTANG IV attacked the railway line in several locations but was either killed or captured six days after being inserted. On the night of 13/14 May the ten-man strong MUSTANG V was dropped near Kanggye, a town in the far north of central North Korea situated on the main railway line and main supply route between Man'ojin on the Yalu and Anju on the Yellow Sea. MUSTANG VI, another ten-man team, was inserted on the following night. Both teams disappeared without trace and were presumed killed or captured.

Two more teams, MUSTANG VII and VIII, five- and six-strong respectively, were dropped into North Korea on the night of 30/31 October. The former, inserted in the same area as MUSTANG V and VI, subsequently made radio contact and reported having destroyed a train but then all contact was lost with it. MUSTANG VIII, dropped near the town of Kuni-ri, on the Ch'ongch'on River 25 miles north of Anju, also made contact and, like MUSTANG VII, reported the destruction of a train. There were no further transmissions from the team and it, too, was presumed to have been killed or captured.

Early February saw four operations, BOXER I, II, III and IV, conducted on the east coast by a JACK unit, the Special Operations Group, whose teams comprised Koreans led by Americans. BOXER I and II were dropped on the night of 6/7 February, BOXER I near Yongdae-ri, a town on the coast some 30 miles north-east of Hungnam, and close to a railway line and main supply route. BOXER II's DZ was in an area farther along the same line close to Tong-ni, another coastal town 23 miles north-east of Yongdae-ri. Two nights later, BOXER III landed 20 miles to the north-east near Tanch'on, while BOXER IV was dropped 30 miles farther up the coast near Songjin which lay less than 70 miles from the border with the Soviet Union. Nothing more is known about these four operations although Ed Evanhoe states that he was informed by an unidentified source that they were successful and that all four teams were extracted without having suffered any casualties.

In operation HURRICANE, a five-man team was dropped on the night of 30/31 March to set up a partisan base in the mountains south-east of

Anju. Radio contact was established soon after the drop but two days later the team reported that it had been compromised and requested extraction by helicopter. This was refused due to the high risk of the aircraft being shot down. Contact was maintained with the team until 5 April when it ceased.

Two much larger operations, RABBIT I and II, were also mounted. RABBIT I comprised two 20-man teams dropped on the night of 31 March/1 April north of the railway lines linking P'yongyang to Wonsan and Hungnam. One team was dropped 30 miles west of Hungnam, close to the town of Kwanp'yong-ni, and the other near the railway line linking P'yongyang and Wonsan, outside the town of Sgo-ri, some 53 miles north-east of P'yongyang. RABBIT II was inserted on the night of 7/8 April near the town of Kangdong. No contact was established with any of the three teams and it was presumed they had been lost.

All in all, the record of airborne operations by Baker Section was disastrous. During the period from September 1950 to April 1953, 393 partisans and agents were dropped into North Korea in 22 separate operations. Of those, 389 were inserted in 19 operations by Baker Section from mid-March 1951 onward, all of which were failures. Considerable resources in terms of aircraft, equipment and money were devoted to the section which proved to be an expensive failure. Most important of all, however, was the high cost in terms of manpower and human lives, as few of those dropped behind enemy Korean lines survived capture. The majority of those who did, and returned to recount their experiences, told of how they were pursued from almost the minute they landed.

Whereas Baker Section proved such a dismal failure with its airborne operations, the same cannot be said of DET 2 of the USAF's 6004th AISS which met with considerable success in inserting parachute teams behind North Korean lines. By July 1952, it had 23 teams sending back a constant stream of intelligence; by the end of the year that figure had increased to 32 teams. In addition to dropping its agents by parachute, DET 2 also used the alternative method of infiltration by sea. For this it possessed a fleet of vessels of various types and sizes which, numbering 30 by the end of 1952, were also used for extracting personnel returning from a mission once they had left their target areas for the coast. In the main, these were locally manufactured craft, of the type used by local fisherman, specially modified for DET 2's purposes.

In the early stages of the war USAF special operations, involving air-borne intelligence-gathering missions and dropping of personnel and supplies into North Korea, were flown by Unit 4, an ad hoc detachment formed shortly after the beginning of the war and initially based at Kimpo Airfield. As described by Colonel Michael Haas in his book, during the weeks following the Chinese invasion of South Korea in early December 1950, Unit 4 moved on to Taegu South Airfield where on 20 February 1951 it was redesignated the Special Air Missions (SAM) Detachment. Commanded by Captain Harry 'Heinie' Aderholt, it was equipped with three C-47 transports together with a C-47 and a B-17 Flying Fortress converted for use as VIP transports. The detachment also carried out psychological warfare operations and was thus also equipped with two C-47s fitted with loudspeaker systems. In April 1952, it was replaced by B Flight, 6167th Operations Squadron. Based at Seoul City Airfield, this unit was equipped with unmarked black-painted C-47 and C-46 transports, and B-26 Invader light bombers converted to carry parachutists.

In 1951 the USAF created its first special operations formation, the 581st Air Resupply and Communications Wing (ARCW) based at Clark Air Base in the Philippines. This consisted of three units: the 581st Air Resupply Squadron, equipped with B-29 Superfortress heavy bombers for leaflet dropping, C-119 Flying Boxcars, C-118 Liftmasters, C-54 Skymasters, SA-16 Albatrosses and Sikorsky H-19 Chikasaw helicopters; the 581st Holding and Briefing Squadron, whose role was to train, brief and supply personnel of other services and agencies for operations behind enemy lines; and the 581st Reproduction Squadron, which was responsible for the production and printing in large quantities of leaflets for psychological warfare operations. A small number of personnel from the wing were attached to CCRAK, B Flight and the 6004th AISS's DET 2. Also attached to B Flight were two of the wing's four black-painted SA-16 Albatross amphibians which, along with the four H-19 Chikasaws based at Seoul City Airfield, were used for covert insertions and extractions of agents at night, flying in at almost wavetop height to avoid detection by enemy radar. In addition, the helicopters had a secondary role of combat rescue of downed aircrew.

Late in 1953, the 581st ARCW's C-119 transports were deployed to Indochina to support French forces in their ongoing battles against the Viet Minh in the northern Vietnam region of Tonkin. Such was the demand for airlift support that the United States mounted a top-secret operation, codenamed SWIVEL CHAIR, in which additional C-119s were flown from Japan to the Philippines where they were attached to another unit also based at Clark Air Base, the 24th Depot Air Wing. There they were repainted with French markings before beginning their supply missions in Indochina. On completion of their tasks, the aircraft flew back to the Philippines to have their USAF markings replaced before returning to Japan. At the same time, the 581st ARCW was conducting a C-119 aircrew training programme for civilian pilots employed by Civil Air Transport (CAT), a company owned by the CIA. The programme was highly intense, lasting a mere three days, at the end of which the CAT personnel were despatched to Indochina to carry out their missions which ended in May 1954 following the fall of Dien Bien Phu. Later that year, the 581st ARCW was transferred to Okinawa where it was disbanded in 1955.

By the beginning of 1952, JACK's BLOSSOM teams had suffered a high rate of attrition to the point where it was considered that the remainder had been captured or turned by the communists. In April, however, it launched a new programme comprising three separate operations. The first was a continuation of the BLOSSOM mission: the establishment of cells throughout central and north-eastern North Korea as the nucleus for a resistance movement. The second entailed the infiltration of teams for intelligence-gathering and the pre-positioning of supplies in hidden caches for subsequent use in escape and evasion operations, these teams being extracted by sea after completing their missions. The third was the conduct of amphibious operations for raiding, sabotage and intelligence- gathering along the east coast.

By the summer of 1952, however, it had become apparent that the first two operations of the new programme had been extensively penetrated by the North Koreans who had either turned a number of the teams after infiltration or, having had prior knowledge of the programme, had planted its own agents among Koreans recruited by JACK. During the latter part of 1952, with increasingly high losses among teams inserted by air, it was evident that the communists exercised complete control over the whole of their area of deployment. By the end of the year the CIA had concluded that its operations in North Korea had been thoroughly penetrated and would have to be terminated.

On 11 November 1952, the guerrilla operations element of FEC-LD(K), AU 8240 was redesignated the United Nations Partisan Forces Korea (UNPFK), AU 8240. At the same time LEOPARD, WOLFPACK and SCANNON were redesignated the 1st, 2nd and 3rd Partisan Infantry Regiments (PIR) respectively. Baker Section's Mustang Raiders parachute unit meanwhile became the 1st Partisan Airborne Infantry Regiment (PAIR).

At the end of December 1st PAIR carried out three operations code-named JESSE JAMES I, II and III, all totally unsuccessful. Three ten-man teams were dropped in the mountains south-east of Sariwon, close to the railway line and main supply route linking P'yongyang and Kaesong. JESSE JAMES II and III were inserted on the night of 27/28 December, I being dropped two nights later after a delay caused by a mechanical fault with its aircraft. None of the three teams made contact with their base, leading to conclusions that all had been killed or captured.

A much larger operation, GREEN DRAGON, was mounted when a force of 97 partisans of 1st PAIR, together with 1,500 lbs of weapons and ammunition, was dropped on the night of the 24/25 January from three C-119s preceded by a B-26 pathfinder aircraft which marked the DZ. GREEN DRAGON's mission was to set up a partisan base deep inside North Korea to form the nucleus for a popular uprising against the communists. Almost two months went by before contact was made, the force reporting that its strength had been severely reduced by enemy action and desertions from its ranks. This aroused suspicion that the communists had captured the unit and were attempting a deception operation. Contact, however, was maintained and towards the end of April GREEN DRAGON reported that it was sheltering five members of the crew of a downed B-29 bomber and requested that they be extracted by helicopter. The decision was taken, however, to drop another 57 partisans instead and thereafter recover the airmen by using a low-flying aircraft to snatch them from the ground. The drop took place on the night of 18/19 May.

On 24 May, a C-47 Skytrain of B Flight flew to the area and in its first pass dropped the special equipment that would enable it to retrieve the aircrew from the ground. Each man would wear a T7-type parachute harness connected to a nylon line, secured in a coil by elastic bands, which in turn was connected to a cable strung between two vertical poles. Flying at almost stalling speed and very low on each subsequent pass, the aircraft was to snag the cable with a trailing hook and pull the man up into the air, the elasticity of the coiled nylon line absorbing the shock of sudden acceleration. While airborne, he would be lifted to the aircraft's cargo door by an electric winch before being hoisted into the aircraft.

The pilot of the B Flight aircraft was in radio contact with the B-29 pilot, Lieutenant Gilbert Ashley, who advised him that all was ready for the retrieval of the first man to proceed. As the C-47 approached, however, it encountered heavy fire from the pick-up location and received several hits. The mission was immediately aborted and the aircraft flew back to base. Three days later, however, it returned to the area and established radio contact again with Ashley who continued to insist that all was well.

The mission was promptly aborted and no further attempts were made to rescue Ashley and his crew who had obviously been acting under duress. It was apparent to the operation's controllers that the partisans had been captured and GREEN DRAGON was considered to have taken over by the communists. Radio contact was nevertheless maintained for the following six months during which it was emphasised to those manning the partisans' radio that the aircrew were to be returned at the end of hostilities. After the war, however, none of the GREEN DRAGON partisans reappeared and Lieutenant Ashley and his crew were never repatriated from North Korea.

March 1953, meanwhile, had seen preparations for the withdrawal of LEOPARD units of the 1st PIR from the islands on the west coast north of the 38th Parallel in the light of an impending armistice and ceasefire. At the same time, to the south, WOLFPACK units of the 2nd PIR were maintaining a high tempo of operations from their island bases to the south of the parallel. Likewise, those of the 3rd PIR still remained active on the east coast. That same month saw the arrival in Korea of a 64-strong contingent of the US Army's newly formed 10th Special Forces Group (Airborne), its members being assigned as advisers to the three partisan infantry regiments and the 1st PAIR.

In April 1953 there was further reorganisation among the partisan units of CCRAK which on 27 September 1952 had been redesignated Army Unit 8242. The 1st PIR was divided into two new regiments, the 1st and 6th PIR being based on the islands of Paengnyong-do and Sok-do respectively, while the 2nd PIR was similarly split in two, becoming the 2nd and 5th PIR based on Kanghwa-do and Yonp'yong-do. Each regiment's numbered LEOPARD and WOLFPACK sub-units became battalions of their respective regiments.

Despite the approaching ceasefire, many members of the two west coast partisan regiments were determined to continue the fight against communism and the decision was taken by CCRAK to support them. The partisans were divided into three groups: those of the 1st PIR, codenamed MOOSE, were assembled on the island of Wollae-do; while those of the 2nd PIR, organised into two groups codenamed BEEHIVE and CAMEL, were located on Kyodong-do.

On the night of 12 May 1953, MOOSE was landed on the mainland in the area of Changyon and reached some mountains to the north from where it made radio contact with CCRAK on 28 May. By that time, however, its strength had been reduced by desertions to 28 men. It made contact for the last time on 3 November, reporting that it comprised only five men and that it was going to abandon its mision and exfiltrate overland. There was no further report from MOOSE and the operation was terminated officially at the end of February of the following year.

Prior to launching BEEHIVE, the 2nd PIR conducted a large reconnaissance-in-force and a series of raids in the area where BEEHIVE would subsequently be landed. Eight days later, on the night of 25/26 May, BEEHIVE went ashore on the Ongjin Peninsula and infiltrated inland to the mountains in the area of Haeju and Ongjin without encountering any opposition. The relatively peaceful aftermath of the raids had apparently resulted in the communist forces in the area lowering their guard. CAMEL landed on the coast at a location north-west of Kyodong-do on the night of 27/28 July, following the ceasefire and conclusion of an armistice, and also advanced inland unopposed, reaching the mountains in the area of Haeju and Kaesong. It did not remain undetected for long, however, and reported to CCRAK that its numbers had been reduced by enemy action and desertions. In January, the decision was taken to withdraw both groups who were instructed to combine forces. On the night of 20/21 February 1954, 32 BEEHIVE and CAMEL survivors were extracted by two CCRAK vessels from a beach at Haenam-ni.

The ceasefire in late July 1953 was followed by the demobilisation of CCRAK's guerrilla forces. Those partisans who elected to do so joined the

ROK Army or were absorbed into the United Nations Partisan Infantry Korea (UNPIK), Army Unit 8240 which had been formed from the 1st and 2nd PIR on 23 September 1953. On 30 April 1954, however, UNPIK was disbanded and its assets dispersed.

While it is accepted that in general they had no major impact on its outcome, special operations played a valuable role during the three years of the Korean War. During the first six months, TLO and SALAMANDER teams provided useful intelligence while warning of Chinese intervention in early December 1950 came from KLO agents six weeks beforehand. Similarly, from early 1951 onward, the USAF's SAU 1 and subsequently the 6004th AISS'S DET 2 enjoyed singular success in inserting and maintaining teams of agents inside Korea, these numbering 32 by the end of 1952.

Moreover, successful seaborne raiding operations caused major problems for the communists in their rear areas, obliging them to divert large numbers of troops which would otherwise have been deployed against UN forces. A good example is DONKEY 1's Operation SHINING MOON on the west coast during the period from March to July 1951; despite the failure of radio communications and absence of contact with their base, the partisans caused considerable disruption and damage, and by the time they withdrew the enemy had been obliged to increase its forces in the area by 28,000 troops. Moreover, on the east coast, missions carried out by the Special Operations Group, 41 Independent Commando RM and Task Force Kirkland caused great disruption to enemy lines of communication and supply, as did raids by LEOPARD and WOLFPACK partisans during the latter part of 1952.

CHAPTER SIX

ALGERIA 1954–1962

No sooner had the war in Indochina ended in 1954 than France found itself faced with another colonial conflict, this time in Algeria.

Situated on the Mediterranean coast of the north-west African area known as the Maghreb, Algeria is the second largest country on the continent, stretching some 1,250 miles from north to south and 1,120 from east to west. It is bordered on the east by Tunisia and Libya, and on the north-west by Morocco. To the south-east lies Niger with Mali, Mauritania and Western Sahara to the south-west. Almost 85 per cent of the country is taken up by the Sahara desert, the remaining northern inhabited region comprising plains and mountains of the Atlas range which includes, from north to south, intermittent coastal massifs and plains which divide and extend southward: the forest-clad Atlas Tellien, part of the range, extending east and west into Tunisia and Morocco; the semi-arid grasslands of the Hauts Plateaux; and the Atlas Saharien which divides the Maghreb from the Sahara. Approximately four-fifths of the population is Arab, with Berbers making up the principal ethnic minority and comprising Kabyles, Chaouïas, M'zabites and Tuareg, the last being a nomadic tribe inhabiting the oases in the south-west of the country and in the mountains of the south-east.

Algeria fell under France's domination after an invasion in July 1830 although resistance continued under two leaders, Ahmad Bey in Constantine (now Qacentina) in the east of the country and Abdel Kader in the west. In 1837, Ahmad Bey was driven out of his stronghold but it was not until 1844 that Abdel Kader was defeated and allowed to go into exile. Although his departure marked the end of national resistance, smaller uprisings continued in some of the Saharan oases and eastern Kabylia until the late 1850s, followed by a major revolt in Kabylia as a whole which was suppressed in 1871.

Declared a French territory in 1848, Algeria remained under French military administration until 1870 with the majority of Algerians, excluding French settlers, being subject to the rule of military officers of the Bureaux des Arabes, established by Marshal Bugeaud. All of these

211

possessed an extensive knowledge of local affairs and customs as well
as being fluent in the languages of those they administered. By 1870,
the number of settlers or pieds noirs, as they were known, had reached
over 200,000 and their increasing opposition to military government
resulted in France permitting a degree of autonomy. Overall authority
was invested in a governor-general who reported to the Ministry of Interior in Paris. Under him were three prefects who were responsible for
Algiers, Oran and Constantine, each being 'départements' of France
and thus entitled to be represented by senators and deputies in the
French parliament.

Initially only the European or *pied noir* element of the population
was entitled to vote but subsequently a double electoral college system
was introduced, one college comprising Europeans plus a limited number
of selected Muslims and the other the entire Muslim population, each
electing eight senators and fifteen deputies to the National Assembly
in Paris. The inequality of enfranchisement in this system was such that
one million *pieds noirs* had equal voting rights to eight million Muslims.
Moreover, there was no legislative assembly in Algeria, only the Délé-
gations Financières which, composed of Europeans and Muslims, was
only responsible for financial budgets.

While the area of the Sahara remained under military administration,
local government throughout the rest of the country was effected through
two types of community. For the *pieds noirs* it was the *communes de
plein exercice* which were established in those areas where Europeans
were in the majority. Based on the system of local government in France,
these were run by municipal councils, headed by mayors, in which three-
quarters of the seats were reserved for Europeans. The *communes mixtes*
controlled the Muslim areas, each headed by a European administrator who governed through a number of officials known as caids.
Appointed by the governor-general, the latter were either trusted elders,
many of whom had fought for France and were highly decorated, or
had achieved their position through family influence or paying large
bribes.

In the aftermath of the First World War, in which 173,000 Algerians
fought for France, suffering 25,000 killed, attempts were made at political reform in Algeria but this met with strong opposition from the *pieds
noirs* who were fearful of any change. In 1930, the rumblings of

Equipment put on display by the MGB after it captured a group of SIS agents. Items shown include a Sten Mk. V silenced 9mm submachine-gun, Browning Hi-Power 9mm pistols, two HF radio transmitter/receivers, medical equipment and currency. (Tom Bower)

The S208, a converted wartime E-Boat used by the SIS for clandestine deliveries of agents along the coastlines of the Baltic states. (Tom Bower)

Former SIS officer and traitor Kim Philby, *left*, with former KGB General Janis Lukasevics in Moscow, November 1987. Philby was blamed for the betrayal of SIS and CIA operations in the Ukraine, Poland and the Baltic. (Tom Bower)

OPPOSITE PAGE
Four of the first group of 'pixies' to be landed on the Albanian coast on 3 October 1949 by Britain's Secret Intelligence Service during Operation VALUABLE. *Second-from-left to right:* Hysen Lepenica; Zogoll Sheno; and Sami Lepenica. Ambushed by Albanian troops within hours of the landing, these three were killed while the fourth member of the group, on the extreme left, succeeded in escaping. (Colonel David Smiley)

The schooner *Stormie Seas*. Crewed by two former Royal Navy officers, it was used to land teams of British-trained guerrillas in Albania during Operation VALUABLE. (Colonel David Smiley)

A group of partisans of the CARDAMONE maquis in Tonkin, photographed in 1953. They are shown here armed with a 50mm light mortar, Sten 9mm submachine-guns and a variety of rifles including the Garand M1 .30-06. (Private collection)

A T'ai partisan radio operator establishing contact with his base, power for his radio being provided by a hand-operated generator strapped to a tree. ANGR-9 or SCR-694 HF radios were among those sets employed for long-range communications. (Private collection)

Members of the CARDAMONE maquis in Tonkin after an airdrop of arms and
equipment. The weapons shown here include Bren .303 light machine-guns,
Sten 9mm submachine-guns and Lee Enfield No.1 SMLE .303 rifles.
(Private collection)

A GCMA commando trained and equipped to reinforce maquis groups. All
members of these units underwent instruction and qualified as parachutists at
the GCMA training centre at Cap St. Jacques in southern Vietnam. They are
seen here armed with the US M3 'Grease Gun' .45 submachine-gun.
(Private collection)

Four members of the GCMA team responsible for the SANGSUE maquis on the Laos-Tonkin frontier during 1953-54. *Left to right*: Sergent Chef Loiseau, Lieutenant Geronimi, Sergent Chef Morcrette and Sergent Martin. (Private collection)

Parachutists of a GCMA Hmong commando unit en route to reinforce a maquis in Laos. They are shown here equipped with the US T7 parachute and Sten 9mm submachine-guns. (Private collection)

A GCMA partisan of the centaine based on the Observatory islet in Tourane in central Vietnam, shown here armed with a French MAS 49 rifle fitted with a telescopic sight. (Private collection)

A GCMA team and montagnard tribesmen crossing a river during an operation. On the right is the commander of the GCMA in the Plateaux Montagnards, Capitaine Pierre Hentic. (Private collection)

The GCMA centaine base on the island of Cu Lao Re, off the coast of central Vietnam, from which maritime raiding operations and surveillance of coastal traffic were carried out. (Private collection)

OPPOSITE PAGE
Members of a GCMA centaine provide cover for the remainder of their group carrying out sabotage of a bridge inside Viet Minh-held territory. (Private collection)

The GCMA training centre at Cap St. Jacques (later Vung Tau) on the coast of southern Vietnam. (Private collection)

Members of the 1st New Zealand SAS Squadron on patrol in Malaya during the Emergency. (Defence Picture Library)

The *USS Perch*. With her two forward engines and all torpedo tubes removed, and fitted with a watertight hangar for a tracked amphibious vehicle on her rear casing, she was specially adapted for raiding operations and could carry 110 fully equipped troops. (M.E. Kebodeaux & Mike Haas)

The *USS Horace A. Bass* (APD-124), a high-speed transport specially designed and equipped with four landing craft to carry and deploy an amphibious raiding force of up to 160 troops. (US Navy)

Royal Marines of 41 (Independent) Commando disembarking from the *USS Horace A. Bass* (APD-124) into the vessel's landing craft prior to a raiding operation. (US National Archives)

The scene of a railway line on the east coast of North Korea after it had been blown up by UN raiding forces attacking enemy lines of communication. (US National Archives)

Members of a US Navy underwater demolition team (UDT) bring their inflatable boat ashore. UDTs carried out reconnaissance and sabotage tasks during coastal raiding operations in North Korea. (US Navy)

US advisers with a unit of UN partisans on an island off the west coast of North Korea. (Charlie Norton & Mike Haas)

Members of 41 (Independent) Commando RM prior to embarking on a raiding operation in North Korea. They are armed with American weapons comprising *from left to right*: .30-06 Browning Automatic Rifle (BAR); .30 M1 carbine; Colt M1911A1 .45 pistol; 3.5 inch rocket launcher; and M3 'Grease Gun' .45 submachine-gun. (US National Archives)

A 22 SAS patrol is debriefed following an operation during the Borneo confrontation. (Defence Picture Library)

A patrol of No.1 (Guards) Independent Coy PARA after returning from an operation during the Borneo Confrontation in 1964. *Left to right*: Capt Algy Cluff, Gdsm Rowley, a 7 Fd Amb medic, Gdsm Gee, Gdsm Handley and the company commander, Major John Head. (Lord Patrick Beresford)

An aerial view of a jungle LZ in Borneo cleared by a patrol of No. 1 (Guards) Independent Company PARA in 1964. (Major Charles Fuglesang)

Members of the Gurkha Independent Parachute Company on patrol in the Third Division of Sarawak in 1965 during operations in Borneo. *Front to rear*: Rfm Kajiman Gurung, Rfm Omprasad Pun, Lt Mike Callaghan and Sig Rudranarayan Limbu. (Major L.M. Phillips)

A 22 SAS patrol unloading stores from a Wessex Mk. V helicopter of No. 845 Naval Air Squadron in Borneo. In the foreground are a number of Ibans. (Defence Picture Library)

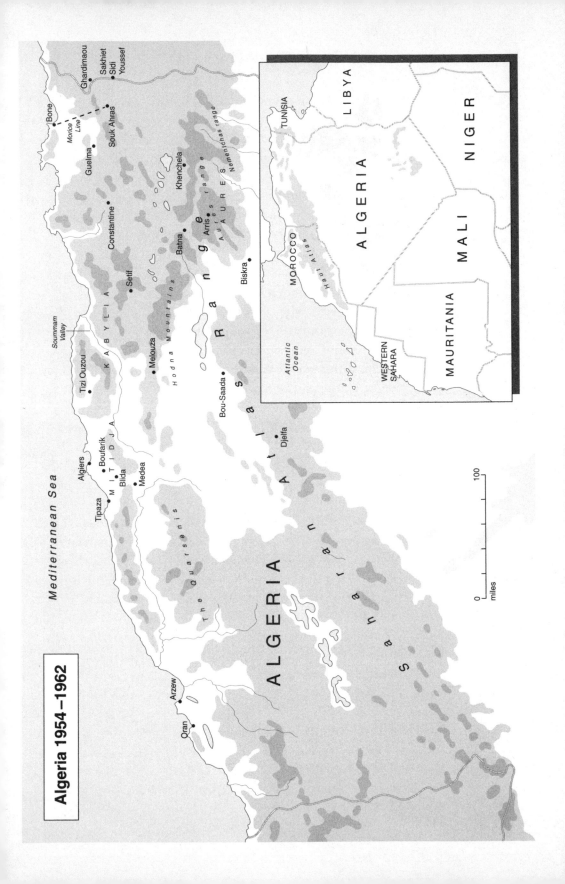

Algeria 1954–1962

Mediterranean Sea

Ghardimaou
Sakhiet
Sidi
Youssef
Bone
Morice
Line
Guelma
Souk Ahras
Constantine
Khenchela
Nememchas range
A U R E S
Aurès range
Arris
Batna
Biskra
R a n g e
Setif
Hodna Mountains
Melouza
K A B Y L I A
Soummam
Valley
Tizi Ouzou
Bou-Saada
Algiers
Boufarik
Tipaza
Blida
Medea
M I T I D J A
The Quarsenis
A t l a s
Djelfa
S a h a r a n
ALGERIA
Arzew
Oran

100

0
miles

LIBYA

TUNISIA

NIGER

ALGERIA

MOROCCO

MALI

Haut Atlas

Atlantic
Ocean

WESTERN
SAHARA

MAURITANIA

discontent among the Muslim population were such that Maurice Violette, a former governor-general, predicted that within twenty years grave difficulties would beset North Africa. Five years later, in the National Assembly in Paris, he tabled the Blum-Violette Bill which proposed a series of reforms but once again strong opposition from the *pieds noirs* doomed it to failure.

The first elements of Muslim nationalism began to surface in the early 1930s with the formation in 1931 of the Associations des Ulemas (ULAMA) led by Sheikh Abdulhamid Ben Badis. A Berber and deeply conservative theologian, Ben Badis believed that the rebirth of Algeria as a nation could only result from a return to the basic principles of Islam. Four years earlier, in 1927, Messali Hadj, an Algerian and member of the French Communist Party (PCF), into which he had been recruited by his French wife, was appointed as president of the Etoile Nord-Africaine, a political association of workers from North Africa. In 1933, the Etoile declared its support for an independence struggle for Algeria, Tunisia and Morocco, universal suffrage and confiscation of all property in the hands of the French and the *pieds noirs*. In 1937, it was renamed the Parti Progressive Algérien (PPA) and thereafter concentrated its attentions on Algeria alone, being banned by the French two years later.

Another, far more moderate, nationalist was Ferhat Abbas. The son of a caid, he had first appeared in the political arena while at university where he had been the president of the Muslim Students Association. Married to a Frenchwoman, he did not believe in Algeria as a separate state but rather as an entity assimilated on a equal footing with metropolitan France. Unlike Ben Badis and Messali Hadj, he and his fellow moderates had welcomed the proposals put forward in 1935 by Maurice Violette in the Blum-Violette Bill which had advocated assimilation. When the bill collapsed, however, they had found themselves vilified as renegades by the PPA and the Ulemas on one hand, and rejected by the French on the other. This resulted in Abbas and his followers gradually discarding assimilation as an ideal, replacing it with some form of autonomy.

The outbreak of war in 1939 was followed a year later by Germany's humiliating defeat of France, this drastically reducing the latter's standing within its colonies where the myth of French invincibility was destroyed forever. Among the colonies, those in Equatorial Africa transferred their allegiance to the Free French while Indochina and Algeria remained loyal to the Vichy regime in southern France of Marshal Philippe Pétain. In November 1942, however, following the Allied landings in North Africa, Pétain secretly ordered the French forces in Algeria, under Admiral François Darlan, to join the Allied side while publicly protesting against the landings.

During 1943, Ferhat Abbas published his *Manifesto of The Algerian People* in which he called for Muslim participation in government and a constitution guaranteeing equality and rights for all Algerians. Shortly afterwards, he was arrested but was later released after pledging his support for France. In March 1944, however, he and Messali Hadj agreed to bury their differences and formed a new movement, the Amis du Manifeste et de la Liberté (AML) which declared its aim as the establishment of an autonomous republic federated with France.

The end of the war, however, brought no prospect of political reforms for Algeria, only the return of French forces and an administration which continued to support the *pieds noirs*. The first signs of impending trouble surfaced in May 1945 in the market town of Sétif, situated eighty miles west of Constantine in the north-east corner of the country. Relations between the largely Muslim community and French settlers had been deteriorating for several weeks and graffiti had appeared on walls, threatening violence and calling on Muslims to rise up against their French oppressors. Moreover, economic conditions in the area were bad, Algeria having suffered from shortages caused by the war and two years of crop failures, added to which the Vichy French authorities had previously handed over the country's emergency stocks of food, normally preserved in case of famine, to their German allies.

The situation came to a head on the morning of 8 May, during celebrations of the Allied victory in Europe. A crowd of Muslims appeared with green-and-white flags, which would subsequently become all too familiar in years to come, and banners bearing slogans calling for an independent Algeria. Among them were a number of activists of the PPA, including Messali Hadj, who was imprisoned along with other senior members of his organisation, the remainder fleeing into exile. His sentence of sixteen years hard labour was subsequently commuted to house arrest.

Sétif's chief of police attempted to seize one of the banners and in the ensuing mêlée was hit by a stone and knocked to the ground. PPA gunmen in the crowd opened fire and the town's small force of twenty gendarmes returned it but was quickly overwhelmed as the demonstrators ran amok. The violence spread swiftly through the town and the surrounding countryside as Muslim pent-up resentment and anger exploded. At Chevreul, French colonists suddenly found their servants turning on them and fled to the local gendarmerie post for protection; at Périgotville, meanwhile, Muslims captured an armoury and turned their weapons on the French. During the next five days 103 colonists were slaughtered and a similar number wounded.

The French authorities responded massively, a number of Army units being rushed to the area. Among them were Senegalese troops who were unleashed on the Muslim population which was also subjected to air attacks and bombardment by a French Navy warship. At the same time, the colonists sought revenge, rounding up Muslims and either hanging or shooting them. The numbers of Muslims killed in the backlash has never been accurately confirmed but has been estimated as between 3,000 and 15,000. A total of 4,500, of which 3,700 were from the department of Constantine, were arrested, and 2,000 of these were later tried and convicted, 151 receiving death sentences, of whom 28 were executed.

In addition to the banned PPA, which operated under cover of a legal organisation called the Mouvement pour le Triomphe des Libertés Démocratiques (MTLD), the nationalists were represented by two other organisations: Messali's and Abbas's AML and Ben Badis's ULAMA. Another revolutionary movement in Algeria was the Parti Communiste Algérien (PCA), some elements of which were also members of the AML.

In December 1947, a small hard core of left-wingers within the PPA/MTLD formed a paramilitary organisation known as the Organisation Secrète (OS), headed by a Kabyle called Hocine Ait Ahmed. Two years later, he was replaced by an Arab named Ahmed Ben Bella. On 28 March 1950 the existence of the OS was discovered by the French authorities who arrested Ben Bella and other members in different parts of the country. It was organised, however, on a cell basis and other elements of it survived intact, some going underground. Among those who did so were Mohamed Boudiaf, Mourad Didouche, Ben M'Hidi, Rabah Bitat, Ben Tobbal, and Abdelhafid Boussouf, all of whom would in due course become prominent figures. Meanwhile, Hocine Ait Ahmed and another, Mohammed Khider, fled to Egypt.

In May 1952, Ben Bella, accompanied by another prominent member of the OS, Ali Mahsas, escaped from prison in Blida. Shortly afterwards Mostefa Ben Boulaid broke out of jail in Bône and fled to Egypt where he joined Hocine Ait Ahmed and Mohammed Khider in Cairo. That same month saw the deportation of PPA/MTLD leader Messali Hadj from Algeria to France following an attack on police by members of his organisation.

In April 1953, the PPA/MTLD suffered a split. During a party conference, a new central committee was elected. While Messali Hadj retained his seat, some of those closest to him were ousted. His strong objections to this led to fighting between rival factions on the streets of Algiers, the authorities looking on with evident satisfaction at this split within the nationalist movement.

Early in the following year, the four nationalist leaders in exile in Cairo and France, Ahmed Ben Bella, Mohamed Khider, Mohamed Boudiaf and Hocine Ait Ahmed, decided that the time had come for more militant action. In collaboration with their five counterparts in Algeria, Mustapha Ben Boulaid, Mourad Didouche, Rabah Bitat, Mohammed Larbi Ben M'Hidi and Belkacem Krim, they formed a new body, the Comité Révolutionnaire d'Unité et d'Action (CRUA). The creation of the CRUA, whose nine leaders were known collectively as the *neuf historiques*, aroused a violent response from the MTLD which was already torn by rivalry between different factions led respectively by Messily Had and Hoken Lahouel. Shortly after the creation of the CRUA, Boudiaf and Rabah Bitat were attacked in Algiers by supporters of Hadj, Boudiaf being left for dead and spending several weeks in hospital. This in turn led to a retaliatory attack on the MTLD headquarters. The CRUA later attempted to heal the rifts with Hadj and Lahouel but neither was interested in reconciliation.

The CRUA meanwhile pressed ahead with its plans for armed insurgency. In early 1954, Mohamed Boudiaf travelled from France, where he had been in exile, to Switzerland where he met Ben Bella, Khider and Ait Ahmed. During this meeting, the decision was taken to launch an armed insurrection in Algeria. Boudiaf was given the task of carrying out the initial stage, namely the creation of a guerrilla force from the various armed gangs and members of the OS in the country. Clandestinely re-entering Algeria in March, he set to work establishing six 'wilayas' or military provinces, each under the command of a leading nationalist: Wilaya I, including the Aurès and Nementchas mountain ranges, was under the command of Mostefa Ben Boulaid; Wilaya II, comprising the northern half of the department of Constantine, was commanded by Mourad Didouche; Wilaya III, consisting of the region of Kabylia, was under Belkacem Krim; and Wilaya IV, comprising Algiers itself, was the responsibility of Rabah Bitat; while Wilaya V, the department of Oran, was placed under Larbi Ben M'Hidi. No commander was nominated for Wilaya VI. In Cairo, meantime, Ben Bella was also hard at work; with the assistance of the Egyptian intelligence service, he was forming a staff to direct military operations in Algeria.

Within each of these wilayas, the CRUA established cells of four to five men who knew only one another. A number of bomb factories were established in the Muslim quarter of Algiers and at Souma, some 30 miles away. These were under the control of a senior member of the CRUA in the Algiers area, Zoubir Bouadjadj, and produced crude but effective explosive devices of black powder and sodium chlorate packed into sections of iron pipe or tin cans. At the same time, weapons were collected and stored in caches throughout the six wilayas. These comprised an assortment of German and Allied weapons, collected during the wartime years, and a large number of sporting guns and rifles, some of them ancient and of dubious quality. Only a small quantity of more modern weapons was obtained from abroad.

In July, a conference of the CRUA and representatives of other revolutionary groups in Algeria was held at Clos Sambier, near Algiers, at which a body called the Committee of the Twenty Two was formed. The conference decided that the coming armed insurgency would not be a limited operation designed to wring concessions out of the French but a full-scale revolution with the aim of winning independence for Algeria. This was followed on 10 October by the establishment of a new revolutionary movement called the Front de la Libération Nationale (FLN). It was on that day that the decision was taken to launch the revolution in the early hours of 1 November, All Saints Day, when the French and colonist elements of Algeria's population would be celebrating the festival and the authorities' guard was likely to be at its lowest.

The French authorities in Algeria, meanwhile, were aware of the existence of the CRUA but had done nothing about it. The Sûreté, the principal government security agency in the country, was receiving a constant stream of intelligence which included details of camps in neighbouring Libya where Algerians were reported as undergoing training. In August its director, Jean Vaujour, attempted to seek advice and assistance from the French government during a visit to Paris but, in the absence on holiday of the Minister of the Interior, François Mitterand, was forced to deal with officials who paid little attention to his warning of impending trouble. His warnings also fell on deaf ears within Algeria where the Governor General, Roger Léonard, declined to take them seriously. During a meeting on 29 October of police, military and Sûreté officials, a report of 100 armed guerrillas observed in the Aurès region was dismissed as nonsense by a senior Army officer. Throughout Algeria, no measures were taken to place the Army or police on alert. Yet such were the signs of impending trouble that the French Defence Minister, Jacques Chevallier, a former mayor of Algiers, decided to travel on 1 November to Algeria to investigate the situation.

AT EXACTLY ONE MINUTE past midnight on 1 November, groups of FLN guerrillas launched approximately 70 attacks throughout Algeria, half of them in the Tell, the area situated between the plateaux stretching from west of Oran to east of Constantine and the coastal plain. Most of the attacks were on government buildings and installations, six members of the security forces being killed and four wounded. In the Aurès region of Wilaya I, a bus was stopped on the highway between the large garrison town of Biskra and Batna by a group of guerrillas under a terrorist named Bachir Chihani. A local caid, Hadj Sadok, was shot and fatally wounded, and a young French couple, both schoolteachers, badly wounded, the husband, Guy Monneret, subsequently bleeding to death on the roadside.

At Biskra, guerrillas attacked the police station 30 minutes before the deadline, resulting in an alert being telephoned to the sub-prefecture office in Batna. This was passed on immediately to the gendarmerie barracks where the alarm was sounded ten minutes before a group of guerrillas, under an individual named Hadj Lakhdar, was about to launch its attack. Disconcerted, Lakhdar gave the signal to abort the assault and his group merely withdrew, gunning down the two guards at the gates of the barracks. At Khenchela, on the road leading eastward through the Nementchas mountains, an attack was mounted at 3.00 a.m. on the garrison in the town, its commander being killed in the battle which followed, during which two guerrillas were wounded. At Ichmoul, meanwhile, a raid mounted on an explosive store at a lead mine failed when a solitary night watchman opened fire with his rifle on the guerrillas, who fled. At T'kout, a gendarmerie post came under attack, its defenders putting up a stout resistance as guerrillas lay siege to it.

In the coastal region of Mitidja within Wilaya IV, meanwhile, unsuccessful attacks were mounted on barracks in Boufarik and Blda. These were carried out by 200 guerrillas from Kabylia in Wilaya III, as the FLN organisation in Mitidja had virtually ceased to exist thanks to the influence of the MTLD faction led by Hocine Lahouel. In Boufarik, Wilaya III deputy commander Omar Ouamrane was forced to launch his attack 35 minutes before the deadline following the premature demolition of nearby bridges by other guerrillas. His force of 100 managed to penetrate the barracks with the help of a Muslim soldier but was driven off after a fierce battle in which the guerrillas captured a small number of weapons. At Blida, meanwhile, an attack by another force of 100 was also driven off, the guerrillas losing three men killed and several wounded.

In Oran, guerrillas of Wilaya V also suffered casualties after an attack on a car which chanced upon them as they were moving into an ambush position The driver survived the attack and succeeded in reaching the gendarmerie post at Cassaigne where he raised the alarm. The security forces in the area reacted swiftly and in the ensuing follow-up operation eight guerrillas were killed. In Kabylia, too, attacks were launched by the Wilaya II of Mourad Didouche on barracks, gendarmerie posts, telephone communications and warehouses.

In Algiers, meanwhile, a series of attacks were launched on a number of targets including the capital's radio station, its telephone exchange, a petroleum storage depot, a gasworks and a large warehouse. All were unsuccessful, largely because the crude bombs used by the guerrillas lacked sufficient explosive power.

The immediate response of the authorities was to launch a massive dragnet. While this undoubtedly succeeded in catching some of those responsible for the All Saints Day attacks, among them Zoubir Bouadjadj and 38 guerrillas in Oran, large numbers of innocent Muslims were rounded up and imprisoned. Their treatment at the hands of the authorities was such that many subsequently joined the FLN.

At this juncture, there were 57,000 French troops in Algeria, the majority forming the country's garrisons with the remainder in transit to Indochina. Of those only 3,500 were available for operations against the guerrillas. Moreover, they were totally untrained and ill-equipped for counter-revolutionary warfare. On the advice of the Army commander-in-chief in Algeria, General Paul Cherrière, the Governor General, Roger Léonard, appealed to the French government for reinforcements, namely the 25ème Division de Parachutiste.

The leading element of the division arrived by air at Bône on 2 November. It comprised the 18ème Régiment de Chasseurs Parachutistes (18e RCP) commanded by Colonel Ducournau and was composed largely of veterans of the Indochina War. Together with the remainder of the division which arrived during the following weeks, it was deployed immediately to the Aurès region where a relief operation had been given priority. Initially, troops were hindered by blocked roads and blown bridges, and the lack of sufficient helicopters hampered moves to supply the colonists' settlements, some of which were cut off for several days.

On 21 November, the French followed the example of the British in Malaya by setting up protected areas known as 'security zones' in which villages were established in the Aurès region with the aim of resettling the local population, thus depriving the guerrillas of its support. Here, however, resettlement was not compulsory and the lack of enthusiasm among the people was reflected in the fact that only 239 families, totalling 2,000 members, out of a total population of 250,000 moved into the security zones. Among these there was an almost total absence of able-bodied men between the ages of 18 and 35; while some were working in France, most of the remainder had either joined the guerrillas or refused to leave their land.

The FLN continued its attacks, mainly in the Aurès where French forces found themselves outmanoeuvred by the swift-moving guerrillas who struck swiftly before slipping away into the harsh terrain of

mountains, djebels and wadis which they knew intimately. The majority of French units, untrained in counter-guerrilla operations and, in
these early days of the campaign, lacking helicopters to give them the
necessary mobility, enjoyed little success in countering the FLN. Tanks
and armoured personnel carriers proved useless in the hilly and rocky
terrain of the Aurès, being confined to the roads on which they were
vulnerable to ambush, their crews being killed and robbed of their
weapons and their vehicles then set alight. Moreover, the icy winds and
frequent heavy rain made conditions difficult for the troops as they
slogged for miles over the seemingly endless hills in search of an elusive
enemy.

The greatest advantage enjoyed by guerrillas was that of intelligence.
The approach of a French column was soon signalled by fires lit on the
hilltops while the presence of patrols was more often than not given
away by the large groups of pi-dogs which inhabited areas throughout
the Aurès. Moreover, the guerrillas ruled the local population by fear:
any assistance given to the French resulted in a slow and violent death.
Thus virtually all the operations conducted during the first month produced few successes for the frustrated French who withdrew their troops
into fortified bases, leaving the surrounding areas to the guerrillas.

Another equally fruitless tactic employed by the French was the *ratis-
sage*, a cordon-and-search operation in which an area was surrounded
and thoroughly searched and the local people interrogated. In each
instance, however, the guerrillas received plenty of warning, enabling
them to disappear into the hills beforehand. Heavy-handed treatment
by frustrated troops inevitably provoked resentment among the local
population who had adopted a policy of neutrality and wait-and-see,
being understandably sceptical of the French who appeared unable to
counter the guerrillas effectively.

At the end of November, however, one French unit succeeded in
turning the tables on the guerrillas. Colonel Ducournau, the commander
of the 18e RCP based at Arris, a town south-east of Batna on the road
through the Aurès to Biskra, had adopted guerrilla tactics, dividing his
unit into detachments and basing them in the hills among loyal Chaouias
tribesmen who acted as guides and trackers. On 29 November, having
patrolled for almost a month without success, one of his detachments
was ambushed by a large group of guerrillas at a location a short

distance north of Arris. Reacting to its contact report, Ducournau himself immediately headed for the scene of the engagement, in a ravine honeycombed with caves, and took command of the operation. During the ensuing battle, the guerrillas were pinned down by heavy fire while other elements of the 18e RCP surrounded them. Twenty-three guerrillas were killed and eighteen captured, the dead including their commander, Belkacem Grine, a leading member of the FLN whose death was a major blow to the organisation. The paratroops' casualties amounted to four killed and seven wounded.

Following this contact, the 18e RCP kept up the pressure on the guerrillas. A week after the action in the ravine, it killed another senior guerrilla and in February captured Mostefa Ben Boulaid, the commander of Wilaya I. This was a major coup for the French and thereafter the situation worsened for the guerrillas whose active strength was by then down to 350. The FLN also suffered reverses elsewhere. The commander of Wilaya II, Mourad Didouche, was also killed and in Algiers the police managed to break up Rabah Bitat's network. Three months later Bitat himself was arrested.

During February 1955, Roger Léonard was replaced as the Governor General of Algeria by Jacques Soustelle. Aged 43 and an anthropologist by profession, he had served under de Gaulle during the Second World War, being appointed Commissioner of Information in 1942 and thereafter head of the Gaullist intelligence service, the BCRA/DGSS, directing Free French intelligence operations in Algiers during 1943–4. Then, as a member of the Constituent Assembly, he had served successively as Minister of Information and Minister of the Colonies.

Soustelle was appointed in January 1955 by Prime Minister Pierre Mendès-France but national elections in France on 5 February saw the latter ousted from power as a result of his proposed economic reform programme. Léonard had by then left Algeria which was thus without a governor general and it was not until three weeks later, when France had a new government under Edgar Faure, that Soustelle's appointment was confirmed.

Soustelle immediately carried out a tour of Algeria as a result of which he produced plans for extensive reforms. These included the decentralisation of the country's administration with the creation of several more departments that gave Algerians greater local autonomy, the recruitment of more Muslims into positions of responsibility, removal of inequities in the electoral systems, initiation of an agrarian reform programme, doubling of the number of schools under construction, making Arabic the official language in Muslim schools, and increased investment in public works.

In addition, Soustelle initiated a major measure designed to improve relations between French administration and the inhabitants of Algeria's rural areas which were known generally as the bled. This was the formation of an organisation called the Section Administrative Specialisée (SAS). It comprised four-man detachments commanded by officers who were Arabists and had served previously as military administrators with the Service des Bureaux Arabes in the French Sahara or with the Service des Affaires Indigènes, a similar organisation which controlled rural areas in Morocco. In addition to an officer, each SAS detachment included an assistant (generally an NCO who doubled as a secretary/treasurer), an interpreter and a radio operator. Each detachment was assigned a detachment of locally recruited Algerian irregulars known as mazghen whose role was protection of the SAS team and provision of intelligence on ALN guerrillas in their respective areas.

The French, however, were hampered by the lack of an effective intelligence-gathering apparatus. The situation was not improved by the heavy-handed approach of French units towards local populations in retaliation for attacks by the Armée de Libération Nationale (ALN) – as the military wing of the FLN was by then known – and in particular by the torture of those suspected of being guerrillas. The result was a lack of co-operation and, consequently, of information. Inevitably, such measures also led to a swelling of the ALN's numbers: by May 1955, it was estimated that the ALN comprised 8,500 full-time guerrillas supported by some 21,000 auxiliaries who provided logistical and intelligence support.

At the outbreak of the insurgency, the principal intelligence- gathering agencies in Algeria were the Service de Liaisons Nord-Africaines (SLNA), a organisation headed by Colonel Paul Schoen, and the Foreign Legion's Bureau de la Statistique de la Légion Etrangère (BSLE) under Colonel Henri Jacquin. The SDECE's presence at that time consisted only of a counter-espionage station tasked with monitoring any external interference, principally from the British and Russians. Internal security was the responsibility of the French security service, the Direction de la Surveillance du Territoire (DST), which liaised closely with its headquarters in Paris. In due course, though, the DST would find itself being overshadowed by the Army as the latter devoted increasing resources to the gathering of intelligence and the conduct of urban counter-revolutionary warfare.

In June 1955, the SDECE expanded its presence in Algeria with the despatch to Algiers of Lieutenant Colonel Germain (a pseudonym) who during the Second World War had served in the BCRA in Algeria as deputy head of the counter-espionage branch. His task was to establish an organisation entirely independent of the SDECE's intelligence-gathering apparatus in North Africa and report directly to the Deputy Director-General of the service in Paris, Louis Lalanne. During the previous month, the French government had tasked the SDECE with neutralising the leaders of the FLN. Six men were targeted for an operation codenamed OUT, responsibility for which was passed to the Action Service of Colonel Henri Fille-Lambie who used the alias of 'Colonel Morlanne'. Two of the men would be dealt with by the service in Paris while Germain's organisation was to handle the other four. To assist him, Germain would have available elements of the 11ème Bataillon Parachutiste de Choc (11e Choc), the politico-military special forces unit which, as described in Chapter 3, had played a central role in the organisation and operations of the GCMA in Indochina.

A detachment of the 11e Choc had been among the reinforcements despatched to Algeria from France, embarking at Marseilles on 9 December and arriving in Algiers next day. It was commanded by Lieutenant Colonel François Decorse who had taken over command of the battalion at the end of 1952. Prior to his departure, he had been briefed on his unit's mission by Colonel Fille-Lambie who had summed it up with the words, 'Sow terror in the FLN's ranks!'

Comprising 300 all ranks, the detachment operated under the cover name of the Groupement de Marche (GM) and was deployed to Kabylia. Throughout the duration of the conflict, its activities would be controlled by the Action Service headquarters in Paris, known throughout the battalion as the 'Box', and be administered by its own base, initially located at Perpignan, in the Languedoc-Roussillon region of southern France, and subsequently at Calvi on the island of Corsica.

On reaching the southern part of Kabylia, the GM was divided into two detachments designated Sub-Groups 1 and 2, although subsequently they were named LE GRAND and BOURDONNAYE after the captains commanding them. Located at Dra El Mizan and Tizi Reniff respectively, each sub-group comprised two 'centaines' which equated to infantry companies in strength and were commanded by veteran lieutenants. These in turn were organised into small operational commando groups which, commanded by young subalterns or second lieutenants, were deployed at locations throughout Algeria, including Bône, Fort-de-l'Eau, Tipaza, Colomb-Béchar and Oran. Each group, containing some 40 men, would conduct strike operations against the FLN, concentrating in particular on hunting down and destroying the headquarters of each wilaya.

An additional 11e Choc unit was formed in December by Captain René Krotoff who, prior to arriving in Algeria, had been commanding the Action Service's training school at Cercottes, in the Loiret in central France. A member of the Free French BCRA during the Second World War, he was among the first to be recruited for the Action Service after its formation in 1946. The two officers who arrived with him from the unit's base at Perpignan were Lieutenant Ade and Second Lieutenant d'Anglade, the latter a graduate of Saint Cyr who had subsequently joined a parachute unit before being posted to the Action Service and the 11e Choc.

Krotoff formed a small 40-man unit called the Groupement Léger d'Intervention (GLI), each man being carefully selected and undergoing a harsh regime of training designed to equip him with skills to operate on his own as well as a member of a team. This included instruction in intelligence-gathering, demolitions and radio communications, as well as combat survival to enable him to survive in the harsh and inhospitable terrain of the mountains. Each was also given a change of identity supported by authentic documents provided by the SDECE.

Within a few weeks the GLI was ready for action and towards the end of February 1956 left Kabylia for the Aurès where it arrived on 2 March and established itself at a base at Menaa, close to its intended area of operations. In order to conceal its identity from the legionnaires of the 13ème Demi-Brigade de la Légion Étrangère (13e DBLE), also based at Menaa, and from others, the GLI assumed the cover of a signals company composed of reservists. Such was its extent that the members of Krotoff's unit received mail generated by the SDECE and addressed to them under their *noms de guerre* from non-existent families and friends.

At this juncture, only Krotoff knew the purpose of the operation. It was in fact aimed at the FLN command element in Wilaya I, in particular Mostefa Ben Boulaid who, having been captured in February 1955 and condemned to death, had escaped from prison in September and had then disappeared. Some reports stated that he had taken refuge in Tunisia, others that he had returned to his lair in the Aurès. The GLI's other targets included Ben Boulaid's three lieutenants: Adjel Adjoul, Abbès Laghrour and Bachir Chihani.

Krotoff had selected an unorthodox method of attack on Wilaya I's headquarters, one that explained the choice of a signals company as a cover for the GLI. He had arranged for a specially adapted SCR 694 transmitter/receiver to be produced by the technical section at the Action Service headquarters in Paris. Modified so that it would only work on main electricity, it contained a two-kilogram charge of plastic explosive which would detonate immediately the set was activated. Krotoff intended that the set should be delivered as part of a resupply parachute drop, its container being dropped last of all after a delay, seemingly due to a last-minute hitch, so that it landed outside the intended drop zone (DZ). On 6 March, two days after the GLI arrived at Menaa, the 11e Choc base at Tipasa reported to Krotoff by radio that the set had arrived.

The operation was scheduled to start on 10 March. Two days before-hand, however, intelligence was received that a large group consisting of some 100 guerrillas was crossing the valley of Oued Bouzina, heading south-east for Tagoust. The entire 13e DBLE was deployed immedi-ately in response but left the 'signals company' in reserve; ignorant of the GLI's true identity, its commander had no confidence in what he perceived to be a unit of communications specialists who were, more-over, only reservists.

It was not until the early evening that the 1st Battalion of the 13e DBLE made contact with the guerrillas but by then it was too late to exploit it. Approaching darkness prevented the use of air support which would be needed to strafe the guerrillas who by this time had taken refuge on areas of high ground behind dry stone walls. An hour later, the headquarters of the 13e DBLE at Menaa received a signal reporting that six German members of the unit had deserted to the guerrillas who earlier had offered to repatriate legionnaires to their home countries if they abandoned the fight and left their units. Exhausted and demoralised after six months of seemingly endless and non-productive operations in the Aurès, and far from the bright lights and distractions of Biskra, the nearest large town, the young legionnaires had quit.

During the night, Legion scouts reported that the guerrillas had moved on after the deserters had joined them. By dawn on the following day, 9 March, the 13e DBLE was in pursuit. At just before midday the GLI, still at the base at Menaa, received a radio signal reporting that the Legion units were in contact with the enemy and ordering Krotoff to deploy his unit by helicopter to create a diversion in the rear of the guerrillas. Lightly equipped, each man carrying only his weapon, ammunition, water-bottle and iron rations comprising a ball of rice and a raw onion, the 40-strong GLI emplaned in two teams aboard two Vertol H-21 Shawnee helicopters, known to French forces as 'La Banane' because of their distinctive banana shape, and took off for the area where a battle was raging between the legionnaires and the guerrillas who were in positions on a plateau, bringing fire to bear on the 13e DBLE units below.

The two helicopters flew to a location behind the area from which the guerrillas were engaging the 13e DBLE. On landing some 300 metres away from its objective, the leading 20-man team under Lieutenant Ade came under heavy fire but succeeded in working its way forward, bringing fire to bear on the guerrilla positions. At the same time, air support arrived in the form of T-6 Texan ground attack aircraft which engaged the guerrilla positions with rockets. Suddenly the resistance slackened and shortly afterwards ceased altogether, some 20 guerrillas surrendering as Ade's team stormed their positions.

Ade and his men were joined shortly afterwards on the plateau by the elements of the 13e DBLE who were somewhat astonished by the swift and brutally efficient assault carried out by the 'signals company'. But soon they came under fire from an automatic weapon on an outcrop on a cliff on the other side of a wadi. A small team of five guerrillas had been left behind as a rearguard, covering the withdrawal of the rest of the band as it headed for the cover of the forests which lay approximately one hour's march away. Under covering fire from an 11e Choc machine-guns and those of the 13 DBLE, one of Ader's men crossed the wadi to the foot of the cliff. An experienced mountaineer, he climbed to the top unseen by the five guerrillas on the outcrop and eliminated them with fragmentation grenades.

As Ade and his team crossed the wadi and reached the foot of the cliff, however, another automatic weapon opened fire along the wadi, pinning them down. At that moment, the GLI's second team appeared in the wadi, led by Captain Krotoff. Seconds later, a guerrilla opened fire with an automatic weapon and Krotoff fell dead, hit in the heart. Beside him fell his radio operator, Corporal Fosset, hit in the top of his spine. After another fierce firefight, the battle petered out as the guerrillas made their escape, taking their wounded with them. Meanwhile, the 13e DBLE withdrew by helicopter, carrying out the bodies of Captain Krotoff and Corporal Fosset. Lieutenant Ade and the GLI followed later, reportedly having summarily executed the 20 prisoners.

Command of the GLI was assumed by an 11e Choc officer, using the pseudonym of 'Captain Puig', who had been involved in the planning of the operation against the headquarters of Wilaya I. On 14 March, after a postponement of five days, Puig relayed orders from Paris to the commander of the sector in which the retaliatory operation was to take place, ordering him to refrain from any action and to place his forces at Puig's disposal for 24 hours from the evening of the next day.

On the morning of 15 March, Puig cancelled his previous orders for the operation, much to the surprise and resentment of his men who were keen to avenge the deaths of Krotoff and Fosset. Instead, at 5.00 p.m., he issued orders for preparations to be made for a parachute resupply drop at 6.00 p.m. The aircraft, a Dakota, duly appeared and the pilot established radio communications with members of the GLI on the DZ, announcing that he would have to make three passes as the zone was too short. On the first pass, the containers landed on the DZ but on the second the wind blew the parachutes into a nearby valley. The situation became even worse on the third pass as the final container failed to be dropped at all, the aircraft carrying out various manoeuvres before it was finally released some eight kilometres from the DZ. A patrol was despatched immediately to the nearby valley where it found that the local population had already retrieved and hidden the two containers of rice which had landed there. After interrogation, an elderly man indicated where they had been hidden.

On the following day, the Dakota returned, searching for the missing container which contained a high-powered radio set, none other than the lethally modified SCR 694 mentioned earlier in this chapter. Throughout the previous evening, guerrilla scouts had observed the seemingly chaotic resupply drop and had noted the landfall of the third container. Now they watched as the Dakota searched for it, joined on the ground by Legion troops from Khenchela. Meanwhile Captain Puig found signs indicating that the guerrillas had, as intended, discovered the container and spirited it away. In order to allay any suspicions on their part, another radio was dropped by parachute two days later, on that occasion without any problems. Thereafter, the 'signals company' continued with its routine operations until the end of March when it left the area and returned to its base at Tipasa.

It would be another three months before it was known whether or not the operation against Wilaya I had succeeded. In fact, it had achieved complete success. On 17 March, the radio set had reached the head-quarters of Ben Boulaid who had heard that the French were search-ing for a radio that had gone missing during a parachute drop. As the Action Service planners had predicted, he had ordered that the set be brought to him. He and three other members of his staff were standing next to the radio when it was connected to an electrical power source and switched on. There was a loud explosion and Ben Boulaid and his three companions had been killed immediately. His death had been fol-lowed by a power struggle for command of Wilaya I between Abbès Laghrour and Adjiel Adjoul, resulting in the defection of the latter to the French. It was not until August that Zirout Youcef was named by the FLN as Ben Boulaid's successor.

IN EARLY 1956, AN element of the GM was detached to take over control of a counter-guerrilla unit, one of a number formed from Alger-ian irregulars called harkis. The first such units had been recruited by officers of the SAS in the early part of the war, their role being that of militias, commanded by SAS officers, to protect villages against guer-rilla attacks and to provide intelligence. From 1957 onward, they were developed into companies of semi-guerrilla troops, always based in their home areas on the grounds that if deployed elsewhere their families would be under threat from nationalist guerrillas. ALN attempts to infiltrate the SAS harkis proved unsuccessful, largely because their tightly knit composition was such that an SAS officer would quickly become aware of any stranger appearing in his unit.

While their effectiveness and reliability depended largely on the qualities of the individual SAS officers under whom they operated, the harkis proved a formidable weapon in the war against the ALN. Familiar with every inch of their own territory, they were able to track the guerrillas through the harsh terrain of the hills and forests of the bled. On some occasions, however, they were completely misused by French units to whom they were attached. In one instance, the SAS officer in charge of a harki unit had been dismissed by a French area commander who had not appreciated his modus operandi. His men had thereafter been employed as porters instead of scouts by a French artillery unit operating in the infantry role. While conducting an operation in the mountains, the unit was attacked by the ALN and suffered heavy losses, one group of gunners being butchered after surrendering to the guerrillas. The harkis, however, fought to the last man, one of them killing fourteen guerrillas. Had they been employed in their normal reconnaissance and scouting role, it is likely that such a débâcle would never have taken place.

In early 1956, a harki unit was formed in Kabylia in an operation codenamed OISEAU BLEU, the brainchild of several unidentified individuals among the French hierarchy inspired by the accounts of the exploits of the GCMA maquis in Indochina. Unfortunately, none of those involved had served in the GCMA and thus had no knowledge of the concept of forming a counter-guerrilla unit. They sought to play on the ancient enmity between the Kabyle and the Arab. In their eyes, it was sufficient that the highly individualistic Kabyles were traditionally anti-Arab and wore their religious faith lightly. So it stood to reason that they would have little sympathy for the FLN which was a collectivist organisation controlled by highly religious Arabs.

Instead of handing the task of forming the new unit, designated Force K, to the SDECE Action Service and the 11e Choc at the very start, it was given to an officer in the DST, an Algerian named Hachiche, who had considerable experience in dealing with the Kabyle community in Paris. Flown to Algeria and installed in his native village of Azazga, at the foot of the Massif Djurdjura, he set about recruiting men for Force K. Despite the very high level of secrecy accorded to the project, Hachiche confided in a close friend, an innkeeper named Za, and revealed that the project had official support at the highest levels and thus the unit would be well supplied with arms and funds. This was indeed the case as Governor General Jacques Soustelle had personally sanctioned the operation.

Zaïded had assured Hachiche that he knew of men who would be prepared to take up arms against the FLN and would approach them on his behalf. In fact he contacted Belkacem Krim, one of the FLN's five senior leaders inside Algeria, and provided him with full details of OISEAU BLEU. After due consideration, the latter decided to play a double game, providing the unsuspecting Hachiche with some of his best guerrillas and allowing them to be armed and paid by the French. Responsibility for running the FLN end of the operation was given to two of his lieutenants, Mohamed Said and Slimane Dehiles (alias Si Sadek).

Before giving OISEAU BLEU his blessing, Soustelle had neglected to check that suitably qualified personnel would be running the operation and that the necessary precautions, vetting and checks would be in place to ensure that OISEAU BLEU could not be penetrated by the FLN. Substantial numbers of weapons and large sums of money were consequently handed over to men vouched for solely by a small town innkeeper in Kabylia. Needless to say, such appalling negligence on the part of those responsible for the operation would prove to be a recipe for disaster.

The first group provided for Force K numbered fifteen men. On the following day, a van arrived in Azazga with a consignment of nine Garand M1 30.06 rifles and ammunition, and funds totalling two million francs. Weeks passed during which the French became impatient for the fledgling Force K to initiate operations against the ALN. The response from Zaïded, who had been appointed as his liaison with the unit, was that the men were still carrying out training. Shortly afterwards, however, a French post in the mountains heard the sounds of a gun battle and next day found the bodies of six men. There was much rejoicing in Algiers at the 'blooding' of Force K. The reality, however, was very different. The six men had been members of Messali Hadj's Mouvement Nationaliste Algérienne (MNA), formerly the MTLD until renamed shortly after the outbreak of the revolution. Previously captured and held prisoner by the ALN, they had been executed to provide 'evidence' of Force K's first operation.

During the ensuing months, similar episodes were staged by Mohamedi Said and Slimane Dehile, Force K being rewarded with further supplies of arms and money. At the same time, the ranks of the unit were swelled by more recruits until by August 1956 it numbered some 1,500 men. Meanwhile, it was apparently exercising complete control of a region in the mountains north of Tizi-Ouzou, Dellys and Port-Gueydon where the FLN would no longer dare to operate. Evidence of this was that there had been no attacks on French military convoys in the area ever since Force K had established itself there. French operations had meanwhile been terminated in the region where Force K guerrillas had complete freedom of movement, having been issued with documents with which they could identify themselves to any French patrol. Such was the total deception of the French that the apparent success of Force K led to suggestions that it could be repeated in other areas of Algeria.

Ironically, the success of Beltacem Krim's double game unnerved the hierarchy of the FLN which believed that OISEAU BLEU was a diabolical plot on the part of the French who were playing a 'treble game'. So anxious were the leaders of the organisation that, at the Soummam Conference, a major summit held on 20 August 1956 in the Soummam Valley, situated between Greater and Lesser Kabylia, they ordered Krim to terminate his double game and send all 1,500 members of Force K back to the ALN.

Some months earlier, information about the existence of OISEAU BLEU and Force K had reached the ears of Captain Pierre Hentic who was attached to the GM's Sub-Group 1. As described in Chapter 3, Hentic had distinguished himself during three years with the Montagnard tribes in Indochina and was an acknowledged expert in the manipulation and winning over of local populations. On joining Sub-Group 1 in Kabylia, he had soon familiarised himself with the terrain and people of the region, and had set up a small team with which he disappeared into the wilds. He and his men lived as natives, dressed in djellabas and living off dried dates. Their targets were the FLN/ALN's political commissars who spread its gospel of nationalism and terror among the local population. These were identified, tracked down and eliminated.

When subsequently investigated by the gendarmerie, the killings were all attributed to the ALN.

From the moment when he first learned of OISEAU BLEU in early 1956, Hentic had harboured grave doubts and suspicions about the operation, his misgivings being based on his firm belief that the formation of a counter-guerrilla unit was a highly specialised task requiring experienced personnel. In his view OISEAU BLEU had been carried out with a lack of expertise and a high degree of irresponsibility on the part of all concerned. Moreover, he had serious doubts about Force K itself, these being reinforced by the apparent lack of information available about the unit's operations against the ALN, all of which appeared to be just too successful with little or no tangible evidence. His requests to visit Force K and offer assistance were met with refusals which only served to increase his already grave suspicions.

Determined to judge matters for himself, he ventured into the area held by Force K in an operation lasting five days. Expecting it to be free of the FLN, he and his group found themselves under heavy attack in the very area of Ali Bou Nab occupied by Force K, being ambushed on their return route. On his return, Hentic submitted a report to the 'Box' in Paris, expressing his misgivings about Force K. This had immediate repercussions which resulted in his being called to Algiers where none of those responsible for OISEAU BLEU would accept his findings. Moreover, the commanders of the sectors within Force K's area still maintained that it was free of guerrillas. Hentic riposted by demanding that he should be allowed to investigate the 'pseudo-maquis' fully. This was agreed by the authorities in Paris who, having called the staff in Algiers to account, decreed that the operation should continue while Hentic carried out a full investigation.

At the beginning of June, Hentic formed a special 30-man detachment for his new task, designated Groupe Léger d'Intervention No. 2 (GLI 2), composed mostly of veterans of GCMA maquis operations in Indochina. He then established a base at Tigzirt, an isolated town with a French garrison on the coast at the eastern end of the Ali Bou Nab mountains, setting up his headquarters in an isolated house on the outskirts of the town. Mysteriously, when Hentic and his men moved into Force K's area, there were no attacks on them, leading Hentic to suspect that the guerrillas had been warned.

Eventually, however, the commander of Force K made contact with Hentic who proceeded to establish good relations with the guerrillas. During this period, he called on the services of Jean Servier, a French anthropologist who had formed some of the first harkis. At gatherings with members of Force K arranged by Hentic, Servier engaged many of them in lengthy conversations in which he spoke to them in their respective Kabyle dialects. As a result, he ascertained that the guerrillas were lying, not being members of the douars (villages) to which they claimed to belong.

Shortly afterwards, GLI 2, under the command of Hentic's second-in-command, Lieutenant d'Aurelles, took to the djebels, Hentic himself being prevented by an old wound from taking part in the operation. Leaving Tigzirt in a convoy heading for Azazgar and dropping off unseen en route, d'Aurelles and his men gathered in an area of forest before making for an area where they were certain to encounter elements of Force K. That night, they set up an ambush on a track and at 10.00 p.m. eliminated a group of four guerrillas who entered their killing area. With no further contacts that night or the following day, they headed north and met elements of Force K who told d'Aurelles that a small ALN group was in the area and that they would track it down and destroy it. Affecting belief, GLI 2 took its leave of the guerrillas and disappeared from the area before swiftly doubling back to observe their actions. They were soon observed following up on the trail of GLI 2 which immediately set up an ambush.

At the same time, d'Aurelles made radio contact with the 11e Choc base at Tipasa, reporting the situation which was relayed to the French headquarters in Algiers. It soon became apparent that Force K had already been in touch with its controllers as d'Aurelles was contacted on the radio by a senior officer at the French headquarters at Tizi Ouzou, controlling the entire area. The latter ordered him to avoid all contact with Force K which was engaged in hunting down a group of ALN. When d'Aurelles remonstrated, pointing out that it was his group that Force K was pursuing, he was ordered to terminate his operation immediately as it was causing confusion between the French and Force K. On returning to Tigzirt, d'Aurelles learned from Hentic that the 11e Choc had been barred from operating in the area.

In August events took a different turn when a patrol of the 151ème

Regiment d'Infanterie was ambushed, suffering 35 killed. Hentic and d'Aurelles visited the site of the ambush, a search of which revealed spent .30-06 calibre cartridges of the type used by the M1 Garand rifles with which Force K was equipped. Despite this evidence, the general commanding the area refused to be convinced of Force K's treachery.

Frustrated to the point of despair, Hentic secretly deployed his unit on to the jebels once more, this time communicating only with the 11e Choc base at Tipasa. During the following days GLI 2, organised in two groups, ambushed tracks and attacked the homes of well-known guerrillas in an effort to collect as much intelligence as possible. While searching the body of a dead ALN guerrilla, one of Hentic's men discovered a photograph in which a member of Force K was clearly identified among a group of FLN guerrillas. All too soon the dreadful truth was revealed: from the very beginning Force K had been a double game perpetrated by the ALN which had used it to acquire arms and funds as well as establishing an area free from interference from French forces. These revelations caused consternation in Algiers where those members of the general staff responsible for OISEAU BLEU found it almost impossible to admit that they had been instrumental in creating a well-armed 1,500 strong unit for the ALN.

The initial attempt by the French to exact retribution on Force K was a shambles. Mountain troops were deployed in the area, only to lose 40 men killed after a company of the 15ème Régiment des Chasseurs Alpins was ambushed by a force of heavily armed guerrillas. The decision was then taken to destroy Force K completely and a huge operation was mounted by two divisions and two airborne units, the 3ème Régiment de Parachutistes Coloniaux (3e RPC), commanded by Lieutenant Colonel Marcel Bigeard, and the 1er Régiment de Chasseurs Parachutistes (1er RCP) under Lieutenant Colonel Albert Meyer.

The GLI 2 was given the task of protecting an artillery command post, evidence that those in Algiers responsible for the OISEAU BLEU fiasco had little liking for those who had exposed the entire sorry affair. Hentic, however, had other ideas and offered the services of GLI 2 to Lieutenant Colonel Bigeard who deployed its 30 members as guides for his companies. Hentic led the 3e RPC to the east beyond Azazga where the paratroops soon made contact with the guerrillas. During the following four days of almost constant fighting, the 3e RPC accounted for 600 of

Force K. The remainder, numbering some 900, made good their escape and were lost to the ALN.

At the beginning of 1957 the GM left its base at Tipasa, situated on the coast at the foot of the Chenoua Massif, and moved inland to the Ouarsenis. Meanwhile the ALN, after the departure of GLI 2 and well armed as a result of OISEAU BLEU, once again began to assert its influence throughout Wilaya I. In neighbouring Wilaya III, the newly appointed commander, Mohammed Said, decided to eliminate the presence of the MNA in his area and launched a series of attacks. The latter retaliated, carrying out massacres of FLN groups. The French looked on, content to watch such a bitter conflict being fought between two principal elements of the nationalist revolution.

The MNA forces, however, were less well armed than their opponents and it was not long before their commander, Mohammed Bellounis, began making overtures to the French who previously had considered using his forces in a counter-guerrilla role against the FLN. But on this occasion the French, still smarting from the fiasco of OISEAU BLEU, made it clear that they would only provide support if the MNA fought openly alongside their troops. Bellounis was reluctant to make any such open declaration of assistance for the French as it would weaken his authority in the huge area under his control which extended from the edge of the rich farmlands of the Mitidja towards Djelfa and Bou-Saada.

Bellounis, however, was under serious threat from the FLN whom he had good reason to fear. Two years previously, in the summer of 1955, ALN forces under Ait Hamouda (alias Amirouche), a leading member of the ALN in Wilaya III renowned for his brutality and cruelty, had attacked the MNA base at Guenzet, besieging it for 48 hours. Bellounis's force had suffered heavy casualties and he had only succeeded in escaping with a handful of his followers. This effectively had ended the MNA's challenge to the FLN's rule in Kabylia and heralded the beginning of its decline as a rival throughout Algeria. Bellounis thereafter had made his way to the area of Mélouza, an arid and inaccessible region in the southern Sahara inhabited by the Beni-Illemane tribes who were strong supporters of the MNA.

On 28 May 1957, an officer of the SAS, Captain Combette, learned of a massacre that had taken place at a small village in his area of responsibility. On arrival, he was met by a scene of carnage: some 300 people lying amidst the ruins of the village. The FLN had struck once again.

Immediately following the massacre, Bellounis made contact with Combette and repeated his request for French support, this time undertaking to rally to the French cause. Despite the fact that they had few illusions concerning his loyalty, the French agreed. Those who had been responsible for OISEAU BLEU and had escaped censure were determined to exercise strict control over Bellounis's force; in their opinion, the strong anti-FLN sentiments of the MNA meant that infiltration by the latter would not be a threat. Personnel of the Deuxième Bureau, however, tasked with ensuring liaison between the new counter-guerrilla unit and the military authorities in neighbouring sectors, did not share this view. Among them was the former 11e Choc officer and Indochina veteran, Captain Freddy Bauer. From the very beginning, he and others warned that the majority of Bellounis's troops were divided between their fear of FLN reprisals and of Bellounis himself. Indeed, just prior to the massacre at Melouza, a number had deserted from the MNA's ranks and joined the FLN.

On the insistence of the French, Bellounis moved his force of 500 south-west from Wilaya III and deployed it in an area between Bou-Saada, Dejelfa and the Hauts Plateaux of the Atlas mountain range, within the region of the FLN's Wilaya VI which was under a senior guerrilla named Si Haouès. Comprising for the most part bare terrain, it was populated by nomadic goatherds and shepherds who followed their flocks over the sparse grassland and rocky scrub of the hills.

With French support, Bellounis eventually increased the strength of his force to some 1,500 men who at this early stage were only lightly armed with carbines. From June onward, he engaged the FLN in a series of skirmishes and during the next four months slowly but surely succeeded in forcing the FLN out of his area. This led to his demanding better weapons, including machine-guns, along with ammunition, clothing and vehicles. Despite the warnings of the Deuxième Bureau liaison officers, who warned that he was untrustworthy and that French authority no longer ruled in his area, his demands were met by the general staff in Algiers, supported by Governor-General Robert Lacoste, who had succeeded Jacques Soustelle in February 1956, and the Ministry of Interior in Paris.

Eventually it became apparent, however, that the Deuxième Bureau liaison officers no longer had any influence over Bellounis and once again the 11e Choc was detailed to solve the problem. In September, in an operation codenamed OLIVIER, a centaine commanded by Captain Pierre Rocolle was despatched from France with the task of taking Bellounis in hand and converting his force into a harki.

Bellounis was not at all happy at the arrival of Rocolle who made it abundantly clear to the guerrilla leader that the latter was in the service of France. Rocolle distributed groups of his men among the katibas (company-size units) of Bellounis's force which they accompanied thereafter on operations. They soon discovered, however, that the so-called counter-guerrillas had little appetite for fighting, preferring instead to terrorise defenceless villages and thus avoid antagonising the FLN commander of Wilaya VI, Si Haouès. Indeed, Rocolle began to suspect that the latter had succeeded in subverting key members of Bellounis's force.

Despite the adverse reports about Bellounis received from Rocolle, the Governor-General acceded to the former's demand that France should officially recognise his forces which he had named the Armée Nationale Populaire Algérienne (ANPA). He had appointed himself as a two-star general and demanded that he should be accorded equal standing with that of the commander-in-chief of French forces in Algeria, General Raoul Salan. This met with prevarication on the part of Lacoste who did little more than order Rocolle to keep an even tighter eye on his increasingly arrogant charge.

By the beginning of 1958, however, Bellounis was secretly preparing to take control of the French-held sectors which bordered his own. Rocolle was aware of this and kept a close watch as the APNA inserted its politico-administrative structures and began recruiting in the areas concerned. Alerted by Rocolle, officers of the Deuxième Bureau arrested several key individuals in each sector. Bellounis resorted to guile, launching harassing attacks on French posts while leading them to believe that they had been carried out as part of a resurgence of activity by the ALN. These were followed by demands for more weapons to enable the APNA to assist the French in driving off the enemy.

The deception lasted until May, by which time Rocolle had decided that measures should be taken to force Bellounis into line. At the end of that month, he held a meeting at which it was made clear to Bellounis that if he wished to continue enjoying French support, the APNA would no longer be a 'third force' to counter the FLN but would be converted into harki units to fight under the direct command of French forces. Bellounis accepted this proposal but there was a mixed response from the rank and file of the APNA: while some units were happy to serve as harkis, others made it clear that they would defect to the FLN.

Rocolle transmitted a warning to Algiers, requesting that airborne units be despatched immediately to deal with the rebellious elements of the APNA. The 3ème Régiment Parachutiste d'Infanterie de Marine (3e RPIMa), commanded by Colonel Roger Trinquier, the former commander of the GCMA in Indochina, was deployed to Djelfa along with a Foreign Legion regiment and a unit of air force commandos. Unfortunately they arrived too late as on the previous evening the units that had decided to defect to the FLN had attacked Bellounis's headquarters which, defended by Rocolle and his centaine who were short of ammunition, had eventually been overrun by the rebels. The latter, having bound and murdered 300 of their former comrades who had opted to serve as harkis, then disappeared into the hills. When the troops of the 3e RPIMa arrived on the scene, they were confronted by a scene of horrific slaughter. Among the bodies were those of Captain Rocolle and his men who had fought to the last. Mohammed Bellounis was also there, having been killed by his bodyguard who had turned on him just prior to the attack.

DURING 1958, THE 11e Choc became involved in another major embarrassment for the French when the ALN managed to convince them that one of their counter-guerrilla units was disloyal. Based in the area of Orléansville, within the region covered by the ALN's Wilaya IV, it was led by an individual named Belhadj Djillalli, alias 'Kobus', who had been arrested in 1950 as a member of the OS and, despite having a reputation for being duplicitous and unreliable, had thereafter become an informer.

The unit had been formed in August 1957 under the auspices of the DST which, despite Djillalli's dubious past, was convinced that he was trustworthy, an opinion shared by officers of the Deuxième Bureau and the SAS stationed in the region. Such faith appeared to be justified when

Djillalli's force started operations, clearing the FLN from his area. By the end of October, the unit numbered some 300 men organised in a battalion of three companies. All Djillalli's officers had been trained secretly in the skills of winning over local populations, psychological warfare and brain-washing by experts of the French Army's Cinquième Bureau at Arzew. Such was his apparent success in rallying the populace throughout the French military zone of West Algeria that its commander, General Gracieux, was convinced that the entire region had been won over.

In reality, it had rallied not to the French but to Djillalli who was playing a double game to further his own ends. By this time, however, there were increasing doubts at high level as to his motives and following a series of disagreements concerning the status of his unit, the staff of the sector headquarters decided to wash their hands of him. Once again, the 11e Choc was called in to clear up the mess. Its initial reaction was one of disbelief and anger at the evident stupidity of yet another attempt by untrained personnel to create a counter-guerrilla unit. Captain Pierre Hentic refused the assignment, as did other 11e Choc officers who were only too familiar with the disasters of OISEAU BLEU and the APNA. Eventually, it was given to a young officer, Lieutenant Val, whose detachment was despatched from Calvi shortly afterwards.

Djillalli's apparent success in winning over the local population inevitably had made him and his unit, which by the spring of 1958 numbered 900 men, targets for the ALN. Instead of mounting direct attacks against them, the political head of Wilaya IV, Ahmed Bougarra (alias Si M'hamed), and its intelligence chief, Omar Oussedik, set out to discredit them with the French by staging a number of incidents which were subsequently laid at the door of Djillalli. These began in January 1958, the first being the mining of a track patrolled regularly by Djillalli's unit. One morning, a patrol was seen to pass along the track without incident but shortly afterwards an 11e Choc vehicle hit a mine. Although unable to confront the guerrilla leader, Lieutenant Val suspected treachery and proceeded discreetly to lay ambushes in the area of the track, keeping a close eye on the counter-guerrillas and monitoring their radio traffic.

Upset by Val's evident suspicion, Djillalli moved his headquarters farther away to a farm on a mountainside from where he could keep the 11e Choc detachment under observation. Val responded by moving his base to a location below that of Djillalli. He also deployed teams among the counter-guerrilla companies active in the south of the region, accompanying them on missions in neighbouring sectors in an effort to split them from Djillalli. Val's plan was to disband the entire force so that it could be integrated among the harkis and local self-defence units already under the Army's control.

Bougarra and Oussedik meanwhile staged the second incident designed to discredit Djillalli. One night, a group of ALN attacked a harki post on the edge of Djillalli's sector while others stole a large flock of sheep, ensuring that their tracks would be easily visible to the French on the following day, herding it past Djillali's headquarters to an area near by. Although the latter denied any involvement in the theft of the sheep, Val's mistrust deepened, and during April 1958 the French gradually withdrew support from Djillalli.

In the meantime, Bougarra and Oussedik approached the senior members of the unit, promising to spare their lives if they went over to the ALN; at the same time, however, they stipulated that Djillalli must be delivered to them alive or dead. His deputy decided on the latter option and, immediately after Djillalli's return from a visit to Algiers, murdered him. Having decapitated the corpse, he took the head with him as he and some twenty other senior colleagues presented themselves to Bougarra. The latter, however, reneged on his word and all of them were executed three weeks later. Djillalli's force was disbanded, most of its strength being absorbed into harki units; the remaining 200 or so men vanished and joined the ALN.

In July 1957, all intelligence gathering in Algeria had been placed under a coordinating body, the Centre de Coordination Interarmées (CCI) under Colonel Léon Simoneau who during the Second World War had served as an intelligence officer with the Resistance, subsequently heading the post-war French Army's Service de Renseignement Opérationnel (SRO) (Operational Intelligence Service). Later he had served in the research branch of the SDECE before being appointed head of the Deuxième Bureau's Russian section, and then of its section attached to the French General Staff. He was then selected to set up the CCI which was formed from the intelligence section of Major General Jacques Massu's 10ème Division de Parachutiste.

The CCI's activities were overseen by the division's chief of staff,

Colonel Yves Godard, who had commanded the 11e Choc during its five years of operations in Indochina. Divided into different sections, covering operational intelligence, counter-intelligence, technical and executive action, it employed 400 officers, some deployed with units such as the 157ème Régiment d' Infanterie at Constantine and the 61ème at Oran, to provide tactical intelligence.

One of the intelligence units functioning under the aegis of the CCI was the Dispositif de Protection Urbaine (DPU), formed by Robert Lacoste, who had replaced Jacques Soustelle as Governor General, and commanded by Colonel Roger Trinquier of Indochina and GCMA fame. Operating in Algiers, the DPU divided the city into sectors, sub-sectors, blocks and individual buildings, each allocated a code number. Within each block, it appointed a Muslim 'responsable' or warden who was required to report all activities and comings-and-goings within his area of responsibility. The DPU oversaw the activities of a number of small teams known as Détachements Opérationnels de Protections (DOP) whose tasks included the interrogation of suspects arrested at night, the latter often being confronted by hooded informers, themselves Muslims who had already broken under interrogation. DOP methods more often than not included the use of torture in order to ensure the swift extraction of information leading to arrests of further suspects by dawn.

A key unit closely linked with the DPU was the Groupement de Renseignement et d'Exploitation (GRE), formed by Trinquier and commanded by Captain Christian Léger, an officer in the Zouaves. A veteran of the GCMA in Indochina who had served as an instructor at the training school at Cape Saint Jacques, he had then been assigned to the SDECE's North African Section before being posted in March 1957 to take command of the newly formed GRE with the task of infiltrating the ranks of the FLN and ALN. Potential recruits were provided by the DOP which, having arrested a suspect with potential as an agent, would inform Léger who would then set out to 'turn' him or her. In due course, he set up a network of high-level agents and informers within the FLN/ALN which remained totally unaware of the GRE operation.

A primary target for Léger was Saadi Yacef who had replaced Rabah Bitat as head of the FLN/ALN network in Algiers after the latter's arrest in the spring of 1955. During the second half of 1956, Yacef had launched a blitz of bomb attacks and shootings in the capital in reprisal for the executions on 19 June of two members of the ALN sentenced to death for murder. These had included, on 28 December, the murder of the Mayor of Algiers, Amédée Roger, by a member of the ALN, Ali La Pointe. Yacef had declared previously that 100 French and colonists would die for each member of the FLN executed by the French. This, together with the retaliatory attacks launched by colonist counter-terror groups and ultimately the occupation of Algiers on 15 January 1957 by the 10ème Division de Parachutiste, had culminated in the Battle of Algiers during which the division's commander, Major General Jacques Massu, had assumed all civil powers. The FLN had called for a general strike to begin on 28 January but two days beforehand Yacef initiated a series of three bomb attacks in bars and cafés in the city, killing 60 people and wounding five. Two weeks later, another two attacks left ten dead and 45 injured.

The French response was swift and effective. On 15 February, one of Yacef's bomb factories was located by the paratroops of the 3e RPC who four days later uncovered a large cache of explosives. On 23 February, acting on intelligence provided by Colonel Trinquier's DPU, the 3e RPC arrested Larbi M'hidi, one of the original six leaders of the FLN in Algeria and its political chief in Algiers. By this time, a number of suspects, all identified by the DPU, had been arrested and interrogated by members of the DOP. Those identified as potential informers were passed on to the GRE.

Léger formed a special group of four agents to entrap Yacef. This comprised an Algerian, a French Army veteran of Indochina, identified only by his alias of 'Surcouf'; a Muslim woman with the alias of 'Ourhia-le-Brune' who was an FLN courier in Algiers, continuing to carrying messages under Léger's control; Hani Mohamed, the commander of the ALN in western Algiers until his capture in August 1957; and the chief of the FLN in eastern Algiers, known only by his alias of 'Safy-le-Pur'.

During the latter part of 1957, Yacef was arrested by troops of the 1er Régiment Etranger de Parachutiste (1er REP) commanded by Lieutenant Colonel Pierre Jeanpierre. This was thanks to the GRE having pinpointed his whereabouts at a house at 3 Rue Caton, in the Algiers casbah. Two weeks later, the 1er REP also cornered Ali La Pointe who had been tracked down by Safy-le-Pur. He had been in the building next door when Yacef was caught but had escaped and made his way to a safe house in the Rue des Abderames. On the night of 8 October, Lieutenant Colonel Jeanpierre's legionnaires surrounded the house. Demands for him to surrender met with no response and so the paratroops set off explosive charges against a wall behind which was a concealed compartment containing not only La Pointe and two others but also a cache of explosives. These, too, were detonated, killing La Pointe and his two companions while destroying the entire house and adjacent buildings.

Prior to his capture, Yacef had appointed Safy-le-Pur as commander of the ALN in Algiers and had informed Amirouche, leader of Wilaya III, of the appointment. On the orders of the Comité de Coordination et d'Exécution (CCE), the FLN's controlling body in exile in Tunis, Amirouche began to reconstruct the networks in Algiers through Safy-le-Pur. Thus the GRE found itself in control of the remaining FLN/ALN elements in the city, playing a 'double game' with the aim of penetrating FLN networks in the rest of Algeria. This extended to allowing, and indeed assisting, the new fledgling network in the capital to carry out some harmless bomb attacks.

Hani Mohamed, meanwhile, was in touch with Amirouche through whom he had made contact with senior members of the Wilaya III command structure. Unfortunately, the entire operation was put at risk when he was arrested by an Army unit. In view of this, and the possibility that the entire GRE operation might be 'blown', it was decided to launch an attempt to ensnare the whole command structure of Wilaya III as quickly as possible. Towards the end of January 1958, Hani Mohamed arranged to meet the entire staff of Wilaya III, with the exception of Amirouche, at a predetermined location. The rendezvous took place one night at the end of the month, with Hani Mohamed accompanied by Captain Léger and members of his unit, all suitably disguised. The Wilaya III leaders arrived at the rendezvous suspecting nothing, only to find themselves under arrest and subsequently imprisoned.

The outcome of the operation had devastating effects on the FLN/ALN, causing rifts and splits within Wilaya III where Amirouche launched a series of raids not only in Kabylia but also in Algiers where he executed the newly established network's command element which had been operating unknowingly under the control of the GRE. The situation was exacerbated by documents, forged by the GRE and planted on the bodies of dead guerrillas, which appeared to identify loyal members of the

FLN/ALN as traitors, all of them falling victim to further purges carried out by Amirouche. Moreover, Léger played upon the hatred and distrust which had existed for centuries between the different ethnic factions in Algeria.

So successful was his deception operation against Wilaya III that Léger increased the number of 'turned' guerrillas whom he sent back into the FLN equipped with false information carefully crafted to sow more discord within the organisation. The possibility of one of his agents defecting back to the guerrillas caused him little anxiety as such an event would only cause further mayhem, increasing the paranoia and distrust already rampant throughout the FLN. On one occasion, a young female suspect from Kabylia was arrested and subsequently handed over to the GRE. While questioning her at his headquarters in Algiers, Léger quit the room on a pretext, leaving on the table some documents which apparently named a senior member of the FLN as an informer. Unaware she was being watched, the suspect had swiftly read them by the time that Léger returned. As he expected, no sooner had the woman returned to Kabylia than she defected back to the ALN, passing on the information in the documents. Once again, this led to another purge and the deaths of those named as collaborating with the French.

The French made extensive use of electronic intelligence in their operations against the ALN who began to use radio communications from 1956 onward. In early 1957, radio intercepts had given warning of guerrilla attacks on the Morice Line, a major barrier of electrified wire fences, minefields and electronic sensors which stretched 100 miles from Bône, on the coast, to Souk Ahras, dominating the Medjerda corridor, to south of Tebessa on the edge of the Sahara. Named after André Morice, the Minister of Defence, it was designed to block off the wilayas from the ALN's headquarters, supply dumps and training camps in neighbouring Tunisia. A similar barrier had meanwhile been constructed along the border with Morocco. In addition to listening to ALN transmissions, the French also pinpointed the transmitters and thus the locations of the headquarters of guerrilla units.

Since 1955, the French had made much use of helicopters and therefore could deploy and manoeuvre forces swiftly in response to information giving details of guerrilla locations. A good illustration of this took place in May 1957 when intelligence reports indicated that two katibas comprising 300 men of Wilaya IV, under a guerrilla with the alias of 'Si Lakhdar', were making their way westward through the mountains towards Médéa, a town in the Atlas some 50 miles south-west of Algiers. They were to rendezvous with another guerrilla unit, commanded by Rabah Zerrari, which had ambushed a French infantry unit a few days beforehand. During the night of 22/23 May, Lieutenant Colonel Marcel Bigeard's 3e RPC was deployed in ambush positions across the guerrillas' route in the area of the village of Agounennda. At dawn on the 23rd, Zerrari's unit encountered No. 3 Company which had been deployed in a location to the north of the 3e RPC's main positions. Si Lakhdar's force also made its appearance and a battle ensued in which the guerrillas succeeded in surrounding the isolated company whose commander requested assistance. Fortunately, helicopter support was on call and within 30 minutes Lieutenant Colonel Bigeard had redeployed two companies swiftly on to high ground overlooking the guerrillas' positions. The ensuing battle lasted three days during which the ALN lost 96 dead and nine taken prisoner, the 3e RPC having suffered eight killed and 29 wounded. The rest of the guerrillas made good their escape.

In addition to waging its secret war against the guerrillas within Algeria, the French intelligence apparatus also conducted operations against the FLN outside the country, its efforts being concentrated largely on the organisation's sources of funds. In France, the Algerian community was just one source of vast sums of money collected, or extorted, by the FLN. An SDECE operation carried out by Service 7, a department specialising in surveillance of foreign embassies and gaining illegal access to diplomatic pouches, resulted in the discovery inside the Egyptian Embassy of documents giving details of payments made to FLN representatives in France. In addition, there were a number of networks throughout France which also provided support for the FLN. One of these was headed by an individual named Jean Jeanson which reportedly smuggled several billion francs from France to Switzerland on behalf of the FLN.

Because these and other funds were used primarily for the purchase of arms, the French also turned their attention on any sources identified as suppliers to the FLN. The first known consignment was delivered to the FLN in February 1955 aboard the Queen of Jordan's personal yacht, the *Dina*, which landed them on the coast of Morocco, all traces of the operation being removed by local peasants organised to herd their flocks of goats up and down the beach immediately afterwards.

At the beginning of October, the French received information concerning a shipment of arms destined for the FLN. Arranged by the Egyptian intelligence service, it was to be transported aboard a former British minesweeper, the *Athos*, sailing from Beirut for Alexandria, where the arms would be loaded aboard the vessel. From there it would sail under a Sudanese flag for Morocco where it was to land the consignment on 16 October off the coast of the Spanish Sahara at Nador. It would be met there by none other than the overall head of the FLN, Ahmed Ben Bella. A close watch was kept on the ship, its departure from Beirut being reported immediately by the SDECE station there. On 4 October, the loading of the weapons in Alexandria, personally supervised by the Egyptian intelligence officer in charge of the operation, was kept under surveillance. At the same time, the SDECE in Berne, Switzerland, reported that a large sum of money had been transferred to the account of the vessel's Sudanese owner. In Morocco, meanwhile, members of the Deuxième Bureau in Rabat were keeping a close eye on Ben Bella.

In due course, the *Athos* sailed from Alexandria, being shadowed by French aircraft, and on 15 October was intercepted by a French warship off Algiers. It was found to be carrying over 70 tons of weapons and ammunition, including: 2,300 rifles, 74 automatic rifles, 240 submachine-guns, 40 machine-guns, 600,000 rounds of small arms ammunition, 72 mortars and 2,000 mortar bombs. The capture of the consignment was a major blow for the FLN which was in sore need of the weapons.

A few days later, the FLN suffered another major setback when the French succeeded in capturing Ben Bella himself. Seven months earlier, in April, a meeting had taken place in Cairo between Mohamed Khider, one of the six leaders in exile of the FLN, and a secret representative of the French government of Guy Mollet, which had been elected into office in January. This led to five more talks during the next five months at various locations, the last being held in Rome in September. It was planned that a further meeting should take place during the following month at which an announcement concerning peace negotiations would be made.

Despite these contacts between the FLN and Mollet's administration, Ben Bella was still regarded by the French as a major menace. As mentioned earlier in this chapter, in May 1955 the SDECE had targeted the leadership of the FLN and in particular Ben Bella himself. The decision had been taken to assassinate him and the service had accorded the highest priority to doing so. In December 1955, an unsuccessful attempt was made to shoot him in Cairo, the gunman being a member of a secret counter-guerrilla organisation headed by a Frenchman named André Achiary. He had been Sub-Prefect of Guelma in Algeria in 1945 during the period of the Sétif massacre that year, and prior to the war had been head of the DST in Algiers. This attempt was followed by another in early 1956 with a bomb planted outside Ben Bella's office in Cairo. Later in the year, a member of an organisation called Main Rouge, which reportedly had links with French intelligence, attempted to shoot him in the Libyan capital of Tripoli; his assailant was later killed while attempting to escape over the border from Libya into Algeria.

Following the meeting between the FLN leadership and Mollet's secret representative in September, the SDECE learned that Ben Bella and four companions, Mohamed Boudiaf, Mohamed Khider, Hocine Ait Ahmed and an Algerian professor named Mostefa Lacheraf, were due to travel by air on 22 October from Rabat, the capital of Morocco, directly to Tunis. There they were to participate in an FLN summit conference to be attended by the leaders of Tunisia and Morocco, as well as secret representatives of the French government. Initially, it had been planned that they would fly aboard the personal aircraft of King Mohammed V of Morocco, who was also attending the summit, and on the morning of 22 October details of the aircraft's flight plan were passed to Algiers by Colonel Jean Gardes, head of the Deuxième Bureau in Rabat. Subsequently, however, it was announced by the royal palace that there would be insufficient space aboard the King Mohammed's aircraft for Ben Bella and his companions and that a DC-3 of Air Maroc, flown by a French crew, would be made available to them instead.

The plane's journey took it via Mallorca where it was due to make a refuelling stop. As it was approaching the island, the pilot, Commandant Gellier, a reserve officer in the Armée de l'Air, received orders from the air traffic control at Oran, to fly to Algiers rather than Tunis. Gellier was initially somewhat reluctant to obey but, after contacting the Air

Maroc headquarters in Rabat which told him to comply, eventually agreed. On leaving Mallorca, the aircraft headed for Algiers, the stewardesses distracting the attention of Ben Bella and his companions from noticing the change in direction and, during the normal pre-landing procedures in the passenger cabin, announcing that the aircraft was landing at Tunis. It was not until the aircraft had landed and they observed the French troops that the five Algerians realised that they had been duped and were in the hands of the French. They were arrested and taken away into captivity, being imprisoned without trial.

THE EXTERNAL WAR AGAINST those supporting or supplying the FLN continued. Considerable amounts of money continued to pour into the organisation's coffers and towards the end of 1957 it was estimated that some seven thousand million francs had been raised in that year alone. The international arms trade by this time had realised that there were considerable profits to be made in supplying arms to the FLN which thus had little difficulty in finding alternative sources of supply, some of them in Eastern Europe. Evidence of this surfaced in January 1958 when a Yugoslav freighter, *Slovenija*, was intercepted off Oran and found to be carrying 148 tons of arms, including 12,000 weapons manufactured in Czechoslovakia.

One of the FLN's principal conduits for arms was West Germany where there were few restrictions and where dealers were only too willing to satisfy the FLN's requirements; among the arms shipped from Hamburg was a consignment of flame throwers shipped as crop-spraying equipment. Supplies were also arranged by a group of former members of the Nazi SS who had fled to Egypt following the collapse of Hitler's regime, among them Ernst-Wilhelm Springer, who had been instrumental in the formation of the Muslim Legion, a wartime SS formation.

The SDECE proceeded to target those who supplied the FLN. The operation was carried out by an Action Service department called 'Bureau 24' which, commanded by an officer known as 'Colonel Lamy', worked closely with elements of the 11e Choc. A West German dealer named Otto Schlüter was the target of four bomb attacks during the period 1956–8, finally severing his connections with the FLN after a remote-controlled car bomb attack which injured him and killed his mother. Others included Dr Wilhelm Beisner, a former member of the Sicherheitsdienst, the wartime SS security service, who narrowly escaped death when a shrapnel bomb exploded under his car, and a dealer named Hans Paulman who was seized with a consignment of weapons, being flown to North Africa from Italy, when his aircraft was intercepted and forced to land in Algeria. Senior members of the FLN involved in procuring arms in Europe were also targets: in November 1957, the head of the FLN in West Germany, Ait Ahcène, was shot dead in Bonn.

One of Bureau 24's principal targets was Georg Puchert, a German living in Tangiers who appeared to be unswayed by threats on his life. Puchert was supplying the FLN with Czech-manufactured copies of the Mauser 98K 7.92mm rifle which had been the principal infantry weapon of the wartime Wehrmacht. The initial operation by Bureau 24 was a bomb attack in Tangier harbour on some speedboats used by Puchert to smuggle cigarettes and alcohol. When this failed to dissuade him from continuing his business with the FLN, the SDECE chose more drastic methods. In September 1958, one of his explosives experts, a Swiss named Marcel Léopold, was found dead in a hotel in Geneva, having been shot in the neck with a poisoned dart fired from an airgun fashioned like a bicycle pump. When this failed to have the desired effect, Bureau 24 targeted Puchert himself: in March 1957, in Hamburg, a bomb containing ball bearings exploded under the driver's seat of his Mercedes, killing him instantly.

Bureau 24 also resorted to other less aggressive measures to stem the flow of arms to the FLN. One of these was to gain control of two arms factories in Switzerland and Spain, supplying faulty weapons and grenades, the latter fitted with instantaneous fuses which caused them to detonate immediately they were thrown, injuring or killing the user. On other occasions, consignments of explosives were intercepted and their contents replaced with harmless substitutes such as cheese.

Despite the best efforts of the SDECE and Bureau 24, however, the FLN managed to transport large quantities of arms to Tunisia during the winter of 1957–8. These consisted of 17,000 rifles, 380 machine-guns, 296 automatic rifles, 190 rocket launchers, 30 mortars and over 100 million rounds of ammunition. With this arsenal at its disposal, the ALN turned its attention to breaching the Morice Line.

In addition to its three parallel electrified fences, minefields and electronic sensors, the line was equipped with 105mm howitzers sited in strongpoints every 2,000 yards so that they could bring fire to bear on any point under attack. Along its entire length ran a road, linking the strongpoints and patrolled by armoured vehicles and troops with tracker dogs, and a railway line along which ran armoured trains equipped with searchlights and carrying troops. The line was garrisoned by some 80,000 troops comprising mechanised, armoured and parachute units, the latter being deployed by helicopters which also assisted in locating those guerrilla units which did succeed in getting through and making off into the mountains. Between the line and the border with Tunisia was an area of no man's land, fifteen to thirty-five miles in width, in which were located some two dozen outposts reminiscent of the isolated bases constructed by the French forces in Indochina. Manned by companies of troops and SAS teams working among the Muslim communities in the area, these outposts served as observation posts and bases for intelligence and counter-intelligence operations.

The guerrillas employed a variety of techniques to penetrate the line. While diversionary attacks were staged at night in other locations, a team would use long-handled rakes to feel their way through the minefields before blowing the three electrified fences with bangalore torpedoes. The main body of guerrillas would then have to move its caravan of mules, carrying arms and other supplies, swiftly through the gap and make good its escape before the arrival of French troops, heading for the mountains. The guerrillas would need to be under cover before dawn and the arrival of French aircraft searching for them. If they were spotted, paratroops would be deployed by helicopter into ambush and cut-off positions.

Casualties incurred by the guerrillas during attempts to breach the line between January and April 1958 were heavy, with 292 killed and 215 weapons lost. Towards the end of April, the ALN decided to mount an all-out offensive and on the night of the 27th a force of 820 guerrillas attacked the sectors of the line north and south of Souk-Ahras. The battle raged for nearly a week during which a large number of guerrillas who had managed to penetrate the line were blocked and surrounded by paratroops deployed by helicopter. By the end, the ALN had lost 620 killed or taken prisoner, and 416 weapons captured. This was a major defeat for the ALN, bringing its total losses, during the seven months since the completion of the Morice Line, to 6,000 men and 4,300 weapons. The battle at Souk-Ahras marked the end of any serious attempts to breach the line and thus ensured that the ALN's units inside Algeria remained cut off from external support in Tunisia.

By early 1958, the French forces in Algeria had reason to claim that they were winning the war against the ALN. There was massive resentment, nevertheless, against the government of France where an economic crisis had resulted in cutbacks in military expenditure. On 15 April, the government of Félix Gaillard fell on a vote of confidence. On the night of 9 May the Governor General, Robert Lacoste, left Algeria ostensibly to return home but secretly having decided not to do so. Like France, the country had been left in a political vacuum.

On 13 May, *pied noir* resentment over the government's lack of response to demands for integration of Algeria with France boiled over into insurrection, as a mob seized public buildings in Algiers, calling for integration of Algeria with France and demanding the return to power of General Charles de Gaulle who had resigned from the presidency in January 1946, after becoming disillusioned with the coalition government which became the Fourth Republic in November of that year. The Army in Algeria was sympathetic to the *pieds noirs*, paratroops of the 3e RPC standing by and watching as the mob stormed the Gouvernement-Générale. In the absence of a government, General Jacques Massu and other senior French officers formed a body called the Committee of Public Safety to maintain order and avert bloodshed. The commander-in-chief, General Raoul Salan, assumed the powers of de facto civil governor.

Plans, meanwhile, were being laid for a military *coup d'état* in France. These called for a force of 5,000 paratroops to land at Villacoublay, southwest of Paris, while armoured troops from Rambouillet would enter the capital in support. The intention was that de Gaulle would then take power with the support of the Army. On 24 May, there was consternation when it was announced that paratroops had seized power on Corsica; among them were the Calvi-based elements of the 11e Choc. For the next few days, France was on the edge of civil war. On 27 May, de Gaulle announced that he had begun the process of forming a government and made clear his opposition to any threat to law and order. On 1 June, he presented himself to the National Assembly and was voted into power. On the following day, he was invested as Prime Minister of France.

Two days later, de Gaulle arrived in Algiers where he received a rapturous welcome. On three occasions during May he had published statements which had appeared to support their cause and during his visit uttered the words, 'Je vous ai compris!' which the *pieds noirs* took as confirmation of his support for the concept of Algérie Française'. But they were to be bitterly disillusioned.

The FLN, meanwhile, had for some time been working on the framework of a government-in-exile and on 19 September 1958 announced the formation of the Gouvernement Provisoire de la République Algérienne (GPRA). It was headed by a president, Ferhat Abbas, and comprised fourteen ministers including Lamine Dabaghine as Foreign Minister; Belkacem Krim, Minister of the Armed Forces; Ben Tobbal, Minister of Interior; Abdelhafid Boussoif, Minister of Communications; Mohammed Yazid, Minister of Information; and Ben Youssef Ben Khedda, Minister of Social Affairs.

December 1958 saw the arrival in Algiers of Paul Delouvrier as Delegate-General (the title of Governor-General having been dispensed with) and General Maurice Challe who replaced General Raoul Salan as commander-in-chief of all French forces in Algeria, the latter returning to France as military governor of Paris. For an airman, Challe possessed a rare understanding of land warfare and very soon had reorganised the Army in Algeria and instilled in it a renewed vigour and optimism. His measures included replacing nearly half of the colonels commanding the 75 sectors, into which the country was divided, and a highly mobile formation called the Réserve Générale consisting of parachute and Foreign Legion units. In addition, irregular harki tracker units, designated 'commandos de chasse', were formed, their role being to locate ALN units which would then be attacked in force by elements of the Réserve Générale. Led by French officers and NCOs, the commandos would deploy into the djebels for prolonged periods during which they were in constant radio contact as they sought out the guerrillas. Once contact was made, they would seek to maintain it while paratroops and legionnaires were brought in by helicopter. By that time, the French possessed enough H-21 and H-34 helicopters to transport two battalions in a single lift.

By the beginning of 1959, the 11e Choc was undergoing consider-able reorganisation. In addition to conducting operations, it had over a period of time been tasked with providing specialist training for per-sonnel of other units, among them members of CCI teams deployed in the large towns and cities. Consequently, it was decided to expand the unit which was redesignated the 11ème Demi-Brigade de Parachutiste de Choc (11e DBPC). Thereafter, it comprised two units with a per-manent base re-established at Tipasa. The first, the 1er Régiment de Parachutiste de Choc (1er Choc) was a training unit; originally formed during the Second World War, it had been disbanded at the end of the conflict. Reformed in 1957, it was based on the island of Corsica where the mountainous terrain and harsh conditions were very similar to those encountered in the djebels and deserts of Algeria. The 11e DBPC's second, entirely operational, element was the original 11e Choc, its cover name of Groupement de Marche changed to Détachement de Sécurité 111 (DS 111).

In January, DS 111 began an operation in the zone of no-man's-land between the Morice Line and Algeria's border with Tunisia. The task was to establish a number of bases within the zone under the guise of the SAS in the hope that the ALN, expecting little risk, would mount attacks on them. From 20 January onward 'SAS bases' were established by three DS 111 centaines in the area of Souk Ahras. The first was located near an area of terrain known as the 'Duck's Beak', which projected like a finger into Algeria, while the second, commanded by Captain Bozon, was on a plateau dominating the Medjerda Valley. The third, led by Lieu-tenant Pieroni, was situated at Sakhiet Sidi Youssef. In addition, two further 80-man groups, given an interception role and commanded by Lieutenants Campana and Daniel Berson, were deployed, the latter located in the Duck's Beak. Meanwhile the headquarters of DS 111, under the unit's commander, Major Ignace Mantéï, was positioned in the centre of the area in the hilltop village of Zarouria.

The first base to be attacked was that of Lieutenant Pieroni at Sakhiet Sidi Youssef which was subjected to machine-gun fire from guerrillas on the Tunisian side of the border. Pieroni and his men were forbidden to indulge in any act of aggression against targets inside Tunisia, as a result of a major incident in February 1958 when French aircraft had bombed the Tunisian village of Sakiet in reprisal for attacks on French troops by guerrillas crossing the frontier from Tunisia, and the shooting down of a French aircraft by a machine-gun in the village. The bombs had unfortunately hit a school and hospital and some 80 people, including women and children, had been killed. Pieroni thus resorted to unconventional means for dealing with the ALN machine-gunners. The DS 111's technical section adapted six 81mm parachute-illuminating bombs by removing the parachute and flare, and substituting condoms filled with human excrement. On the next occasion that the post came under fire, the guerrillas, accustomed to the illuminating bombs, failed to take cover and looked skywards, waiting for the flares. Instead, they received a liberal and unpleasant dousing, following which there were no further attacks on the post from inside Tunisia.

A far more serious threat, however, was posed by the ALN units based to the north of Ghardimaou in Tunisia and operating in the Duck's Beak. Led by Mahmoud Chérif, a former officer in one of the French Army's regiments of Spahis, they continued to harass the Morice Line although, since the casualties incurred in the spring of the previous year, they were careful to avoid any further risk of heavy losses.

The interception group in the Duck's Beak, under Lieutenant Campana, had established its base in the village of Toustain. From there it set out to familiarise itself with the difficult terrain in its area, notably hills clad with thick forests and overgrown plantations of oak trees teeming with game, including wild boar. Its operations consisted of lengthy patrols and ambushes frequently carried out in freezing winds and heavy rain. Contacts with the guerrillas were infrequent but fierce. The first took place on 10 February, followed by another on 10 March in which four guerrillas were killed and a number of weapons captured, among them a 50mm light mortar.

Over the next two months there were no further contacts with the guerrillas. Campana was convinced, however, that this was a deliberate ploy on the part of the ALN to allow the situation in the area to calm down before carrying out a large infiltration. He therefore maintained the same level of patrol activity and on the night of 3 June, the entire group embarked on an operation, setting up an area ambush on the Djebel Ensour, a range that stretched to the south-east.

Campana deployed his force in three sections which were in radio contact with one another. Two of these comprised the main ambush force whose killing area was a track junction, in a valley below, known to be used by ALN couriers; above and behind them was his command post, while his third section was sited farther back on high ground in support. The entire ambush faced east towards the Tunisian frontier, ready to intercept any guerrillas heading for the Morice Line. No enemy showed up during the night and at 6.00 a.m. next morning Campana radioed his three sections, ordering them to withdraw. No sooner had he done so, however, than a contact took place between his command group and a large force of guerrillas which appeared suddenly from the west, rather than the east. Numbering some 160 heavily armed men, it had been on a harassing operation and was now on its way back to Tunisia via the Duck's Beak.

Campana's command group numbered only ten men: himself, two radio operators, a medical officer, two medical orderlies and four stretcher bearers. Realising that his two sections below were unable to assist and that it would take the third at least half an hour to reach him, Campana led his group in a charge through the guerrilla positions to the valley below, in order to link up with the sections there, and got through without any casualties. When he reached the valley floor, however, he discovered that his sections were 500 yards away, held up by a guerrilla reconnaissance group which had preceded the main body.

Alerted that Campana was in trouble, Major Mantéï despatched reinforcements by helicopter. Meanwhile, Campana's command group was under heavy fire from the guerrillas who had by this time taken up positions in the rocks above. Realising that to remain there would be lunacy, Campana launched an assault up the almost sheer slope, his men fighting their way through undergrowth and heavy fire to close with a forward enemy position which was cleared. They continued to press on upward, reaching a point halfway up the slope where they were subjected to three counter-attacks by the guerrillas, all of which were driven off. A fourth, however, resulted in three of Campana's men being wounded and captured; only one man would be found later, having been executed by his captors.

At just after 7.00 a.m., as the battle continued, Campana himself was wounded by a bullet in the chest. His second section had meantime made its way on to high ground and brought heavy fire to bear on the guerrillas who were forced to begin a withdrawal. Minutes later, the first and third sections also joined the battle, the latter wiping out one group of guerrillas. Shortly afterwards, Campana, having regained his feet, was hit again as he prepared to lead his men in another assault, and died a few minutes later. The reinforcements duly arrived on the scene and exacted revenge by wiping out the entire guerrilla force.

March 1959 had meanwhile seen the 11e Choc involved in a mission that resulted in the defection of an ALN unit. It was one result of an operation that had taken place in October of the previous year when a four-man team of GLI 1 was infiltrated into the region of Mac Mahon, to the south of Batna. Led by Lieutenant Varennes, its task was to eliminate a senior ALN intelligence officer, named Si Hacène, known to be returning from a liaison visit in the Aurès to his base in the Hodna mountains.

An ambush was laid but by dawn on the following day Si Hacène had failed to appear. Soon afterwards, however, a member of the team spotted ALN guerrillas moving in haste through a nearby olive grove. An hour later, firing broke out in the area and the team found itself in the middle of a battle between guerrillas and troops of a French parachute unit. Unfortunately for Varennes and his men, the commander of French forces in the southern zone had neglected to give notice of a major operation in the Aurès–Nementchas region. All four members of the team were dressed in the green combat dress worn by the ALN and were in danger of being caught up in the sweep of the area being conducted by the paratroops who would undoubtedly have shot them on sight. Varennes decided to find a place where he and his three companions could lie up until the operation had passed them by but stumbled upon an ALN guerrilla who was also attempting to avoid the paratroops. Offering no resistance, he was swiftly taken prisoner and accompanied the team when it exfiltrated from the area later that day.

The prisoner, known only by the alias of Makhlouf, proved to have been forcibly recruited by the ALN in 1957. Trained as a medical orderly, he had been promoted to the rank of sergeant. In due course, he had been assigned to an ALN unit, commanded by a guerrilla named Ali Hambli and located in Tunisia, near the border with Algeria, on a plateau called the Djebel Harraba. Ali Hambli, like many senior members of the ALN, had by this time become disenchanted with the political elements within the FLN, notably its external front, the Gouvernement

Provisoire de la République Algérienne (GPRA). Eventually, relations had deteriorated to the point that there was open warfare between Ali Hambli and 'loyalist' ALN forces in the region led by Mahmoud Chérif. During these hostilities, Makhlouf had been captured and forced to serve in a loyalist unit. Eventually assigned as a trainee medical officer to an ALN unit in Wilaya I, he had been en route to his new post when captured by Varennes's team.

Makhlouf was happy to throw in his lot with the 11e Choc. In due course, he was interviewed by Colonel Léon Simoneau, commander of the CCI, who decided to mount an operation to persuade Ali Hambli and his unit to defect. Accordingly, at the end of December 1958, Makhlouf was sent into Tunisia and in early February 1959 made contact with Ali Hambli. The Djebel Harraba, however, was surrounded by loyalist ALN forces and it required an operation mounted by Ali Hambli to enable Makhlouf to reach the guerrilla commander.

Colonel Simoneau's proposal for a defection or 'rallying' to the French side met with a mixed reaction from Ali Hambli and senior members of his unit who were concerned by the fact that their men had committed bombings, sabotage attacks and assassinations during the years of the conflict. Simoneau had foreseen this, however, and agreed that they would be pardoned. Ali Hambli himself had other concerns, notably the loss of his command and influence, and thus placed conditions on his rallying to the French. First, he would be paid 1,580,000 francs; there being 158 men in his unit, this was based on the sum of 10,000 francs offered by the French for a guerrilla captured alive. Second, he was to be given politico-military responsibility for the region of Montesquieu of which he was a native and which he intended to rule as his fiefdom. Third, he would retain his captain's 'galons, badges or rank, albeit only those of an auxiliary.

Lieutenant Varennes, who had by then established a base in the area of no-man's land between the Morice Line and the Tunisian frontier, was given authority to negotiate with Ali Hambli and proceeded to the Djebel Harraba. At the ensuing talks, although he was reassured by the presence of Varennes, the guerrilla leader was not convinced that the French authorities would keep their word. Varennes therefore arranged for direct radio contact between Ali Hambli and the controller of the operation, a CCI officer identified only as 'Donald'. Eventually, agreement was reached and on 12 March Ali Hambli announced that he would rally to the French side. The date for the defection was set for the night of 15 March. The weather on the 13th, however, was bad and Ali Hambli feared that the wadis would become flooded and thus impass-able, enabling the ALN to corner and destroy his force. At dawn on the 14th, however, the weather was fine and Varennes made radio contact with his base, confirming that the operation would take place that night.

Twenty of Ali Hambli's men had opted not to rally. Despite an under-taking given to Varennes that their lives would be spared, he executed them before his departure. The guerrillas set off at 4.00 a.m. on the morning of the 15th and at dawn, led by a group of eight machine-gunners, punched a breach through the positions of the loyalist forces and Tunisian National Guard surrounding the Djebel Harraba. Flank protection groups protected the main body of the unit as it rushed pell-mell through the breach and down into the valley below while a rear-guard dealt with any follow-up. The Tunisians reacted swiftly, deploying units by vehicle to fight a delaying action in an attempt to allow other ALN forces to carry out an encircling movement to block Ali Hambli's route. After a delay of 30 minutes, however, the latter succeeded in breaking through, crossing an 800-metre-wide stretch of ground to a river bed which provided cover. Thereafter, led by Varennes, the fleeing guerrillas made good their escape towards the barrier of the Morice Line where they were met by French infantry and armour which had been alerted by the firing.

Such was the secrecy of the CCI's involvement in the operation that Varennes, whose dark features and ability to pass himself off as an Arab were the reason for his being selected for this type of mission, was not permitted to identify himself to the French troops at the barrier. He and Makhlouf were consequently rounded up with Ali Hambli and his men with whom they remained until the arrival of 'Donald'. Ostensibly taken away for interrogation, Varennes and Makhlouf were flown by helicopter to the 11e Choc base at Tipasa.

While the defection of Ali Hambli and his unit was of great propa-ganda value to the French, the psychological warfare specialists of the Cinquième Bureau exploiting it to the full, the aftermath posed con-siderable problems. Regarding them with disfavour, the SAS was unwill-ing to allow Ali Hambli and his men to settle in the Souk-Ahras area, seeing them as troublemakers. Once again, the problem was handed to the 11e Choc and DS 111 to resolve. The latter responded by reorganising the 130 guerrillas into two counter-guerrilla units, the first based at Ain Zana while the other, judged to be the better of the two, was under the command of Ali Hambli and was given the role of conducting operations against the ALN in Tunisia.

Ali Hambli's unit, given the codename ALIAS, did not perform well on its first mission which was aimed at the headquarters of the ALN's East Base in Tunisia, on the outskirts of Ghardimaou. The counter-guerrillas proved completely ineffective and were forced to withdraw, pursued by companies of ALN, towards the border where a DS 111 team was waiting to recover them. But before reaching it, they were heavily attacked and fled in panic. It took some time for the DS 111 team to reach them and air support had to called in to cover their withdrawal to the Morice Line. As a result of this fiasco, Major Ignace Mantéï took the decision to disband ALIAS which was eventually dispersed throughout the Constantine area. As for Ali Hambli, he was despatched into retirement, no longer needed by the French, sentenced to death by the ALN and rejected by his own men who blamed him for having failed to obtain the right for them to become civilians. In November 1959, he died in a traffic accident while driving from Montesquieu to Clairefontaine, his car colliding with a telegraph pole after apparently skidding off a very straight stretch of road.

By the beginning of 1960, it had become apparent to the *pieds noirs* and the Army in Algeria that de Gaulle had made clear his support for independence for Algeria. In September of the previous year, he had broadcast a speech advocating 'self-determination' for the country. This had resulted in swiftly mounting disaffection within the Army in Algeria, particularly among the parachute units which had borne the brunt of the fighting against the ALN since the arrival of General Challe. In January the much respected General Jacques Massu was removed by de Gaulle and despatched to France as the commander of the garrison of Metz, after stating to a journalist, ' I myself, and the majority of officers in a position of command, will not execute unconditionally the orders of the Head of State.'

Massu's departure enraged the *pieds noirs*, and those plotting against de Gaulle took the opportunity to use it as an excuse to launch a further outburst of insurrection. On 24 January a general strike took place, accompanied by a mass demonstration in the Plateau des Glières in Algiers. Army units, principally the regiments of the 10ème Division de Parachutiste withdrawn from the djebels by General Challe to help in the maintenance of public order, refused to deploy against the *pieds noirs*. The latter became involved, during the following days in what became known as 'Barricades Week', in running battles with gendarmes and the much-hated paramilitary troops of the Compagnies Républicaines de Sécurité (CRS). On the evening of 29 January, however, de Gaulle appeared on television and addressed France and the Army in Algeria, appealing for the latter's loyalty and obedience. He succeeded totally and the insurrection in Algeria ended two days later.

The fall-out was considerable and de Gaulle set out to purge those elements within the Army known or suspected of involvement in the plots against him. Among them was General Challe, now appointed commander of French forces in NATO, his place being taken by General Jean-Albert-Emile Crépin who had replaced Massu but had since been promoted to take over his new appointment. They also included some of those fighting the secret war against the FLN, one of whom was Colonel Léon Simoneau, the commander of the CCI, who was transferred back to France. The CCI itself was disbanded, its role being assumed by the Bureau des Etudes et des Liaisons (BEL) under Colonel Henri Jacquin, formerly head of the Foreign Legion's BSLE and of the Deuxième Bureau in Algiers. During 1959, the BEL had absorbed Captain Christian Léger's Groupement de Renseignement et d'Exploitation (GRE), continuing its deception and misinformation operations which by the end of 1960 would result in the ALN executing nearly 5,000 guerrillas suspected of collaborating with the French. This figure has never been substantiated but undoubtedly large numbers of guerrillas arrested and subsequently released by the French were purged, leading to further defections from the ALN by guerrillas who not only sought to escape retribution but also were losing faith in the revolution. Yet such results were not without their drawbacks; on occasions, the purges inspired by them resulted in the deaths of agents controlled by other intelligence units.

Others similarly removed from Algeria, because of their known or suspected involvement in the conspiracies and plotting, included former

11e Choc and Cinquième Bureau commander Colonel Yves Godard, Colonel Antoine Argoud, who had succeeded Godard at the Cinquième Bureau, and 3e RPC commander and counter-insurgency expert Colonel Roger Trinquier. Several renowned members of the 11e Choc left its ranks, among them Captains de la Bourdonnaye-Montluc, Michel Badaire and Ade. Along with Trinquier, several duly reappeared as mercenaries in the secessionist Zairean province of Katanga, in Central Africa, and later in the Middle East where they fought alongside Yemeni royalists against the Egyptian forces of Colonel Gamal Abd al-Nasser. The 11e Choc itself, however, retained its presence in Algeria with the DS 111 which was now under the direct control of the commander-in-chief himself.

Meanwhile, the war against the ALN continued unabated. At the end of January 1960, a BEL officer, Captain Heux, made contact with certain senior figures led by Si Lakhdar, the intelligence chief of the ALN's Wilaya IV. The guerrillas intimated that they wished to see an end to the war and accept the 'Peace of the Brave' advocated by de Gaulle, hinting that many in the ranks of the ALN had become disenchanted, blaming the GPRA for letting them down. As a relatively junior officer, Heux could only report these facts to his superiors in Algiers, which he did and thereafter occupied himself with other matters. This was as well for him, as the affair was to have dire consequences for those embroiled in it.

On 17 March, Si Lakhdar, accompanied by Halim and Abdellatif, respectively the political and military heads of Wilaya IV, made their way to Médéa where they appeared at the house of the local caïd to whom they announced that Mohamed Zamounn, alias Si Salah, the leader of Wilaya IV, wished to negotiate peace with the French. They insisted, however, that he would only do so with the French government in Paris.

News of the Wilaya IV delegation's appearance was transmitted immediately to Colonel Jacquin of the BEL who relayed it to Paris and President de Gaulle. The latter responded by despatching two emissaries, his personal aide, Bernard Tricot, and Colonel Mathon, a member of staff of the Prime Minister, Michel Debré, who met the three guerrillas at the Médéa prefecture on 28 March. Three days later another meeting took place. Having satisfied themselves that the guerrillas were genuine, Tricot and Mathon, accompanied by Colonel Jacquin, then attended a series of discussions in which Si Salah's spokesmen put forward their proposals and demands. The latter included two that were unacceptable: the three guerrillas wished to seek the opinion of Ben Bella, still imprisoned by the French, and wanted to travel to Tunis to lobby the FLN leadership there. It was agreed that there should be a breathing space of eight weeks while Lakhdar and his companions sought further support for their proposals, during which the French would cease all operations in Wilaya IV. Fears of possible duplicity on the part of the guerrillas were allayed by Colonel Jacquin whose radio interception service confirmed that the Wilaya IV hierarchy had broken away from the GPRA.

In May, matters took a major leap forward when the French issued an invitation for the Wilaya IV leadership to attend a meeting in Paris. On 9 June, Si Salah, his deputy Si Mohammed, and Si Lakhdar flew to Paris accompanied by Bernard Tricot and Colonel Jacquin. On the following day, the three men were taken to the Elysée Palace where they attended an interview with President de Gaulle who informed them that he would shortly be appealing to the GPRA to declare a ceasefire; if this met with refusal, he would be adopting the proposals discussed and agreed during the meetings in Algeria.

De Gaulle's appeal to the GPRA was broadcast on 14 June. Rather than calling for a ceasefire, however, it extended an invitation to the GPRA to open negotiations with him in Paris. This outraged the Army and in particular those senior officers, such as Colonel Jacquin, who were well aware that Si Salah had gone to Paris on the basis that the French would not resume contact with the GPRA. Nevertheless, on 18 June, Jacquin accompanied Si Salah to Kabylia where the latter was due to meet Mohand Ou El-Hadj, the commander of Wilaya III, to elicit his support. Two days later, the GPRA announced that it would accept de Gaulle's invitation.

In Si Salah's absence, meanwhile, Si Mohamed had shown his true colours. Returning to the fold of the GPRA, apparently under threat of death, he had Si Lakhdar executed along with Abdellatif, Halim and others who had knowledge of the talks with the French and the secret trip to Paris. He went on to capture and imprison Si Salah after the latter's return from Wilaya III. A year later, on the orders of the GPRA, Si Salah was summoned to appear before it in Tunis and set off with an escort of twelve guerrillas. En route, however, while passing through the Djurdjura, he and his companions encountered a patrol of the Chasseurs Alpins and in the ensuing contact he was shot dead.

Of those who had met de Gaulle in Paris, only Si Mohamed remained alive and thus was an embarrassing witness to what became known in high-level French military and government circles as the 'Si Salah Affair'. The decision had been taken at the highest level that the entire affair should be covered up and indeed President de Gaulle himself was quoted as warning, 'Personne ne parlera de l'affaire Si Salah. Et celui qui en parlera n'en parlera pas longtemps' (No one will speak of the Si Salah affair. And he who does speak of it will not speak for long). Moreover, the BEL was determined to make Si Mohamed pay dearly for his treachery. But he had disappeared and evaded several traps set for him. In August 1961, however, the BEL's radio interception service picked up a transmitter in the area of Blida in southern Algeria.

At this juncture, Colonel Jacquin turned to the 11e Choc and handed it the task of eliminating Si Mohamed. A fifteen-man detachment, commanded by Captain Bréval and comprising three teams of three men equipped with radio direction-finders (DF) and one assault team, was despatched from the 11e Choc base on Corsica and deployed in Blida. During the following days, the three DF teams monitored the transmissions which were too short in duration for bearings to be fixed by the direction-finders. On several occasions they were resumed two hours later from different locations.

Bréval and his men kept a listening watch 24 hours a day, the three DF teams criss-crossing Blida and its outskirts, each dressed as troops apparently going about their everyday duties. Eventually, their patience paid off. Some ten days after their arrival, one of the DF teams picked up the signal from Si Mohamed's transmitter, recognising the distinctive hoarse tones of the Wilaya IV leader who was issuing a series of orders. On this occasion, for some unknown reason, he appeared to have abandoned his usual security precaution of minimising the length of his transmissions and remained on the air sufficiently long for the three DF teams to obtain bearings. When plotted on Captain Bréval's map, the intersection of the three lines indicated the location of Si Mohamed's transmitter in a group of three buildings in a village on the outskirts of Blida.

Under cover of darkness, Bréval and his men travelled to the area by vehicle, carrying out their final approach on foot. While observing one of the three buildings, Bréval himself spotted a radio antenna cable fastened to a piece of wood projecting from the roof. Deploying his three DF teams in positions where they could block anyone attempting to escape, he prepared to lead his assault team across twenty metres of open ground to the main entrance to the building. As he did so, however, a guerrilla sentry opened fire from an area of open ground between the building and its neighbour. With surprise lost, Bréval ordered his vehicles to switch on their headlights, illuminating the building. At the same time, he ordered his second-in-command, a lieutenant, and three other members of the assault team to move round to the other side of the house to create a diversion. As the four men moved round the opposite side of the house, the young officer was hit by a burst of fire from a window which killed him instantly. The soldier behind him responded swiftly by lobbing a grenade into the room, silencing all further opposition. Bréval and one other man meanwhile had reached the main entrance to the building. Firing as they went, they entered swiftly and found Si Mohamed and a young guerrilla lying dead in one room. In another, they found three more guerrillas: one had been killed and two wounded by the grenade thrown through the window.

A search of the building revealed a cache of documents, two radio sets, three carbines, three machine-pistols and a quantity of ammunition. Just as Bréval and his men were regrouping, however, there was a burst of fire as a hitherto unobserved guerrilla fled for his life, followed by Master Sergeant Bièvres who pursued him into a nearby automobile scrapyard and municipal rubbish dump. A fire fight ensued but eventually Bièvres succeeded in shooting dead his adversary. Thus the 11e Choc eliminated the last of those who were witnesses to the 'Si Salah' affair. On the following day Captain Bréval and his detachment left Algiers and returned to their base on Corsica.

In the meantime there had been yet another uprising. In April 1961, an attempted putsch was mounted in Algeria and France by four generals, Raoul Salan, Maurice Challe, Edmond Jouhaud and André Zeller, the latter two having retired as Chief-of-Staff of the Armée de l'Air and Chief-of-Staff of France's ground forces respectively. Once again France, which was suffering from increasing industrial and social unrest at the time, appeared to be under threat of civil war with elements of the Army, notably elements of its airborne forces, supporting the idea of a *coup d'état*. Moreover, it was subjected to attacks by the Organisation Armée Secrète (OAS) which was continuing the fight for 'Algérie Française' through the use of terrorism, and whose shootings and bombings, known as 'plastiquages', became almost nightly events on the streets of Algiers. The irony was that the leaders of the OAS were none other than those who only shortly beforehand had been orchestrating French counter-terrorist operations throughout Algeria. In addition to Generals Salan (the organisation's chief), Challe, Jouhaud and Zeller, they included General Paul Gardy, former Inspector-General of the Foreign Legion; Colonel Yves Godard, former commander of the 11e Choc and chief of the Cinquième Bureau; Colonel Antoine Argoud, Godard's successor at the Bureau; and Colonel Jean Gardes, former chief of the Deuxième Bureau at Rabat. In effect, the counter-terrorist 'gamekeepers' had become 'poachers', adopting the very methods of terrorism to pursue their cause.

After four days, however, the putsch failed as the population and the Army responded to an appeal for loyalty and support from de Gaulle. Some parachute regiments, including the Foreign Legion's renowned 1er REP, had sided with the plotters and subsequently were punished with disbandment.

On 18 March 1962, the long-running negotiations between the French and the GPRA over a ceasefire and independence culminated in the signing of an agreement. The ceasefire took effect on the following day and on 3 July France recognised Algeria's independence.

After the war ended, the 11e DBPC de Choc regrouped in Corsica. Despite the brutally efficient and dedicated way in which it had disposed of France's enemies in Indochina and Algeria, the writing was on the wall and it was not to escape de Gaulle's purge of those units he considered to be suspect. Colonel François Decorse, who had been in command for some eight years, was promoted to general and posted elsewhere. Meanwhile, the officers and men of the 11e Choc were subjected to in-depth scrutiny and vetting by the French Army's notorious Securité Militaire. One long-serving and highly distinguished officer was removed on the grounds that a general known to be a vehement opponent of independence for Algeria was godfather to his son.

Colonel Decorse was replaced by Lieutenant Colonel Albert Merglen, a committed Gaullist, whose brief was ostensibly to reorganise the 11e Choc. In fact, he oversaw the dismantling of the entire demi-brigade which had ceased to exist by the end of the year. Many officers and men were discharged, their services no longer required. Those personnel considered totally reliable politically were posted to Lorraine in the Moselle, in north-eastern France, where they formed the initial core element of the 13ème Régiment de Dragons Parachutistes (13e RDP). This unit was in the process of becoming one of the military elements of the SDECE's Action Service, a role that it continues to carry out today for the Direction Générale de Sécurité Extérieure (DGSE) which replaced the SDECE in April 1982. Others were assigned to four newly created training establishments, the Centres Nationaux d'Entrainement Commandos (CNEC). By the end of 1962, the 11e Choc had disappeared completely, suffering the same fate as the CCI, BEL, GRE and other elements of the secret war in Algeria.

Twenty-three years later, the 11e Choc rose like a phoenix from the ashes. On 1 November 1985, it was reformed on the orders of President François Mitterrand as the 11ème Bataillon de Parachutiste de Choc but was subsequently redesignated the 11ème Régiment de Parachutiste de Choc (11e RPC). A decade later, however, it met its final demise when, on 30 June 1995, it was disbanded again and its functions replaced by three 'stations': the Centre Parachutiste d'Entrainements Specialisés (CPES) in Cercottes, the Centre Parachutiste d'Instructions Specialisés (CIPS) in Perpignan and the Centre Parachutiste aux Opérations Maritime (CPEOM) in Roscanvel, the last subsequently being moved to Quellern in Brittany.

CHAPTER SEVEN

BORNEO 1962–1966

Although Malaya attained full independence in 1957, Britain had retained its forces in the country and in neighbouring Singapore. These consisted mainly of 17 Gurkha Division, comprising 63 and 99 Gurkha Infantry Brigades based respectively at Seremban, in Negri Sembilan, and in Singapore, and 28 Commonwealth Brigade at Terendak in Malacca. Singapore also still accommodated extensive dockyards and airfields belonging to the Royal Navy and Royal Air Force.

With the United States engaged in a major conflict against communism in South Vietnam, and secretly so in Laos, the late 1950s had seen the beginning of the period of the 'domino theory' and the fear that the fall of South Vietnam would result in the rest of South-East Asia falling under the communist yoke. Communism was spilling over from North Vietnam into Laos and Cambodia, and it was feared that Thailand would be next. All British threat assessments and planning with regard to Malaya were thus concentrated towards the north of the country and its northern neighbour. In fact, a far more imminent threat was beginning to fester in a wholly different direction, from Indonesia to the south across the Straits of Malacca.

Indonesia is an archipelago of 13,670 islands extending some 3,200 miles from the island of Sumatra in the west to New Guinea in the east, and approximately 1,000 miles from north to south. The southern side of the island chain includes Sumatra, Java, Bali, Lombok, Sumbawa, Flores and Timor. North of these is Borneo, the third largest island in the world, which at the beginning of the 1960s comprised Indonesian Kalimantan and the British colonial territories of Sarawak, Brunei and North Borneo.

The country's population in the early 1960s numbered some 80 million, its ancestors having migrated from mainland Asia prior to 1000BC. It is predominantly Muslim, Islam having been brought to northern Sumatra by Indian traders in the thirteenth century and then spreading throughout the other islands in the archipelago with the exception of Bali which remained Hindu. In 1511, the Portuguese arrived in the Spice Islands (now the Moluccas) being followed by the Spaniards,

Dutch and British. Subsequently the Dutch East India Company, with its headquarters in Batavia (now Djakarta), established colonial control over Java, Sumatra and the Spice Islands. By the end of the seventeenth century, it had extended it to most of the archipelago which was by then known as the Dutch East Indies.

In 1927, the Indonesia Nationalist Party (PNI) was formed under Ahmed Sukarno with the aim of pursuing independence from the Netherlands. Two years later, however, he and other PNI leaders were arrested and imprisoned for two years at Bandung, the capital of Jawa Barat province on the island of Java, before being sent into exile for eight years on Flores and Sumatra. In 1942, the Dutch East Indies were invaded by the Japanese who, having interned all Dutch administrative personnel, appointed Indonesians to some of their positions instead. Sukarno was among a number of nationalist and Islamic leaders who accepted appointments. In March 1943, having convinced his new masters that Indonesian support could best be mobilised by an organisation which represented genuine Indonesian aspirations, he formed a party called Pusat Tenaga Rakjat (Centre of the People's Power) which proved an effective platform on which to establish himself as leader of the Indonesian nation. In March 1944, however, the Japanese, who felt that it was serving Indonesian interests rather than their own, replaced Sukarno's organisation with the Dkawa Hokokai (People's Loyalty Organisation) which was kept under tight control. In September, they announced that they were preparing to grant independence.

On 14 August 1945, however, Japan surrendered unconditionally to the Allies and on the 17th Sukarno proclaimed independence for Indonesia, establishing his seat of power at Jogjakarta on Java. But in early December, British troops of the 23rd Indian Division entered the Javanese capital of Batavia to restore law and order and protect the thousands of civilian internees and prisoners-of-war who had been incarcerated by the Japanese. Dutch forces then arrived in February 1946 and during the following four years attempted to regain control of the country, but failed to do so. On 27 December 1949, independence was formally granted to Indonesia, with the exception of Irian Bayat (West New Guinea – now called Irian Jaya) which remained under Dutch control.

Sukarno was installed as the country's first president. The next six

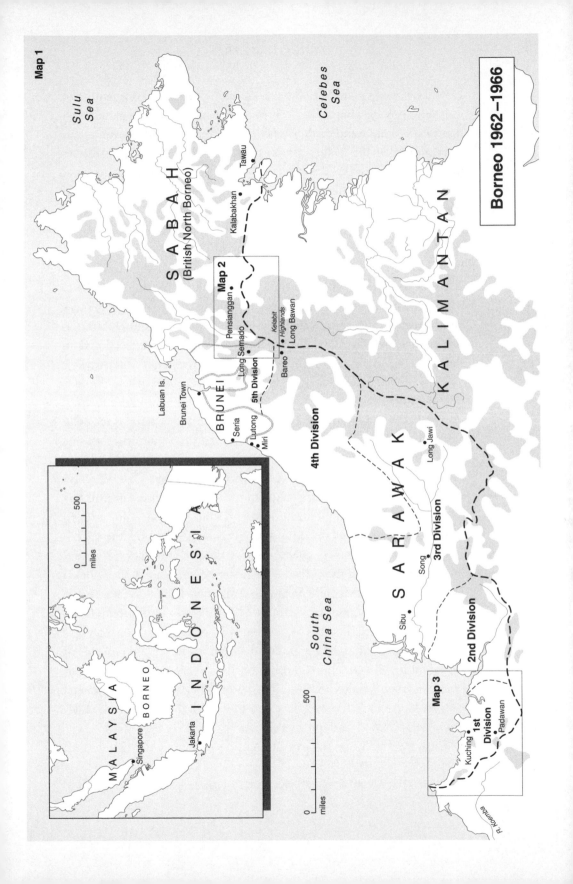

Map 1

Borneo 1962–1966

Sulu Sea

Celebes Sea

SABAH
(British North Borneo)

Tawau

Kalabakhan

Map 2

Pensianggan

Long Semado

Kelabit Highlands

Bareo

Long Bawan

5th Division

Labuan Is.

Brunei Town

BRUNEI

Seria

Lutong

Miri

4th Division

KALIMANTAN

Long Jawi

SARAWAK

Song

3rd Division

Sibu

South China Sea

2nd Division

Map 3

Kuching

1st Division

Padawan

R. Koemba

500

miles

0

MALAYSIA

Singapore

BORNEO

INDONESIA

Jakarta

500

miles

0

500

0

miles

years, however, saw little in the way of a much-needed programme of reorganisation, administration, rehabilitation and development although there were, admittedly, gains in health and education. The economy was in a parlous state but that did not prevent Sukarno from launching extravagant projects with the aim of encouraging cultural self-awareness and self-expression as part of a programme to promote the new national identity. In this he succeeded but at a ruinous cost.

The first general election to be held in Indonesia took place at the end of September 1955 and was won narrowly by Sukarno and the PNI which secured 57 seats in the House of Representatives. Among the other parties gaining seats was the Indonesian Communist Party (PKI) which won 39 and thereafter wasted little time in expanding its power base throughout the country. In provincial elections held in July 1957, the communists won 34 per cent of the total votes, a larger proportion than that achieved by any one of the country's other three political parties.

In early 1958, while Sukarno was out of the country, a group of senior military officers and politicians formed a new government, the Revolutionary Government of the Indonesian Republic (PRRI) under the country's vice president, Mohammad Hatta, and shortly afterwards insurrection broke out on Sulawesi and Sumatra. By the middle of the year, these had been put down by the Army whose position within the country was thereafter strengthened, with Lieutenant General Abdul Haris Nasution emerging as the most powerful military leader. In order to offset the Army's power, Sukarno strengthened his ties with the PKI.

In July 1960, he issued a decree dissolving the House of Representatives and marking the introduction of a system known as 'Guided Democracy'. In March of the following year, a new legislature, the House of People's Representatives – Mutual Self-Help was established. Of its 238 seats, 154 were allocated to members of so-called 'functional groups' including the military whose political element was named Golkar. All representatives were appointed rather than elected, with 25 per cent being reserved for the PKI. Another body, the 616-strong Provisional People's Consultative Assembly, was formed, with the leader of the PKI, Dipa Nusantara, as its deputy chairman.

The early 1960s saw Sukarno attempting to remove the Dutch from Irian Bayat, the western half of New Guinea. The eastern part was an Australian trust territory; so it appeared that there could also be a threat

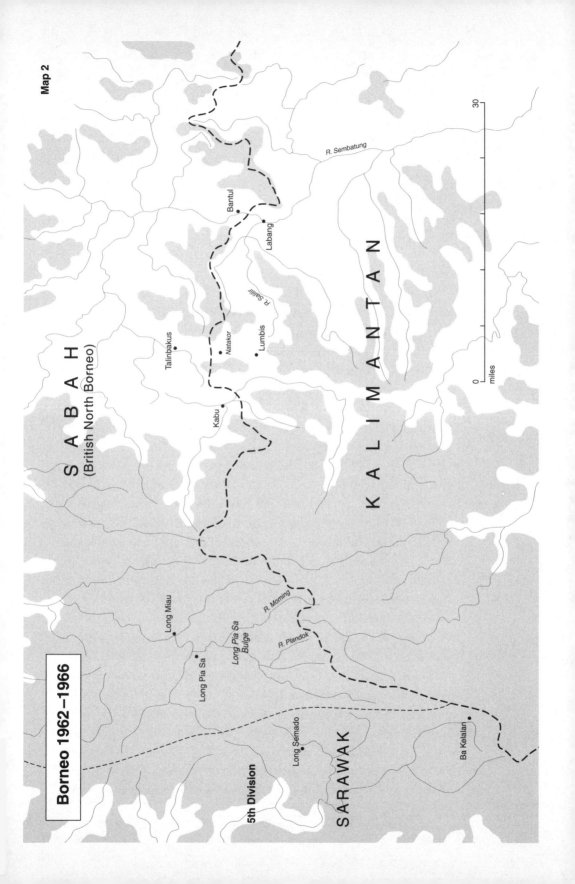

Map 2

Borneo 1962–1966

SABAH
(British North Borneo)

KALIMANTAN

SARAWAK

5th Division

R. Sembatung

Bantul
Labang

R. Salilir

Talinbakus
Natakor
Lumbis

Kabu

Long Miau

Long Pia Sa
Bulge

R. Morning

R. Plandok

Long Pia Sa

Long Semado

Ba Kelalan

miles

0   30

to Commonwealth interests. During 1962, however, the Netherlands agreed to transfer transitional responsibility for Irian Bayat to the United Nations. Sukarno, who by this time was enjoying huge popularity, recognised this as a victory on his part and on 17 August proclaimed 1962 as a 'year of triumph'.

In neighbouring Malaya, meanwhile, the end of 1961 had seen the Prime Minister, Tunku Abdul Rahman, announce plans for a Federation of Malaysia incorporating Malaya, Singapore, Sarawak, Brunei and North Borneo. All but one of the states were receptive to this proposal, as was Britain whose Conservative government under Harold Macmillan was seeking to divest itself of the country's remaining colonies. The exception was the oil and gas-rich British protectorate of Brunei whose ruler, the Sultan, Sir Omar Ali Saifuddin, wished Britain to continue maintaining responsibility for its defence and foreign affairs.

Sukarno, however, had his own plans for Malaya, Singapore and the entire island of Borneo, incorporating them with Indonesia and the Philippines in a federation named 'Maphilindo' which, with a population of 150 million and unlimited natural resources, he foresaw as being a bloc capable of rivalling in economic power the United States, the Soviet Union and China. His plan included the removal of British forces, a proposal unwelcome not only to the British themselves but also to Tunku Abdul Rahman and Lee Kwan Yew, Prime Minister of Singapore, who feared the threat of communism to the north. The Tunku's proposal threatened to thwart the ambitions of Sukarno, who attacked it bitterly, condemning it as a neo-colonial stratagem by imperialists attempting to encircle Indonesia. In Kuala Lumpur and London, however, while there was some concern at the growth of communism in Indonesia, Sukarno's aggressive rhetoric was not taken seriously. Moreover, he appeared to be primarily occupied with recovering Irian Bayat from the Dutch. There was thus no inkling of any impending trouble.

In December 1962, however, insurrection suddenly exploded without warning in Brunei. A British protectorate from 1888 until granted independence in January 1984, Brunei is located on the north-west coast of Borneo. Although covering only some 2,200 square miles, it possesses huge resources of oil and natural gas as well as minerals. In the early 1960s its population numbered some 85,000 of which just over a half was Malay and a further quarter Chinese, the remainder comprising

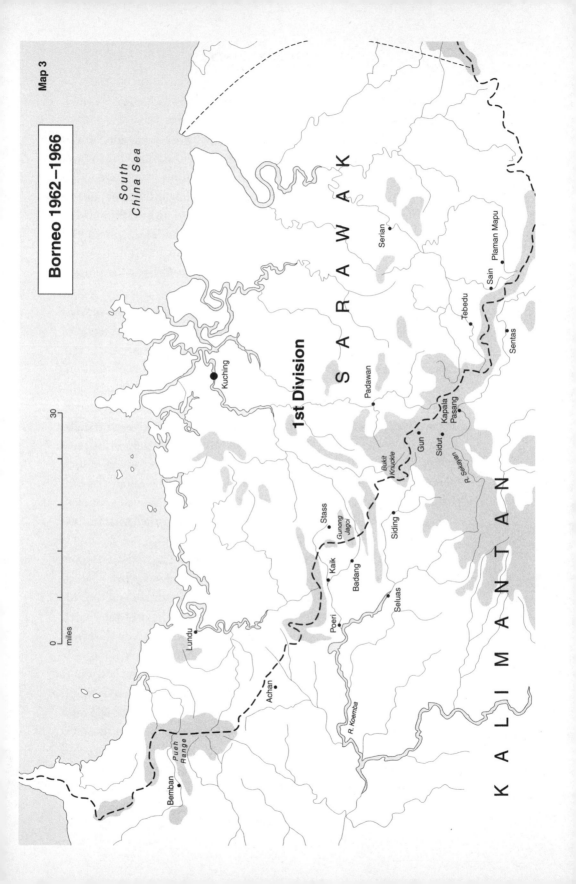

Map 3

Borneo 1962–1966

South
China Sea

30

0

miles

Kuching

1st Division

S A R A W A K

Serian

Padawan

Sain

Plaman Mapu

Tebedu

Sentas

Kapala
Pasang

Gun

Sidut

R. Sekayan

Bukit
Knuckle

Siding

Stass

Gunong
Jagoi

Kaik

Badang

Seluas

Poeri

Lundu

Achan

R. Koemba

K A L I M A N T A N

Pueh
Range

Bemban

Iban, Punan and other tribes inhabiting the jungle-clad interior, primarily along the banks of the Brunei, Tutong and Belait Rivers.

Oil had been discovered in 1929 but despite the huge income derived by the Sultan from the concession granted to the Shell Petroleum Company, there was little benefit to the population which depended principally on agriculture. The country suffered from insufficient housing as well as inadequate health and education services, the situation being exacerbated by the inefficiency and corruption endemic among the ruling element who enjoyed fabulous wealth. This inevitably caused resentment which in 1953 boiled over into a revolt which was suppressed without difficulty.

The Sultan enjoyed absolute rule and it was not until 1962, in what was perceived to be a half-hearted attempt to introduce a façade of democracy, that he permitted elections for a legislative council. He did, however, place a limitation on this by decreeing that he would nominate more than half the members for the new body, the rest to be contested. The election took place in September and all contested seats were won by the Partai Ra'ayat (People's Party) which advocated unification with Sarawak and North Borneo, followed by federation with Malaysia. The idea behind this proposal was that such a combined state would be sufficiently powerful to resist domination by Malaya or Singapore. The Sultan, somewhat naturally, was opposed to such a scheme, feeling little inclination to share his massive oil revenues with his two neighbours.

The Partai Ra'ayat possessed a secret military wing named the Tentera Nasional Kalimantan Utara (North Kalimantan National Army), better known by its initials of TNKU. Headed by an individual named A. M. Azahari, who had fought alongside the Indonesians against the Dutch after the return of the latter in 1946, it enjoyed close links with Sukarno's regime in Indonesia which provided guerrilla warfare training for TNKU officers, including their commander Yassan Affendi. By the latter part of 1962, the TNKU numbered some 4,000 men. Of these only 2,250 were fully trained, being organised in fifteen companies of 150 men each. They were, however, poorly armed, being equipped with only a small quantity of modern military small arms, some 1,000 shotguns and large quantities of spears and parangs (jungle knives similar to machetes).

An initial indication of trouble appeared in April 1962 in the form of a report in a local newspaper about training being conducted in the jungle by rebel groups, and bulk purchases of olive drab cloth being made in the bazaars. This went unheeded. A further warning came in early November in neighbouring Sarawak, which was divided into 'divisions' for administrative purposes. Richard Morris, the British Resident responsible for the Fifth Division, received information that trouble was brewing in Brunei and passed it to the authorities in Sarawak's capital of Kuching. A Special Branch investigation, however, revealed no real evidence of a planned insurrection. On 23 November, however, Morris passed on further information which stated that an uprising would occur after 19 December. Although, once again, no firm evidence of such was forthcoming, a warning was passed to the Commander-in-Chief Far East, Admiral Sir David Luce, who instructed his Chief of Staff, Major General Brian Wyldbore-Smith, to assess contingency plans for counter-insurgency operations in Brunei and to update them in view of the reports of impending trouble.

On 6 December, a further report was received from Morris in Sarawak that the rebellion was due to begin on the morning of the 8th. On the following day, the Resident of the Fourth Division was warned that trouble was imminent. The authorities in Brunei and throughout Sarawak were alerted and a detachment of the Sarawak Police Field Force (PFF) was despatched to the coastal town of Miri, some 20 miles west of the border with Brunei. At the same time, the commander of an RAF detachment on the island of Labuan, situated six miles off the north-western coast Borneo in the South China Sea, flew a PFF platoon from the North Borneo capital of Jesselton to Brunei Town to reinforce the police there.

The insurgency began at 2.00 a.m. on the morning of the 8 December, with attacks throughout Brunei. In the capital, Brunei Town, assaults were mounted by 300 rebels on the Sultan's palace and the Prime Minister's residence. These were beaten off but the TNKU captured the capital's power station and cut off all electricity. At the same time, raids were launched on police stations in the towns of Tutong and Seria, and in the district of Temburong. Outside Brunei, further attacks took place in the western region of North Borneo and in the Fifth Division of Sarawak where the rebels captured the capital town of Limbang.

First reports of trouble reached Singapore and Admiral Luce's headquarters in the early hours of 8 December and at 4.00 a.m. Headquarters

99 Gurkha Infantry Brigade was ordered to place its stand-by unit, the 1st Battalion The Queen's Own Highlanders (1 QOH), on 48 hours' alert to deploy to Brunei. The highlanders, however, were training on the west of coast of Malaya and so the 1st Battalion 2nd Gurkha Rifles (1/2GR), based at Slim Barracks in Singapore, was detailed for the task instead. That afternoon a force comprising C and D Companies and a small tactical headquarters took off from Singapore in three RAF Beverley transports, a Britannia and a Hastings, and flew to Brunei via Labuan. From there they were ferried to Brunei Town whose runway could only accommodate the Beverleys.

During that night, opposition was encountered and cleared by D Company in Brunei Town where at least 24 rebels were killed. Meanwhile C Company drove west to Seria, encountering opposition beyond Sengkurong and at Tutong where the rebels suffered seven killed, 20 wounded and 100 captured. On the following day the commanding officer, Lieutenant Colonel Gordon Shakespear, and his battalion headquarters arrived from Singapore while A Company was flown ten miles down the Sarawak coast where it secured the oilfield installations and airfield at Lutong and the oilfield at Miri. On the morning of 10 December, Headquarters 99 Gurkha Infantry Brigade landed at Brunei Town. On the 11th, 1 QOH landed at Anduki Airfield, recapturing it from the rebels and subsequently mounting an attack on Seria. That same day saw the arrival at Anduki of B Company 1/2GR which cleared the remaining town of Kuala Belait where four rebels were killed and sixteen wounded.

Elsewhere, other British units were also involved in tackling the rebels. In Sarawak's Fifth Division, 42 Commando Royal Marines recaptured the town of Limbang after sailing up the Sungei Limbang in two lighters, while in the Fourth Division the TNKU was routed by the 1st Battalion The Royal Green Jackets (1 RGJ).

Within a week, the rebellion had been crushed and British forces were in full control of Brunei and Sarawak. The security troops had lost seven killed and 28 wounded while rebel losses totalled 40 killed, 1,897 captured and detained, and 1,500 supporters packed off to their homes. The remainder of the TNKU either fled into the jungle, intending to carry on their struggle from there, or returned to their homes ready to take up arms again once the British had departed. Some of those seeking to cross the border from Sarawak into Kalimantan were intercepted by an irregular force of Kelabit tribesmen, led by the curator of the Sarawak Museum, Tom Harrisson, who had served with SOE's Force 136 during the Second World War, raising the tribes against the Japanese. Meanwhile, the two leaders of the rebellion, Azahari and Yassan Affendi, remained at large.

Any hopes Sukarno may have harboured of a rapid British withdrawal, however, were soon dashed. On 19 December, Major General Walter Walker, hitherto the commander of 17 Gurkha Infantry Division, arrived in Brunei as Commander British Forces and Director of Operations in Borneo. He swiftly set out to mop up all remaining elements of the TNKU by August 1963, that being the date set for the creation of the Federation of Malaysia. Three weeks after the rebellion British forces had been increased throughout the region. Brunei and eastern Sarawak became the responsibilities of 99 Gurkha Infantry Brigade which comprised 1/2GR (relieved in early February by the 1st Battalion 7th Gurkha Rifles (1/7GR)), 1 QOH, 1 RGJ, and 40 and 42 Commandos RM (the latter less one company). Headquarters 3 Commando Brigade, plus a company of 42 Commando and a Royal Artillery battery in the infantry role, was deployed in western Sarawak. Meanwhile, a company of 1 QOH was stationed in the area of Tawau in North Borneo. Local forces comprised the Royal Brunei Malay Regiment, the Sarawak Rangers, the police constabularies of each territory and an irregular force of 4,000 tribesmen under Tom Harrisson.

On 18 May in Brunei, troops of the 2nd Battalion 7th Gurkha Rifles (2/7GR) were led by an informer through a mangrove swamp to an area where a rebel camp was located. Mounting an attack on it, the Gurkhas flushed out the occupants towards a number of ambushes laid by other elements of 2/7GR. Ten rebels were killed or captured. Among those taken prisoner was Yassan Affendi, his capture effectively bringing to an end the rebellion in Brunei. It was later discovered that Azahari was in Indonesia and thus well out of reach of the British.

As further troops were committed to the theatre, Walker's forces were subsequently reorganised into three brigades. Central and East Brigades were responsible for Brunei, part of Sarawak's Fifth Division and Sabah, while West Brigade covered the remaining four divisions of Sarawak. Central and East Brigades were initially commanded by Walker's deputy,

Brigadier Jack Glennie, who hitherto had been the Brigadier General Staff at Headquarters Far East in Singapore, while West Brigade was under Brigadier F. C. 'Billy' Barton, commander of 3 Commando Brigade. In January 1964, however, the latter handed over to Brigadier A. G. 'Pat' Patterson of 99 Gurkha Infantry Brigade.

RAF air support consisted of medium-range transports in the form of Hastings and Beverleys, the latter capable of operating from jungle airstrips, and short-range Single and Twin Pioneers. In addition, helicopter support was provided by RAF Belvederes, Sycamores and Whirlwinds, and by the Wessex and Whirlwinds of the Fleet Air Arm's 845 and 846 Naval Air Squadrons. The last two arrived with the commando carrier HMS *Albion* which was accompanied by a number of frigates and inshore minesweepers, the latter being of limited use due to their top speed of fifteen knots. Although the Royal Navy had disbanded its Coastal Forces at the end of the Second World War, it still possessed motor torpedo and gun boats of the Brave and Dark classes but there would have been major problems in transferring them to the Far East. In the event, however, the initially feared threat posed by the Indonesian Navy's fast patrol craft did not arise.

Undaunted by the failure of the rebellion in Brunei, Sukarno set out to sabotage Tunku Abdul Rahman's plans for the establishment of Malaysia. His initial idea was to separate Sarawak and North Borneo from any federation by using a combination of political and military measures, the latter to include guerrilla warfare.

Situated in the northern and north-western areas of Borneo, the state of Sarawak (now called East Malaysia) occupies some 47,000 square miles. As mentioned earlier, it was at that time divided into five divisions for administrative purposes, each under the authority of a British Resident and comprising a number of districts, each with its own district officer. North Borneo, meanwhile, was divided into four residencies. The coastal area of the entire region, including Brunei, is flat and consists of low-lying plains where the major centres of population are situated. Inland, the terrain is covered in dense tropical rain forest, while along the 1,000-mile-long frontier with Kalimantan, mountains clad with thick jungle rise to heights of up to 8,000 feet. There are few roads through the inland areas, communication being principally via the numerous rivers which intersect the country or by air. The populations of all three states comprise a mixture of Malays, Chinese and indigenous tribes, the latter including Iban, Punan, Murut, Kelabit, Kayan and others.

Contrary to majority opinion that the rebellion in Brunei would be over once mopping-up was complete, and despite little evidence of further activity on the part of the Indonesians, Major General Walter Walker was convinced that Sukarno had far from given up. Moreover, he was well aware that there was already an organisation that shared the Indonesian dictator's desire to sabotage any plans for the federation of Malaysia. This was the Clandestine Communist Organisation (CCO), a large body predominantly based on the large Chinese immigrant community in the towns of Sarawak. It had for some years been expanding its influence and strength which by 1963 comprised a hard core of approximately 1,000 activists organised in 250 cadres, with a further 3,500 available. Of these, some 1,000 had undergone weapon training by the Indonesian army inside Kalimantan. Furthermore, the CCO could call on the assistance of some 25,000 supporters. Such was Walker's concern about the organisation that, following the rebellion, 300 leading members were arrested in western Sarawak as a precautionary measure.

In addition to the CCO, another threat was posed by a force of irregulars whom the British designated Indonesian Border Terrorists (IBT). Numbering some 1,500 and supported by regular troops, they were organised in eight operational units along the length of the border. Six of these were targeted on Sarawak's First and Second Division, the other two on the Fifth Division and North Borneo.

Walker knew full well that his forces would be hard-pressed to contain any large-scale insurgency supported by Indonesian troops. Indeed, Sukarno's defence minister, General Abdul Haris Nasution, had previously published a book in which he postulated that the British-held states in Borneo could be taken by guerrillas operating from sanctuaries inside Kalimantan. Crossing the border at will, they would operate with the support of the Indonesian army, inciting rebellion and causing major disruption. Walker was therefore determined that the CCO had to be deprived of any support from the Indonesians but, in order to achieve this, he would have to ensure that his forces dominated the jungle throughout the length of the 1,000-mile-long frontier. To do so with only six battalions of infantry, plus some local units, would be impossible and he would have to rely heavily on intelligence to enable him to deploy them where necessary.

Shortly after his arrival, Walker requested the presence in Borneo of the commanding officer of 22nd SAS Regiment (22 SAS), Lieutenant Colonel John Woodhouse, who arrived early in January. Although he originally had a different mission in mind, Walker accepted Woodhouse's suggestion that SAS patrols would be best employed by being positioned along the border to make contact with the indigenous populations and monitor Indonesian activities. Shortly afterwards A Squadron, commanded by Major John Edwardes, flew out from Britain and deployed to Borneo.

The squadron was spread over a wide front. The First Division was the responsibility of 1 Troop, commanded by Captain Ray England, which set up its base at Padawan, a village situated at a river junction and possessing a school, medical dispensary and chapel run by its Anglican community. Its four four-man patrols were deployed some 25 miles apart, each having some 25 villages in its area. Captain Bill Dodds's 2 Troop was allocated the border area of the Fourth Division in northern Sarawak, home of the Kelabit tribe, while 3 Troop, under Sergeant Ian 'Tanky' Smith was responsible for that of North Borneo.

The patrols of all three troops remained in their locations for no less than three months during which they formed close relations with the local people whom they eventually persuaded to gather intelligence on the Indonesians in their respective areas. At the same time, they gathered topographical information, which was of great value in improving the detail shown on maps, which featured little more than contours and river-lines, as well as recording possible ambush positions, crossing points along the border, and suitable sites for dropping and landing zones for parachute resupply missions and helicopter operations.

Although Walker remained suspicions of Sukarno's intentions, there was little evidence of impending trouble and in April he was ordered by the Commander-in-Chief Far East to withdraw his headquarters. He was on the point of departing when on 12 April a force of 30 Indonesians attacked a police post at Tebedu, some 20 miles east of Padawan, killing an NCO and wounding two constables before turning their attention to the local bazaar which they looted before withdrawing. Unfortunately, the village lay only two miles from the border and there was no time for early warning to be given of the incursion. In the aftermath of the raid, however, local people supplied 1 Troop with information concerning the presence of Indonesian units of approximately company strength at the border villages of Gun, Sidut and Kapala Pasang situated over the border, just inside Kalimantan, between eight and thirteen miles due south of Padawan.

Despite the discovery of documents left at Tebedu, designed to give the impression that the raid had been carried out by TNKU guerrillas, it later proved to have carried out by regular troops. Although the unit was never identified, it subsequently became known that the Indonesian Army's para-commandos (RPKAD), the Navy's marines (KKO) and the Air Force's paratroops (PGT) were training and leading IBT units on operations in Sarawak. Further attacks followed, all being aimed at isolated police posts where arms and ammunition could be captured. The British countered by constructing a number of forts, located near the border in the vicinity of kampongs (villages), for use as patrol bases. Constructed by sappers, each was heavily fortified and equipped with a helicopter landing pad.

On 17 May, the Indonesians changed their tactics and attacked a civilian target, presenting further problems for Major General Walker who would now require additional troops if the Indonesians were no longer limiting their attacks to the security forces. As a result, the 1st Battalion 10th Gurkha Rifles (1/10 GR) was deployed to the Third Division while the 2nd Battalion (2/10GR) was despatched to the Second Division.

Shortly after the Tebedu raid in April, D Squadron 22 SAS, commanded by Major Tom Leask, had relieved A Squadron which returned to Britain. Just over two weeks later, however, tragedy struck when the second-in-command of 22 SAS, Major Ronald Norman, along with the regiment's operations officer, Major Harry Thompson, and a signaller, Corporal M. P. Murphy, died when the RAF Belvedere helicopter in which they were travelling crashed into the jungle, killing all nine people aboard.

In addition to deploying patrols throughout Sarawak and North Borneo, D Squadron was given the task of training the Border Scouts, an irregular force formed in July 1963 from local tribesmen. Commanded by Major John Cross of the 7th Gurkha Rifles, the scouts' role was principally one of intelligence- gathering while also acting as a screen to detect Indonesian incursions. Organised in sections commanded by

NCOs of the Gurkha Independent Parachute Company, formed six months earlier, they were based either in tribal communities or in security force bases along the border. Initially, a large number of unsuitable tribesmen were recruited, many of them being from urban communities rather than the jungle, and Cross had considerable problems in reorganising the scouts and rebuilding them into a unit capable of performing its intended role. By the time he completed his task a year later, there were 1,500 Border Scouts in Sarawak and a further 1,000 in North Borneo

During this period 22 SAS possessed only two sabre squadrons; so A Squadron, commanded by Captain Bill Dodds, returned to Borneo in August to relieve D Squadron, by then commanded by Major Roger Woodiwiss, which had completed its six-month tour of operations. On this occasion, operations took place in the north of Sarawak with Captain Ray England's 1 Troop being deployed to Long Semado in the Fifth Division, near the border with North Borneo, while 2 Troop under Captain Iain Jack went to Bareo in the eastern corner of the Fourth Division. 4 Troop, commanded by Sergeant Maurice Tudor, was meanwhile despatched to Ba Kelalan, situated in the south-east corner of the Fifth Division, between Long Semado and Bareo. 3 Troop had not accompanied the squadron to Borneo, being employed on a task elsewhere.

Early in August, a tripartite summit meeting was held in the Filipino capital of Manila at which every effort was made by Tunku Abdul Rahman to reach a peaceful solution. He agreed to a visit by United Nations (UN) observers to Sarawak and North Borneo as a measure to determine the wishes of their respective populations with regard to federation with Malaya. The Indonesians meanwhile continued their incursions into Sarawak. During the second week of August, a force of 60 IBT, reinforced by regular troops, crossed the border near Sungei Bangkit in the Third Division and headed towards Song on the Rajang River. Towards the end of the month, another of similar size carried out an unsuccessful attack at Gumbang in the First Division. In both cases they were intercepted by Gurkha units.

On 16 September 1963, the Federation of Malaysia came into existence, following United Nations confirmation of the fact that it accorded with the wishes of the majority of the people of Sarawak and North

Borneo, the latter being renamed Sabah following federation. Sukarno, however, refused to recognise Malaysia and stepped up his efforts to destroy it.

His first response was a major raid carried out some 30 miles inside the Third Division at the village of Long Jawi. Situated on the upper stretch of the Rajang River, it comprised a large longhouse several huts and a school. Its inhabitants were Kenyans and Kayans, many of whom originated from Long Nawang, a large village over the border in Kalimantan. A Border Scout post had been established at Long Jawi, with another post at Long Linau, 50 miles to the north-west as the crow flies.

The post was manned by two Gurkha NCOs and two riflemen of 1/2GR (one of them a signaller), two PFF radio operators and a detachment of 21 Border Scouts. On 25 September, the post received a visit from Captain John Burlison of 1/2GR, the unit responsible for the Third Division, who brought with him a two-man LMG group and a corporal to relieve the post NCO. Unknown to Burlison, who departed two days later, a large force of Indonesians was hiding in the village. On the following morning one of the scouts, who against the corporal's orders had slipped away to visit his wife who was ill, returned and reported that the post was about to come under attack.

At dawn, the Indonesians launched their assault with small arms and 60mm light mortars, a battle ensuing as the six Gurkhas and the Border Scouts put up a stout defence. As the Gurkha signaller attempted to make contact with 1/2GR at Sibu, the two PFF radio operators tried frantically to raise their base at Belaga, situated some fifteen miles north of Long Linau at the junction of the Rajang and Belaga rivers. Shortly afterwards, however, a group of enemy succeeded in approaching the post's signals centre unseen and opened fire on the signallers, killing all three. Meanwhile some of the Border Scouts slipped away down the opposite side of the hill in an attempt to escape. All but one were caught, disarmed and tied up by the Indonesians, the survivor returning in haste to the post.

The battle raged for another two hours during which the Indonesians suffered several casualties. By this time the only surviving members of the post were five Gurkhas (a rifleman having been killed) and the remaining Border Scout. Two of the Gurkhas had been wounded and each man was down to a few rounds of ammunition. The NCO, Corporal Tejbahadur

Guring, therefore decided to withdraw. Dragging the two wounded Gurkhas with them, the survivors managed to escape into the jungle from where Tejbahadur watched the enemy attack the post an hour later. Finding it deserted, the Indonesians spent the rest of the day spraying the surrounding area with automatic and mortar fire. On the following day, having administered emergency first aid to the two wounded men and concealed them in the jungle, Tejbahadur, the other two Gurkhas and the Border Scout set off for the nearest village. Four days later, having travelled by foot and long-boat, they reached Belaga and raised the alarm.

An immediate follow-up operation was mounted by 1/2GR, commanded by Lieutenant Colonel Johnny Clements, who moved his troops by helicopter to ambush points on the routes most likely to be used by the raiders as they withdrew towards the border. During the following weeks, the battalion accounted for approximately half of the Indonesians, the rest escaping back over the border into Kalimantan.

After the Long Jawi raid, A Squadron, having been rejoined by 3 Troop, was redeployed to the Third Division where it soon located the large base just inside Kalimantan from which the raid had been mounted. 4 Troop was despatched to Sabah, spending six weeks in an area known as the Gap with the task of dealing with any infiltration there.

In December, D Squadron arrived back in Borneo to relieve A Squadron. Major Roger Woodiwiss was informed that his primary task was to detect and report incursions that were continuing to take place, one in December involving a large force of Indonesians who attacked Kalabakhan on the Sungei Serudong in the south-east of Sabah; they were subsequently intercepted and virtually wiped out by troops of 1/10GR. D Squadron's secondary role was to assist infantry units to intercept the raiding groups, guiding them to suitable locations where the enemy could be ambushed.

On 22 January 1964, in the Long Pa Sia Bulge, a wild, mountainous and unpopulated area in the south-west corner of Sabah adjoining Sarawak's Fifth Division, a patrol commanded by Sergeant Bob Creighton discovered tracks left by a group of twenty men heading north from the border. On the following day, further tracks of another group of twenty were found by a team of Border Scouts to the east of Long Miau. The scouts had followed these northward and came upon a camp where more than 200 men had halted for two nights before continuing their march on the morning of the 22nd. It was known that there were three battalions of Indonesian troops in the area of Long Bawan in the Kelabit Highlands to the south of the Bulge and it appeared that a major incursion had taken place.

On receipt of these reports, the commanding officer of the 1st Battalion Royal Leicestershire Regiment, Lieutenant Colonel Peter Badger, deployed his companies and platoons to cover the most likely withdrawal routes. Among these was a ten-man patrol of No. 6 Platoon commanded by a young officer, Second Lieutenant Mike Peele, which was flown from Long Semado into Long Pa Sia where it was joined by another nine men from No.6 Platoon. Ordered to pick up the Indonesians' tracks and follow up with all speed, Peele and his men reached the enemy camp at 9.00 a.m. on 24 January and discovered tracks leading east. An hour and a half later they came across a camp for some 80 men and about two hours later heard shots fired as signals. Moving closer, they spotted an enemy camp positioned alongside a stream.

At 1.00 p.m. Peele despatched a cut-off group comprising eight men with a light machine-gun (LMG) to work its way round to the rear of the enemy camp. Meanwhile, the remainder of the patrol worked its way towards the camp to a point from where its could launch its assault. After some twenty minutes, however, when the assault group was about 40 yards away, an Indonesian soldier appeared and spotted the assault group which came under fire from an LMG and four riflemen. Peele and his men immediately attacked the camp, killing the enemy machine-gunner and four other Indonesians. Another Indonesian who offered resistance was also killed. The remainder of the enemy fled, abandoning the camp together with a large quantity of arms and equipment. Two of them were captured by a D Squadron patrol under Sergeant Bob Creighton which arrived in the area on the following day. Under questioning, the prisoners revealed that their objective had been Brunei where they were to carry out a series of raids.

During February a patrol commanded by Sergeant 'Smokey' Richardson was detailed to reconnoitre along the border of the Bulge from Ba Kelalan to the Sungei Plandok where it was to rendezvous with Sergeant Bob Creighton's patrol. Given the mountainous nature of the terrain, the task was long and arduous, with accurate navigation proving very difficult. On 12 March, two days after receiving a helicopter resupply, the patrol reached the Sungei Plandok and headed north to make the rendezvous. Within a few hundred yards, however, the lead scout, Corporal Tony 'Lofty' Allen, spotted footprints on a sandbank and an hour later Richardson observed a man fishing. The man fled after Allen called to him in Malay and, on following up, the patrol discovered a sentry position and tracks which led to two large camps, each capable of accommodating up to 100 troops, and evidently abandoned several days earlier. Further reconnaissance of the area revealed a large track heading northward from the main camp.

Richardson's signal, giving details of his find, placed all forces in the area on the alert. In the meantime, however, it was apparent that the patrol had been compromised; fresh prints on the track indicated that the sentry had been one of a three-man group left behind to keep an eye on the camps whose members would undoubtedly be en route to warn the raiding force of British troops in its rear. Next morning, having received orders during the night from Major Roger Woodiwiss to follow the raiders' track, the patrol set off northward, using the same track, as movement through the jungle was impossible without chopping, the noise of which would have carried far and alerted the enemy.

That evening, Richardson received a signal from Woodiwiss, ordering him to halt for the night and then return south on the following day. Woodiwiss was concerned that the patrol might inadvertently bump into one of the ambushes laid by infantry units. Richardson, however, was unsure of his exact position and had begun to suspect that the camps were not in Malaysia, as he had reported, but in Kalimantan. If that was the case, then to proceed south would result in the patrol moving deeper into Kalimantan. After due consideration, it turned back and by the afternoon had reached the area of the camps.

The patrol then headed east, seeking an area to lie up for the night but at dusk it encountered four Indonesian soldiers. Two were shot dead and the patrol promptly scattered and made for its emergency RV. Dawn on 15 March found Richardson, Corporal Allen and Trooper John Allison hiding in a clump of bamboo. The fourth member of the patrol, however, its signaller Trooper Paddy Condon, was missing along with his vital 128 set. The patrol remained waiting while Richardson and Allen searched for him throughout the area despite the presence of the enemy. Next day, they found his bergen rucksack, looted and slashed.

Because the patrol had twice failed to make scheduled radio contact with the squadron base, Major Roger Woodiwiss had meantime taken off in a helicopter and was flying over the area. Hearing the aircraft, the patrol headed for the landing point (LP) which they had cleared earlier for their resupply on 10 March. Leaving Allison with their rucksacks, Richardson and Allen continued their search for Condon but their efforts proved fruitless. Two days later the patrol was picked up by Woodiwiss who overflew the area again and spotted the LP. It subsequently transpired that Trooper Condon had been wounded and captured by Indonesian para-commandos of the RPKAD. Having interrogated him, they had killed him after finding that his groin injury made it impossible for him to walk.

On 27 May, Woodiwiss led a team of nine men, including himself, Richardson and Allen, back into the area to determine on which side if the border the two camps were located and to discover whether the 150-man enemy force had withdrawn or was still inside Sabah. Four days later, on the morning of 1 June, the team approached the camps where it came under fire from a sentry. Withdrawing, Woodiwiss set about determining the exact locations of the camps. On the morning of 2 June he and his team pinpointed the enemy track leading north into Sabah and showing signs of further use by a large number of men. On the following day, Woodiwiss divided his team into two patrols. Sergeant Richardson took four men with him eastward to locate a long-established route leading north along the Sungei Plandok to Long Pia Sa, while Woodiwiss and the remainder followed the enemy tracks.

Examination of the trail revealed to expert tracker Sergeant Bob Creighton that it was in regular use by the Indonesians and that a group of ten men had occupied one location a week beforehand. Another stretch revealed fresh tracks and at that juncture Woodiwiss called for infantry support. Heading east, he and his patrol made their way to an LP where on the morning of 6 June helicopters flew in a reinforced platoon of 2/7GR, commanded by Major Brian Watkinson.

Woodiwiss headed south towards the incursion track. On the next day, his force reached it and turned north, Sergeant 'Buddha' Bexton in the van as lead scout, following slowly and cautiously in the tracks of the enemy raiding force. Moving at a distance behind Woodiwiss and his signaller, Trooper 'Dicky' Bird, came Watkinson and his platoon.

Suddenly, Sergeant Bexton was killed by a burst of automatic fire as he was ambushed by a twenty-strong force of Indonesians who fled immediately, seeking to avoid contact with the Gurkhas who mounted an immediate assault. A search of the area revealed a camp at which 90 men had stayed during the previous night. Meanwhile, heading south, the enemy escaped over the border.

A week later, on 14 June, another incursion took place when a group of 40 Indonesians appeared south-west of Kabu but fled three days later when a Gurkha unit was deployed to intercept them. On 22 June, fresh tracks were observed near Kabu again and the LP there came under mortar fire when helicopters arrived with Gurkha troops. They followed up and four days later a major engagement took place, the enemy suffering casualties and retiring over the border.

At the end of June, D Squadron was relieved by A Squadron, commanded by Major Peter de la Billière. It had by now become apparent, given the regiment's commitments in the Middle East as well as in Borneo, that two squadrons were no longer sufficient for the task. In January, authority had been given for the reformation of B Squadron which had been disbanded in 1959 after the end of operations in Malaya and the Jebel Akhdar in Oman. Despite this welcome addition to the regiment's establishment, it would be months before the new squadron had been recruited and trained and therefore further manpower obtained elsewhere.

In early February 1964, No. 1 (Guards) Independent Company The Parachute Regiment, the pathfinder unit of 16th Parachute Brigade, had been on internal security operations in Cyprus when it was ordered, without warning, to return to Britain. Not until its arrival at its base at Pirbright, in Surrey, was it learned that 22 SAS required an additional squadron for its operations in Borneo and that the company had been selected for the role.

Until then the company, commanded by Major John Head of the Irish Guards, had been organised into four patrols, each mounted in four Ferret scout cars, and an anti-tank troop equipped with Wombat 120mm recoilless anti-tank guns mounted on long wheelbase Land Rovers. The company had left these and its vehicles behind in Cyprus and was now reorganised into four troops, each of sixteen men, and a company headquarters. Every man was required to undergo training in languages, signals, demolitions and field medicine, as well as in the tactical skills required for the new role. After two months spent at the 22 SAS base at Hereford, the company flew out to Malaysia where it underwent a six-week jungle warfare course conducted by 22 SAS instructors and culminating in a rigorous ten-day exercise carried out under the critical eye of the regiment's commanding officer, Lieutenant Colonel John Woodhouse.

On 8 May, having been passed fit for its new role, the company moved to Borneo and deployed to Sibu in the Third Division where it was responsible for the entire 300-mile stretch of border. On 16 May, sixteen patrols were flown in by helicopter, eleven being positioned on the most likely crossing places while a twelfth was attached to the nomadic Punan Busang tribe which roamed throughout a border area called the Ulu Danum. The remaining four patrols were deployed in depth, moving among the villages and longhouses and conducting 'hearts and minds' operations, including the provision of medical assistance, while also gathering intelligence.

Those patrols covering the border remained in the jungle throughout the company's tour of operations, being extracted only once for a week's rest and recuperation. Life was an unremitting round of moving through often difficult terrain for up to eight hours a day, clearing LPs, laying ambushes, mapping previously uncharted terrain and coping with the difficulties of communicating by radio over distances of up to 250 miles.

A Squadron, meanwhile, had been busy on 'hearts and minds' missions in Sabah's Long Pa Sia Bulge, restoring morale among the Murut tribesmen in the areas of Kabu and Saliliran whose faith in the British had been shaken by the Indonesian incursions. Accompanied by sections of Border Scouts, the squadron's patrols conducted regular visits to villages where the medics treated injuries and ailments, and villagers were paid to perform tasks such as clearing LPs. Patrols departed before dusk, camping out in the jungle before moving on to other villages on the following day. But it was Major Peter de la Billière's idea of using 'Step-Up', the system by which the SAS squadrons called for immediate infantry support, which restored the tribes' faith. He promised them that any sighting of Indonesians would result in the immediate appearance of large numbers of British troops. A demonstration was provided and the Muruts' trust and confidence was regained.

At the village of Talinbakus, some three miles north of Saliliran, the highly inventive Sergeant Phil 'Gipsy' Smith achieved similar results by manufacturing a hydroelectric generator from a bicycle dynamo connected to a paddle wheel mounted on a frame installed in a nearby river. A length of D10 cable led to a bicycle headlight hung in the house of the penghulu (headman) house, making it the only building in the entire border region to enjoy electric lighting. The penghulu's standing, and that of his community, was enhanced to record levels and the entire area won over to the British at a stroke.

A Squadron achieved similar results elsewhere but in certain areas, notably those near the border and more remote mountainous locations, the local people remained nervous, understandably so, given the Indonesians' readiness to use intimidation and to carry out reprisals on those they suspected of helping the British. In some cases, there was no alternative but to establish a small permanent garrison to deter any further incursion, thus reassuring the people and guaranteeing their support.

It should not be imagined, however, that the SAS squadrons had it all their own way. The Indonesians were not to be underestimated, as was illustrated by a contact that took place in early August. On the morning of the 6th a patrol of 4 Troop, commanded by Lance Corporal Roger Blackman, was in the area of the Sungei Moming following a report on the previous evening of the noise of firing coming from the area.

Blackman's lead scout was Trooper Billy White who led the way up a ridge. Sensing that there was something untoward afoot in the area, the patrol was moving slowly and cautiously – so silent was its approach that an Indonesian soldier quietly cooking a meal behind a large tree never heard White, who suddenly stepped out from behind it. White had no option but to shoot the man dead while Lance Corporal Blackman shouted at his patrol to take evasive action. As he did so, a platoon-sized force of Indonesians opened fire from an ambush position at close range immediately to White's front. White returned the enemy fire while Blackman and his signaller, Trooper Jimmy Green, discarded their heavy bergen rucksacks (one of which contained the patrol's radio), and ran off to the left, carrying out the well-rehearsed tactic of 'shoot-and-scoot'. The fourth member of the patrol, Australian Lieutenant Geoff Skardon, an officer in the 1st SAS Company (Royal Australian Regiment), on attachment to 22 SAS, meanwhile started to cover White's withdrawal but saw him fall after being hit.

Although under fire, Skardon managed to reach White and eventually pulled him into a hollow where he attempted to carry out emergency first aid. White, however, had suffered a massive wound which had ruptured his femoral artery, causing him to bleed to death rapidly. Realising this, Skardon took to his heels, firing at five enemy running towards him. He eventually made his escape but not before he had been forced to discard his belt and pouches, containing his survival kit, map and compass, which had been caught on a length of 'Wait Awhile', a trailing plant with long tendrils bearing backward-facing barbs.

On the morning of 7 August, Lance Corporal Blackman and Trooper Green reached the LP from which they had started their patrol on the previous day. There they encountered another patrol, under Corporal Wally Poxon, who had reported the sounds of the battle and had been ordered to secure the LP pending Blackman's return. Lieutenant Skardon arrived two hours later, having navigated himself back to the LP despite the loss of map and compass. Blackman, Green and Skardon were extracted by helicopter shortly afterwards and were flown to the squadron base. On the following day, they returned with a company of 1/2GR to search the area where they discovered Trooper White's body, and that of the Indonesian killed by him, as well as their rucksacks. They also found the ambush positions, marked by spent cartridges, of 30 enemy who apparently had occupied them for some days. Evidently the Indonesians had left the area immediately after the contact, withdrawing south over the border.

It was during this period that the Director of Operations, Major General Walter Walker, received permission from the British government to conduct operations over the border into Kalimantan up to a distance of 3,000 yards. The aim of these operations, codenamed CLARET, was to unsettle and unbalance the Indonesians who were escalating their campaign, not only intensifying their attacks along the Sarawak and Sabah borders but also mounting sea and airborne attacks on the Malaysian mainland.

On 17 August, an Indonesian force of over 100, comprising marines of the KKO, RPKAD para-commandos and CCO irregulars, crossed the Straits of Malacca in boats and landed on the coast of south-west Johore.

This was intercepted by Malaysian troops who killed or captured most of them, hunting the rest as they fled into the jungle. Two weeks later, 200 paratroops of the Air Force's PGT embarked in four transports at Djakarta. One aircraft, however, was unable to take off and of the remaining three, one crashed into the sea while flying at low level to avoid detection by radar. The two surviving transports encountered an electric storm over Labis and scattered their sticks over an area of five miles, these being hunted down by troops of 1/10GR and the Gurkha Independent Parachute Company.

The first cross-border operation was carried out from Sabah by an A Squadron patrol of 1 Troop under Captain Ray England. Its mission was to carry out an observation task along the Sungei Sembakang, southeast of Labang, a supply route for the Indonesian bases along the Sungei Salilir which forked westward from the Sembakang, flowing parallel to the border toward Lumbis where there was a company base. The patrol was to observe the volume of traffic on the river, reconnoitre ambush positions and gather intelligence about the local topography and population. The operation was preliminary to a cross-border strike to be conducted by A Company 1/2GR and the patrol was accompanied by Lieutenant (QGO) Manbahadur Ale, one of its platoon commanders.

The patrol was deployed by helicopter to Bantul on 13 August and crossed the border two days later. Such was the need for silence and caution, given the extreme political sensitivity of the operation, that the pace was slow. On the afternoon of 18 August, the patrol reached the banks of the Sembakang and established a lying-up place (LUP) among the roots of a fallen tree on a slope above the river, with a separate OP position near by. During the following days, it watched local people fishing and observed boats passing up and down the river, one of them containing six Indonesians. At one point, two soldiers caused some alarm when they halted and stared upward at the position before continuing to walk along the bank. On 25 August the patrol withdrew and made its way back to the border from where it was extracted.

The ensuing cross-border strike was aimed at the evacuated village of Natakor, situated at a stream junction north of Lumbis, which had been occupied and fortified by a platoon of Indonesian troops. On 4 September, A Company 1/2GR, commanded by Major Digby Willoughby and comprising a reinforced company headquarters and an assault force of 45, was lifted to the nearest village on the Sarawak side of the border and next day was led over the border by Murut guides. On the morning of 6 September, the company attacked the enemy base, the Indonesians putting up stiff resistance with heavy fire from medium and light machine-guns and mortars. By the time the battle was over some seventeen Indonesians had been killed including the enemy commander, and an estimated twelve wounded. A Company suffered four wounded and Major General Walker gave permission for a helicopter to cross the border and evacuate them. Having destroyed large quantities of equipment and stores, and razing the base to the ground, A Company set off for the border which it reached and crossed without incident.

A Squadron conducted further CLARET operations, although local people twice stumbled upon its patrols. On the second occasion, the Indonesians were informed and attacked the patrol's position which fortunately had been vacated two hours earlier. At the end of October, the unit handed over to B Squadron and returned to Britain.

Towards the end of its tour of activities, the Guards Independent Parachute Company was also tasked with conducting CLARET operations. One of these, Operation ANNABEL'S (named after the London nightclub frequented by officers of the Household Brigade) entailed making contact with members of the Punan Busang tribe in Kalimantan who inhabited an area called Long Kihan where an Indonesian base for approximately 600 men was located. Captain Algy Cluff's patrol, which had been living with the Sarawak-based element of the Punan Busang, was given the task of linking up with the other half of the tribe at Long Kihan with the purpose of obtaining information on the Indonesian base. A problem soon arose, however, as the Sarawak-based Punan, somewhat shy and retiring people who avoided involvement with either side, were reluctant to lead British troops over the border into Indonesia.

The situation was resolved by the company's second-in-command, Captain the Lord Patrick Beresford, who persuaded the Punan that the 'Great White Queen' would be greatly pleased if they were to render assistance to her soldiers. This statement greatly impressed the tribesmen who regarded the British royal family with great reverence, and responded by presenting Beresford with a rotan mat as a gift for Her Majesty. This posed another problem, as he would obviously have to provide the Punan with some proof that the gift had been delivered. Accordingly, he contacted his family in England who, at his urgent request, rapidly despatched to him a large photograph of himself shaking hands with the Queen after a polo match. The Punan were extremely impressed, none of them questioning the fact that it had taken only a few days for their rotan mat to be presented to the 'Great White Queen' by Beresford on the other side of the world and for him to rejoin them in the jungle.

Two patrols, commanded by Beresford and Cluff, were subsequently led over the border and after five days' march into Indonesia reached a track on which lay a broken branch. This was a sign left by the chief of the Sarawak-based tribe who had gone ahead to warn those at Long Kihan of the troops' arrival, indicating to the patrols' guides that they were expected. After the two patrols met up with the tribesmen, the Indonesian base was reconnoitred but found to be unoccupied.

Towards the end of the company's tour of duty, another CLARET mission was carried out by a patrol commanded by Captain Charles Fuglesang. Crossing the border near the boat station at Balui, the same crossing point as was used by the large Indonesian force which had attacked the 1/2GR and Border Scout post at Long Jawi in the Third Division in September of the previous year, the patrol reconnoitred an area up to a depth of 3,000 yards from the border. The nearest enemy positions, however, were well into Kalimantan and the patrol saw nothing except items of discarded equipment.

Subsequent to the arrival of B Squadron, the end of October 1964 also saw the appearance of the Gurkha Independent Parachute Company which had also been reorganised and retrained in the SAS role. Commanded by Major L. M. 'Phil' Phillips, it relieved the Guards Independent Parachute Company at Sibu. In addition to deploying patrols in the Third Division, it had four more in the Fifth Division, attached to a Gurkha battalion. Over the next six months, the company patrolled constantly with patrols being rotated to allow them rest and recuperate at periodic intervals at the base in Sibu, the longest period spent in the jungle being twelve weeks. Despite a request from Phillips, Major General Walker refused to allow the company to take part in CLARET operations. Nevertheless, some of its patrols did make unauthorised forays across the border.

In mid-December the commander of B Squadron, Major Johnny Watts, was summoned by Major General Walker who told him that the 3,000-yard limitation on CLARET operations was being increased to 10,000 yards to augment their deterrent effect. At the same time, Walker informed him that the main threat was in the First Division where the enemy had concentrated a division of regular troops. Moreover, it had been reported that the Indonesians had brought an airborne force to a state of combat readiness and it was feared that an operation could be mounted against Sarawak's capital of Kuching. In contrast to Sabah, the terrain in the First Division was flat and much of it under cultivation, with a road running the length of the division with branch roads to towns throughout the region. It therefore lent itself to an invasion by large formations, Kuching itself being situated only 25 miles from the border.

As part of Walker's counter to this new threat, B Squadron was to move from Sabah to the First Division where it would operate under command of West Brigade, commanded by Brigadier Bill Cheyne (who had taken over from Brigadier 'Pat' Patterson in November), which comprised three infantry battalions covering a 150-mile-wide front. The squadron's tasks would be to conduct cross-border operations to locate targets for the infantry.

Having moved its base to Kuching, where it was located above a brothel, B Squadron commenced its first CLARET operation on 29 December when three patrols crossed the border and carried out reconnaissance tasks, one watching a track in the area of Gunong Jagoi while another reconnoitred the area surrounding Badang and Stass. The third scouted around the village of Kaik situated on the Separan tributary, found enemy tracks leading to the border and heard the sounds of mortar fire. The entire area, much of it comprising open, flat terrain given over to cultivation, did not lend itself to this type of operation and the latter two patrols were unable to carry out their primary tasks of watching tracks for enemy movement. The frequent presence of local people also caused problems, as was the case with two further patrols deployed in the areas of Bukit Knuckle and between Gunong Jagoi and Gunong Brunei.

Towards the end of January 1965, the squadron reconnoitred areas farther to the north-west, particularly around Poeri on the Sungei Koemba which appeared to be on the Indonesian line of communications.

Reconnaissance by three patrols offered no sightings of Indonesian troops, although tracks and the sounds of mortars provided evidence of their presence, but revealed that the terrain in the area of the river was impassable swampland. One patrol, commanded by Sergeant Dave Haley and deployed farther downstream, penetrated to the 10,000 CLARET limit where it also found signs of activity but saw no enemy.

Major Johnny Watts then turned his attention northward to the areas of the Sungei Bemban and Sempayang which was threatened by an Indonesian presence along the Pueh Range and by a substantial number of communists, supported by the PKI, known to be living in the port of Lundu. A track followed the Sempayang upstream, then turned north over a jungle-clad spur of the Pueh range to the town of Bemban which was believed to be garrisoned by the Indonesians. Patrols commanded by Captain Angus Graham-Wigan and Sergeant 'Tanky' Smith were sent to reconnoitre the stretch of track crossing the spur and at first found much evidence of activity, followed by sightings of small groups of enemy. Other patrols, under Captain Alec Saunt and Sergeant Dick Cooper, discovered that the Lower Sempayang could only be navigated with difficulty, this explaining why the track, rather than the river, was the Bemban garrison's main line of communication and supply.

Also active in this area were the Cross-Border Scouts, a 40-strong unit of Ibans formed in mid-1964 by a 22 SAS officer, Major Muir Walker. They had conducted their first missions in July, one being an ambush which resulted in the deaths of two Indonesians. Command of the unit had subsequently been taken over by Major John Edwardes who was assisted by two members of B Squadron, Lance Corporal Jim Penny and Trooper Dave Abbott. During this period, Edwardes was searching for an Indonesian training camp believed to be located beyond the Sungei Bemba. Crossing the border in force with 30 scouts, he established a base camp from which he despatched patrols which came across tracks but failed to find any enemy encampment.

Just before the squadron handed over to D Squadron there was a first sighting of enemy troops in force. Patrols had been deployed farther south-east into the area of the Sungei Sekayan where the Indonesians had established a main base at Balai Karangan. Seven miles east of the town was the village of Jerik and, another four miles to the east, that of Segoemen, the two being connected by a track running parallel to the border and traversing a spur leading south from the border ridge-line. Two patrols, commanded by Sergeant Dave Haley and Corporal Joe Little, were sent to reconnoitre the area, the latter finding a deserted camp for 80 troops. Haley's patrol established an OP near the track and an LUP on the spur. On the following day, a small body of enemy scouts were seen heading west along the track. Minutes later, a very large contingent of well-armed troops appeared from the direction of Jerik and two groups were sighted climbing the spur to the east and west of the patrol. Haley and his men, however, withdrew from the area undetected and headed north-east, hearing signal shots fired by the enemy from every direction. They later surmised that the track of the inward leg of their journey must have been discovered, alerting the Indonesians to their presence.

February saw the return of Major Roger Woodiwiss and D Squadron, relieving B Squadron which returned to Britain. Its first two operations were to deploy three reconnaissance patrols into the mountainous watershed area between Koemba and Sakayan, searching unsuccessfully for a route that would lead down to the Indonesian side of the border. Three other patrols, under Squadron Sergeant Major Bob Turnbull, crossed into Kalimantan farther north along the Gunong Brunei to reconnoitre a track between Seluas, on the Sungei Koemba, and Badang some seven miles to the north-east, as well as the upper reaches of the river itself to Siding.

Meanwhile, two patrols under Captain Gilbert Connor and Sergeant 'Blinky' Townsend attempted to reach the Lower Koemba, from where they could hear the noise of marine engines, but were frustrated by an impassable barrier of swamp. At the same time, a patrol under Sergeant Alf Gerry was despatched to the north-west of the First Division to reconnoitre the village of Batu Hitam which lay at the western foot of the Pueh Range. Consisting of little more than a single longhouse, this had been visited in February by a B Squadron patrol, under Corporal Arthur Bigglestone, which had found no sign of an enemy base but had encountered local people whose behaviour, despite assurances that there were no enemy in the area, had aroused his suspicions. Sergeant Gerry received a similar response from a hunting party he encountered, the latter insisting vehemently that there was no Indonesian camp in the vicinity.

A deserted Indonesian training camp had in the meantime been spotted one evening by an eight-man patrol, commanded by Sergeant Eddie Lillico, which was en route to the Sungei Sekayan, some 3,000 yards over the border, to set up an OP to watch the river which was known to be the Indonesians' main line of communication in the area. Next morning, Lillico decided to inspect the camp more closely and, leaving four men in an LUP at the location on a ridgeline where the patrol had spent the night, headed off towards a spur leading to it. He and his companions were travelling light, having left their bergen rucksacks at the LUP.

The camp was made up of several lean-to shelters or 'bashas' interspersed between clumps of bamboo. The patrol approached it with utmost caution, observing the area for ten minutes before the lead scout, Trooper Ian Thomson, moved out of cover. As he did so, he and Sergeant Lillico came under fire from Indonesian troops at short range, both being hit by a burst from a light machine-gun. Thomson was badly wounded in the left thigh, his femoral artery being ruptured. On falling, he landed two yards from an Indonesian, shooting him dead instantly with a burst from his Armalite assault rifle. Crawling to cover, he applied a tourniquet to staunch the massive flow of blood from his wound.

Lillico, meanwhile, had been hit in the front of his left hip, the bullet leaving a large exit wound in his buttock and rendering him immobile. Nevertheless, he managed to extract the two shell dressings he always carried and crammed them down the back of his trousers into the wound.

On an order from Lillico, who was under the mistaken impression that he could walk, Thomson withdrew, pulling himself along by his elbows. As he did so, Lillico provided covering fire, hitting two of the enemy who appeared in the open. Thomson succeeded in crawling to the top of the ridge-line from where he fired several bursts into the clumps of bamboo and any other cover in the area of the camp. After a while, hearing no further firing from Lillico and receiving no answer after twice calling his name, he set off again, crawling a foot at a time in the direction of the LUP. Eventually, he took shelter in a pig-hole under a fallen tree where he spent the night.

The two other members of the patrol had taken cover and then headed back to the LUP which Lillico had designated an emergency RV. From there they reported the contact by radio to the squadron base at Kuching and then set off towards the border and the infantry company base at Sain, some two miles north of it, reaching it after a march of several hours. Later that day the patrol led a rescue force of a platoon of the 1st Battalion 6th Gurkha Rifles 1/6GR back into Kalimantan.

Satisfied that the enemy had withdrawn from the area, Lillico had meanwhile crawled 500 yards towards the ridge, making his painful way through an area of thick undergrowth, known as 'beluka', and unknowingly following Thomson's example by also taking refuge in a pig-hole. There he remained for the rest of the day and that night. He awoke next morning to find a patrol of Indonesians some 30 yards from his position, one of whom subsequently climbed the tree above his pig-hole. Fortunately, however, the sound of an approaching helicopter caused the patrol to move off in its direction. Shortly afterwards, Lillico heard two bursts of fire and assumed the Indonesians had caught Thomson.

The latter, meantime, had continued his crawl towards the border and by the evening of the second day had covered a distance of 1,000 yards. Hearing the helicopter, and believing that it was a hostile aircraft bringing in Indonesian reinforcements, he opened fire through the jungle canopy in its direction, happily without any adverse effect. During the afternoon, he decided to fire three signal shots and these, fortunately, were heard by the Gurkha platoon which arrived at his position shortly afterwards.

Following the departure of the enemy patrol, Sergeant Lillico had likewise resumed his crawling and eventually reached the border ridgeline. There he awaited the return of the searching helicopter. As dusk was beginning to fall, he heard its approach and switched on the SARBE search and rescue beacon carried by every member of a patrol. The weather had been deteriorating fast and at that point a heavy storm erupted. The helicopter pilot, Flying Officer David Collinson, who had spent two days searching for the two men, had earlier been foiled by the height of the trees in his attempts to lift Thomson out of the jungle. Having located Lillico, he was determined to extract him. Descending into the clearing clear of the canopy and then hovering, he reversed his Whirlwind until its tail was between two trees; at this point he was low enough to lower his winch cable with a strop which Lillico was able to place around his shoulders. Safely extracted, he was flown to hospital at

Kuching where he was later joined by Thomson, both subsequently making a full recovery from their wounds.

MARCH 1965 SAW THE arrival in Borneo of C (Independent) Company of the 2nd Battalion The Parachute Regiment (2 PARA), commanded by Major Peter Herring. Despite the conversion of the Gurkha and Guards Independent Parachute Companies to the SAS role, and the reformation of B Squadron, 22 SAS was still overstretched due to its increasing commitments elsewhere in the world. It had thus been decided late in 1964 that The Parachute Regiment would form independent companies as further reinforcements.

Drawn from selected volunteers from throughout 2 PARA and supplemented by signallers and medics from 216 Parachute Signals Squadron and 23 Parachute Field Ambulance, C Company arrived at Nee Soon in Singapore. Coincidentally, 2 PARA itself was there, en route to Borneo as 'Spearhead' battalion, the British Army's unit on standby in Britain to deploy at short notice worldwide. The company then moved to Brunei to carry out jungle training. After an initial week's introduction for patrol commanders, all members embarked upon a concentrated month of training in jungle warfare skills provided by SAS instructors, fresh from operations in Sarawak. The three troop commanders, Lieutenants Simon Hill, Chris Johnson and John Winter, all undertook two-week operations in the Fifth Division before being given the go-ahead.

In March the company moved to Sibu where it relieved the Gurkha Independent Parachute Company. A forward administrative base was established at Nangga Gaat, a village situated a day's journey up the Sungei Rajang, which was also the base of the Fleet Air Arm's No. 845 Naval Air Squadron. Commanded by Lieutenant Commander 'Tank' Sherman, the squadron would provide C Company with helicopter support, ferrying patrols from Nangga Gaat to their operational areas. Sadly, the month following the company's deployment was marred by a tragic accident. Two of 845 Squadron's Wessex helicopters, having extracted patrols commanded by Lieutenant Chris Johnson and Sergeant McNeilly, were returning to Nangga Gaat one evening when they collided in the gathering gloom, all on board perishing in the crash. The eight members of C Company and the aircrew are commemorated by a memorial erected by the villagers.

A task inherited from the Guards and Gurkha Independent Companies was to send a patrol to live with the Punan Busang. The tribesmen were nomadic, living in a hutted village for weeks or months, hunting in the local areas for wild pig, monkey and sometimes toucan, and moving on when game became scarce. Lieutenant Winter's patrol became C Company's Punan specialists, spending twelve weeks with them during one operation.

Towards the end of its tour, by which time it had established its credentials with 22 SAS, C Company took part in CLARET operations. Four patrols, under Lieutenant Simon Hill, were detached to A Squadron, in Kuching, under Major Peter de la Billière. Hill developed his own unconventional style of tactics. He and his signaller, Lance Corporal Burston, would cross the border on their own, leaving behind the two other members of the patrol to secure the crossing point. They would then disappear into Kalimantan, re-emerging anything up to ten days later after completing their task. No direct contact had been made with the enemy by the time C Company's four-month tour of operations came to an end. In July, it returned to Britain and 2 PARA.

By this time, 22 SAS had established a theatre headquarters alongside that of the Director of Operations on the island of Labuan, headed either by the Commanding Officer, Lieutenant Colonel Mike Wingate-Gray, or the Second-in-Command, Major John Slim. Previously its headquarters in Borneo had been located in Brunei at the Haunted House, a building belonging to the Sultan of Brunei. Inhabited during the Second World War by the Kempetai, the Japanese secret police, it was reputedly haunted by the ghost of a young girl murdered by brutal interrogators. After the move to Labuan, it became a base for one of the SAS squadrons or independent parachute companies on operations in Borneo.

When Major General Walter Walker departed in April 1965, he was succeeded as Director of Operations by Major General George Lea who had commanded 22 SAS in Malaya for three years during the Emergency. Not long after Lea had taken over, the Indonesians launched a major incursion into the southern area of the First Division with an attack by a battalion on a base at Plaman Mapu held by B Company of 2 PARA.

At 4.45 a.m. on 27 April, in pitch darkness and heavy rain, the base came under heavy fire from artillery, mortars, rocket launchers and small arms. With most of the company out on patrol, it was held by an under-strength platoon of young soldiers, who had recently completed their basic training, and a further 34 men comprising the company commander, Major Jon Fleming, his company headquarters, an artillery forward observation officer (FOO) and two 3-inch mortar crews.

Enemy sappers blew holes with Bangalore torpedoes in the barbed wire defences and, advancing through the breaches, the Indonesians overran one of the 3-inch mortar positions but were driven out in a counter-attack by a section which lost three or four men wounded. Meanwhile Company Sergeant Major (CSM) John Williams asked the FOO to call down fire on the area of the base held by the enemy. Followed by the platoon commander, Captain Nick Thompson, and one section, Williams led another counter-attack but a mortar bomb exploded among his small force, killing all but himself and two others. On his orders, a section under Corporal Baughan then drove the enemy back to a nearby gully. Another Indonesian assault was beaten back by the fire from the section's general purpose machine-gun (GPMG).

Heralded by heavy supporting fire and the detonations of Bangalore torpedoes, another attack was made on the same sector of the base but B Company's remaining 3-inch mortar, manned by Sergeant McDonald at maximum elevation, dropped bombs on the enemy only 30 yards away while Corporal Baughan's section laid down heavy fire. At the same time, 105mm pack howitzers at Gunan Gajak responded to the FOO's call for supporting fire and shells started to fall among the enemy.

CSM Williams had by this time been wounded and was blind in one eye, hit in the left side of his face and head by shrapnel from a mortar bomb, with bullet grazes on his skull. Nevertheless, he led a patrol of three volunteers to clear the enemy from the base perimeter, encountering one Indonesian who was quickly killed. At that moment helicopters arrived, bringing in reinforcements in the form of 2 PARA's quick reaction force company. Meanwhile three platoons had been despatched by helicopter to block the most likely enemy withdrawal routes while two companies of Gurkhas were flown into Plaman Mapu to follow up the enemy force.

B Company had evidently been attacked by a battalion of RPKAD para-commandos. Two companies had carried out the assault, a third having set up a firm base for the attack. A fourth company was meanwhile in ambush position on the Indonesian side of the border to counter any follow-up by British forces. Whereas B Company had suffered only two killed and seven wounded, the enemy casualties had been very heavy, numbered at some 300, although no bodies were found. This mystery was solved some ten years later when an Indonesian officer who had taken part in the battle attended a course in Britain. He explained that the absence of bodies was due to the many dead and severely wounded having been thrown into the nearby river flowing towards the border.

The last week of April also saw an encounter in the area of the Ayer Hitam involving a D Squadron patrol, commanded by Captain Robin Letts, which was reconnoitring 9,000 yards into Kalimantan in an effort to glean information concerning Indonesian lines of communication up the Sungei Sentimo to the forward bases of Berjongkong and Achan. The patrol had crossed the border on 20 April and on the morning of the seventh day, having moved through a large area of swamp, came upon a stream. Close inspection revealed that undergrowth below the surface of the water had been cleared, leading Letts to believe that it was in use as a thoroughfare. Having already established an LUP on a small island in the swamp, he set up a two-man OP inside a sharp bend in the stream from which he could observe a stretch of approximately 90 yards. Towards evening, four boats carrying Indonesian soldiers were observed travelling downstream.

That night, Letts sent a signal to the squadron base, requesting permission to attack the next boats to appear. Shortly after dawn on the morning of the 28th, he established an ambush position in the area of his OP of the previous day and settled down to wait. At 8.15 a.m., three boats appeared, the first two each carrying three armed soldiers. Letts engaged the second boat, killing two Indonesians, while Corporal 'Taff' Springles turned his attention to the first craft, overturned by its two occupants, whom he shot. Meanwhile Trooper Taff Brown had opened fire on the third boat, killing all three occupants. At that point the fourth member of the patrol, Trooper Pete Hogg, spotted a fourth boat appearing from downstream and opened fire but its crew succeeded in gaining the cover of the stream bank and disappearing unscathed. The entire action had lasted only four minutes.

Withdrawing immediately to the LUP, the patrol collected its bergen rucksacks and headed swiftly towards the border. The Indonesians were slow to react and not until an hour and a half later did they mortar the area. By that evening, Letts's patrol had reached the border where, after establishing an LUP, it received a signal giving permission to attack any targets seen on the stream.

During the second week of May, D Squadron scored another success against a riverborne target. On 10 May, a patrol commanded by Sergeant Don 'Lofty' Large headed across the border to reconnoitre the area of the Sungei Koemba in the area of Poeri, on the northern bank, to ascertain whether the river was being used for as a line of communication and supply. His destination was a spur that ran south from the border to the river. On the second day, he was forced to make a detour after spotting a platoon of Indonesians establishing a camp. Two days later, the patrol ran into a huge swamp and had to wade through it for the next few days, heading west in search of the spur. A tall man, Large was in water up to his chest while his companions, Troopers Pete Scholey, Paddy Millikin and Kevin Walsh, were up to their necks. At night, the four men took shelter on islands of mud on which they erected their bashas.

On their long trek through the swamp, the patrol could hear the sounds of engines coming from the direction of the river. Finally they found the spur and, passing through some jungle and a rubber plantation, reached the Koemba which swept round in a sharp bend in front of them. Although the rubber trees were obviously not being tapped, a reconnaissance of the area revealed fresh tracks. Large therefore set up an OP near the river bank, in a ditch hidden by bushes on all sides.

On the first day, two enemy soldiers in a canoe were observed hauling up a fish trap, and on the second several launches passed upstream, returning later after discharging their cargoes. It appeared that the Indonesians were indeed using the river as a supply line.

The patrol's secondary task was to disrupt any military traffic found on the river, so Large signalled D Squadron's base, requesting and receiving permission to engage any opportunity targets. Although several launches were observed, Large held his fire as they were either too small or moving fast downstream. He was waiting for a bigger boat, heading upstream and forced to slow down to negotiate the sharp bend, the plan being to open fire on its stern with the aim of putting the engine out of action. During the afternoon, just such a target appeared, flying the Indonesian flag. Naval and army officers could be seen on her deck but once again Large held his fire as he also observed a young woman. Several years later, Large learned that the commanding officer of the RPKAD, Colonel Leonardus 'Benny' Moerdani, had been among those aboard the craft.

Rain was falling heavily and a storm had broken out overhead when another launch, some 40 feet in length, appeared, heading upstream. Large could see Indonesian troops seated underneath its canopy whose canvas sides had been unrolled to provide protection against the rain. As the craft slowed and rounded the bend, the patrol opened fire. The launch duly stopped dead in the water and started to drift back downstream, listing to starboard as a fire broke out amidships.

The patrol withdrew under cover of the heavy rain, heading swiftly up the spur with the aim of clearing out of the area as quickly as possible before the arrival of enemy troops. On the way, Large had a heart-stopping encounter with a king cobra which reared up at him before backing down and slithering away. The patrol broke track at dusk and established its bashas in a patch of thick jungle for the night.

Next day, Large and his men headed east through terrain which offered good going. When they reached the border, they found themselves south of their original crossing point. Having sent a signal requesting a helicopter, the patrol was in due course extracted. Soon afterwards, D Squadron's third tour in Borneo came to an end and it flew back to Britain, having been relieved by A Squadron.

In April, meanwhile, further reinforcements for 22 SAS had arrived in the form of 1 Detachment, 1st Ranger Squadron New Zealand SAS, commanded by Major Bill Meldrum. Forty strong, the detachment had reached Borneo around the end of February and had spent a month training at Tutong in Brunei. Thereafter it moved to Sarawak, to join D Squadron in Kuching.

A Squadron arrived in May to carry out its fourth tour of operations in Borneo, this time exclusively in the First Division where the threat was greatest. This was emphasised by another incursion by two groups of Indonesian troops who penetrated to the road linking Kuching and Serian to the south-east where they linked up with CCO guerrillas to mount an attack on a police station. This had major repercussions, not least the intimidation of the local Chinese population, some of whom had also been attacked.

After the squadron's arrival, Major Peter de la Billière attached three members of 2 Troop, Corporal Rob Roberts and Troopers Rover Slater and Jimmy Green, to Major John Edwardes and his Cross-Border Scouts who had continued operations against the Indonesians. All three men, accompanied by eighteen scouts, were soon despatched by Edwardes on a mission to locate and attack a CCO camp believed to be situated some 10,000 yards across the border, in the area of Gunong Kaliman-tan on a bend in the Sungei Bemban, west of Bemban itself.

Two days after crossing the border, having set up a firm base on the lower slopes of the Gunong Kalimantan, the patrol began its search for the camp. Two armed CCO terrorists were observed and three days later a major track was discovered leading north-west towards the mountain. Reconnaissance to the south-east revealed a bridge across the river, on the far side of which were number of huts and, most surprisingly, given this was in the middle of the jungle, a telephone line. By dawn on the following day Corporal Roberts and the entire patrol were in positions surrounding the huts. Recognising a relative among the inhabitants, one of Roberts's scouts made contact and learned that there was a CCO camp on the mountain itself, while the nearest Indonesian base was six miles upstream.

Withdrawing his men to the western bank of the river, Roberts placed himself, Slater and nine scouts in ambush 800 yards from the river to prevent any CCO approaching from the direction of the mountain camp. The rest of his force, under Green, took up positions covering the bridge. The telephone line was duly cut in a move designed to force the Indone-sians to send men to investigate the problem and repair the line. Six hours later, a patrol of seven men appeared on the bridge and Green sprang his ambush, killing six of the enemy and wounding the seventh who escaped into the jungle.

The patrol withdrew and headed north. Shortly afterwards, a larger group of Indonesians, which had been following a short distance behind its seven-man advance element, opened fire with a mortar which brought down bombs in pursuit of Roberts and his men. No casualties were caused, and the patrol continued its march north, eventually crossing the border in darkness and returning to its base.

Following this operation, air photographic reconnaissance by the RAF revealed a camp in the jungle high up on the Gunong Kalimantan. Plans were laid by Major John Edwardes to attack it, with members of 1 and 2 Troops, including the latter's commander, Captain Malcolm McGillivray, being called in to augment his force.

McGillivray set out on 9 July, his group consisting of ten SAS and 21 scouts. Five days later, he and his men reached the foot of the mountain, beginning their search for the camp on the following day. When all attempts proved unsuccessful, McGillivray decided to lay an ambush on the track found by Corporal Roberts on the earlier operation, selecting a position some 2,000 yards north-west of the Sungei Bemban. It covered a gully, bridged by a log, which opened out on its northern side into a semicircular area which provided good cover. While McGillivray and Slater, accompanied by two scouts, were carrying out a reconnaissance of the position, they observed an eleven-man Indonesian patrol, confirming their decision that the position ideal for an ambush.

McGillivray positioned Corporal Roberts, Trooper Franks and four scouts as the killer group covering the log, with an early warning/cut-off group comprising Corporal Bill Condie and Troopers Steve Callan and George Shipley, together with three scouts, on the right flank. On the left were Troopers 'Jock' Henry and 'Taff' Bilbao and two scouts. McGillivray, together with Slater and the rest of the scouts were 200 yards to the rear in the patrol's LUP where the three groups would rendezvous before withdrawing from the area.

The ambush was set by 1.00 p.m. and two and a half hours later, in the midst of heavy rain, five enemy soldiers appeared and were swiftly dispatched as they crossed the log. They were, however, an advance group and no sooner had the ambush been sprung than a second, larger force deployed on the right flank of the ambush and opened fire. Corporal Condie's group promptly withdrew out of the enemy's line of fire to lower ground to its rear. In the absence of a follow-up and the three groups pulled back unhindered to the LUP and eventually withdrew, making their way back across the border without further incident.

In May 1965, 22 SAS in Borneo was augmented by 1 Squadron of the Australian SAS Regiment (SASR) which had been formed on 4 September of the previous year from the 1st SAS Company (Royal Australian Regiment). Based at Swanbourne near Perth, the capital of

Western Australia, it consisted of a headquarters and two squadrons, each of the latter composed of 92 all ranks plus attached specialists such signallers for rear-link communications.

In February 1 Squadron arrived in Brunei, establishing its head-quarters in the Haunted House. On 28 March, it sent its first patrols to the south-east area of the Fourth Division, in the valley of the upper Sungei Batam Baram, and then dispatched others to Sabah, to the area of Pensiangan and ultimately to the Gap. These early ventures were designed to familiarise the patrols with operating in Borneo and their tasks were principally to collect topographical information, conduct 'hearts and minds' operations among the local indigenous people who included Dyaks and Punan, oversee crossing points on the border and report on incursions by Indonesian troops.

In the first of its CLARET operations, 1 Squadron sent a patrol from Sabah over the border into the area of Labang, some 3,000 yards inside Kalimantan, on the Sungei Sembatung. The patrol was led by Major Alf Garland, being lifted on 2 May by helicopter from Pensianggan to a border LP from which it made its way to the east bank of the river. It was spotted on two occasions by local people and forced to move to another location. On 7 May, it took up a position from where it could observe Labang. By now, however, Garland's second-in-command, Lance Corporal Fred Grosewich, had succumbed to fever and the mission had to be aborted. Arriving back at the border LZ on 11 May, the patrol was extracted on the following morning.

Another patrol, similarly tasked with carrying out surveillance of Labang, enjoyed more success. Commanded by Lieutenant Tom Mar-shall, it was inserted a few hours later into the same LP as Garland's patrol and established an OP from which it observed fifteen Indonesian soldiers around the village's principal longhouses. On 13 May, another patrol, under Lieutenant Peter McDougall, came across eight enemy soldiers in the Labang area; later that month further patrols were dispatched from Sabah across the border. Sergeant Roy Weir recon-noitred possible enemy incursion routes north from Labuk on the Sungei Sembatung, while Sergeant Chris Pope carried out a similar task farther to the east in the area of the Gap.

On 4 June, a patrol commanded by Corporal John Robinson was dropped by helicopter into an LP near the border south-west of Saliliran to locate an enemy force believed to be in the area of Lumbis, some 5,000 yards south of the border. Three days later, it reached the Sungei Salilir and set up an LUP from where it kept watch on several villages on the far side of the river, estimating that there were approximately 20 Indonesians in the area. Meanwhile, at Talisoi some twelve and a half miles to the east, another patrol, under Second Lieutenant Peter Schuman, also carrying out a surveillance task on the Salilir, observed enemy troops in boats heading downstream towards Labang.

Following its reconnaissance of Lumbis, Corporal Robinson's patrol returned to the area during the latter part of June, now accompanied by B Company 2/7GR and a section of two 81mm mortars which were to mount an attack on the Indonesian force sighted earlier. Crossing the border on 21 June, Robinson and the Gurkhas reached a point three days later from which he went forward to carry out a final reconnaissance. In the early hours of the following day, B Company moved into position for its attack with all of its eight GPMGs lined up on a ridge overlooking the objective.

At 9.00 a.m., as the Indonesian troops were eating breakfast, the Gurkha machine-guns and mortars opened fire. The battle lasted approximately three-quarters of an hour, during which several enemy were killed and a 60mm light mortar was put out of action, before the company withdrew under covering fire from a Royal Artillery 105mm pack howitzer at Kabu, some 11,000 yards to the north-west, which brought down fire on the objective. B Company and Corporal Robinson's patrol headed swiftly back while the Gurkhas ambushed the track from Lumbis, but the enemy did not follow up and the entire force crossed the border without incident.

During this period the major element of 1 Squadron had been active in the area of Central Brigade, commanded by Brigadier Harry Tuzo. Four patrols, however, had been attached to A Squadron 22 SAS which was operating in the First Division under West Brigade. On 11 June a sixteen-man patrol, commanded by Lieutenant Peter McDougall, deployed to the north-west area of Sarawak's First Division, being inserted by helicopter close to the border. Thereafter, it headed for the Sungei Bemban and a track that led south to Sawah, on which it was to lay an ambush.

McDougall and his men reached their objective on 17 June and early on the following morning set up the ambush. Seven M-18A1 Claymore anti-personnel mines, covering a frontage of some 75 yards, were sited to the front of the killer group while early warning/cut-off groups, each with a Claymore to its front, were sited on each flank. Meanwhile, a protection group was positioned to the rear. During the next couple of days, small groups of Indonesian troops and local people were observed using the track. At just after 11.00 a.m. on 21 June, one of McDougall's early warning groups signalled that a group of fourteen Indonesians was approaching. As the enemy entered the killing area, the firing lever on the electrical initiator to detonate the Claymores was pressed but the system malfunctioned. The patrol withdrew after dusk and subsequently reached the border. After its return to Kuching and A Squadron's base, it discovered that the system had insufficient electrical power for the length of cable linking the initiator to the Claymores.

In July, two ambushes proved more successful. On 3 July, a four-man patrol commanded by Sergeant John Pettit crossed the border from Sabah and headed south to the Sungei Salilir to establish an OP and report on enemy traffic on the river. Pettit was also authorised to ambush an opportunity target during the last 48 hours of his operation. A number of boats were observed passing in both directions but at 5.00 p.m. on 5 July, the patrol spotted a boat with nine men aboard approaching upstream. As it neared the OP, it swung towards the patrol which opened fire at some ten yards' range, hitting all aboard the craft. A report, received on 17 July, confirmed that five enemy had been killed with three more later dying of their wounds.

On 21 July a ten-man patrol, commanded by Second Lieutenant Trevor Roderick, was in an ambush position on the northern bank of the Sungei Salilir. It had been there since the previous day, watching boats passing up and down the. Just after midday, a boat containing six men approached from upstream. As it neared the patrol's position, weapons and equipment were observed in the bottom and Roderick initiated the ambush, all six Indonesians dying in a hail of automatic fire. As the patrol withdrew, firing was heard from the earlier ambush position and at night mortars brought down fire to the north of the patrol's location. On 24 July, Roderick and his men reached the border and were duly extracted by helicopter.

On 2 August, 1 Squadron completed its tour, returning to its base at

Swanbourne in Western Australia. Its area of operations was taken over by the Guards Independent Parachute Company which, having left its No. 1 Troop behind in Britain to carry out pathfinding duties with 16 Parachute Brigade, could field only twelve patrols. During this second tour, patrols were mostly deployed for short periods on 'hearts and minds' missions, intelligence-gathering or border surveillance. The company also carried out a number of CLARET operations, having established a forward operating base at Pensianggan which lay less than twelve miles from the border. Patrols were flown in RAF Twin Pioneer or Army Air Borps Beaver aircraft from the company's base at the Haunted House in Brunei to Sepulut, some sixteen miles north-east of Pensianggan, and from there were lifted by helicopter to the forward operating base.

Four CLARET operations were carried out by Captain Charles Fuglesang's troop, the first involving a search for an Indonesian base established north of the Sungei Salilir. The patrol given the task was unable to locate it and, its rations exhausted, was forced to return to the border. After two days back at the Brunei base, it was reinserted and successfully located and observed the enemy base before withdrawal.

The next operation proved more fruitful. A patrol under Captain Fuglesang crossed the border east of Bareo, situated in the eastern corner of Sarawak's Fourth Division, some 70 miles south-west of Pensianggan. Its task was to observe an Indonesian airfield and bring down fire from a 105mm pack howitzer sited on a ridge-line to shell both the airfield and track junctions in the area. At one point, as the patrol directed the howitzer's fire from their position, the Indonesians attempted to reinforce the airfield's garrison by dropping paratroops from a C-130 transport. The defenders, however, under the impression that they were being bombed, opened fire on the aircraft with 12.5mm anti-aircraft machine-guns, hitting it and causing it to crash.

The third operation by Fuglesang's troop lasted ten days. Accompanied by a platoon of Gurkhas, it crossed the border to lay an ambush on a track behind the base which had been located on the first operation. The Gurkhas were to set up a base while Fuglesang and his men advanced further into Kalimantan to establish their ambush. After three days, having failed to locate any tracks, Fuglesang was convinced that he must be nearing his objective. Taking three Gurkhas and two members of his patrol, he went forward while the remainder of his force established an LUP. After about an hour, he discovered a track and halted to consider his options when one of the Gurkhas opened fire, killing two Indonesians moving south along it. It was obvious there were other enemy in the area and therefore, having been compromised by the sound of the firing, Fuglesang had no choice but to withdraw. Rejoining the rest of his force as quickly as possible, he headed back to the border and reached it two days later by way of a river crossing made hazardous by two days of heavy rain.

The fourth and final CLARET operation was the ambushing of a track, between 9,000 and 10,000 yards over the border, believed to be in use by Indonesian units. Having crossed into Kalimantan, Fuglesang's troop navigated with difficulty through terrain which was very badly mapped and where there was very little 'pattern' to the hills. After ten days or so of searching, he and his men were unable to locate the track and returned to their border LP from which they had been inserted earlier by helicopter.

The most serious of several contacts between the company's patrols and the Indonesians occurred on 15 September. A patrol had located a large enemy base, estimated to hold up to a company, and a company of Gurkhas was detailed to attack it. The company commander, Major John Head, decided to insert two patrols, under Sergeant William McGill, to the rear of the enemy position to lay an ambush on a river track. They were to destroy any enemy retreating after the Gurkha attack.

The two patrols were inserted four days before the start of the main operation. At approximately 9.00 a.m. on 15 September, a group of six enemy was seen approaching the ambush area. It was moving cautiously, searching the ground carefully, and obviously the advance element of a large force. Some ten minutes later, the leading Indonesian encountered McHill's right-hand early warning/cut-off group of two men. He was shot dead immediately whereupon the remaining five Indonesians charged the ambush position, four being killed at point-blank range. There was a brief lull during which the main enemy body of some 50 men could be heard and eventually seen advancing to attack and out-flank the ambush position. Meanwhile, very heavy small arms and light mortar was brought down. Anticipating the enemy's next move, McGill withdrew both his patrols and eventually broke contact. The two patrols then dispersed, making for their respective emergency rendezvous (RV) locations. One man, Guardsman Shepherd, realised that he was being followed and swiftly took up an ambush position. As his pursuers came into view, he opened fire and killed two of them before continuing on his way.

On receiving Sergeant McGill's contact report, Major John Head had flown by helicopter from Brunei to the company's forward operating base at Pensianggan. There he waited anxiously for news of the two patrols whom he knew would be heading for their emergency RVs as the first step in withdrawing towards the border. The Gurkha company based at Pensianggan had meanwhile deployed patrols forward as a defensive screen. To the relief of all concerned, however, both patrols appeared and next morning moved safely through the Gurkha positions.

At the end of October, the Guards Independent Parachute Company completed its second tour of operations and left Borneo, handing over to the Gurkha Independent Parachute Company.

TWO MONTHS PREVIOUSLY, A Squadron, had been engaged in several CLARET operations as part of an intensified series of strikes designed to discourage the Indonesians from further incursions into Sarawak and to increase feelings of insecurity on their side of the border.

The most ambitious of these actions was launched in close conjunction with the 2nd Battalion 2nd Gurkha Rifles (2/2GR), commanded by Lieutenant Colonel Nick Neill. Codenamed KINGDOM COME, it involved six large ambushes by 2/2GR on the Sungei Koemba and Sungei Sentimo while A Squadron's 1 and 3 Troops, under Captains Mike Wilkes and John Foley, were employed in stirring the enemy into action. The operation, however, was hampered by heavy rain which fell unceasingly for five days, rendering four of the 2/2GR ambushes and all the A Squadron actions unsuccessful. The remaining two Gurkha ambushes, carried out by A and Support Companies on the Koemba and Sentimo respectively, resulted in boatloads of four and ten Indonesians being killed. KINGDOM COME was followed by BLOOD ALLEY in which C Company 2/2GR, commanded by Major Geoff Ashley, and 1 Troop accounted for six Indonesians in an ambush between Poeri and Kaik, on a tributary of the Koemba, and then a further 21 in a fierce battle following the arrival of an enemy force.

After this came JACK SPRAT, mounted by 1 and 4 Troops with the aim of stirring up the enemy along the Sungei Sentimo and its tributary, the Sungei Ayer Hitam. On 1 September, Captain Mike Wilkes's 1 Troop took up an ambush position to the north of Babang Baba on the north bank of the Ayer Hitam while 4 Troop, under Sergeant Maurice Tudor, did likewise 5,000 yards away on the south bank. At 1.45 p.m., two boats entered 4 Troop's killing area, each carrying eight Indonesian soldiers. All sixteen died in a heavy volume of fire but troops from another two boats landed upstream and advanced swiftly towards 4 Troop which withdrew swiftly as mortar bombing followed. Three days later, Tudor and his men reached the border and crossed back into Sarawak.

At the same time, HELL FIRE was being mounted by Support Company 2/2GR, commanded by Major Christopher Bullock. It was accompanied by Squadron Sergeant Major Lawrence Smith of A Squadron who led it to its objective, the tributary of the Sungei Poeteh along which ran the Indonesian supply route between Babang Baba and a base south of Berjongkong located by Smith during a previous operation.

The SAS aim of stirring up trouble succeeded as, on the day following 4 Troop's ambush, the leading platoon of an Indonesian company, following the track from Berjongkong to Babang Baba, fell into Bullock's ambush. The ensuing battle was fierce, the enemy outnumbering the Gurkha company by three to one. Bullock, however, had anticipated the enemy's reaction and had sited his GPMGs accordingly. When the Indonesians mounted a flanking attack, they were met by a heavy volume of fire; nevertheless they pressed home their assault, following up as the Gurkhas fell back through a checkpoint as part of the laid-down procedure for a withdrawal.

By this stage, the company was in dire need of covering fire support. It was accompanied by an artillery forward observation officer (FOO), Captain John Masters of the Royal New Zealand Artillery, but he, together with his signaller and Bullock's company sergeant major, had failed to appear at the checkpoint. Fortunately, Squadron Sergeant Major Smith stepped into the breach and, having produced a fire plan, contacted by radio the guns on the border which were on call. Shortly afterwards the first shell landed and, following corrections, the resulting support fire kept the Indonesians at a distance. Major Bullock, meanwhile, accompanied by two of his Gurkhas, went back to search for the three missing men. Encountering a large group of enemy, they killed several in the ensuing skirmish.

Support Company continued its withdrawal before halting for the night. On the following day, it resumed its journey towards the border, with artillery fire support being augmented during the final stages by that of 2/2GR's 81mm mortars. At the border was the missing signaller who had avoided capture after his position was overrun and made his way 10,000 yards back to the border without either map or compass.

Later in the day, Captain John Masters appeared. He and the company sergeant major had become separated from the rest of the company by the heavy fighting during the withdrawal to the checkpoint. The sergeant major had been wounded in the leg and was unable to walk and so, heading for the border, Masters had carried him for a distance of 6,000 yards. Overcome with exhaustion, he had then been forced to leave him in a carefully concealed position before continuing his journey to the border. Led by Major Bullock, and accompanied by Squadron Sergeant Major Smith, a search party set off to look for the sergeant major who was duly found and evacuated by helicopter to hospital where he recovered fully from his wounds.

In September A Squadron turned its attention again to locating the elusive CCO base in the area of Batu Hitam, on the south-western edge of the Pueh Range on the border of the north-west of the First Division. Communist subversion was on the increase in the area of Lundu and the base at Batu Hitam was providing support for it. Working on the theory that the CCO base was situated between the Sungei Sempayang and the Sungei Bemban, Major Peter de la Billière deployed 1, 3 and 4 Troops, along with himself and a three-man headquarters element, giving him a dozen patrols plus his own; 2 Troop, meanwhile, was still detached to Major John Edwardes and his Cross-Border Scouts.

On 10 September, the squadron crossed the Pueh Range, each troop making for its respective area to be searched. Captain Mike Wilkes's 1 Troop headed for the area north of the Sungei Bemban, and east of Bemban itself, while Captain John Foley and 3 Troop made for the area in the centre between the Bemban and the Sungei Batang Ayer. Sergeant Maurice Tudor's 4 Troop meanwhile headed farther south to the area bordered by the Batang Ayer and the Sungei Sempayang. Great caution had to be exercised as patrols advanced, skirting areas under cultivation where local people were at work during the day.

All three troops had been instructed to snatch a prisoner, with a view to obtaining information as to the camp's location. With this in mind, 3 Troop made its way to the track linking Bemban with Sawah to the south. Captain Foley, accompanied by Troopers 'Lofty' Blackburn and 'Jacko' Jackson, went forward to reconnoitre the track at a point where it crossed a ridge-line and to find a suitable place for an ambush. While they were observing it from a spot just inside the jungle, a platoon of Indonesian troops cautiously appeared and halted for a while before moving off. Later in the day, while Foley and his companions were still in position, the same platoon returned and once again halted in full view of the three men.

Minutes later, four of the Indonesians approached Foley's position. Apparently suspicious, one of them raised his weapon and Foley had no option but to open fire, as did Blackburn and Jackson. All three then withdrew at speed, pursued by a heavy volume of fire from the enemy platoon who followed up immediately. Foley and Jackson managed to reach the troop RV but Blackburn had become separated from them and failed to appear. Having waited for him for as long as possible, Foley had to leave without him as he withdrew his troop from the area. A search operation mounted by a company of 2/2GR made its way to the Bemban-Sawah track without finding any sign of the enemy or Blackburn. The latter had succeeded in shaking off his pursuers and, despite losing his belt kit in the chase, eventually crossed the border a week later.

3 Troop continued its task, meanwhile, searching along the Batang Ayer where it located the area of an Indonesian camp from which could be heard the sounds of activity, including the firing of small arms. Before it could move into observation positions, it heard the sounds of more troops approaching and was obliged to withdraw and leave the area.

In the meantime, 1 Troop had also discovered an enemy base, albeit not the one it was seeking. Corporal Bill Condie's patrol suddenly found itself on the edge of an area of cleared jungle facing a hill surmounted by a large fort which inexplicably was deserted. Close inspection showed it to be well constructed, with positions for machine-guns and mortars, and so sited as to provide observation over the border to the east. It proved to be an Indonesian, rather than a CCO, base and thus was not the squadron's objective.

Even less success was enjoyed by 4 Troop which was prevented by large areas of cultivation from making progress, let alone snatching a prisoner.

After nineteen days, as there was still no sign of the CCO base, A Squadron withdrew across the border and returned to Kuching. In early October, it was relieved by B Squadron and went back to Britain.

SEPTEMBER SAW THE Gurkha Independent Parachute Company in Borneo once more, this time deployed in the Fifth Division. During this second tour the company, commanded by Major John Cross, took part in CLARET missions across the border.

One such operation was carried out by two patrols, one led by Cross himself, which were flown by helicopter to an LP a mile from the border. From there they climbed through the jungle until, at 2.00 p.m., they reached the border ridge-line. Advancing into Kalimantan, Cross and his men broke track and took up positions for the night. Next morning the two patrols headed south to examine an area for signs of Indonesian activity. They subsequently discovered an enemy camp which apparently had been abandoned only the previous day.

On another occasion, Cross led a group of four patrols on a task to reconnoitre a track that ran parallel to the border. There was an enemy base in the area, occupied by a force of between 400 and 500 troops, from which the Indonesians had been mounting attacks across the border. Cross's mission was to determine whether the track was being used as a route from the camp to points on the border from which the incursions were being launched. His four patrols were to spend two days reconnoitring in four different directions, after which they would concentrate at an RV and set up an ambush on the track. The enemy camp lay only some three miles to the west, and Cross hoped that sooner or later some Indonesians would approach along the track and run into his ambush. He had catered for such an eventuality by equipping all four patrols with Claymore mines.

After the patrols had crossed the border, but before they separated to carry out their individual reconnaissance tasks, misfortune struck when a local inhabitant was encountered coming from the direction of the enemy camp. After some deliberation, Cross decided to let the man continue on his way but decided that his patrols would spend only one day reconnoitring, gathering at the RV during the evening and not on the following day as originally planned.

Cross led his patrol to the east, following the local who had indicated that there were tracks in the area and that there was a longhouse frequented by Indonesians. When it was time to head for the RV, Cross realised he was lost and there was no sign of any such tracks. As the afternoon wore on, he and his three Gurkhas came upon a longhouse. They had bypassed it at a distance and climbed a rise when Cross noticed a tree with the initials RPKAD and the previous day's date carved low down on the trunk. Although unable to determine his exact position on his map, he was certain that he and his men were between the enemy camp and the ambush location. By then it was getting late in the day and, rather than risk walking into his own ambush, he moved his patrol into an LUP under cover of darkness. That evening he sent a signal to his other three patrols, instructing them to make their way to his location by 8.00 a.m. next morning.

Dawn revealed the patrol's position to be in a clump of trees surrounded by a large expanse of open terrain. By 10.00 a.m. Cross was becoming anxious as there was no sign of the other patrols. Eventually he resorted to making cuckoo calls, a method of signalling he had used eighteen years previously during the Malayan Emergency after learning that there were no cuckoos in Malaya. This ruse worked and twenty minutes later the three patrols arrived, having been waiting half a mile away. They had guessed that Cross would use the cuckoo call and had been listening for it. Without further ado, Cross moved his force into the cover of the nearby jungle and decided to have a look at the longhouse which he had passed on the previous day. Approaching it cautiously, he found it to be inhabited by elderly locals who made him and his men welcome.

On the following day, all four patrols began the march back to the border. Late that afternoon, they camped on a ridge-line above an area which had been the scene of an action between the Indonesians and 1/2GR some months previously, and which featured a large and apparently well-maintained LP. As they were eating their evening meal, an

Indonesian troop-carrying helicopter, escorted by fighters, suddenly appeared overhead and flew on in the direction of the LP. From the noise of its engines, Cross could tell that the helicopter had landed, and guessed that it was disembarking troops. A few minutes later, it reappeared and flew away. Meanwhile the four patrols had stood-to, ready to engage any enemy who appeared, but none did so. Cross subsequently led his men his men back across the border without any contact taking place.

B Squadron's arrival at Kuching in early October had coincided with an attempted *coup d'état* in Indonesia by dissident army officers who killed six generals. This was put down by loyal troops under Generals Kemusu Argamulja Suharto and Abdul Haris Nasution, but chaos reigned during the following weeks. In Djakarta, mobs burned down the headquarters of the PKI while in central Java the commander of Indonesian forces there made clear his sympathies for the communist cause. On the island of Sulawesi, meanwhile, the communists turned on the army.

There was no indication as to the new regime's intentions and the secret war in the jungles of Kalimantan continued, albeit with a temporary lull in Indonesian operations. This ended, however, with an incursion into the Third Division, in the area of the Sungei Katibas.

B Squadron, commanded by Major Terry Hardy, began operations by mounting a major ambush on the far side of the Pueh Range. Meanwhile, a patrol of 9 Troop under Captain Alec Saunt set off in yet another effort to locate the elusive CCO base in the Batu Hitam area.

Crossing the border, the squadron headed over the Pueh Range and three days later had taken up an ambush position on the Bemban-Sawah track where it crossed the spur running westward to Gunong Kalimantan. The centre of the position was on a track junction, extending over a 50-yard front. Captain Richard Pirie's 7 Troop, reinforced by a patrol of 9 Troop and nine scouts, was on the right with a similarly strengthened 8 Troop, commanded by Sergeant Arthur Bigglestone, on the left. Captain Andrew Styles's 6 Troop defended the rear. Elements of 7 and 8 Troops were positioned to counter any assault from the flanks which were also protected by Claymore mines. Behind 6 Troop was the squadron headquarters with a checkpoint through which each man would pass in the withdrawal phase of the operation.

The first signs of activity were two locals carrying bananas, followed by a man and a boy who, alerted by a slight noise from the rear of the ambush position, paused before continuing their journey south. As they did so, however, the man cut a blaze on a tree at the left-hand end of the ambush. This information was relayed to Major Terry Hardy's position between 7 and 8 Troops and he guessed that it would not be long before enemy troops arrived to investigate. Indeed, some hours later a force of Indonesians suddenly attacked the left flank of the ambush, several being shot dead and others falling prey to the Claymore mines guarding 8 Troop's flank. Hardy had positioned two more Claymores farther down the track, covering dead ground, and these were also initiated, causing additional casualties among a second enemy force approaching the ambush position. A light mortar began to bring down bombs to the rear of 7 and 8 Troops but ceased fire after its position was spotted and one of its crew shot dead.

The squadron then pulled back quickly, 6 Troop covering the withdrawal of the other two troops before passing through the checkpoint. Making their way back up the spur, Hardy and his men headed east 10,000 yards across the Pueh Range to the border back into Sarawak. Twenty Indonesians had reportedly died in the action.

Captain Alec Saunt's patrol was still busy hunting for the CCO base near Batu Hitam, its hopes being raised after spotting fourteen armed Chinese heading west along a track over the Pueh Range. A subsequent follow-up operation by the whole of 9 Troop, however, failed to locate the base and another by 6 Troop west of the Sungei Bemban produced similar results. The base thus remained as elusive as ever.

B Squadron had meanwhile been joined by 2 Detachment of the 1st Ranger Squadron NZSAS, under Major Rod Dearing, which arrived on 6 October following completion of a month's jungle training in Brunei. One of the New Zealand patrols mounted a river-watch operation, being authorised to carry out an ambush should a suitable opportunity target come to light. The position selected by the patrol commander was on a high bank which afforded excellent observation along the river and good fields of fire.

On the morning of the second day, a boat carrying Indonesian marines of the KKO and a large quantity of stores headed upstream. Filming them as they passed, the patrol commander noted that the enemy were well armed with Armalites and were very obviously alert. Assuming that the craft had been on a resupply mission, he decided to ambush it on its return journey. At about 11.00 a.m. next day, an outboard engine could be heard in the distance approaching from upstream and shortly afterwards the boat came into view. Opening fire, the patrol killed two of the KKO and wounded a third as they attempted to swim to the far bank.

Abandoning its position, the patrol withdrew swiftly from the area and put as much distance as possible between it and the river. Breaking track at dusk, it camped overnight and on the following morning continued its journey to the border where it was extracted by helicopter.

A few days later, a B Squadron patrol, withdrawing from an area under fire from Indonesian mortars, ran into marines of the same KKO unit, who opened fire on the lead scout; he responded swiftly, killing one of the enemy. The patrol withdrew, mounted a swift snap ambush and killed two more of the enemy as they followed up in pursuit. Breaking contact, the patrol then made good its escape.

Another lull occurred during December, reflecting the seemingly chaotic political situation in Djakarta as the Indonesian army attempted to unseat Ahmed Sukarno who, despite increasing opposition to the communists, refused to ban the PKI. In Sarawak, meanwhile, the CCO was still very active and the Director of Operations, Major General George Lea, was well aware that whereas the end of the Confrontation would see an end to incursions by the Indonesian army, the PKI would continue its subversive operations in Sarawak and Sabah.

Towards the end of January 1966, reports were received of an impending incursion in the area of Tebedu, in the south-east of the First Division. It was to be launched from Kampong Sentas, a village some 3,000 yards south of the border on the southern bank of the Sungei Sekayan. Major Terry Hardy's B Squadron was given the task of carrying out a pre-emptive strike.

The 53-strong squadron set off on 30 January. With 9 Troop detached elsewhere, the squadron was reinforced with five members of the NZSAS detachment and four of 2 Squadron Australian SASR, the advance party of which had arrived at Kuching on 18 January with the main body following ten days later. In addition, it was accompanied by a Royal Artillery FOO and a platoon of the 1st Battalion Argyll and Sutherland Highlanders whose role would be to secure and hold the point at which the squadron would cross the Sungei Sekayan 1,200 yards upstream from the enemy camp on the far bank.

On the third evening of the operation, the final approach to the river was made under cover of darkness. One man swam across to the far bank, taking with him the loose end of a rope which was secured before the rest of the force, having left their rucksacks with the Argylls, pulled themselves across to join him. Running along the river was a track, and above it a telephone line which was promptly cut.

Captain Andrew Styles and 6 Troop, together with Major Terry Hardy, set off east along the track, followed by Captain Wilf Charlesworth and 8 Troop with Captain Richard Pirie and 7 Troop bringing up the rear. Hardy's plan was to surround Sentas under cover of darkness and attack at first light on the following morning. Before reaching the village, however, the squadron had to cross a creek by a log bridge and then make its way past two hills; in a clearing on the first was a group of huts belonging to what was believed to be a pepper farm while on the second was an enemy heavy machine-gun position. Accompanied by members of 6 Troop, Hardy climbed the first hill and, moving into the clearing, approached the huts with the intention of persuading the farmer and his family to remain inside and not raise the alarm. In fact, the huts were not those of a pepper farm but a military camp.

At that juncture Trooper Ken Elgenia, sheltering with some others behind a hut that was open from waist-height upward, lobbed a No. 80 white phosphorus grenade at the main hut with the intention of setting it alight and illuminating the enemy positions. Unfortunately his aim was not true and the grenade struck an upright, bouncing back inside the hut and exploding. Sergeant Dick Cooper was covered in burning phosphorus, setting his clothing alight and burning him badly, as was Sergeant John Coleman, one of the Australians attached to B Squadron, who suffered burns to his head, back and hands. As the rest of the men by the hut continued to return the enemy fire, Coleman dashed down to a ditch to the rear, followed by Sergeant Lou Lumby and Trooper Ginger Ferguson who helped him try to extinguish the flames.

The remainder of the squadron was now withdrawing and Lumby, Ferguson and Coleman found themselves on their own as they headed for the river along the ditch. Eventually, heavy undergrowth forced them out on the eastern side of the hill with the huts and they came under fire from the heavy machine-gun on the second hill. Charging along the hillside of the hill, with Coleman still alight from the burning phosphorus, they returned further fire from the area of the huts before reaching the river. Here they encountered a group of enemy pursuing the squadron which was by then heading westward to recross the river. After a brief skirmish with the enemy, the three men headed east and managed to ford the river farther downstream in an abandoned canoe. Before they reached the northern bank of the Sekayan, however, artillery fire, called down by the FOO, started landing on the enemy camp and in the river. Leaving the area as rapidly as possible, the three men turned west but, after coming across a longhouse, veered north for the border.

B Squadron meanwhile crossed the river to the northern bank and moved to the emergency RV where it waited for Lumby, Ferguson, Coleman and a fourth man who was also missing, Trooper Elgenia. When none of them had appeared by 10.00 a.m. Hardy gave the order for the squadron to withdraw to the border. There he found Ferguson, Lumby and Coleman awaiting him.

Like the other three, Elgenia had not heard the order to withdraw and had continued to do battle with the enemy until he suddenly realised that he was alone. Retreating down the hill, followed by some enemy who apparently were under the impression he was one of their number, he succeeded in reaching the river-bank track and headed west, still followed by the Indonesians. After some 200 yards, however, he was caught in the blast of a Claymore mine initiated by members of the squadron who had observed the pursuing group. Unbelievably, Elgenia survived unscathed, being blown into the river and surfacing downstream. Despite having lost his weapon and belt kit, and suffering from phosphorus burns, he headed for the border which he reached three days later.

Ten days afterwards, a 30-strong force under Captain Wilf Charlesworth returned to the area but was unable to cross the river which was in spate due to heavy rain. In the meantime, the Indonesians had launched their planned incursion from another base farther downstream. A 70-strong force of regular troops and CCO guerrillas crossed the border into the First Division but eventually found itself blocked by companies of 2/7GR, flown in by helicopter, who inflicted heavy casualties.

At the end of February, B Squadron completed its tour of operations and returned to Britain, being relieved by 2 Squadron Australian SASR.

JANUARY 1966 HAD meanwhile witnessed the arrival of D (Patrol) Company 3 PARA, the second of the independent companies raised by The Parachute Regiment for special operations in Borneo. The company, under Major Peter Chiswell, had been formed in July 1965 from volunteers from throughout the battalion. Competition had been fierce and a selection course had been held in Wales, after which those fortunate enough to have won places in the company underwent intensive training in the required skills.

Like its 2 PARA equivalent, the company was organised into four platoons, each consisting of four four-man patrols, a company headquarters and a base communications section provided by 216 Parachute Signals Squadron. In addition to Major Chiswell, officers in the company included Captain Jeremy Hickman, the Operations Officer, and three subalterns – Lieutenants David Chaundler, Alec Honey and David Hanmer.

Major Chiswell was given four and a half months to train his company to the operational standards required by the new role. He was fortunate in that his company sergeant major, WO2 Arthur Watchus, had just completed a tour of duty with 22 SAS. Basic skills training began in Aldershot. The signallers were introduced to the 125 set, an HF CW only transmitter/receiver used by agents of the Special Operations Executive during the Second World War. Despite their age, these radios were robust although difficult to keep dry in damp conditions. The company's medics were trained by 23 Parachute Field Ambulance to an advanced standard and in the communications skills required for consultations with a doctor via radio. By means of a special code, professional medical advice could be obtained for a sick and wounded member of a patrol. Meanwhile, those selected to be linguists flew out to the Far East to learn Malay and subsequently, on their return, carried out a demolitions course with 9 Parachute Squadron Royal Engineers. At the same time, all officers, patrol commanders and NCOs underwent intensive training with 22 SAS at its base at Hereford, as well as extensive briefings at the Intelligence Corps Centre at Ashford, in Kent. Platoon and patrol training in Wales followed, culminating in a series of exercises in Scotland.

Early in January 1966, the company arrived in Singapore. Following acclimatisation and having drawn its equipment, it underwent further training at the Jungle Warfare School at Johore Bahru in Malaysia before being flown to the island of Labuan and the 22 SAS theatre headquarters. From there it travelled by landing craft to Brunei where, before becoming operational, it was required to complete a period of work-up training with 22 SAS at a jungle base. There all the tactics, techniques and skills assimilated during the previous months were put into practice under the close supervision of SAS instructors. In late March, after completing its final training, the company moved to the 'Haunted House' where it relieved the Gurkha Independent Parachute Company. There it became the patrol unit of Central Brigade, commanded by Brigadier David House.

The company's principal operational role was to maintain depth surveillance forward of the border ridge, providing patrols to perform in-depth close reconnaissance tasks on selected targets. It worked closely with Headquarters Central Brigade and with 22 SAS headquarters on Labuan. While the number of contacts with the enemy were few, a mass of valuable intelligence was obtained. A number of CLARET operations were carried out, the first of these taking place soon after the company became operational.

D (Patrol) Company completed its six-month tour of operations in July, following which it returned to Britain. The intention had been to replace it with a patrol company from 1 PARA but in the light of the apparently declining threat from the Indonesians, the decision was taken not to do so.

From March onward, 2 Squadron Australian SASR and 2 Detachment NZSAS were the only SAS units in Borneo, the latter being replaced by 3 Detachment under Major David Ogilvy that same month.

Patrols of 2 Squadron continued to carry out CLARET operations along the Sungei Sekayan, spotting small groups of Indonesian troops in the area of Serankang. On 17 March, a patrol commanded by Sergeant Peter White and accompanied by Major Charles McCausland, a company commander in 2/7GR, and one of his platoons, crossed the border and made its way to the Sekayan. Its aim was to enable McCausland to carry out a reconnaissance of Sentas prior to an attack by his company. A crossing point just upstream of Sentas was secured by the Gurkha platoon, following which White's patrol and McCausland crossed to the south bank and moved up a nearby creek which they found to have been cleared for use as a concealed line of communication. Here they encountered a local who, when questioned by McCausland, revealed that an Indonesian patrol was following behind him. McCausland and the patrol returned to recross the river and, together with the Gurkha platoon, swiftly left the area which was subjected to a mortar attack by the Indonesians a few minutes later.

On 10 April, two patrols under Sergeant Peter White crossed into Kalimantan as part of a surveillance operation by 2 Squadron. Once an LUP had been established, White despatched two three-man patrols: one to reconnoitre Siding, on the Sungei Koemba, and the other to investigate the Sungei Pawan which flowed north-west into the Koemba to the south-east of Siding.

Five days later, the second patrol was spotted by local people but despite the possibility of having been compromised, White decided to continue his surveillance. On the morning of 16 April, a force of some fifteen Indonesians was heard approaching the LUP and White withdrew his two patrols, booby-trapping the LUP area with a grenade before moving off to the north-east. At this point, he realised that four of his men had become separated from the rest; having failed to locate them White decided to head for the pre-selected patrol RV on the border. Not long afterwards, the patrol heard the booby trap explode.

Next morning, unexplained small arms fire was heard to the rear of the patrol and the Indonesians began to mortar the area in a desultory fashion. The patrol was unaffected by this and reached the RV on the border where it was extracted by helicopter and lifted to Gumbang which was a 1/10GR company base. The missing four members also arrived at the RV and were flown to the 2 Squadron base at Kuching.

In May, an incident occurred which resulted in a contact. On 16 May a patrol commanded by Sergeant Barry Young crossed the border and reconnoitred an area of swamp along the Sungei Poeteh in the area where Captain Robin Letts's patrol of D Squadron had carried out its successful ambush in April of the previous year. On the sixth day of the operation the patrol moved north, away from the river but heading parallel with it in the direction of Berjongkong. On 23 May, having established an LUP, Sergeant Young, accompanied by Private Alan Easthorpe, moved forward to observe the Poeteh. While photographing the river to the south, Young was spotted by five Indonesian soldiers who suddenly appeared from the north in a canoe. Opening fire, he hit the first three men while Easthorpe engaged the other two, hitting both.

Withdrawing rapidly, the patrol left the area and headed north. After some twenty minutes, a mortar opened fire from the south. Young now turned east towards the border but during the early afternoon was forced to alter course again after hearing sounds of enemy activity on a spur ahead of him. Halting just before dusk, the patrol heard shots fired as signals to the east and west as Indonesian troops continued their search. Moving off at first light, Young decided against returning to his original crossing point for fear the enemy might have backtracked to it, and instead headed east in the direction of Kampong Munti. On the evening of 24 May, the patrol established an LUP near the village and was extracted by helicopter next day.

On 25 May, a delegation of eight Indonesian army officers flew to Kuala Lumpur and three days later, all CLARET operations ceased after the start of negotiations between Malaysia and Indonesia. Thereafter, the Indonesian delegation travelled to Bangkok for the drafting of proposals to end the conflict, returning to Djakarta on 1 June. During the rest of the month, however, intelligence reports revealed that the Indonesians were planning to send two groups, designated MANJAP 1 and 2, into the First Division to carry out intelligence-gathering and subversive operations. Patrols of 2 Squadron were deployed to help intercept these groups which were eventually accounted for by companies of the 4th Battalion Royal Australian Regiment and 2/7GR.

In June, it was reported that a force of some 50 Indonesian troops, commanded by a Lieutenant Sumbi, was making its way towards the border with the Fifth Division. Previous reports had indicated that Sumbi's objective might be the Shell oil installations at Seria, in Brunei, and it was thought that he planned to cross the border by way of a remote, jungle-covered ridge-line between the villages of Ba Kelalan and Long Semado. The battalion in whose area Sumbi's probable crossing point lay was 1/7GR. Providing a forward screen were patrols of the Gurkha Independent Parachute Company.

329

First evidence of Sumbi's force having crossed the border came on the morning of 29 July when one of the company's patrols, commanded by Corporal Singbahadur Gurung, found a small piece of silver foil smelling of coffee. As there were no British troops in the area and as the Gurkha ration pack did not contain coffee, it was concluded that the foil had been dropped by an Indonesian. Further careful examination of the area revealed tracks made by three men heading north over the border into the Fifth Division. Having followed these for three days, the patrol found three pairs of discarded British-pattern jungle boots and pieces of sacking used by 45 men who had tied them over their boots to prevent any tracks being made on the ground.

The pursuit was then taken up by five more of the company's patrols, 1/7GR and other units. A number of contacts took place with Sumbi's force over the following two months, during which some of his men were captured while others surrendered or died of starvation. Sumbi himself was caught on 3 September, after the Confrontation campaign had officially ended, the so-called Bangkok Accord having been signed by Malaysia and Indonesia on 11 August. Apparently he had attended the British Army's Jungle Warfare School where he had been awarded a 'B' grading for his performance as a student.

On 21 July, D Squadron 22 SAS relieved 2 Squadron which returned to its base at Swanbourne in Western Australia. That same month also saw the arrival of 4 Detachment NZSAS under Major David Moloney which, having relieved 3 Detachment, remained at Kuching until 9 September when it returned to New Zealand. Shortly afterwards D Squadron returned to Britain, ending three years of SAS operations in Borneo.

During the three years of the campaign, British and Commonwealth casualties numbered 114 killed and 181 wounded. Of those, the 22 SAS squadrons suffered three killed and two wounded by enemy action, while the Australian SASR lost three dead – one killed by a rogue elephant and two drowned during a river crossing. None of the independent parachute units attached to 22 SAS sustained any casualties. Indonesian forces, on the other hand, were known to have suffered 590 killed, 222 wounded and 771 captured, these figures excluding those killed and wounded across the border who could not be counted.

A brief assessment of the attempt by Indonesia to achieve domina-

tion of South East Asia, and of the successful campaign which thwarted
Sukarno's ambitions for Maphilindo, was made some years later by Major
General George Lea:

> Tactically she [Indonesia – author] tried to do it by armed subversion
> and infiltration to establish cells of terrorists and saboteurs, while
> strategically she built up considerable forces and threatened to use
> them. Such activity amounts not merely to an internal security
> problem: it is aggression. It was beaten by reacting promptly and very
> firmly by matching the strategic threat with Navy, Army and Air Force
> [assets], and by inflicting disproportionate casualties until Indonesia
> was convinced that her aim of crushing Malaysia was unattainable.
>
> Success therefore was first and foremost a military one. It has been
> argued that the new regime in Djakarta, coupled with the parlous
> state of the Indonesian economy, brought about the Bangkok Accord;
> those were certainly important factors, but the significance of our
> military contribution can best be judged by asking what would have
> happened if we had not given it. There can be no doubt that Borneo
> certainly and Malaya possibly would now be under complete control
> of the Indonesians.

A final verdict on the Confrontation in Borneo is best left to the words
used by Denis Healey, the Secretary of State for Defence at the time,
in his statement to the British Parliament shortly after the end of the
campaign:

> When the House thinks of the tragedy that could have fallen on a
> whole corner of a continent if we had not been able to hold the
> situation and bring it to a successful termination, it will appreciate
> that in the history books it will be recorded as one of the most efficient
> uses of military force in the history of the world.

CHAPTER EIGHT

TIBET 1956–1974

In 1956, while Britain was winning the war against the communists in the jungles of Malaya, the United States was about to become embroiled in a secret war which had started six years earlier on the 'roof of the world', in the hidden kingdom of Tibet.

Situated to the north of India, Tibet comprises a high plateau surrounded by formidable mountain ranges. The northern area of plain, called the Chang-tang and inhabited by nomadic tribes, is bordered by the Kunlun Mountains and the Chinese province of Sinkiang (now Xinjiang). In the east, during the period covered by this chapter, the Tibetan regions of Amdo and Kham were bordered by the Chinese provinces of Gansu and Sichuan; today Amdo comprises China's Tsinghai Province while Kham has been absorbed into that of Szechuan. Amdo in the north-east consisted of extensive plains while Kham, in the south-east, was characterised by mountain ranges, intersected by high-altitude passes and powerful rivers, and vast plateaux broken by coniferous forests and valleys with whitewashed villages and pastures giving the region its name of 'the Land of Flowers'. The inhabitants of Amdo, namely Amdowa and Golok tribesmen, and those of Kham, known as Khambas, comprised a total of 23 tribes. Proud and highly independent by nature, all were expert horsemen, being mounted on small but sturdy and surefooted ponies. Proficient in the use of small arms and swords, the tribesmen learned to shoot from a very early age, not only for the purpose of hunting game but also to defend themselves and their families from marauding bands of brigands.

Southern Tibet exhibits fertile valleys growing rice and barley, which are the Tibetans' staple food, and plateaux clad with forests and pastures. The great Brahmaputra River flows across the region whose southern frontiers are the ranges of the Himalayas; along its southern slopes are strung, from east to west, the Indian state of Arunachal Pradesh (previously the North East Frontier Agency) and the hill kingdoms of Bhutan and Nepal respectively. In the west, Tibet is bordered by the Himalayas, faced to the south by north-western India and Kashmir.

It was during the nineteenth century that Tibet closed its doors to outsiders and in particular to the British who saw it as a trade route to China. Britain eventually resorted to force and the Tibetan ruler, the Dalai Lama, fled to China but returned after a treaty signed between Britain and Tibet in 1904. Two years later, however, Britain and China also signed a treaty which recognised the latter's suzerainty over Tibet. In 1910, the Chinese attempted to take direct control by force and once again the Dalai Lama was forced to flee, on this occasion to India. Until then, the Tibetan attitude towards China had been one of indifference but this latest attempt by the Chinese to subjugate their country caused the Tibetans to regard them thereafter as enemies. During the Chinese Rebellion of 1911–12, Tibet expelled all Chinese and declared itself an independent nation, the Dalai Lama returning to his country in 1912.

This coincided with renewed Chinese attempts to reoccupy parts of eastern Tibet. That same year, a force of 5,000 troops recaptured Tachienlu, Batang and Chamdo and by 1914 had largely gained control of Tibet's frontier regions. Tibet responded by despatching troops and soon a war over the disputed border areas developed between the two countries.

In October 1913, a tripartite conference between Tibet, China and Britain was held at Simla, in north-western India, to resolve the dispute and other matters concerning Tibet. This proved a lengthy process, the conference lasting until April of the following year. After claims made by both Tibet and China, and protracted negotiations, Britain produced a compromise solution. In addition to designating specific areas to be placed under Tibetan or Chinese rule, Tibet itself would be divided into two parts: Inner and Outer Tibet. Chinese suzerainty over the whole of Tibet would be acknowledged, as would the autonomy of Outer Tibet which would be administered by the Tibetan government from its seat in Lhasa. Tibet's territorial integrity was to be recognised by both Britain and China who would not interfere in the administration of Outer Tibet. Furthermore, Chinese troops or government officials would be barred from entering Outer Tibet, with the exception of a Resident who would be based in Lhasa with a military escort not exceeding 300 troops. China would undertake not to colonise Tibet nor to absorb it as a province.

In April 1914, a draft convention was initialled by the delegates representing all three countries. Two days later, however, the Chinese renounced its plenipotentiary and refused to sign the convention. Britain and Tibet nevertheless signed it and thereafter regarded it as binding.

During the following year violence broke out when Khamba tribesmen attacked Chinese garrisons in eastern Tibet and, having reclaimed the entire area, began advancing farther east to reclaim territory formerly belonging to them up to and including Tachienlu. At this point, the British intervened at the request of the Chinese and persuaded the Khambas to call a halt to the fighting. The Lhasa government, whose relations with the highly independent Khambas and their northern Amdowan neighbours had always been poor, instituted a retrospective demand for taxes due for the period during which eastern Tibet had been under Chinese occupation. This resulted in a worsening rift between both regions and the government in Lhasa.

Between 1920 and 1930, relations between Britain and Tibet grew more distant, the latter turning to China which at that time was weak and divided. Inevitably, however, trouble flared up again in eastern Tibet when Chinese troops from the garrison at Sikang intervened in a local dispute in Kham. This led to the entire region rising in revolt. In 1932, a Khamba leader, Kesang Tserim, expelled the Chinese troops and declared most of Kham to be an autonomous region.

Tibet's ruler at this time was the Thirteenth Dalai Lama. On 17 December 1933, he died. Next month, pending the discovery of his successor, a regent, Reting Rimpoche, abbot of the monastery at Reting near Lhasa, was appointed. Meanwhile, a struggle for power began between Kunpel-La, a favourite of the late Dalai Lama, and the latter's nephew. The situation in Lhasa began to look dangerous, heightened by the deteriorating situation in eastern Tibet where during 1934 a rebellion took place, led by the military governor of Kham, Topgyay Pandatsang and his elder brother Rapga. In addition to his official position, Topgyay was also the head of one of the four wealthy and powerful families who owned large trading houses in Kham, the others being the Andutsangs, Gyadutsangs and Sadutsangs.

The two brothers amassed a force of Khambas and headed for the regional capital Chamdo, from where they intended to march on Lhasa. They were confronted by a force of Tibetan troops who forced them to retire, only to be met by Chinese troops advancing from the east. The latter had been despatched to Tibet by the nationalist Chinese leader,

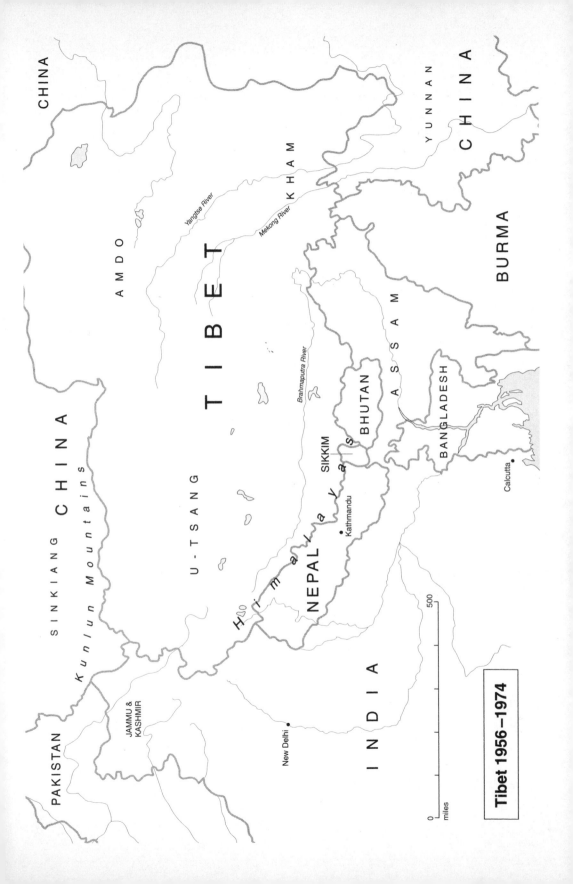

Tibet 1956–1974

Generalissimo Chiang Kai Shek, as a result of increasing fears over a large Tibetan force operating unchecked on China's borders. The Khambas were defeated by the combined Tibetan–Chinese forces and the Pandatsang brothers were compelled to flee to India.

July 1937 saw the start of the war between China and Japan which had invaded northern China and seized the north-eastern provinces of Manchuria in 1931, thereafter showing further designs on the rest of China. Eight months earlier, in December 1936, in what became known as the Sian Incident, Chiang Kai Shek had been kidnapped by one of his own generals, Chang Hsüeh Liang, commander of Chiang's Manchurian forces who were based at Sian in north-western China. Concerned for his Manchurian homeland, Chang had demanded that Chiang cease fighting the communists, led by Mao Tse Tung, and form a united front against the Japanese. Having agreed to his subordinate's demands, Chiang Kai Shek had been released and, keeping to his word, had subsequently joined forces with the communists. But he also arrested Chang Hsüeh Liang, keeping him imprisoned until 1949.

By October 1938, the nationalists had been forced by the Japanese to retreat westward to Chungking where Chiang Kai Shek established his government and military headquarters. It was during this period that he conceived the idea of using Amdo and Kham as a last bastion of defence. To that end, he enlisted the aid of the Pandatsang brothers, who had returned from India, and two Amdoan chiefs, Lobsang Tsewong and Geshi Sherab Gyaltso. The four leaders, all appointed as senior officers by Chiang, agreed to collaborate with the nationalists in fighting the Japanese if the need arose. In the meantime, their appointments and positions with the nationalists gave them access to large quantities of weapons which could be used to overthrow the government in Lhasa. They planned for the Khambas under Topgay Pandatsang to seize control of the whole of Kham while Lobsang and Geshi did likewise in Amdo. A message would then be sent to Lhasa, demanding that it recognise the two regions as parts of Greater Tibet and offering to join in a united war against the Chinese for Tibet's independence. Should the government refuse, the Khambas and Amdowas would march on Lhasa.

In February 1940, a four-and-a-half year old boy, Lhamo Dhondrub, was discovered and enthroned as the Fourteenth Dalai Lama. Next year the Regent, Reting Rimpoche, retired to his monastery for a period of

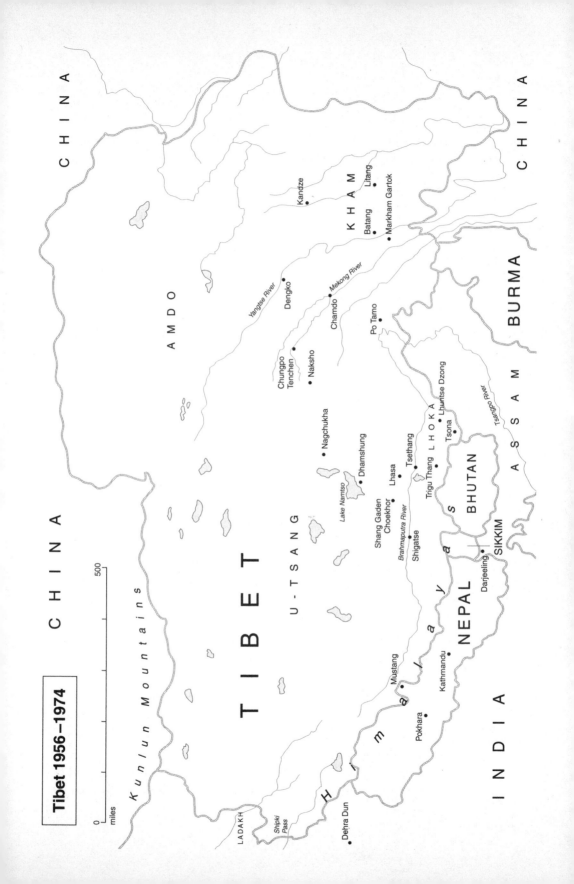

Tibet 1956–1974

CHINA

CHINA

CHINA

CHINA

BURMA

INDIA

NEPAL

SIKKIM

BHUTAN

ASSAM

LADAKH

TIBET

AMDO

KHAM

U-TSANG

LHOKA

Kunlun Mountains

H i m a l a y a s

miles
0
500

Kandze
Litang
Batang
Markham Gartok

Dengko
Yangtse River
Mekong River
Chamdo
Po Tamo

Chungpo
Tenchen
Naksho

Nagchukha
Dhamshung
Lake Namtso

Shang Gaden
Choekhor
Lhasa
Tsethang
Trigu Thang
Tsona
Lhuntse Dzong
Tsangpo River

Shigatse
Brahmaputra River

Mustang

Pokhara

Kathmandu

Darjeeling

Dehra Dun
Shipki Pass

meditation and handed over the reins of power to his appointed stand-in, Takta Rimpoche, the young Dalai Lama's tutor.

The Western world, meanwhile, was locked in war with Nazi Germany and Japan. During the conflict, Tibet maintained a position of neutrality while agreeing to allow the transit of supplies from the Allies to China through Tibetan territory. In addition, it authorised a reconnaissance mission by the United States which was carried out by two officers of the Office of Strategic Services (OSS) during the period from October 1942 to June 1943.

After the conclusion of the Second World War in 1945, Tibet decided to end its policy of isolation from the rest of the world and dispatched a delegation to India and China, ostensibly to congratulate the wartime Allies on their victories over Germany and Japan but in reality to discuss Tibet's future position with China. It travelled to New Delhi in March 1946, and then to Chiang Kai Shek's headquarters in Nanking. The delegation delivered a letter to him which included a statement of Tibet's claim to independence and a request that no more Chinese diplomats be posted to Lhasa, with all further communications to be conducted by radio. Needless to say, the Chinese paid little attention to the Tibetan demands and instead tried to persuade them to sign a document declaring that they were subjects of the Chinese Kuomintang government. Chiang Kai Shek, however, soon had more pressing matters for his attention when in April 1946 civil war broke out between his nationalist forces and those of the communists of Mao Tse Tung.

In April 1947, as the long-running struggle for supremacy in Lhasa continued, Takta took steps to ensure that the Regent, Reting Rimpoche, would not return to power. He sent troops to the monastery to arrest the Regent and two close associates, all three being charged by the National Assembly with plotting to kill Takta and seeking assistance from Chiang Kai Shek to overthrow the government. Reting's two associates confessed but he himself admitted to nothing more than approving their opposition to Takta's regime. All three were found guilty but before being sentenced, Reting died; it was subsequently rumoured that he had been poisoned. His associates received death sentences later commuted to life imprisonment.

The Pandatsang brothers and the two Amdowa leaders meanwhile were progressing in their plans for a rebellion against the government in Lhasa. In July 1949, however, the authorities announced without warning that all Chinese personnel in the capital were being expelled. This caused considerable dismay among the four plotters who suspected the hand of Britain, India and possibly the United States behind this announcement. If this was the case, they feared their Khamba and Amdowan tribesmen could find themselves facing forces from those three countries rather than those of the Lhasa government. Discretion being the better part of valour, they decided to postpone the uprising for the time being.

In October 1949, the nationalist forces of Chiang Kai Shek, defeated by the communists after some three years of civil war, withdrew from the Chinese mainland to the island of Formosa (now Taiwan). On 1 October, Mao Tse Tung proclaimed his new government of the People's Republic of China in Peking and six weeks later reports arrived in Lhasa of Chinese troops moving into areas of the frontier with eastern Tibet. On 7 January 1950, China's intentions towards Tibet were further clarified in an announcement by General Liu Bo Cheng that the People's Liberation Army (PLA), having annihilated all resistance in south-west China, would begin to 'liberate our compatriots in Tibet'.

The Pandatsang brothers and the two Amdowa leaders had meanwhile received a message from the new regime in Peking. In it, the communists announced that all of Tibet was to absorbed into China within a year, to be followed over the following five years by Nepal, Sikkim, Bhutan and India. Aware, too, of the plan to overthrow the government in Lhasa, they would support it fully by supplying weapons and money.

The four leaders were in a quandary. They realised it would be fruitless to send a warning to Lhasa since the government was well aware that rebellion was brewing in Amdo and Kham and would surely regard such a message as some form of ruse. They decided, therefore, to contact the governments of Britain and India, advising them of the Chinese intentions. Rather than take the message himself, Topgyay retired to a mountain stronghold north of Chamdo and despatched an emissary to India. He was a young Scotsman named George Patterson, who had arrived in Tibet as a medical missionary in 1947. As a friend of Topgyay, he was now entrusted with delivering warnings of Chinese intentions to the British and Americans.

Patterson's journey, by way of Assam, took him two months. His first destination was Calcutta where he called on the British High Commissioner, David Anderson, who took the matter sufficiently seriously to arrange a meeting, over dinner at his apartment, with an officer of the Central Intelligence Agency (CIA), Robert Lynn, who was based at the US Consulate, and an Indian security official. Patterson's information was passed to London and Washington but because neither Britain nor the United States possessed full diplomatic representation with China, it was left to India to make the necessary investigations in Peking. Inevitably, the Chinese persuaded the Indian ambassador, Sardar Pannikar, that it was untrue and that any troop movements on China's western borders were part of routine deployments.

In Washington, meanwhile, the possibly of a Chinese invasion of Tibet had been taken seriously to the extent that a meeting took place at the State Department on 16 June, being attended by representatives of the British Embassy. The purpose of the meeting was to discuss US proposals to 'encourage and support Tibetan resistance to Communist control'. A document produced by the State Department concluded that only a comparatively small amount of assistance, in the forms of arms and equipment, would result in any such resistance being reinforced to the point where it would be able to inflict considerable losses on the Chinese, thus making any invasion too costly. The Americans proposed that such assistance should be provided by India, under persuasion from the British. But Britain, having left India only two years previously, had little interest in South Asia and expressed no enthusiasm for the American proposals.

In August, the United States intimated to the Tibetans that US assistance would be forthcoming in the form of secret financial aid to buy arms from India, without the latter knowing the source of the funds. Next month the Tibetans made their initial request for arms to the Indians who had been warned by the British beforehand to expect such an approach.

FIRST SIGNS OF CHINA'S real intentions towards Tibet had, in fact, come in July 1950 when a force of 500 troops of the People's Liberation Army (PLA) crossed the upper reaches of the Yangtse River and occupied the small border town of Dengko situated on the west bank, some 120 miles north-east of Chamdo. The governor of Chamdo, Lhalu Shape, who had earlier sent a two-man radio team to Denko to provide early warning of any Chinese attack, dispatched two scouts to ascertain the size of the Chinese force while a messenger was sent to summon Muja Dapon, the commander of a force of 400 Tibetan regular troops located on the Kham–Amdo border north of Chamdo. The scouts returned after four days, reporting that the Chinese numbered between 500 and 700, and two days later Muja and his force arrived.

While Lhalu placed Chamdo in a state of defence, Muja and his troops, reinforced by 200 Khamba tribesmen on horseback, marched north-east to Dengko. Keeping the latter in reserve, he launched an assault with his regulars on the Chinese whose machine-guns caused heavy casualties among the Tibetans who nevertheless pressed home their attack. That evening, when it appeared that the battle had reached a stalemate, Muja committed his 200 mounted tribesmen who broke into the centre of the Chinese positions in the village and set about slaughtering the PLA troops. By the time the fighting was over, the entire enemy force had been massacred.

The battle at Dengko received no publicity abroad as the attention of the rest of the world was focused on Korea where war broke out on 25 June. Meanwhile, Chinese forces assembled elsewhere in eastern Kham and from the higher reaches of the Mekong River came news of a large force entering Batang, situated to the south-east of Chamdo on the east bank of the Yangtse. Tension was increased further by news from Amdo of the sacking of the great monasteries at Serten and Shatsong. On 6 August, a further blow fell in the form of a massive earthquake, the worst in Central Asia in 50 years, which caused devastating damage in Chamdo and the towns of Kandze, Litang, Dergue and Batang, destroying thousands of houses and many monasteries.

The rest of Tibet meanwhile awaited the expected Chinese onslaught, the government in Lhasa despatching more troops from its tiny 10,000-strong army to Kham. To the east, PLA forces numbering some 120,000 were poised to invade. Some 50,000 troops were at Yaan, a town in China's Szechwan province, situated near Kanting east of Chamdo on the Kham–China border. Another 40,000 were to the north in Amdo, while a third force of 30,000 was 2,000 miles away to the north in Sinkiang.

On the night of 6 October 1950, China launched its invasion with over 80,000 troops of General Liu Ba Ting's First and Second Field Armies. At Dengko, Muja Dapon's force came under fire from artillery east of the Yangtse, responding with Bren .303 light machine-guns (LMG), the heaviest weapons it possessed. About 60 miles to the south, PLA troops silently crossed the river and annihilated the 50-man Tibetan detachment guarding the ferry at Markham Druga. Thousands more were ferried across, subsequently advancing on the Tibetan garrison at Rangsum which lay 25 miles away. Some 130 miles farther south, 2,000 PLA troops crossed the Yangtse before dividing into two columns, one heading north for Chamdo while the other attacked the garrison at Markham Gartok where 250 Tibetan troops and Khamba irregulars put up a stout resistance before being overrun and wiped out.

On 7 October fighting continued in the north where, despite being heavily outgunned, Muja Dapon's small force had prevented the Chinese from crossing the Yangtse. By this time, however, the 300-strong garrison at Rangsum was under heavy attack, eventually withdrawing to the first mountain pass on the road leading to Chamdo where it made a stand. Next day, the PLA launched wave after wave of assaults which were repulsed by the gallant Tibetans who mowed down the Chinese as they stormed forward. Sheer weight of numbers, however, eventually forced back the defenders who suffered heavy casualties from artillery fire as they crouched behind rocks for cover. At nightfall, the Tibetan commander realised that the situation was hopeless and ordered his force to disperse, leaving the road to Chamdo open.

In the Khamba capital, the 300-strong garrison had deployed to cover the main approaches, being reinforced by tribesmen armed only with flintlock rifles and swords but prepared to fight to the death in resisting the invaders of their country. But the newly arrived governor of Chamdo, Ngabo Ngawang Jigme, who during August had replaced Lhalu Shape, was not made of such stern stuff. In disguise, he and his officials, together with 700 troops, fled the town and headed west, much to the anger of the Khambas.

Muja Dapon, meanwhile, continued to stand alone against the Chinese, defending Dengko until he was forced to pull back after the PLA had crossed the Yangtse 20 miles to the north. Withdrawing in good order to Chamdo, he and his force set off on 16 October to locate Ngabo whom he found at a monastery only a day's march from Chamdo. The cowardly governor had halted there after learning that the road to Lhasa had been cut by the Chinese forces which had advanced south from Amdo. Despite Muja's assurances that their combined forces could break through to Lhasa, Ngabo refused to move and on the following day surrendered to the Chinese. After resistance lasting ten days, Tibet had fallen.

The Tibetans appealed to the United Nations but initially found none who would champion their cause. In January 1951 the sixteen-year-old Dalai Lama, who had retired with his government to Yatung in the south of the country, received assurances from the Chinese, through their ambassador in New Delhi, that no further invasion of Tibet would take place if he conducted negotiations with the government of Mao Tse Tung in Peking. A delegation, headed by Ngabo Ngawang Jigme and including one of the Dalai Lama's elder brothers, Gyalo Thondup, was despatched and talks were held during the following months.

On 23 May, the Chinese announced that the Seventeen Point Agreement had been signed, even though the Tibetan delegation had not been authorised by the government in Lhasa to do anything more than discuss the new situation with China. In fact, the delegation had been bullied and coerced by the Chinese into accepting their terms and signing the agreement which declared that 'the Tibetan people shall unite and drive out imperialist aggressive forces from Tibet and shall return to the big family of the Motherland – the People's Republic of China'. The agreement undertook to retain Tibetan autonomy, maintaining the internal authority of the Dalai Lama and the status quo of the system of regional government within Tibet. At the same time, however, it called on the government in Lhasa to assist Chinese forces in entering Tibet. A military and administrative committee would be established in Lhasa, as would a military area headquarters. All Tibetan forces would be incorporated into the People's Liberation Army (PLA), China assuming all responsibility for national defence and foreign affairs. The Seventeen Point Agreement effectively ratified the Chinese occupation of Tibet and ended the country's de facto independence.

On 1 July, a Chinese delegation, together with members of the Tibetan delegation to Peking, arrived in India at the West Bengali capital of Calcutta en route to Yatung for negotiations with the Dalai Lama. By this time, the latter had decided that he was prepared to agree to the Chinese controlling his country's foreign relations and defence but that if they insisted on control of Tibet's internal affairs, he would leave and go into exile. This decision had been made known to the United States with whom the young ruler had been in secret communication through the US Embassy in New Delhi. The US State Department, with the support of the CIA, had been actively encouraging the Dalai Lama to go into exile in India, Ceylon or Thailand, agreeing to support him in the event of his doing so and to provide limited military assistance for any Tibetan resistance movement through the supply of small arms and light weapons. In addition, the Americans had expressed support for a plan, ultimately rejected by His Holiness, for him and a small group of his followers to be spirited away into the neighbouring country of Bhutan from where they would be flown to safety.

Despite the attempts of the United States and others to persuade him to go into exile, the Dalai Lama returned to Lhasa on 17 August 1951 after a month's journey from Yatung. Just prior to his arrival, the commander of the occupying Chinese forces, General Zhang Jingwu, had established his headquarters in Lhasa and a month later the first units of the PLA arrived. In late October, the Dalai Lama formally accepted the Seventeen Point Agreement signed in Peking in May. The subsequent continuing influx of PLA forces in Tibet inevitably placed a heavy burden on the local population, resulting in food shortages and rising prices for essential items in Lhasa and the surrounding villages, and causing further resentment among the Tibetans. The Chinese responded by devoting considerable efforts to winning the hearts and minds of the disgruntled Tibetans: a hospital and clinic were opened in the city, offering free medical treatment, while a mobile cinema team provided free entertainment.

During the invasion, the Chinese had been forced to commit the majority of their available aircraft to supporting the PLA forces on the ground, and it had become obvious that the country could never be dominated fully without the existence of strategic roads for use by vehicles. So they lost little time in constructing two major highways, one leading from Lhasa to Lake Kokonor in the far north-east of Amdo, while the other ran 1,400 miles from Lhasa across Kham to Kanting on the Chinese border. Completed in 1953, this second route crossed fourteen mountain ranges, at altitudes of up to 13,000 feet, and seven major rivers. Both highways were constructed ostensibly for purposes of economic development but no one in Tibet was under any illusion that they had been built for any other purpose than to allow swift movement and reinforcement of Chinese forces.

After the first few months following the occupation, the Chinese mask of benevolence began to slip as Peking instituted so-called 'democratic reforms' designed to cause internal dissent among Tibetans and thus enable the Chinese to increase their grip on the country. Meanwhile, they maintained an uneasy relationship with the Tibetan government, promising autonomy for the country and respect for Tibetan institutions and customs yet at the same time seeking to destroy the very roots of Tibetan culture. Public assemblies were held in villages at which the Chinese announced that the population comprised five classes: capitalists, landowners, the middle-class bourgeoisie, peasants, and labourers and servants. The last were told to denounce their employers and masters but failed to do so, there being no discontented proletariat in Tibet and thus no 'class hatred'. The Chinese therefore resorted to new tactics, including the bribing of beggars to make allegations against the wealthy, which proved equally fruitless.

Eventually, having made no progress in persuading the Tibetans to accept their reforms, the Chinese turned to more brutal methods against the populations of Amdo and Kham. Among these were execution of members of the upper three classes; in the Amdo town of Doi, 300 were executed in front of a crowd as a lesson to those who refused to bow to Chinese demands. At the same time, thousands of Chinese settlers were imported into eastern Tibet to 'colonise' the region. This was followed in early 1954 by the establishment of cooperatives in the Litany and Kandze areas of Kham, with cattle and land being confiscated from Tibetans.

This was the final straw and several Khamba tribes made preparations for rebellion, their leaders looking to Lhasa for support, which was not forthcoming. The unscrupulous Ngabo Ngawang Jigme, by now a minister, was firmly under the influence of the Chinese and the Dalai Lama appeared to be enjoying good relations with the government of Mao Tse Tung in Peking. Under the influence of Ngabo, he acceded to the requests of the PLA commander in Tibet, General Zhang Jingwu, and even dismissed his prime minister, Lukhangwa, at the demand of the Chinese.

In late 1953, the Chinese had issued an 'invitation', which in reality was more of a demand, to the Dalai Lama to visit China and to attend the first Chinese Peoples National Assembly due to take place the following September. Eventually, despite pleadings and petitions from his people not to go, he accepted in the belief that he might be able to influence the Chinese in their policy towards Tibet. He left Lhasa in the middle of 1954, accompanied by an entourage of approximately 500 and was joined en route at Sian by the Panchen Lama, the next most senior religious leader in Tibet.

The journey took some weeks, the final parts being completed by train and air. Two days after his arrival in Peking, where he and the Panchen Lama were welcomed with great ceremony, the Dalai Lama was involved in a series of lengthy discussions with Mao Tse Tung who so impressed the young Tibetan leader that at one point he admitted, 'Every time I saw Mao, he inspired me again.'

The Chinese went to great lengths to persuade the Dalai Lama and his followers of the great wonders of Marxism, and described to him in detail the new systems of government to be adopted in Tibet, the Preparatory Committee for the Autonomous Region of Tibet (PCART). This, they claimed, would enhance his authority and increase the number of Tibetans in his government. They omitted to mention, however, that as an autonomous region Tibet was merely a province of China and an integral part of the People's Republic.

On 12 March 1955, the Chinese State Council announced that it had passed a resolution concerning Tibet. Under its terms, the PCART would consist of 51 individuals: fifteen from the Tibetan government; ten from a body called the Panchen Kanpo Lija (Committee on Historical and Unsettled Problems); ten from the People's Liberation Committee of Chamdo (which was under the control of a Chinese general); five members of Chinese Cadres of the Central People's Government working in Tibet; and eleven representatives of public bodies, religious sects and monasteries. The Dalai Lama would be director of the PCART, while the Panchen Lama and the senior PLA officer in Tibet, General Chang Kuo Hua, would be vice-directors. The secretary general of the organisation would be Ngabo Ngawang Jigme.

The resolution also stated that the Tibetan government, the Panchen Kanpo Lija and the People's Liberation Committee of Chamdo would be directly responsible to the Chinese State Council for administrative matters. It further stipulated that all measures approved by the State Council to be undertaken by the PCART should also be observed and carried out by the PLA Tibetan Military District Command. By these measures, China steadily reduced the powers of the Dalai Lama and placed the government of Tibet firmly under the control of the PLA in Tibet. Within the PCART itself, the Chinese would control at least half of its membership as well as its agenda.

A few days later the Dalai Lama left Peking. It was while bidding farewell to his guest that Mao Tse Tung stated: 'Religion is poison. Firstly it reduces the population, because monks and nuns must stay celibate, and secondly it neglects material progress.' These words obviously caused the scales to fall from the eyes of the Dalai Lama, who later wrote of the Chinese leader: 'You are the destroyer of the Dharma [the Buddhist Law of all things] after all.'

The Dalai Lama returned to Tibet in June, interrupting his journey to Lhasa at Chamdo where he urged the Khambas to take a moderate stance in their dealings with the Chinese. His pleas fell on deaf ears, particularly after the PLA troops stationed in Chamdo began abusing the monks and attempting to prevent the local people from visiting the monasteries. In October, large PLA forces arrived at Batang, Litang, Kandze and Dergue and announced that all Khambas were required to surrender the weapons they habitually carried. They also proclaimed that henceforth the Tibetan religion was to be regarded as poisonous, that all monasteries and monks were to be 'eliminated' and that 'God and gods are the instrument of exploitation'.

This was the match that lit the flame of rebellion throughout Kham, the tribes in the hills being joined by almost the entire able-bodied male populations of towns and villages. In Chamdo, however, the Chinese succeeded in luring over 150 officials and local leaders of the region to the fortress of Jomdho, some 40 miles from the capital, where they found themselves suddenly surrounded by PLA troops. After fifteen days of attempted indoctrination, the Khamba leaders managed to overpower their guards at night and disappeared into the darkness to join their compatriots in the mountains.

By 1956, however, the Chinese were well ensconced in eastern Tibet. Large garrisons had been established at Batang, Litang, Kandze and Dergue, and fortified outposts located every twenty miles along the two highways that spanned Kham. PLA troops in the region numbered some 40,000, being reinforced by approximately 20,000 trained militia recruited from the Chinese 'colonists'. Further reinforcements could be summoned from Szechuan only two days travel away via newly constructed roads.

Undeterred, the Khambas launched a series of attacks on the highways, cutting off the lines of supply to the Chinese garrisons. Litang was first, falling after its garrison fled, followed by Batang. Kandze, Chamdo and Dergue were also attacked and captured, along with a number of other minor garrisons. Chinese 'colonists' were evicted from their settlements, being expelled in large numbers eastward back into China. The Chinese regional headquarters at Yaan, near Kanting, received a stream of frantic radio transmissions reporting Khamba attacks. From the regions of Amdo and Golok came similar reports of garrisons and isolated units being overrun by Amdowan and Golok tribesmen who showed no mercy in slaughtering the enemy. The Goloks were reported as wiping out three PLA regiments, an estimated 7,000 Chinese being killed in the process. All roads into Tibet had been cut with the exception of one, a long, circuitous and highly secret route, completed that year, which led from China west through Sinkiang and across the Aksai Chin desert to provide better communication between Sinkiang and western Tibet. The Aksai Chin, however, lay inside the Indian state of Kashmir and the stretch of road across it was built without India's knowledge.

IT WAS IN DECEMBER 1956 that the first steps were taken towards creating a national resistance movement. At that time, the only such body was a loose alliance of two dozen Khamba and Amdowa clans grouped together as the National Army of the Defenders of the Faith (NADF). A Khamba leader named Gompo Tashi Andrugtsang, a member of one of Tibet's four powerful trading families, had travelled throughout southern and eastern Tibet, his activities as a trader covering the real purpose of his journeys which was to contact other leaders and assess their readiness to fight the Chinese. Earlier, he had dispatched emissaries throughout Kham, urging the Khambas to mount attacks against the oppressive occupiers of their country. In some areas, his approaches fell on fertile ground as tribal chiefs expressed their willingness to join a national resistance under his leadership. Others proved less amenable, regarding him as their social inferior and thus being reluctant to subjugate themselves to him.

In early 1957, communicating with utmost secrecy, Gompo Tashi raised the subject of armed resistance with the Dalai Lama through the head of the latter's personal staff, an abbot named Thupten Woyden Phala. He asked the Dalai Lama to consider granting military assistance to the resistance movements in preparation for a national uprising to eject the Chinese from Tibet. While sympathetic to the trials and tribulations of his people, the Dalai Lama was a man of peace, unable to condone the use of force against the Chinese. Moreover, he was convinced that any uprising was doomed to failure. He thus turned down Gompo Tashi's request for assistance.

Unknown to the Dalai Lama, however, Gompo Tashi had already obtained a limited amount of military assistance from an external source, the United States, and in particular the CIA. Six Tibetans were handpicked for specialist training by Gyalo Thondup and Thubten Jigme Norbu, the Dalai Lama's elder brothers, Tsipon Shakabpa, (former chief financial officer of the Tibetan government who had headed the trade mission to India, China and the United States in 1947-8), Lhamo Tsering, a senior member of the resistance movement, and a Khamba monk named Gyatotsang, whose nephew Wangdu, also a nephew of Gompo Tashi, was among those chosen. Selected from a number of candidates proposed by Gompo Tashi, they made their way to India and East Bengal from where they were flown to Saipan, one of the Northern Mariana Islands in the Western Pacific. Captured from the Japanese in 1944, Saipan had become an important American air base during the latter part of the Second World War and since 1953 had been under US naval jurisdiction.

This was to be the start of a long-running operation, codenamed ST CIRCUS, which would provide arms and training for the Tibetan resistance. Initially, it was headed by John Regan, an officer in the Directorate of Plans, the division of the CIA tasked with the conduct of covert operations. He was subsequently succeeded by Frank Holober, who during the period 1951-2 had been involved in covert operations on the south-eastern coast of China, carrying them out with nationalist Chinese guerrillas based on Quemoy and other islands lying off the mainland.

At a training camp established by the CIA, the six Tibetans, who had been given the *noms de guerre* of 'Walt', 'Dick', 'Dan' 'Tom', 'Sam' and 'Lou', underwent four and a half months of extensive instruction in guerrilla warfare conducted by another officer in the Directorate of Plans, Roger E. 'Mac' McCarthy. In addition to small arms, they were trained in the use of light support weapons, including the 57mm recoilless rifle and 60mm mortar, and well schooled in tactics, fieldcraft, map-reading, navigation, demolitions, mine-laying, sabotage, booby traps and first aid. They also received instruction in intelligence-gathering skills and in the operation of the RS-1 crystal-controlled HF transmitter/receiver, a set used by the OSS during the Second World War, along with the use of one-time pads and a Tibetan telecode for encryption and decryption of messages. Furthermore, the Tibetans were trained in the selection and marking out of dropping zones (DZs) for the dropping of parachutists as well as arms and equipment.

The final part of their training was a parachute course, conducted at Kadena Air Force Base (AFB) on the Japanese island of Okinawa, during which they underwent ground training and carried out three descents using modified steerable T-10 parachutes especially designed for use at high altitudes. The descents were made from a converted B-17 Flying Fortress, taken over by the CIA from the US Air Force (USAF). Stripped of any identification markings, the aircraft was operated by Civil Air Transport (CAT), a subsidiary of a CIA-owned company named Pacific Corporation. Formed by General Claire Chennault in China in October 1946 as CNRRA Air Transport (the name being changed to Civil Air Transport at the beginning of 1948), CAT had begun its existence flying aircraft supplied by the US government to transport refugees and relief supplies in China. From 1948 onwards, it had transported supplies for the nationalist Chinese forces of Chiang Kai Shek by then engaged in the civil war against the communists.

Leaving China in 1949 along with the nationalist forces, CAT had transferred its base to Taiwan and next year had been purchased by the CIA. Equipped mainly with C-47 Douglas Skytrains and C-46 Curtiss Commandos, it had carried out covert missions over southern China and Burma in support of nationalist Chinese forces attempting a reconquest of China. In 1953, flying C-119 Flying Boxcars supplied by the USAF, it had supported French forces in Indochina, assisting in the airlift of 16,000 French troops into the ill-fated base at Dien Bien Phu and carrying out resupply missions.

The late 1950s saw CAT aircrews in Indonesia flying Douglas B-26 Invader light bombers, modified as ground attack aircraft, in support of rebels seeking to overthrow the pro-communist regime of President Ahmed Sukarno. The shooting down of one of its aircraft and the capture of the pilot had exposed the CIA's role in the insurrection. From late 1959 onward and for the following six years, CAT would also be involved in Operation ST BARNUM, the air operations element of ST CIRCUS.

On completion of their parachute training, the two-man team of Athar Norbu and Losang Tsering was flown to a Second World War airfield at Kurmitola, east of Dacca in East Pakistan (now Bangladesh) which had been adopted by the USAF's Strategic Air Command (SAC) as an emergency landing field and now acted as a forward staging base for ST BARNUM. This phase of the operation was the responsibility of a special USAF Unit, Air Force Detachment 2, based at Kadena Air Force Base. During a full-moon period in October 1957, the two Tibetans boarded the B-17 which was flown by a USAF pilot, Major Robert Kleyla, who had previous experience of flying B-17s, to Kurmitola. From there it was flown by a CAT aircrew of Polish and Czechoslovakian exiles who had previously flown missions deep into Soviet-occupied eastern Europe. Athar and Losang Tsering were subsequently dropped into Tibet, in an area on the banks of the Brahmaputra River to the south of Lhasa. Accompanying them was a container holding a Lee Enfield ..303 rifle and ammunition for each of them; two radios and hand-cranked generators, complete with duplicate sets of ancillaries; clothing; money, in Tibetan and Indian currencies; rations, in the form of tsampa (roasted barley flour) and dried salt beef; medical kits and other miscellaneous equipment. In addition, each man jumped with a personal weapon and equipment container holding a Sten 9mm submachine-gun, ammunition and rations. Losang Tsering also carried the signal plans vital for maintenance of radio communications with the ST CIRCUS forward base on Okinawa.

The two men landed without mishap and, having cached most of their equipment, headed for Lhasa on their initial task which was to deliver a message for the Dalai Lama from the United States government offering to provide assistance if His Holiness requested it. This was delivered to Gompo Tashi who passed it to the head of the Dalai Lama's staff,

Thupten Woyden Phala. The Dalai Lama, once again refusing to condone the use of violence, refused to make such a request to the Americans. The US State Department nevertheless decided to drop the second team into eastern Kham during the full-moon period in November. Three of its members, including the leader Wangdu Gyatotsang, landed nine miles from their home area near Litang. The fourth had passed out in the aircraft and was unable to jump; he was subsequently despatched overland to rejoin his comrades but was intercepted and killed en route.

Soon after landing, Wangdu and his two companions encountered a Khamba resistance unit and made their way to a guerrilla base commanded by one of Wangdu's brothers, signalling to the CIA that they had arrived safely and had made contact with local resistance forces. Wangdu then set about contacting other resistance groups in Kham. He was to assess and report by radio their respective strengths and capabilities, while passing on to the guerrillas the skills imparted to him and his men by their CIA instructors. He would also report on operations conducted against the Chinese and on the order of battle of PLA formations and units in its area.

Gompo Tashi, meantime, had been busy persuading the chiefs of the 23 or so Khamba, Amdowan and Golok tribes to form a national resistance movement. He had assembled them at Lhasa through the ruse of suggesting to the Tibetan government that special ceremonies be held in honour of the Dalai Lama, the highlight being the presentation to His Holiness of a magnificent throne of solid gold encrusted with diamonds, pearls and other precious and semi-precious stones. Thousands of Tibetans flocked to the capital prior to the ceremonies which were held in July, the throne being set in place at the Dalai Lama's Norbulingka Palace, his summer residence. During the lengthy preparations and under cover of the actual celebrations, the leaders of the various resistance factions had meetings with Gompo Tashi at which the formation of a national resistance movement was discussed. The Chinese remained completely unaware of these, but when they later discovered what had taken place under their very noses, they summoned the Lhasa government's entire cabinet, the commanders of the Tibetan army and the abbots of the three largest monasteries and warned them that anyone discovered helping the resistance would be executed, proclamations to that effect being published throughout Tibet.

In early 1958, a further meeting was held in Lhasa, at Gompo Tashi's home, when all but a few of the chiefs agreed to form a movement named the Chushi Gangdrug, a collective term referring to the four rivers and six mountain ranges of the region of Kham. Agreements were reached on the areas in which different groups would operate, appointments of individuals to positions of command, acquisition of arms, horses and mules, allocation of resources and selection of targets to be attacked. News of the formation of the Chushi Gangdrug was conveyed secretly to the Dalai Lama by Thupten Woyden Phala who actively supported the idea of armed resistance.

Athar Norbu and Losang Tsering, who were still in Lhasa, had meanwhile received two more messages from the US State Department, transmitted via THE ST CIRCUS forward base on Okinawa, urging the Dalai Lama and his government to make a formal request for American assistance. Although the Dalai Lama again refused, President Dwight D. Eisenhower gave his approval for the CIA to provide support, including the delivery of arms and provision of training, for the Tibetan resistance.

In April, while Lhasa was again filled with throngs of Tibetans attending a Buddhist festival, Gompo Tashi convened another meeting attended by 300 members of the Chushi Gangdrug. The gathering was given the choice of either remaining in the capital to challenge the Chinese as and when the necessity arose to protect the Dalai Lama, or to confront the PLA in battle elsewhere throughout the country. Each alternative course of action was written on a piece of paper which was inserted in a ball of dough, both balls then being put into a cup which was placed in front of a statue of the Buddha and spun clockwise. The first ball to fall out contained the piece of paper giving the confrontation alternative and thus the die was cast: the Chushi Gangdrug would sally forth and do battle with the PLA.

Shortly afterwards, Gompo Tashi and the 300 who had attended the meeting left Lhasa and made their way to Trigu Thang, in the region of Lhoka, south of Lhasa, where the Chushi Gangdrug had established its tactical headquarters. It was there on 16 June 1958 that the organisation's military wing was formed under the name of the National Volunteer Defence Army (NVDA) under the overall command of Gompo Tashi. The adoption of the new name was for diplomatic reasons. Although the NVDA was recruited mainly from the eastern regions of

Tibet, its leaders were keen for it to be seen as a national force and to bear a name that reflected such. Not long afterwards, the NVDA moved its headquarters farther east to Tsona, south of the Tsangpo River and some 120 miles from the Indian border to the south.

Gompo Tashi had already devoted much of his family's wealth to purchasing weapons for the resistance, these being a mixture of Russian, Czech, German, British and Canadian small arms and ammunition acquired primarily from India. The rapidly expanding NVDA needed more, however, and in the middle of August, he and a force of 750 guerrillas left Tsona and set off for Shang Gaden Choekhor where it was known that the Tibetan army had a depot containing a large armoury as well as considerable amounts of grain and forage for horses. By this time Athar Norbu had left Lhasa and made his way to India where he was coordinating the first of the arms drops to be carried out by the CIA. Gompo Tashi, however, had decided not to wait for these but to proceed with his plan of seizing the arms and ammunition held at Shang Gyatso Dzong, after which he would begin operations against the Chinese.

Ahead of his main force went a reconnaissance group of 150 guerrillas who headed for Chu Shur where PLA forces had been reported as active. Unfortunately, a Chinese collaborator had informed the PLA of the guerrillas' intentions and routes; on 26 August, the latter were ambushed on a road at Nemo Lhokhar, coming under heavy small arms and mortar fire which pinned them down. Fortunately, Gompo Tashi and the main force heard the firing in the distance and moved up into the hills overlooking the area. In the ensuing battle, lasting two days, the PLA force was routed by a charge of mounted guerrillas. Chinese casualties were heavy, amounting to some 200, while NVDA losses numbered 40 killed and 68 wounded, with the loss of 50 horses and mules.

Short of ammunition after the heavy fighting, the guerrillas continued their march north with all haste but on arrival at Shang Gaden Choekhor discovered that the contents of the army depot's armoury had been transferred to the monastery of Shang Gadhen Choling, situated some ten miles away, on the orders of the government in Lhasa. It took three days of diplomatic pleading and argument before the monks, under strict instructions from the government in Lhasa not to surrender the arms to the guerrillas, could be prevailed upon to hand them over. In addition to 385 Lee Enfield rifles, there were ten Bren LMGs, eighteen Sten guns, two 60mm light mortars, two 80mm medium mortars, 108 80mm and 288 60mm mortar bombs, and large quantities of .303 and 9mm ammunition. In order to enable the monks to convince the Chinese that they had been forced to surrender the arms under duress, three of their number were taken hostage but were released on the evening of the guerrillas' departure.

Gompo Tashi and his men continued to head north. A reconnaissance force pushed on ahead to Wuyk Zomthang and Takdru Kha to look for any signs of a PLA presence, being followed close behind by another 100 guerrillas who would provide immediate support in the event of trouble. A PLA convoy was ambushed, all eighteen Chinese drivers and troops being killed in the process. Having liberated seven horses, together with quantities of arms and ammunition, the reconnaissance force retraced its tracks south to rejoin Gompo Tashi and the main body.

Another group of 50 guerrillas, meanwhile, was despatched to Wuyk Zomthang and Takhdru Kha to check for any Chinese presence there. A similar-sized group then set off to reconnoitre the banks of the Nemo River but as they approached Nemo Shung, they encountered a PLA unit and a fierce action ensued in which they suffered one man killed and another wounded. Withdrawing, they encountered other PLA units and sustained further casualties. The fighting spread as more of Gompo Tashi's force moved up to engage large numbers of Chinese who brought heavy small arms and mortar fire to bear. Once again, though, a mass cavalry charge by the guerrillas routed the Chinese troops who broke and fled rather than face the razor-sharp swords of the Khamba horsemen. Having regrouped, the NVDA then cleared the villages throughout the area, rooting out pockets of resistance and setting fire to buildings in which some Chinese took refuge and refused to surrender.

Gompo Tashi's losses in this battle were surprisingly light, numbering twelve killed and some twenty wounded, while the PLA lost some 700 killed and many wounded. The guerrillas captured large quantities of arms and ammunition but had little time to savour their victory as reports arrived of the approach of another large PLA force. Withdrawing that evening and preceded by an advance guard of 50, Gompo Tashi and his men carried out a forced march east towards Nemo Junpa where they encountered some 1,000 PLA troops. Avoiding contact, they bypassed the enemy force but shortly afterwards met another, larger body approaching from the opposite direction. In the ensuing fighting, the guerrillas killed some 200 Chinese, wounded many more, and then withdrew.

Continuing their journey, the guerrillas made for Jang Yangpa Chen but their leading element was warned of the presence of a large PLA force numbering some 10,000 troops in the area. A subsequent reconnaissance revealed the presence of some 200 PLA trucks but no sign of any force of such size. Aware of the danger of being trapped, however, Gompo Tashi decided to mount an attack on Jang Yangpa Chen without delay. Complete surprise was achieved with a cavalry charge which routed the PLA troops in the town, whose numbers were larger than expected and who suffered heavy casualties. Having seized large quantities of arms and ammunition, the guerrillas pressed on to Jang Namtso where they regrouped and rested for several days.

During this period, enemy aircraft were observed searching for the guerrillas. Scouts reported, too, not only that a PLA force of 1,000 was following up behind but also that other Chinese units were moving into the area. Gompo Tashi had already sent additional scouts forward to reconnoitre mountain trails and these now led the guerrillas, in groups of 100 or so, travelling approximately ten miles apart, through very difficult terrain where the PLA would be unwilling to follow.

Gompo Tashi's next objective was an airfield and depot at Dhamshung, his force being short of food and other supplies. Having slaughtered the garrison there, the guerrillas replenished their stocks of food and arms before setting the depot ablaze and leaving for Nakchukha, thereafter heading south for De Gung Drakhe. As they did so, they laid an ambush for a small PLA unit which had been following them, killing all but a few of its members. Shortly afterwards, however, Gompo Tashi's advance element of 100 men was ambushed and pinned down by a larger enemy unit, the battle lasting throughout the day and that night. At dawn next day he prepared his main force for an assault, but suddenly the Chinese, who had suffered a number of casualties including eighteen killed, broke and fled.

There was little respite for the guerillas. No sooner had they regrouped and resumed their advance than news arrived of a large force of 10,000 PLA troops, supported by 400 vehicles, deploying into positions blocking Gompo Tashi's planned line of march. Shortly afterwards, heavy enemy mortar bombardment and machine-gun fire were directed on to the plateau where the NVDA had taken up positions. Six guerrillas were killed and twenty-two wounded, Gompo Tashi himself being among the latter, while twenty horses and mules were lost. Fortunately the barrage resulted in a massive dust cloud which acted as a smokescreen in covering the guerrillas' withdrawal during the late afternoon, enabling them to escape just before the enemy encircled the plateau. The Chinese attempted to follow but soon gave up after losing some four vehicles full of troops which skidded off the narrow trails, tumbling down the mountainsides to the valleys far below.

Next day found Chinese aircraft searching for the guerrillas but hampered by low cloud. During the following two days and nights, Gompo Tashi and his men continued their march until they reached Kong Tse La where they were able to rest while sending out groups on foraging and reconnaissance tasks. But when a large PLA force was observed approaching their location, they were obliged to carry out a fighting withdrawal, losing fifteen men in this skirmish. Shortly afterwards, the guerrillas suffered a major blow when a company, 100-strong, was captured after running out of ammunition. The remainder meanwhile managed to get away by a very difficult route, travelling for several days and nights in an effort to shake off their pursuers.

Eventually, Gompo Tashi arrived at Japho Jakey where he divided his force into three groups which rested for two days before laying a large ambush and sending out reconnaissance patrols. These reported the presence of a 3,000-strong PLA force at nearby Ahtsar Lake and he was about to prepare an attack when he received reports of the arrival of enemy reinforcements. At this juncture the guerrilla ambush was sprung and a PLA patrol of eighteen men was wiped out. The firing, however, attracted the attention of the main enemy force and soon the guerrillas were once again under heavy small arms and mortar fire. The battle lasted throughout the day, the guerrillas withdrawing under cover of darkness, suffering only two men wounded but inflicting heavy casualties on the Chinese, although these were never quantified. Moving on, after a warning of a large Chinese force of 5,000 troops waiting to intercept his force near Jang Lhari, Gompo Tashi headed via Jang Methika for Naksho.

At Naksho, his men were able to rest for four days and replenish their food stocks before moving on to Dramthang and ultimately Sarteng.

Here the guerrillas learned of the atrocities being carried out against Tibetans by the Chinese. These included destruction of monasteries with monks being imprisoned or forced into hard labour, public executions or beatings and the rape of women and nuns.

Some weeks earlier, three groups of 40 guerrillas had deserted from the ranks of Gompo Tashi's force. One group had made its way west to Nepal which it reached after several skirmishes with the Chinese. The other two, commanded respectively by two individuals named Zenang Ahker and Relpa Bhuchung, had set about committing crimes against local people. Such acts were highly detrimental to the reputation of the NVDA and Gompo Tashi decided to deal with the renegades at the earliest opportunity. Before doing so, however, he was obliged to replenish his stocks of arms, ammunition and food by attacking a PLA supply depot near Sarteng Galton. The small garrison of 40 troops was quickly overrun and the depot emptied of its contents. A detachment of 100 guerrillas was promptly despatched to Chukhor where it arrested the two renegade guerrilla leaders who were tried, condemned and executed. Their followers were disarmed and either fined or whipped, some of the more stubborn receiving both punishments or losing an ear or a finger for particularly severe offences. All were then branded and cast out into the wilds to survive as best they could.

On 6 December, Gompo Tashi's force left Sarteng Galton and marched to Chakra Pelkhar in north-western Tibet. By this time, it had become apparent to him and his commanders that the increasing use of airborne surveillance by the Chinese meant that it was no longer possible for the NVDA to operate in large numbers. It would have to rely more on increased mobility and the use of guerrilla tactics, such as ambushes, rather than large- scale attacks. At a conference of commanders on 8 December, it was therefore decided to split the force into smaller groups. The main mounted unit of 500 tribesmen would be located in the Lhoka region while two groups of 30 men would be moved to Tsethang and Dre to carry out operations in those areas. The remaining elements, including those troops who had been left behind at Lhoka at the start of Gompo Tashi's expedition and who were now summoned to join him at Chakra Pelkhar, would be divided into two divisions each operating in company-sized groups of 100 men. These would be augmented by volunteers recruited from local people.

On 25 December, the guerrillas launched an attack on the town of Po Tamo, a town on the Lhasa–Sichuan highway which was a vital Chinese line of supply that Gompo Tashi aimed to cut. Unfortunately, the force summoned from Lokha was unable to reach Chakra Pelkhar in time for the battle which lasted a fortnight. Nevertheless, the guerrillas eventually carried the day, killing over 550 Chinese troops while only suffering only twenty killed and nine wounded. Shortly afterwards, a small force of 29 guerrillas, reinforced by 400 local people, attacked a nearby Chinese base. This battle lasted another ten days during which heavy casualties were inflicted once again on the Chinese by the guerrillas and locals who set fire to the base, destroying its buildings and a large number of vehicles.

The end of December 1958 found guerrilla reconnaissance units at Naksho Tsogu, Lho Dzing and Tsawa Pesho. Their tasks were to reconnoitre each area, acquire further supplies of arms and ammunition, as supplies were by then running low, and to recruit young men to swell the guerrillas' ranks.

WHILE GOMPO TASHI HAD been taking the war to the enemy, the United States had been continuing to provide support. In February 1958, a second group of Tibetans, selected by Gyalo Thondup and Lhamo Tsering, had been sent from Tibet via India to the United States for training in guerrilla warfare. On this occasion, it was to have been carried out at a CIA facility on the eastern seaboard of the United States, on the coast of Virginia; but the climate there proved unsuitable for men used to living in mountainous areas at high altitudes and thus the Agency had been forced to seek a more suitable location. The solution was produced by the US Army which offered the use of Camp Hale, the former wartime base of the 10th US Mountain Division located at 10,000 feet near the town of Leadville in the mountains of Colorado.

The first group of Tibetans to be trained at Camp Hale arrived there at the end of May 1959. Training was provided by a team of instructors selected by Roger McCarthy who subsequently succeeded Frank Holober as head of OPERATION ST CIRCUS. Each of the instructors was known to the Tibetan trainees only by his first name. In charge of the camp was 'Mr Tom', a former member of the US Army's airborne forces named Tom Fosmire, who was assisted by 'Mr Zeke', in reality Albert W. Zilaitis who two years later succeeded Fosmire as head of training and commander of the camp.

Training was conducted six days a week, each day lasting ten to twelve hours and incorporating exercises by day and at night. On some occasions, Sundays were also used for training if necessary. Radio communications, covering the use of the RS-1 HF transmitter/receiver, transmission of messages at speeds of up to twenty words per minute and encryption/decryption of them, were taught by 'Mr Ray' while logistics was the specialist subject of 'Mr Al'. Instruction in field medicine and first aid was provided by 'Mr Harry', who also provided medical treatment. 'Mr Ken', operations officer John Kenneth Knaus, lectured on the history of communism and propaganda and also trained the Tibetans in the use of a portable mimeograph machine and the production of leaflets and pamphlets.

Out on the training areas and ranges, 'Mr Bill' provided instruction in the use of small arms comprising handguns, sub-machine-guns and rifles, the last consisting of the Lee Enfield No. 4 .303, Springfield M1917 .30 and Garand M1 .30/06, including sniper variants. In addition, the Tibetans were trained to use support weapons comprising 3.5 inch rocket launchers, 60mm light and 81mm medium mortars and 57mm and 75mm recoilless rifles. Meanwhile, 'Mr Roy' taught them minor unit tactics, including ambushes, and how to select and mark DZs for the reception of parachute resupply and personnel insertion drops. Other subjects included fieldcraft, map-reading and navigation, demolitions, sabotage, booby traps, mine-laying, combat survival, psychological warfare operations, field medicine and first aid, establishment of intelligence and underground networks, and the driving of wheeled and tracked vehicles. Each man also underwent parachute ground training provided by Mr 'Jack', before carrying out three descents at Butts Field Air Force Base in Colorado.

Throughout its seven years' duration, the ST CIRCUS training programme at Camp Hale was carried out under maximum security with all unauthorised personnel banned from the camp and surrounding training areas which were patrolled by military police. The sounds of explosions emanating from the area caused rumours of an atomic weapons test programme, a misconception fostered by a report planted by the CIA which resulted in a front-page story in a Denver newspaper to that effect. On their arrival, the Tibetans had been flown into Peterson Air Force Base near Colorado Springs from which they were transported in buses with blacked-out windows to Camp Hale. Later, after a traffic incident which resulted in local civilians catching sight of some of the trainees, rumours of 'unidentified orientals' reached the local press and ultimately the *New York Times*. The CIA moved quickly to clamp down on the story which was suppressed by the newspaper after the personal intervention of the Secretary of Defence, Robert McNamara.

When training was complete, each group of Tibetans waited at Camp Hale for deployment back into Tibet. Air drops were scheduled to take place during the full-moon phase of each month. A week to ten days prior to the date of a drop, a group would be flown to Kadena AFB on Okinawa where it would be equipped with the Tibetan clothing its members were to wear in Tibet. It was also issued with personal weapons, maps, compasses, binoculars, signal plans, first aid equipment, survival gear and any other equipment required for its tasks. Thereafter, the group would undergo detailed briefings on its mission before being flown to the ST BARNUM forward staging base at Kermitola in East Pakistan.

The CIA, meanwhile, had commenced dropping consignments of weapons into Tibet. The first drop had taken place in July 1958, a month after Gompo Tashi's departure for Shang Gyatso Dzong, with a small consignment of weapons being dropped at Trigu Thang where it was received by Losang Tsering, one of the first two-man teams, whose companion Athar Norbu had coordinated the drop from India. Shortly afterwards, the leader of the second team, Wangdu Gyatotsang, appeared at Trigu Thang. Some time earlier, misfortune had befallen him and his men when the guerrilla base at which they were located had come under heavy attack by PLA troops. During the ensuing action Wangdu's two companions, one of them the team's radio operator, had been killed but Wangdu himself had managed to escape. Subsequently, he made his way south from Trigu Thang to India where he would re-emerge to play a major role in the resistance.

The second delivery of weapons did not take place until 22 February 1959, by which time Athar had rejoined Losang Tsering at Trigu Thang. These first two drops provided a total of 403 Lee Enfield rifles, 20 Bren

LMGs, 60 grenades and 26,000 rounds of .303 ammunition, a mere drop in the ocean compared to the quantities of weapons required by the thousands of Tibetans who had flocked to join the NVDA in Lhoka since June 1958.

Prior to these first two drops, it had been realised that the B-17 used in the transport of the initial two teams was unsuitable for dropping large quantities of arms and equipment, and that CAT's C-46s and C-47s did not possess the range to carry out operations over Tibet. The CIA thus used the only other suitable aircraft in its inventory, the Douglas C-118 Liftmaster. Aircrew were selected from volunteers among CAT personnel who had experience of carrying out clandestine flights for the CIA in other regions. Parachute despatch officers (PDO), who were responsible for despatching men and containers from the aircraft over the DZ, were recruited from members of the US Forestry Service whose 'smoke jumpers' were highly skilled in parachuting into remote areas of the United States to put out forest fires.

Missions were planned in response to requests from a resistance group for arms and equipment. The guerrillas would select and nominate a DZ, each of which was photographed in May 1959 by a U-2 high-altitude reconnaissance aircraft belonging to the Development Projects Division of the CIA's Directorate of Plans. These photographs, together with others taken in subsequent U-2 missions during September and November 1959, were used to create the first accurate maps of Tibet. Routes to and from the DZ would be planned in detail, with factors such as weather conditions, terrain, the threat of interdiction by enemy aircraft and payload being taken into account. Much of the final planning for missions was also carried out by Major Lawrence Ropka, a USAF officer seconded to the CIA.

The C-118, however, was soon found to be far from suitable for the task. Its maximum operating range was only 3,000 miles from Okinawa, requiring the aircraft to land and refuel at Kermitola before flying on over Tibet. Furthermore, powered by four Pratt & Whitney 2,500 hp engines, it was unable to operate at altitudes which would have enabled it to fly above the Himalayas. Pilots were therefore forced to navigate their way through the mountains, a potentially hair-raising experience as one pilot in particular discovered when forced to take violent evasive action on being confronted by a peak of over 25,000 feet which did not feature on his chart. The aircraft's other drawbacks included lack of an adequate radar and the inability for its cargo door to be opened in flight, requiring its removal beforehand and thus the use of oxygen by all those aboard for much of the flight. Moreover, the small size of the doorway required more than one pass for all personnel and containers to be dropped, increasing the possibility of the location of the DZ and those on it being compromised, as well as making the aircraft a potentially easy target for hostile fire from the ground. Finally, the high altitudes and weather conditions over Tibet, including winds of over 100 mph, were such that payloads for the C-118 had to be limited to a maximum of 12,000 lbs.

Larger loads and improved performance in such conditions would require the use of an aircraft such as the larger C-130A Hercules transport whose turbo-prop engines possessed double the horsepower of the C-118 and would allow operation at considerably increased altitudes. It had, however, only recently entered service with the US Air Force (USAF), the first having appeared in Tactical Air Command (TAC) squadrons at the end of 1956. Nevertheless, on being approached by the CIA, the USAF agreed to assist by providing unmarked C-130As, albeit the absence of markings would be of little import as the aircraft at that time was in American and Australian service only.

The aircraft were supplied for each mission by the 315th Troop Carrier Wing (TCW) at Naha AFB on Okinawa. On each occasion, they were flown to Kadena AFB where containers of arms and equipment were loaded by members of the CIA's aerial resupply section of ZR BLUSH, the Agency's principal East Asian logistics base which also located at Kadena. Each container was a load weighing some 85 lbs which could be carried by pack mules or ponies and, prior to each mission, the resistance group due to receive the drop would be advised by radio of the number of containers so that it would have the requisite number of animals waiting near the DZ.

Once loaded, each C-130A was flown by a CAT crew, comprising pilot, co-pilot, a navigator (on occasion two), flight engineer and three parachute despatchers, to the ST CIRCUS forward staging base. Initially, as mentioned earlier, this was situated at the USAF SAC emergency landing field at Kermitola in east Pakistan. Later, due to increasing political problems between India and Pakistan, this was relocated to Takhli in Thailand, an SAC base some 130 miles north of Bangkok. Also on board the air-craft was a 315th TCW pilot who ensured that his CAT counterpart was fully familiar with the aircraft prior to the commencement of the mission.

The forward staging base was operated by the 1045th Operational Evaluation and Training Group (OETG), the USAF cover name for a unit providing specialist support for CIA covert operations throughout Central and South-east Asia and which was responsible for operational oversight and planning of ST BARNUM operations. On arrival, each air-craft was stripped by 1045th OETG personnel of its USAF markings and completely 'sanitised' for any compromising indications of USAF origin. Thereafter, the crews awaited an alert message from the ST CIRCUS forward base on Okinawa which would give 24 hours notice of a mission launch. Subsequent affirmation messages would be issued twelve and six hours prior to take-off, followed by another one hour beforehand. Final confirmation for the mission to proceed would be given at time of scheduled take-off.

The decision to proceed with, or abort, a mission was primarily dependent on weather conditions in Tibet and particularly over the DZ. These were reported by the resistance group due to receive the drop, its operator sending messages in morse which related to images printed on cards, supplied by the CIA, showing various types of weather condi-tions. Each three-digit code referred to a particular situation regarding cloud coverage, winds and other weather characteristics in the area. This simple but highly effective method of meteorological reporting even-tually proved more effective than the sophisticated systems normally employed by the USAF.

The first C-130A missions, dropping arms and equipment only, took place in July 1959. On 19 September, the first group of Tibetans who had undergone training at Camp Hale were dropped back into Tibet (details of its tasks being given later in this chapter). Between nine and twelve missions were scheduled for the full-moon phase in each month but during November and December less than half of these were carried out due to problems with the aircraft. Foremost among these was the APN-59 radar set with which the C-130A was equipped as a navigation aid but which suffered from a high failure rate resulting in a large number of aborted missions. In addition, the very large fuel load of 40,000 lbs restricted the aircraft's passenger and equipment payload to 26,000 lbs.

These and other problems were solved by Major Harry 'Heinie' Aderholt, a USAF officer who previously had commanded the Special Air
Missions Detachment in Korea and subsequently had served two tours
of duty on secondment to the CIA, initially as head of its air training
branch and then as an unconventional warfare planning officer. In
January 1960, he took over command of the 1045th OETG and responsibility for ST BARNUM. He addressed himself swiftly to the problems
plaguing the airdrop programme and at his request the CIA's own elec-
tronics specialists investigated the recurring fault with the APN-59, soon
identifying it as being caused by the aircraft's electrical system. As to
the limitations on payload, discussions with the C-130A's manufacturer,
Lockheed, revealed that while the maximum gross take-off weight was
124,000 lbs, under emergency wartime conditions this could be increased
to 135,000 lbs. The lower figure was based on the side-loads affecting
the aircraft's undercarriage during taxiing, when steering exerted a side-
ways strain, and thus had no relevance with regard to performance of
the aircraft when airborne. Aderholt solved the problem by taxiing each
aircraft to its position at the end of the runway from which it would take
off, at which point it was fully fuelled. As a result, each C-130A was able
to carry an additional 11,000 lbs of payload.

Each mission normally involved up to three aircraft which would take
off just before nightfall from Takhli at fifteen-minute intervals, subsequently climbing to an altitude of 35,000 feet and heading north-west
across Thailand to Burma and beyond to India. They then headed north
across eastern India towards the Brahmaputra River, the radio operator signalling the aircraft's progress along a series of checkpoints with a
series of three-digit morse transmissions to Takhli. Flights were of six
to seven hours' duration and the principal problem facing the navigator was the inaccuracy of the charts covering Tibet. In order to verify
his position, the navigator took shots of three stars with a periscopic
sextant fitted in the roof of the cockpit. Two minutes were required for
each shot with a minute between each; with computing time added, the
entire process took some fifteen minutes. The task was not simple as it
required the aircraft to be flying straight and level, which was seldom
the case because, in most instances, pilots were flying as low as possible to avoid detection by Chinese radar and thus were forced to weave
their way through mountains.

As missions were only carried out in periods of full moon and in fine conditions, visibility was always crystal clear and guerrilla reception parties on the DZs could be seen quite clearly as the drops were carried out from an altitude of 1,000 feet. On those occasions when personnel were also being dropped, they normally numbered up to twelve and were despatched in twin 'sticks' from the two side doors in the rear of the fuselage, the equipment containers having already been dropped from the cargo ramp which was lowered as the aircraft approached the DZ. In those instances when a single parachutist was dropped, he would be despatched from the ramp after the cargo.

Despatching of parachutists and loads was the responsibility of the aircraft's three PDOs who also checked, prior to a mission, the rigging of loads and the parachutes attached to them, as well as those worn by personnel being dropped. Since they were not used to operating at such high altitudes, each PDO was equipped with an oxygen mask and three portable oxygen bottles for use when the aircraft hold was depressurised prior to the drop.

Although the majority of missions were completed without incident, there were instances where aircraft came under fire from Chinese anti-aircraft artillery, but none was hit. The planes, however, were operating at maximum range and there was very little margin for problems caused by unforeseen circumstances. On one occasion, a navigational error combined with bad weather caused two aircraft to become lost and, unable to find the DZ, to head south out of Tibet back into Indian airspace. The pilot in command of the second aircraft, William Welk, decided to land at the SAC emergency landing field at Kermitola as he was running low on fuel. Despite heavy rain, a 30-knot crosswind and no runway lights, and with only a non-directional radio beacon to guide him in, he succeeded in doing so. Meanwhile the leading aircraft, commanded by M. D. 'Doc' Johnson, had continued the flight back to Takhli but as it approached the base, warning lights indicated that there was only a few minutes of fuel left in the aircraft's tanks. Furthermore, there was thick fog over the base. With only sufficient fuel for one attempt, 'Doc' Johnson brought his aircraft in for an approach, spotting as he did so one of a number of flares fired by Major 'Heinie' Aderholt and Major Lawrence Ropka who had positioned themselves at the approach end of the runway. At that juncture, two of the C-130A's four engines died.

Descending in a spiral to avoid the hills surrounding the air base, Johnson spotted the runway while at 200 feet and had only enough time to line up with it before his remaining engines cut out, leaving him to glide into a safe landing.

There were other occasions when aircraft were forced to land in India, much to the dismay of the Indian authorities who were concerned that news of the landings would reach the ears of the Chinese. Nevertheless it was to the great credit of the crews, as well as those responsible for the planning of the missions, that not one aircraft or aircrew member was lost throughout the duration of ST BARNUM.

From July 1959 to May 1960, 40–45 drops were carried out with about 85 trained guerrillas and some 800,000 lbs of arms, equipment and medical supplies being delivered to the resistance. On 1 May 1960, however, a U-2 was shot down over Sverdlovsk (now Ykaterinburg) while on a reconnaissance mission deep inside the Soviet Union. Four days later, the affair was made public by the Soviet premier Nikita Khruschev who declared the flight to be an 'aggressive act' by the United States. On 7 May, he revealed that the U-2 had taken off from an air base at Peshawar, the capital of Pakistan's North West Frontier Province, with the mission of flying across the Soviet Union via the Aral Sea, Sverdlovsk, Kirov, Archangelsk and Murmansk to a military airbase at Bodö in Norway. Furthermore, Khruschev stated that the pilot, Gary Powers, had admitted working for the CIA.

Naturally, the United States denied all responsibility, stating that no authorisation had been given for any such flight albeit a U-2 might have strayed into Soviet airspace. The Soviets refused to accept this or to believe that the US government had no knowledge of such flights, sending protest notes to Turkey, Pakistan and Norway, all of which were cowed into protesting to the United States while seeking assurances that no US aircraft would be deployed from their territories for such unauthorised purposes. Khruschev was determined to obtain the maximum benefit from this affair, declaring that the Soviet Union would not take part in an impending summit unless the United States immediately ceased all such flights over Soviet territory, apologised for those already carried out, and punished those responsible.

President Dwight Eisenhower acceded to one of Khruschev's demands by promising to suspend all such flights during the remaining period of his administration. At the same time, he suspended all further missions over Tibet (details of which appear later in this chapter). Although two or three additional flights took place during the following year under the newly elected Kennedy administration, the U-2 incident effectively ended ST BARNUM operations over Tibet.

IN TIBET, MEANWHILE, THE beginning of 1959 found the NVDA actively carrying the war to the enemy. On 24 January, a force of 130 guerrillas attacked Chinese forces at Tenchen, overpowering them and subsequently laying siege to a number of outposts whose water supplies were cut off. The Chinese, however, responded with the use of aircraft which strafed and bombed the guerrillas, forcing them to withdraw in late February.

Between 29 January and 4 February, the main element of Gompo Tashi's force had been participating in religious celebrations at Lho Dzong. It left the town on the following day and marched to Shodor, where it set about recruiting to fill the gaps in its ranks; it also dispatched five-man groups of experienced guerrillas to twelve areas with the task of forming, training and leading additional resistance groups in operations against the Chinese.

By now it was clearer than ever to Gompo Tashi Andrugtsang and the other guerrilla commanders that the increasing use of airpower by the Chinese was making travel by horseback increasingly hazardous and that they would have to operate in smaller numbers, using guerrilla tactics rather than attacking the PLA in force. On 21 February, a council of war was held at which commanders and guerrillas alike were allowed to express their opinions. It was unanimously agreed that the NVDA units should withdraw from Shodor to Lokha and join the main guerrilla forces there. With two 50-man scout groups deployed in front and on its flanks for protection, the 500-strong main force and its train of wagons set out in a series of small convoys for Lokha, which was reached without incident. The NVDA then began guerrilla operations in central Tibet, its principal targets being the Chinese garrisons guarding the PLA's main supply routes.

In Lhasa, in early March, the Dalai Lama received a demand from the Chinese political commissar in the capital, General Tan Kuan Sen, that he attend an operatic performance to be held on 8 March in the large PLA camp outside the city. Playing for time, he replied that he could only attend on the 10th. The general had stipulated that His Holiness, who was normally escorted outside his palace by a 25-strong armed bodyguard, should be unaccompanied. Furthermore, he insisted that PLA, rather than Tibetan, troops would be posted along the route to be taken to the camp, and that the bridge between the PLA camp and the capital would be closed to all Tibetans except those attending the opera. These demands, along with the insistence by Tan Kuan Sen that His Holiness's visit to the camp should be kept secret, inevitably raised strong suspicions that the Chinese intended to kidnap the Tibetan ruler, these being strengthened by reports that three aircraft had arrived at the PLA airfield outside Lhasa.

It was not long before details of the Chinese demands leaked out and spread like wildfire, resulting in a mob of 30,000 surrounding the Norbulingka Palace with the aim of preventing His Holiness from being kidnapped by the Chinese. Meanwhile, the response on the part of the Tibetan government was similarly hostile and a week later it issued a proclamation of independence from China. On 17 March, by which time there was increasing unrest among the capital's population and the large numbers of pilgrims present in the city to celebrate the festival of Monlam, the cabinet and national assembly decided that the Dalai Lama should leave Lhasa and seek safety elsewhere. Their decision had been expedited by the firing that afternoon of two mortar bombs by the PLA, albeit these had landed harmlessly in a pond beyond the northern perimeter of the palace. During the previous day, artillery surveyors had been observed taking readings on the Norbulingka Palace with their instruments.

Contingency plans for the evacuation of His Holiness had been drawn up in early 1959 by the head of his personal staff, Thupten Woyden Phala, the commander of the Tibetan Army's 2nd Regiment, Colonel Tashi Para, and a senior commander in the NVDA, Ratuk Ngawang. These called for three groups to leave the capital, one comprising the Dalai Lama and members of his family and personal entourage, the other two consisting of guerrillas and Tibetan troops disguised as traders, monks and pilgrims who would head in different directions, acting as decoys to confuse any pursuing Chinese forces.

Preparations for the Dalai Lama's escape that night were put into immediate effect. First to leave at 9.00 p.m. were his mother, elder sister and younger brother with an escort, all disguised as Khambas. Next went His Holiness accompanied by his brother-in-law who commanded his bodyguard, Thupten Woyden Phala, another senior abbot and two soldiers; all six were dressed as members of a patrol apparently carrying out an inspection of the palace's security measures. The third party, consisting of two long-serving tutors, four members of the Lhasa government cabinet and a small group of officials, was smuggled out of the palace in the back of a truck escorted by Tibetan troops. All three groups subsequently made their way to a rendezvous a short distance south of Lhasa where they crossed the Kyichu River, being met by a 30-strong unit of Khambas, who had brought ponies for the entire entourage, and the two-man CIA radio team of Athar Norbu and Losang Tsering.

In haste, the Dalai Lama and his companions, escorted by the Khambas and the Tibetan troops who had left with them, headed south undetected by the Chinese who were still ignorant of the escape venture. Meanwhile, the two decoy groups left the capital and headed towards the border with India by other routes, in the hope of drawing off any pursuers. During the following days, having crossed over the mountain pass at Che-La and subsequently the Brahmaputra River, the Dalai Lama's entourage headed south-east over the mountains for the Sabo Pass, constantly alert for Chinese aircraft. Fortunately, the cloud cover was thick and low, thus hindering any search from the air.

The intention of the Dalai Lama was to reach Lhuntze Dzong which featured a large fortress and where he intended to form a new government and open negotiations with the Chinese. On 24 March, however, a messenger arrived with news that banished any ideas of such discussions. Four days earlier, the PLA had attacked Lhasa, killing many thousands of Tibetans and destroying many buildings. The attack on the capital had begun in the early hours of the morning with the shelling of the Norbulingka Palace, followed by similar treatment of the Potala Palace, the Dalai Lama's winter residence. The Jokhang Monastery, Tibet's oldest and most revered monastery where all major religious celebrations are held, and others nearby, had also been attacked by artillery and mortars, as had other areas of the capital. Armed only with rifles and swords, Tibetans had rallied on the Iron Hill, a feature of high ground on which was situated the city's Chakpori medical school. At first they had achieved some success, counter-attacking and overrunning a force of PLA troops at Shukti Lingba, a small hamlet at a ferry point across the Tsanpo River behind the Ganden Monastery, and even knocking out a tank with petrol bombs.

After two days of fighting, however, the Tibetans were overwhelmed and on 22 March the quisling Ngapo Ngawang Jigme, who had come to an understanding with the Chinese soon after the occupation of Tibet, had broadcast orders to all Tibetans to cease resistance and surrender to the Chinese. Subsequent reports revealed that the Chinese had imprisoned virtually all those who had not been killed in the fighting, including those who had travelled to Lhasa for the religious celebration and Tibetan New Year, among them more than 25,000 monks who were confined to their quarters.

The Dalai Lama resumed his journey south-east to Lhuntze Dzong by way of Chongay Rewu Dechen, Thosam Dargyaling and E-Chudo-gyang. Progress was difficult, the entourage having to make its way along narrow and slippery mountain trails and snow-clad mountain passes. Eventually it reached Shopa Nup, thereafter heading east towards Lhuntze Dzong. Just before his arrival, however, the Dalai Lama learned that the government in Lhasa had been dissolved by the Chinese and replaced with a new regime led by the Panchen Lama, assisted by Ngapo Ngawang Jigme and three PLA generals. Furthermore, the Seventeen Point Agreement of 1951 had been torn up by the Chinese who had annexed Kham and Amdo, absorbing Amdo into the province of Tsing-hai and Kham initially into Sikang which in turn became part of Szechuan.

It was now obvious that the Dalai Lama had no alternative but to go into exile in India. Throughout the journey, Athar Norbu and Losang Tsering had maintained radio contact with the CIA, keeping the ST CIRCUS controllers apprised of the entourage's progress south. Now it transmitted a formal request to the Indian government for asylum, this being passed on to Washington from where it was relayed to the US Embassy in New Delhi, which in turn delivered it to the Indian government. Within 24 hours a response was received from Prime Minister Jawaharlal Nehru, granting the request.

There was acute anxiety in Washington and New Delhi that the Dalai Lama would be intercepted before reaching the border as by this time reports had been received that the Chinese, enraged by his escape, were actively searching for him. Aircraft were observed in the skies above and at one point a plane flew low over the party, fortunately failing to spot it. Messages were transmitted from Washington, urging His Holiness to proceed with all haste. Leaving Lhuntze Dzong, he and his entourage headed south-west for Tsona-Dzong and beyond to the Indian border.

The latter stages of the journey were particularly arduous. The weather was bad, with sleet, snow and ice making progress difficult over the mountains. The ten days of travel had taken their toll on the entire group, and all the ponies which were suffering from lack of fodder and fatigue. The Dalai Lama himself was exhausted and ill by the time he and his companions reached the village of Mangmang which was the final halt before India and sanctuary. Having rested there for a day, they pressed on southward and on 31 March reached the Indian border where they were met by paramilitary border troops of the Assam Rifles and a group of Indian officials. In two weeks they had travelled a distance of almost 300 miles over difficult terrain.

Gompo Tashi, meanwhile, had learned from an All-India Radio broadcast on 22 March of the uprising in Lhasa. Initially, he had immediately moved the majority of his forces to Ahzar Lake and thereafter to Chaksam Chupo while at the same time despatching reconnaissance groups to monitor any movements by the Chinese. Then a message arrived from the Dalai Lama, announcing that he had escaped from Lhasa and was in Lhuntze Dzong. Fearful that the pursuing Chinese, whose aircraft could be observed criss-crossing the skies, would capture His Holiness, Gompo Tashi and those guerrillas with him headed for Lhuntze Dzong. Arriving at Azhar Lake on 3 April, however, he had received a message informing him that the Dalai Lama had already reached India.

Next day, Gompo Tashi and his men marched to Kongpo Gyatha but moved on immediately after learning that a large force of Chinese troops were near by. Making their way to Drephur, they met another NVDA force which had brought up supplies on pack animals from Tsomo Rak. Shortly afterwards, however, a large force of Chinese from Lhasa arrived in a large convoy of some 300 vehicles and a fierce engagement ensued, the outnumbered guerrillas eventually retiring after abandoning their supplies. Large numbers of enemy troops, supported by aircraft,

A 14-strong Khamba raiding party in the Dzum Valley in Nepal prior to setting out on an operation to ambush a Chinese PLA convoy on the road from Lhasa to Kathmandu, between the Chinese garrison towns of Dzonkar and Kyeron, on 6 June 1964. (Adrian Cowell)

The raiding party climbing up towards the 20,000 foot Khojang Pass over the Himalayas. (Adrian Cowell)

The party's commander, Tendar, giving final orders to his scouts prior to the ambush. (Adrian Cowell)

The raiding party's commander and one of his men clean their M1 Garand .30-06 rifles as they prepare for the ambush. (Adrian Cowell)

A member of the raiding party, armed with a Lee Enfield No.1 SMLE .303
rifle, in his position awaiting the arrival of the PLA convoy. (Adrian Cowell)

A Khamba guards the raiding party's escape route. (Adrian Cowell)

The site of Camp Hale, Colorado, where the selected Tibetan guerrillas underwent training by the CIA. (John K. Knaus)

The compound at camp Hale. Inset: one of the signs discouraging visitors to the area. (John K. Knaus)

OPPOSITE PAGE
Troops of 22 SAS on the Jebel Akhdar in late January 1959. (Colonel David Smiley)

A village on the top of the Jebel Akhdar. (Colonel David Smiley)

WARNING
THIS AREA MAY CONTAIN
EXPLOSIVE ORDNANCE.
DO NOT MOVE OR MOLEST
ANY METAL OBJECT.
NOTIFY RANGE OFFICER,
FORT CARSON, COLO.

A BATT of D Squadron 22 SAS deploying for a search of a wadi in early 1971. (Major General Tony Jeapes)

Members of the Firqat Salahadin, including the original 23 who came across from the PFLOAG with Salim Mubarrak in January 1971. (Major General Tony Jeapes)

D Squadron 22 SAS and the Firqat Salahadin embarked on a dhow en route
to the landing prior to the operation at Sudh in February 1971. (Major
General Tony Jeapes)

A member of a D Squadron 22 SAS BATT in a position on the Eagle's Nest in
the eastern area of the jebel in Dhofar in mid-March 1971. (Major General
Tony Jeapes)

Members of G Squadron 22 SAS take a break during an operation in the Wadi Jardoom on the jebel in western Dhofar in late 1974. (Major General Tony Jeapes)

A GPMG gunner of B Squadron 22 SAS scans the hillside at Point 985 during the Sherishitti Caves operation in 1975. (Major General Tony Jeapes)

OPPOSITE PAGE
A firqat poses with captured enemy weapons after a successful wadi search. (Major General Tony Jeapes)

A large quantity of captured enemy weapons and ammunition on display in Salalah. (Major General Tony Jeapes)

The 'One-Zero' of MACV-SOG's Reconnaissance Team New York, John St. Martin, shown here fully equipped for an operation. He carries a Claymore anti-personnel mine in the pouch on his chest and a length of detonating cord for quick demolition ambushes. Inset: the golf-ball-sized V40 mini-grenade carried by MACV-SOG personnel. (Frank Greco and Ben Baker)

Two members of MACV-SOG, Sgt Maj Billy Waugh, *left*, and Sfc Melvin Hill come under fire from NVA troops as they disembark from a helicopter at a location some fourteen miles north-west of Khe Sanh. (Billy Waugh)

Captain Mecky Schuler and members of his MACV-SOG Hatchet Force company at an NVA way station on the Ho Chi Minh Trail 25 miles north-west of Khe Sanh. (Mecky Schuler)

A Montagnard member of Hatchet Force Company B MACV-SOG Command & Control North after returning from Operation TAILWIND, carrying satchels of captured NVA documents which were among the most important ever brought out of Laos. (Gene McCarley)

A mujahid radio operator of the Jamiat-i-Islami establishes communications from a mountain-top position above the Panjshir Valley in northern Afghanistan in January 1981, power for his radio being provided by a generator operated by a second guerrilla. (Associated Press)

Mujahidin of the Jamiat-i-Islami search bodies of Afghan government troops following a guerrilla ambush in the Panjshir Valley in December 1985. A knocked-out armoured vehicle is in the middle of the road while the remains of another burn in the background. (Associated Press)

OPPOSITE PAGE
Members of a mujahidin unit wind their way along a mountain trail in the Kunar Valley in 1985. (Associated Press)

A group of guerrillas receive instruction in the 75mm recoilless rifle at a mujahidin base near Lowgar, south-west of the capital Kabul in June 1987. (Associated Press)

A patrol of the GRU's 157th Spetsnaz Brigade in Paktia Province prior to embarking on an operation in Afghanistan in 1987. (James G. Shortt)

A member of a patrol of the GRU's 157th Spetsnaz Brigade holds a Stechkin pistol to the head of a captured guerrilla while interrogating mujahidin captured during an operation in Afghanistan's Paktia Province in 1987. (James G. Shortt)

Two members of the GRU's 157th Spetsnaz Brigade in Afghanistan's Paktia Province in 1988. Both dressed as mujahidin, one being armed with a suppressed Stechkin pistol, they are members of a Karavan Ohotniki (Caravan Hunters) unit whose role was the interception as well as the capture of westerners crossing into Afghanistan. (James G. Shortt)

A guerrilla of the Jamiat-i-Islami undergoing counter-sniping training by a team of British instructors in 1988, one of whom can be seen in the background. (James G. Shortt)

A mujahidin Stinger SAM team with an RPG-7 providing local protection. (James G. Shortt)

Members of a mujahidin unit with a heavy machine-gun mounted on a captured Soviet light vehicle. On the right is another, equipped with a multi-barrelled rocket launcher. (Defence Picture Library)

continued to pour into the area as the Chinese stepped up their hunt for the Dalai Lama. On 12 April, Gompo Tashi arrived at Lhuntze Dzong. He planned to make his way to Tsona and establish a base there but was informed that it had fallen to the PLA. At a conference of his commanders, he raised the idea of mounting an attack to recapture Tsona, where the NVDA had been formed during the previous year, but it was apparent to all present that their force of 2,000 guerrillas was powerless against such overwhelming odds. By this time, the Chinese had committed a further 100,000 troops, plus supporting armour, artillery and aircraft to put down the rebellion in Tibet. After lengthy discussion, it was decided that the entire guerrilla force would seek sanctuary in India. On 21 April 1959, Gompo Tashi led his men over the border into exile.

IN KHAM AND AMDO, other resistance groups fought on to keep the spirit of resistance in Tibet alive, while in the United States the training of guerrilla teams continued in Colorado. On 19 September 1959, the first group of Camp Hale-trained Tibetans was despatched back into Tibet. Nine men were dropped blind in the area of Ringtso, near Lake Namtso, some 200 miles to the north-west of Lhasa. Their mission was to establish contact with a resistance leader named Natsang Phurpo, who had been reported as leading a force of 4,000 guerrillas, and persuade him to mount a series of raids on convoys of vehicles transporting borax from mines in his area. Unfortunately, on arrival in the area where it expected to make contact with Phurpo, the team ran into Chinese forces who had been informed of its presence by a collaborator within the guerrillas' ranks. Forced to flee, the team headed south after caching its radio and trekked 350 miles to the area of Mustang in western Nepal which was already home to a large number of Khambas and guerrillas who had fled Tibet previously. From there it made its way to Darjeeling before being extracted from India by the CIA and transported back to Camp Hale for debriefing and preparation for another mission.

During the same full moon period in September, a group of nine guerrillas was sent into Tibet, followed later in the month by three other teams, numbering eighteen men in all, who were dropped in the area of Pembar, some 200 miles north-east of Lhasa, in the centre of the mountainous region of Shotalasum, where a number of Khamba resistance groups had regrouped. The first of these teams, comprising seven men, was to provide training for these groups, and to equip them with weapons which were to be dropped in due course. The ultimate objective was for the resistance to seize control of Shotalasum which lay between the northern and southern highways leading from Lhasa to Sichuan, guerrilla bases being established from which these two major supply lines could be cut.

The second team of six men was to assist in the reception of the arms drops which began in October. The first drop contained 370 M1 Garand rifles, four LMGs, 75,000 rounds of ammunition and two RS-1 transmitter/receivers. The second took place in November, delivering a similar quantity of small arms and ammunition as well as three recoilless rifles and 150 rounds of ammunition. December saw the delivery of a much larger consignment of arms comprising 800 M1 Garand rifles, 113 M1 .30 carbines, a large quantity of grenades and 2,000,000 rounds of ammunition. The final drop to the resistance groups in Pembar took place on 6 January 1960, three C-130As dropping arms, equipment, food and medical supplies.

By this time, the mass concentration of resistance groups in Pembar was causing the CIA serious concern. About 12,500 guerrillas, together with some 30,000 to 37,500 dependants, as well as large herds of animals, were living there in large camps. This was contrary to the policy agreed by Gompo Tashi and the commanders of the NVDA who had recognised that the increasing use of air power by the Chinese, along with the increasing use of artillery and armour and enhanced mobility of PLA forces, meant that the days of large formations and units of resistance fighters were over.

The Chinese soon became aware of the flights over Tibet and of the large numbers of resistance groups in the Pembar area. A month after the last supply drop, they attacked with a series of air strikes on the guerrilla camps, bombing and strafing them to devastating effect. These were followed up by columns of PLA troops in trucks and armoured vehicles supported by mortars, artillery and cavalry.

Many thousands of guerrillas and their dependants died in the air attacks and in subsequent engagements with PLA troops who encircled the area, bringing heavy mortar and artillery fire to bear before launching their assaults. Many guerrillas, along with several but not all of the

Camp Hale team members, escaped the Chinese net but found themselves having to fight their way out as they headed north or west. Forced to travel at night, avoiding the roads being used by the enemy, they made their way along mountain trails pursued by PLA cavalry units, laying ambushes as they went, but those who collapsed from exhaustion or starvation were hunted down.

The third team dropped into Pembar, numbering five men, had meantime reached southern Amdo where it had made contact with several resistance groups, the largest of which, numbering over 4,000 men, was located at Nira Tsogeng, just south of the Thangla Pass in the southwest of the region. It was planned that these groups should mount a series of attacks on convoys using the Lhasa–Quinghai highway, another major Chinese supply route; and in response to a request from the team for arms, two C-130As carried out a drop on 13 December 1959, delivering 1,680 rifles and 368,800 rounds of ammunition. Another consignment was brought in by two aircraft on 10 January 1960, although only one aircraft was able to drop its load. This was followed by further drops by four aircraft on 15 January. An eighth drop was made shortly afterwards, the arms being accompanied by sixteen men led by Ngawang Phuljung, a nephew of Gompo Tashi Andrugtsang.

Phuljung and his men, who were organised in three teams, had been given the task of persuading the guerrillas to split up into smaller units before embarking on operations against the Lhasa–Sichuan highways. Unfortunately, their pleas fell on deaf ears. As at Pembar, the guerrillas were accompanied by large numbers of dependants and herds of animals and were unwilling to leave them. Once again, it was not long before the Chinese struck. On 22 February, enemy aircraft attacked the resistance camps while PLA troops, supported by armour and artillery, began to surround the area to cut off any escape attempts by the guerrillas.

The pattern of slaughter and destruction was similar to that during the assault on Pembar. Vast numbers of guerrillas and dependants died in the onslaught while many who escaped subsequently perished while being relentlessly pursued by PLA armour and cavalry units. Of the eighteen Camp Hale-trained team members, only one, a radio operator, survived to make his way back to India.

The ST BARNUM flights into Tibet continued in early April 1961 when two ten-man teams were dropped into Kham and a third seven-man team into the area of Markham. This last team was led by Yeshe Wangyal, who had been a member of the first Camp Hale team dropped at Ringtso in September 1959. His father was commander of a resistance group and the team's mission was to link up with it and two other groups in the Markham area, and then to organise supplies of arms for them. Although on the day following the drop Wangyal discovered that his father had been killed some months earlier, he went on to meet the other two guerrilla leaders who headed a force of some 80 men and their dependants. It was soon apparent, however, that the Chinese had achieved total control over the entire area and that there was little prospect of any real success being achieved by resistance operations. Wangyal and his team were under orders to abandon their mission in the event that the odds proved overwhelming; so they decided to make for India, using a route along which it was less likely they would meet Chinese forces.

Accompanied by the guerrillas and their dependants, Wangyal and his men set off but almost immediately encountered PLA troops with whom they fought a series of running battles as they sought to escape. One of the team was killed while only 40 of the guerrillas survived. The remaining members of the small force were cornered and made a stand; but by the time they were overrun by vastly superior numbers, only one member of the team, Nemyo Busang, and fifteen guerrillas were still alive. Busang would spend the following eighteen years without trial in a Chinese prison, being released in 1979.

The demise of this last team signalled the end of Operation ST BARNUM flights into Tibet. From 1957 to 1961 a total of 88 Tibetans out of the approximately 200 trained at Camp Hale were dropped by parachute into Tibet. Twelve survived: ten made their way out to India, one was captured and one surrendered. The rest died during encounters with Chinese forces.

Resistance in Tibet, nevertheless, was far from over. In early 1960 the Dalai Lama's second elder brother, Gyalo Thondup, accompanied by Gompo Tashi and Lhamo Tsering, approached the CIA with the suggestion of establishing a major resistance base in the Nepalese region of Mustang. Ruled by a maharajah known as the King of Lo and located in north-western Nepal, north of the western urban centre of Pokhara, Mustang is a mountainous area of several hundred square miles jutting northward into Tibet. To its south lie the mountain ranges of Annapurna and Dhaulagiri, while running north to south through its centre is the Kali River which subsequently turns east to join the Trisuli River to flow into the Gandruk. The capital of the region is Lo Mantang which, situated on a plateau, is some twenty miles from the border with Tibet.

After their arrival in India the previous April, Gompo Tashi's forces had been disarmed and disbanded. As refugees, his men had found themselves working on road gangs in Sikkim or carrying out similar work in the border regions of India. At the meeting with CIA officers in the spring of 1960, Gompo Tashi suggested reforming the NVDA which would operate from a base in Mustang. While this appeared to be an attractive proposition, the CIA was well aware that the US government would not sanction it without permission from the Nepalese government. But since security and political considerations excluded any approach to the latter, the decision was taken to proceed regardless on the basis that the project should be kept entirely secret; in the event of it being compromised, it would be abandoned immediately.

As a first step, a group of 26 men selected by Gompo Tashi was despatched from India to the United States for training at Camp Hale. Among these was a Khamba named Lobsang Champa who would take charge of the new force on completion of his training, the other trainees being destined to be commanders of guerrilla companies under him. Meanwhile, a small seven-man advance element, including two radio operators trained at Camp Hale, was sent to Mustang, with the task of establishing the base area and coordinating logistical support for it. It was under the command of another Khamba, Baba Yeshe, who had been leader of the NVDA element left at Lhoksa when Gompo Tashi set off to fight the Chinese in eastern Tibet in August 1958. On arrival in Mustang, Yeshe established a base some fifteen miles south of Lo Mantang and 25 miles from the Tibetan border.

It had been agreed between the Tibetans and the CIA that the force should number no more than 300 men, these being infiltrated into Mustang without the knowledge of the Nepalese government. Those recruited initially had been given strict instructions not to divulge the reasons for their impending departure nor details of their destination. Inevitably, however, news of the newly reformed Chushi Gangdrug leaked out and spread like wildfire through all the Tibetan communities in northern India. Large numbers of former NVDA guerrillas made their way from Sikkim to Gompo Tashi's home in Darjeeling where they volunteered their services. Although this led Sikkim's ruler to complain to Gyalo Thondrup about the likely effects on road maintenance of the roads throughout his small country, the latter was powerless to halt the flood of volunteers. This inevitably attracted the attention of the Indian press which published a series of articles about the mass exodus of Tibetans from India.

The political fall-out over the U-2 debacle in 1960 had placed even greater importance on the maintenance of secrecy concerning the presence of the new resistance force in Mustang, and particularly with regard to the covert flights by CAT which by this time had been renamed Air America. In the United States, there was growing concern within the CIA about the rapidly growing guerrilla army which by the autumn of 1960 numbered over 2,000 men plus their dependants. Threats from Washington to cancel the project proved fruitless, as did demands that Baba Yeshe send back most of his men to India. In Mustang, meanwhile, there was growing hostility from the local population which resented the continual demands for food from the Tibetans. The problem of feeding his men and their families was such that Baba Yeshe sent a stream of signals to the CIA, urgently requesting food as well as arms.

November 1960 saw John F. Kennedy elected as the 35th President of the United States. Kennedy was well aware of the communist menace in South-east Asia where Laos and South Vietnam were under threat from North Vietnam, backed by China and the Soviet Union. Despite the fiasco of the Bay of Pigs invasion of Cuba, which resulted in a humiliating failure for the United States, Kennedy gave his approval in mid-March 1961 for the CIA to continue its support for the Tibetan guerrillas. This was in the face of strong opposition from the new US ambassador to India, John Kenneth Galbraith, who feared that the operation would be compromised and adversely affect relations between his country and the Soviet Union.

Kennedy's view prevailed, however, and the first arms drop for the Mustang guerrillas took place on 15 March with C-130As from Takhli delivering a consignment of arms to a DZ over the border into Tibet south of the Brahmaputra River. It contained sufficient weapons to equip approximately half of Baba Yeshe's force which was by then organised in sixteen companies of 100 men each. Thereafter, Baba Yeshe lost little time in launching operations against the Chinese, despatching 50-strong units to attack PLA garrisons and convoys travelling along the main highway between Lhasa and Sinkiang. This forced the Chinese to increase its forces in the region and to divert supply convoys via the Qinghai–Sinkiang highway some 190 miles farther to the north.

Summer of 1961 saw the arrival in Mustang of Lobsang Champa who had completed his training at Camp Hale and was now returning to take command of the guerrillas. By this time, however, Baba Yeshe, who had set up the base and transformed a motley crowd into a disciplined, well-trained body, had established himself firmly as the overall commander and somewhat understandably refused to hand over command despite an order from the CIA for him to do so. After some dispute, Yeshe prevailed and Lobsang had to content himself with commanding a company.

Baba Yeshe was by now pressing for the delivery of further arms with which to equip the remainder of his force which was continuing its activities against the Chinese. Ambassador Galbraith, however, had persisted in his opposition to the operation and eventually President Kennedy agreed to the diplomat's proposal that further air drops could only be made with the agreement of the Indian government (which was already aware of the operation and, as far as the CIA was reportedly concerned, had given its tacit approval to it). The decision was taken however, to reroute the aircraft to minimise the amount of time they spent in Indian airspace.

During that summer, the CIA submitted a request for the agreement of the National Security Council (NSC) Special Group to obtain clearance for further drops to take place. No speedy response was forthcoming, as the request was debated at length for several months. In October, however, a guerrilla group led by Ragra Jetar, one of those trained at Camp Hale, ambushed a PLA convoy, killing all those aboard it. Among the dead the guerrillas found a deputy regimental commander in possession of a number of highly classified documents. These were despatched to the United States where they proved to be of utmost importance, providing intelligence on a wide variety of political as well as military matters.

The arrival of this material in Washington was fortuitous, coinciding as it did with a renewed onslaught by Ambassador Galbraith in his efforts to have ST CIRCUS closed down. In November the Director of Central Intelligence, Allen Dulles, appeared before the NSC Special Group armed with the documents with which he was able to prove that the CIA operation in Tibet was providing intelligence of good quality as well supporting the Tibetan resistance. President Kennedy therefore authorised a further drop of arms which took place on 10 December.

During 1962, while Baba Yeshe's guerrillas continued their raiding operations into Tibet, relations between India and China deteriorated as a result of a long-running dispute over delineation of the border in three sectors between India and Tibet: in the east, the area known as the North East Frontier Agency (NEFA), now called Arunachal Pradesh, situated north of Assam in north-eastern India; in the centre, two areas of over 7,700 square miles either side of the Himalayan watershed; and in the north-west, the Aksai Chin plateau in the area of Ladakh on the north-eastern edge of the state of Jammu and Kashmir, bordering Tibet and the Chinese province of Sinkiang.

In the east, the line of the border between Tibet and India's NEFA was delineated by the McMahon Line, named after Sir Henry McMahon, the chief British negotiator at the Simla Conference of 1913–14. Representatives of Britain, Tibet and China had agreed during this conference that the border should follow the crest of the high Himalayas which was proposed as the natural, ethnic and administrative boundary. Following India's independence in 1947, however, China had laid claim to an area comprising the districts of East and West Kameng, Lower and Upper Subansiri, East and West Siang, and Lohit, on the grounds that it had never accepted the McMahon Line. India was adamant in its refusal as the border proposed by the Chinese would follow the line of the Assam Plain which would be almost indefensible.

In the north-west, Kashmir had been an area of dispute between India and neighbouring Pakistan since 1947 when Indian troops entered it on operations against Pushtun tribesmen who had invaded the district of Barramulla, after which the Maharajah of Kashmir, Hari Singh, acceded to union with India. Pakistan had always refused to accept the accession, pressing for a plebiscite which it was confident would be in its favour due to the large number of Muslims within Kashmir's population. China did not take sides, having its own claims to Ladakh and the Aksai Chin Plateau where it subsequently conducted military

manoeuvres during the 1950s and through which it proceeded to con-
struct the Sinkiang Road without India's knowledge.

At the end of April 1954, India and China signed an agreement under
the terms of which passes at Shipki La, Mana Niti, Kungribini, Darma
and Lipu Lekh were specified as recognised border crossing points to
be used by 'traders and pilgrims of both countries'. Shortly afterwards,
however, China protested when India stationed troops at an outpost at
Barahoti, situated south-east of the Niti Pass, insisting that the post was
north of the pass and thus that the Indians should withdraw from Chinese
territory. Despite India pointing out the error in this statement, China
refused to admit its mistake and continued to claim the area concerned.

Tension between India and China increased after the Dalai Lama's
flight into exile in March 1959, and a number of clashes took place along
the border during the rest of the year. In the east, on 7 August, some
200 Chinese troops crossed the border into India at Khenzemane in the
Kameng frontier division east of the Thagla Ridge which lies at the junction of Tibet, eastern Bhutan and NEFA. A small ten-man patrol of
Indian troops attempted to confront them but was pushed back to the
bridge at Drokung Samba which the Chinese maintained was in Chinese
territory. On 26 August, a PLA force of approximately 300 men crossed
the McMahon Line into the Longju region of the Subashin frontier division and attacked an isolated Indian outpost at Longju, a few miles south
of the line. Manned by only a dozen or so men and being dependent on
aerial resupply, there being no roads leading to it, the post was one of a
number established by India's intelligence-gathering organisation, the
Intelligence Bureau, which was responsible for operations within the
border regions. Each was manned by Intelligence Bureau personnel,
fluent in Chinese and Tibetan dialects, who monitored Chinese communications throughout southern Tibet.

Further cross-border incursions took place later during 1959 and this
resulted in responsibility for operations in the NEFA border region
being transferred from the Intelligence Bureau to the Indian Army
whose 4th Infantry Division was switched from the Punjab to Assam,
being tasked with the defence of the entire McMahon Line from the
Tibet–eastern Bhutan–NEFA border junction to the Burmese border.

In early November, Chinese premier Chou En Lai suggested demil-
itarisation by both India and China of the entire length of the border

between India and Tibet to a depth on both sides of twelve and a half miles, using the McMahon Line in the east and the 'line of actual control' in the west. India would not accept this as it would have lost defensible areas in the east while China would have gained territory in the west. The Indians produced a counter-proposal under which Indian troops would withdraw behind the border claimed by China while the PLA would pull back behind that claimed by India. This was turned down by the Chinese who protested it was 'unfair'.

In November 1961, the Indian Army's General Officer Commanding (GOC) Eastern Command, Lieutenant General S. P. P. Thorat, recommended the establishment of a line of additional forward posts along the border, their role being to give early warning of any border incursions; to its rear would be a second line of strongly defended posts designed to retard any Chinese advance. Behind these would be a line of defences intended to halt the Chinese and from which counter-attacks would be launched, supported by reinforcements brought up from farther south.

The Indian Army, however, faced major problems in defending the border in the NEFA area. The lack of adequate roads and infrastructure meant that posts had to be resupplied by air which proved unreliable, with up to 70 per cent of supplies being lost in some drops. Helicopters purchased from Russia proved unsuitable for use at such high altitudes, while the troops of the 4th Infantry Division lacked clothing and equipment and training for high-altitude warfare. Furthermore, the small arms and support weapons in service at that time were of Second World War vintage, while the lack of transport meant that the division had to leave much of its artillery on the plains to the south.

Following Prime Minister Jawaharlal Nehru's agreement to the siting of more posts along the border, one was established during the first half of 1962 at Dhola on the Thagla Ridge, overlooking a key PLA garrison at Leh. Located at an altitude of 13,000 feet, it was six days' march from the nearest road, making logistical support difficult. On 8 September, the Chinese responded by deploying a small force of 60 troops in positions dominating the Indian post.

The Indians reacted immediately by despatching troops of the 9th Battalion The Punjab Regiment (9 PUNJAB), one of three battalions of 7 Infantry Brigade, which arrived at Dhola on 15 September. Two days later the brigade commander was ordered to recapture the Thagla Ridge but refused to do so as he realised it was indefensible. On 20 September, another confrontation took place at the bridge at Namka Chu with a small number of casualties being incurred on both sides. As the fighting escalated, 7 Infantry Brigade was reinforced by two battalions, the 1st Battalion 9th Gurkha Rifles (1/9 GR) and the 2nd Battalion The Rajput Regiment (2 RAJPUT). Both units, however, were understrength and ill-equipped to carry out missions at altitudes of 16,000 feet, being equipped for operations in the warm climate of the Indian plains. Furthermore, each soldier was issued with only 50 rounds of ammunition.

On 10 October, just as the Indians were preparing for an operation to expel the Chinese from their positions overlooking the post, the latter struck first. At 5.00 a.m. some 800 PLA troops attacked two platoons of 9 PUNJAB at Tseng Jong, killing six, wounding eleven and capturing fourteen. No supporting fire was forthcoming from 7 Infantry Brigade as its 'artillery' comprised two 3-inch medium mortars with 60 bombs each and two machine-guns with 12,000 rounds of ammunition.

Over the next few days, the brigade was reinforced by the 4th Battalion The Grenadier Regiment (4 GRENADIERS). Like the earlier reinforcements, however, they were equipped only with warm weather clothing and 50 rounds of ammunition per man. Other arrivals included 450 men of a pioneer unit detailed to assist in the collection of airdrops and carrying supplies forward.

On 20 October, the Chinese unleashed their first large-scale assault, commencing with bombardments by 76mm and 120mm mortars. These were followed by attacks launched by an infantry division, with one brigade advancing on Tsangdhar while others carried out encircling movements cutting off the withdrawal routes of Indian units. Both 2 RAJPUT and 1/9 GR were trapped in this manner and fought on to the last man; by 9.00 a.m. both battalions had been wiped out. Meanwhile the headquarters of 7 Infantry Brigade was overrun and its commander captured while leading a small group of his men in an attempted break-out.

Because the threat from Pakistan precluded withdrawal of any of its divisions on its western border, India had to call on reinforcements for deployment in NEFA from elsewhere. Battalions were summoned from other areas of the country as two strongpoints were established by 4th

Infantry Division whose headquarters was at Dirang Dzong along with 65 Infantry Brigade. These were sited on two major ridge-lines situated one behind the other. The forward position at Se La was manned by 62 Infantry Brigade, comprising five battalions, while the other at Bomdilla, 60 miles to the rear, was defended by 48 Infantry Brigade with three battalions. The total strength of the two garrisons was between 10,000 and 12,000 men.

The Chinese launched an assault on Se La from the north-west and north-east on 16 November. Although 62 Infantry Brigade put up a stout defence, and despite its commander's insistence that he was confident of holding out, the commander of 4th Infantry Division overruled him and ordered the brigade to fall back to Dirang Dzong. By that stage, however, the Chinese had encircled Se La and the brigade suffered heavy casualties as it withdrew towards Bomdilla.

Two days later, 48 Infantry Brigade at Bomdilla was also attacked. During the battle, the commander received orders to despatch two companies, supported by two of the brigade's four tanks and two mountain guns, to Dirang Dzong. Protests that his entire force was already heavily committed in driving off the Chinese were ignored and at 11.15 a.m. that morning the column set off from Bomdilla. No sooner had it done so than it was ambushed and cut off by the Chinese. By 4.00 p.m., with the Chinese having overrun several sectors of the strongpoint, the brigade carried out a fighting withdrawal from Bomdilla towards Rupa where it intended to regroup. This never materialised, however, and two days later the remnants of the brigade were finally annihilated at Chaku, south of Rupa.

By this time the PLA lines of communication and supply were fully extended and the Chinese called a halt to their advance, declaring a unilateral ceasefire on 22 November and stating that they would withdraw their forces to the pre-hostilities boundaries north of the McMahon Line by 1 December. Meanwhile, in Ladakh in the north-west, they seized an area of some 14,670 square miles up to their line of actual control. This would be increased by a further 1,000 square miles handed over to China by Pakistan during the following year.

When the conflict was over, there was much public criticism in India of the chaos and ineptitude demonstrated at high levels during the defence of the NEFA frontier area. It was recognised that, among a number of measures to be taken to strengthen its defences, India would have to give swift consideration to improving its defences throughout its entire northern regions bordering Tibet. A mission, headed by leading US diplomat Averill Harriman, arrived shortly from the United States in response to a request from Prime Minister Nehru for assistance. Among its members were the chief of the CIA's Near East and Far East divisions, James Critchfield and Desmond Fitzgerald, and the head of the Agency's Tibetan Task Force, John Kenneth Knaus.

As a result of this mission, it was agreed that military assistance to a total value of $120 million would be provided by both the United States and Britain. At the same time, the CIA would establish an intelligence-gathering capability in India to determine Chinese dispositions within Tibet with the ultimate aim of conducting guerrilla operations there. More Tibetans would be trained at Camp Hale and the CIA would renew its support for the force in Mustang.

The Agency would also provide support for a new paramilitary force formed on 14 November by the Intelligence Bureau, to be recruited entirely from Tibetans. The brainchild of the Intelligence Bureau's chief, B. N. Mullik, it was initially known as Establishment 22, a name coined by its first Inspector General, Major General Uban, who had commanded the 22nd Mountain Regiment of the Royal Indian Artillery during the Second World War, but was subsequently designated the Special Frontier Force (SFF). Its base was established at Chakrata in the Himalayas, home to a large Tibetan refugee population and just over 60 miles north of the city of Dehra Dun, in the north-western state of Uttar Pradesh, and 75 miles from the Tibetan border.

As had happened during the re-formation of the Chushi Gangdrug in Mustang, word soon spread of the creation of the SFF and there was a mass exodus of Tibetans from all over India to Dehra Dun from where they were transported by road to Chakrata. The initial strength of the force was approximately 6,000 men organised in a headquarters wing and six battalions, each comprising six companies of 120 commanded by Tibetan officers. In due course, signals and medical companies were also formed, each including women in their ranks. All recruits initially underwent six months of basic training based on that of the Indian Army, followed by training in guerrilla warfare skills provided by CIA and Indian Army instructors. From 1964 onward, this entailed parachute training conducted at Agra during which each individual carried out five descents to qualify for his parachutist's wings.

Deployed in bases along the entire border, including one accommodating two companies on the Siachen Glacier in Kashmir, the SFF was to carry out reconnaissance and intelligence-gathering operations in Tibet. These included the planting of sensors to monitor Chinese nuclear and missile tests.

In Washington and Mustang, meanwhile, efforts were being turned towards resolving the future of Baba Yeshe's guerrilla force. In mid-1963 a meeting took place in Mustang between the guerrilla commander and representatives of the CIA. The latter began by insisting that the guerrillas should move their base from Nepal into Tibet while Baba Yeshe countered with the argument that he still possessed insufficient weapons for all of his sixteen companies, only half of whom were armed. The Americans responded by declaring that it would be difficult to obtain authorisation for further supplies until the guerrillas had left Mustang. Baba Yeshe then proposed a compromise whereby four of their groups would be based in Tibet while another three, one led by him, would remain in Mustang. In the event, however, this issue remained unresolved as the guerrillas subsequently reported to the CIA that they had been unable to find suitable locations for bases inside Tibet.

The CIA was also giving consideration to the future of 133 Tibetans who were at that juncture undergoing training at Camp Hale. It was decided that these would not join the force in Mustang but would instead be used to set up an intelligence network inside Tibet.

In late 1964, the CIA and India's Intelligence Bureau formed a combined operations centre in New Delhi to coordinate and control the activities of the Mustang guerrilla force and the 133-strong Camp Hale group. The former, however, had no clearly defined role and control from New Delhi proved to be difficult. The guerrillas themselves were used to making decisions and conducting action on a unilateral basis, these being geared to one sole objective, namely the expulsion of the Chinese from Tibet. Thus, they had no interest in making any concessions either to Indian or American political objectives. On a number of occasions, the combined operations centre only learned of guerrilla operations after they had been carried out.

The CIA considered Baba Yeshe to be out of control and therefore proposed that he should be replaced as commander of the Mustang force. This was opposed by the Dalai Lama's elder brother, Gyalo Thondup, who had succeeded Gompo Tashi as head of the movement seeking freedom for Tibet after the latter's death in the autumn of 1963. Gompo Tashi had supported Baba Yeshe's position as commander and Gyalo was reluctant to move him. The Indians took Gyalo's side but made it clear that they expected him to bring Baba Yashe and his men under control. In view of this the CIA backed down on their demands. Meanwhile, Baba Yeshe was still requesting a further supply of arms and in May 1965, with the agreement of the Indians, a drop took place in Mustang, delivering 250 rifles, 36 Bren LMGs, 42 Sten guns, six 57mm recoilless rifles, 75 hand-guns, 72,000 rounds of ammunition and 1,000 grenades.

During the following year, however, the combined operations centre in New Delhi received a number of complaints from the Camp Hale-trained company commanders with regard to Baba Yeshe who was becoming increasingly autocratic. Lhamo Tsering, the operations officer at the centre, was sent to carry out an investigation. There he learned that Baba Yeshe was refusing to delegate any of his authority and was keeping a tight grip on the CIA-supplied funds for which he kept no accounts. Allocation of missions and supplies to his guerrilla companies was entirely at his whim and he appeared increasingly to be less concerned with operational matters than with lining his own pockets, including the acquisition of valuable antiques from Tibetan refugees passing through his area. On touring the guerrilla camps, Lhamo Tsering also discovered that only half of the Mustang force was armed, despite the third arms drop carried out during the previous year. Nevertheless, he found the discipline in the guerrilla companies to be good and the men themselves well trained. Using a great deal of tact and diplomacy, he managed to defuse the situation and settle the disputes between Baba Yeshe and his company commanders. At the same time, he set up a finance unit to manage the force's funds.

The combined operations centre, meanwhile, had been engaged in despatching the Camp Hale-trained intelligence agents into Tibet. On being flown from the United States to India, they underwent a period of 'acclimatisation' in small camps in the Kumaon Hills of the northern Indian state of Uttar Pradesh where they soon learned to forget the comforts of Camp Hale, growing accustomed again to eating Tibetan

food and living in spartan conditions. On completion of this final phase
of their preparation, they were led to the border by Intelligence Bureau
officers based along the frontier, the majority being despatched into
western and central Tibet. A few teams achieved some success, one
operating for two years in the area south of the Brahmaputra, in the area
of Dinggye, while others in areas south of Shigatse succeeded in doing so
for only a few months. Others encountered lack of support from local
people who voiced little enthusiasm for resistance against the Chinese
after discovering that the teams could provide virtually no assistance in
ridding them of the hated occupiers. Several teams returned to India
after only a few weeks in the field.

Losses among the intelligence teams were light, with only five men
captured. The Chinese attempted to turn one of these but his arrest was
detected immediately when he used his real name instead of his *nom
de guerre* in his first radio transmission. The combined operations centre
then proceeded to 'play' the apparently turned agent, feeding him doctored information. Eventually, however, this radio game was discontinued for fear of the Chinese pinpointing the location of the centre's
transmitter. By 1967, it was apparent that the entire operation was producing little in the way of worthwhile intelligence and the remaining
agents were recalled to India.

By 1968, however, problems had arisen again in Mustang where Baba
Yeshe had returned to his autocratic ways, having disbanded the finance
unit and regained control of the funds. The combined operations centre
was determined now to solve the problem once and for all and during
the summer sent Lhamo Tsering back to Mustang where he was joined
by a representative of the Tibetan government-in-exile, Phuntso Tashi,
the Dalai Lama's brother-in-law. There the two men discovered that a
serious rift had developed between Baba Yeshe and his recently
appointed deputy commander, Wangdu Gyatotsang, who had been the
leader of the second CIA-trained team dropped into Tibet in November 1957. As recounted earlier, following the demise of his team as a
result of enemy action, he had made his way to the NVDA main headquarters at Trigu Thang in southern Tibet before subsequently travelling on to India. There he worked with Gyalo Thondup and Lhamo
Tsering for ten years before eventually being appointed as the deputy
commander of the force in Mustang.

The Mustang force had felt the benefits of Wangdu's experience and knowledge which soon manifested themselves in the formation of a training centre and the foundations of an underground organisation inside Tibet, as well as in the efficient tasking of the guerrilla companies. By now, however, it was evident that the Chinese grip on Tibet was such that guerrilla action was of little further use. The role of the guerrillas was thus switched to intelligence-gathering, with small teams being despatched into Tibet along a 350-mile-wide front along the border with south-eastern Tibet, these reporting back to five radio teams positioned just inside Nepal. A network was eventually established throughout Tibet, many of its agents being among those Tibetans ostensibly collaborating with the Chinese but passing information via a chain of couriers. Among the intelligence acquired by this organisation was the transfer by the Chinese of their main nuclear base from Sinkiang to a new location north of Lhasa.

Baba Yeshe had by now come to resent and dislike his highly efficient deputy and relations between the two men soon deteriorated to the point where it was decided that steps would have to be taken to remove Baba Yeshe. In February 1969, he was invited to attend celebrations in Dharamsala, the seat of the Tibetan government-in-exile, marking the tenth anniversary of the Tibetan uprising. From Mustang, he travelled to New Delhi and reported to the combined operations centre where he was informed by Gyalo Thondup that he had been relieved of his command. Instead of proceeding to Dharamsala, however, he returned to Mustang where he found some of his supporters plotting to kidnap Lhamo Tsering, who was on a visit to Mustang at the time, and hold him hostage. Forbidding any such measure and having gathered a 200-strong group of those loyal to him, Baba Yeshe left Mustang ostensibly for Dharamsala but in fact travelled only a few miles eastward to Mamang where he established his own base. Hostilities broke out between the two groups, ending only after the intervention of the Nepalese who summoned Baba Yeshe to Kathmandu where he was granted protection and political asylum in exchange for providing information on the Mustang force, its strength and dispositions.

Early 1969 saw the CIA announce that it was withdrawing its support for the Mustang force. As John Kenneth Knaus explains in his book *Orphans of The Cold War – America and the Tibetan Struggle*, those in the Agency who had advocated support for Tibetan resistance, among them Desmond Fitzgerald, the head of the Agency's Far East Division, who had since died, were no longer in key positions. Their successors regarded ST CIRCUS with little enthusiasm and advocated winding up the operation. Moreover, in addition to experiencing internal political problems, the guerrillas had been unable to establish bases inside Tibet and this factor alone prevented them from mounting any really effective action against the Chinese whose domination of the country was complete. Moreover, US policy towards China, which by this time was in the grip of the Cultural Revolution launched by Mao Tse Tung three years earlier in August 1966, was changing with the first tentative moves being made by the new administration of President Richard Nixon towards re-establishing relations with Peking.

The disbandment of the 1,800-strong guerrilla force was not an easy proposition, as it had to be achieved by gradual dismantlement without news of the CIA's decision leaking out to the guerrillas. Lhamo Tsering was given the task and produced a plan by which 1,500 men would be resettled in Nepal and India during the following three years, the remaining 300 being retained for the time being with support from both the United States and India. Much effort went into developing projects in Nepal for employment of the former guerrillas, the most successful of these being rug-weaving factories in Pokhara and Kathmandu, a transport company operating trucks, buses and taxis between the two, and a hotel in Pokhara. Of those initially selected for resettlement, 300 were offered the opportunity of enlistment in the SFF but only 120 opted for this choice.

The disbandment was not without its problems, some of them caused by the force's former commander Baba Yeshe and his supporters who continued to be a thorn in the side of the Tibetan government-in-exile. The situation was made all the worse following a visit to Peking by the Nepalese monarch, King Birendra, who was threatened by Mao Tse Tung with military action unless he closed down the Mustang base. Faced with such a threat, the Nepalese complied and in early 1974 a 10,000- strong force of police and troops was despatched to Mustang. At the same time, they offered the guerrillas $500,000 in rehabilitation aid and land rights in exchange for them laying down their arms and surrendering.

At a meeting with the Nepalese Home Minister, however, Wangdu Gyatsotsang explained that he was unable to order his men to surrender without some form of guaranteed arrangements for resettlement for them. The Nepalese asked Wangdu for proposals and he turned to Lhamo Tsering for assistance. The latter travelled to Kathmandu in March but was promptly arrested and placed under house arrest in Pokhara by the Nepalese who had been tipped off about his arrival by Baba Yeshe who was still smarting from his removal from his position of command and was seeking revenge. Shortly afterwards, the Nepalese demanded that the guerrillas surrender their weapons by 30 July or face expulsion from Mustang by force. In Dharamsala, meanwhile, it was recognised that there was no option but to yield to this ultimatum and the Dalai Lama's brother-in-law, Phuntso Tashi, together with His Holiness's chief of security, P. T. Takla, was sent to Mustang via Kathmandu to deliver the message to Wangdu and his men. Lhamo Tsering was permitted to accompany the two emissaries only as far as Jomosom in Mustang where he was held in custody as the Nepalese had learned of a plan by the guerrillas to rescue him.

Phuntso Tashi and P. T. Takla travelled an hour and half farther north to the nearest guerrilla base where they were met by Wangdu and a large gathering of Khambas. They were equipped with a tape recording of the Dalai Lama instructing Wangdu and his men to lay down their arms. In late July, the majority began complying with His Holiness's command, long columns of mules carrying weapons accompanying the guerrillas heading south into western Nepal. At this juncture, however, the Nepalese reneged on their deal of rehabilitation in exchange for surrender and launched a major operation, arresting the guerrillas and marching them to Jomosom.

News of the Nepalese treachery soon reached Wangdu who, with a small group of 40 men, fled on horseback towards the border, taking with him the Chushi Gangdrug's operational records. On reaching it, he subsequently joined forces with one of the guerrilla radio teams positioned there as part of the Mustang force's intelligence-gathering operations. Using the radio, he sent a message to the combined operations centre in New Delhi, proposing that he should set up a new force for future operations in Tibet. This proposition met with a flat refusal and an order for him to make his way to India.

During the following two weeks, Wangdu and his men repeatedly crossed into Tibet and back into Nepal as they headed for the Indian border some 200 miles away. Both the Chinese and the Nepalese, however, were determined to prevent his escape and he encountered ambushes on both sides of the border. One night a mule carrying the group's food was lost and Wangdu sent two men to retrieve it; but one of them made his way to Jomosom and gave himself up, earning a reprieve in exchange for divulging Wangdu's planned escape route. The Nepalese despatched a large body of troops to establish an ambush at the 18,000-feet-high Tinker's Pass, towards which the fugitives were heading, while sending a 40-strong party of Baba Yeshe's group to follow up from the rear.

Wangdu reached the Tinker's Pass, which lies some twenty miles from the Indian–Nepalese border, at the end of August. As he and five others went forward to reconnoitre the track leading through it, they were caught in the ambush. Moving up to join them, the remainder of the group arrived in time to see Wangdu charging a Nepalese position, his five companions having already been killed. The ensuing battle lasted throughout the rest of the day with the Nepalese incurring heavy casualties before the rest of Wangdu's men succeeded in escaping by scaling the surrounding cliffs and making their way to the Indian border which they crossed a few hours later. Next day, Baba Yeshe was flown by helicopter from Kathmandu to the Tinker's Pass to identify Wangdu's body.

Wangdu's death marked the end of active armed resistance by the Tibetans against the Chinese occupiers of their country. In their desire to ingratiate themselves further with their northern neighbours, the Nepalese supplied Peking with details of the Mustang intelligence network inside Tibet, all provided by Baba Yeshe. Lhamo Tsering was held in prison without charges by the Nepalese for five years until he was put on trial in 1979 with six other former Mustang guerrillas. One of these was Ragra Jetar, the commander of the team which had captured the valuable haul of intelligence documents in October 1961; his role as one of the ringleaders of the plot to rescue Lhamo Tsering had incurred the wrath of the Nepalese. Two others were former company commanders, while a fourth was a radio operator. The sixth member of the group was a guerrilla who had been caught attempting to escape from Mustang to join Wangdu.

All seven were charged with resisting Nepalese demands to surrender and being involved in the armed activities of an illegal and unfriendly force. In their defence, lawyers produced evidence, including photographs, of a visit by the Nepalese monarch, King Birendra, to the guerrilla base in Mustang where he was presented with a horse by Baba Yeshe, while also pointing to the good relations between the guerrillas and the local Nepalese security forces. Moreover, all had surrendered before a deadline of 31 July 1974 laid down by the Home Minister who had declared that those who did so would not face prosecution. The court disregarded these arguments, however, and all seven were found guilty. Lhamo Tsering and five others received sentences of life imprisonment while the sixth was sentenced to death for resisting arrest. Appeals for pardons were submitted to King Birendra but it was not until 1981, following an appeal by the Dalai Lama, that the seven were released.

The rapprochement between China and the United States, which had begun in 1971 with a visit to Peking by US Secretary of State Henry Kissinger, followed by an official visit by President Nixon in February 1972, had meanwhile resulted in the Americans quietly dropping the Tibetans' cause in the United Nations and terminating any further support from the CIA. In 1971, the Nixon administration requested that the Tibetans close their office in New York, which had been opened along with one in Geneva in 1964, its presence being seen as an embarrassment and possible obstacle to the further improvement of Sino–US relations. This drew an indignant refusal from Gyalo Thondup. In the summer of 1974, the United States terminated the financial support it had been providing for the Dalai Lama and his government-in-exile since the latter's flight to India in 1959. This was understandably regarded by the Tibetans as the final betrayal of the undertakings given to them in 1951, who saw themselves as being discarded by the United States which no longer needed them now that they had served their purpose. They had no choice but to accept, resolving that in future they would continue the struggle for the freedom of their country on their own.

CHAPTER NINE

OMAN 1958–1976

In the late 1950s, no sooner had Britain, assisted by Commonwealth forces, defeated the forces of communism in the jungles of Malaya than it found itself caught up in a long-running conflict in the harsh desert and mountains of the Sultanate of Oman in the Persian Gulf.

The largest state in the Gulf, covering an area of some 120,000 square miles, Oman occupies the south-eastern coast of the Arabian Peninsula. It is of strategic importance since its Musandam Peninsula overlooks the Straits of Hormuz at the mouth of the Gulf. The north of the country features the Al-Hajar Mountains, running south-eastward parallel to the coast of the Gulf of Oman and reaching a height of over 10,000 feet on the plateau of the Djebel Al-Akhdar. These are split by a great central divide, the Wadi Sama'il, which separates them into western and eastern ranges. To the north-east of the Al-Hajah is the Al-Batinah coastal plain on which the country's capital, Muscat, is located. East of the mountains are the sandy plains of Ash-Sharqivah while to the south-east, to the south of Ra's Al-Hadd looking out over the Arabian Sea, is the region of Ja'lan. To the south-west a plateau leads away from the mountains to the foothills and valleys of Al-Jaww, Oman's heartland, while to the west is the semi-desert area of Az-Zahirah and the border with the United Arab Emirates. Until 1971, this comprised the Trucial Oman States, made up of the seven small emirates of Abu Dhabi, Dubai, Sharjah, Ajman, Um Al-Qaywayn and Ra's Al-Khaymah and Al-Fujayrah, thereafter becoming the United Arab Emirates. Beyond Al-Jaww and Az-Zahirah lies the desert of the Rub' al-Khali (Empty Quarter) through which runs the border with Oman's western neighbour, Saudi Arabia.

Covering some three-quarters of the country is a large expanse of desert which stretches away 400 miles to the mountainous region of Dhofar in the south-west. This consists of a narrow coastal plain, on which is located the provincial capital of Salalah, dominated by the crescent form of the djebel massif of the Al-Qara Mountains which rise to between 3,000 and 4,000 feet. Beyond the djebel is a flat and featureless region known as the negd. Covered with shingle and rocks and intersected by large sandy wadis, it extends northward to a gravel plain and subsequently to the sandy wastes of the Rub' al-Khali and Saudi Arabia. Its sole inhabitants are the Mahra, a warlike nomadic tribe who wander the expanse of the region with their herds of camels and goats.

To the south-west of Dhofar is Oman's other neighbour, the Republic of Yemen which was formed in 1990 from the People's Democratic Republic of Yemen and the Yemen Arab Republic, also known respectively as South and North Yemen. Offshore, Oman possesses two territories in the form of the islands of Masirah, to the east, and Al-Hallaniyah, the largest of the five Khuriya Muriya Islands, 25 miles off its south coast.

The climate in Oman is generally dry and hot in the interior areas, with a high level of humidity along the coast. The dominating factor in Dhofar is the south-west monsoon, known locally as the *khareef* which, lasting from the beginning of June to the end of September, makes the region's climate more moderate and the area of the coastal plain fertile.

OMAN WAS SETTLED SOME 4,000 to 5,000 years ago by migrants from Egypt; and the origins of the Omani tribes are traced back to the immigration of Arab tribes from South Arabia into the region of Ja'lan during the second century AD. These tribes then moved northward into the area of Mazun where they encountered others moving in from the north-west.

Arab dominance of the country began with the introduction of Islam in the seventh century but not until the following century did any form of national unity emerge. This arrived with the Ibadites, an extremist Islamic sect introduced to Oman by the Kharejites, survivors of the army of Ali, Mohammed's son-in-law, and proclaimed at Nizwa at the end of the seventh century by Abdullah bin Ibadh. The Ibadhis, who regarded the Koran as the only source of authority and followed the Sharia law of Islam, were headed by an Imam elected to serve as both their spiritual and secular leader. Selection of a new Imam was based on agreement among the religious leaders and chiefs of the principal tribes, in particular those of the two major tribal groupings, the Ghafiris and the Hinawis.

Eventually, however, elected Imams gave way to hereditary dynasties. Meanwhile, Oman suffered invasion and occupation by a number of foreign powers, including the Portuguese and Persians. The Portuguese sacked Muscat in 1507 and exercised control over the entire coast until the next century when they were driven out by the Al-Yaarabah dynasty whose base was the ancient fortress of Rostaq situated on the northern edge of the western range of the Al-Hajar. The Al-Yaarabahs recaptured Muscat in 1650, subsequently building a powerful navy and securing Portuguese settlements along the coasts of Persia and East Africa. In the eighteenth century, however, the Al-Yaarabahs fell from power and the following 25 years saw a long-running civil war over succession between two rival Imams supported respectively by the Ghafiris and Hinawis. It ended with victory on the part of the latter whose candidate, Ahmad ibn Sa'id, proceeded to defeat and eject the Persians who, under their ruler Nadir Shah, had invaded Oman in 1737.

Elected Imam in 1749, Ahmad ibn Sa'id thus established the Al Bu Sa'id dynasty which has been in power in Oman since then. In due course, however, his grandson, Sa'id bin Sultan, who ruled Oman during the period 1806–56, gained control of the island of Zanzibar and transferred his place of residence there. On his death, his realm was divided between his two sons.

The fortunes of the dynasty waned during the latter half of the nineteenth century and would have collapsed altogether but for the assistance of Britain which supported the Al Bu Sa'id Sultans against the periodic threats of the Ibadhi Imams who continued to hold sway over the tribes in the interior, a number of attacks being mounted on Muscat and the coastal town of Matrah during 1895 and 1915. In 1920 an agreement between the tribes and Sultan Taymur bin Faysal, known as the Treaty of Al-Sib, was negotiated by the British whose connections with Oman dated back to the seventeenth century and the East India Company. It recognised the supremacy of the Sultan but granted a degree of autonomy to the tribal leaders, including permission to elect their own Imam, and his right to appoint local governors, known as walis, in the tribal areas. While the boundaries of such areas were never formally delineated, the Imam's walis exercised their authority within the interior while those of the Sultan did likewise in the coastal areas.

The treaty brought peace to Oman for the next 30 years until the death in 1954 of Muhammad al-Khalili who had been Imam since 1920. Trouble soon arose, principally stirred up by Saudi Arabia which since

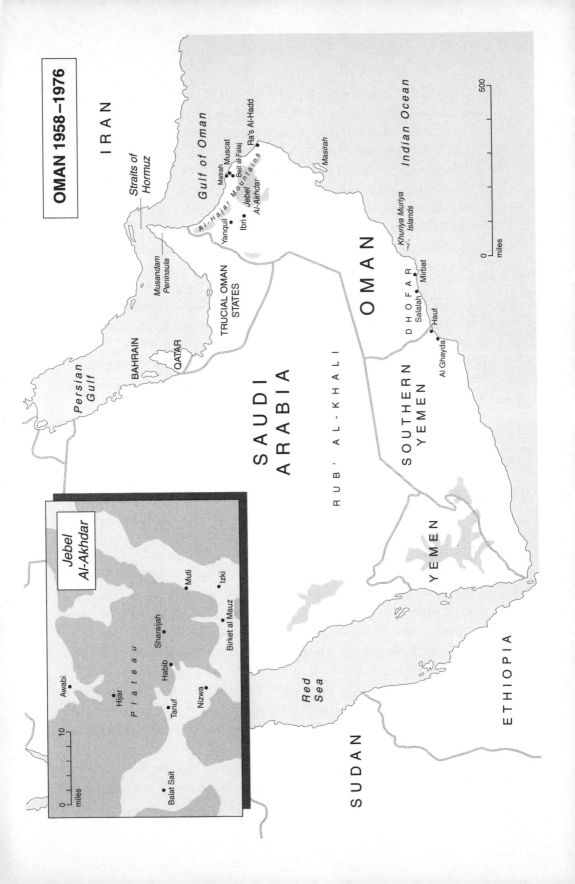

OMAN 1958–1976

IRAN

Straits of Hormuz

Gulf of Oman

Musandam Peninsula

BAHRAIN

QATAR

TRUCIAL OMAN STATES

Persian Gulf

SAUDI ARABIA

RUB' AL-KHALI

Matrah
Muscat
Belt al Falaj
Al-Hajar Mountains
Yanqui
Ibri
Jebel Al-Akhdar
Ra's Al-Hadd

Masirah

O M A N

Indian Ocean

Khuriya Muriya Islands

D H O F A R
Salalah
Mirbat
Hauf

Al Ghayda

SOUTHERN YEMEN

0   500
miles

Red Sea

YEMEN

ETHIOPIA

SUDAN

Jebel Al-Akhdar

Awabi
Hijar
Plateau
Sharaijah
Habib
Tanuf
Nizwa
Muti
Izki
Birket al Mauz

Balat Sait

0   10
miles

1937 had been attempting to push its southern frontiers southwards and south-eastwards beyond the Rub' al-Khali and over the borders into Oman, the Aden Protectorate and the Trucial Oman States. In 1952, the Saudis had occupied the Buraimi Oasis, the joint property of the Trucial state of Abu Dhabi and Oman. A force of 8,000 tribesmen, rallied by the Imam in the name of the Sultan, had begun moving to eject the Saudis but were forestalled from doing so by the British who intervened. This was a grave error on the part of the latter as the expulsion of the Saudis would have been a severe blow to their standing while increasing the loyalty of the Omani tribes to the Sultan.

The dispute was referred to international arbitration by a tribunal in Geneva, during which the Saudis were reportedly busy bribing representatives with offers of large sums of gold. This eventually came to the notice of the president of the tribunal and the British delegate, both of whom resigned in protest. By the end of 1955, however, no settlement had been achieved and Britain's patience ran out. Shortly afterwards, the Saudi troops at the Buraimi Oasis were ejected by the Trucial Oman Scouts, an Arab force commanded by British officers and NCOs, who established their own garrison there alongside that of a force of Omani troops.

The Saudis, nevertheless, had succeeded in spreading their influence in Oman, subverting the tribes with gifts of money and weapons. They were encouraged in their efforts not only by Russia, which was pursuing its own long-standing imperialist aims in the region, but also by the United States whose interest centred on the discoveries of oil in the region and who were keen to see British influence diminished. Furthermore, Muhammad al-Khalili's successor as Imam was a weak character named Ghalib bin Ali who had not been elected to his position but merely appointed by three tribal chiefs. Completely under the influence of the Saudis, Ghalib was also dominated by his brother Talib, the wali of Rostaq, a forceful and ambitious character, and two of the latter's henchmen. The first of these was Suleiman bin Himyar, leader of the Beni Riyam tribe who rejoiced in the title of 'Lord of the Djebel Akhdar' the great plateau of the Al-Hajar which had been occupied for centuries by the Nebahina dynasty who had little regard for the rule of Sultan or Imam. The other was Sheikh Salih bin Isa, leader of all the Hinawi tribes, from the southern Omani province of the Sharqiya.

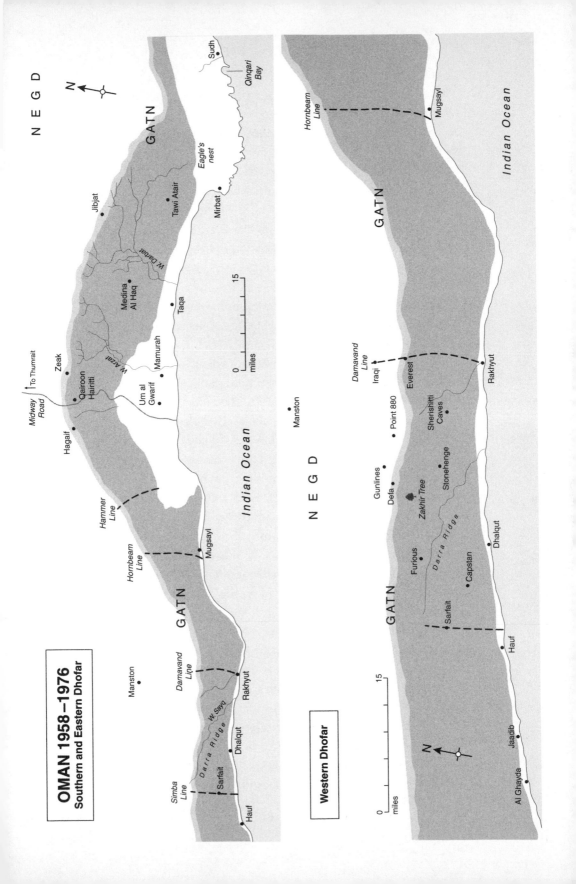

OMAN 1958–1976
Southern and Eastern Dhofar

Western Dhofar

N E G D

N

GATN

Midway Road
To Thumrait

Hagaif
Zeak
Qairoon Hairitti
Jibjat

W. Arzat

Um al Gwarif
Medina Al Haq
Tawi Atair

W. Darbat

Mamurah
Taqa
Mirbat

Eagle's nest

Qingari Bay

Sudh

Indian Ocean

Hammer Line
Hornbeam Line
Mugsayl

Manston

Damavand Line

W. Sayq
Darra Ridge
Rakhyut

Simba Line
Sarfait
Dhalqut
Hauf

GATN

0   15
miles

N E G D

GATN

Hornbeam Line
Mugsayl

Indian Ocean

GATN

Damavand Line
Iraqi
Everest
Rakhyut

Gunlines
Defa
Zakhir Tree
Point 880
Sherishitti Caves

Stonehenge
Furious
Darra Ridge
Capstan
Sarfait
Dhalqut

Manston

Hauf
Jaadib
Al Ghayda

N

0   15
miles

Immediately after Ghalib's appointment, he and Talib had travelled around the interior, establishing garrisons of tribesmen at Nizwa, his main seat of power, and in other major towns and villages. Shortly afterwards, a dispute arose between the Sultan and Ghalib over oil concession rights in the western desert, in the area of the Djebel Fahud, where a British oil company had expressed a wish to drill. The Sultan claimed that under the terms of the Treaty of Al-Sib he possessed sole rights to negotiate and grant such rights as it was an external affair. Ghalib, however, encouraged by the Saudis and the United States, insisted that it was an internal matter and thus any such negotiations were within his jurisdiction.

The Sultan was not prepared to countenance any such view and in December 1955 settled the dispute by force, despatching troops of the Muscat and Oman Field Force to occupy Nizwa. It was a bloodless operation which resulted in the abdication of Ghalib and his retirement to his home village, while Talib and Sheikh Salih fled to Saudi Arabia. Suleiman, having declared his loyalty to the Sultan, retreated to his fastness on the Djebel Akhdar, and peace was restored to Oman.

In Saudi Arabia, however, Talib was soon at work planning a rebellion in Oman. It would be headed in the centre of the country by Ghali and himself while Sheikh Salih's brother, Ibrahim bin Isa, would lead it in the south. Throughout 1956, he raised a guerrilla force from among Omanis employed as labourers in Saudi Arabia, these being trained by Saudi army instructors in the use of small arms, mortars and mines. The rebellion was scheduled to take place in May 1957. Talib and his guerrilla force were landed on the Al-Batinah coastline, made their way into the mountains to join Ghalib and declared their opposition to the Sultan. But the latter had not been idle and had imprisoned Ibrahim bin Isa who had initiated his part of the rebellion a day too early. He had also lured Suleiman bin Himyar down from the Djebel Akhdar to Muscat and placed him under house arrest. Suleiman, however, escaped and returned to his mountain fastness from which, having joined forces with Ghalib and Talib, he declared war.

The Sultan responded by dispatching the Muscat and Oman Field Force from its headquarters at Firq to attack Ghalib's village of Balat Sait, but it was ambushed by rebel forces who inflicted very heavy losses, forcing it to withdraw. The Sultan immediately turned to Britain for military assistance and the latter responded swiftly, sending a company of the 1st Battalion The Cameronians (Scottish Rifles). Together with the Trucial Oman Scouts and the remnants of the Muscat and Oman Field Force, supported by RAF Venom fighters, it recaptured Nizwa and attacked Suleiman's home at Muti and his large fort at Birket al Mauz, forcing him, Ghalib and Talib to retire to the Djebel Akhdar.

Measuring some 40 to 50 miles in length and approximately ten in width, the Djebel Akhdar is a limestone massif with a plateau at a height of some 6,000 feet and mountain peaks rising to about 10,000 feet. The land on the plateau is highly fertile, readily supporting the tribes living on it. The only routes to the top are narrow tracks leading through steep ravines, easily held by relatively small numbers of tribesmen in defence against an army. Caves provided good protection against air attack and also provided locations for caches of arms smuggled in from Saudi Arabia by land and sea.

Having built up a considerable arsenal of weapons and increased their strength on the plateau, the rebels opened a guerrilla campaign against the Sultan. Groups of rebels descended from the plateau to carry out attacks, lay mines and ambush convoys of vehicles.

During the latter half of 1958, after a visit by the Sultan to Britain, the British government agreed to provide further military assistance. Following the rebels' rout of the Muscat and Oman Field Force, the Omanis had been reorganised into a force that comprised the North-ern Frontier Regiment, of some 450 all ranks, based at Nizwa; the Muscat Regiment, numbering approximately 250 men deployed on garrison duties at Beit al Falaj, situated just outside Muscat, and in the capital itself; an artillery troop equipped with two 5.5 inch guns and two 75mm howitzers; and a training depot located about fifteen miles from Muscat. All officers within these units, with the exception of a small number of Arabs and Pakistanis in junior positions, were British – either seconded from the British Army or serving under contract – while the other ranks were Arabs and Baluchis. The latter were recruited from Gwadar, an area on the coast of Baluchistan, in the far south-west of Pakistan, which belonged to Oman until 1958 when the Sultan sold it to Pakistan while retaining the right to muster troops.

All units came under the command of the Headquarters Sultan's Armed Forces (SAF), headed by a colonel and situated at Beit al Falaj.

Dhofar was the responsibility of a 200-strong independent unit commanded by a British contract officer and comprising a mixture of Arabs,
Djebali tribesmen from the mountains inland from Salalah, and a few
Baluchis. Known as the Dhofar Force, it came under the direct command
of the Sultan himself.

In addition, British units from Bahrain and the Aden Protectorate
were deployed on attachment to SAF. These consisted of two squadrons
of the Trucial Oman Scouts, one based at Ibri and the other at Izki; two
troops of Ferret scout cars of the 13th/18th Royal Hussars based at
Nizwa; a Royal Signals detachment providing communications between
all units throughout Oman; a Royal Marine training team of an officer
and eight sergeants attached to the Northern Frontier Regiment; Royal
Engineer survey parties, and a small number of RAF pilots and ground
crew responsible for operating the two Single Pioneer aircraft which
made up SAF's air arm.

In-mid 1958, Colonel David Smiley arrived in Oman to take up the
appointment of Commander SAF. As mentioned in Chapter 2, he had
served during the Second World War with the Special Operations Executive in Yugoslavia, and later in Thailand. After the war he had been
attached to the Secret Intelligence Service (SIS) and was responsible
for training anti-communist guerrillas for operations in Albania.

It soon became clear to Smiley that his forces would be unable to
capture the Djebel Akhdar and eliminate the increasing threat of the
guerrillas, notably their mining of roads. The British government agreed
to provide further assistance and in August, while on leave in England,
Smiley was advised that 22nd SAS Regiment (22 SAS) was due to withdraw from Malaya later in the year and that a squadron would be available for operations. His request for a full squadron of Ferret scout cars,
as opposed to just two troops, was granted.

In October, operations against the rebels on the Djebel Akhdar began
in earnest. D Squadron of The Life Guards, commanded by Major
Kenneth Diacre, had arrived during September to replace the 13/18th
Royal Hussars, and three of its five troops, each of four Ferret scout
cars, were deployed to Nizwa, Izki and Awabi respectively as part of a
blockade on the mountain. A company of the Northern Frontier Regiment attacked and captured the village of Tanuf, where Talib had positioned his headquarters in a cave, and a squadron of Trucial Oman Scouts

occupied Yanquil at the north-western end of the Al-Hajar range, sealing off all approaches. Meanwhile, SAF units carried out fighting patrols to seek out the enemy while Shackleton bombers and Venom fighters attacked targets on the plateau.

The rebels responded with night attacks on Tanuf, supported by mortar bombardments, but these were repulsed after fierce fighting. It became apparent that Smiley's tactics were proving successful when Ghalib sent a message requesting a truce to negotiate an agreement between the Sultan and the rebels. This, however, was merely a ploy by the rebels to buy recovery time and the fighting resumed after two weeks, albeit hampered by torrential rain.

At the end of October, Lieutenant Colonel Tony Deane-Drummond, Commanding Officer of 22 SAS, accompanied by Major Frank Kitson of the Planning Branch at the War Office, arrived in Oman to carry out their own reconnaissance to ascertain whether the task was suitable for an SAS squadron. After reconnoitring the foothills of the Djebel Akhdar and carrying out an air reconnaissance of the plateau itself, they returned to England, Deane-Drummond recommending that one of his squadrons should be employed in the assault.

D Squadron 22 SAS, commanded by Major Johnny Watts, arrived in Oman during the third week of November. It had spent the immediate period prior to its departure from the Far East retraining for its new task and on arrival, having established a base at Beit al Falaj, was given four days to acclimatise to the fierce dry heat of the desert after the humid swamps and jungles of Malaya. On the fifth day it travelled to Nizwa and then Tanuf where it was split, with the 21 men of 16 and 17 Troops being despatched under Captain Muir Walker, the commander of 16 Troop, to reconnoitre the northern side of the Djebel Akhdar. Accompanied by a SAF officer, Major Tony Hart, and a platoon of the Muscat Regiment, Walker and his men made their way undetected from Awabi up a narrow track to the edge of the plateau, passing deserted rebel posts, and setting up a base 3,000 yards from an enemy position at a place called Aqbat al Dhafar. They then attempted to work their way round the position but the rebels had reinforced it. Colonel David Smiley was unwilling to commit the two troops to a frontal assault and concentrated instead on reinforcing his foothold on the plateau with more troops of the Muscat Regiment.

Meanwhile 18 and 19 Troops had remained at the south side of the mountain whose slopes were vast slabs of smooth rock rising for thousands of feet to further slabs. Patrols were sent up the mountain, lying up during the day in positions from which they would observe rebel movements, and descending back to base on the following night. The heat during the day was intense, the rocks in which the patrols concealed themselves becoming too hot to touch. Water had to be carefully rationed during the 24 hours of each patrol and it was common for men to be completely dehydrated by the time they returned.

On 26 November, two five-man patrols of 19 Troop were in positions some 600 yards apart on the mountain. The patrol commander of one of them, Sergeant Ian 'Tanky' Smith, observed a rebel approaching his post and at a range of 200 yards shot him dead. The patrol immediately came under heavy fire from some twenty rebels. The second patrol prepared to move up to provide fire support but as one member, Corporal Duke Swindells, stood up, he was shot dead.

Four days later, a force of 40 rebels, supported by mortars, mounted an attack on the Northern Frontier Regiment company and the troop of 5.5 inch guns at Tanuf. At one point it looked as if they might overrun the SAF positions but the Omani troops rallied under the members of the Royal Marine training team until reinforcements arrived in the form of a troop of The Life Guards who inflicted heavy casualties on the enemy and helped drive them off.

On the night of 30 November, 18 and 19 Troops set off up the mountain. The former, commanded by Captain Peter de la Billière, was to mount an attack on a number of caves being used by the rebels. Set in a sheer rock face, they were unassailable and could only be attacked by fire from an outcrop some 200 yards away. Covering fire would be given from higher up by 19 Troop positioned on another outcrop. The ascent took nine hours, navigation being difficult and the gradient of the slopes steep, and 18 Troop reached its fire position at 5.30 a.m. on the morning of 1 December. Just after dawn, as the figures of rebels appeared at the mouths of the caves, the troop opened up with rifles, machine-guns and a 3.5 inch rocket launcher which fired rockets into the caves. Almost immediately, other rebels in caves higher up the rock face returned the fire and a fierce battle ensued. At that point, RAF Venom fighters joined the fray, scoring a direct hit on a rebel mortar crew firing from a crevice, and 18 Troop withdrew under covering fire from 19 Troop. Enemy casualties were initially claimed as eight dead but subsequent interrogation of prisoners revealed that only two had been killed and three wounded.

That same night, on the northern side of the Djebel Akhdar, a six-man patrol of Captain Muir Walker's force, commanded by Sergeant Herbie Hawkins, came under an attack from some 40 tribesmen armed with rifles but supported by two light machine-guns (LMG). Waiting until they approached to within 150 yards, he and his patrol opened fire, killing five rebels and wounding four before the remainder withdrew.

During the following weeks, Colonel David Smiley reinforced the positions on the northern edge of the plateau. On 27 December, Captain Walker led a reconnaissance in force by 16 and 17 Troops on a feature of twin peaks codenamed SABRINA. That afternoon, however, 16 Troop was spotted just as it was ascending the right-hand feature by climbing a rope. The rebels opened fire and the ensuing battle ensued lasted all night. At one point the two sides were only a short distance apart. Eventually, the SAS took the right-hand peak, killing nine rebels.

The positions on the northern side were reinforced at the end of December with two troops of Trucial Oman Scouts, from the squadron based in the village of Hijar, a platoon of the Northern Frontier Regiment and a troop of The Life Guards in the infantry role, armed with eight Browning .30 machine guns dismounted from their Ferret Scout cars.

By this time it had become apparent to Colonel Smiley and Major Watts that a second SAS squadron would be required to storm the Djebel Akhdar. The request for reinforcement was transmitted to the 22 SAS base at Hereford, in England, and Lieutenant Colonel Deane-Drummond agreed, saying that he would accompany it with a small tactical headquarters to command both squadrons. Political sanction was granted by the Foreign Office and War Office, but with the proviso that all British troops must leave Oman by the first week of April 1959. This was because the United Nations were due to discuss the situation in the Middle East, with Oman high on the agenda, and the British government was anxious not to suffer any embarrassment by the presence of its troops in the country.

Deane-Drummond arrived in Oman on 1 January 1959 and established his headquarters with those of Colonel Smiley at the Northern

Frontier Regiment's base at Nizwa. On 12 January A Squadron, commanded by Major Johnny Cooper, arrived from Malaya and five days later, having acclimatised, relieved D Squadron which returned to Beit al-Falaj for a few days of rest and recuperation. On 24 January A Squadron mounted an attack on SABRINA and captured the entire feature.

The Foreign Office deadline left only three months for the capture of the Djebel Akhdar. Smiley and Deane-Drummond had agreed that any attack would have to be launched at night during a full-moon period, which occurred at the end of each month. The date for the operation was thus set for the night of 25 January.

Air reconnaissance flights over the Djebel Akhdar indicated that the rebels' main strongholds were at Habib, Saiq and Sharaijah which were too far from the Aqbat al Dhafar position; and since this was in any case held by a strong enemy force, no approach could be made from that direction. Eventually, Deane-Drummond decided to launch his assault by way of a buttress on the eastern side of the Wadi Kamah, due north of Nizwa. This route was apparently unguarded and could be climbed in approximately nine and a half hours, enabling the assault troops to be in position on the edge of the plateau by dawn. Moreover, although there was no track, it was felt that the slope was negotiable by donkeys carrying up water and food in the event that a planned air drop, due to take place at 6.45 a.m. following the attack, could not take place.

The assault would be led by A and D Squadrons as Colonel Smiley had received orders from British headquarters in Aden that all other troops, British and SAF, were only to be used in support. The operation consisted of three phases. In the first, to be completed before first light on 26 January, A Squadron, less 4 Troop, would capture a crest, code-named VINCENT, approximately one third of the way up the mountain. Meanwhile D Squadron would secure three features: a prominent peak, known as PYRAMID; the top of the plateau, named BEERCAN; and a peak beyond it designated COLIN which overlooked the enemy-held village of Habib. The two squadrons would be accompanied by a 50-strong irregular force of Beni Ruawha tribesmen under the command of an SAF officer, Major John Clarke. During this phase, 4 Troop, along with a platoon of the Muscat Regiment and a force of 200 Abryeen tribesmen commanded by an SAF officer, Major Jasper Coates, would mount a diversionary attack on Aqbat al Dhafar. In the second phase, C

Company Northern Frontier Regiment would relieve A Squadron on VINCENT while The Life Guards' dismounted troop would take over PYRAMID from D Squadron which would move on to BEERCAN. In the third and final phase, A Squadron was to move up on to BEERCAN and regroup, with D Squadron doing likewise on COLIN.

RAF air support would be available with Venom fighters on station from first light, while Valetta transports from Bahrain would carry out resupply drops on BEERCAN once it had been secured. Meanwhile, two helicopters were to be positioned at Nizwa to evacuate any casualties.

Smiley and Deane-Drummond were well aware that the rebels would be expecting an attack and thus it was imperative that they should be deceived as to the direction from which it would be made. Prior to the operation, therefore, a number of diversionary attacks were mounted in different areas of the Djebel Akhdar. During the period 8 to 22 January, D Squadron and A Company Northern Frontier Regiment conducted fighting patrols from Tanuf, ejecting some rebels from a feature of high ground where they had established an observation post (OP). Between 18 and 22 January, A Squadron, with the squadron of Trucial Oman Scouts based at Hijar in support, carried out exploratory attacks on Aqbat al Dhafar. On 23 January, it withdrew, leaving 4 Troop behind, and rejoined D Squadron at Tanuf. On the night of 24 January, A Company Northern Frontier Regiment was involved in an action with rebels near Tanuf while C Company carried out an attack from Izki. As a final deception ploy, the handlers of the donkeys due to bring up supplies after the securing of BEERCAN were told in strictest confidence, being threatened with the direst consequences should they break it, that a feint attack was to be mounted via the Wadi Kamah while the real assault would be made up the track from Tanuf. This was done in the full knowledge that such information would soon find its way to the rebels.

The operation began at 7.30 p.m. after last light on the night of 25 January. A and D Squadrons were transported in trucks from Tanuf to Kamah from where, preceded by two lead scouts, they began the long climb up the mountain. Each man was very heavily laden with a rucksack weighing some 90 lbs, belt kit and personal weapon. In the distance to the north could be heard the sound of firing as 4 Troop, the Muscat Regiment platoon and Abryeen tribesmen started their diversionary attack. At about 4.00 a.m., however, the climb was halted following the discovery by members of 16 Troop of a heavy machine-gun in a cave covering the track. The weapon, a .50 Browning on an anti-aircraft mounting, was in position but there was no sign of the crew. In order to maintain surprise, there was no question of attacking the cave. At the same time, the slow pace of the climb was such that there was a danger that D Squadron would not reach BEERCAN before dawn. The problem was resolved by the squadron caching its rucksacks on a narrow ridge, codenamed CAUSEWAY, which linked PYRAMID and BEERCAN, and continuing the climb with each man carrying his belt kit, weapon and as much ammunition as possible.

Leaving 16 Troop to cover them and deal with the machine-gun crew, 17, 18 and 19 Troops made their way silently past the cave and down a 40-foot cliff face to a narrow track which led up a wide wadi. A short while later came the sound of some shots and the explosion of a grenade indicating the demise of the rebel machine-gun crew at the hands of 16 Troop. This alerted some rebels to the east who opened fire on 16 Troop with an LMG but this was quickly suppressed by some accurately placed fire before the troop set off to rejoin the rest of the squadron.

After another long, hard climb up the wadi, D Squadron reached the edge of the plateau and Major Watts swiftly established a defensive perimeter. By now it was dawn and shortly afterwards the three Valetta transports appeared and dropped a resupply which included jerricans of much-needed water. Meanwhile, there was no rebel activity as D Squadron collected its cached rucksacks and sent patrols to reconnoitre further out on to the plateau.

In the meantime, A Squadron had encountered some rebels during its approach and casualties had been incurred by a bullet which hit a No. 94 Energa rifle-launched grenade in Trooper 'Nanto' Carter's rucksack, causing it to explode; he had been seriously wounded, along with the two men behind him. Despite all three being evacuated by helicopter to hospital, two of them died 24 hours later. Rebels had also opened fire with mortars and machine-guns on C Company Northern Frontier Regiment but these had been silenced by SAF's troop of 5.5 inch guns at Tanuf.

The deception plan and diversionary attacks, however, had proved successful as the majority of the rebels had now moved to the area of plateau overlooking the Tanuf track. They had also strengthened their forces at Aqbat al Dhafar in the north where they had been kept occupied by the diversionary attack mounted by Major Coates's force.

That afternoon, the village of Sharaijah was captured and the battle for the Djebel Akhdar was over. As in the other villages, only women, children and elderly people were found there, the young men remaining in hiding in the caves and rocks surrounding the area. Having regrouped his forces, Colonel Smiley sent out his irregulars to make contact with the villagers and persuade them to surrender and lay down their arms. Patrols were also despatched to hunt down the rebel leaders and to search all villages and caves for weapons. These located a considerable quantity of weapons which included twelve Bren LMGs, six .50 Browning heavy machine-guns, eight mortars, Czech and Polish grenades and a large amount of American ammunition and mines, all bearing markings which indicated that they had been supplied by the Saudi Arabian Army. A number of prisoners were taken and one of these revealed the location of Suleiman's personal cave situated in the hills on the plateau. A search of this revealed, in addition to quantities of arms, ammunition and food, a quantity of documents and approximately 1,000 letters giving details of the rebel organisation and its network of supporters throughout Oman. These included prominent individuals, sheikhs, village headmen and rebels involved in mine-laying and smuggling of arms.

Ghalib, Talib and Suleiman had meanwhile fled, escaping with a small band of followers through the SAF cordon around the mountain and making their way to the Sharqiya in the south of the country. Eventually, they made their way to the coast and boarded a dhow which took them to Saudi Arabia.

The end of the rebellion was followed by a 'hearts and minds' campaign to win over the inhabitants of the Djebel Akhdar. British sappers were sent to repair the buildings, reservoirs and other facilities that had been damaged by bombing and shelling. During this period there was no trouble as the rebels lay low but in the summer of 1959 they resumed the mining of roads and began sniping at military camps.

DURING THE EARLY 1960s, another threat to Oman emerged in Dhofar, to where Sultan Sa'id bin Taymur had moved permanently in 1958 when the mountain tribes rebelled against his restrictive and repressive regime.

The insurgency began in 1962 with the mining of an oil exploration vehicle and occasional attacks on SAF vehicles. These were carried out by a group of dissidents, headed by Musallim bin Nufl, who in June 1965 formed the nucleus of the Dhofar Liberation Front (DLF). Under the slogan 'Dhofar for the Dhofaris', and while opposing the rule of the Sultan, its viewpoint was conservative, maintaining the traditional tribal structures and the practice of the Islamic religion.

To the west of Dhofar, the latter part of 1967 saw the withdrawal of British forces from the neighbouring Aden Protectorate which became the independent Marxist state of the People's Republic of South Yemen. Already active there was a Marxist revolutionary movement called the Popular Front for the Liberation of the Occupied Arab Gulf (PFLOAG) which was receiving support from China and the Soviet Union. After the British withdrawal, it approached the DLF and suggested that the two organisations join forces. The latter was initially reluctant but was eventually persuaded by promises of money and arms. A headquarters and base were established at Hauf and Al Ghayda, just over the border from Oman. Within a short period of time the conservative traditionalists of the DLF had been ousted by the hard-line Marxists of the PFLOAG who immediately began establishing cells along classic communist lines throughout the entire djebel area of Dhofar and indoctrinating the population. Dhofari children were abducted and spirited away to Hauf for indoctrination while adults were sent to the Soviet Union and China for intensive courses in Marxism and guerrilla warfare. At the same time, guerrilla groups were formed to enforce the organisation's will through the use of terror. Those who resisted were tortured or killed; on one occasion, five men were pushed off the top of a cliff while in on another incident, a man and his sons were shot with a machine-gun.

The djebel of Dhofar's Al-Qara Mountains lies some ten miles inland from the area of plain north of Salalah and extends westward some 150 miles to the Yemeni border. To its north are the featureless wastes of the negd. With its flat northern rim, known as the gatn, reaching heights of between 3,000 and 4,000 feet, the main part of the djebel is a plateau of approximately nine miles width in the centre but narrowing both to the east and west. The most fertile area is in the central, main plateau which features rolling grasslands stretching north to the gatn; during the *khareef* these become lush and green, gradually becoming dried up throughout the rest of the year. In the plateau's easternmost area, the terrain consists of open, stony terrain with little in the way of vegetation or water resources, while from the central area to the west large areas are covered by woods and thick scrub. In the far west, the djebel peters out into an escarpment at the eastern end of which is the Darra Ridge which curves round south-east towards the coastline and the town of Dhalqut.

Stretching for thousands of yards southward from the central area of the djebel plateau to the plain are a number of wadis, the largest being the Wadis Arzat, Darbat or Sayd. Beginning as shallow gullies, these increase in size, in some instances becoming steep-walled, deep valleys of several hundred yards in width. Joined by smaller, secondary wadis from the east and west which link them with others, these large wadis are filled with thick bush and vegetation, providing good cover for those seeking concealment, and contain sources of water in the form of water-holes, pools or running streams.

The inhabitants of the region, known as djebalis, which means 'people of the mountains', comprise several different semi-nomadic tribes who are ethnically different from the coastal Arabs. Among them are the Bait Kathir, Bait Ma'asheni, Bait Umr and Bait Gatun. Believed to be descended from inhabitants of the mountainous regions within Yemen, they speak southern Arabic dialects which are largely unintelligible to speakers of standard Arabic. Their main livelihood is the breeding and herding of cattle, sheep and goats. During the months following the end of the *khareef* at the end of September, when water is plentiful, they live on the plateau in their houses but as supplies dry up they and their families are forced to move down to the water sources in the wadis where they live in caves. They remain there through the return of the *khareef* at the beginning of June, emerging and returning to the plateau once it is over.

Blame for the underlying cause of the unrest in Dhofar can be laid at the door of Sultan himself, Sa'id bin Taymur. Although an educated man, he was an autocratic and repressive ruler determined to protect his country from what he perceived as the evils of modernisation and progress, viewing education and modern medicine as sources of potential threat to his regime and thus denying his people schools and modern healthcare. This resulted in a large number of Omanis leaving the country and seeking employment abroad where they established themselves as businessmen, teachers, doctors, soldiers, and professionals of various kinds. Some returned in due course, increasing awareness and resentment among the population at the country's backward state.

Sharia law was administered throughout all of Oman's provinces by the Sultan's walis and qadis with offences such as murder and adultery being punishable by death, drunkenness by flogging and smoking by imprisonment. Muscat possesses two great forts which overlook its harbour, Fort Mirani and Fort Jilali. The latter, guarded by troops of the Muscat Regiment at the time, was used for the incarceration of criminals who were shackled with iron fetters around their ankles and forced to sleep on the stone floors of their cells while existing on a bare minimum of a diet and little water.

One individual who was well aware of the problems being caused by Sa'id's refusal to countenance any development in Oman was his son Qaboos bin Sa'id. Educated privately, he had undergone training at the Royal Military Academy Sandhurst in Britain, subsequently being commissioned into The Cameronians (Scottish Rifles). Thereafter he had received a grounding in civil affairs, spending a further period in Britain studying government and civil administration before returning to Oman. No sooner had he arrived than he was placed under house arrest in Salalah by Sa'id who, having overthrown his own father, apparently feared that Qaboos would do likewise. During the following seven years, the latter remained a virtual prisoner in his own home.

By 1970 the PFLOAG controlled the whole of the djebel area of Dhofar, with SAF in charge only of the capital of Salalah and the towns of Taqa and Mirbat along the coast to the east. The situation was becoming increasingly grave and was of growing anxiety to the British whose principal concern was that if a hostile regime took power in Oman, it would gain control of the entrance to the Gulf and thus exercise a stranglehold on oil supplies to the West. Moreover, if Oman fell, the oil-rich Trucial Oman states would inevitably come under threat. The situation had not been improved by the announcement by the British government that it would be pulling out its forces from the Persian Gulf; it had resulted in several Soviet- or Chinese-backed movements in the region manoeuvring to take advantage of the potential vacuum that would inevitably follow such a withdrawal.

In early 1970, the British made their first move to resolve the situation by planting rumours among the press that the Sultan was intending to abdicate. At the same time, SAF's chief of intelligence, Major Malcolm Dennison, established contact with prominent Omanis who were living in exile after fleeing from Sa'id's repressive regime. According to Stephen Dorril in his *MI6 – Fifty Years of Special Operations*, Dennison suggested to Qaboos that, in the event of a successful coup to overthrow the Sultan, he should appoint his own brother Tariq bin Taimur, who would otherwise be a contender for the throne, as Prime Minister. Dennison subsequently travelled to Dubai, apparently with Qaboos's agreement, where he elicited the agreement of Tariq and other dissidents.

Another figure who allegedly played an indirect part in events at that time was Timothy Landon, a former British Army officer who had been a cadet at the Royal Military Academy Sandhurst with Qaboos and had served on secondment in Oman during the mid-1960s. On leaving the Army, he had reportedly been trained by the Secret Intelligence Service (SIS) and two years later had returned to Oman where by July 1969 he was responsible for all military intelligence operations in Dhofar. During the following twelve months, he allegedly attended a series of secret meetings with Qaboos, as well with Sheikh Baraik bin Hamood, the Wali of Salalah, and the Sultan's secretary, Hamad bin Hamud al Bu Said whom he had also known as a cadet at Sandhurst. Among others whose support was said to have been sought by Qaboos and Landon was Mr F. Hughes, Managing Director of Petroleum Development Oman (PDO), a subsidiary of Shell.

On 12 June, troops were attacked by PFLOAG guerrillas at a SAF camp near Izki, in northern Oman, near a PDO installation. This resulted in Shell applying pressure on the British government to take action. Eight days later in Britain, the Labour government of Harold Wilson was defeated in a general election and replaced by the Conservatives under Edward Heath who shortly afterwards gave his approval for the coup to take place. On the afternoon of 23 July, SAF troops surrounded the Sultan's palace in Salalah. A small ten-man group, reportedly led by Landon and Sheikh Baraik bin Hamood, entered but came under fire from loyal guards. Sheikh Baraik then made his way to the Sultan's apartments where the latter produced a pistol, wounding Sheikh Baraik and shooting himself accidentally in the foot. Eventually, the Sultan capitulated and agreed to abdicate in favour of Qaboos. After medical treatment in Bahrain, Sa'id bin Taymur was subsequently flown to London where he lived in comfort until his death there in 1972.

Qaboos immediately set to dragging his country into the twentieth century, much to the approval of the Omani population who greeted the announcement of his plans for development with much delight. He also granted an amnesty for the guerrillas which was accepted by a number of the original members of the former DLF but ignored by the hard-line PFLOAG. Indeed, it resulted in a split within the organisation, with the PFLOAG element attempting to disarm the DLF in the eastern area of Dhofar. A battle ensued after the latter refused to surrender their weapons and subsequently a group of 24 former DLF guerrillas left the djebel and surrendered to SAF.

At this juncture the British took further steps to assist Qaboos in dealing with the insurgency. Prior to the coup, the commanding officer of 22 SAS, Lieutenant Colonel Johnny Watts, and his Operations Officer, Captain Ray Nightingale, had been despatched to Oman to examine how the SAS could help counter the guerrilla threat in Oman, and in particular in Dhofar. Their recommendation for the raising and training of a force of loyal Dhofaris to resist the PFLOAG had been turned down, however, by the Sultan. After his removal, a four-man team was dispatched by 22 SAS to Oman to carry out an assessment task. This was followed by a fifteen-man team, under Captain Tony Linnington, which arrived in Oman in September under the cover name of the British Army Training Team (BATT). Based in the town of Mirbat, its task was to plan the defence of the Salalah plain area and to gain the confidence of the local inhabitants by carrying out 'hearts and minds' operations in Mirbat and Taqa. These included the establishment of clinics to provide medical treatment, and a small number of minor construction projects which included improvement of water supplies.

This was the beginning of an operation, codenamed STORM, which would see elements of 22 SAS deployed in Oman for the following six years. It was based on the assessment carried out by Lieutenant Colonel Watts who had produced a plan based on five elements:

1. An intelligence cell
2. An information team

3. A medical officer – with SAS medics in support

4. A veterinary officer

5. The recruitment and training of a Dhofari irregular force to operate in support of SAF

Watts had emphasised that the SAS could only provide a short-term means to an end in countering the PFLOAG in Dhofar as eventually Omanis would have to be trained to undertake these roles themselves. The ultimate solution could only be provided by the Sultan and his government in the provision of facilities in the form of hospitals, clinics, schools, roads and all the infrastructure of a modern Islamic society.

During the latter part of 1970, the British received intelligence reports in Sharjah and Dubai that Iraq was taking an unhealthy interest in Oman, reportedly training guerrillas in the north of the country, recruiting them from among the Shihoo tribe who inhabited the strategically important Musandam Peninsula overlooking the Straits of Hormuz.

The decision was taken to counter this threat and 22 SAS was given the task of dealing with it. An operation, codenamed BREAKFAST, was mounted on 12 December 1970 with three troops of G Squadron, reinforced by members of A and B Squadrons, being landed with a force of Trucial Oman Scouts from a Royal Navy minesweeper at a place called Jumla. Meanwhile the squadron's free-fall parachute troop, also reinforced by members of A and B Squadrons, had emplaned at Sharjah. At 4.00 a.m. it dropped from 11,000 feet over the Wadi Rawdah, a deep valley stretching inland from the coast and terminating in a large bowl surrounded by steep walls of some 7,000 feet in height. The troop's mission was to cut off any insurgents withdrawing inland after the coastal landing. Unfortunately one of its members, Lance Corporal Paul Reddy, apparently became unstable while in free-fall and suffered an entanglement with his parachute as it deployed. Unable to open his reserve in time, he hit the ground and was killed instantly.

Despite this setback, the troop continued with its tasks, establishing OPs and watching for insurgents. None were seen although evidence of their presence, in the form of indentations in the ground made by the baseplates of mortars when fired, was discovered. In due course, the troop made contact with Shihoo tribesmen in the area. Meanwhile, the remainder of the squadron had discovered that it had landed at the wrong location, having confused the name Jumla with that of their objective, a village called Gumla, situated a few miles farther along the coast. Having arrived at Gumla, the squadron found possible traces of the Iraqi training team who had, however, disappeared.

When the operation ended, the squadron remained on the Musandam Peninsula for a month, carrying out 'hearts and minds' missions among the Shihoo. The operation had highlighted the need for a military presence to be maintained in the area; elements of a SAF unit were deployed there shortly afterwards and construction of an airstrip was begun in the Wadi Rawdah.

In February 1971, D Squadron 22 SAS, commanded by Major Tony Jeapes, arrived in Oman to take over from Captain Linnington and his BATT who had established a main base at a SAF camp at Um al Gwarif, a short distance to the north-east of Salalah.

According to the account given later by Major General Jeapes in his book *SAS – Secret War*, one of the first tasks facing him was the recruitment and training of Dhofari irregular units, known as firqats. The first was the Firqat Salahadin, a 32-strong group named after the great Muslim warrior leader, led by an individual named Salim Mubarak who had previously been second-in-command of the PFLOAG in the eastern area of Dhofar and had undergone training in China. The firqat was trained at Mirbat by 17 Troop commanded by Captain Ian Croker.

On 23 February, the firqat underwent its baptism of fire at Sudh, a town on the coast 20 miles east of Mirbat, which was occupied by a 50-strong group of guerrillas. Together with 17 Troop, which was D Squadron's boat troop, and 18 Troop, commanded by Captain Peter Phelps, it sailed from Mirbat in a dhow during the afternoon and that night arrived at Qinqari Bay, some 4,000 yards to the south-west of the town. Major Jeapes had learned that the guerrillas were apparently expecting an assault from the sea and thus decided to attack from inland. After 17 Troop had reconnoitred and cleared the landing beach, the remainder of the force was ferried ashore in two Gemini inflatable assault craft. Shortly afterwards, it set off on the approach march to its objective and by 1.00 a.m. on the following morning had reached its lying-up position (LUP) in the Wadi Sudh which lay some 1,000 yards north of Sudh itself.

Before dawn, the force took up its attack positions. Two sections of firqats made their way along high ground on either side of the wadi while the rest of the force moved along the bed of the wadi itself. By half an hour before dawn, all were in their respective positions. Just after dawn, at 6.30 a.m., a ten-man firqat reconnaissance group moved down the wadi and entered the town. Shortly afterwards, however, one of its members returned to report that there were no guerrillas to be seen.

Jeapes lost no time in securing Sudh and, having positioned pickets on the high ground overlooking the town, constructed defensive positions in the form of sangars. Later that morning, the firqat made its way through Sudh, gathering all the male inhabitants and shepherding them to the largest house in the town, belonging to the wali, where they were addressed by Salim Mubarak who lectured them on the evils of communism and described the improvements that would come under the new Sultan's rule.

During the afternoon, a group of 24 guerrillas were spotted a short distance from the town. They made no effort to mount a counter-attack, although one or two moved up to open fire with their Kalashnikov assault rifles at the small fort in the centre of the town. They were discouraged from any further acts of aggression by return fire from the fort which included a well-aimed round from one of the squadron's Carl Gustav 84mm shoulder-fired medium anti-tank weapons (MAW) which impacted on the crest of the hill held by the guerrillas.

On the following morning, a SAF infantry company arrived in a dhow and took over responsibility for the town from Jeapes's force. Meanwhile, Salim Mubarak had established communication with the commander of the guerrilla force, Ahmed Mohammed Qartoob, and during the rest of that day messengers went to and fro between the two men as Mubarak attempted to persuade Qartoob to defect from the PFLOAG to the Sultan's cause. The guerrilla leader, however, stood firm, accusing Salim of having been seduced by the Sultan's false promises and offering him amnesty if he and his men would revert to the PFLOAG cause. While delivering one such message, however, Qartoob's messenger inadvertently revealed the whereabouts of the guerrilla hideout in a wadi. The Firqat Salahadin promptly surrounded it and presented Qartoob with the ultimatum of agreeing then and there to negotiate, or die. Qartoob wisely chose the former course and, accompanied by his second-in-command and political commissar, Salim Said Dherdhir, and five other senior members of his group, accompanied the firqat back to Sudh where he negotiated and argued at length for two days with Salim Mubarak. Eventually, Qartoob and Dherdhir were won over and by 28 February, the day on which D Squadron withdrew, leaving behind a BATT, they and 36 members of their group had come over to the government side.

The next operation was to be mounted on the djebel in eastern Dhofar. It would involve 17 and 18 Troops, together with the Firqat Salahadin, carrying out a night ascent of the 3,000 feet high cliffs prior to attacking On the night of 6 March, a patrol of 19 Troop, D Squadron's mountaineering and climbing specialists, accompanied by six members of the firqat, set off for a reconnaissance of an area called the Eagle's Nest which consisted of a semicircular ridge honeycombed with caves surrounding a flat plateau, its open side facing the escarpment. The patrol was led by Captain Peter Phelps, in the absence of 19 Troop's commander, Sergeant Bill Connell. Phelps's task was to reconnoitre a route up on to the djebel and to discover whether the guerrillas had established a picket on the heights. By dawn on the following day, he and his men were in an LUP on a cliff ledge where they remained until dusk when they continued their ascent, reaching the plateau shortly afterwards. Having found no evidence of an enemy presence, the patrol withdrew during the night and returned to Mirbat.

The operation proper began on 13 March, having been delayed as a result of the sudden death of Salim Mubarak, apparently from angina. The entire force, commanded by Captain Ian Croker and comprising the two troops and 60 men of the Firqat Salahadin, under Mohammed Said, Salim Mubarak's successor, climbed the steep escarpment of the djebel which they reached by dawn on the following day. Once again, there was no indication of an enemy presence and a helicopter brought in an 81mm mortar, ammunition, and a water resupply. On the night of 17 March, Croker's force moved farther west on to the djebel with the firqat moving ahead, reconnoitring and picketing the route ahead. Just before dawn on 18 March, it reached its objective, a long, low hill feature running east to west, where Croker established a defensive position.

Just after dawn, three enemy were spotted some 300 yards away. Oblivious of the SAS and the firqat, they moved off to a nearby wadi into which they disappeared. A party of the firqat set off in pursuit and returned after a brief engagement, victoriously carrying three captured Type 56 assault rifles.

The sound of the firing alerted other guerrillas in the area and some twenty minutes later they opened desultory fire at long range. Shortly after Croker's own 81mm mortar and its bombs had been delivered by helicopter, the enemy opened fire with a 60mm light mortar and thereafter kept up a steady and very accurate fire on the two troops' positions, one bomb scoring a direct hit on the sangar occupied by Captain Phelps and his signaller only seconds after they had vacated it in a hurry after watching the previous bomb explode only yards away. Two weeks later, the enemy mortar man surrendered himself at Taqa; it transpired that he had previously served as an officer in the Trucial Oman Scouts and had been trained in Britain.

With no further resupply available by helicopter, the only source of water was a well 400 yards away to the north at the bottom of a huge cavern, 150 yards in radius and 300 feet in depth, called Tawi Atair (The Well of Birds). The sole access to the water at the bottom was a precarious spiral path which wound around the sheer sides of the cavern. While members of the firqat and the two troops did reach the well, the effort required to climb to the top again was so exhausting that they consumed most of the water they had collected. Dehydration thus became a major problem, only being alleviated slightly by a resupply dropped by parachute from a Sultan of Oman's Air Force (SOAF) Shorts Skyvan transport.

By this time, Croker's force had been reinforced by a further 35 members of the Firqat Salahadin who had been under training at Mirbat. While en route to join him, they had encountered some guerrillas and killed six of them. But the lack of water was proving a major problem; after twelve days the position was abandoned and Croker's force withdrew south to another location on the high ground above the Wadi Hinna from where it eventually returned to Mirbat. This had been the first operation by D Squadron and a firqat unit on the djebel, achieving success in that nine enemy had been killed on their own territory and demonstrating to the guerrillas that they could no longer operate on the djebel with impunity. Equally importantly, it was realised that a permanent presence would have to be established on the djebel before support could be elicited from the local djebali population.

Meanwhile, Major Tony Jeapes had been busy forming two more

firqats. The first of these was the Firqat Al A'asifat, made up of Mahra tribesmen and led by Musalim Qaraitas. He had joined the Firqat Sala-hadin on deserting from the PFLOAG. When some of his former com-rades decided to surrender, he had returned to them and two days later led them to a rendezvous in a wadi where Jeapes was waiting with food and water. Then Qaraitas had led them to Barbezum, a location in the featureless wilderness of the negd, to the north of the djebel, where he established a base. Having agreed to form a firqat, they were joined soon afterwards by a BATT from 16 Troop under Captain Clive Fairweather, and then by more Mahra who had also deserted the guerrillas' ranks, increasing the firqat's strength to 38 men.

In the meantime, other firqats had been created. The first was the Firqat Al Nasr formed from the Bait Kathir tribe. Led by Musalim bin Tufl, it was based at Mamurah, to the east of the SAS main base at Um al Gwarif, where it was being trained by a small BATT commanded by a corporal. Another, the Khalid bin Waalid, was being formed from the Bait Ma'asheni tribe. Led by Mohammed Musalim Ahmed, it was based at Taqa. A third firqat, the Tariq bin Zeead, was created from the Mahra and, like the Firqat Al Nasr, based at Mamura.

Considerable effort was meanwhile being devoted to psychological operations which were the responsibility of a small team commanded by a 22 SAS NCO, Corporal John Wright, who proved to be a master of his task. Equipped with broadcasting equipment and printing presses, the team was detailed to disseminate truthful information among the Dhofari population. This was achieved by distributing large numbers of cheap Japanese transistor radios free of charge among the djebalis when they came down from the djebel to trade. The guerrillas, however, retaliated by confiscating and destroying them when the villagers returned to the djebel. Wright then put the sets on sale in the souk (market); he believed that, having paid for them, the djebalis would not be so inclined to hand them over on demand. This proved to be the case and sufficient numbers of radios reached the djebel for news broadcasts to be spread among the population.

Radio broadcasts were backed up by a weekly newspaper produced by Corporal Wright and his team, along with a system of notice boards placed at entry points in the defensive perimeters which surrounded Salalah, Mirbat and Taqa. Like the newspaper, these proved popular, featuring photographs and news sheets giving details of the developments taking place throughout the region.

The SAS civil action teams at Mirbat, Taqa and Sudh were also carrying out sterling work providing medical treatment for the local population which resulted in considerable improvements in the general standard of health.

During the latter part of April, however, major problems occurred within the Firqat Salahadin which took in members of more than one tribe. An inter-tribal dispute arose with a faction of Bait Umr and Bait Ma'asheni tribesmen, led by Ahmed Mohammed Qartoob, rising in mutiny against Mohammed Said, who was a member of the Bait Gatun. Despite the best efforts of Major Jeapes and Sergeant Connell, who was commanding the 17 Troop BATT in the absence of Captain Croker, who had been evacuated to Britain after falling victim to jaundice, the dispute was not resolved. On 22 April, all 68 members of the firqat paraded in front of Jeapes who gave them the choice of remaining in service or surrendering their arms and departing. Forty of them chose the latter course, leaving to join other firqats.

In May, an operation was mounted to capture a 75mm recoilless rifle which had been shelling Taqa from the djebel, killing one person and wounding several others. In addition, it had scored a hit on the building accommodating the BATT. Air strikes by SAF Strikemaster ground attack aircraft proved ineffective in locating the weapon and it was beyond the range of the BATT's 81mm mortar.

The weapon was being fired from a feature called the Djebel Aram, a 7,000-yard-long feature which ran from the Wadi Darbat in the east to the Wadi Ethon in the west. While its southern face was sheer, its northern face, most of which fell away into the Wadi Ethon, was steep but could be climbed. Air reconnaissance by Major Jeapes and the commanding officer of the Muscat Regiment battalion, Lieutenant Colonel Fergus Mackain-Bremner, revealed two possible approach routes: one from the west, running parallel to the Wadi Ethon; and the other from the east via a narrow pass, the Aqbat Aram. Jeapes selected the latter.

The operation was conducted by a force comprising two SAS troops, the Firqat Salahadin, the Firqat Khalid bin Waalid and a battalion of the Muscat Regiment. Having assembled at Mamurah, the entire force was moved by truck to a point three miles south of the Wadi Ethon from where it moved off on foot towards the djebel seven miles to the north, the SAF battalion in the lead. Then the long climb began. On reaching a ridge leading to the Aqbat Aram, the force turned west towards the Djebel Aram. By half an hour before dawn, the two SAS troops and firqats had reached a small plateau where they paused to wait for dawn before advancing any farther in order to avoid an accidental contact with the SAF battalion which was due to seize the peak of the Djebel Aram. Shortly after dawn, however, Jeapes and his men came under fire after a member of the Firqat Salahadin unexpectedly ran into a small group of enemy who subsequently withdrew to a wadi where it became pinned down by one of the SAS general purpose machine-guns (GPMG).

Meanwhile, before dawn, the SAF battalion had despatched a patrol to the peak of the Djebel Aram. Finding it unoccupied, and instead of securing it, the patrol had returned to make its report. Advancing some twenty minutes later, Lieutenant Colonel Mackain-Bremner and his men came under fire from guerrillas, who had occupied the peak immediately after the patrol's withdrawal, one soldier being killed and three wounded by a burst from an LMG. Nevertheless the battalion took the feature and was joined shortly afterwards by Jeapes and his men.

Leaving the firqat, which was by this time showing signs of fatigue, the two SAS troops then proceeded to clear an area of thick bush to the north-west of the SAF battalion's positions. As they did so, the leading troop came under fire and a brief engagement took place, the enemy withdrawing, hotly pursued by the second troop. Both troops then regrouped and, rejoined by the firqat, established defensive positions. Thereafter, a SAF company, with firqat and SAS support, attempted to advance into the Wadi Ethon but came under heavy machine-gun and mortar fire and was forced to retreat. Soon afterwards, a combined SAS/firqat patrol headed off towards the djebel's southern escarpment and discovered the position from which the 75mm recoilless rifle had been shelling Taqa; hidden there was a small quantity of ammunition for it. This find subsequently led to the conclusion that the guerrillas' fierce defence of the Wadi Ethon had in fact been covering the evacuation of the weapon itself.

During the second night, Major Jeapes mounted an operation to prevent an expected guerrilla counter-attack, positioning five ambushes on a spur, north-east of the SAS/firqat positions, running east for 300 yards and then north for a further 400 yards down to a saddle between the Wadi Darbat and Wadi Ethon. Three ambushes, manned by the two SAS troops, were sited at the top of the spur, at the point where it turned north and at a spot 100 yards down the northern arm. The remaining two were located 100 yards apart farther down the northern arm, and were the responsibility of the firqat.

The initial contact took place on the lower part of the northern arm as the second firqat ambush group was en route to its position. It encountered part of a guerrilla group moving up from the Wadi Darbat on its way to link up with another from the Wadi Ethon. A short but fierce engagement broke out, with the guerrillas suffering a number of casualties. As they were withdrawing, the enemy from the Wadi Ethon opened fire on the firqat ambush group whose commander was killed. The Wadi Darbat guerrillas then returned to the fray and the second firqat ambush group, carrying the body of their commander, retired 100 yards to the ambush position above under supporting fire from the SAS. Despite heavy fire from the SAS GPMGs and SAF mortars, the latter called down by Major Jeapes from his position at the top of the spur, the guerrillas continued to press forward while the two firqat ambush groups drew back to the SAS position at the bend in the spur from where Sergeant Connell was controlling the situation. Eventually, the guerrillas' advance was halted and they withdrew, taking their dead and wounded with them.

At dawn, a combined force of SAS and members of the firqat moved down to clear a small village situated to the north-east of the SAS/firqat main position. A brief engagement took place and fifteen guerrillas were seen withdrawing. At just after midday, the entire force of the SAF battalion, SAS troops and firqat began to retire from the djebel, moving as swiftly as possible over the plateau and down the steep escarpment via a narrow track, eventually reaching the plain across which the entire force headed three miles to Taqa.

This was the last operation carried out by D Squadron which was relieved during May by B Squadron, commanded by Major Richard Pirie. Jeapes and his men had achieved much during their tour of operations as by this time there were six firqats either in existence or being formed, the Salahadin, A'asifat, Al Nasr and Khalid bin Waalid having been joined by the Tariq bin Zeead and the Gamel Abdul Nasr.

FROM JUNE TO SEPTEMBER the *khareef* covered the djebel plateau in mist. During this period, B Squadron concentrated on training the firqats and bringing them up to strength in time for operation JAGUAR, to commence early in October. This would be on a large scale involving B and G Squadrons, with five firqats – the Khalid bin Waalid, A'asifat, Salahadin, Gamel Abdul Nasr and a newly formed firqat named the Al Umri – totalling 300 men. These would be reinforced by a SAF force comprising two infantry companies, a pioneer platoon and a platoon of Baluch irregulars. Air support would be provided by SOAF helicopters and Strikemaster ground attack aircraft. The entire force would be led by the Commanding Officer of 22 SAS, Lieutenant Colonel Johnny Watts.

Two weeks prior to the operation, a deception plan was put into effect to convince the guerrillas that an action was being mounted from the south against their stronghold in the Wadi Darbat. One of the SAF 5.5 inch guns was deployed at Taqa, facing north, while on the day before the operation began, a force of the Firqat Al Umri and a BATT, commanded by Captain Sean Broderick, made its way up on to the djebel to the east of the Eagle's Nest and headed west. This concentrated the attention of the guerrillas to the south while JAGUAR itself was mounted from the negd in the north.

The aim of the operation was to capture and hold a disused SAF airstrip, called Lympne, situated on the gatn, some four miles east of Jibjat. On the afternoon of 29 September the majority of B and G Squadrons, together with the Firqat A'asifat, Firqat Salahadin and the platoon of Baluch askar irregulars, were flown into an airstrip at an abandoned oil exploration camp, known as Midway, which lay some 55 miles north of the djebel. Numbering approximately 250, these would make an approach on foot, the remainder of the assault force being brought in by helicopter once the airstrip had been secured and the firm base established. On 30 September, the first stage of the approach south-east across the negd was carried out in a convoy of trucks which delivered the SAS and firqats at the mouth of a wadi. From there on the night of 1–2 October began a long, hard climb up the steep northern slopes of the djebel to the Mahazair Pools, an open flat area where the force halted for a while before resuming the seemingly endless ascent to the top. The terrible conditions of heat, high humidity and steep, rough terrain, combined with a lack of water, took their toll and it was only approximately half the force which, as dawn broke at around 6.30 a.m., reached the airstrip and secured it. Fortunately there were no enemy in the area and from dawn onward, SOAF Skyvan transports and helicopters brought in the two SAF companies, the Firqat Khalid Bin Waleed, two 75mm guns, mortars, supplies and much-need water. Meanwhile, there was no activity on the part of the enemy until the late afternoon when a probing attack was mounted by a force of some 30 guerrillas on the western side of the defensive perimeter.

It soon became apparent, however, that the airstrip was disintegrating rapidly from the large number of aircraft using it. On the afternoon of the second day, therefore, Lieutenant Colonel Watts decided to move the firm base to Jibjat, 7,000 yards away to the west, which possessed a stronger runway. This was duly secured by three firqats and a BATT who went ahead of the main body, clearing the route. By mid-morning on 4 October, following a brief but fierce skirmish with the enemy, Jibjat had been secured and during the following 72 hours more aircraft arrived with further supplies of defence stores, ammunition, rations and water.

Having set up the firm base, Watts divided the SAS elements of his force into two groups: East Group with the Firqat A'asifat and West Group with the Firqat Khalid bin Waalid and the Firqat Salahadin. Thereafter, he launched a two-pronged attack into the enemy-held areas down the eastern and western sides of the Wadi Darbat. Over the next five days, both groups experienced heavy fighting as they gradually gained control of the area, during which three men were severely wounded. One of them, Sergeant Steve Moores, died shortly afterwards from his wounds, becoming the first member of 22 SAS to be killed on operations in Oman since the Djebel Akhdar campaign of early 1959. On the afternoon of 5 October, the guerrillas launched a fierce counter-attack on Captain Sean Broderick's force, which had linked up on the previous day with elements of the East Group, but this was driven off. By 9 October, the guerrillas had ceased their attacks and had withdrawn from the plateau to the wadis.

By 12 October, another firm base, nicknamed WHITE CITY, had been established by West Group and a SAF infantry company some fifteen and a half miles inside guerrilla-held territory. As information was received of some 200 guerrillas in the Wadi Darbat, a strong force under

Captain Broderick was dispatched, on 20 October, to the village of Shahait, on the edge of the wadi, which was seized after a brief engagement which saw two guerrilla couriers killed, the documents found on their bodies providing valuable intelligence.

Soon afterwards, Watts moved his headquarters from Jibjat to WHITE CITY. By this time it was clear to him and Colonel Mike Harvey, SAF's Commander Dhofar, that the guerrillas' main line of supply from the Yemen had to be interdicted. Accordingly, they established three fortified strongpoints, known as the Leopard Line, from which the SAS and firqat carried out patrols. The northernmost was located north of the gatn, above the Djebel Khaftawt, and all three were heavily protected by barbed wire and minefields and garrisoned by SAF troops, while mines were also laid on the likely enemy routes between them. Although the Leopard Line did not cut the enemy supply route, it certainly hindered it, and the reaction of the guerrillas, who mounted heavy bombardments on all three strongpoints with recoilless rifles and mortars, was testimony to that fact.

Increasing priority was being given meanwhile to creating a permanent administrative presence on the djebel to persuade the local population to come across to the government side. At WHITE CITY, a programme of construction of permanent buildings and drilling of wells for water was soon under way. The firqats moved their families, along with their herds of goats and cattle, into WHITE CITY and soon Watts was facing demands from them for the government to buy their livestock. Indeed, the situation by 27 October had become so crucial that the firqats were refusing to undertake any operations until the goats were sold. This threat was reinforced by 45 members of the Firqat A'asifat who handed in their weapons and resigned. It was at this stage that Sheikh Baraik bin Hamood, who had been appointed wali of Dhofar following Qaboos's coming to power, interceded and gave orders that SOAF aircraft should fly the goats from the djebel to Salalah to be sold.

The enemy, meantime, were far from idle. During the middle of November, fierce fighting broke out on the ridge to the north of the head of the Wadi Arzat, which lay to the west of the Wadi Darbat. It was occupied by North Group (formed by Lieutenant Colonel Watts from a BATT), the Firqat Salahadin and a SAF company of the Djebel Regiment. Together with West Group, which had occupied a waterhole to the west of WHITE CITY, North Group came under heavy attack, as did the Leopard Line which was shelled by 75mm recoilless rifles. Eventually, West Group was forced to abandon its positions at the waterhole and carry out a fighting withdrawal to WHITE CITY.

On 28 November, following the airborne transportation of the firqats' goats to Salalah, an operation codenamed TAURUS was mounted to drive their herds of cattle, totalling 500 head, down from the djebel to Taqa and then on to Salalah. A graphic description of the scenes that took place is given by Major General Tony Jeapes in his book:

> Next day saw what must surely be unique in military history: a Texan-style cattle drive supported by jet fighter cover and 5.5-inch artillery. Amidst scenes like shots from a Boulting Brothers comedy mixed with a John Wayne western, fire fights between pickets and adoo [enemy] on the high ground, whoops of delight from the firqat and expressions of amused disbelief by the SAF and SAS, 500 head of cattle were driven across the plateau and down the Djebel to Taqa. Most of the animals were owned by firqat families, but many of them had also been owned by men serving in the adoo and were 'confiscated' by the firqat during the drive. Next day the herd, surrounded by armoured cars, arrived at Salalah to be met by the rejoicing inhabitants. As one SAS soldier described it, 'Salalah looked like Abilene.'

The movement of the herds to Salalah did much to destroy the myth that the guerrillas ruled the djebel, while also rectifying the problems with the firqats, in particular the Firqat A'asifat. The latter had earlier insisted on observing the Muslim festival of Ramadan, which had begun on 20 October, despite dispensations from the Qadi, Oman's senior religious leader, and the Sultan who ruled that those members of SAF and the firqats involved in Operation JAGUAR need not fast from sunrise to sunset on the permissible grounds that they were involved in a jihad (holy war).

By the end of 1971, the eastern area of the djebel was in the main dominated by SAF units, the firqats and A Squadron which arrived in Oman at the end of the year to relieve B and G Squadrons, who returned to Britain. Similarly, the coastal plain area of Dhofar was under government control and much work was being done to provide medical treatment and other civil aid for the local population. Lieutenant Colonel

Watts's five-point plan had proved remarkably effective in countering the PFLOAG in Dhofar but the guerrillas were far from beaten, as they would demonstrate during the following year.

A Squadron spent the four months of its tour in Oman on the eastern part of the djebel, patrolling from Jibjat and White City as part of an operation to ensure domination of the area and keeping a close eye on the Leopard Line. In the spring of 1972, SAF mounted a major mission, codenamed SIMBA, in which the Desert Regiment, commanded by Lieutenant Colonel Nigel Knocker, carried out a heliborne operation to establish a base at Sarfait, in the south-west of Dhofar near the border with Yemen, situated on a guerrilla supply route. Complete surprise was achieved and the battalion set up its firm base on a feature of high ground where it remained for the next three years, becoming a major thorn in the side of the guerrillas who were forced to divert their supply route farther south.

Spring of 1972 also saw the return of B Squadron which was soon deployed in BATTs on the djebel and the coastal plain. One of these, comprising eight men under Captain Mike Kealy, commander of 8 Troop, was at Mirbat. It was based in a building known as the BATT House, located to the north of the town on the far side of a wadi running east to west. To the north-west of the BATT House was an old fortified building, the home of the town's wali guarded by 30 askars, while to the north-east was a fort manned by a 25-strong detachment of the Dhofar Gendarmerie, a locally recruited auxiliary force. Dug-in a short distance to the west of the fort was a 25-pounder field gun manned by a single SAF gunner; and about 500 yards from the three buildings and the town was a perimeter fence of barbed wire encompassing the entire area. To the north, at the foot of the main djebel, was a feature of high ground called the Djebel Ali on which was an outpost manned by the gendarmerie detachment.

By the latter part of July, B Squadron was in the process of handing over to G Squadron. The successes of the government forces during the previous months had spurred the PFLOAG into mounting a major operation in order to counter the erosion of its support among the local population which was gradually defecting to the government's side. Several major contacts took place between groups of guerrillas and the B Squadron BATTs on the djebel, the latter warning more than once that there were indications that either Mirbat or Taqa would be attacked in strength in the near future and that they should therefore be reinforced.

These warnings were apparently ignored at higher level, unfortunately so as the guerrillas were indeed planning a major attack with Mirbat as its target. On 17 July, they employed a group to show itself on the plain in an effort to lure some of the town's garrison into pursuing it up on to the djebel. This ploy proved successful. The major part of the Firqat Al Umri, led by Ahmed Mohammed Qartoob and based in the town, was dispatched in pursuit, leaving the defence of Mirbat to its remaining members, the eight-strong BATT, the gendarmerie detachment and the askars.

In the early hours of 19 July, having moved undetected across the djebel in six or so groups, some 250 guerrillas infiltrated down to the plain under cover of darkness. They were heavily armed with Type 56 assault rifles, RPD LMGs, and Shpagin DShK 38/44 12.7mm heavy machine-guns, and were supported by 81mm and 82mm medium mortars, 60mm light mortars, Carl Gustav 84mm shoulder-fired medium anti-armour weapons (MAW), and two 75mm recoilless rifles.

The initial phase of the enemy assault on Mirbat was an attack against the gendarmerie outpost on the Djebel Ali. The enemy had intended to neutralise the section of gendarmes silently but matters did not go according to plan and shots were fired, raising fears among the guerrillas that their presence had been compromised. Shortly afterwards, at about 5.00 a.m., their mortars opened fire.

The skirmish on the Djebel Ali, however, had gone undetected by those in Mirbat and the first indication the members of the BATT had of the impending attack was a series of explosions as a salvo of mortar bombs exploded just outside the perimeter fence. Captain Mike Kealy and his men stood-to immediately, Corporal Bob Benson bringing the team's single 81mm mortar into action as the BATT House and gendarmerie fort came under fire, while the BATT signaller, Trooper Pete Wallace, established radio contact with B Squadron's headquarters at Um al Gwarif. Meanwhile Corporal Talaisi Labalaba, one of a small number of renowned Fijians serving with 22 SAS, sprinted 500 yards to the 25-pounder position and brought the gun into action, firing over open sights at the enemy as they approached the perimeter fence and made for the gendarmerie fort which came under fire from a Carl Gustav

84mm MAW and RPG-7 rocket-propelled grenades. From the BATT House came supporting fire as Corporal Roger Collins and Trooper Pete Wallace brought the BATT's GPMG and Browning .50 heavy machine-gun respectively to bear, causing casualties among the guerrillas who nevertheless continued to press home their assault. Also entering the fray were those members of the Firqat Al Umri left in the town.

At this juncture, Trooper Jim Takacece, another Fijian, ran the 500-yard gauntlet from the BATT House to the 25-pounder position to join Corporal Labalaba who had by this time been wounded in the chin. Sprinting under heavy fire from machine-guns and mortars, he swerved and dodged across the flat and open ground, launching himself into the gun-pit. Seconds later, responding to shouts from Takacece, the 25-pounder's Omani gunner emerged from the fort and attempted to join the two Fijians in the gun pit but was hit as he did so and fell. Takacece thereafter acted as loader, ramming in the shells as fast as Labalaba could fire them, but minutes later he, too,was hit and collapsed, being grazed on the head by another bullet as he did so. Despite his serious wounds, however, he propped himself against the wall of the gun-pit sangar and engaged the enemy with his rifle. At that point, Corporal Labalaba, unable to find any further ammunition for the 25-pounder and aware that by that time the enemy had in any case advanced too close for it to be effective, moved out from the cover of the 25-pounder's shield and reached for a 60mm light mortar to bring into action instead. As he did so, however, he was hit and killed instantly.

It was now about 7.00 a.m. and, concerned at the 25-pounder falling silent and the loss of radio contact with its crew, Captain Mike Kealy decided to find out the situation there for himself. Leaving Corporal Bob Benson in command at the BATT House, and accompanied by Trooper Tommy Tobin, one of the team medics, he ran to the wadi. Unseen by the enemy, the two men managed to reach a point halfway to the fort before they were spotted. The guerrillas immediately brought heavy fire to bear as they raced for the gun-pit which, miraculously, they reached unharmed. Kealy then dived into the 25-pounder ammunition bunker, situated a few feet away, while Tobin immediately began check-ing Labalaba for signs of life. Takacece meanwhile kept up a steady fire with his rifle on some 40 guerrillas who were heading for the shelter of the northern side of the fort. Seconds later, however, Tobin was hit and seriously wounded. In the meantime, under cover of the blind side of the fort, the leading guerrillas had broken through the perimeter fence and closed to within yards of the 25-pounder position; seconds later they threw a number of grenades at the gun-pit and ammunition bunker. Fortunately, these either exploded without effect or failed to detonate.

Meanwhile, an SAF helicopter appeared in response to the BATT's call for casualty evacuation and Corporal Roger Collins ran to the BATT's landing zone (LZ) some 200 yards away to the south-west, throwing a green smoke grenade to signal that it was safe to land. At that moment, however, the LZ came under heavy fire from an enemy heavy machine-gun and both the aircraft and Collins were forced to beat a hasty retreat.

In the 25-pounder position, with the enemy at close range and in danger of being overrun, Captain Kealy called on his radio to Corporal Bob Benson for supporting fire. At the BATT House, however, Lance Corporal Austin 'Fuzz' Hughes had already cranked his 81mm mortar to maximum elevation in order to drop its bombs on the ever-nearing enemy. The 25-pounder position was inside the mortar's minimum range and thus he was forced to pull the weapon back off its bipod and hold the barrel to his chest while another member of the BATT dropped the bombs down it. With Benson calling corrections and Hughes adjusting his position accordingly, bombs began to rain down on the enemy in the vicinity of the 25-pounder position, forcing them back.

Trooper Pete Wallace had already transmitted two requests for air support and minutes later two Strikemasters hurtled in at very low level, strafing the guerrillas with cannon and rockets before dropping 500 lb bombs on a group assembling in a wadi to the east of the fort. On its last pass, however, one plane was hit in the tail by a burst from a heavy machine-gun and disappeared into the cover of the low cloud, heading back to Salalah. The other aircraft, having expended all its ordnance, followed it soon afterwards.

At Um al Gwarif, meanwhile, the news of the attack on Mirbat had resulted in the mounting of a relief operation. By a stroke of good fortune, a 23-strong party of G Squadron, comprising the squadron commander, Major Alastair Morrison, his squadron sergeant major and 21 junior NCOs and troopers, were still at Um al Gwarif, the remainder of the squadron having already deployed to various locations to take them over from B Squadron. Morrison and his party had been about to set off for the ranges to zero their weapons when the BATT's contact report was received. Armed with nine GPMGs, in addition to their self-loading rifles, an M-79 40mm grenade launcher and a large amount of 7.62mm ammunition, they were driven to the SOAF base at Salalah where B Squadron's commander, Major Richard Pirie, had already established a joint operations centre. There Morrison and his men emplaned aboard two SAF Agusta Bell 205 helicopters and were flown to a landing zone (LZ) on the beach some 3,500 yards to the south-east of Mirbat, landing there some twenty minutes later at around 9.15 a.m. just as a second air strike, guided in by Corporal Bob Benson via his SARBE ground-to-air radio, was taking place. While one Strikemaster concentrated its attacks on the enemy in the area of the fort, the other attacked guerrilla heavy machine-gun positions on the Djebel Ali with cannon and rockets. The latter then joined the first aircraft in attacking the enemy near the fort who by this time were beginning to withdraw.

Meanwhile, while one group of six secured the landing zone, Major Morrison and his remaining sixteen men advanced towards Mirbat. Successively, they encountered a group of three guerrillas, all of whom were killed, and another group in a wadi where three were killed and the remaining two wounded. They then came under fire from six guerrillas in a position among some rocks, all of whom were shot dead. As G Squadron continued its advance, mopping up further groups of enemy, reinforcements in the form of a platoon of SAF's Northern Frontier Regiment arrived by helicopter. Eventually, Morrison and his men reached the BATT House where they found a scene of carnage which was later described by Trooper Pete Wallace in Michael Kennedy's book *Soldier I: SAS*:

> I thought that I had stumbled into an abattoir refuse-room. The whole area was covered with wounded men, either lying down or propped up against the walls. The floor was littered with bloodstained shell dressings. The stench of blood, sweat and urine was everywhere. Clusters of flies buzzed frenziedly around, feeding greedily on open wounds and bits of flesh and bone. Roger knelt trying to force a drip into the trembling arm of a man with a gaping hole in his throat. The man's rapid breathing made a terrible whistling and bubbling noise.

Captain Kealy, meanwhile, was attempting to arrange the evacuation of the wounded in the 25-pounder position and the fort, discovering that the only means of transport, a gendarmerie Land Rover parked inside the fort, had been hit several times and rendered immobile. At that juncture, however, members of G Squadron appeared at the fort, followed by a helicopter which evacuated the dead and wounded. The BATT had suffered one killed, Corporal Labalaba, and three seriously wounded; one of the latter, Trooper Tobin, died soon afterwards from his wounds.

By this time, the fighting had died down and the enemy were withdrawing in small groups along the wadis up to the djebel, leaving behind them 38 dead, along with large quantities of weapons and equipment scattered over the entire area. Many seriously wounded later died on the djebel and it was later reported that the total number of deaths numbered just under 100 men.

During the immediate aftermath of the battle, Captain Kealy's immediate concern was the Firqat Al Umri up on the djebel whom he feared would meet the retreating guerrillas. His fears appeared justified when the sound of firing could be heard from beyond the Djebel Ali which by this time was occupied by the Northern Frontier Regiment platoon. Despite his exhaustion, he insisted on leading a patrol up on to the djebel where he eventually met the members of the firqat, who had suffered a number of casualties, making their way down to the town.

The battle of Mirbat was a turning point in the war in Dhofar. Three prisoners had been taken during the battle and interrogation of them revealed that the PFLOAG's plan had been to occupy the town for a few hours, execute the wali and other local leaders, and subject the community to a haranguing before disappearing back on to the djebel. In so doing, the guerrillas' ultimate intention had been to terrorise the population throughout Dhofar into withdrawing its cooperation with the government. Although they had timed the operation to take place during the last part of the *khareef*, when cloud cover and mist were such that air support was normally impossible, they had reckoned without the skill of the SOAF Strikemaster and helicopter pilots who came to the BATT's rescue. Furthermore, the timely arrival of G Squadron had enabled a relief force to be quickly deployed for a counter-attack. Inevitably, there were recriminations within the guerrilla groups over the failure of the operation, the finger of blame being pointed at those considered responsible. The PFLOAG leaders on the djebel resorted to terror tactics in an attempt to reassert their authority but this proved counter-productive and led to many guerrillas surrendering to government forces during the following two months.

DESPITE THIS MAJOR SETBACK, the PFLOAG still posed a major threat, as was illustrated later in the year when guerrillas launched a 122mm Katyushka rocket at the SOAF base at Salalah. Fortunately, damage was slight although ten people were wounded. The result was an operation in which four heavily fortified bases, known as the 'Dianas' and each manned by a SAF platoon, were established at locations on high ground dominating the area from where the rocket had been fired. These subsequently came under heavy and frequent attack by the PFLOAG which, nevertheless, was unable ever again to launch a rocket at the SOAF base.

Just before the establishment of the Dianas, another defensive barrier had been installed by sappers of the Royal Engineers and the Jordanian Army. Named the Hornbeam Line, it stretched northward from Mugsayl on the coast to a point 40 miles inland and featured fortified positions every 2,000 yards, linked by barbed wire fences and minefields, these being manned by SAF units and the Firqat Al Nasr. Stationed at Oven, at the northern end of the line, was an SAS BATT. In early 1973, reinforcements arrived in the form of an Iranian special forces battalion, the first element of a task force sent by the Shah of Iran to assist the Sultan in the war against the PFLOAG, which during the following year changed its name to the Popular Front for the Liberation of Oman (PFLO).

Elsewhere, an SAS BATT and a firqat were positioned north of Salalah at Qairoon Hairitti, on the Midway Road which led from the Dhofari capital to Thumrait in the negd and then north-eastward to Northern Oman. Other BATTs and firqats were stationed at Hagaif, which was situated on the gatn to the west of the Midway Road; Zeak to the east of Qairoon Hairitti; Medina Al Haq; Jibjat and Tawi Atair. By early 1974, the number of firqats had increased to sixteen, with a total strength of some 1,000 men; to take over the burden of administering them from the SAS, SAF formed Headquarters Firqat Forces. A Squadron, commanded by Major Paddy Kingston, took over from G Squadron in providing the BATT for the first part of that year and it was during this period that another member of 22 SAS was killed in operations against the PFLO.

On 12 April, an eight-man BATT of 4 Troop and the Firqat Al Umri, the entire force under Captain Simon Garthwaite, was taking part in an action to clear a wadi in the area of the Tawi Atair prior to a SAF unit attacking and seizing a feature called Atair Hill. Five members of the BATT remained on the lip of the wadi while the rest of the force, led by the commander of the firqat, Ahmed Mohammed Qartoob, his sergeant major, Mohammed, and one of his NCOs, Corporal Salem, entered a narrow part of the wadi in single file. Threading its way through bushes and scrub strewn with boulders, it headed for a number of caves with the aim of searching and clearing them. Shortly afterwards, it surprised a group of guerrillas and a fierce firefight ensued with both sides taking cover.

The enemy reacted swiftly, mounting a counter-attack during which Qartoob, Mohammed and Salem were wounded. Seeing them pinned down, Captain Garthwaite went forward to extricate them, bringing fire to bear with his rifle and an M79 40mm grenade launcher. Coming under heavy fire himself, however, he was hit and killed, as were Qartoob, Mohammed and Salem. The action, which lasted only a few minutes, took place in the depths of the wadi, out of sight of the other members of the BATT and a SAF company positioned on the opposite sight of the wadi. In due course, the second-in-command of the BATT, Corporal Jimmy Bonham, led a patrol down into the wadi and eventually recovered the bodies of Captain Garthwaite and his men.

The latter part of 1974 saw the PFLO under considerable pressure from SAF's Dhofari Brigade, commanded by Brigadier John Akehurst, as well as from the BATT and firqats who dominated the eastern and central areas of the djebel. Another defensive barrier, the Hammer Line, was established on the Djebel Khawtawt; this followed roughly the same route as the Leopard Line which had been abandoned in mid-1972 as its fortified positions could not be resupplied during the monsoon season. The Iranian special forces battalion, too, was reinforced by a second 1,200-strong unit and a battery of artillery which were deployed in bases along the Midway Road to keep it clear of any enemy. During November, however, the entire Iranian force was airlifted westward into the negd to an airstrip called MANSTON which was rapidly transformed into a major base featuring a tarmac runway, capable of use by C-130 transports, and accommodating both Iranian battalions, a large headquarters and the task force's own helicopters and transport aircraft.

On 2 December, the Iranians launched a major operation to establish another defensive barrier. Called the Damavand Line, it would stretch from a place named Iraqi, situated some thirteen miles to the south-west of MANSTON, southward on to the djebel to a base called EVEREST from where it would continue approximately three miles to the enemy-held town of Rakhyut on the coast. Both battalions, each accompanied by firqat units and SAF liaison officers, were to take part. One Iranian battalion would advance from MANSTON to Iraqi and then to EVEREST which comprised a spur from which two ridges continued south to Rakhyut. The second Iranian unit would meanwhile move to a base called GUNLINES, situated some fifteen miles south-east of MANSTON, from where it would advance south to a ridge above an area called the Sherishitti Caves which was to be seized. This complex of caves – which had been the subject of a study by 22 SAS two years earlier – was known to be used by the PFLO as a major storage facility, holding tons of arms, ammunition and equipment, and therefore was a major target. Both battalions were then to continue south to Rakhyut, the capture of which would also be a major blow to the PFLO which had held it since 1969, using it as its principal support base in western Dhofar.

The operation began on 2 December and both battalions reached and occupied their initial objectives, EVEREST and GUNLINES, unopposed. Next night, however, the guerrillas infiltrated up a wadi between two Iranian companies at GUNLINES and opened fire. In the darkness there was chaos as the latter returned fire at each other, albeit without causing any casualties to themselves or the enemy who withdrew shortly afterwards. On 5 December, the GUNLINES battalion sent a company to occupy a wooded feature called Point 880 which lay two miles to the south. Attached to the 190-strong company was a firqat detachment accompanied by a SAF liaison officer, Major Johnny Braddell-Smith. Having occupied its objective during the morning, the company came under fire from a hill to the south and a few minutes later the sangars forming the south-western part of its position were attacked by guerrillas who worked their way up to them and overpowered the occupying troops, killing them all and taking their weapons. That night, the enemy launched a mortar attack and at 8.00 a.m. next morning a small group of guerrillas launched another assault on the south-western sector of the position, this being repulsed without casualties.

As a result of these attacks, the Iranian battalion refused to advance farther south from GUNLINES and was ordered to join the other battalion in advancing down the ridges leading south from EVEREST to Rakhyut. It took two weeks for the redeployment of this battalion to become the right-hand unit for the advance on Rakhyut which did not begin until 25 December. The left-hand battalion, led by a firqat group under a SAF liaison officer, Captain Mike Lobb, encountered no opposition and reached a point halfway to Rakhyut. The right-hand battalion, led by its firqat and Major Braddell-Smith, initially made good progress but after about a mile and a half was ambushed by a large force of guerrillas. While taking cover, the firqat's sergeant major was killed and Braddell-Smith went forward to recover his body. In so doing, however, he was also killed. Both bodies were recovered two weeks later. The Iranian battalion meanwhile was also suffering casualties but held its ground. Despite this setback, the operation continued and on 5 January Rakhyut was captured by the Iranians, who eventually established the Damar-vand Line.

ATTENTION, MEANWHILE, HAD been turned to the task of capturing the Sherishitti Caves, situated at the head of the Wadi Sherishitti which ran north to south. The sole access to them was by way of two tracks: one descended to them from above while the other ran along the foot of the topmost of several escarpments. The wadi ran up these, mounting the final escarpment before turning north-west through an area of thick bush. Thereafter, it passed through a large 500-yard-long by 200-yard-wide clearing above the caves, subsequently dividing into a series of smaller wadis running south on a long ridge stretching east to west. Another large ridge lay along the northern side of the wadi.

Codenamed DHARAB, the operation to seize the caves was to be carried out in three phases by a SAF battalion, the Djebel Regiment with Red Company of the Desert Regiment attached, B Squadron 22 SAS and the Firqats Tariq bin Zeead and Southern Mahra. Also taking part were

members of G Squadron which, commanded by Major Neville
Houghton, was due to take over the BATT role from B Squadron within
a couple of weeks. In the initial phase of the action, an airstrip at Defa,
situated on the gatn just over two miles south-west of GUNLINES, would
be seized and secured by the SAF Armoured Car Squadron and the
entire assault force and all necessary weapons, ammunition, equipment
and stores flown in by helicopter and Skyvan transports in the early hours
of 4 January. Then the assault force would advance from Defa 3,000
yards south-west along the gatn to a place called Zakhir Tree, named
after an enormous tree on the feature, before turning south-east along a
heavily tree-clad ridge to two clearings in the bush known as Point 980,
that being the height in metres above sea level. The third phase would
consist of the advance north-eastward along a series of ridges towards
the caves.

The entire force was assembled at MANSTON by the evening of 3
January 1975. Defa was secured and by 7.30 a.m. next morning all was
ready to commence the advance to Zakhir Tree. It was led by a group
comprising the main firqat element accompanied by 6 and 8 Troops
under B Squadron's commander, Major Andrew Turner. It had been
given the task in view of the firqats' knowledge of the ground which, it
was assumed, would enable them to make the best progress over difficult
terrain, much of which was covered in thick bush. The members of G
Squadron, along with 7 and 9 Troops, were split into four-man BATTs
accompanying the firqat guides attached to each SAF company.

Before reaching the area of bush, resistance was encountered from
a dozen or so guerrillas armed with RPG-7s and a machine-gun which
caused problems among the firqat, the latter refusing to advance any
further without heavy supporting fire from SAF Saladin armoured cars,
SAF artillery and SOAF Strikemasters. This inevitably destroyed any
chance of surprise but nevertheless B Squadron's two troops under Major
Turner and the rest of the force, led by No. 1 Company of the Djebel
Regiment under its acting commander Captain Nigel Marshall, pushed
on regardless of whether the firqats were accompanying them or not,
fighting their way through the thick bush to Point 980 which was reached
at around 3.30 p.m. On arrival, Marshall and his men discovered a large
unexploded SOAF bomb dropped during an earlier operation and a protective sangar had to be built around it before the position could be

occupied. An hour later, helicopters arrived with the necessary stores for the construction of a defensive position as, in view of the time of day, the third phase of the operation had been postponed until the following morning. That afternoon, Brigadier John Akehurst gave orders that the defensive perimeter was to be expanded and a spur two miles to the south of Point 980, known as STONEHENGE, was to be secured during the night.

That evening, however, a small group of guerrillas attacked a group of soldiers laying mines and trip-flares, wounding three of them and losing three of their own number killed. During the night, no attempt was made to follow Akehurst's orders and when he returned on the following day, he found that STONEHENGE had not been taken. For reasons unexplained, the commanding officer of the Djebel Regiment had hitherto not been present throughout the operation. Summoning him by helicopter, Akehurst relieved him of his command and appointed Major Patrick Brook, commander of the Armoured Car Squadron, to take over. The most experienced SAF soldier present, he knew the area well.

The advance on the caves began at dawn on the following day. No. 1 Company remained at the Point 980 base to hold it while Nos 2 and 3 and Red Companies, each accompanied by a BATT, set off for the objective. No. 2 and Red Company were to proceed north-east, subsequently turning east across the wadi and heading south-east to take up positions on the ridge to the north of the caves from which they could dominate the southern side of the horseshoe-shaped escarpment. No. 3 Company would remain on the western side of the wadi, taking up a position from which it could observe and dominate the mouths of the caves and the open area of ground on the northern side of the escarpment. The task of attacking the caves themselves had been allocated to B Squadron and the firqats who would approach along the track down into the wadi and down the escarpment. Should any resistance be encountered, fire support would be provided by SAF mortars and artillery, and by SOAF Strike-masters.

At 11.00 a.m. the Djebel Regiment's tactical headquarters, accompanied by B Squadron's two troops and the firqats, set off after the three companies. By that time Red Company, commanded by Major Roger King, should have crossed the wadi but had moved too far to the south while following the firqat guides. Navigation in the thick bush was very difficult with commanders having to rely on compass bearings, time and pacing of distances. Despite a number of anxious radio messages from the battalion headquarters querying his exact location, King firmly believed that he was heading north-east and would soon cross the wadi. But he had turned east too soon and he and his company eventually found themselves emerging from the bush on the western side of the wadi, in the position allocated to No. 3 Company, overlooking the large 500-yard-long clearing above the caves. Deploying his company there, King notified Major Brook who agreed that Red Company should remain there while No. 2 Company moved through it to cross the wadi and clearing on to the high ground beyond.

The acting commander of No. 2 Company, Captain Nigel Loring, prepared to cross the wadi. Before setting off, however, he went forward with his four-man BATT to a point from where they could observe the 200-yard-wide clearing to their front. The commander of the BATT, Corporal Willie Williams, strongly advised Loring against crossing it, pointing out the folly of any such move unless the ridge on the other side of the wadi was secured beforehand. He also pointed out the possibility of the high ground already being in enemy hands, and recommended that the company should pull back and work its way round to the north to the high ground under cover of the thick bush.

Unfortunately, Williams's advice conflicted with the orders given earlier to Loring who decided to follow them. Before No. 2 Company set off, however, the second-in-command of Red Company, Captain David Mason, moved one of his platoons 200 yards to the north to a position on a small hill from which it could observe the full length of the clearing. Once all were in their respective positions, No. 2 Company's first platoon advanced into the clearing with Captain Loring, accompanied by his radio operator and an NCO, leading the way. It had almost reached the halfway point when it came under fire from a single guerrilla firing a burst from his AK-47. Loring and his men immediately went to ground in the clearing while an air strike was summoned. Unhappily, due to the directions not being clear or the pilot misunderstanding them, when it arrived minutes later the aircraft strafed the area occupied by Red Company's headquarters, wounding two men.

After the air strike, No. 2 Company resumed its advance. On the far side of the clearing, Captain Loring, his radio operator and accompanying NCO reached a small knoll and were just disappearing over it out of sight of Red Company when a large body of enemy, later conservatively estimated at 200, opened fire with an array of weapons, subsequently identified as including RPG-7s, Type 56 assault rifles, RPK and RPD LMGs, Goryunov GPMGs and at least one Shpagin DShK heavy machine-gun, causing heavy casualties.

The noise of the firing was deafening and from his position with the platoon on the hill to the north, Captain Mason could see members of No. 2 Company dropping as they were hit. Moving forward on his own and under heavy fire, he sprinted to some rocks some 50 yards out from the thick bush where he found the members of Corporal Williams's BATT who subsequently withdrew to join the remainder of No. 2 Company in the area of Red Company's positions. There they met Sergeant Jim Vakabale who had been sent forward with 8 Troop by Major Andrew Turner to coordinate the BATT's actions. Shortly afterwards, however, the troop became pinned down by heavy fire.

Under cover of smoke from a white phosphorus grenade, Mason ran forward to a large rock some 200 yards beyond the far side of the clearing. There he found members of No. 2 Company's headquarters, which had been following the leading platoon, lying dead or wounded. He also discovered the body of Captain Ian MacLucas, the company's artillery FOO, lying in a large fissure in the rock. Near by lay the latter's radio operator who had been badly wounded.

During the next two hours Mason set about discovering whether there were any survivors from the leading platoon, assisted by two soldiers of No. 2 Company he found there – Private Saoud Said who was unhurt but badly shocked, and Private Hamid Khalfan who had suffered a severe wound in the chest but insisted he was still capable of helping and operating his GPMG. The three men searched the area thoroughly and found eleven more survivors, carrying them back to the rock. It was at this juncture that Mason discovered Captain MacLucas was still alive, although very seriously wounded. Having injected him with morphine and applied first aid, he used MacLucas's radio to call for artillery support and for stretchers to be brought forward to evacuate the wounded. Thirty minutes later, as smoke and high explosive shells landed around the enemy's positions, he and his two companions began carrying some of the survivors to a small valley between Red Company's main position

441

and its platoon on the small hill to the north, and continued doing so under constant heavy fire. At that point, some twenty guerrillas attacked the platoon from the north but were repulsed after suffering a number killed and wounded.

Mason, in the meantime, had called for air support and SOAF had responded swiftly with pairs of Strikemasters, guided by him on his SARBE ground-to-air radio, attacking the guerrilla positions with 2-inch SURA rockets and cannon. At the same time, SAF artillery at Defa was laying down a constant barrage of high explosive and smoke on the guerrillas, these being directed by Red Company's FOO, Captain Douglas MacLaine, with whom Mason was in contact by radio. Already precarious from the heavy volume of enemy fire, the situation in the area of the rock was made all the more so as the dry grass and scrub were set ablaze by the 25-pounder smoke shells.

Suddenly, Mason and his two soldiers came under attack from a dozen or so enemy and a fierce skirmish took place in which the guerrillas were beaten off after losing several of their number killed. At this point, realising that he had still not accounted for Captain Loring, Mason went forward alone some 100 yards in search of him, moving over the knoll and down to the nearside slope of the wadi. There he found Loring, who had been killed instantly on being hit several times. At that moment, however, he came under further heavy fire and was forced to retire rapidly back over the knoll.

Some 30 minutes later, in response to Mason's urgent requests for assistance, Captain Michael Shipley, second-in-command of No. 3 Company, came forward with a platoon equipped with stretchers to carry back the dead and wounded. He was accompanied by Red Company's BATT under Lance Corporal Mel 'Taff' Thompson and Sergeant Jim Vakabale who applied emergency medical treatment to Captain MacLucas and the other wounded. Because of the continuing weight of enemy fire, Vakabale made contact with B Squadron's mortar detachment, which was under the command of Corporal Pete Donnelly, calling for twelve rounds from each of the six mortars which were laid in parallel. Shortly afterwards, a total of 72 81mm high explosive bombs impacted on the enemy positions with devastating effect, notably reducing the volume of fire and allowing the evacuation of the wounded across the clearing to Red Company's position and safety. Last to withdraw from the area of the area of the rock were Captains Mason and Shipley, together with Privates Hamid and Saoud.

As SAF artillery and B Squadron's mortars continued to bring down effective fire on the enemy, the three companies and B Squadron started pulling back from the area at around 5.30 p.m. Shots were then heard from the direction of the wadi. Believing the guerrillas to be firing into the bodies of the twelve dead, Major Andrew Turner immediately responded by calling down ten rounds from his mortars on the area. There was no further firing.

The entire force then withdrew to Point 980 where it regrouped. It had been a bloody repulse for SAF whose casualties numbered twenty-two wounded and thirteen killed. One of the latter had been carried back to Red Company's position but the bodies of the other twelve could not be reached due to the constant barrage of enemy fire; it would be some months before their remains were eventually recovered. Known PFLO casualties numbered fourteen killed, with an additional twenty estimated later, while numbers of enemy wounded were never discovered.

At dawn on the following day, Brigadier John Akehurst arrived by helicopter, accompanied by the Commanding Officer of 22 SAS, Lieutenant Colonel Tony Jeapes, who had flown from Britain immediately after hearing of the action on the previous day during which a small number of the BATT had been wounded. They were followed by helicopters bringing in ammunition, mines, stores and other materials necessary for the establishment of a strongly fortified position.

Having spoken to his officers and soldiers, Akehurst immediately turned his mind to his next move. As he states in his book *We Won a War*, he decided that he could not risk any further reverse for the Djebel Regiment whose morale, while still good given the circumstances, needed nurturing even though the officers and men were willing to make another attempt to capture the caves. It was now that a member of the BATT suggested the use of heavy firepower, rather than a frontal assault, to evict the guerrillas from the caves. The idea was taken up, the first step being the capture of STONEHENGE. This was achieved without any trouble and on the next day two 106mm recoilless rifles were positioned there. At the same time, an SAF bulldozer ploughed a track through the bush to STONEHENGE, enabling a Saladin armoured car to be driven on to the position from which the caves were subsequently shelled. Although this denied the enemy its refuge, it would be almost a year before the Sherishitti Caves yielded up their contents.

Attention once more was turned to the guerrillas in the area of Zakhir Tree, who were subsequently dispersed. A search of the area uncovered a large arms cache containing large quantities of mortar bombs, RPG-7 rockets, ammunition, food, medical stores and other equipment. On 19 January, all SAF units, the BATT and firqats withdrew from the area.

Despite the setback at Sherishitti, the following months saw considerable progress in the war against the PFLO. The war moved gradually westward and the SAS handed over their bases to SAF. During late June, A Squadron deployed a four-man BATT under Corporal Wally Potter to the island of Al-Hallaniyah, one of the five forming the Kuria Muria group off the Omani coast, to provide medical assistance for the inhabitants and improve the airstrip so that it could be used by SOAF Skyvan transports. In addition, it was to carry out a census of the population, examine problems with regard to food and water, and produce a report on the measures necessary to improve the poor standards of living.

During the following weeks Corporal Potter and his companions managed to improve the health of the islanders considerably and to teach them the rudimentaries of hygiene. In due course the recommendations in their report were implemented by the Omani government which built houses, a community centre, clinic and radio communication post. It also drilled new wells for water and established regular weekly visits by medical personnel.

During September, a BATT provided by 16 Troop of D Squadron was deployed on an operation to set up a firqat base on the western area of the djebel. It was also to take part in one of three diversions designed to divert the enemy's attention from a major SAF operation, codenamed HADAF, during which another defensive barrier would be established from a place called FURIOUS, situated to the east of Sarfait, southward to the town of Dhalqut on the coast. The aim of the diversionary operations, codenamed BADREE, WAAGID BADREE and KUHOOF respectively, was to set up a new position at Gunlines to convince the guerrillas that another assault was being mounted against the Sherishitti Caves.

BADREE entailed an attack on 14 August by a company of the Northern Frontier Regiment, the BATT and its firqat, a troop of the Armoured Car Squadron and a troop of 25-pounder guns. The objectives were

GUNLINES and then Defa, both of which were occupied without resistance; WAAGID BADREE, consisting of a heliborne attack by a SAF company on a high feature near Bait Handob, east of the Damavand Line, had been mounted on the previous day to distract attention from the advance on Gunlines.

On 17 August, the enemy began firing Katyushka rockets against GUNLINES and Defa and continued to do so for the next three weeks. Thereafter, whenever the mist lifted, both came under further bombardment. In mid-October, 16 Troop's commander, Captain Cedric Denton, requested clearance from Major Clive Fairweather, commanding D Squadron, to mount an attack on the Katyushka launching position. Permission was granted and, having deployed a forward support group of a platoon of the Northern Frontier Regiment and the armoured car troop, 16 Troop set off south-west from Defa at 4.00 a.m. on 19 September with two firqat guides to the Zakhir Tree, the suspected location of the Katyushka launcher or its forward observer.

Navigation was very difficult, because of thick mist caused by the *khareef*, and the firqat guides proved highly unreliable. Eventually, the troop found itself on a spur at the head of the wadi to the west of the Zakhir Tree. Sergeant Roger Slatford, six members of the troop and the two firqat guides moved further down the ridge to a point from where they could observe down the wadi, while Captain Denton and the remainder stayed on the spur. Just as dawn was breaking, Slatford and his patrol moved again, making their way 200 yards to the north-east to a better position on the side of the wadi. At that point, Corporal Danny Weekes moved off with one of the firqat guides to locate the Zakhir Tree. Having crossed the wadi and moved up on to the ridge on the other side, he observed the recent tracks of a group of four or five men heading north while at the same time detecting a faint smell of cooked meat. Following his nose and ignoring his very nervous companion who was quietly beseeching him to turn back, Weekes made his way forward and shortly afterwards spotted the Zakhir Tree through a small gap in the mist. Retracing his footsteps, he reported back to Sergeant Slatford who contacted Captain Denton on the radio.

At that point, Slatford observed a figure some 70 yards away, heading north parallel to the wadi. No sooner had Denton received his warning over the radio than three guerrillas appeared out of the mist and a member of the group opened fire with a GPMG, hitting all three. One, however, returned fire at the same time, hitting Lance Corporal Geordie Small in the thigh and rupturing his femoral artery. Denton called for assistance and a Saladin armoured car came forward to evacuate Small to Defa from where a request for a 'casevac' by helicopter was requested. Small's injury, however, was more severe than had been realised and by the time the aircraft had arrived he had bled to death.

Sergeant Slatford and his patrol meanwhile were heading north to rejoin Captain Denton and his group. While advancing up the wadi, however, they came under fire from the rear and Lance Corporal Tony Fleming fell wounded. A fierce engagement then ensued at close range in the thick bush while, under covering fire from the remainder, two members of the patrol dragged Fleming up the wadi to the cover of some rocks. Meanwhile Denton called for supporting fire and shortly afterwards artillery shells and mortar bombs began exploding on the ridge to the west and in the wadi to the south. At that moment, a line of infantry appeared to the west and Sergeant Slatford, believing it to be the Northern Frontier Regiment platoon, stood up to attract the troops' attention. In fact they were guerrillas who immediately opened fire, hitting him three times. With Slatford out of action, Corporal Weekes took over command as the action continued with the enemy continuing to put down heavy fire.

Just as it looked as though the patrol would be overrun, the guerrillas began to withdraw, having already recovered their casualties which were heavier than Slatford and his men realised at the time. At that point, the armoured car troop and the Northern Frontier Regiment platoon came forward down the eastern ridge of the wadi and opened fire on the western ridge. As they did so, Captain Denton and his group moved down to Sergeant Slatford's position from where the entire troop withdrew shortly afterwards, Slatford and Fleming being evacuated to Defa on the back of a Saladin armoured car.

The finale to the campaign in the western area of the djebel followed this action, and together with the other diversions, convinced the PFLO that SAF's main thrust would come from the north-east. Having been pushed back westward, the guerrilla forces were by this time deployed on either side of the Wadi Sayq which was too wide and deep to allow the rapid redeployment of troops from one side to the other. If SAF forces were to attack on one side or the other, only those guerrilla groups on that side could be deployed to face them. Faced with the choice of concentrating their forces on one side or dividing them equally either side of the wadi, the PFLO took the latter course.

Two further diversionary operations had meanwhile been launched. During the nights of 13 and 14 October, undetected by the enemy, SAF engineers cleared mines along three routes leading south from the rear of the SIMBA base at Sarfait, situated to the west of the Wadi Sayq. On the night of the 14th a reinforced company of the Muscat Regiment, commanded by Major Ian Gordon, exfiltrated down the Wadi Sarfait and by dawn on 15 October had occupied a position on a plateau called CAPSTAN situated to the south of the Darra Ridge. After its insertion in the spring of 1972, SIMBA had been subjected to sporadic attacks from PFLO 85mm guns positioned at Hauf just over the Yemeni border. The intensity of these had increased during the first half of October and by the 15th had become heavier still with CAPSTAN also coming under fire following its occupation. The PFLO shelling was answered by three 5.5-inch guns flown into SIMBA two months earlier. In addition, SOAF carried out a series of retaliatory air strikes at dawn on 16 October, these being conducted by Hawker Hunter fighter-bombers presented earlier to Oman by King Hussein of Jordan; armed with 30mm cannon and 1,000 lb bombs, they carried a far more powerful punch than SOAF's Strike-masters. The strikes took place at Hauf and at Jaadib, the latter situated farther to the west along the coast, destroying an 85mm gun and severely damaging both PFLO headquarters.

The Iranian task force meanwhile advanced westward from Rakhyut in a heliborne assault to secure a ridge which overlooked some of the routes leading to the Sherishitti Caves to the north, the assault being preceded by a heavy naval bombardment from three Iranian Navy warships lying offshore. This operation served further to convince the guerrillas that an attack on the caves was imminent and they engaged the Iranians heavily.

The original plan for HADAF had been for the Frontier Force and the Armoured Car Squadron to move south-west from Defa to FURIOUS which would have been secured earlier by a heliborne assault. From there they would then have headed south to the heights above the Wadi Sayq. At dawn on the second day, three companies of the Frontier Force would have carried out a heliborne assault across the wadi, under supporting fire from artillery at Defa, GUNLINES, FURIOUS and SIMBA, two then moving south to seize the cliffs overlooking Dhalqut. Such was the degree of success achieved against the enemy so far, however, that Brigadier John Akehurst decided to modify his plan. First, he decided to thrust south to the coast in order to cut the PFLO lines of supply in an attempt to bring the conflict to a close as swiftly as possible. On the night of 16 October two companies, one of the Frontier Force and the other from the Kateebat Janoobiya, another SAF regiment, advanced south from Sarfait to the coast and secured their objectives without meeting any resistance.

The Baluchi soldiers of the Frontier Force, however, having spent the previous year and a half at Sarfait or on the Hornbeam Line, were unused to operating in the thick bush of the western Djebel. Akehurst therefore postponed HADAF, giving Lieutenant Colonel Jonathan Salisbury-Trelawney nine days to retrain his battalion in the area of Qairoon Hairitti and Wadi Naheez.

On the morning of 26 October, the final operation to clear the PFLO from the western djebel began. Under supporting fire from artillery and mortars, the leading Frontier Force company advanced to the Zakhir Tree where a party of guerrillas had been observed laying mines, subsequently being driven off by shellfire. Having secured the area, the rest of the battalion advanced to FURIOUS with a bulldozer making the track passable for armoured cars and trucks. Once the objective had been secured and cleared of any mines, SOAF Skyvans began flying in supplies for the battalion.

A company of the Frontier Force, supported by elements of the Armoured Car Squadron, then advanced south towards Point Alpha, a large spur extending into the northern side of the Wadi Sayq. So far there had been little in the way of enemy activity but as the company crossed over a ridge en route to Point Alpha, the commander, Major Michael Deacon, his FOO Captain Nigel Gershon and the commander of the D Squadron BATT attached to the company, came under fire from the objective as they descended a forward slope towards it. The latter swiftly called down supporting fire from the BATT mortars on the objective and shortly afterwards the guerrillas withdrew, enabling the company to occupy the spur.

The second day of HADAF was spent consolidating and preparing for the next phase, the enemy meanwhile shelling FURIOUS with mortars and recoilless rifles. On the morning of the third day, operations recommenced with the clearing of wadis and spurs back towards Point 980 and STONEHENGE, both of which were captured and secured. Thereafter, a company headed for the heights above the Sherishitti Caves, covered by the Armoured Car Squadron. Halfway to the objective, however, it came under fire from a recoilless rifle and halted as SOAF Hunters attacked the suspected location of the weapon with 1,000 lb bombs. As one aircraft made a low pass over the area, the guerrillas launched a SA-7 Grail shoulder-fired surface-to-air missile. All the aircraft in the area took evasive action and fortunately avoided being hit. Soon afterwards, the Sherishitti Caves were captured and found to contain large quantities of weapons, ammunition, clothing, food and medical supplies. Some of the caves were mined and while they were being searched a SAF officer was severely wounded when stepping on an anti-personnel mine.

The final phase of the operation saw Major Michael Deacon's company of the Frontier Force dispatched to secure an LZ on a large hill at the eastern end of the Darra Ridge. Setting off under cover of darkness, it headed south to the coastline and made its way to the southern end of the Wadi Sayq; then it climbed the hill, securing it before first light after encountering no opposition. At dawn, the battalion headquarters and two more companies were flown in by helicopter, followed by Brigadier John Akehurst and the Commander of the Sultan's Armed Forces, Major General Kenneth Perkins. The Frontier Force then advanced westward along the Darra Ridge to a point overlooking Dhalqut which was occupied on the following day, 1 December, by which time the guerrillas in the area had withdrawn.

Abandoning their heavy weapons and equipment, the remaining PFLO forces in the western djebel retired at night towards the Yemeni border. Boxed in to the north, east and west, and with the SON patrolling offshore to the south, there was only one route left open to them: across the northern end of the Wadi Sayq and round to the north of SIMBA. Ten days later, on 11 December, the conflict was officially declared at an end. It was not until 30 April of the following year, however, that the Yemeni army and the PFLO ceased their shelling of SIMBA.

In the eastern djebel, however, several groups of guerrillas were still at large and continued to pose a threat. In February 1976, the SAS returned to the east and, with the firqats, began assisting SAF operations to pacify the region. At the same time, development throughout Dhofar was proceeding apace and by September several schools had been built, administrative centres established and supplies of water further developed. This was not lost on the guerrillas and during this period an increasing number gave themselves up.

In September, Operation STORM came to an end and the last SAS squadron left Dhofar and returned to Britain. It left behind the firqats who, with a strength of 2,500, were handed over to Headquarters Firqat Forces. The latter subsequently recruited a number of Firqat Liaison Officers, several of them former members of 22 SAS, who operated with the firqats in the same way as before. During the six years of the conflict, 22 SAS and its BATTs had played a major role not only in helping the Sultan's Armed Forces to fight the PFLO, the regiment losing twelve of its number in the process, but also in winning the hearts and minds of the Dhofari population by providing civil aid, an equally important task, as had proved to be the case previously in Malaya and Borneo.

CHAPTER TEN

VIETNAM, CAMBODIA AND LAOS 1954–1971

Following the end of the First Indochina War in 1954, Vietnam was divided in two – the communist north, comprising the newly created Democratic Republic of Vietnam under Ho Chi Minh, and the south, under its French-backed puppet premier Bao Dai, the former emperor. A fourteen-mile-wide demilitarised zone (DMZ), following the 17th Parallel, was established and an international control commission (ICC), made up of representatives from Canada, Poland and India, was given the responsibility of ensuring that the terms of the Geneva Accords were complied with by both sides. The ICC was also responsible for monitoring foreign advisory missions and policing military activities on both sides of the DMZ.

Almost 900,000 refugees, in the main staunchly anti-communist Catholics, left the north and resettled in the south while some 100,000 Viet Minh troops marched northward where they were absorbed into the 324th and 325th Divisions of the newly created People's Army of Vietnam, to become more familiarly known in the West as the North Vietnamese Army (NVA). Meanwhile, approximately 10,000 communists remained in the south as 'sleepers', ready to be activated when required, while sufficient weapons for up to 6,000 guerrillas were hidden in caches throughout the south.

On 24 October 1954, President Dwight D. Eisenhower informed Ngo Dinh Diem that the United States would supply military aid directly rather than via the French. Just over six months later, on 10 May 1955, South Vietnam formally requested US military assistance and on 20 July refused to participate in the all-Vietnam elections stipulated under the Geneva Accords on the grounds that it would be impossible for them to be held in the communist north. On 23 October, a national referendum resulted in the ousting of Bao Dai and the creation of the Republic of Vietnam under a government headed by Ngo Dinh Diem. Meanwhile, on 25 September, Cambodia also declared itself an independent state.

On 28 April 1956, the US Military Assistance Advisory Group (MAAG), commanded by Lieutenant General 'Iron Mike' O'Daniel, took over responsibility for the training of the newly formed Army of the Republic of Vietnam (ARVN) and French troops began to leave the country. In June 1957 the last of them departed and in September South Vietnam held its first democratic elections, Diem being elected as President.

Under the Geneva Accords, the MAAG was limited to a total strength of 342 but, in order to deal with the logistical problems caused by the French withdrawal, was permitted a further 300 personnel designated as a Temporary Equipment Recovery Mission (TERM). The Americans used this as a cover to introduce additional military and intelligence personnel into the country. Among the latter was a CIA unit designated the Saigon Military Mission (SMM). Based in the US Embassy and headed by US Air Force Colonel Edward Lansdale, it had appeared shortly after the fall of Dien Bien Phu in May 1954 with the task of assisting in paramilitary and psychological warfare operations against the Vietminh. Even before the departure of the French, however, the SMM was concentrating on the organisation of covert action teams for deployment in the north where they would carry out sabotage, assassinations and other clandestine missions.

These teams were infiltrated into the north with the assistance of Civil Air Transport (CAT), the CIA's own airline, which had been contracted to evacuate refugees from the north to the south. The ferrying tasks provided cover for the shipment of arms and explosives from Saigon to Hanoi where they were received by an SMM team operating under MAAG cover and commanded by Major Bob Conein. A US Army officer who had served in the OSS during the Second World War, his apparent official role was the coordination of the evacuation operation. His real mission, however, was the organisation of a covert action team codenamed BINH whose role would be to carry out sabotage attacks on North Vietnam's road and rail transport system. Another team, designated HAO and commanded by Major Fred Allen, had been allocated the mission of organising a resistance movement in the southern half of North Vietnam.

In February 1956, the SMM formed the first ARVN unconventional warfare unit, the 1st Observation Group. Three hundred strong, it was trained to operate in fifteen-man teams inside North Vietnam. In the event of a communist invasion of the south via the DMZ, the unit's role was to provide 'stay-behind' teams which would form resistance groups

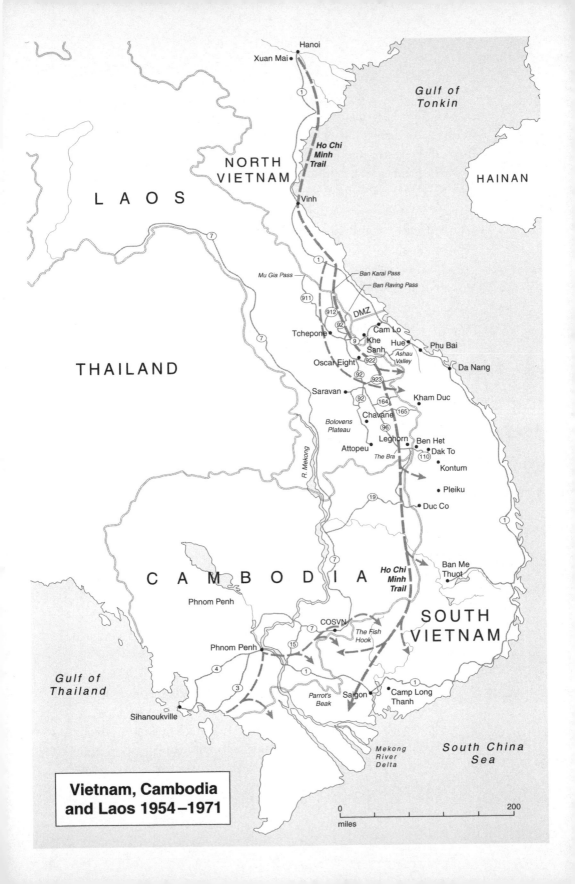

Vietnam, Cambodia
and Laos 1954–1971

along the lines of the GCMA maquis of the First Indochina War and harass NVA lines of communications and supply.

In Laos, meanwhile, where 7,000 Viet Minh troops had remained secretly in contravention of the Geneva Accords, the communists were taking advantage of a deteriorating political situation to seize control of the Laotian 'Panhandle'. During 1957, Communist Pathet Lao guerrillas and NVA troops took the strategically important town of Tchepone situated at a crossroads of a network of trails leading to the Central Highlands of South Vietnam and the Mekong Delta. The capture of the town gave the communists control over the entire heartland and the ability to carry out infiltrations along the length of South Vietnam's long border.

The United States was prevented by the Geneva Accords from stationing a large military MAAG in Laos, and thus in 1958 the CIA established the Program Evaluation Office (PEO) as a front for covert operations against the Pathet Lao and NVA. One of the first tasks of the PEO was to establish good relations with the Montagnard tribes who inhabited the mountainous region which spanned the Lao–Vietnamese border. The initial response from the tribes was sceptical as they remembered only too well their abandonment by the French and their subsequent treatment at the hands of the communists. This was particularly the case with the Hmong and their chief Vang Pao, who demanded guarantees from the CIA that he and his people would not suffer a similar fate if they agreed to support the United States against the communists. These were readily forthcoming from the Americans, who were only too keen to convince him.

In July 1959, a force of 107 US Special Forces personnel, commanded by Lieutenant Colonel Arthur 'Bull' Simons, arrived in Laos under PEO cover to train Royal Laotian Army battalions and irregular units in unconventional warfare in a CIA operation designated WHITE STAR. Its original mission soon changed and during the next twelve months, based on the Bolovens Plateau in southern Laos and assisted by a unit of Thailand's paramilitary Border Police, WHITE STAR trained over 9,000 Hmong tribesmen who were later deployed to harass the Pathet Lao and NVA, attacking their lines of communication and supply. Eventually, the CIA's Hmong army would number over 40,000, being resupplied and supported by aircraft flown by crews belonging to Air America, as CAT had become known by then.

In South Vietnam, the period of 1959–60 saw the appearance of increasing numbers of known members of the Viet Minh who had moved north in 1954 after the First Indochina War. In mid-1959, the communists dispatched a secret unit, the 559th Transportation and Support Group, commanded by General Vo Bam, to make preparations for a large-scale invasion of South Vietnam via Laos. In close cooperation with the North Vietnamese intelligence service, the Trinh Sat, the 559th trained large numbers of communists for infiltration into South Vietnam. During the following five years, approximately 44,000 would outflank the DMZ via Laos, travelling along the network of trails which would become notorious as the Ho Chi Minh Trail.

The large-scale infiltration of the south was accompanied by Trinh Sat assassinations of many South Vietnamese government officials and during November 1960 members of the ARVN's 3rd Airborne Brigade staged an unsuccessful coup against President Diem.

Early 1960 saw the reappearance of Brigadier General Edward Lansdale who, dismayed at the worsening situation in South Vietnam, made recommendations for large increases in US military aid to strengthen the ARVN. These fell on fertile ground with the newly elected President John F. Kennedy who, on his inauguration in early 1961, authorised plans calling for increases in the strength of the ARVN and local defence forces. Four hundred extra members of the US Special Forces were allocated to South Vietnam to carry out a newly conceived operation, the Civilian Irregular Defense Group Program, aimed at establishing areas which were secure from communist influence and helping local communities to develop their own self-defence capabilities. In September 1961, the 5th Special Forces Group (Airborne) was activated in South Vietnam, thereafter being the unit which provided Special Forces personnel for operations in that theatre.

Kennedy's enthusiasm for counter-insurgency and unconventional warfare also resulted in the expansion of the CIA's covert operations in Vietnam, orchestrated by the station chief in Saigon, a former OSS officer named William Colby. He received authorisation to use Special Forces personnel and members of the US Navy's SEAL (Sea, Air, Land) teams as instructors and advisers to South Vietnamese personnel to be employed on covert operations. Based on the coast at Nha Trang, and working under the innocuous cover name of Combined Area Studies

(CAS), these trained members of the ARVN's 1st Observation Group in the skills and techniques of long-range deep penetration reconnaissance. During 1961 and 1962, the 1st Observation Group conducted 41 operations into Laos, reconnoitring the principal North Vietnamese infiltration routes, but these yielded little in the way of intelligence primarily because of excessive caution on the part of the reconnaissance teams.

The SEAL element of CAS also formed and trained a reconnaissance and raiding unit called the Sea Commandos whose role was coastal raiding in junks. After several such raids, however, the members of the unit found themselves being intercepted by heavily armed North Vietnamese Swatow class gunboats, and the CIA replaced the junks with Norwegian-built *Nasty* class fast attack craft originally designed for actions in the Norwegian Sea against warships of the Soviet Red Navy. Heavily armed and with a maximum speed of 47 knots, they soon proved they could outrun and outgun the North Vietnamese boats.

The CIA also established a clandestine air arm to support its covert operations in the field. This was formed from a squadron of the Vietnamese Air Force (VNAF) commanded by Colonel Nguyen Cao Ky, with training being provided by Nationalist Chinese pilots who were highly experienced in conducting covert missions over China for the CIA. Responsibility for planning of air operations into North Vietnam and Laos was given to the USAF's 1045th Operational Evaluation and Training Group (OETG) which, as mentioned in Chapter 8, was a unit providing specialist support for CIA covert operations throughout Central and South-east Asia. While still involved in Operation ST BARNUM in Tibet, the 1045th OETG carried out aerial support of CIA operations in North Vietnam and Laos. Once again, planning for such was carried out by Major Lawrence Ropka who routed flights into North Vietnam via Laos, whose mountainous regions made detection difficult.

The first team of four agents to be dropped into North Vietnam was trained at Camp Long Thanh, 25 miles north-east of Saigon, and by the late spring of 1961 had completed its training. Codenamed ATLAS, it was flown in March to Thailand from where it was inserted by helicopter just over the border into Laos, in Khammouan Province close to the North Vietnamese province of Nghe An. Unfortunately, it had been compromised, and NVA forces had already surrounded the drop zone (DZ) when the team landed. Two of its members were captured and two were killed immediately after landing. Three months later, the two survivors were put on trial in Hanoi.

May saw a second team dropped into Son La Province in the west of North Vietnam. Codenamed CASTER, it comprised four sergeants from the ARVN's 22nd Infantry Division who were all natives of Son La. Radio contact was maintained by the team with its base in Saigon but it soon became apparent to the CIA that the team had been captured and 'doubled', its radio operator working his set under control of the North Vietnamese. Contact was maintained with CASTER until July 1963 when it was lost. In the meantime, two more teams, ECHO and DIDO, had also been dropped. ECHO was inserted on 2 June into the district of Lam Trach in the coastal province of Quang Binh but all three of its members were captured shortly afterwards, the three radio sets in their possession also being put to use in an already expanding North Vietnamese deception operation. The CIA maintained contact with ECHO until August 1962 after which it was terminated.

DIDO was also dropped during June 1961, four men being inserted into the northern part of Lai Chau Province, in the north-west of North Vietnam, of which they were natives. Shortly after landing, however, all four were captured when one of them made contact with members of his family from whom he obtained food. DIDO was thereafter 'doubled' by the North Vietnamese under whose control it operated thereafter until contact was terminated by the CIA.

In 1962, other teams were inserted, the first being TARZAN with whom the CIA maintained radio contact until June 1963. On 20 February EUROPA was dropped just inside the border with Laos. Two days later, however, it was captured near its DZ and in due course joined the ranks of those already operating under North Vietnamese control. On 16 April REMUS, comprising four men, was inserted into an area not far from Dien Bien Phu. On 12 August it was reinforced with two more men.

Insertions continued during the rest of the year and by the end of 1963 a total of 26 teams and a single agent had been dropped or landed in North Vietnam. Of those, nearly all had been captured by the North Vietnamese, with at least three known to have been 'doubled'. Aware of what had befallen them, the CIA nevertheless continued to maintain communications with those radios operating under North Vietnamese control as part of its own deception programme.

Eighteen months earlier, in April 1961, the Kennedy administration had suffered a disaster with the failure of the invasion of Cuba by CIA-supported anti-Castro exiles at the Bay of Pigs. This led to the appointment of a commission, headed by General Maxwell Taylor, to investigate the reasons for the plan's failure. Its findings stated that the operation had grown to proportions beyond those manageable by the CIA and recommended that other covert programmes being undertaken by the Agency should be reviewed; it also recommended that those which had expanded beyond the role of intelligence operations should be transferred to the US Army. As a result, it was agreed by the CIA that its covert operations in South Vietnam would be handed over within eighteen months, the procedure for doing so being codenamed SWITCHBACK. This was due to be completed by the end of 1963 but was delayed by two major events: the overthrow on 1 November of South Vietnamese President Ngo Dinh Diem and the murder three weeks later of President John F. Kennedy.

The steady increase in communist infiltration of the south, meanwhile, had led to the United States mounting covert operations against North Vietnam. The decision was now taken to escalate these and during December an operational plan, jointly conceived by the CIA and the Department of Defense, and designated Operational Plan 34A (OPLAN 34A), was submitted to the Joint Chiefs of Staff for their approval. On 21 December 1963, US Secretary of Defense Robert MacNamara briefed President Lyndon B. Johnson on its details. On 16 January 1964, the Department of Defense directed that responsibility for OPLAN 34A be assigned to the US Military Assistance Command Vietnam (MACV), commanded by General Paul Harkins, which had replaced the MAAG in early February 1962. Three days later, the plan was formally activated in a joint signal from the State Department, Department of Defense and CIA to their respective elements in Saigon.

On 24 January 1964, MACV formed a special unit to take over the CIA's covert activities within Vietnam. Initially called the Special Operations Group, it consisted of members of all three armed services, including US Special Forces, US Navy SEALs and USAF special operations personnel. Within a few months, however, its name would be changed to the innocuous-sounding Studies and Observation Group (SOG). As recounted by John Plaster, author of the authoritative history

SOG: The Secret Wars of America's Commandos in Vietnam, and a former member of SOG, it was not under the command of MACV but reported directly to the Joint Chiefs of Staff in Washington from whom it received its directives. In Saigon, only five individuals outside SOG were privy to information concerning its activities: the commander-in-chief of US forces in South Vietnam; his chief of staff; his intelligence officer; the commander of the USAF's Seventh Air Force; and the commander of US naval forces.

Appointed as Chief of MACV-SOG was Colonel Clyde R. Russell who had served with the 82nd Airborne Division during the Second World War and in the 1950s had commanded the 10th and 7th Special Forces Groups (Airborne) respectively. Having taken over the CIA's base at Camp Long Thanh north-east of Saigon, he organised his new unit into four components. The first of these was the Airborne Operations Group, located in Nha Trang and specialising in intelligence and airborne insertion of SOG personnel and agents into enemy-controlled areas. It was initially commanded by Lieutenant Colonel Edward Partain, who had previously served with the 10th Special Forces in West Germany,.

Air support for SOG was planned by its Air Studies Branch. Air operations, codenamed MIDRIFF, were the responsibility of the Air Studies Group which provided aircraft in support of all elements of SOG. Under its command were the 20th 'Green Hornets' Special Operations Squadron (SOS), flying UH-1F transport helicopters and UH-1P gunships armed with two GAU-2B pintle-mounted 7.62mm miniguns and two XM-157 seven-shot rocket pods; the VNAF 219th Helicopter Squadron, equipped with H-34 Kingbee helicopters; and the First Flight, a unit comprising four C-123 Provider transports flown by Chinese Nationalist pilots who had served previously with the Republic of China's 34th Squadron, a highly secret unit which conducted missions on behalf of the CIA over mainland China.

Seaborne operations, codenamed PLOWMAN, were the responsibility of the Maritime Operations Group with its Naval Advisory Detachment (NAD) comprising twelve SEALS from Detachment Echo of SEAL Team One, a number of personnel from Boat Support Unit One and five members of the USMC's Force Recon. The NAD took over responsibility for the Sea Commandos and the *Nasty* class fast attack craft.

Psychological warfare operations, conducted under the codename of HUMIDOR, were meanwhile handled by the Psychological Operations Group whose role would include broadcasting of 'black' propaganda from secret radio transmitters, some purporting to be inside North Vietnam, and 'grey' Voice of Freedom propaganda from two transmitters at Hué and Tay Ninh.

Logistical support for SOG was provided by its Logistics Division which was able to call for support on the US Army's Counter-Insurgency Support Office (CISO) and the CIA's highly classified Far East logistics base at Camp Chinen on the island of Okinawa.

Radio communications played a vital role in all SOG operations and these were the responsibility of the Communications Division, which provided all operational elements with radios and cryptographic equipment for use on operations as well as maintaining communications with them in the field.

In addition to Camp Long Thanh, SOG found itself inheriting from the CIA over twenty agents still undergoing training. By this stage, the number of teams inserted into North Vietnam numbered more than twenty; of those only four, BELL, EASY, REMUS and TOURBILLON, were believed to have survived, along with a single agent codenamed ARES. According to John Plaster, few were of suitable quality and the decision was taken to 'get rid of them'. Those considered of dubious mettle were formed into teams codenamed BOONE, BUFFALO, LOTUS and SCORPION, and during the period May to July 1964 were dropped into North Vietnam where they were all captured. The small number deemed to have potential were despatched as reinforcements for the three surviving teams. Meanwhile, SOG had begun recruiting new agents.

Colonel Russell was under pressure to begin operations and within three weeks of SOG's formation, the Maritime Operations Group launched its first mission. On 16 February, three of the NAD's *Nasty* class boats attempted to land Sea Commando combat swimmers to carry out a demolition task on a bridge. Heavy fire from NVA coastal batteries, however, forced the boats to withdraw and the mission to be aborted. A similar operation mounted a few nights later also failed, eight Sea Commandos being lost in the process.

Some successes, nevertheless, were achieved by the NAD, which destroyed five targets and carried out two raids. On 30 July, five of its

Nasty boats attacked enemy coastal radar sites near Haiphong. On 2 August, the North Vietnamese retaliated by attacking the destroyer USS *Maddox* with motor torpedo boats (MTB) in the Gulf of Tonkin. On the following day, NAD *Nasty* boats carried out another attack on a coastal radar. On 4 August, despite a warning from the United States that any further attacks on its warships would result in serious repercussions, North Vietnamese MTBs attacked USS *Turner Joy*. On 5 August, aircraft of the US Navy's Seventh Fleet carried out retaliatory attacks against the enemy MTB bases and other military targets in North Vietnam. Two days later, the US Congress adopted the Tonkin Gulf Resolution, endorsing any measures taken by the President to repel attacks on US forces and prevent further aggression.

Other elements of SOG were busy meantime on land. In April, during a visit to Saigon, Defense Secretary Robert MacNamara had demanded that ARVN forces should carry out reconnaissance tasks west of Khe Sanh. He recognised, however, that the Vietnamese would be incapable of producing results unless Americans accompanied them and so gave his approval for Special Forces personnel to take part in missions code-named Project LEAPING LENA. He stipulated that these operations should begin within a month but in the event the first reconnaissance team was not inserted until 24 June. During the following week five more teams, each comprising eight Vietnamese, were dropped into Laos. Out of a total of 48 men, only four returned, the remainder having been killed or captured. The survivors, however, had discovered the Ho Chi Minh Trail which they described as a network of roads and tracks, heavily camouflaged against observation from the air, along which convoys of trucks and large numbers of NVA troops were moving unhindered.

In early 1965, evidence of expansion of the Ho Chi Minh Trail was produced in photographs of a newly constructed road taken by the pilot of an Air America aircraft flying over the Mu Gia Pass between North Vietnam and Laos. On 8 March, SOG received the long-awaited authorisation to deploy its Special Forces personnel on reconnaissance operations against the Ho Chi Minh Trail.

At this juncture, Colonel Clyde Russell handed over as Chief of MACV-SOG to Colonel Donald Blackburn who was no stranger to the world of unconventional warfare. During the Second World War, after the Japanese occupation of the Philippines, Blackburn and others had

escaped from Bataan to the mountains of northern Luzon where he had
organised a resistance force of 20,000 men made up of five regiments,
one consisting of Igarote tribesmen renowned in the past for being headhunters. Dubbed 'Blackburn's Headhunters', the guerrillas had acted
as scouts and guides for US forces after the invasion of Leyte in 1944,
while also carrying out other missions such as target location for USAF
bombers and search-and-rescue for downed aircrew. At the end of the
war, Blackburn, now a full colonel at the young age of 29, was posted as
an instructor to the military academy at West Point where he lectured
in unconventional warfare. He was later posted to Vietnam as an adviser,
following which he commanded the 77th Special Forces Group (Airborne) at Fort Bragg, North Carolina.

SOG'S FIRST MAJOR OPERATION under Blackburn's command
was SHINING BRASS – the conduct of reconnaissance tasks in Laos by
teams of mercenaries led by Special Forces personnel. This was carried
out by a new component of SOG, the Ground Studies Group headed
by Colonel Arthur 'Bull' Simons, who had commanded the WHITE STAR
teams in Laos in 1959–62. An initial sixteen volunteers to lead five teams
were recruited from the 1st Special Forces Group (Airborne) on Okinawa
where they carried out training for the mission. On completion, they
were flown to South Vietnam where they were allocated on the basis of
two or three to a team comprising nine Nung tribesmen. Originally of
Chinese ethnic origin from the southern province of Kwangsi, thereafter having emigrated to Vietnam, the Nungs were renowned as formidable fighters and had already proved themselves ideal for clandestine
operations under the CIA. Each American member of a team had a code
number denoting his position: the commander was known as One-Zero,
his assistant being One-One and the team's radio operator One-Two. In
addition, each was also allocated a codename to be used over the radio,
while the team was given an overall codename of an American state.

The initial phase of SHINING BRASS was targeted on southern Laos
where teams were to locate and identify NVA bases and concentration
areas to be engaged by USAF air strikes. The second phase would see
the raising and training of special mobile strike companies, known as
'Hatchet Forces', whose role was the conduct of heliborne hit-and-run

attacks on NVA lines of communications and supply. The third and ultimate phase was the recruitment of large numbers of hill tribesmen and their formation into irregular units similar to those raised by the French GCMA some fifteen years earlier. SOG, however, encountered opposition from the US ambassador in Laos, William Sullivan, who insisted on confining its operations to limited areas along the Laos–South Vietnam border and restricting use of helicopters to emergency evacuation only.

Colonel 'Bull' Simons, meanwhile, had established the SHINING BRASS command and control centre under Lieutenant Colonel Ray Call within the giant US airbase at Da Nang. A forward operating base (FOB) from which operations would be launched into Laos, as well as providing accommodation for reconnaissance teams and refuelling facilities for helicopters, was then installed at an isolated Special Forces base at Kham Duc, in the jungle some 60 miles south-west of Da Nang. It was under the command of Lieutenant Colonel Charlie Norton, a Special Forces officer who had served with UN partisan units during the Korean War, while operations launched from it were under the direction of Major Larry Thorne. One of the most remarkable characters ever to have served in the US Special Forces, Thorne was a Finn who had fought against the Soviets in 1940, commanding his own guerrilla group and conducting raids behind enemy lines; during one action, an ambush on an enemy convoy, he and his men killed 300 Russians without incurring any casualties of their own. Following Finland's surrender to the Soviets in 1944, he joined the German armed forces and, having undergone training in guerrilla warfare, served for the rest of the war with a unit of marines. Wanted by the Soviets, he was arrested on his return to Finland but succeeded in escaping to the United States where, with the help of former OSS chief General 'Wild Bill' Donovan, he became a US citizen. Thereafter, he enlisted in the US Army as a private soldier and volunteered immediately for special operations. In due course, he joined the 77th Special Forces Group and in 1956 received his commission as a first lieutenant.

Thorne's assistant at Kham Duc was Major Sully Fontaine who during the Second World War had enlisted in the British Army as a sixteen-year-old and had then been parachuted into France to fight alongside the resistance. Enlisting in the US Army during the Korean War, he had subsequently joined the Special Forces and during 1963 had commanded a 5th Special Forces Group CIDG base.

The first SHINING BRASS operation was launched at dusk on 18 October 1965. Reconnaissance Team IOWA, under its One-Zero Master Sergeant Charles Petry, was lifted forward from Kham Duc by two H-34 King-bees of the VNAF 219th Helicopter Squadron to a landing zone (LZ) on the border. A third Kingbee, with Major Larry Thorne aboard, followed to retrieve passengers and crew of either of the leading two aircraft in the event of their being shot down. Fire support for the insertion was provided by Green Hornet' UH-1P gunships with further air support on call via a USAF forward air controller (FAC) who was already airborne in a Cessna O-1 Bird Dog.

IOWA's LZ was some twenty miles to the north-west of Kham Duc, in an area cleared previously by tribesmen for growing crops and then abandoned after the soil had become exhausted. En route, the aircraft encountered bad weather and occasional heavy machine-gun fire from the ground which was avoided without difficulty. As dusk fell, the two leading Kingbees disembarked the team and departed, followed by the FAC and the gunships, the third Kingbee remaining briefly in the area, in case Petry and his men ran into trouble, before also turning for home. On the way back, however, it disappeared and no trace of the aircraft, its crew or Major Larry Thorne was ever found. SOG had already suffered its first casualties.

The weather deteriorated sharply as IOWA headed for its objective, a location on the Laotian Highway 165 where it met the South Vietnamese border in the northernmost of the two areas in which SOG was permitted to operate inside Laos. Codenamed TARGET D-1, it was suspected as being an area from which NVA mortars and rocket launchers were bombarding Da Nang.

On reaching D-1, Petry and his men found it to be a hive of enemy activity with a number of NVA camps, roads and trails in the area. On the third day of the operation, they could hear the noise of vehicle engines and set off to investigate. But they soon made contact with an NVA patrol and one of Petry's Nungs was killed. The enemy reacted swiftly as IOWA took evasive action and made its way out of the area. Weather conditions were still bad and it was not until two days later that they broke, enabling Petry to call in air support and permitting the team to be extracted by helicopter. On returning to Kham Duc, Petry immediately flew back to the area with an FAC and helped to direct air strikes on targets found during his three days in the area, among them several large munitions dumps.

On the evening of 2 November, Reconnaissance Team ALASKA, commanded by Master Sergeant Dick Warren, was inserted into an LZ on the border, its objective being an NVA concentration area used as a base for attacks into South Vietnam. Comprising a large expanse of flat terrain, it was covered in elephant grass growing to head height through which passage for a team was difficult without leaving tracks. The enemy in the area were aware that an insertion had taken place and the team was forced repeatedly during the next three days to take evasive action to avoid meeting patrols in search for it.

On the fourth day, an encounter took place during which the team killed several enemy before making its escape, pursued by NVA troops. Leading his team to the top of a high hill, Warren made radio contact with an FAC as the enemy surrounded the feature and set fire to the grass in an attempt to flush the team from cover. At that point, help arrived in the form of F-105 Thunderchief fighter-bombers which proceeded to strafe and bomb the NVA as the team was extracted by a Kingbee. On reaching Kham Duc, Warren returned to the target area in an FAC aircraft to assist in directing air strikes against a bridge and various buildings, secondary explosions indicating that these had contained munitions.

After these two missions, it became standard practice for FACs, identified by the radio callsign COVEY, of the USAF's 20th Tactical Air Support Squadron to provide cover on a daily basis for SOG teams. They were accompanied by a member of SOG whose role was not only to assist in searching for targets and selecting LZs for insertions and extractions, but also to remain in radio contact with teams so as to respond immediately to requests for assistance.

On 11 December 1965, the USAF carried out its first bombing raid into Laos when 24 B-52 Stratofortress heavy bombers attacked the area reconnoitred by Reconnaissance Team IOWA. By that time SHINING BRASS had turned its attention farther south to the second area in which SOG was permitted to operate in Laos, that bordering the Central Highlands of South Vietnam. Operations were launched from an airfield at Dak

To to reconnoitre NVA camps and trails in the area of Highway 110. The first two teams, KANSAS and IDAHO, both encountered enemy forces, the latter having one Nung killed and one American wounded.

By the end of December, SHINING BRASS had mounted eight operations, with six teams returning after locating major NVA bases, supply routes and dumps. The information they brought back enabled an accurate picture to be assembled of the NVA's logistics operation in Laos. The Ho Chi Minh Trail comprised a network of major roads designed for use by convoys of Soviet-supplied trucks. Heavily camouflaged, these travelled at night in groups of up to 100 vehicles when the sky was overcast and rendered surveillance and attack from the air virtually impossible. Branching off from the main routes were numerous trails used by NVA porters carrying loads on their backs or on specially designed heavy duty bicycles fitted with balloon tyres. All roads and trails were camouflaged by a lattice of branches and twisted their way through gaps in trees, allowing as many of them as possible to be retained. NVA camps, way stations and transport parks were sited at intervals along the major routes and it was these that SOG reconnaissance teams came across as they probed their way slowly and carefully through the thick jungle.

Such was the previous lack of knowledge among the US intelligence community in Saigon that SOG reconnaissance reports initially were disbelieved. On one occasion, a report of tracked vehicles was received with derision, only to be confirmed a few days later by photographs taken by an airborne FAC. It was not long, however, before SOG intelligence was recognised as being sound and utterly reliable.

In early 1966, the restrictions on SOG in Laos were relaxed by Ambassador Sullivan who agreed to operations being launched along the entire 200-mile length of the Laotian border and up to a depth of twenty miles. In addition, he gave authorisation for insertions by helicopter. As a result, the number of SOG reconnaissance teams was increased from five to twenty. In order to man them, SOG turned to the Montagnards of the Central Highlands. Colonel 'Bull' Simons gave responsibility for recruiting from various tribes, including the Rhade, Jarai, Sedang and Bru, to Major Sully Fontaine who was adept at the task.

Following the lifting of restrictions, Colonel Donald Blackburn produced a three-phase programme for SOG: first, reconnaissance to locate and confirm targets such as NVA bases, concentration areas, depots, munitions and supply routes; second, insertion of strike teams, supported by air power, to exploit such targets; and third, organisation of local indigenous forces for harassment operations along the Ho Chi Minh Trail.

By July, SHINING BRASS had carried out 38 reconnaissance missions inside Laos. At that point, it deployed some teams to a Special Forces base at Khe Sanh for operations inside the DMZ and to the west of it inside Laos along Highway 9, a disused road leading across the border and 30 miles along a valley to Tchepone which was a major NVA terminus.

During the weeks after operations started from Khe Sanh, SOG suffered its first major losses. The first involved an H-34 Kingbee of SOG'S VNAF 219th Helicopter Squadron. The aircraft had originally been designed for naval use and thus was equipped with a tail which could be folded for parking below decks on an aircraft carrier. The Kingbee was flying Reconnaissance Team NEVADA to Kontum when its tail became unfastened and swung round into the main fuselage, causing the aircraft to disintegrate in mid-air and disgorge all aboard to their deaths below. All the bodies were subsequently recovered except for that of the team's One-Zero, Master Sergeant Ralph Reno.

Three weeks later another team, commanded by Sergeant Major Harry D. Whalen, was inserted to the west of Khe Sanh. By the third day of the operation, it was running short of water and halted near a river. Covered by the rest, the team's One-One, Sergeant First Class Delmer Laws and two Nungs went forward to fill their waterbottles. As they did so, enemy troops lying in ambush opened fire. The team dived into the river and headed downstream, except for Sergeant Major Whalen who, prevented by heavy enemy fire from following them, moved upstream. Spotting an overhang in the river bank, he dived underneath it and hid. Seconds later, NVA troops waded to and fro past him, searching the river and firing bursts into the water.

Whalen escaped being hit but shortly afterwards had to listen to screams of agony as captured members of his team were tortured only yards from him. The NVA were aware that one member of the team had escaped and were attempting to goad him into making a rescue attempt which, given the large numbers of enemy present, would have been suicidal. Eventually, they tired of their efforts and, having shot their prisoners and stripped Sergeant First Class Laws and the team's radio operator, Specialist 4 Donald Sain, of their weapons, radio, maps and signal codes, left the area. It was not until long after nightfall, however, that Whalen was able to leave his hiding place and move upriver to a location from which he was able to call for assistance on his personal ground-to-air radio/beacon. He was subsequently extracted by helicopter.

Two days later, an SOG team led by Major Gerald Killburn and Master Sergeant Billy Waugh was inserted to retrieve the bodies. That of Sergeant Laws was never located while the corpse of Specialist 4 Sain was found booby-trapped with a grenade which had to be disarmed before the body could be recovered

Such was the high-level security surrounding SOG and its operations that the circumstances and locations of the deaths of those killed in action could never be revealed to their families. Similar precautions governed the distribution of the most valuable intelligence gleaned by SOG: a fictitious Laotian guerrilla group was generally credited as the source.

Late in 1966, SOG was ordered to provide reconnaissance support for the 3rd US Marine Amphibious Force which had been involved in operations against two NVA divisions, pushing them northward to the DMZ. The marines had taken up positions just south of the DMZ at Con Thien, on a feature of high ground nicknamed the Rockpile. There they were subjected to constant attacks and artillery bombardments by the two enemy divisions whose exact positions were unknown.

The first SOG operations in support of the marines around Khe Sanh and in the DMZ began in the autumn, the teams being equipped with 'wiretap' equipment for monitoring conversations on enemy telephone lines along roads and trails. Such tasks were extremely hazardous as the presence of such lines normally indicated the presence of a regiment or division; moreover, the NVA possessed electronic monitoring equipment which would eventually detect the existence of a tap. The initial missions proved unsuccessful, with the first three teams being deployed for less than three days due to large numbers of enemy in their areas. On 28 September, a team was almost overrun and suffered the loss of an American NCO, Staff Sergeant Danny Taylor, and two Nungs.

On 3 October, Reconnaissance Team COLORADO, commanded by Sergeant Ted Braden, was inserted near Khe Sanh, not far north of the Ben Hai River at the western end of the DMZ. Meanwhile a second team, ARIZONA, was also inserted near Khe Sanh. No sooner had its helicopter lifted off, however, than the team came under heavy fire from all sides; it had landed in the middle of a major NVA unit position. Attempts to extract it failed due to the volume of fire; of the seven helicopters which attempted to land, six were hit. Eventually the team's One-Zero, Master Sergeant Ray Echeverria, announced over the radio that the situation was hopeless and gave instructions that no further attempts at extraction should be made; instead, an air strike was to be put in immediately on the team's position. Minutes later, A-1 Skyraider fighter-bombers blasted the entire area with bombs.

Incredibly, some members of the team did survive the bombing. Three days later one of its Montagnards was extracted and told how he and the team's signaller, Sergeant Eddie Williams, had escaped after Master Sergeant Echeverria and his One-One, Sergeant Jim Jones, had been killed. Williams had been wounded in the thigh and eventually the two men had hidden in cave. Too weak to go on, Williams had told the Montagnard to fetch help. The latter set off but minutes later heard gunfire and the sounds of grenades exploding from the direction of the cave, followed by silence. It was later discovered from an NVA prisoner that Williams had been captured and, after being led through villages in the area until he collapsed, was executed.

Reconnaissance Team COLORADO, meanwhile, had achieved considerable success. In addition to locating a number of NVA base camps, it had managed to place a wiretap undetected and had returned with several cassettes of recorded conversations.

During 1966, the North Vietnamese denied vehemently that NVA forces were in South Vietnam. They were proved to be lying by Reconnaissance Team IOWA which was deployed on a road-watch operation on Highway 110E where it observed large numbers of NVA troops and porters moving past. Crawling forward to a position closer to the road, the One-Zero, Master Sergeant Dick Meadows, proceeded to film them with an 8mm cine camera as well as photographing them. After the team's extraction, the films were flown to Washington where they were shown in secret to members of Congress who had hitherto accepted North Vietnam's denials.

IN SEPTEMBER 1966, SOG was assigned an additional role. Earlier in the year, consideration had been given to the problem of locating and rescuing downed aircrew after SAF search-and-rescue (SAR) missions had failed to recover them. Colonel Harry Aderholt, tasked by the commander of the USAF's Pacific Air Force to come up with a solution, felt that this was a role for SOG, an opinion shared by the Chief of MACV-SOG, Colonel John Singlaub, who had succeeded Colonel Donald Blackburn in April. A former member of the OSS during the Second World War, he had served in France in 1944 as the commander of a JEDBURGH team before being transferred to Asia. He had been seconded twice to the CIA, conducting operations in Manchuria and then in Korea with JACK. Thereafter he had served on the G-3 (Operations) staff of the 101st Airborne Division.

On 16 September 1966, a new section of SOG, OPS-80, with Aderholt as its head, was formed. Its role was to locate US personnel reported as missing in action (MIA), identify North Vietnamese prisoner-of-war (PoW) camps, and effect rescues either through direct action or through the bribery and suborning of communist officials. Because it would be in contact with several organisations outside SOG, OPS-80 adopted the cover name of the MACV Joint Personnel Recovery Centre (JPRC). Its operations were given the codename of BRIGHT LIGHT.

The first took place during the following month, after the shooting down of an A-1 Skyraider on the late afternoon of 12 October. The pilot, US Navy Lieutenant Dean Woods, had succeeded in baling out, landing on a ridge in thick jungle between Hanoi and Vinh to the south. From his position, he could see that he was in an area between two highways leading from the port of Haiphong to the Mu Gia Pass and the Ho Chi Minh Trail.

Woods had travelled as far and as fast as he could from his parachute which was firmly caught up in a tree and thus a clear indicator to any enemy searching for him. The approach of nightfall, however, precluded any rescue attempt and it was not until next day that he switched on his emergency radio/beacon to call for extraction. Before long, he had been located by a US Navy SH-3C Sea King SAR helicopter escorted by A-1 Skyraiders and F-4 Phantoms. Enemy forces were seen approaching and these were engaged by the Skyraiders while the Sea King hovered above Woods and attempted to winch down an extraction harness through the jungle canopy high above him. Unfortunately, it kept becoming tangled in branches and foliage and eventually the aircraft was forced to fly off to its parent vessel offshore to refuel. There was insufficient daylight left for the plane to return and guide Woods to an area where it could land, and a second rescue effort had to be postponed until the following day.

Bad weather conditions, however, prevented any further attempt being made by the Navy. Moreover, the NVA had been observed moving anti-aircraft artillery into the area, ready to ambush the helicopter when it made an expected appearance. The task was therefore handed to SOG which allocated it to Reconnaissance Team IOWA and its One-Zero Dick Meadows, by then commissioned and promoted to the rank of captain. On the night of 14 October, the thirteen-strong team was flown aboard the aircraft carrier USS *Intrepid* but it was not until the morning of 16 October that the weather cleared sufficiently for it to be deployed ashore by helicopter. Just before dawn, two Sea Kings lifted off from *Intrepid* and headed for the North Vietnamese coast. One carried IOWA while the other was a decoy aircraft whose role would be to draw the enemy's attention by making sham landings.

As expected, the two aircraft came under heavy anti-aircraft fire as they neared the shore, heading for the ridge-line where NVA troops could be seen approaching Lieutenant Woods's position. Thanks to the skill of the Navy pilots, however, both escaped unscathed and the second Sea King succeeded in inserting Meadows and his men some 800 yards from Woods's position. Moving swiftly, IOWA headed for the ridge-line and was nearing it when Meadows was informed by radio that Woods had been captured.

At that juncture, the team came upon a large trail and Meadows decided to set up a quick ambush to catch a prisoner. Shortly afterwards, an NVA officer and three soldiers, walked into the area and were challenged by Meadows who emerged from cover. All four reacted swiftly, raising their weapons, but Meadows was faster and shot them all dead. Having searched the bodies, the team left the area and was duly extracted by one of the Sea Kings. On the return journey to USS *Intrepid*, however, the aircraft came under enemy fire and received a large number of hits, eventually being forced to ditch close to a US warship.

According to author John Plaster, Lieutenant Dean Woods spent the next six years in captivity in North Vietnam. After the war, he met Dick Meadows who presented him with a Tokarev pistol taken from the body of the NVA officer.

During October, SOG mounted a second but much larger BRIGHT LIGHT operation. Information had been received some weeks earlier from a defector from the Viet Cong, the popular name for the Viet Nam Cong San, the guerrilla organisation formed in 1960 as the military arm of the communist National Liberation Front in South Vietnam. Its nucleus comprised former members of the Viet Minh subsequently reinforced by some 2,000 NVA who had infiltrated from the north during the previous year. Questioning of the defector had indicated that the pilot of a USAF C-123 shot down in June of the previous year, Captain Carl E. Jackson, was being held prisoner at a PoW camp in the Mekong Delta, at a location approximately 90 miles north of the southernmost tip of South Vietnam.

Codenamed CRIMSON TIDE, the operation was to be carried out by a company-sized SOG force of three platoons of Nungs commanded by Special Forces NCOs, all under the command of Captain Frank Jaks. The latter was another of those who had found their way into the US Special Forces in the 1950s. During the Second World War, he had been a member of the resistance in Czechoslovakia but had left his country in 1948, following its take-over by the communists, and had emigrated to the United States.

On 18 October, Jak's force was flown from the SOG base at Kontum to Soc Trang where it transferred to twelve UH-1 helicopters which would insert it into the target area. Jaks himself was not happy with the operation: not only was it six weeks since the defector had made his appearance but there had been no proper briefing for Jaks who merely had been shown a map of the area of the PoW camp. Moreover, he had been informed that the camp itself was lightly guarded and that the mission should take no more than twenty minutes or so. With mounting unease, he ordered his men to carry double their normal loads of ammunition.

Twenty minutes after lifting off from Soc Trang, the leading four helicopters, carrying a platoon commanded by Sergeant First Class Charlie Vessels, approached their LZ but, finding it too small for all twelve helicopters, began to land the platoon on the other side of a canal on the edge of the PoW camp. At the same time, Captain Jaks and the other two platoons were landed on the planned LZ. Suddenly, the entire force came under very heavy fire. The aircraft carrying a squad of Vessels's Nungs and Sergeant First Class Fred Lewis was hit by heavy machine-gun fire, with the latter falling mortally wounded from the aircraft which crashed seconds later. Sergeant Vessels and the rest of the platoon were meanwhile pinned down, as were Captain Jaks and the other two platoons. The latter called for air support but instead of the highly effective propeller-driven A-1 Skyraiders, F-100 Super Sabres arrived overhead. Their bombing, hindered by low cloud, was inaccurate and caused a number of casualties among Jaks's force. It was not until that evening and the approach of dusk that Skyraiders appeared but by then it was too late.

The battle continued throughout the night with Jaks and his men repelling a number of attacks. It was not until the following morning that they managed to fight their way across the canal to the third platoon. There they found the bodies of Sergeant Lewis and his Nungs and further away, in a small cemetery, those of Sergeant Vessels and the remainder of his men who were either dead or seriously wounded.

It was later discovered that the CRIMSON TIDE company had encountered two VC battalions numbering 1,000 men and equipped with mortars and heavy machine-guns. Captain Jaks's premonition of trouble had been well justified.

It was not long, however, before BRIGHT LIGHT scored its first success. A week after CRIMSON TIDE, an F-105 Thunderchief was shot down over North Vietnam and its pilot was observed baling out by an SOG observer, Major Frank Sova, who was airborne with a COVEY FAC over Laos at the time.

The task of recovering the pilot went to SOG's JPRC which in turn allocated it to Captain Frank Saks, who realised that the distance to the target area was some 70 miles, beyond the Ho Chi Minh Trail and the range of SOG's UH-1 helicopters. After due consideration by the aircrews, the problem was resolved by loading an extra aircraft with drums of fuel and a hand pump. As dusk approached, Saks and his team lifted off from Dak To and headed for the downed pilot's location. Darkness was approaching as the planes made their final descent but NVA forces were spotted nearing his position. Guided in by flares, the aircraft landed and the pilot leapt aboard as enemy troops appeared only 100 yards away. The return flight, including a landing in a Laotian field to refuel the aircraft, was uneventful, and thus SOG celebrated not only its first successful BRIGHT LIGHT operation but also the first ever recovery of a downed pilot at night.

Many BRIGHT LIGHT recoveries were carried out throughout the rest of the war. Regarded as the most hazardous of all SOG operations, they were conducted in areas where large numbers of enemy and anti-aircraft defences were usually present, the latter including not only guns and surface-to-air missiles (SAM) but on occasions MiG-21 fighters. The latter posed a potent threat and on at least one occasion caused a BRIGHT LIGHT mission to be aborted. Moreover, the enemy, aware that the shooting down of an aircraft would inevitably result in the appearance of an SAR team, would set an ambush for it, sometimes using a captured radio/beacon or air marker panel to draw the rescue force into the trap. In some instances, enemy posed as the downed aircrew; a soldier, dressed in the captured pilot's flying suit and helmet, would fire flares to guide in a rescue helicopter which was engaged with an anti-armour weapon as it made its final approach. On other occasions, pilots were forced at gunpoint to lure in the aircraft but managed to warn the rescue team in time for the attempt to be abandoned; history does not relate what happened to them afterwards.

SINCE APRIL 1964, SOG had also been inserting teams of agents into North Vietnam in an operation codenamed TIMBERWORK. With one exception, such missions were carried out by the Air Studies Group, teams being dropped by the C-123 transports of First Flight. From April to December of that year a total of twelve teams had been dropped. Of those, five (ATTILA, LOTUS, SCORPION, BUFFALO and BOONE) were believed to have been captured and one, EAGLE, to be under enemy control. Another, CENTAUR, had been wiped out on 14 November when its C-123 transport crashed on to Monkey Mountain near Da Nang.

During 1965, fewer teams were introduced. Nine men of HORSE were dropped in May to reinforce EASY. The latter had been inserted in August 1963 and then been reinforced in July 1964 with the six-strong PISCES. A further nine men of DOG were dropped as reinforcements for EASY in

September. Two months later, in November, two more teams were also inserted. An eight-strong VERSE was dropped as reinforcements for TOUR-BILLON, and to provide instruction in road-watch techniques, two of these being killed in the drop. Ten men of ROMEO were inserted by helicopter later in the month.

There were five insertions in 1966, the first, in early March, being KERN, in which one of its nine members was killed in the drop. This was followed in June by the fifteen-strong HECTOR which was inserted by helicopter; a further eleven men, in the form of HECTOR-BRAVO, were dropped as reinforcements for HECTOR in September but the two teams failed to link up. In early October, eight men of SAMSON were inserted by helicopter into Laos and on 24 December two men, TOURBILLON-BRAVO, were dropped as reinforcements for TOURBILLON, taking in with them wiretap equipment and electronic movement sensors.

Five more teams and a single agent were despatched into North Vietnam during 1967. On 26 January, eleven men of HADLEY were inserted by helicopter but were believed to have been captured shortly afterwards. On 22 April, HANSEN, seventeen-strong, was also inserted but requested extraction shortly afterwards due to the presence of enemy in the area of the LZ. On 21 August, two men were dropped as rein-forcements for REMUS, which had been in the field since April 1962, and on 13 September a single agent was landed from the sea by the Mar-itime Operations Group's NAD. Eight days later, the seven men of RED DRAGON were dropped but became separated during the infiltration stage of their mission. After making radio contact with the team, there were suspicions that it was operating under North Vietnamese control.

Although SOG had a high success rate for insertions, with only a few individuals being killed or injured during parachute drops, there was much doubt within the organisation as to whether agent teams were trustworthy. In a conversation with the author of this book, John Plaster, who served three tours with SOG, confirmed that it was eventually assumed that those teams not captured were working under control of the North Vietnamese. Even when it was known that a team had been cap-tured, however, radio contact was maintained as part of SOG's decep-tion operations up until 1969.

In December 1966, SOG's Air Studies Group and BRIGHT LIGHT capability was enhanced with the arrival of the USAF's 90th Special

Operations Squadron (SOS), hitherto based on Taiwan at Ching Chuan Kong Air Force Base. This unit was equipped with the MC-130 Black-bird, a special operations variant of the C-130 Hercules equipped with highly sophisticated electronic countermeasures (ECM), computerised navigational systems and Forward-Looking-Infra-Red (FLIR) enabling it to fly nap-of-the-earth and avoid enemy radars and anti-aircraft defences. Assigned solely to SOG, the 90th SOS's MC-130s were also fitted with the Fulton STAR Recovery System designed to permit the aerial retrieval of downed aircrew from the ground.

The system comprised a hydraulically operated yoke whose two 20-foot-long prongs, when not in use, were folded back along either side of the aircraft's nose. Prior to an extraction, a canister containing a balloon with 1,500-foot-long cable, two cylinders of helium gas and a special combination suit/harness, was dropped from the aircraft. Having donned the suit and attached himself to the cable, the individual on the ground would inflate the balloon before releasing it. The MC-130, with its yoke swung forward in a V-shape, would then fly in and snag the cable, snatch-ing the man off the ground, and winching him up to the open tailgate of the aircraft. The system was proven, having been used by the CIA during several operations in other parts of the world, including the Arctic. But it was only suitable for covert extractions in areas where there were no enemy nearby, and in North Vietnam and Laos that was never the case. Although a number of such rescues of pilots were attempted by the 90th SOS Blackbirds, none were successful as on each occasion, enemy troops, guided to the pilot's location by the balloon, arrived before he could be snatched to safety.

In March 1967, SHINING BRASS was redesignated PRAIRIE FIRE as it had been recognised by then that the original codename had become compromised. In January of that year the US commander-in-chief in Vietnam, General William Westmoreland, had proposed that the oper-ation should be expanded to include long-range deep penetration oper-ations inside Laos. The US ambassador, Henry Cabot Lodge, had agreed to assess the political implications but was replaced by Ellsworth Bunker before doing so. The proposal was taken no further and was never put into effect.

By mid-1967, the NVA had adopted effective countermeasures against PRAIRIE FIRE reconnaissance teams in Laos which found themselves encountering enemy defences in considerable depth. Moreover, it had taken to reconnoitring likely areas for LZs, keeping them under surveillance from observation posts (OPs) positioned on high ground and in trees. In many instances, 12.7mm heavy machine-guns were sited to cover more than one LZ. In the event of a helicopter approaching, OPs communicated with nearby camps by telephone, runners or banging a gong to sound the alarm. The NVA also positioned watchers on trails to discover where they had been crossed. Every evening, areas on either side of roads being used by convoys were swept by troops to clear them of any ambushes.

At the same time, hill tribesmen were employed to track PRAIRIE FIRE teams while radio direction-finding (DF) equipment was used to locate their positions. Any encounter with a team resulted in a swift reaction with large numbers of troops being deployed to sweep the area and to man blocking positions along all possible escape routes. Meanwhile, heavy machine-guns would be resited swiftly to cover likely extraction LZs.

In mid-July 1967 came evidence that the NVA was also employing specialist troops in Laos to hunt down and destroy PRAIRIE FIRE missions. A team, commanded by Master Sergeant Sam Almendariz, was reconnoitring near Highway 922, approximately 60 miles west of Hué, when it was ambushed by NVA troops who leaped from cover and closed with its three Americans. Almendariz was shot dead, as was his One-One, Master Sergeant Robert Sullivan, whose CAR-15 carbine was wrestled from him by an enemy soldier who then opened fire on the team's One-Two, Sergeant First Class Harry Brown. The latter, however, succeeded in breaking away and escaping with the team's five Nungs to a point where he was able to radio for assistance and extraction. A Kingbee of SOG's VNAF 219th Helicopter Squadron, carrying three members of SOG, Captain Oliver Brin, Sergeant Major Billy Waugh and Master Sergeant Charles Minnicks, responded but was forced to withdraw due to enemy fire. After refuelling at Khe Sanh, however, the aircraft returned with just the pilot, a fearless Vietnamese known only as 'Cowboy', and Master Sergeant Minnicks aboard. Under fire, Cowboy lowered his aircraft into the seemingly impossible LZ, hovering just above the ground as Minnicks dragged Sergeant Brown and his Nungs aboard the plane. Although hit in the neck by a bullet, Cowboy flew the aircraft out of the area and back to Khe Sanh.

The troops who had ambushed Almendariz and his team were former members of the NVA's 305th Airborne Brigade, which had been formed in 1965 but was disbanded at Son Tay in North on 19 March 1967. On that same day the NVA created from it a new special operations formation, the 305th Sapper Division.

The members of the 305th were the NVA's elite troops. Soviet-trained, they were better equipped than the rest of North Vietnam's forces and were politically the most reliable. Following the brigade's disbandment, half of its former members became sappers, trained to infiltrate targets inside South Vietnam and attack them with explosive charges. The other half formed a specialist counter-reconnaissance regiment comprising three battalions, trained to track down and eliminate SOG teams along the same lines as the Viet Minh's 421st Intelligence Battalion which had operated in a similar fashion against the French GCMA and its Montagnard maquis during the First Indochina War. Each battalion was allocated its own area of operations, the first active to the west of Khe Sanh and Tchepone while the second was deployed between the Ashau Valley in South Vietnam and the areas containing a number of major NVA base areas twenty miles to the west. The third battalion meanwhile covered the area of southern Laos and northern Cambodia.

Each battalion possessed its own trackers who were stationed at strategic points along the Ho Chi Minh Trail from which they could be summoned swiftly as soon as the presence of an SOG team had been detected. Some were accompanied by tracker dogs; apparently limited in number, they were based in the more important of the NVA base areas.

These counter-reconnaissance troops made life more difficult for SOG teams and on two occasions located the latter in their lying-up positions (LUPs). In both instances the raids took place at night, as the enemy infiltrated the LUP and attacked the American members of the team. On the first occasion all three were killed and after the second all were missing, subsequently declared MIA.

One team had a close encounter with counter-reconnaissance troops which lasted three days. Reconnaissance Team MAINE, commanded by Staff Sergeant David Baker, was reconnoitring within an NVA base area when it realised that it was being tracked. Despite taking evasive action such as doubling back and sideslipping, Baker and his men failed to shake off the enemy trackers who were eventually joined by a counter-reconnaissance company, carrying out a sweep of the area which MAINE successfully dodged. On the following day the enemy repeated the process but once again the team escaped detection. After a while, however, Baker realised that the enemy were attempting to drive him and his men eastward to a point where they would either be trapped against the foot of a steep ridge or be forced into open ground.

At dawn on the third day, the enemy continued to push eastward as MAINE tried unsuccessfully to worm its way through the counter-reconnaissance company, whose two leading platoons were deployed in the form of a 'V' with the third platoon following up behind in reserve, ready to deploy in the event of the SOG team breaking through.

Rapidly considering the three courses open to him – be trapped against the foot of the ridge, be pushed out into the open or attack – Staff Sergeant Baker opted for action. During the late morning he spotted a suitable site for a linear ambush on the edge of a wood-line covering an open expanse which the enemy would have to cross. Taking up positions, the team awaited the appearance of the enemy. The latter, however, advanced to the far side of the clearing, just out of sight of the team, with one platoon moving along it almost up to MAINE's position. Shortly afterwards, to the amazement of Baker and his men, nine enemy appeared and sat down some ten feet away from the ambush position and began eating their midday meal. As they watched, the members of the team realised that the group in front of them was none other than the command element of the counter-reconnaissance company, consisting of the commander, his three platoon commanders and two Chinese advisers who were officers of the People's Liberation Army (PLA).

Baker and his men continued to watch the nine men for some 40 minutes until the faint sound of one of the team's five Montagnards quietly cocking his .45 pistol alerted the group to the team's presence. As two of them reached for their weapons, MAINE opened fire, killing all nine before taking to their heels under a murderous hail of fire. Fortunately, the deaths of all their officers and the two PLA advisers caused such confusion in the enemy ranks that MAINE was able to move sufficiently far to be extracted an hour later.

A NUMBER OF CHANGES HAD taken place in SOG from 1966 onward following the arrival of Colonel John Singlaub. Its strength was increased to 2,500 American personnel and over 7,000 Vietnamese and indigenous troops. Special mobile strike companies, known as 'Hatchet Forces' and normally comprising up to four Special Forces personnel and 120 indigenous soldiers, were formed for offensive tasks.

One major change affected the organisation of the Ground Studies Group. Until 1966, SOG operations had been coordinated and controlled from Command and Control at Da Nang with teams being launched from four FOBs at Kontum, Khe Sanh, Da Nang and Phu Bai. Singlaub rearranged the Group into three elements: Command and Control North (CCN) at Da Nang, covering North Vietnam and Laos; Command and Control Central (CCC) at Kontum, allotted the tri-border region of South Vietnam, Laos and Cambodia; and Command and Control South (CCS) at Ban Me Thuot, responsible for operations in Cambodia.

The North Vietnamese had been functioning from sanctuaries inside so-called neutral Cambodia since the early 1960s when they had established the 'Sihanouk Trail', a network of roads and trails running north and east from the Cambodian port of Sihanoukville (later Kompong Som) to South Vietnam. In due course it featured, like the Ho Chi Minh Trail, way stations, rest areas and supply dumps. The Cambodians, meanwhile, were supplying over 150,000 tons of rice annually to the North Vietnamese and were permitting shipments of Chinese-supplied arms through Sihanoukville. In 1965, after the severing of diplomatic relations with the United States by the Cambodian premier, Prince Norodom Sihanouk, North Vietnam had stepped up its incursions into South Vietnam from its sanctuaries over the border in Cambodia. By 1966, although there was no definite proof, MACV estimated that 1,000 tons of Chinese arms had made their way through Sihanoukville to NVA supply dumps in Cambodia.

Sihanouk's relations with Hanoi had fluctuated somewhat and from 1963 onward there had been a number of clashes between units of the Viet Cong and Cambodian, several hundred Cambodians being killed or wounded. In 1966, he admitted publicly that the NVA and Viet Cong had established bases along the border. Until then the Johnson administration, keen to woo the Cambodian leader away from the communist camp, had avoided confronting him over the issue, choosing instead to

ignore the increasing evidence that the NVA and Viet Cong were operating from inside Cambodia. In early 1967, however, after requests from
General William Westmoreland and the Commander-in-Chief Pacific,
permission was finally given for SOG to conduct reconnaissance operations, codenamed DANIEL BOONE, inside Cambodia.

There were, however, severe limitations imposed by the State Department. The operation had to be totally deniable: air support for reconnaissance teams in trouble would be restricted to helicopter gunships,
these only being permitted to open fire in self-defence or to assist a team
in breaking contact; combat dress was to be plain jungle-green with all
weapons and equipment being of foreign manufacture and untraceable;
teams would be restricted strictly to intelligence gathering and were
permitted to engage the enemy only in self-defence; and prisoners could
be taken but their numbers were to be limited to two or three at a time.

The area of Cambodia most heavily occupied by the North Vietnamese
was the far north-east of the country, the tri-border region formed by
the northernmost part of Ratanakiri Province which protrudes between
southern Laos and South Vietnam. In the north-east, opposite the South
Vietnamese city of Pleiku, in the area of Highway 19, lay a 50-mile-long
area known as the Wasteland. Totally lacking in sources of water, it was
a barren wilderness where US forces were unable to operate but through
which the NVA and Viet Cong passed when infiltrating southward. In
the south-east, between the two capitals of Saigon and Phnom Penh,
lies an area known as the Parrot's Beak, to the north of which the border
between Cambodia and South Vietnam, unmarked in many areas and
mostly poorly defined, runs through areas of thick jungle. Heading north-
east around an area dubbed the 'Dog's Face', it curves ten miles back
into Vietnam in an area called the 'Fish Hook' before resuming its north-
eastern course. To the south of the Parrot's Beak the border runs westward across the Mekong River which descends through Cambodia from
the north to Phnom Penh, where it swings south-east through Vietnam
to the Mekong Delta. Large NVA and Viet Cong sanctuaries were situated in the border region in the areas of the Mekong, the Parrot's Beak
and Fish Hook, while smaller bases were located along the border in
the north-east, just inside Cambodia and Laos.

Initial DANIEL BOONE operations were concentrated on the thick jungle
in the far north-east of Cambodia which adjoined the Central Highlands

of South Vietnam. The first mission proved uneventful but the second, launched on 15 June 1967, was observed by the NVA while being inserted by a Kingbee on a ridge only 100 yards over the Vietnamese border into Laos. The team, commanded by Sergeant First Class Lowell Stevens, and comprising his One-One, Sergeant Roland Nuqui and four Nungs, went to ground as enemy troops swarmed into the area. Establishing radio contact with a COVEY FAC accompanied by an SOG observer, Stevens requested immediate extraction. Unfortunately, the observer, an inexperienced SOG officer, hesitated for several minutes, asking for further details before recalling the Kingbee and summoning four gunships to the LZ. As the Kingbee, carrying another SOG NCO, Master Sergeant Ben Snowden, hovered over the steeply sloping LZ, it was subjected to a hail of fire from an enemy machine-gun which killed Snowden and badly damaged the aircraft which nevertheless succeeded in lifting off and flying back to Dak To where it crash-landed.

A second Kingbee appeared shortly afterwards and touched down after a series of passes over the LZ, Stevens and his team scrambling aboard immediately. No sooner had it lifted off, however, than the NVA machine-gun opened fire again, shooting off the tail rotor and causing the aircraft to go into a wild spin before crashing on its side. Amazingly, all six members of the team and the three aircrew survived, only the helicopter's door gunner being seriously wounded. Pulling the others from the wreckage, Stevens and Nuqui led the way as the group crawled under fire into the nearby jungle. Stevens's call for air support was soon answered by an A-1 Skyraider which dropped napalm on the machine-gun position but was itself shot down. Almost immediately a third Kingbee appeared, supported by gunships which laid down very heavy suppressive fire, and extracted the team.

During the following months, DANIEL BOONE teams located a large number of NVA roads, trails, base camps and supply dumps, enabling a picture to be compiled of the North Vietnamese military infrastructure in the Cambodian border regions. One particularly heavily occupied area in the south-eastern border region of Cambodia was the Fish Hook where the headquarters of the Viet Cong, the Central Office of South Vietnam (COSVN), was reportedly located. In early 1967, a combined US/ARVN operation, codenamed JUNCTION CITY, had been mounted in the South Vietnamese province of Tay Ninh near the

Cambodian border. Involving 22 US and four South Vietnamese battalions, its aim had been the capture of COSVN and the location and destruction of Viet Cong bases in the area. While the operation had resulted in over 2,700 enemy killed and quantities of arms, food and documents captured, a large number of Viet Cong and COSVN had escaped into Cambodia.

The autumn of 1967 found SOG concentrating its teams on Cambodia's far north-eastern border region. To the east of the border, five miles inside South Vietnam, lay Dak To where US forces were heavily engaged in one of three diversionary battles staged by the North Vietnamese, the other two being at Song Be and Loc Ninh. A number of DANIEL BOONE teams were inserted over the border to discover whether the NVA was reinforcing and to locate a reported road which was a major enemy supply route. A team under Sergeant First Class Lowell Stevens located the road on the third day of its mission and that night observed from a nearby bamboo thicket as NVA troops cleared trees from the path of a convoy of Soviet-manufactured trucks carrying loads of rice and ammunition towards the enemy lines near Dak To. Six hours later they returned, carrying the bodies of numerous enemy dead. As Stevens and his men watched, NVA troops reappeared just before dawn on the next day and replaced the trees, camouflaging the road once again. Having photographed the road, the team was about to reconnoitre a trail when it encountered four NVA soldiers moving in advance of a long column of troops. Reacting swiftly, Sergeant s Stevens shot all four as the team took evasive action and withdrew before the enemy could react.

Inevitably, however, there were casualties, the first when an SOG team commander, Sergeant First Class Charlie White, fell from an extraction rig while he and his team were being winched out of thick jungle under fire in north-east Cambodia. A BRIGHT LIGHT team was dropped on the following day but found no trace of him. A few months later Reconnaissance Team HAMMER, comprising two Americans and four Nungs commanded by First Lieutenant Harry Roske, set off to reconnoitre the Fish Hook area to locate the elusive COSVN. Inserted not long before dusk, the team came across three NVA soldiers and Kroske was shot dead while attempting to take one of them prisoner. The four Nung team members escaped and throughout that night the team's One-One, Specialist 4 Bryan Stockdale, found himself evading a large force of

NVA troops who at one point set fire to a large expanse of head-high grass in an attempt to flush him out.

Two hours before dawn, Stockdale established radio contact with an FAC directing an air strike over South Vietnam who relayed his request for assistance to the SOG base 80 miles away at Ban Me Thuot. The response from the 'Green Hornets' of the 20th SOS was immediate: a Huey UH-1F troop carrier, escorted by six UH-1P gunships, lifted off before dawn and made for Stockdale's location. They arrived over his position just as an NVA platoon, whose two trackers he had just killed, was preparing to attack and overrun his position. Such was the strength of the enemy in the area that it took three hours of successive attacks by the gunships before he could be extracted.

While SOG's Air Studies, Maritime Operations and Ground Studies Groups engaged the enemy in the jungle and on the sea, its Psychological Operations Group was spreading deception through the use of black propaganda and various 'dirty tricks' projects. The most secret element of SOG, it was composed of some 150 personnel, approximately half of them Vietnamese, including a small number of CIA officers. According to John Plaster, the group's budget for 1967 alone was $3.7 million.

The largest, most elaborate project involved the construction of a fake North Vietnamese fishing village on the island of Cu Lao Cham, off the South Vietnamese coast near Da Nang. Fishermen were intercepted while fishing in North Vietnamese waters by *Nasty* boats of the NAD whose crews, after blindfolding them, abducted them to the island, known to those conducting the operation as 'Paradise Island'. Here they were given a friendly welcome. Treated as honoured guests, they were informed that they were on the North Vietnamese mainland, in territory liberated and held by the Sacred Sword of the Patriotic League (SSPL). Over the following two weeks, along with copious quantities of food, they were fed hints and clues about the SSPL, its other coastal enclaves and protected villages deep in the mountains. They were also made to memorise recognition signals and how to listen for orders via radio broadcasts over transistor radios given to them with other gifts before their departure and return, blindfolded, to the North Vietnamese coast.

All such material was of course fictitious and designed for the ears of North Vietnamese counter-intelligence officers who would also listen to the broadcasts transmitted to non-existent agents by SOG's clandestine radio stations. Meanwhile, aircraft of the Air Studies Group's First Flight dropped leaflets to non-existent resistance groups.

Other Psychological Operations Group projects included POISON PEN, which entailed the mailing from overseas of letters implicating North Vietnamese officials in acts of disloyalty or espionage. In some cases, they contained microdots with instructions designed to make even the most innocent of actions look suspicious. In some instances, the typeface of a particular official's typewriter would be duplicated, with incriminating letters subsequently being produced and mailed.

Another project involved the forging of North Vietnamese documents printed with the correct inks, papers and watermarks. Complete with signatures from SOG's extensive library of those belonging to North Vietnamese and Viet Cong officials, these were introduced by the CIA into the enemy's distribution system, causing confusion and in some cases allowing manipulation.

Radio also played a major part in SOG's black propaganda operations. As mentioned earlier in this chapter, SOG possessed a number of clandestine radio stations at secret locations in South Vietnam, at least one of which purported to be in North Vietnam. Other SOG broadcasts were made by a US Navy EC-121 Warning Star aircraft flying off the coast of North Vietnam, confusing NVA radio direction-finding units who were unable to pinpoint its location. These broadcast to large numbers of transistor radios, codenamed PEANUTS, which were dropped by the Blackbirds of the 90th SOS, floated ashore from *Nasty* boats, or planted in enemy base camps or left along trails by reconnaissance teams. The PEANUT set was designed so that broadcasts from SOG's 'Radio Hanoi' station could be received loud and clear while those of the genuine Radio Hanoi and other stations were obscured by static.

A rather more deadly type of gift was inserted into the NVA logistics system under a project codenamed ELDEST SON. Chinese small arms and 82mm mortar ammunition was doctored so that it would explode in the breech of a weapon or the barrel of a mortar when fired. Reconnaissance teams carried single rounds or full AK-47 magazines for planting on the bodies of dead NVA troops, while cases of four 82mm bombs were 'discarded' at suitable locations. On one occasion a large quantity of ELDEST SON ammunition was dumped in a sampan by members of

SOG's NAD who proceeded to riddle it with small arms fire and cover it with chicken blood before setting it adrift upstream of a village known to be occupied by the Viet Cong. The latter apparently swallowed the bait whole and the ammunition disappeared into the Viet Cong supply system. Most of the doctored ammunition and bombs, however, were left in bogus caches constructed by specialist teams based at Ban Me Thuot and Da Nang.

In early June 1968, the effectiveness of ELDEST SON became evident when bodies of NVA soldiers were found lying beside their shattered AK-47 assault rifles. On another occasion, troops of the 25th US Infantry Division discovered a complete NVA mortar battery with dead soldiers sprawled around their burst mortars. Meanwhile forged North Vietnamese documents, inserted via CIA agents, were fed into the NVA and Viet Cong distribution systems, admitting that there had been problems with the quality of ammunition supplied from China but that efforts were being made to solve them. Evidence that the North Vietnamese believed the problem to be one of quality control in China came through NSA radio intercepts. SOG reinforced this by issuing press releases to US armed forces television and radio stations in South Vietnam, warning that there had been several incidents in which injuries and deaths had been caused by poor quality enemy weapons and ammunition malfunctioning.

These and other SOG psychological warfare projects served to cause considerable damage and confusion within the NVA and Viet Cong command structures. An indication of their value came in May 1968 when North Vietnamese negotiators insisted, as a pre-condition for peace negotiations to be held in Paris, that the United States terminate its psychological operations campaign forthwith.

Meanwhile, in April 1968, a re-evaluation was conducted of SOG's long-term agent programme which was not enjoying success. Most if not all teams had been captured, some undoubtedly having been turned. Evidence of this was forthcoming shortly after the capture of a NVA prisoner who revealed that a team inserted in 1962 had been operating under North Vietnamese control ever since. It was identified almost immediately as REMUS. A few weeks later, the North Vietnamese announced the capture of REMUS, wrecking an SOG plan to 'triple' it. This gave rise to suspicion that there was a North

Vietnamese 'mole' among the South Vietnamese personnel in SOG's headquarters.

In August, the Vietnamese revealed that they had captured a further three teams which had in fact also been under their control since insertion. While maintaining normal communications with the remainder, SOG plotted its revenge. One team, expecting a resupply drop by F-4 Phantoms delivering canisters containing supplies, received instead a stick of bombs which killed the North Vietnamese impersonating its members. Other resupply drops were made, their contents included radios and weapons modified to explode when operated. One drop comprised containers filled with explosives rather than supplies; on the following day aerial photographic reconnaissance of the DZ revealed vehicle tracks and large craters where the containers had exploded on being opened.

Short-term SOG agent programmes, however, appeared to have avoided North Vietnamese penetration. Among these was STRATA (Short-Term Roadwatch & Target Acquisition) which was targeted on the network of roads and trails which led through the Mu Gia and other passes leading from North Vietnam to the Ho Chi Minh Trail. Trained separately at the SOG base at Camp Long Thanh, and dressed and equipped as NVA troops, STRATA teams were launched from Nakhon Phanom in eastern Thailand and inserted up to 150 miles north of the DMZ. They reportedly achieved limited results in their primary missions of road watch and reconnaissance, being seldom able to approach sufficiently close to a road to observe traffic or identify targets for air strikes. They did, however, succeed in leaving leaflets and other psychological operations material relating to non-existent resistance groups in areas through which they passed. A total of 26 STRATA operations were carried out by fourteen teams over a period of thirteen months, each lasting no more than two weeks. Twenty-six agents out of a total of 102 were lost, all subsequently being declared MIA.

Other short-term agent teams also inserted in the guise of NVA troops were EARTH ANGELS. About a dozen teams, each of two or three former NVA personnel, were sent to reconnoitre enemy supply routes in Laos and Cambodia. Posing as NVA couriers, they mingled with NVA units travelling south. Each mission lasted approximately a week with teams being extracted at predesignated points. Like STRATA, EARTH

ANGELS apparently avoided penetration by the North Vietnamese.

At the beginning of November 1968, on the eve of the elections in the United States which resulted in President Richard Nixon assuming office in January of the following year, SOG was ordered to terminate its agent programmes in North Vietnam. It thus switched to running false networks in three operations codenamed Projects URGENCY, BORDEN and OODLES, these forming the principal elements of a major deception operation codenamed FORAE.

URGENCY involved the planting of money, messages and other incriminating 'evidence' on unwitting North Vietnamese, among them a number of the fishermen temporarily kidnapped and entertained by the 'Sacred Sword of the Patriotic League', incriminating them and strengthening the belief among the North Vietnamese that there were extensive SOG networks which had not been located and penetrated.

BORDEN meanwhile used NVA prisoners who were known to be hardline communists but who were led to believe that they had hoodwinked SOG. Fed with false information about non-existent SOG networks, they were then inserted into North Vietnam. Some were flown as members of a team to be dropped, with the BORDEN agent being the first to jump; instead of being followed by his companions, parachutes with harness strapped round blocks of ice were despatched after him, to be found hanging from trees on the following day. The NVA would expend much time and resources searching for the non-existent team. Some BORDEN agents dropped into Laos unknowingly carried electronic homers concealed in their equipment which would enable B-52 ARC LIGHT raids to be carried out on the NVA headquarters where they were being questioned after surrendering themselves.

OODLES concentrated on deceiving the North Vietnamese that a further network was at large in North Vietnam. Radio messages were transmitted and supplies dropped to fourteen non-existent teams. with BORDEN agents subsequently being inserted as reinforcements. The result was the same: North Vietnamese counter-intelligence devoted considerable time and resources to hunting down a phantom network.

Mid-1968 saw the departure of Colonel John Singlaub as Chief of MACV-SOG and his replacement by Colonel Steve Cavanaugh who had served with the 11th US Airborne Division during the Second World

War and later had commanded the 10th Special Forces Group (Airborne). Shortly after taking command, Cavanaugh began to reduce SOG missions inside South Vietnam and instead concentrated on cross-border operations into Laos and Cambodia. The exception was the Ashau Valley on the Laotian border. Extending some 25 miles north-east to south-west, and up to approximately two miles wide, it was an area of grass-land which previously had accommodated two airfields and three bases that eventually had been abandoned. By 1968 it was the terminus of some 40 trails and roads, leading from NVA bases inside Laos, and a hive of enemy activity.

As mentioned earlier in this chapter, in 1966 Colonel Singlaub's enhancements of SOG's capabilities had included the formation of 'Hatchet Forces'. Under restrictions laid down by the US ambassador in Laos, these had been limited to platoon-sized operations. In 1969, however, all such constraints had been removed and SOG was permitted to deploy up to a Hatchet Force company, comprising three Special Forces personnel and 126 indigenous troops, with authorisation from the US Commander-in-Chief Pacific in Hawaii.

By that time SOG had formed four such companies based at Kontum, Da Nang and Ban Me Thuot. The principal handicap on their deployments, however, was the limited amount of helicopter support available, each Hatchet Force operation requiring twelve aircraft devoted to its support. Moreover, immediate extraction had to be guaranteed in the event of a company encountering strong enemy opposition and thus operations could only be conducted during periods of good weather. Nevertheless, despite these restrictions, Hatchet Force operations, along with reconnaissance team missions, forced the NVA to allocate increasing manpower resources to the security and protection of the Ho Chi Minh Trail. It is estimated that by 1969 some 70,000 enemy troops were employed along the trail, about 30,000 of whom comprised three infantry divisions responsible for rear area security. Against them were ranged approximately 50 Americans plus indigenous troops of SOG.

In June 1967, a Hatchet Force operation was mounted in Laos against a target designated OSCAR EIGHT, an area in South Vietnam approximately 25 miles north-west of the Ashau Valley featuring a road junction where Highway 922 turned off from Highway 92. It was a hilly region suspected as being the location of the forward headquarters of the NVA's 559th Transportation and Support Group. USAF intelligence had discovered, too, that the area, which was heavily defended by anti-aircraft batteries, accommodated the largest NVA storage depot outside North Vietnam. Moreover, during the weeks prior to the raid there was an unprecedented volume of enemy signals traffic, giving rise to speculation that a major NVA formation headquarters was also located in the area.

The planned LZ for the operation was far from ideal but was the only one considered suitable, being located in a bowl surrounded by jungle-clad hills occupied by anti-aircraft batteries and infantry in well-emplaced bunkers. The raid began at dawn, preceded by an attack by nine B-52 Stratofortresses which dropped almost 1,000 500 lb and 750 lb bombs over the entire area. These initiated many secondary explosions and SOG's Sergeant Major Billy Waugh, who was airborne with the COVEY FAC, observed NVA troops emerging from bunkers to roll fuel barrels away from an area which was ablaze.

As soon as the bombing ceased, the Hatchet Force company, comprising four Special Forces personnel and 100 Nung irregulars, was inserted by helicopter. No sooner had it landed, however, than it was surrounded by a large force of NVA troops. Seeking cover in bomb craters on the LZ, the company fought desperately while calling for air support. A-1 Skyraiders and helicopter gunships responded but encountered heavy flak from the enemy anti-aircraft batteries which had largely escaped the bombing.

The battle lasted throughout the day and that night, the company holding off hundreds of enemy seeking to overrun its position. At dawn on the following day, air support arrived in the form of fighter-bombers which dropped cluster bombs and used their cannon in attempts to drive back the surrounding enemy. Two gunships and an H-34 Kingbee were shot down as USMC CH-46 Sea Knight helicopters arrived to extract the company. One succeeded in lifting off with a platoon but a second was hit as it ascended, crashing to the ground from a height of 100 feet. By the time the remnants of the company had been extracted, 23 Americans, comprising Special Forces personnel as well as USAF and USMC aircrew, had been lost. Of those, six were subsequently declared MIA.

One member of the company, Sergeant First Class Charles Wilklow, who had been in the shot-down Sea Knight, was captured and, seriously wounded, was left to die. Lying unconscious, he awoke next day to observe two Caucasians, later thought to be Soviet advisers, and a NVA officer watching him. On the night of the fourth day, despite his maggot-infested wounds and suffering from hypothermia, Wilklow dragged himself out of the area under cover of darkness. It was not until the following morning that the enemy noticed his disappearance and launched a search for him. Fortunately, they were unsuccessful. Using an air marker panel he found in his pocket, Wilklow had by then attracted the attention of an aircraft carrying an SOG BRIGHT LIGHT team which extracted him soon afterwards. He was the only American member of SOG ever to return from Laos after being declared MIA.

Early in 1969, a particularly bold operation, codenamed SPINDOWN, was carried out by a Hatchet Force company inside Laos in an effort to disrupt an NVA attack on a Special Forces base at Ben Het in South Vietnam, some three miles from the junction of the borders with Laos and Cambodia. The base was manned by a garrison comprising twelve Special Forces personnel and 1,500 Montagnards who had been reinforced earlier by several Special Forces Mobile Strike (MIKE) companies, a battery of 8-inch howitzers and four tanks. Facing them were two NVA regiments, the 28th and 66th, supported by artillery and a company of Soviet-supplied PT-76 tanks, who were subjecting the base to a ceaseless bombardment. The single road to the base had been cut and a large number of anti-aircraft guns were making resupply by air hazardous.

On the evening of 3 March, the NVA launched its attack which was led by ten PT-76 tanks. These soon encountered the minefields while coming under fire from the base's 8-inch howitzer battery and strikes from aircraft dropping cluster bombs. Although this initial assault was beaten off, the beleaguered garrison observed the appearance of further enemy troops.

On 4 March, CCC's Hatchet Force Company A, commanded by Captain Bobby Evans, was inserted from Kontum and immediately dug in on a slope 300 yards above and to the north of the highway. Its mission was to block Highway 110 and thus prevent enemy reinforcements and supply convoys from getting through to Ben Het. The position dominated the surrounding area and there was no way for convoys to circumvent it. The enemy soon reacted, however, bringing down mortar fire which had little effect on the solidly constructed bunkers. That night, they attempted to run convoys past the position but these were spotted and immediately attacked by AC-130 Spectre and AC-119 Stinger gunships loitering on-call above. An attempted night attack met with similar lack of success. On the following night, another convoy attempted to run the gauntlet but the lead truck received a direct hit from the company's 90mm recoilless rifle while the remainder were blasted by machine-gun and mortar fire.

Company A remained in position for six days during which it successfully prevented use of Highway 110, the NVA's principal supply route through Laos. It was credited with destroying six trucks while at the same time creating a backlog of traffic and supplies which provided excellent targets for air strikes. The operation was highly successful, causing disruption in the enemy's logistics system and forcing the NVA to divert to the rear manpower resources sorely needed at Ben Het which it failed to overrun.

BY EARLY 1969 THE Cambodian port of Sihanoukville had become a major North Vietnamese conduit for supplies of arms shipped from Eastern Europe. Consignments were moved from the port by large numbers of trucks, belonging to a transport company owned by the Trinh Sat, the North Vietnamese intelligence service, to a storage depot on the outskirts of the Cambodian capital of Phnom Penh. Convoys then carried them north-west along Highway 7 to the area of the Fish Hook where they were delivered to Rear Transportation Unit 70 which provided logistical support for the NVA's 5th and 7th Division and the Viet Cong's 9th Division. The Fish Hook contained several base camps, the largest of which was situated only three miles inside the Cambodian border and 30 miles north-east of Tay Ninh in South Vietnam.

In the United States, considerable evidence of these violations of Cambodia's so-called 'neutrality' had been provided by US intelligence sources, among them SOG. President Richard Nixon, who had assumed office in January 1969 and was engaged in peace negotiations with North Vietnam in Paris, was shown the evidence and in late February 1969, plans were laid for bombing raids by B-52s, to be carried out against NVA sanctuaries in Cambodia. During March, Nixon issued two warnings to the North Vietnamese that the United States would retaliate against any attacks causing casualties among US personnel at a time when efforts were being made to find a peaceful solution to the conflict. The North Vietnamese ignored these warnings and proceeded to attack Saigon with 122mm rockets. Three days later, B-52 Stratofortresses bombed NVA bases in the Fish Hook, a number of secondary explosions indicating that munitions dumps were among the targets hit.

A month later, a second bombing raid was planned; the target on this occasion was COSVN whose location had been given by a NVA deserter as being fourteen miles south-east of the Cambodian town of Memot and only a mile inside the border. It was decided that a force would be inserted immediately after the raid to put in a ground attack on COSVN. The task was allotted to CCS's 100-strong Hatchet Force company of Montagnards commanded by Captain Bill O'Rourke. By this time, the DANIEL BOONE programme had been given a new codename of SALEM HOUSE following exposure in an article in *Newsweek* magazine reporting on US Special Forces personnel infiltrating into Cambodia.

On the morning of 24 April 1969, the company lifted off from Quan Loi, some 20 miles and ten minutes flying time south-east of its objective. Due to limited availability of helicopter support from the 20th SOS 'Green Hornets', the company was being flown by five helicopters in two lifts, two of its three platoons being inserted in the first lift. During the flight, however, one aircraft, with Captain O'Rourke aboard, developed mechanical problems and was forced to turn back, leaving the other four to fly on.

Minutes later, as the last of the B-52s' bombs exploded on the target area, the remaining four helicopters touched down on the LZ. The moment they landed, they came under a massive volume of fire on all sides from NVA troops in bunkers. Taking cover in nearby bomb craters, the Hatchet Force fought back. First to be killed among its Special Forces personnel was Sergeant Ernest Jamison who was shot while attempting to reach a wounded Montagnard. Soon afterwards, Captain James Cahill, to whom command had devolved when Captain O'Rourke's helicopter was forced to turn back, was hit in the mouth and severely wounded. Meanwhile, the commander of the company's 2nd Platoon, First Lieutenant Greg Harrigan, directed fire support from the Green Hornet gunships who brought their 7.62mm miniguns and rocket launchers to bear on NVA positions. Forty-five minutes later, however, Harrigan was killed.

At this point, Captain O'Rourke arrived and vainly attempted to land and reach his men, but his aircraft was driven off by heavy fire. Other Green Hornets made several efforts to extract the beleaguered force but were also unsuccessful. The battle raged on with the Hatchet Force suffering mounting casualties. The end suddenly came, however, when a Royal Australian Air Force Canberra bomber, of 2 Squadron RAAF based at Phan Rang, arrived on the scene and carried out a bomb attack. Listening on the emergency radio frequency, the pilot had realised that the Hatchet Force was in a dire situation and, without bothering to request clearance to cross the Cambodian border, had flown to its assistance.

The Canberra's attack proved highly effective, providing the breathing space needed for the Green Hornets to race in and extract the surviving members of the Hatchet Force. Meanwhile, the commander of the 1st Platoon, First Lieutenant Walter Marcantel, directed continuing air support; so close were the enemy that he and his nine surviving Montagnard irregulars were themselves wounded by fire from the aircraft. Eventually all survivors, including the wounded, were evacuated. Of those left behind, one man was declared MIA: Sergeant First Class Jerry Shriver, who had last been seen charging an enemy position with some of his Montagnards. According to John Plaster, a declassified report published in 1993 indicated the possibility that an American had been captured but that has never been confirmed.

The most successful Hatchet Force operation in Laos took place during the latter part of 1970, when the CIA requested support for an operation, codenamed HONOURABLE DRAGON, in which a large force of the Agency's Hmong irregulars were attempting to recapture a strong-point called Pakse Site 26 in the south of the country on the south-eastern edge of the Bolovens Plateau. The NVA was putting up a fierce resistance and the Hmong were suffering heavy casualties. The CIA's concern was that should HONOURABLE DRAGON fail, there would be little to prevent complete communist domination of southern Laos.

The CIA asked SOG to insert a Hatchet Force company near Chavane, an important NVA rear base area, with the aim of causing as much trouble as possible. Chavane was 20 miles beyond the maximum distance that SOG was permitted to operate inside Laos but on this occasion the restriction had been lifted by the US ambassador in the Laotian capital of Vientiane.

The operation, codenamed TAILWIND, was allotted to CCC Hatchet Force Company B based at Kontum and commanded by Captain Eugene McCarley. On the morning of 11 September, he and fifteen other Special Forces personnel, together with their 110 Montagnard irregulars, were lifted in three USMC CH-53 Sea Stallion helicopters and, escorted by twelve AH-1 Cobra gunships, flown to Dak To where the aircraft refuelled. At 12.00 midday, they took off again and headed south parallel to the border for 50 miles before swinging west towards Chavane. As soon as they reached the high mountainous plateau of the Bolovens the aircraft came under heavy fire and took several hits, one Montagnard being seriously wounded.

The three Sea Stallions nevertheless reached the pre-designated LZ and landed McCarley and his men who headed north-west. As they left the LZ, they heard the sounds of telephones ringing and made for them. Only a quarter of a mile away, they found a major NVA supply area comprising bunkers full of 122mm and 140mm high explosive rockets. These were blown up, causing a large number of secondary explosions as the company pressed on. A NVA platoon was encountered and after an action lasting an hour, Captain McCarley called in an air strike. Some of his men had been wounded and after their evacuation by helicopter, he continued his advance westward. Nightfall found the company still on the move, any opposition being overcome either by a quick assault or by massive firepower from an AC-130 Spectre gunship circling overhead.

Dawn on 12 September found nine of the Special Forces personnel and eleven Montagnards wounded but still the company pressed on towards the west. At midday, from a spot inside the edge of the jungle, McCarley and his men saw a large convoy of twelve trucks and large numbers of NVA troops half a mile below them on Highway 165. McCarley immediately called in an airstrike of A-1 Skyraiders which destroyed the trucks and routed the enemy who fled in all directions.

By this time, however, twenty or so more members of the company had been wounded and required medical evacuation (medevac). A Sea Stallion arrived and, hovering low, was embarking the first casualty when it came under fire and was forced to lift off. As it did so, it was hit by an anti-tank rocket which failed to explode but passed through the aircraft, rupturing a fuel tank. The aircraft succeeded in clearing the area but was forced to land five miles away. Shortly afterwards, a second helicopter landed at the medevac LZ but came under fire from enemy heavy machine-guns and was forced to withdraw; badly hit, it landed some five minutes later.

The company dug in on high ground overlooking Highway 165 and that night repelled several attacks with Claymore mines and fire support from an AC-130 Spectre gunship. Before dawn on 13 September, McCarley and his men were on the march once more and three hours later encountered a bunker complex. Having first attacked it with air strikes, the company then put in an assault, forcing the NVA battalion occupying the bunkers to retire. A search of the complex revealed it to be a major logistical headquarters; in one large bunker deep underground, a vast quantity of documents was found stored in boxes and bags. This haul, combined with the fact that nearly half of the company had now been wounded, persuaded McCarley that the time had come to withdraw. Moreover, the COVEY FAC overhead advised him that NVA units were converging on his location.

Getting out as quickly as possible, McCarley called for extraction. Heading for one LZ, he switched to another at the last moment to deceive NVA anti-aircraft artillery, on the high ground above him, which was attacked by Skyraiders with cluster bombs containing tear gas. The first Sea Stallion lifted out a platoon with the bulk of the captured documents. As it did so, the LZ came under fire from enemy mortars which were quickly neutralised by an F-4 Phantom dropping napalm. Meanwhile, McCarley was heading for another LZ where, once again having deceived the enemy as to his intentions, his second platoon was evacuated successfully.

By now the third helicopter was nearing the point at which it would have to return to Dak To to refuel. McCarley, warned that the aircraft had only sufficient fuel for one extraction attempt, headed with his remaining platoon for an area of elephant grass which they reached just as the Sea Stallion made its final approach to the LZ. Without further ado the platoon clambered aboard, followed by McCarley in observance of the rule that the One-Zero of any SOG team or force was always the last to board an aircraft on extraction.

Despite the casualties suffered by Company B, three Montagnards killed and 33 wounded, together with all sixteen Americans wounded, TAILWIND had been a huge success. Not only had it thrust deep into enemy-held territory and struck a highly damaging blow at the NVA's logistical command structure, it had resulted in the deaths of over 400 enemy and the destruction of a large amount of NVA ordnance. More importantly, however, the haul of captured documents yielded a vast amount of extremely valuable intelligence. Among them were not only detailed records of NVA arms shipments and codebooks but also a 400-page document providing detailed information on the NVA's 559th Transportation and Support Group.

Despite such success, however, and as part of its increasing policy of 'Vietnamisation', in which responsibility for operations was being transferred gradually to the ARVN, Washington directed that there should be no further Hatchet Force operations in Laos.

ONE OF THE MAJOR PROBLEMS confronting SOG throughout much of its existence was the compromising of its operations. Its first BRIGHT LIGHT operation, CRIMSON TIDE, in October 1966 had seen the rescue force encountering two NVA battalions where there should have been only a small number of troops guarding a PoW camp. In June 1967, the Hatchet Force raiding the forward headquarters of the 559th Transportation and Support Group at OSCAR EIGHT had been confronted by a large force of NVA troops as soon as it landed. Yet again, two years later in April 1969, the Hatchet Force company landing to attack COSVN had found itself ambushed on its LZ.

Checks on SOG's internal operational security revealed no leaks and thus the finger of suspicion pointed at a mole at a high level within the ARVN. This was strengthened in early 1970 when the NSA intercepted radio messages from Hanoi to NVA field formations, giving details of SOG deployments and targets. To counter this, SOG began to provide misleading information to the ARVN but this measure was of only limited effect as once a team was deployed it was a simple process for a 'mole' to check VNAF air strike reports. SOG was therefore forced to look for alternative solutions to protect its teams.

On 29 April 1970, 12,000 ARVN troops with US advisers crossed the

Cambodian border and attacked the Parrot's Beak. Two days later, on 1 May, US forces also advanced into Cambodia, their targets the NVA and Viet Cong sanctuaries, many having been pinpointed previously by SOG. Airmobile units of the 1st US Cavalry Division, along with the 11th Armoured Cavalry Regiment and the ARVN 3rd Airborne Brigade, attacked the Fish Hook where an estimated 7,000 enemy were reportedly located. To the south-west of Pleiku, units of the 4th US Infantry Division discovered a large and well-equipped NVA hospital and captured 500 tons of rice. On 7 May, the NVA's largest base in Cambodia fell to troops of the 1st US Cavalry Division who captured 1,484 weapons, 1.5 million rounds of small arms ammunition, 22 cases of anti-personnel mines, and 30 tons of rice. Known as 'The City', this was the supply base for the NVA's 7th Division. On 8 May, the 1st US Cavalry Division's 2nd Brigade also captured a large NVA depot known as 'Rock Island East' and containing over 1,000 weapons and 329 tons of ammunition and explosives, all of which were blown up. A further massive supply dump, containing 203 tons of ammunition and supplies, was located beside Highway 14.

B-52 Stratofortresses were meanwhile on the hunt for COSVN once again. Some weeks prior to the invasion, they had struck before dawn at an area believed to be its location. Now they attacked its suspected escape route and one morning bombed a camp north-west of Mimot. After the attack, troops of the 25th US Infantry Division found 101 corpses and a document bag imprinted with the Vietnamese characters for COSVN.

The invasion of Cambodia resulted in strong opposition throughout the United States and ultimately led the Nixon administration to order the withdrawal of all US forces from Cambodia, the last leaving by 30 June. According to John Plaster, who was One-Zero of Reconnaissance Team CALIFORNIA, one of a number of teams deployed by SOG during this operation, the vast haul of captured ordnance totalled 23,000 assault rifles and submachine-guns, 2,500 machine-guns and mortars, 62,000 grenades, fifteen million rounds of small arms ammunition, 143,000 mortar bombs and rockets, and 79,000 tons of rice. In addition, 435 vehicles were captured or destroyed. US and ARVN casualties totalled 1,084 killed, 5,749 wounded and thirteen missing. NVA and Viet Cong figures were 11,349 killed and 2,328 captured.

The majority of the enemy, however, had fled beyond the eighteen-mile limit laid down for the incursion into Cambodia and thus escaped the US/ARVN onslaught; and even as the invasion took place, the NVA was already moving west and establishing new base areas deeper inside Cambodia and southern Laos.

During June 1970, Colonel John Sadler replaced Colonel Steve Cavanaugh as Chief of MACV-SOG. Like the latter, he had served with the 11th US Airborne Division in New Guinea and the Philippines during the Second World War. After the war he had served as a parachute instructor at the US Army's airborne school at Fort Benning, Georgia, and had subsequently become one of its leading experts on parachuting. Temporarily assigned to the CIA as a parachute specialist, he had served with JACK in the Korean War during which he had experimented with early military free-fall parachuting techniques. Then he had served with Special Forces and in 1958, the year following the commencement of HALO (High Altitude Low Opening) training by the US Special Forces, had qualified as a free-fall parachutist. Subsequently, he had served with the WHITE STAR teams in Laos.

On assuming command and learning of the operational security threat facing SOG, Sadler decided to introduce HALO as a method of insertion. A six-man team, codenamed FLORIDA and comprising Staff Sergeant Cliff Newman, Sergeants First Class Sammy Hernandez and Melvin Hill, an ARVN officer and two SOG Montagnards, was formed and immediately sent to Okinawa for basic HALO training in a high security area. A month later the team returned to South Vietnam and the SOG base at Camp Long Thanh for further training. In November it carried out a night descent followed by a two-day exercise at the end of which it was declared operational.

The team's first mission was in an area of Laos west of Kham Duc, tapping a telephone along a road under construction by the NVA. Before the mission, SOG arranged with the NSA for monitoring of enemy radio communications for mention of any word connected with the forthcoming operation. This proved a wise move as a signal from Saigon to Hanoi was intercepted; it gave not only the names of the six team members but also the map coordinates for their planned DZ.

The mission went ahead on the night of 28 November, the team dropping from a 90th SOS Blackbird on to an alternative DZ whose location was kept a closely guarded secret within SOG. All six men landed safely and spent the next four days searching for the telephone wire. NVA troops were observed in the area but it was clear that they had no inkling of the team's presence. On the fifth day, the team was extracted by helicopter to Nakhon Phanom in eastern Thailand, on the border with Laos, before being flown back to South Vietnam. The world's first operational HALO entry had been carried out.

Early 1971 saw the training of a second four-man all-American HALO team which carried out an operation in May in an area between the Ashau Valley and Khe Sanh. One man was injured during the descent, when an anti-personnel mine exploded in his pack, and another on landing. Both were evacuated while the remaining two members carried out the reconnaissance task before being extracted on the fifth day.

A third team had meanwhile been formed, likewise consisting of four Americans: Sergeant Major Billy Waugh, Staff Sergeant James Bath and Sergeants Jesse Campbell and Madison Strohlein. After completion of its training, the team was assigned a mission in an area 60 miles south-west of Da Nang near the Laotian border where there were indications of a heavy NVA presence. Dropped on the night of 22 June, the four men became dispersed during the descent, Staff Sergeant Bath and Sergeant Strohlein both being injured on landing. NVA troops were in the area and Sergeant Campbell was soon on the run. A BRIGHT LIGHT operation was launched to rescue the team but the helicopters were unable to locate Strohlein who, having thrown a coloured smoke grenade to indicate his position, warned them off after observing NVA troops approaching. Having extracted Waugh and Campbell, the aircraft were forced to withdraw because of the onset of dusk. Returning on the following afternoon, the BRIGHT LIGHT team extracted Bath but there was no sign of Strohlein. A Hatchet Force Platoon was inserted on the following morning, finding his CAR-15 carbine and signs that he had put up a fierce resistance before being taken prisoner.

The fourth HALO operation carried out by SOG was the most successful. A four-man team under Captain Jim Storter and comprising Staff Sergeant Miller Moye, Sergeant First Class Newman Ruff and Sergeant Jim Bentley, dropped into the Plei Trap Valley, north-west of Pleiku, in early September. The mission had originally been scheduled for two days earlier but once again a radio message from the North

Vietnamese 'mole' in Saigon, giving their names and location of the DZ, had been intercepted by the NSA. Apart from Sergeant Ruff going into a flat spin in free-fall after his rucksack worked itself loose, the descent proceeded without problems and the four men landed on the DZ within 30 yards of each other. During the following four days, they reconnoitred the Plei Trap Valley without the NVA becoming aware of their presence before being extracted on the fifth day.

A final HALO operation took place a month later as a four-man team was dropped on the Cambodian border in the Ia Drang Valley, approximately 25 miles south-west of Pleiku. The team became scattered during the descent with one member, Sergeant First Class Mark Gentry, landing away from the rest. Having established radio contact with him, One-Zero Sergeant First Class Dick Gross and Staff Sergeant Howard Sugar heard NVA troops searching for them near by and went to ground. Next morning, as he set off to rejoin the rest of the team, Gentry suddenly encountered a squad of NVA eating breakfast. Swifter in his reactions, he shot them all dead before leaving the area as fast as possible. Two hours later, the entire team was extracted without further problems.

Following its invasion of Cambodia, the United States escalated the withdrawal of its forces from South Vietnam, pulling them back to defensive areas in the areas of major cities, airbases and along the coast. As US formations and units left the Central Highlands, the DMZ and areas along South Vietnam's borders, their places were taken by ARVN units. The latter, however, were unable to stem the progress of the NVA which soon advanced into these areas while extending its lines of communications and supply from Laos into South Vietnam.

On 21 January 1971, the 5th Special Forces Group (Airborne) handed over the last of its bases to a unit of the ARVN special forces shortly before withdrawing from South Vietnam. After its departure, SOG's CCN and CCC were redesignated Task Force 1 Advisory Element and Task Force 2 Advisory Element respectively, these providing covers for those members of US Special Forces still serving with SOG.

SOG continued to be fully operational and up until the beginning of February was still despatching teams into Laos. On 6 February, however, Chief SOG was ordered to terminate all operations in Laos and was allotted an area of activity comprising a six-mile-deep strip along the Laotian border and the DMZ. Meanwhile, the NAD was once again active in its *Nasty* boats. On 19 February, four of them attacked and sank two North Vietnamese fast-attack craft and damaged two gunboats.

SOG operations continued until the autumn of 1971 with teams reconnoitring and reporting on the continuing increase in VVA forces. On several occasions their intelligence was initially disbelieved, particularly a report on the presence of NVA armour in southern Laos. The final operation took place in December 1971 in the Ashau Valley where a reconnaissance team located tanks and other armoured vehicles, calling in air strikes on a large concentration of vehicles before it made good its escape.

In March 1972, the MACV Studies and Observation Group was disbanded. Its missions had undoubtedly been highly successful in forcing the NVA to devote large numbers of troops to rear area security in Laos and Cambodia rather than operations in South Vietnam. It was later calculated that on average each American member of a reconnaissance team or Hatchet Force unit tied down 600 NVA soldiers. In addition, the destruction by SOG Hatchet Forces of large quantities of arms, munitions and supplies prevented their use in South Vietnam and thus inhibited the enemy's capability to conduct operations there. Moreover, the thousands of NVA troops who were killed in Laos and Cambodia by SOG and its air support never reached South Vietnam and thus could not be deployed against US and ARVN forces.

While its effects could not be measured in the same way as its air, maritime and ground operations, SOG's psychological warfare programme also proved highly effective, causing considerable confusion throughout the enemy chain of command and forcing the NVA to devote significant resources to countering it. Its long-term agent programme, however, had a more chequered history, and undoubtedly had been heavily penetrated by the North Vietnamese from its early days under the CIA's Combined Area Studies. As with SOG's reconnaissance teams, it appears that one or more moles in Saigon provided details of agents and their insertion points beforehand. Moreover, recruitment was carried out by the South Vietnamese and thus it would have been almost impossible for SOG to know whether Trinh Sat double-agents were among those it despatched into North Vietnam. Where it became obvious that teams were operating under North Vietnamese control, SOG maintained communications and attempted to 'play' them as part of its FORAE deception programme in which projects such as URGENCY, BORDEN and OODLES resulted in North Vietnamese counter-intelligence pursuing a large number of phantom agents. As recounted earlier, there were occasions when SOG was able to use such projects to take direct action against the enemy and thus exact retribution.

It was not until 1973 that the US government admitted that US troops, predominantly members of the US Special Forces, had been killed on operations in Laos and Cambodia since 1965. The official figure given was 81 but the actual total of American SOG personnel lost on operations was over 300. Fifty-seven of them were recorded as MIA and only one of those returned; the fate of the remainder remains unknown to this day.

CHAPTER ELEVEN

AFGHANISTAN 1979–2001

In Afghanistan on the night of 24 December 1979 a large number of Soviet transport aircraft began landing at the airport outside the capital of Kabul and at an airfield approximately 40 miles to the north at the huge military airbase at Bagram, disgorging paratroops of the 105th Guards Airborne Division reinforced by two regiments of the 103rd and 104th. Similar scenes were meanwhile taking place at the city of Kandahar in the south of the country, Jalalabad in the east and Shindand in the west. By dawn on 27 December, some 5,000 troops had moved into the area of Kabul itself. Meanwhile, two motorised rifle divisions, the 357th and the 66th, were advancing from Kushka, on the border with Turkmenistan, south to Herat and continuing on to Shindand, Farah and Kandahar, occupying each city with a garrison. Simultaneously, the 360th advanced into Afghanistan from Uzbekistan, crossing the border at Termez and advancing south to Mazar-e-Sharif before heading southeast to the Salang Pass Tunnel, arriving at Kabul by the morning of 26 December. To the east, the 201st and 16th Motor Rifle Divisions likewise occupied Kunduz, Badakshan and Baglan. The forward elements of Headquarters 40th Army, under General Vladlen M. Mikhailov, First Deputy Commander of the Turkmen Military District, meantime landed at Bagram to take command of all Soviet forces in Afghanistan.

During the evening of 27 December, paratroops moved from Kabul airport and their other airfield bases into Kabul itself, seizing the capital's telephone exchange and occupying the Ministry of Interior and the city's radio station. Throughout the capital, they took up positions occupying government ministries and key installations.

At the Darulaman Palace, the heavily fortified residence of President Hafizullah Amin, a battle raged between Afghan Army units guarding the palace and a detachment of Soviet special forces. According to writer and Soviet specialist James G. Shortt, this comprised elements of the 1st Battalion 16th Spetsnaz Brigade, based at Chuchkovo in the Moscow Military District. They were reinforced by troops from another spetsnaz formation based at Chirchik and by the Spetsrota (Special

Assignments Company) of the Felix Dzerzhinsky Motor Rifle Division (an Interior Ministry (MVD) formation based in Moscow) under its commander Captain Mal'tsev. Spearheading the force was a team of KGB spetsnaz troops led by Colonel Boyarinov, commandant of the KGB's Special Tasks School at Balashika on the ring road outside Moscow.

Commanded by an MVD officer, Major General Viktor Paputin, the detachment, whose mission was the capture of the palace and the assassination of Amin by the KGB spetsnaz team, had landed with the 105th Guards Airborne Division at Bagram. Accompanied by a battalion of paratroops, it had headed for the Darulaman Palace in BMD-1 armoured personnel carriers (APC) belonging to the airborne division. On arrival at a barrier on the access road to the palace, the leading elements had found their way barred by a solitary Afghan sentry who, on refusing to let them pass, was despatched with a silenced pistol. Reaching the palace, the leading APC attempted to ram its way through the gates but became jammed. The paratroop battalion quickly established a cordon around the area while eliminating the guards stationed around the outside of the palace.

Led by the KGB team under Colonel Boyarinov, the spetsnaz force then stormed the building itself. Details of its interior lay-out had been provided by Lieutenant Colonel Mikhail Talybov, an officer of the KGB's Eighth Department, a division of the S Directorate within the First Chief (Foreign Intelligence) Directorate, which was responsible for the conduct of 'direct action' operations, including assassination. Of Central Asian ethnic origin, Talybov had been infiltrated into the palace, in the guise of a cook, at the end of September with the mission of assassinating Amin by use of poison. Failing twice in his attempts, however, he had then concentrated on transmitting information about the layout of the palace and Amin's movements.

As they entered the palace, Boyarinov and his men encountered heavy opposition from guards inside the building and began to take heavy casualties as they fought their way up the main staircase to the first floor where Amin's KGB-trained bodyguard team was putting up a fierce resistance. When it appeared that the attack was in danger of being repulsed, Boyarinov himself withdrew to summon reinforcements; in so doing, however, he forgot his earlier orders to the paratroops to kill anyone fleeing from the palace and was shot dead as he emerged from the building.

The palace was eventually captured after further hard fighting that day, during which Major General Viktor Paputin was also killed. According to reports, all of which lack detail as the Soviets were careful to leave no witnesses of the ensuing events, the KGB spetsnaz team quickly ran Amin to earth and executed him, his family and all members of his personal entourage and household. Lieutenant Colonel Talybov apparently was not a witness to the killings, only emerging from his hiding place under the stairs once all firing had ceased.

At 9.15 p.m. that night, the inhabitants of Kabul listened to a speech by Babrak Karmal, leader of the communist Parcham faction of the People's Democratic Party of Afghanistan (PDPA), who had been flown in from Tashkent where he had been in exile. Broadcasting over Radio Kabul, he announced that Amin had been tried by a revolutionary tribunal and sentenced to death. He went on to state that he had taken over the country and that the Soviet Union had responded to his request for military assistance.

The Soviet forces, meanwhile, were meeting resistance from the Afghan army. The 8th Division, based near Kabul, put up stout opposition, as did the 15th at Kandahar. Fierce and prolonged fighting also took place at Herat and Jalalabad. In other areas, Soviet troops managed to disarm Afghan units before they could mobilise and all air bases were seized before the Afghan Air Force could take any effective action against the invaders. Although it took several weeks to suppress the initial resistance to the invasion, including a three-day battle inside Kabul itself, by the end of March 1980 the Soviets had secured a firm grip in the capital and the major provincial cities and established their own puppet regime. Little did they realise, however, that they had just entered the beginnings of a war which would last for nine years.

BORDERED TO THE NORTH by Turkmenistan, Uzbekistan and Tajikistan, to the south and south-east by Pakistan, and to the west by Iran, Afghanistan occupies a land-locked position in South-Central Asia. Measuring some 600 miles from north to south, and approximately 800 miles east to west, it consists of three distinct regions: the northern plains, which are the country's principal agricultural region, with much of the border to the north being formed by the Amu Darya River; the central

Afghanistan 1979–1989

highlands which, including the Hindu Kush, are a western extension of the Himalayas; and the south-western plateau, comprising desert and semi-desert terrain which includes the Rigestan Desert. Running from north-east of the central highlands down through the south-western plateau is the 715-mile-long Helmand River.

More than half of Afghanistan's people are Pushtuns who live mainly in the southern and eastern areas of the country. The remainder are Tajiks, who are to be found in the north-east and west, Uzbeks, who are predominantly farmers in the region north of the Hindu Kush, and Hazaras, who are nomadic and inhabit the central highlands. Over four-fifths of Afghanistan's population is based in its rural regions, primarily along the rivers, while the remaining fifth is nomadic. In addition to the capital of Kabul in the east, major urban centres include the cities of Herat, Kandahar, Mazar-e-Sharif, Jalalabad and Kunduz. Most are situated on the main circular highway which runs south-west from Kabul to Kandahar, then heads north-west to Herat before turning north-east to Mazar-e-Sharif from which it veers south back to Kabul.

Originally part of the Persian Achaemenian empire, Afghanistan was conquered by Alexander the Great during the fourth century BC, subsequently becoming part of the Maurya empire of northern India, and then being absorbed by the empire of the Kushan king, Kaniska, during the second century BC. In 1219, the country was invaded by the Mongols of Genghis Khan under whose rule it remained until the fall of his empire. Thereafter it comprised a series of independent principalities until the eighteenth century when it was absorbed by the Mughal empire of India. During the early 1700s, the Persian king Nader Shah wrested control of Afghanistan from the Mughals, being succeeded by Ahmad Shah Durrani who proceeded to unite it as a nation. After his death in 1772, however, a combination of tribal disputes and imperialist machinations on the part of Britain and Russia, the latter attempting to annex northern Afghanistan, caused splits to reappear among the Afghans.

In the course of the nineteenth century, Britain failed in its attempts to conquer Afghanistan but succeeded in subduing Baluchistan and large Pushtun areas which at that time formed part of Afghan territory. In 1893 the British established a boundary, dubbed the Durand Line, which defined the de facto limits of Afghan territory and established

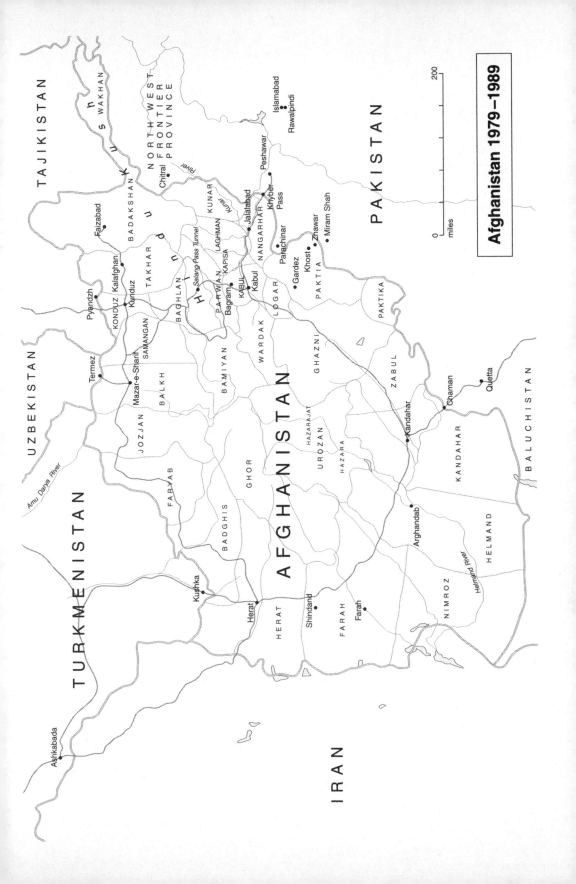

Afghanistan 1979–1989

zones of responsibility for the maintenance of law and order between British India and Afghanistan.

During the First World War, Afghanistan, under King Habibollah Khan, who had succeeded his father Abdor Rahman Khan, remained neutral, having resisted pressure to enter the war on the side of Germany and its allies; but in early 1919 Habibollah was assassinated. He was succeeded by Amanollah, his third son, who immediately launched a month-long but inconclusive war against the British which resulted in Afghanistan winning the right to conduct its own foreign affairs. Amanollah immediately signed a treaty of friendship with the Bolshevik regime in the Soviet Union which evolved into a long-standing relationship which would last 70 years.

For the next ten years Amanollah presided over a series of reforms, some of which – notably constitutional changes, removal of the veil for women and the introduction of coeducational schools – caused offence within the more conservative of Afghanistan's tribal and religious leaders. Civil war, led by a Tajik named Baccheh Saqow, broke out in November 1928 and two months later Amanollah abdicated in favour of his elder brother, Inayatollah, going into exile in Italy. Baccheh Saqow, however, seized the throne instead, crowning himself as Habibollah II, but ten months later he was ousted and murdered by Mohammed Nader Khan who was proclaimed Nader Shah. In 1931 the latter brought in a new constitution designed to appease the country's religious leaders.

In November 1933, Nader Shah, too, was assassinated, being succeeded by his son, Zahir. During the following twenty years, Afghanistan went through a period of internal development and expansion of foreign affairs. In 1953, however, power was seized by the king's nephew, Lieutenant General Mohammed Daoud Khan, a militant Pushtun nationalist who advocated an independent state of Pushtunistan formed from the Pushtun areas given by the British to Pakistan following its creation in 1947 after partition from India.

Daoud turned to the Soviet Union for economic and military aid and from 1956 onward the Soviets, who had coveted Afghanistan since the days of the Bolshevik Revolution of 1917, began training the Afghan army and air force. This was followed by major infrastructure projects which included the construction of a highway leading from the Tajik–Afghan border to Kabul and port facilities along the Amu Darya

River. Daoud meanwhile introduced a series of far-reaching reforms while at the same time maintaining a politically repressive regime which permitted no opposition. His downfall, however, was caused by the issue of Pushtunistan which he continued to pursue vigorously. As a result, Pakistan closed the border in August 1961, forcing Afghanistan to rely largely on the Soviet Union for trade and transit routes. In a move designed to appease the Pakistanis, Daoud resigned in March 1963 and the border was reopened two months later.

The Soviets had by now increased their influence among the Afghan armed forces. This was engineered by the Main Intelligence Directorate of the Soviet General Staff, the Glavnoye Razvedyvatelnoye Upravleniye, better known by its acronym of GRU, which, in September 1964, encouraged Soviet-trained officers within the Afghan army to join an underground body, the Armed Forces Revolutionary Organisation. Zahir Shah, meanwhile, had introduced a new constitution, and the country's first free elections were held in August 1965 with a large number of parties, ranging from Islamic fundamentalist to far left, putting forward candidates for seats in the two houses of legislature, the House of People and the House of Elders. During the elections, the Soviets encouraged Afghanistan's two communist political factions, the Parcham and Khalq, to bury their differences and combine forces. At the same time, they provided support for a third group, the newly formed PDPA, which won three of the five National Assembly seats for Kabul.

As the political situation became increasingly polarised, Zahir Shah appointed five successive Prime Ministers between September 1965 and December 1972. His refusal to promulgate the acts governing political parties, as well as municipal and provincial councils, led to a stagnation of the political process. Moreover, his popularity was waning as a result of his failure to react effectively to Pakistani repression of Pushtun and Baluch ethnic minorities inside Pakistan, and because of his highly unpopular decision to allow Iran access to the Helmand River during a period of drought in Afghanistan. In July 1973, he was overthrown in a bloodless coup led once again by Daoud who was supported by the Parcham and left-wing officers in the armed forces.

Returning to power, Daoud abolished the 1964 constitution, establishing the Republic of Afghanistan, with himself as Prime Minister and Chairman of the Republic's Central Committee, and forming a coalition government with the communists of the Parcham led by Babrak Kamal,who agreed to do so with the encouragement of the Soviet Union. The Khalq, led by Nur Mohammed Taraki and Hafizullah Amin, meanwhile refused to support the new regime, dismissing Daoud's policies as too conservative.

Outside Afghanistan, meanwhile, the growing power of Babrak Karmal and the Parcham began to cause disquiet, no more so than in Iran where during 1974 the Shah, with support from the United States, tried to draw Afghanistan into a pro-Western economic and security bloc which included Pakistan, India and the Persian Gulf states. This took the form of a $40 million credit offered to Afghanistan as the initial element of a ten-year economic aid package totalling $2 billion. The plan, which also included a major road and rail network linking Afghanistan with the Persian Gulf, was for Iran to replace the Soviet Union as the principal supplier of aid to Afghanistan.

The US Central Intelligence Agency (CIA) and the Shah's intelligence service, SAVAK, along with other agencies from Pakistan, India, China and the Middle East, were busy, meanwhile, conducting operations in Afghanistan against their Soviet counterpart, the KGB. The CIA and SAVAK, moreover, were both involved in attempts by Islamic fundamentalist groups to overthrow Daoud in September and December 1973, and in June of the following year.

These combined efforts on the part of Iran and the United States resulted in Daoud shifting further to the right, towards the pro-Western Iranian-led bloc. In July 1974, he removed 200 Soviet-trained officers from the armed forces and during the following year replaced his communist Interior Minister with a committed anti-communist, General Kadir Nuristani. In October 1975, he dismissed a further 40 Soviet-trained officers and, in a move designed to reduce dependency on the Soviet Union, established arrangements for training to be carried out in India, Egypt and the United States.

In November, Daoud began to moderate his policies on the question of establishing an independent Pushtunistan, declaring that Afghanistan would no longer provide a safe haven for the 10,000 or so Pushtun and Baluch guerrillas operating against Pakistan. He caused more outrage by refusing to allow Pushtun refugees fleeing from Pakistan to enter Afghanistan. Shortly afterwards, he announced that he was breaking ranks with the Parcham and setting up his own political movement, the National Revolutionary Front. This caused dismay in the Soviet Union which during the following eighteen months increased pressure on the Parcham and the Khalq to bury their differences and combine forces.

Although, in May 1977, the Soviets finally persuaded the two factions to merge, divisions persisted. Apart from any ideological disputes, there was a fundamental difference between them. The Parcham was recruited predominantly from the country's urbanised upper classes who had little contact with Pushtun tribal affairs; among these the Persian influence was strong, with the majority speaking Dari, an Afghan dialect of Farsi. The membership of the Khalq, however, was drawn from the country's lower middle class from the rural areas and towns who sought Pushtun dominance within Afghanistan and the return of the territories handed over to Pakistan by Britain in 1947.

During 1977, Daoud increased the pace of his efforts to divorce Afghanistan from the Soviet Union. Increased repression of the communists began in February and two months later, while on an official visit to Moscow, Daoud clashed personally with the Soviet premier, Leonid Brezhnev, who demanded that he remove a number of NATO experts working in Afghanistan. The Afghan leader responded by stating that his countrymen would never permit the Soviet Union to interfere in their internal affairs and that decisions on employment of foreign experts would be the exclusive prerogative of Afghanistan alone. On his return, Daoud reinforced that statement by stepping up the number of officers being sent to India, Egypt and the United States and initiated an additional programme for the training of air force officers in Turkey. Furthermore, he negotiated $500 million- worth of aid from Saudi Arabia for the construction of a hydroelectric scheme, and concluded aid agreements with China and Kuwait.

These developments, together with Daoud's increasingly close relations with Iran, Egypt, Turkey and Saudi Arabia were viewed with growing alarm by the Soviet Union and the communists in Afghanistan. Moreover, Pushtun nationalists became increasingly convinced that Daoud was planning to surrender all claims to the territories lost to Pakistan in exchange for further aid from the United States and Iran. Indeed, Pakistan's military ruler, General Mohammed Zia ul-Haq, had made it clear that rapprochement between his country and Afghanistan would be conditional upon the latter ceasing to pursue the matter of Pushtunistan and Baluchistan as well as accepting the Durand Line. In March 1978, at a meeting with Zia in Islamabad, both sides seemed ready to compromise, as Daoud indicated that he was prepared to accept these conditions on the basis that some form of autonomy would be granted to the Pushtun and Baluch areas within Pakistan.

There was suspicion among Pushtun nationalists that Daoud had come to some form of accommodation with the Pakistanis when, after his return, he informed a meeting of Pushtun and Baluch tribal leaders in Kabul that their 10,000-strong force, of insurgents from Pakistan had to leave Afghan territory by 30 April. Word of his suspected deal with Zia spread swiftly through the armed forces, and the communists were quick to take advantage of the situation. Daoud found himself increasingly isolated, with his power base being reduced to a rump of hard-line anti-communist loyalists among the senior echelons of the police and army who stepped up their efforts to eradicate the communists from any positions of authority. These culminated on 17 April with the murder of a senior member of the Parcham, Mir Akbar Khaiber, whose death sparked off a wave of unrest. This in turn resulted on 25 April with the arrests and imprisonment of Nur Mohammed Taraki, Babrak Karmal and five other senior communists.

Hafizullah Amin, however, was merely placed under house arrest and was able to smuggle out a contingency plan, drawn up previously by the Khalq, to overthrow Daoud. Copies were distributed among key air force and army officers and on 27 April a coup took place. It was led by the army's 4th Division which, despite encountering initial resistance from the 7th and 8th Divisions, succeeded in liberating Amin and the other communist leaders. It was joined during the day by other army formations defecting to the rebels. Elements of the air force were also involved in the plot but it was not until late afternoon that half a dozen aircraft from the air base at Bagram attacked the presidential palace. By the end of the day, Amin had gained control and three days later it was announced that a new government, the Revolutionary Council of the Democratic Republic of Afghanistan, had been formed. Daoud and most of his family meanwhile had met their deaths.

Nur Mohammed Taraki and Babrak Karmal were appointed President and Vice-President respectively, while Amin assumed the appointments of First Deputy Prime Minister and Foreign Minister. Major Aslam Watanjar, who as deputy commander of the 4th Division had led the coup, became Deputy Prime Minister, while the air force chief of staff, Colonel Abdul Qader, was appointed Defence Minister.

Amin, however, was soon locked in a struggle for power with all of his former fellow conspirators who were now his rivals. At the end of June, Karmal and six other leaders of the Parcham were sent abroad as ambassadors. In August, Abdul Qader was arrested on a charge of plotting a coup against Amin, while Karmal was summoned from his diplomatic post in the Czech capital of Prague. Neither he, nor his six fellow ambassadors, obeyed the summons but promptly disappeared to avoid arrest and enforced return to Kabul. Meanwhile Aslam Watanjar, who was coveting the post of Defence Minister, was demoted to Communications Minister.

At the same time, Amin pressed ahead with a series of reforms which, although undoubtedly to the benefit of many who were disadvantaged, were over-ambitious and badly planned. Proposals relating to the ownership of land and the status of women, for example, encountered strong opposition from an alliance of those whose interests would have been adversely affected and the more conservative elements of the population, including the mullahs. Despite growing hostility, Amin persisted with his reforms, enforcing them wherever necessary with the assistance of his secret police, who were commanded by his nephew, and military courts. It was not long before Amin's opponents at home began receiving support from Islamic fundamentalist bodies abroad, some of these despatching armed groups into Afghanistan from Pakistan.

The Soviets viewed Amin's rule with growing dismay, their attempts to persuade him to share power with his rivals being ignored. By this time there was growing resistance on several fronts to his regime and in February 1979 a group of Tajik anti-Pushtun separatists, belonging to an organisation called Setam-i-Milli, kidnapped the US ambassador, Adolph Dubs, demanding the release of their leader, Badruddin Bahes, who had been arrested and imprisoned. The Afghan government refused to negotiate with the kidnappers, who were holding Dubs prisoner in a hotel in Kabul, and instead sent in the police. During the ensuing attack on the hotel room, Dubs, along with two of his kidnappers, was killed by the police.

In the aftermath of Dubs's death, Amin claimed that the Setam-i-Milli leadership was closely linked with the Parcham, itself associated with the KGB in Kabul, and that the kidnapping had been designed to damage relations between his regime and the United States. According to a US State Department report subsequently published in 1980, four Soviet advisers had been on hand with the police, three of them with the team which assaulted the hotel room and one reportedly positioned with some of the snipers surrounding the building and directing their fire.

In March, a serious uprising took place in the western city of Herat and fighting erupted between rebel forces and government troops, during which the 17th Division mutinied and defected to the rebels. It took two weeks of fierce fighting before order was restored, by which time some 3,000 people had been killed. Among these were 49 Soviet advisers and their families who were massacred in their homes. It was later discovered that the insurgents had been led by Afghans armed and trained by the regime of Ayatollah Ruhollah Khomeini which had taken power in Iran during the previous month, following the fall of the Shah. Moreover, a large section of the local population, who were predominantly Shi'ite Muslims, had supported the uprising. The revolt in Herat was followed on 23 June by a mutiny of Afghan troops in Kabul and another on 6 August when an Afghan unit attempted to seize the fortress of Balahisar inside the capital which dominates the city.

Meanwhile, Amin and Taraki had asked the Soviet Union to send troops to help counter the ever-growing insurgency. This request was refused, although the Soviets undertook instead to supply further aid in the form of a military mission and helicopter gunships which arrived during the following month. Increasingly alarmed by the deteriorating situation and the mounting strength of the insurgent forces, who by this time were receiving external support from Saudi Arabia, Egypt, the United Arab Emirates and China, the Soviets proposed that Amin should form a coalition government with Babrak Karmal who had remained in Prague under the protection of the Czech government. This met with an angry refusal from Amin, already involved in a showdown with Taraki who had appointed Aslam Watanjar as Defence Minister and another member of the Khalq, Sherjan Mazdooryar, as Interior Minister. Moreover, Taraki had further infuriated Amin by replacing the latter's nephew, Asadullah Amin, as head of the secret police with another Khalqi, Asadullah Sarwari.

The Soviets then decided on an alternative plan which called for Taraki remaining as President and Karmal becoming Prime Minister, while Amin was sent abroad as an ambassador. During a visit to Moscow in early September 1979, Taraki agreed to this proposal but did not reveal that other plans were afoot to assassinate Amin on his way to Kabul airport to receive Taraki on his return. The KGB was apprised of the plot, however, by an informer shortly before Taraki's departure from Moscow. Anxious to avoid a bloody confrontation which would only serve to destabilise Afghanistan, it warned Amin in time.

Relations between Amin and Taraki worsened rapidly thereafter as each demanded the other's resignation. Meanwhile, another plot to assassinate Amin on 14 September had been hatched by Asadullah Sarwari but this failed. Amin reacted quickly by seizing control and dismissing all of his rivals from their posts. An attempt to arrest them, however, failed; they had already sought sanctuary in the house of a KGB agent.

On 10 October, Radio Kabul announced that Taraki had died of a serious illness; the Soviets discovered shortly afterwards, however, that he had been tracked down and murdered on 17 September by three of Amin's men. His death caused high-level reverberations in Moscow where there were growing suspicions that Amin would turn to the United States for support. These were being encouraged by Watanjar, Sarwari, Mazdooryar and a senior member of the Khalq named Syed Gulabzoi; under guard by the KGB in Kabul, they were supplying their protectors with apparent evidence of Amin's increasingly close relations with Washington. This was reinforced by Babrak Karmal and his six fellow ex-ambassadors who had gathered in Moscow and were doing their utmost to strengthen Soviet fears that Amin was indeed turning to the West. It was apparently at this stage that the KGB's agent inside the Darulaman Palace, Lieutenant Colonel Talybov, was instructed to assassinate Amin but failed in his attempt to do so.

Among the Soviets there were divisions between those who advocated military intervention in Afghanistan and others strongly opposed to it. Among the former were the Soviet President Leonid Brezhnev and other influential figures such as Defence Minister Dmitri Ustinov and Viktor Khrychkov, director of the KGB's foreign intelligence department. Opponents included Prime Minister Alexei Kosygin, Foreign Minister Andrei Gromyko and KGB chief Yuri Andropov.

Several factors concerned the Soviets as they argued for and against intervention. Not least was the possibility that Amin might permit the United States to establish electronic intelligence ('elint') monitoring stations to replace two in Iran lost following the Islamic revolution in February. They had been used for monitoring Soviet radio communications and missile telemetry transmissions from the Baikonur missile and space centre, situated on the north bank of the Syr Darya River about 100 miles north-west of Qvzylorda, in south-central Kazakhstan. Another was the possibility, after the sacking of the US Embassy in Teheran and the taking of American hostages, that the United States might take direct military action against Iran.

The Defence Ministry and senior individuals of the Soviet General Staff were divided on the issue. Among those who strongly opposed intervention were the Chief of General Staff, Marshal Nikolai Ogarkov, the First Deputy Chief of Staff, Marshal Sergei Akhromeyev, and the Commander of the Carpathian Military District, General Valentin Varennikov. Others advocated sending in a limited number of troops as a measure to stabilise Afghanistan, stationing them in Kabul and the principal Afghan cities but barring them from becoming involved in combat.

As the end of 1979 approached, the situation was exacerbated by deteriorating relations between the Soviet Union and the United States. Although the second Strategic Arms Limitation Treaty (SALT II), limiting the number of strategic nuclear weapon systems to be possessed by either side to 2,400, had been signed in Vienna on 18 June by Leonid Brezhnev and President Jimmy Carter, the impression that détente was grinding to a halt was reinforced when the US Senate's Armed Services Committee rejected SALT II on 30 November. Moreover, the United States was determined to position intermediate range ballistic missiles in Europe; an announcement that it would deploy Tomahawk cruise missiles and Pershing II tactical nuclear weapons was made on 12 December. This was the final straw. On the evening of the 12th, a meeting of the Soviet Politburo was held at which the decision was taken to intervene militarily in Afghanistan. Two weeks later, the invasion took place.

AS RELATED BY JOURNALIST John K. Cooley in his book *Unholy Wars – Afghanistan, America and International Terrorism*, six months beforehand, on 3 July, President Carter had authorised covert assistance to the resistance in Afghanistan by the Central Intelligence Agency (CIA) through the signing of a presidential finding. The principal advocate of such action was US National Security Adviser Zbigniew Brzezinski who saw an opportunity to end the Cold War by dragging the Soviet Union into a long-running conflict which ultimately would prove insupportable and ultimately bring about its collapse; indeed, after the crossing of Afghanistan's northern borders by Soviet forces, he wrote to the President saying, 'Now we can give the USSR its own Vietnam war.' Years later, he would state, 'This secret operation was an excellent idea. Its effect was to draw the Russians into the Afghan trap.'

According to journalist Selig Harrison in his book (co-authored with Diego Cordovez) *Out of Afghanistan – The Inside Story of the Soviet Withdrawal*, US Secretary of State Cyrus Vance, although not opposed to Brzezinski's policy, had serious reservations and felt that diplomatic efforts should be made to negotiate a Soviet withdrawal since the occupation of Afghanistan was still at an early stage and the United States had yet to respond. His plan called for an agreement between the United States and the Soviet Union, under which both would be prevented from establishing forces, military bases or facilities in Iran or Pakistan. This would assuage Soviet fears of US intentions in South-west Asia and provide the basis for a Soviet withdrawal from Afghanistan. In early February, with President Carter's support, he wrote to his Soviet counterpart, Foreign Minister Gromyko, suggesting establishment of a dialogue on the assumption that 'if there was restraint on both sides and respect for the independence and territorial integrity of the states in the region, our respective interests need not lead to confrontation'. Gromyko's response was positive and Vance requested Carter's approval to arrange a meeting. Brzezinski reportedly was vehemently opposed to the idea and eventually won over the vacillating Carter who instructed Vance not to continue with his initiative.

Grave doubts also existed among those at high level within the CIA, including the Director of Central Intelligence (DCI), Admiral Stansfield Turner. As reported by Bob Woodward in his book *VEIL: The Secret Wars of the CIA 1981—1987*, Turner pondered at length over the question of 'whether it was permissible to use other people's lives for the geopolitical interests of the United States'. He was also concerned that

CIA-supplied arms would be used against Soviet forces and that 'US policy was to fight to the last Afghan'. Eventually, however, he overcame his qualms and gave his support to the operation.

Central to US plans for countering the Soviets in Afghanistan was neighbouring Pakistan, with whom the United States had established an alliance during the early days of the Cold War. At the beginning of the 1950s Pakistan had become an integral part of an intensive US pro-gramme to conduct 'elint' and signals intelligence ('sigint') operations against the Soviet Union. In May 1954, it signed an agreement with the United States under which the latter would provide military aid in exchange for the continued use of intelligence facilities. In September of that year, along with the United States, Britain, Australia, New Zealand and the Philippines, Pakistan became a member of the South East Asian Treaty Organisation (SEATO) which was formed to counter communist expansion as manifested through military force in Korea and Indochina, and through subversion and insurgency in Malaya and the Philippines. In 1955, Pakistan also joined Britain, Turkey and Iran in the Middle East Treaty Organisation, later redesignated the Central Treaty Organisation (CENTO), which was intended to oppose the threat of Soviet expan-sionism into the oil-producing regions of the Middle East.

Pakistan's political scene during most of the 1950s was one of turbu-lence until October 1958 when the country's President, Iskander Mirza, abolished all political parties and abrogated the constitution, placing the country under martial law administrated by General Mohammed Ayub Khan who became Prime Minister presiding over a cabinet consisting of three senior army officers and eight civilians. Mirza himself was dis-missed shortly afterwards by Ayub Khan who thereafter held the appoint-ments of president, commander-in-chief and chief administrator of martial law under which Pakistan remained until mid-1962 when a new constitution introduced a system of federal government headed by a President. In January 1965, Ayub Khan received a new mandate but that year saw Pakistan embroiled in a brief and inconclusive war with India over Kashmir which resulted in a suspension of US military aid and, following internal unrest, a state of emergency under which Pak-istan was governed for the next four years during which there was increas-ing opposition to the government.

In March 1969, by which time he was under considerable pressure to step down, Ayub Khan handed over to the commander-in-chief of the armed forces, General Mohammad Yahya Khan. With internal unrest continuing to plague parts of the country, Pakistan was once again placed under martial law, but in November Yahya Khan declared that a general election would be held in December of the following year. This was duly held and won in West Pakistan by the Pakistan People's Party (PPP) led by Zulfikar Ali Bhutto and in East Pakistan by the Awami League under Sheikh Mujibur Rahman.

Bhutto refused, however, to form a government with the Awami League, this resulting in a nullification of the election which caused rioting in East Pakistan that developed into a full-blown civil war. Units of the Pakistan Army were deployed to suppress the insurgency, their brutality in doing so leading to an influx of some ten million refugees into India. The latter responded by invading East Pakistan and during the ensuing hostilities the Pakistanis were heavily defeated by the Indian Army, while East Pakistan subsequently became the independent state of Bangladesh. This humiliating defeat resulted in the resignation in December of Yahya Khan who was replaced by Zulfikar Ali Bhutto, his Foreign Minister.

After the adoption of a new constitution in 1973, which rendered the presidency largely ceremonial, Bhutto became Prime Minister while also holding the portfolios of Interior, Defence and Foreign Affairs. During the following four years, he began to pursue policies of Islamic socialism which brought few tangible changes. His rule became increasingly autocratic with suppression of criticism of his regime, imprisonment of political opponents and adoption of repressive measures against Pushtuns and Baluchis. At the same time, he sought to move Pakistan up to major power status by initiating the development of nuclear weapons in response to India's first nuclear test in 1974. He also tried to neutralise the Army's role in politics and internal affairs, removing senior officers, restructuring the chain of command and abolishing the post of commander-in-chief. This, together with his demand for deployment of troops to suppress a tribal insurrection in Baluchistan, antagonised the army. Meanwhile, he proceeded to foster closer relations with the Soviet Union and China while distancing himself from the West and the United States.

In January 1977, Bhutto announced that elections would be held within two months. Nine opposition parties combined to form the Pakistan National Alliance (PNA) but the election, which was marked by violence, resulted in a sweeping victory for Bhutto and the PPP albeit there were claims of fraud and vote-rigging. As serious unrest ensued in Karachi and other cities, Bhutto proclaimed martial law, calling out the army to suppress the violence. He attempted to placate the PNA by offering concessions but the latter refused to consider anything short of a new election.

In July, the army, concerned at the mounting chaos reigning throughout Pakistan, moved in and overthrew Bhutto in a coup led by General Mohammad Zia Al-Haq. In early September, Bhutto was imprisoned and charged with the attempted murder of a political opponent in 1974. Subsequently tried and found guilty, he was sentenced to death and executed in early April of the following year.

A zealous Muslim, who immediately imposed Islamic punishment for crimes, Zia had the support of the Muslim League and the Jamaat-i-Islami, the two dominant Islamic movements which have played central roles in Pakistani politics since the country's creation in 1947. Just over a year later, he formed a cabinet drawn from leaders of the Muslim League and other religious parties, as well as civilian administrators and technocrats, assuming the office of President in September 1978. His coming to power was marked by the Army's reasserting its control over much of Pakistan's affairs, both internal and external, and the discouragement of political parties – factors that caused the Muslim League and the Jamaat-i-Islami to withdraw their support for Zia.

This left Zia isolated, a situation made worse by his deteriorating relations with the United States and the Carter administration. The latter was becoming increasingly concerned about Pakistan's nuclear weapons development programme which was placing continued US economic and military aid at risk. By the beginning of 1979, however, the worsening situation in Afghanistan was causing mounting interest in Washington and, as reported by journalist Peter Niesewand in the *Washington Post* of 2 February 1979, Pakistan was by then actively involved in supporting Afghan anti-government guerrillas accommodated in former Pakistan Army bases guarded by Pakistani troops. When initially approached with regard to playing a front-line role in a war to expel the Soviets from Afghanistan, Zia was not slow to seize the opportunity to improve Pakistan's standing with Washington and thus ensure continuing American support.

During the months following President Carter's authorisation for covert support to the Afghan resistance, the CIA's planners produced details of an operation to be conducted by the Agency's secret arm, the Directorate of Operations (DDO), which during the 1960s and 1970s had been deeply involved in covert operations in a number of countries including Cuba, Vietnam, Laos, Cambodia, Angola and Tibet. Cuba and the Bay of Pigs fiasco in particular had resulted in unfavourable publicity for the CIA, as had exposure of its long-standing involvement with Nationalist Chinese forces in Burma who were major producers of opium. With a view to minimising the Agency's direct involvement with the Afghans, the operation would therefore follow a similar pattern to that employed by the CIA in Laos and Tibet, with no Agency personnel participating in missions inside Afghanistan; the plan was to train an army of Muslim extremists to engage the Soviet occupation forces in a protracted and costly conflict which Moscow would ultimately find insupportable. In this instance, however, an added dimension was added in order to avoid any allegation of direct involvement by the CIA in the conflict: officers and men of the Pakistan Army would be trained by US personnel and in turn would provide instruction for the Afghan guerrillas who called themselves 'mujahidin' (Soldiers of God).

To provide such training, the DDO would call on the special operations forces of the US military, notably members of the US Army's 5th Special Forces Group (Airborne), which specialises in activities throughout Asia, and the US Navy's Sea Air Land teams (SEALs). Many of these were veterans of clandestine CIA operations in Vietnam, Laos, Cambodia and elsewhere. On completion of their training, the newly qualified instructors would be flown back to Pakistan where they would thereafter be employed by the Pakistani military intelligence apparatus, the Directorate of Inter-Services Intelligence (ISI).

The ISI was created in 1971, replacing the Directorate of Intelligence Bureau formed in 1948. Headed by a director general and with its headquarters in the federal capital of Islamabad, its functions not only include, as its name suggests, the coordination of the intelligence-gathering functions of the military intelligence services of Pakistan's armed forces, but also the collection of foreign and domestic intelligence. According to certain reports, it is organised into the following six bureaux: Joint Intelligence X (JIX), a secretariat tasked with preparing intelligence estimates and threat assessments, while also providing administrative support to ISI units; Joint Intelligence Bureau (JIB), responsible for gathering of political intelligence and comprising three sections, one of them dedicated to operations against India; Joint Counter-Intelligence Bureau (JCIB), conducting intelligence-gathering operations in the Middle East, South Asia and China, and responsible for surveillance of Pakistani diplomats abroad; Joint Intelligence North (JIN), responsible for covert operations in Jammu and Kashmir; Joint Intelligence Miscellaneous (JIM), tasked with intelligence-gathering and espionage operations overseas; and Joint Signals Intelligence Bureau (JSIB), responsible for 'sigint' operations, for which it maintains a chain of stations along the border with India, and for maintaining radio communications support for Muslim militants in Jammu and Kashmir.

As mentioned earlier, the ISI allegedly had been involved for some time with Pakistan's support for anti-government insurgents in Afghanistan, providing arms and training at former Pakistan Army bases. Immediately after the Soviet invasion General Zia Al-Haq appointed a new director general, Lieutenant General Akhtar Abdel Rahman Khan. When Zia asked his opinion on countering the Soviet threat, the latter proposed that Pakistan should give all possible support to the Afghan resistance movement, thus defending not only Pakistan itself but also Islam. Like his counterparts in the CIA, Akhtar Khan foresaw that a lengthy guerrilla war could prove to be the Soviets' Vietnam. In his opinion, Pakistan should offer not only arms and equipment to the mujahidin but also training, operational intelligence and guidance. He proposed that bases should be established within the NWFP where the guerrillas could be trained and from which they could then operate into Afghanistan.

Zia gave his blessing to Akhtar Khan's ideas and the latter lost little time in handing the task to the ISI's Afghan Bureau whose role would be to coordinate mujahidin operations inside Afghanistan and to provide logistic support. Its headquarters were at Camp Ojhri, a large Pakistan Army base located on the northern outskirts of the Punjabi city of Rawalpindi, on the road leading to the federal capital of Islamabad. Surrounded by high walls and covering approximately 80 acres, it comprised offices, a large warehouse for the storage of arms and equipment, garages containing some 300 civilian trucks and other vehicles, accommodation for up to 500 men and a training area.

According to Brigadier Mohammad Yousaf, its commander from 1983 to 1988, in his book *The Bear Trap* (co-authored with Mark Adkin), the bureau was organised into three sub-units: Operations Branch, responsible for operational intelligence, planning of operations, selection of targets and allocation of operational tasks to individual mujahidin groups; Logistics Branch, tasked with the collection, allocation and distribution of arms and equipment to the mujahidin; and Psychological Warfare Branch, equipped with three radio stations situated on the border of Pakistan's North West Frontier Province (NWFP) with Afghanistan, and responsible for psychological operations. The bureau also possessed two forward bases located at Peshawar and Quetta, the capitals of NWFP and Baluchistan respectively and major garrison towns occupied by formations and units of the Pakistan Army. Another ISI unit, separate from the Afghan Bureau, was meanwhile tasked with the supply and distribution of food and clothing, purchased with CIA-supplied funds, to the mujahidin.

PESHAWAR WAS THE PRINCIPAL base of the Afghan resistance which comprised seven main political factions, all of them Sunni Muslim groups formed after the communist coup in Kabul in 1978 and all but one from the eastern Gilzai or minority Pushtun tribes. Four of the seven were so-called fundamentalists, the first being the Hizbi-i-Islami (Islamic Party), a largely Pushtun group led by Gulbuddin Hekmatyr who was strongly opposed to the United States and the West. Formed in 1968, it split in 1979, a second group being led by a cleric named Mawlawi Younis Khalis, and named after him, made up of tribesmen from the eastern areas of Afghanistan. Hekmatyr's group was the larger and more fundamentalist, its aim being the establishment of a single-party Islamic state in Afghanistan, while also proposing land reform and nationalisation of all industries. Generally anti-West in outlook, it advocated the formation of close ties with the rest of the Muslim world. Its military forces numbered between 15,000 and 20,000, 4,000 of whom were full-time guerrillas. Hekmatyr's main area of operations was in the south-east of the country but he also maintained a strong presence in the provinces of Nangarhar, Konduz, Kunar, Laghman and Baghman.

Khalis's group, also largely Pushtun and likewise favouring the establishment of an Islamic state, was more liberal in outlook and endorsed ties with the West. Its forces also numbered between 15,000 and 20,000 men, 3,500 of whom served full-time, and were under the control of regional commanders, foremost of whom was Jallalladin Haqqani. Khalis's principal area of operations was in the east, in Nangarhar, Paktia, Paktika and Kunar, and in the city of Jalalabad.

The third group, a non-Pushtun body consisting almost entirely of Tajiks from Badakshan and the Panjshir Valley, was the Jamiat-i-Islami (Islamic Society) led by Ustad Burhaneddin Rabbani, a former professor of Islamic law of the Afghan State Facility of Islam and a moderate who was also liberal in his stance towards the West. Based in north-east Afghanistan, with much of its leadership drawn from professional and educated classes, it was well organised, both politically and militarily, with Rabbani regarded by all elements as the overall leader. Its forces, which ultimately numbered some 60,000, of whom 12,000 to 15,000 were full-time, were commanded by Ahmed Shah Massoud. Their main area of operation was the Panjshir Valley but they were also active in the provinces of Badakshan, Baghlan, Konduz, Balkh and Samangan, as well as in Kabul, Herat Faryab, Jozjan and Farah.

The fourth fundamentalist faction was the Ittihad-e-Islami (Islamic Alliance), a Saudi-Arabian supported group of several hundred hardline radicals led by Abdul Rasul Sayyaf. Originally formed as a coalition, it subsequently split into several fundamentalist and moderate groups, one remaining under Sayyaf. Controlled by political and military committees, both under his control, its forces of between 6,000 and 15,000 men were led by regional commanders and operated in Nangarhar, Paktia and Parwan provinces, and in Kabul.

The remaining three factions were commonly referred to as moderates or traditionalists and had been formed in Peshawar after the 1978 coup in Kabul. The first of these was the Mohaz Melli Islami (National Islamic Front of Afghanistan). Formed in 1979 and led by Sayyad Pir Gailani, it favoured the return of the exiled Afghan king, Zahir Shah, as a constitutional monarch presiding over an elected parliament. Its military forces comprised some 2,000 full-time guerrillas with approximately 15,000, largely Pushtun, available on-call.

The second moderate group was the Jebhe-i-Najat-i-Milli Nejad (National Liberation Front), a small faction centred in the south of the country. Formed at the end of 1978 by an Islamic spiritual leader named Sibghatullah Mujadaddi, it advocated a democratic political system governed by Islamic tenets and was pro-Western in its outlook. Its forces of between 8,000 and 15,000 came under the control of regional commanders, operating in Kunar Province and the city of Kandahar.

The largest of the moderate groups was the Harakat-i-Inquilabi-i-Islami (Islamic Revolutionary Movement) formed in late 1978 by Mawlawi Mohammed Nabi Mohammedi, a former member of the Afghan parliament. Comprising a membership of Pushtuns and Uzbeks, it urged a democratic government for Afghanistan and favoured a non-aligned stance with other countries. Its forces, which numbered approximately 30,000, predominantly operated in Logar, Ghazni, Farah, Herat and Kabul, while also being active in Paktia, Helmand and Kandahar.

In addition to the seven main groups, there were a number of small Shi'ite groups, some maintaining links with Iran. First among these was Hizbollah (Party of God) which advocated Afghan union with Iran. Numbering some 4,500 in total, it operated in the west of Afghanistan. Another group which also favoured union with Iran was the Sepha-i-Pasdarae (Revolutionary Guards). Led by Mohsen Reza'i and supported by Iran, it numbered between 3,000 and 8,000 and operated in Herat, Helmand, Jozjan and Bamiyan.

A third Shi'ite group was the Shura which, headed by Sayed Ali Beheshti, proposed autonomy for Afghanistan's central-western region of Hazara. Numbering between 4,000 and 8,000, it was active in the provinces of Balkh, Baghlan, Bamiyan and Ghazni. A fourth group was the Harakat Islami (Islamic Movement) whose aim was the imposition of a Islamic fundamentalist state in Afghanistan. Led by Sheikh Muhsini and numbering some 12,000, of whom about 2,000 were full-time, it was active in the north in Badakhshan, Balkh, Jozjan and Faryab provinces.

There was little if any cooperation between the seven groups, whose tribal allegiances, different degrees of Islamic dogma and differences in social backgrounds all contributed to long-standing divisions, the mujahidin being drawn from every class and background in Afghanistan. It was not until May 1985 that an alliance was formed by the seven groups – the Islamic Union of Afghan Mujahidin – which survived until the end of the conflict.

The majority of the seven suffered from internal rifts, and relations between their respective headquarters and the commanders of the fighting units, who possessed by far the most influence and exercised total control over military operations, were frequently far from smooth.

Early in 1980, an organisation was formed for the recruitment worldwide of Muslims to fight in Afghanistan. Called the Mekhtab al-Khidemat al-Mujahidin (MAK) (Service Office of the Mujahidin), it was formed by a Saudi Arabian named Osama bin Laden, the son of a wealthy construction magnate with close connections to the royal family. Bin Laden was assisted in forming the MAK by Sheikh Abdullah Azzam, a Palestinian and professor of Shari'a law at the University of Jordan. The MAK established offices throughout the world while bin Laden set up a number of camps in the Sudan to which volunteers were sent before being despatched via Yemen to Pakistan. At the same time, he became one of the principal fund raisers for the mujahidin, eliciting money from wealthy sympathisers in Saudi Arabia and throughout the Muslim world. Recruiting also took place in the United States, this being handled by a number of Muslim organisations. Prominent among these was the Al-Kifah Afghan Refugee Centre, known popularly as the 'Al-Jihad Centre'. Based in Brooklyn, New York, and funded by organisations such as the World Muslim League and Tabligh-i-Jamaat, it was headed by Sheikh Abdullah Azzam.

Another organisation which also featured in mustering volunteers was the Tabligh-i-Jamaat which is known to have recruited from the mid-1980s onward in North Africa and Europe. An Islamic missionary group founded by Maulana Mohammad Ilyas, the organisation is based in Pakistan and has branches and schools worldwide. According to author John Cooley in *Unholy Wars*, it began its recruiting operations in Tunisia where its missionaries toured schools and colleges, enrolling some 160 recruits for six weeks of religious studies in Pakistan. At the end of these, ISI officers were introduced to the students, approximately 70 of whom were persuaded to undergo military training at one of the ISI's secret camps. In Algeria, which was suffering from serious internal unrest, the Tabligh recruited some 3,000 deserters from the Algerian army while in Europe it was assisted by extremist Islamic organisations such as the Muslim

Brotherhood which has branches throughout France and Germany.

An attempt was made, in early 1980, to create a unified Afghan resistance movement. During January and February, a number of meetings of Pushtun tribal chiefs, headed by Mohammed Omar Babrakzai, a former judge of the Kabul High Court and leader of the Jadran tribe inhabiting Paktia Province, took place to formulate a response to the Soviet invasion. On 11 May, on the outskirts of Peshawar, a national assembly was convened, attended by 916 delegates representing all provinces throughout Afghanistan, all Pushtun tribes and all non-Pushtun ethnic groups.

Until this point, the Pakistanis, in particular the ISI, and the seven Pakistan-based groups-in-exile had paid little heed to calls for a single resistance movement. The national assembly, however, representing as it did all tribal and ethnic groups within Afghanistan and advocating the establishment of a military and political command and control structures, possibly leading to a government-in-exile, caused considerable alarm. The assembly set up a national commission consisting of 100 members with 51 seats allocated to delegates selected on a provincial basis, the remaining 49 being divided among the seven Pakistan-based groups who were in the minority. It further decided that all commanders for resistance units should be selected by tribal leaders and called for the creation, following the ejection of the Soviets and the end of hostilities, of a federalised Afghan state in which tribes and regions would be granted autonomy. The assembly rejected all fundamentalist doctrine and called for a non-sectarian Islamic state with a foreign policy of non-alignment.

The efficiency and orderly manner with which the national assembly had been held, together with the pronouncements of its policies and decisions, caused much alarm within Pakistan, which saw it as a threat to the seven groups-in-exile through whom it hoped to keep the resistance movement divided and thus the issue of 'Pushtunistan' firmly off the political agenda. The ISI was thus detailed to sabotage the newly formed national commission by sowing the seeds of dissension and strife within its ranks. Meanwhile, it threatened to withhold supplies of arms and funds to the three traditionalist groups. Very soon these had withdrawn from the commission which by the latter part of 1980 had almost ceased to function. This inevitably prevented the resistance movement from producing a properly coordinated strategy throughout the war and providing an effective political alternative to the communist regime in Kabul.

IN JANUARY 1980, ZBIGNIEW Brzezinski travelled to Pakistan for a meeting with General Zia ul-Haq, who insisted that all supplies of arms, funds and training should be supplied to the mujahidin by Pakistan. He reinforced this demand with three conditions: first, all countries involved in the supply and funding of the operation should maintain complete and utter security about shipments, categorically denying any publicised reports of such; second, all consignments were to be trans-ported to Pakistan by the swiftest means available; third, shipments were to be limited to two per week. Zia's demands suited the Carter admin-istration which, together with the CIA, was anxious to ensure that all traces of US involvement in the operation were well concealed. The first consignments of arms for the mujahidin, meanwhile, had arrived in Pakistan on 10 January, soon being followed by others.

Brzezinski then travelled to Cairo where he submitted a request to President Anwar Sadat that the Egyptians supply Soviet-manufactured weapons from their stocks for the mujahidin. Sadat complied and a few weeks later US transport aircraft began flying to Egyptian airbases at Qenas and Aswan to collect consignments which were then flown to Pakistan. The arms were collected by the ISI and taken to Camp Ojhri for subsequent distribution to the mujahidin. Initially, the weapons were drawn from stocks supplied during the period when Egypt had been a recipient of Soviet military aid, many being in poor condition. During 1980, however, the Egyptians reactivated a number of plants set up in 1975 for the production of locally manufactured versions of Soviet small arms and certain surface-to-surface and surface-to-air missiles (SAM). Operating under the name of the Arab Organisation for Industrialisa-tion, this had been a joint venture by Saudi Arabia, Egypt, the United Arab Emirates (UAE), and Qatar who invested some \$1.04 billion in the project. In July 1979, however, they had ceased activities following the withdrawal of Saudi Arabia, the UAE and Qatar in protest at Egypt's growing rapprochement with Israel. With US financial and technical support, all the plants were now reactivated and by the end of 1980 were once again producing copies of Soviet weapons.

One of the requirements for the mujahidin was a man-portable SAM for deployment against Soviet and Afghan Air Force aircraft, in particular helicopters. Among the weapons manufactured at Saqr was the shoulder-fired Grail SAM-7 infra-red guided missile. This, however, together with a version manufactured in China, proved relatively ineffective with only a one-in-ten chance of hitting a target even under perfect conditions. An alternative considered by the CIA was the Redeye, a US-manufactured infra-red-guided SAM which had been in service with the US Army since the 1960s. A consignment of several dozen Redeyes were shipped to Pakistan where trials were carried out in late 1980. But these missiles proved unsuccessful, with a high failure rate.

Training of Pakistani Army personnel had meanwhile begun, earlier that year, at several US Army facilities, including one at Fort Bragg, North Carolina, home of the US Army Special Forces and the John F. Kennedy Centre for Military Assistance. Others included Fort A. P. Hill and Camp Pickett, in Virginia, where instruction was provided in infiltration and exfiltration techniques. Training was also conducted at a CIA facility called Camp Peary, near Williamsburg in Virginia. Some 25 square miles in extent, this was the CIA's principal training base for members of the DDO and others who required the arcane skills necessary for covert operations.

Selected Pakistani officers and other ranks, some of them members of the Special Service Group (SSG), the Pakistan Army's special forces formation, were trained intensively in a wide range of subjects including weapons, explosives, demolitions, sabotage, radio communications, field medicine, guerrilla warfare tactics, and assassination of enemy commanders and leaders. At Camp Peary, they underwent specialist training in intelligence-gathering operations, surveillance, counter-surveillance, report writing, agent and courier recruitment, use of dead-letter boxes and other aspects of intelligence tradecraft.

Having secured Pakistani and Egyptian support for its anti-Soviet coalition, the Carter administration turned to China. Since 1971, when US National Security Adviser Henry Kissinger had paid a secret visit to Peking, paving the way for an official visit by President Richard Nixon in February 1972, the United States and China had been achieving a gradual rapprochement. On 4 January 1980, US Secretary of Defense Harold Brown flew to Peking for meetings with Chinese premier Deng Xiao Ping and senior members of his government. Brown's aim was to enlist China's cooperation in countering the Soviets in Afghanistan, offering in exchange to grant China 'most favoured nation status' and to supply aerospace and communications technology, ostensibly for civil use but easily adaptable for military purposes.

Deng and the Chinese leadership accepted Brown's proposals and, having agreed to supply arms for the mujahidin, the Chinese delivered the first consignment approximately a month after Brown's visit, this being collected by US aircraft and flown to Pakistan. This and other early consignments comprised small arms such as Type 56 7.62mm assault rifles, Type 74 7.62mm general purpose machine-guns, Type 57 12.7mm and Type 54 14.5mm heavy machine-guns, and support weapons such as 60mm and 82mm light and medium mortars and large quantities of ammunition. In due course, 107mm and 122mm rocket launchers, including the Type 63 107mm twelve-tube multiple type, were also supplied by the Chinese.

It was later rumoured but never confirmed that some consignments of arms were despatched overland by way of China's vast province of the Uighur Autonomous Region of Sinkiang, situated north of Tibet, whose westernmost tip, 40 miles wide and 120 miles long, borders the easternmost Afghan province of Wakhan, a narrow mountainous corridor sandwiched between Tajikistan to the north and Jammu and Kashmir in the south. Inhabited by some 3,000 Kirghiz tribesmen, Wakhan was occupied during early 1980 by up to 2,000 Soviet troops in a move to deny the mujahidin access to the Chinese border. It was subsequently absorbed into the Soviet Union after being formally handed over by Afghanistan under coercion from Moscow. Fortified bases were established in the mountains, along with airstrips and helicopter landing zones (LZs). Thereafter the Soviets, with assistance from Afghan government forces, proceeded to drive the Kirghiz south over the border out of Wakhan into Pakistan.

Another route alleged to have been used by the Chinese was the Karakoram Highway which connects Sinkiang with Pakistan and comprises part of the Silk Road. An ancient trade route constructed by China to link it with the Roman Empire, the Silk Road originally stretched 4,000 miles from Sian, the capital of Shensi province, following the Great Wall of China north-westward, bypassing the desert of the Takla Makan and climbing the mountains of the Pamirs before crossing Afghanistan and continuing westward to the Levant. Accounts differ as to the use to which the Chinese put the Karakoram Highway: some state that consignments of arms were dispatched along it while Brigadier Mohammad Yousaf maintains that it was only used for the supply of a large quantity of mules for the mujahidin.

On 25 May, a delegation headed by Geng Biao, China's vice premier for security and the secretary general of the Chinese Communist Party's committee for military affairs, carried out a two-week official visit to the United States during which it was announced that sales of aircraft and air defence radar to China had been agreed. In September that year, a US military delegation paid a visit to Peking, this being followed by another Chinese delegation to Washington shortly afterwards. There were other, well hidden, benefits from this remarkably swift rapprochement between the two countries, the most notable being the establishment of two US 'elint' monitoring posts at Qitai and Korla, in the north-east and centre of Xinjiang Province respectively, to replace those lost in Iran in early 1979. Such facilities were of crucial importance to the United States in its ability to monitor military activities within the Soviet Union.

After the Iranian revolution, the United States had been reliant on those of its other posts based in Turkey. These, however, had been temporarily closed during the 1970s following Turkey's invasion of northern Cyprus in mid-1974 and a retaliatory US embargo on military aid to Ankara which was not lifted until 1978. Although they were subsequently reinstated, their future existence was thereafter considered to be in doubt, particularly as the Turks attempted to link it to continuing US military aid. Thus the agreement of the Chinese to the positioning of the two new posts in Sinkiang was of utmost importance to the United States. Manned by Chinese trained by the Americans in the skills of 'sigint', and operated under the direction of the CIA's Science and Technology Division, both would have the task of monitoring Soviet forces in Afghanistan and Central Asia.

Arms from other sources were also arriving in Pakistan for the mujahidin. By the end of 1980 these included copies of weapons manufactured by Pushtun gunsmiths in workshops in and around Peshawar, and Polish-manufactured copies of Soviet weapons. Among the latter were SAM-7 Grail shoulder-fired surface-to-air missiles although, as with the Egyptian and Chinese manufactured versions, these also proved relatively ineffective. Another source was inside the Soviet occupation forces in Afghanistan, none other than an officer on the logistics staff of the headquarters of the 40th Army in Kabul who sold weapons directly to the mujahidin.

During 1983, a number of consignments of Soviet-made weapons were flown straight from the United States to Pakistan. These had been purchased from the Israelis who had captured them following the expulsion of the Palestine Liberation Organisation in Lebanon. They were of little use to the Israelis, who used either US weapons or their own, and who therefore exchanged them for discounts on the purchase of F-16 aircraft and other arms from the United States. Major General Richard Secord, the Pentagon's Deputy Assistant Secretary of Defense for International Security Affairs in the Near East, Africa and South Asia, was placed in charge of the exchange programme. Arms were shipped from Lebanon to the port of Wilmington, North Carolina, from where they were transported by road to a secret CIA storage facility in San Antonio, Texas. The weapons were then inspected and serviced, their serial numbers being erased. Some were retained for CIA use while the rest were repacked for shipment either to Central America, for use by the Contras in Nicaragua, or to Pakistan where they were handed over to the ISI.

Apart from those consignments flown by US or Saudi Arabian aircraft to the Pakistani Air Force base at Chaklala, near Rawalpindi, all arms were shipped by sea to the port of Karachi. From there they were transported under armed escort by rail north to the ISI headquarters at Camp Ojhri, a proportion on occasions being sent directly to Quetta. On arrival at Rawalpindi, the consignments were broken down and loaded on to the ISI's fleet of civilian trucks for the next stage of the journey north to Peshawar where they were delivered to warehouses belonging to the seven mujahidin groups. These loads were then repacked and loaded aboard trucks which took them to guerrilla bases inside the Tribal Areas, which lie between the NWFP and the border, stretching from north of Peshawar to the south-west, and in Baluchistan.

Here they were met by mujahidin who were waiting to collect their allocated arms and other supplies which were carried by caravans of pack ponies across the border into Afghanistan and on to the forward operational bases in different areas. These normally followed six main routes, the northernmost of which could only be used from June to October as it was closed by snow for the remaining eight months of the year. Starting in Chitral, in northern Pakistan, it led westward across the Hindu Kush to the Panjshir Valley, Faizabad and northern Afghanistan.

The most commonly used route began in the area of Parachinar, to the west of Peshawar, and headed over the border to Ali Khel and the eastern Afghan province of Logar; from there it divided, one leg leading to Kabul or snaking north over the mountains to the plains around Mazar-e-Sharif. Farther south, another route commenced in the area of Miram Shah, heading west via Zhawar and then either north into Logar Province or south via Ghazni.

Baluchistan's capital of Quetta was the start of the fourth route which crossed the border at Chaman, thereafter heading north-west across open areas of terrain for Kandahar and its surrounding areas. The fifth route began over 250 miles farther to the west, at a small base at Girzi-Jungle on the border with the south-western Afghan province of Helmand, leading to Nimroz, Farah and Herat in the west of Afghanistan. As with the route from Quetta, this led across open terrain and thus trucks were used, rather than pack ponies, as speed was of the essence to avoid attack from the air. The sixth route was the longest with convoys having to move consignments along the length of Baluchistan's border, across the frontier with Iran and then north to the border between Iran and western Afghanistan from where the route split before turning east.

Of the seven Pakistan-based groups, that most favoured by the Pakistani government and the ISI was the fundamentalist Hizbi-i-Islami of Gulbuddin Hekmatyr which was allocated over half of the arms and funds supplied by the CIA. Brigadier Mohammad Yousaf admits in *The Bear Trap* that a total of 73 per cent was allocated to the four fundamentalist groups. This displeased the CIA, which favoured the traditionalists of Sayyad Pir Gailani's National Islamic Front of Afghanistan (NIFA) and Sibghatullah Mujadaddi's National Liberation Front, but no effort was made to redress the balance as the Agency had effectively allowed the Pakistanis to have the whip hand. According to the brigadier, the ISI's allocation of arms supplies was made purely on the grounds that the fundamentalists groups were militarily more effective. Others, however, among them seasoned observers with an extensive knowledge of Pakistani politics of the period and with much time spent with the mujahidin during operations in Afghanistan, maintain that it was solely the ISI's and General Zia ul-Haq's political agenda which governed the distribution of CIA-supplied aid in favour of the four fundamentalist groups.

By mid-1980, according to Brigadier Yousaf, the ISI had established two camps, each capable of accommodating 200 men, for training the mujahidin. One was situated in the area of Peshawar in the NWFP and the other near Quetta in Baluchistan, both in secret locations to which the trainee guerrillas were driven under cover of darkness. Staffed by detachments of American-trained ISI personnel, each comprising half a dozen officers and a dozen NCOs, the camps provided a variety of courses which were mostly of two weeks' duration and included tactics; support weapons comprising mortars, anti-armour and anti-aircraft weapons; demolitions and sabotage, including the destruction of strategically important pipelines, electricity pylons and bridges; mine-laying and mine disposal. Training the mujahidin was not without its difficulties as each faction refused to allow its men to undergo training alongside members of another. Moreover, commanders would demand training in certain subjects which their ISI instructors were well aware were of little relevance to their groups' particular operational requirements. Added to this was the problem of keeping the existence of the camps secret, particularly as a considerable amount of live firing was conducted there; on more than one occasion, a camp had to be struck and moved swiftly after its location had possibly been compromised.

During the following years, the ISI expanded its covert training facilities to the point where, by 1984, it was training 1,000 guerrillas per month. Increased resources enabled it to train over 17,500 during 1985 and 19,500 in 1986. By 1987, it was running seven camps, four in the area of Peshawar in NWFP and three around Quetta in Baluchistan. By 1988 over 80,000 mujahidin had received training at the hands of the ISI.

FROM 1981 ONWARD, THE ISI took an even more active role in the war when it began to deploy three-man teams into Afghanistan on special operations. Normally under a major, a team would be given a specific mission. The commander would select a mujahidin group which would then train under the supervision of the team before accompanying it on the operation, the latter thereafter acting in a similar role to that of the BATT teams fielded by 22nd SAS Regiment (22 SAS) in Oman, as recounted in Chapter 9. Dressed and equipped as mujahidin, the ISI teams conducted missions lasting weeks. During that time they would be out of contact with their base as they were not equipped with radios due to the risk of interception and location by enemy direction-finding (DF) units. According to Brigadier Yousaf, by 1984 the ISI had eleven such teams deployed: seven in the area of Kabul, two farther north around the enemy airbase at Bagram and two in the area of Jalalabad to the east of Kabul.

Right from the start, the cost of the entire operation in support of the mujahidin increased dramatically. During 1980 funding came from the CIA, which secured $30 million in appropriations from Congress, and from Saudi Arabia and other sources who contributed approximately $45 million. By the second year, the CIA's share alone had soared to $50 million.

Early 1981 had seen the arrival in office of President Ronald Reagan. His DCI was William Casey, a wartime member of the CIA's predecessor, the Office of Strategic Services (OSS), who had a penchant for covert action. Unlike his predecessor, Casey harboured no such doubts or reservations and soon after taking up his appointment began to press for expansion of the operation and the supply of better arms and equipment. During April 1981, he visited Saudi Arabia to obtain increased Saudi support, overcoming initial reluctance by tabling an agreement by the Reagan administration to sell the Saudis five Airborne Warning and Control Systems (AWACS) aircraft. Later that year, he had managed to get an increase in funding to $80 million for the period 1981–2.

Casey's enthusiasm for the Afghan venture was shared by a number of US politicians who had dedicated themselves to the support of the mujahidin and the secret war in Afghanistan. These included Republican Senator Gordon Humphrey from New Hampshire, Democrat Congressman Charles Wilson from Texas, and Republican Congressmen David Dreier and Bill McCollum from California and Florida respectively. In 1984, Wilson, who admitted to being obsessed with repaying the Russians for Vietnam and the 58,000 US servicemen who were killed there, established a close relationship with Casey and the two men worked closely on the Afghan operation. During that same year, he lobbied the House Appropriations Committee, on which he sat, and the House Intelligence Committee for an increase of $40 million in funds for the undertaking. This came from the Department of Defense's 'Black Budget', the funds allocated for covert activities. While no detailed

figures are available as to the exact amounts devoted to the Afghan operation, an approximate idea of their size can be gauged by the fact that,
whereas the annual allocation for the Black Budget up to and including
1980 was a maximum of $9 billion, from 1981 onward it would total
approximately $36 billion. Like the weapons, the major part of the ISI-
controlled and Arab donated funds tended to be funnelled to the four
fundamentalist groups, the Saudis directing much of their support to
the Ittihad-e-Islami of Abdul Rasul Sayyaf.

In addition to the funds employed for the purchase of arms, the CIA
supplied further amounts to the ISI on a monthly basis. These were
used to pay for the facilities maintained in and around Peshawar by each
of the different mujahidin factions, the salaries of their numerous officials and employees, warehouses for storage of arms and equipment,
purchase of items not supplied by the ISI, such as clothing and food,
and transportation of arms and equipment to the forward bases inside
Afghanistan. This last item was a major expense as the contractors who
supplied the vehicles and pack horse trains were quick to take advantage of every opportunity to make considerable profits from the war. As
Brigadier Yousaf states in his book, the cost of transporting a mortar to the
Mazar-e-Sharif was approximately $1,100 while the cost of each mortar
bomb was $65, so that total monthly expenditure on such transporta-
tion alone was $1.5 million.

Added to the CIA and Saudi Arabian-supplied funds were those channelled to the four fundamentalist parties by individuals and Muslim
organisations worldwide. These, together with the ISI's preferential
treatment of the fundamentalist factions, worked to the detriment of
the traditionalist groups who, burdened with administrative and other
overheads, had less to devote to operational requirements. It was a
vicious circle which enabled the ISI to justify to the CIA its allocation
of larger percentages of arms and funds to the fundamentalists.

In 1987, by which time support for the mujahidin had soared to a
staggering $630 million per annum, suspicions arose in the United States
over mismanagement of funds and equipment, and allegations were lev-
elled at those in Pakistan responsible for funnelling them to the
mujahidin. Some reports alleged that up to 80–85 per cent had been
siphoned off by Pakistani officials. At the end of February of that year
a request was made by William H. Gray, Democratic Representative for

Pennsylvania, that the US General Accounting Office (GAO) investigate the covert assistance being provided by the CIA to the mujahidin to determine whether any of the funding was being diverted. The GAO accordingly began an investigation but it was halted after the CIA and the Congressional intelligence committees refused to open their files.

James G. Shortt, who travelled into Afghanistan on two occasions, spending months with mujahidin units of Sayyad Pir Gailani's NIFA, later recalled senior members of this and other factions complaining of funds and equipment being diverted by Pakistanis. In an article published in the magazine *Special Forces* in August 1988, Shortt reported seeing US clothing and equipment, donated by the United States for the mujahidin, on sale for extortionate prices on merchants' stalls in Peshawar. A standing joke among the mujahidin at that time was that if a guerrilla returned from hospital still ill, he was told that the Pakistanis had not just stolen his money but also his health.

In addition to the United States, Britain, too, was taking an active interest in the conflict in Afghanistan, lending its support to the traditionalist groups supporting the return of King Zahir Shah. Prominent among these was NIFA, its military chief being Brigadier General Rahmatullah Safi. A native of the eastern province of Parwan, Safi attended the Kabul Military Academy before being commissioned into the Royal Afghan Army. In 1956, he was sent to the Soviet Union where he underwent three years of mountain warfare training in Tashkent and Odessa, and then on to the Ukraine, being attached to a spetsnaz unit until his return to Afghanistan where he raised the 30th Mountain Brigade. In 1968, he was sent to the United States for training at the US Army Special Warfare Centre (later the John F. Kennedy Centre for Military Assistance) at Fort Bragg in North Carolina. Between 1970 and 1973, by which time he was a lieutenant colonel, he underwent training in Britain with 22 SAS. On his return to Afghanistan, he raised the 444th Special Forces Brigade, commanding it until the communist coup in 1978. Arrested and tortured, he was imprisoned for three and half years, then placed under house arrest. Escaping from Afghanistan shortly afterwards, he made his way to Italy where he joined King Zahir Shah in exile, remaining with him until 1980 when, at the request of Sayyad Pir Gailani, he travelled to Pakistan to take up arms against the Soviet occupiers of his country.

The early 1980s saw Britain's Secret Intelligence Service (SIS) lending its support to CIA operations in Afghanistan. In his book *Ghost Force*, author Ken Connor, himself a former long-serving member of 22 SAS, recounts how two former members of the regiment were recruited by the SIS to assist in planning an operation against a Soviet air base. Subsequently introduced to a group of CIA officers, they were shown air and satellite photographs featuring 24 MiG-21 'Fishbed' fighter/strike aircraft parked near the perimeter track of the airbase. Two days later, the two men had devised a plan for an attack by a mujahidin unit in which the guerrillas would infiltrate into the base and blow off the tail of each aircraft with explosives. A month later, they were recalled to London and shown satellite photographs revealing all 24 aircraft with their tail sections neatly blown off.

During the previous year the SIS had despatched a team, headed by a former officer of the Royal Marines Special Boat Squadron (SBS), into Afghanistan to provide training for Jamiat-i-Islami mujahidin groups belonging to Ahmed Shah Massoud based in the Panjshir Valley. This was initially conducted in Pakistan but by 1982 was taking place in Afghanistan, with the team and guerrillas infiltrating over the border for training missions. Returning from one such task, however, they were ambushed by spetsnaz troops from a 900-strong brigade based north of Kabul. According to mujahidin sources, the spetsnaz were disguised as guerrillas, the first instance of such a ruse. In the ensuing action, the team's pack horses were killed and all its equipment lost. Although all members of the team escaped unscathed, their passports were discovered in their rucksacks and were later produced at a press conference as evidence that Britain was active in Afghanistan.

The embarrassment caused by this incident resulted in the training operation being transferred to Britain. In 1983, a group of Ahmed Shah Massoud's junior commanders were flown from Pakistan to Britain where they reportedly had several weeks of training under the auspices of an organisation called KMS, a commercial company. Registered in Jersey in the Channel Islands, with offices in Kensington in West London, it was staffed by former British special forces personnel. According to a covering letter sent earlier with a three-page proposal for training in Afghanistan, to be carried out over twelve months by a team of three instructors at a cost of £160,000, KMS by then had been in existence for over ten years during which it had trained special forces and unconventional units in South America, Africa, the Middle East and Southeast Asia.

The object of the exercise for the Jamiat-i-Islami junior commanders was to produce a cadre trained in a number of skills. According to Ken Connor, it took place at three sites: one in the north of England and two in Scotland, the latter located just over the border on the west coast. Among the subjects and skills taught were planning of operations, including attacks on airbases; sabotage of aircraft on the ground and anti-aircraft ambushes; tactics; demolitions; radio communications; and use of support weapons such as mortars and artillery. At the end of their training, the guerrillas were flown to Pakistan and infiltrated back into Afghanistan.

Support for mujahidin groups in central western Afghanistan came from Iran. According to a CIA report published in July 1985, Iranian clerics infiltrated the Shi'ite Afghan population of the semi-desolate region of Hazarajat shortly after the Islamic revolution in February 1979. From the beginning of 1980 to the end of 1982, the Iranians also attempted to court some of the Pakistan-based Sunni groups, notably Gulbuddin Hekmatyr's Hizbi-i-Islami, by supplying them with unspecified quantities of small arms and equipment, including Iranian-manufactured versions of the Heckler & Koch G-3 7.62mm rifle, mines, shoulder-fired light anti-armour weapons and clothing. From mid-1983 onward, however, the Iranians severed all contact with the seven Peshawar-based groups and concentrated on those in the centre and the west. Their support of the Harakat-e-Islami and other Shi'ite groups in the Hazarajat region eventually resulted in interfactional strife which took a heavy toll of guerrilla leaders, significantly weakening the resistance movement in the centre and west of Afghanistan. The bulk of Iranian support was directed towards the Hizbollah and Sepha-i-Pasdara but supplies of arms were limited by Iran's war with Iraq which inevitably claimed precedence.

From early 1981 onward, training of selected Shi'ite Afghan mujahidin took place at a number of establishments in Iran. Principal among these was Manzarieh Park, in the northern suburbs of the Iranian capital of Teheran, which provided training by North Korean and Syrian instructors for Pasdaran (Iranian Revolutionary Guards) as well as for guerrillas and terrorists from the Middle East and North Africa who were later sent to Lebanon. A second was at Eram Park, on the outskirts of the city of Qom, and a third 400 miles east of Teheran at Gorgon Plain. Yet another was situated at Vakilabad, 600 miles east of Teheran.

During the early 1980s, Britain's SIS dispatched a three-man team into Afghanistan to purloin a piece of titanium armour, the control panel and other designated items from an Mi-24 Hind helicopter gunship shot down by the mujahidin. The team, apparently comprising three former members of 22 SAS hired on contract for this specific task, was led in by a group of guerrillas and took with it, strapped to a donkey, a special motorised circular saw capable of cutting titanium. It successfully cut a sample of the armour and extracted other designated items including the control panel. No sooner had the team retired from the location than spetsnaz troops appeared in another two Hinds. Having landed, they placed explosive charges on the wrecked aircraft and blew it up before withdrawing.

In October 1983, the Kabul regime, with Soviet assistance, mounted an attack in the United Nations (UN) against Western interference in the country. At the same time, they published photographs of a 30-year old Briton named Stuart Bodman who, it was claimed, had been killed on 1 July in a spetsnaz ambush. On his body had been found a Motorola URC-10 satellite communications radio, a British passport, an international driving licence and some letters which not only identified him as an employee of Gulf Features Services in London but also indicated that three other individuals, identified only as 'Tom', 'Chris' and 'Phil', would be joining him. On 5 October, Pakistani monitoring of Soviet radio communications had picked up reports of the arrest of six Britons, identified by the Afghan Foreign Ministry as Bodman, his three companions and two further individuals identified as Roderick Macginnis and Stephen Elwick. According to James G. Shortt, two of the men named in the documents found on Bodman's body were subsequently found to be working in Hereford, the base town of 22 SAS; on being questioned, both admitted to having worked in Pakistan and Afghanistan.

Not surprisingly, the Foreign Office in London denied all knowledge of the six men. Meanwhile, investigations by the media revealed that the only 30-year old Stuart Bodman in Britain, tracked down through the national register of births, deaths and marriages, was a warehouseman who was alive and well, and living in Surrey, south of London. It transpired that he had once held a passport in the early 1970s but had destroyed it, and had never travelled further afield than the Channel Islands. The real identity of the individual killed in the Soviet ambush was never revealed and remains a mystery to this day. It was subsequently claimed that he and his five companions were members of a group whose task was to collect Soviet weapons for analysis at specialist defence establishments in Britain and the United States.

The CIA also took advantage of the conflict to lay its hands on the latest developments in Soviet weaponry. At that time, the Agency had a valuable human intelligence ('humint') asset inside the Soviet Union providing first-rate information, including plans, specifications and test data on current systems and others still under development. Identified later as A. G. Tolkachev, he was a member of the Moscow Aeronautical Institute. Another was a senior official in the Indian government who provided information on air defence weapons supplied to India by the Soviets. The Agency, however, needed samples of actual weapons for analysis and testing and thus launched a top-secret operation, code-named SOVMAT, to acquire them. In many cases small arms were taken from the bodies of Soviet troops killed in action, particularly spetsnaz, as such units frequently were issued with the best and most recently issued models. Other types of weapons and equipment were purchased by the mujahidin directly from corrupt Soviet officers in Kabul, among them infra-red flares employed by Soviet aircraft as countermeasures against the SAM used by the guerrillas. Larger and sophisticated weapon systems, including some of the latest types of armoured vehicles and sophisticated radars fitted to aircraft, were acquired through the CIA's long-established worldwide network of front companies and corporations which purchased them from Eastern Bloc arms dealers and, in some instances, government organisations.

It was the ISI, however, which presented the CIA with its greatest acquisition. High on the Agency's list was an intact Mi-24 Hind-D (the export model officially designated Mi-35), but all attempts to persuade an Afghan air force pilot to defect with his aircraft had proved unsuccessful. The commander of the ISI's Afghan Bureau, Brigadier Mohammed Yousaf, then lent a hand by briefing the leaders of the seven mujahidin groups on the requirement. Soon word had been sent to

Kabul and some time later, in mid-1985, two Hind-Ds landed at Miram Shah, just inside Pakistan. A few weeks later they had been spirited away to the United States along with some of the crews. An interesting footnote to this story is that in 1997 a Hind-D with Afghan air force markings was observed in a hangar at the Royal Aeronautical Establishment at Farnborough, in southern England.

PRIOR TO INVADING AFGHANISTAN, the Soviets had laid down a number of principal points governing the action and their subsequent occupation of the country. The initial task of their forces, which would keep a low profile and avoid any direct confrontations with the mujahidin, was to establish garrisons in the major cities while also securing air bases, major highways and other key areas in order to stabilise the country. Afghan army units, freed from such static garrison tasks, would then deploy into rural areas, backed up by Soviet air power, artillery and logistical support, and engage and destroy the mujahidin forces. Once the latter had been defeated, all Soviet forces would be withdrawn.

The Soviets, however, had not counted on the capabilities and strengths of the mujahidin as guerrillas, and on the lack of enthusiasm on the part of the Afghan army in engaging them. Within two months, the Soviets found themselves directly involved in combat operations. With little opportunity to deploy off the roads which wound through harsh mountainous terrain, the troops of the motor rifle divisions, predominantly men from the Soviet Central Asian republics, soon found they were outmanoeuvred and outgunned by the agile guerrillas, heavily armed with RPG-7s and other shoulder-fired anti-armour weapons. Once their ammunition was exhausted, they were slaughtered as they cowered inside their vehicles.

One of the early major Soviet operations took place in March 1980 in the Kunar Valley in the east. After heavy air and artillery bombardments, the 201st Motor Rifle Division advanced up the valley to relieve Afghan army units under attack from the mujahidin. In the face of the armoured threat, the guerrillas withdrew from the valley into the surrounding hills and mountains. Three months later, the Soviets launched another operation to clear a route from the city of Gardez, south of

Kabul, south-eastward to Khost. This ended in disaster when the mujahidin isolated and massacred an entire motor rifle battalion. These and other actions soon impressed upon the Soviet high command in Kabul the urgent necessity of a change in strategy and a restructuring of the occupation force.

Changes in the Soviet order of battle took place during the summer of 1980. Units and formations composed of Central Asian troops, who as Muslims had tended to fraternise with the local population and whose reliability was considered suspect, were sent back to the Soviet Union and replaced with troops from Russia. From 1980 to mid-1982, Soviet forces increased to a total of between 110,000 and 120,000, including air force personnel. Under command of 40th Army, these included three motor rifle divisions: the 5th Guards, 108th and 201st based at Shindand, Kabul and Kunduz respectively. Two more motor rifle divisions, the 54th at Termez and the 346th at Kushka, had a partial training role, while a third, the 280th at Ashkabada, near the border with Iran, was purely a training formation. In addition, there were two independent motor rifle brigades, the 66th and 70th based at Jalalabad and Kandahar respectively, and four independent motor rifle regiments: the 181st based at Bagram, the 187th at Mazar-e-Sharif, the 191st at Ghazni and the 866th at Faizabad. Support troops included an engineer brigade and an artillery brigade.

The large force of airborne troops in Afghanistan came under the command of Headquarters 103rd Guards Airborne Division co-located with the forward headquarters of 40th Army in Kabul. This formation comprised four airborne regiments, drawn from the 103rd, 104th and 105th Guards Airborne Divisions, and three air assault or airmobile brigades, among them the 56th Air Assault Brigade based at Gardez. Another formation, the 345th Guards Air Assault Regiment, was stationed at Bagram as a mobile reserve. Finally, there were two spetsnaz brigades which comprised two types of unit: raydoviki, raiding units; and vysotniki, specialists in long-range reconnaissance and intelligence-gathering as well as direct action.

During 1980, the Soviets decentralised their forces and divided Afghanistan into seven military regions, each with its own headquarters controlling allocated formations and units. Each region possessed its own dedicated helicopter assets as it had soon become apparent to the

Soviets that these would play a major role in the war. The initial number of some 60 aircraft was steadily increased during the first eighteen months to a point where they totalled some 300 by mid-1981. These were deployed in air regiments stationed at Bagram, Kunduz, Kandahar and Shindand, with squadrons deployed to outstations under the command of units they were supporting. Fixed-wing and transport aircraft were also increased in number as the conflict continued, but these remained under control of 40th Army's forward headquarters at Kabul.

Meanwhile the Soviets persisted in employing conventional tactics at brigade and divisional level. Each operation involved between 6,000 and 12,000 troops, including Afghan formations taking part under Soviet command. These would typically begin with prolonged heavy bombardments by artillery, strike aircraft and helicopter gunships, after which armoured columns would advance along main roads in valleys while remaining within range of artillery and air support. More often than not alerted beforehand, the mujahidin would withdraw into the mountains, allowing the Soviets to take control of an area. This would prove only temporary; unable to establish a permanent presence, the Soviets would withdraw to their garrison bases, allowing the guerrillas to return. This meant that operations had to be mounted repeatedly in the same areas, most of them ultimately achieving little in the way of success.

By the end of 1980, however, the Soviets had altered their tactics, using air assault and airborne troops deployed by helicopter along the axes of advance by motorised rifle formations. These were inserted in the rear or on the flanks of known mujahidin concentrations with the task of isolating them, destroying their forward bases and blocking their infiltration and supply routes. As described in *The Bear Went Over the Mountain*, a compilation of accounts of actions by Soviet officers who served in Afghanistan edited by Lester W. Grau, one of the first such actions took place in Kunar Province in December 1980 after the Soviet detection of a 50-strong force of mujahidin which had infiltrated from Pakistan and crossed the Kunar River before making its way to a canyon south-west of Chaghasarai.

An airborne battalion was given the mission of locating and destroying the guerrilla group and deployed to a position north of Chaghasarai. From there a company, less one platoon, was transported by road in the early hours of 15 December to a point just over a mile south of the canyon from where it moved to blocking positions to the south and south-west of the objective. A second blocking force, comprising a platoon plus the battalion's reconnaissance platoon, was meanwhile inserted by helicopter into blocking positions to the north and west. At 5.00 a.m., the remainder of the battalion carried out a sweep of the canyon from the east, an hour later making contact with the mujahidin who with-drew under covering fire, only to encounter the blocking groups who accounted for 28 guerrillas, killing 24 and capturing four.

During 1981, the majority of Soviet operations were primarily intended to ensure the security of Kabul and the major Soviet and Afghan bases. In April, combined Soviet and Afghan troops launched an offen-sive in the Panjshir Valley against the forces led by Ahmad Shah Massoud. Situated astride the route leading from the Soviet border to Kabul, the valley offered ideal bases from which Massoud's men could cut the route leading from Kabul to the Salang Tunnel. It was for this reason that it was to remain the scene of the largest number of Soviet offensives throughout the entire war. During March, Massoud had conducted a raid on the airbase at Bagram, north of Kabul, whereupon the Soviets began the first of several attempts to destroy his bases. Although they were driven out of the valley, he and his men were able to retreat into the safety of the surrounding hills from which they could harass the enemy.

A similar operation took place in April in the Logar Valley, south of Kabul, also failing to achieve its objective; and in August combined Soviet–Afghan forces attempted to entrap and destroy a mujahidin force in the Marmoul Gorge in Balkh Province, but without success.

In late 1981, the Soviets replaced a number of the senior command-ers in Afghanistan and these conceived a new strategy of cutting off the mujahidin from Pakistan. During the period from October to Decem-ber, Soviet and Afghan aircraft carried out a number of incursions into Pakistani airspace, on occasions attacking mujahideen base camps near the border. Some success was also achieved during several operations conducted in Nangrahar Province, near the border, and in Parwan Province, where heavy losses were inflicted on the mujahidin.

At the beginning of 1982, the Soviets resumed their large-scale sweeps which initially brought some degree of success in January in Parwan Province where heavy losses were inflicted on mujahidin forces. Similar

operations were also mounted around Herat, in the west, and Kandahar in the south. Another successful raid by mujahidin on the Bagram
airbase on the night of 25 April, in which over a dozen aircraft were
destroyed, provoked the Soviets into launching another offensive in the
Panjshir Valley with approximately 11,000 troops, reinforced with 4,000
Afghan troops, advancing up it from the south while additional Soviet
troops moved up from the north. Once the valley had been sealed off,
Soviet aircraft carried out saturation bombing of the entire area, devastating a large number of villages albeit these had been evacuated long
beforehand. This was followed by a wave of helicopters bringing in large
numbers of airborne troops. Massoud's forces, however, managed to
escape the dragnet largely unscathed and once again withdrew into the
hills, ambushing any Soviet units which attempted to follow up.

During the rest of 1982, major offensives were conducted in May in
the Ghorband Valley, to the north of Kabul, another in the Panjshir
Valley during September, and a third in the Laghman Valley to the east
of Kabul in November. All proved similarly unsuccessful.

The Soviets altered their strategy once more in 1983. Instead of
seeking to engage the guerrillas, they concentrated on driving the population from the rural areas through the bombing of villages, killing of
livestock, and destruction of fields and crops with incendiaries, denying
their future use through the laying of anti-personnel mines, and con-
taminating whole areas with chemical agents delivered by aircraft. Entire
areas were left uninhabitable by this process, forcing large numbers to
head west to Pakistan and its already overflowing refugee camps.

That year the Soviets yet again modified their order of battle. By this
time they had appreciated that their motor rifle formations and units
were ill-equipped and poorly trained for a war which called for lightly
equipped, highly mobile infantry with effective fire support readily available. So they created a special counter-insurgency force from their airborne and air assault troops which, together with units from the two
spetsnaz formations, were deployed not only in aerial missions by battalions and companies to outflank and block mujahidin groups but also
in operations by small units against guerrilla infiltration routes and lines
of supply, these being carried out by platoons or patrols.

One such operation was carried out at the end of July 1983 by a
20-strong patrol which ambushed a route used by convoys bringing

supplies to mujahidin groups in Helmand Province, the ambush itself being laid by a bridge crossing a canal. As described in *The Bear Went Over the Mountain*, the patrol was inserted by two Mi-8 Hip helicopters approximately three miles south of the area just before dusk, with cover from four Mi-24 gunships. After last light, the patrol moved up to the ambush site and reconnoitred the area, discovering a mujahidin two-man observation post (OP) nearby. Some three-quarters of a mile to the north-east was a village called Anova while half a mile to the west lay another called Marja.

Having positioned two MON-50 anti-personnel mines (the Soviet equivalent of the M-18A1 Claymore) covering the bridge, the patrol had taken up its positions by 9.30 p.m. During the following five and a half hours, however, it observed nothing except for the two mujahidin in the OP signalling to both villages with a torch. The patrol commander, Major V. P. Gladishev, was under instructions to withdraw at 3.00 a.m. but 25 minutes beforehand a truck appeared from the direction of Anova, heading towards Marja. As it crossed the bridge, both mines were initiated and the patrol opened fire; meanwhile, two of its members attacked the OP with grenades. Within two minutes the action was over, all 28 occupants of the vehicle having been killed. After removing a quantity of weapons and documents from the truck, the patrol withdrew and headed for a predetermined landing zone (LZ) from where it was extracted by helicopter before dawn.

Over the next couple of months, the same battalion carried out eighteen similar operations, killing some 200 guerrillas and capturing 20 more. In addition to about 200 weapons and a considerable quantity of ammunition, it discovered a large sum of money in Iranian, Pakistani and Afghan currencies.

Mujahidin operations during 1983 included offensives aimed at besieging and capturing the Afghan garrisons in the cities of Urgun, Khost and Jadji, for which the guerrillas assembled heavy weapons and large stocks of ammunition. A lack of trained sappers, however, restricted their ability to clear minefields laid by Soviet troops. Jadji was relieved in August by a 12,000 strong Soviet–Afghan force but it was not until December that 10,000 Soviet and 7,500 Afghan troops relieved Khost after advancing into the area and forcing back the besieging mujahidin forces. Meanwhile, the siege of Urgun lasted until 22 January of the following year when the garrison was rescued by Soviet airborne troops landed by helicopter.

The mujahidin also devoted considerable effort to penetrating the defences at Kabul. Until then, their attempts had consisted of attacks by small underground groups on Soviet military personnel and barracks within the city but these had proved increasingly difficult to sustain due to improvements in security by both Soviet and Afghan forces. It was thus decided to launch a major assault on the Bala Hissar Fort, a large Soviet bastion just inside the city's defensive perimeter. On 13 August, a large body of mujahidin managed to pierce the perimeter and attack the fort. The battle lasted throughout the night before the guerrillas withdrew.

The attack on Bala Hissar was followed by a raid on a large Afghan army base in the north-east, in which several aircraft and an ammunition depot were blown up, and by a series of assaults against Soviet convoys on main routes leading to Kabul. These provoked a fierce response from the Soviets who proceeded to carry out indiscriminate carpet bombing of three valleys in the area of Shomali, near the main route leading north of Kabul, while also deploying airborne and spetsnaz troops by helicopter to flush out mujahidin groups and destroy their bases.

In 1983, Ahmed Shah Massoud had negotiated a truce with the Soviets and the Kabul regimes. This had held for a year but by March 1984 it was apparent to the Soviets that Massoud would not renew it and by April he had resumed his attacks on the Salang highway. The Soviets therefore launched a major offensive, called PANJSHER VII, which was designed to finish Massoud's forces once and for all. Of the 20,000 troops taking part, most were airborne and air assault units, including 6,000 flown in from the Soviet Union as reinforcements. They included a large proportion of the 103rd Guards Airborne Division, a regiment of the 104th Guards Airborne Division, the 375th Guards Airborne Regiment and a regiment of the 108th Motor Rifle Division. These were reinforced by 6,000 Afghan troops, including elements of the 8th and 20th Divisions, 38th Commando Brigade and tribal militias. In addition, they were supported by 36 Tu-16 Badger bombers and a large number of Su-24 Fencer ground attack aircraft as well as the helicopter gunships and transport helicopters dedicated to the airborne formations. An extensive command and control organisation was established for the operation which was to be controlled from an airborne command post in a specially equipped An-12 Cub transport.

It was not long, however, before Massoud learned of the impending operation and in March he launched a pre-emptive attack against a fuel convoy on the Salang highway. Moreover, he had obtained details of the Soviet plan from sympathisers in the Afghan forces and accordingly evacuated the civilian population and the principal elements of his forces from the main valley. Having laid a number of minefields, he withdrew the remainder of his troops into the mountains.

Before the operation started, the entire area was bombed heavily. On 21 April, preceded by a rolling artillery barrage, 10,000 Soviet mechanised troops, reinforced by 5,000 Afghans, moved into the mouth of the main valley. After some delay caused by Massoud's minefields, they advanced up the valley itself, reaching Rokha on 24 April before progressing to their initial objective of Khenj. During the second phase of the operation, which began at the beginning of May, airborne troops were landed in battalion strength at Dasht-e-Rawat and at the entrance of the main side valley. Fierce fighting occurred here, one airborne battalion being mauled heavily by the mujahidin after it advanced beyond the range of supporting artillery. Elsewhere, a group of guerrillas in the main valley suffered heavy losses from bombing.

The Soviets advanced meanwhile into the adjoining valleys while another column moved from Khinjan via the Salang Pass highway into the Andarab Valley, linking up with an airborne unit. Other columns from Jalalabad probed the southern approaches to the Panjshir Valley, the Alishang and Kantiwar passes, while Afghan militia forces advanced down the Anjuman Valley towards the Panjshir. The Soviets made little headway, however, in the side valleys. Narrow and twisting, they were unsuitable for the deployment of armoured vehicles or helicopters while troops on foot were vulnerable to ambush.

In the meantime, Massoud had received reinforcements from other mujahidin groups who, in a bid to relieve the pressure on him, launched attacks around Jalalabad and Kabul. At the same time, he carried out another raid on the airbase at Bagram, destroying several MiG-21 aircraft.

By the end of June, the operation had ended and the Soviets started to pull back their troops, leaving Afghan units to garrison the Panjshir in a series of fortified bases established for the task. They had failed in their objective of capturing or killing Massoud, and destroying his forces. Indeed, by the end of June he had returned to the Panjshir and had begun attacking the bases in the valley. Soviet losses during PANJSHIR VII were subsequently reported as at least 500 dead plus a large number of helicopters destroyed, while mujahidin casualties were put at approximately 200.

During September, the Soviets mounted another offensive in the Panjshir, this comprising a series of helicopter-borne operations by air assault units in the upper area of the valley, but it achieved only limited success and failed to prevent Massoud re-establishing control over the area.

Soviet emphasis on heliborne operations continued into 1985. During August the mujahidin stepped up their activities in Logar Province, shelling Kabul from the south-east in addition to attacking outposts and convoys. Eventually, reports from the Afghan intelligence service, KHAD, indicated that a force of up to 600 guerrillas, organised in fifteen groups, was located in the area of the three villages of Khurd-Kabul, Malang, Kala and Malikheyl. Another large concentration was based nine to twelve miles farther to the south-east in the area of the village of Tizini-Khash, reportedly the location of a large arms and ammunition dump heavily guarded by 300 guerrillas equipped with DshK 12.7mm heavy machine-guns and mortars.

It was decided that a force of Afghan troops would set up a base in the Logar Valley while the 103rd Guards Airborne Division, commanded by Major General Yuri Yarygin, was given the task of locating and destroying the mujahidin. A composite force of three battalions from two airborne regiments was assembled for the operation, being reinforced by an independent reconnaissance company from the division's third regiment, an engineer battalion, a tank battalion and an artillery regiment less one battalion.

The entire force was to move into the operational area during the period 9–11 August. On 13 August, the two reconnaissance companies would then be lifted just over 30 miles to two positions blocking two canyons south of the Logar Valley. The main force of three battalions would then carry out an air assault into an area north of the village of Khurd-Kabul and engage the guerrillas.

Just prior to the operation, however, the mujahidin groups in the area of Khurd-Kabul, Malang, Kala and Malikhey pre-empted matters by attacking the Afghan army base in the Logar Valley which was abandoned by its garrison. Major General Yarygin therefore altered his plan, combining the two reconnaissance companies into a single force and reinforcing it with an Afghan battalion and a section of sappers. This would now be lifted into a position east of Malikheyl and establish a blocking position at the mouth of a canyon.

On 13 August, after a 30-minute flight in two lifts, the reconnaissance companies and the Afghan battalion were landed on the western slope of the canyon and headed south, eventually becoming pinned down by heavy machine-gun and mortar fire from mujahidin on features dominating the area. At the same time, a large group of some 600 guerrillas was seen withdrawing from the canyon. By then it was dark and thus no air support was available; moreover, the companies were beyond the range of supporting artillery. Unable to enter the canyon because of heavy enemy fire, the companies dug in on a ridge-line and awaited the arrival of the main force which landed next morning after an artillery bombardment of the LZ area. By this time, however, the guerrillas had retired through the canyon and made good their escape.

Yarygin decided to go ahead with the next phase of the operation, the capture and destruction of the mujahidin force and arms dump in the area of Tizini-Khash. At 2.12 p.m. that afternoon, supporting artillery brought down a barrage on the area of four planned LZs, being followed by air strikes. At 2.45, the first of three lifts began as 180 men of the 1st Battalion 350th Airborne Regiment, and 120 men of the 2nd Battalion, were flown aboard 22 Mi-8 Hip helicopters to two LZs from where they deployed into blocking positions. The main force was then flown into the two other LZs under cover of further air strikes.

The reconnaissance group of two companies, which had been part of the second lift, was landed just under four miles to the west of its intended LZ. After a forced march it reached a small village of Tizini-Khash where it found no sign of any mujahidin or any large arms cache. The group commander, Captain V. V. Selivanov, then discovered from his Afghan guide that the names of small villages printed on the map were not necessarily those by which they were known by the local population. The village which was the group's objective was in fact called Zandekhkalai.

Pushing on, Selivanov and his men reached Zandekhkalai where they were joined by the rest of the assault force. According to an account given later by Selivanov, some 150 mujahidin died in the ensuing battle and a search of the village uncovered seven large caches of arms and ammunition.

Missions conducted by airborne and air assault units in Afghanistan frequently laid the burden of responsibility for their success on junior officers commanding companies and platoons, a departure from the norm in the Soviet Red Army where initiative and flexibility were not encouraged at lower levels. A good illustration of this took place in October 1985 during an operation carried out by the 4th Air Assault Battalion attached to the 70th Independent Motor Rifle Battalion based at Kandahar.

Intelligence had been received that the mujahidin had established a base for training guerrillas in the use of shoulder-fired SAM in an area south-west of the city and the battalion was given the task of attacking and destroying it. At 7.00 a.m. on 13 October, the 12th Air Assault Company, commanded by Captain V. G. Istratly, was inserted into an LZ to the south of a hill feature east of the objective, and secured it. The company came under heavy fire and throughout the rest of that day, despite artillery and air support, the rest of the battalion was unable to land.

By dusk the company's ammunition was beginning to run low and Istratly realised that he could not hold out until the battalion broke through to him on the following morning. On his own initiative, he decided to mount a company attack that night. In the early hours of 14 October, his first platoon moved to the west, making its way to a point on the south-west of the training base's perimeter, while the second platoon headed north towards mujahidin positions on the south-east face of the hill feature to create a diversion. Meanwhile, the third platoon advanced towards the southern end of the base, taking up a position just to the south. At 2.30 a.m., all three platoons attacked simultaneously and once the battle was under way the second platoon veered round to the north of the hill feature and mounted an assault on the base from the east. The attack was successful and by 4.00 a.m. the objective had been overrun. The mujahidin mounted a counter-attack two hours later but this was beaten off using captured weapons, including three

DShK 12.7 mm heavy machine-guns. The guerrillas finally withdrew on the arrival of the rest of the 4th Air Assault Battalion.

THE SOVIETS' INCREASING USE of airborne and air assault units, coupled with close air support, increased the pressure from the mujahidin on the ISI to supply an effective countermeasure. The most potent threat was the Mi-24 Hind gunship equipped with a fearsome armament of either a 12.7mm Gatling-type four-barrelled machine-gun or 30mm cannon, 57mm rockets and bombs; in addition, it could accommodate up to ten fully equipped troops in its rear cabin.

As mentioned earlier, the SA-7 Grail SAM supplied by Egypt and China had proved ineffective, as had the US-manufactured Redeye which had entered service with the US armed forces in 1966. In 1984 the ISI approached the CIA with a request for the FIM-92A Stinger, a passive infra-red guided weapon which had replaced the Redeye from 1982 onward. This was turned down as the US Army was reluctant to see its stock of 3,000 missiles depleted and feared, moreover, that the secret technology contained in the missile could fall into the hands of the Soviets who would inevitably copy the weapon through a process of reverse engineering. The US Secretary of Defense, Caspar Weinberger, threw his weight behind the refusal, expressing his concern at the possibility of technology being leaked to the Soviets, while the State Department claimed that the introduction of US high technology weaponry into Afghanistan could provoke a serious response from the Soviets against Pakistan.

In May 1985, the US Undersecretary of Defense for Policy, Fred Ikle, and his Coordinator for Afghan Affairs, Michael Pillsbury, paid a visit to Islamabad and the headquarters of the ISI. There they met its Director General, Lieutenant General Akhtar Abdel Rahman Khan, who stressed the need for effective anti-aircraft weapons while presenting the two Americans with a list of arms requirements which included Stingers. Shortly afterwards, this was despatched by cable from the US Embassy to the Director of Central Intelligence, William Casey. Ikle and Pillsbury also attended a meeting with General Zia ul-Haq, but he was more concerned that Stingers should be provided to the Pakistan armed forces; as regards supplying the missiles to the mujahidin, he confined himself to saying that he would consider the matter.

During their visit, Ikle and Pillsbury received a briefing from a senior Pakistan Army officer, Lieutenant General Mirza Aslam Beg, whose corps was responsible for much of the area along Pakistan's border with Afghanistan. He presented the two Americans with a very sombre picture of events, stating that the mujahidin were being beaten by the Soviets. This, and a subsequent conversation with Lieutenant General Akhtar Abdel Rahman Khan, convinced them that the United States needed to increase its support for the guerrillas, and on their return to Washington they pressed for such. This resulted in a further $200 million being released from secret Defense Department funds but the request for the supply of Stingers was refused once again.

The CIA's head of the Directorate of Operations, John McMahon, meanwhile proposed that the mujahidin should be supplied with the Blowpipe SAM, a heavy and cumbersome shoulder-fired weapon adopted by the British armed forces in 1975. The ISI, however, knew that although the weapon could engage an aircraft head-on, not needing to seek its engine exhausts as a heat source because the missile was guided by radio via a thumb-operated joystick control on the launcher, the operator was required to leave any protective cover to launch it and thus remained exposed while guiding it on to its target. The much sought-after lightweight Stinger, on the other hand, was a passive infra-red-guided 'fire-and-forget' weapon that enabled its operator to take cover and reload immediately after launching his first missile. Moreover, the Pakistanis were also aware that the Blowpipe's performance during the Falklands War, only three years earlier, had proved disappointing; indeed, 22 SAS had resorted to acquiring Stingers at short notice from the US Army and had used them to good effect against Argentinean aircraft. In any case, Blowpipe was almost obsolete as the British had begun replacing it in 1984 with the Javelin, a superior version with an improved rocket motor giving better speed and range and featuring an improved semi-automatic command to line-of-sight (SACLOS) radio guidance system.

The CIA nevertheless insisted on supplying the Blowpipe. On their arrival, however, the first missiles proved to be faulty, being equipped with defective guidance systems that caused them to go into free flight after launching. Modifications were carried out but the weapon still proved to be unreliable, with a high proportion failing during launch. Despite these problems, further Blowpipes were delivered. Four were subsequently captured after a group was forced to withdraw rapidly from the scene of an action, the missiles later being displayed on Soviet television as further proof of British involvement with the Afghan resistance.

Another unsuitable weapon foisted on the mujahidin by the CIA was a 20mm anti-aircraft gun manufactured by Oerlikon-Bührle of Switzerland. With a total weight of 1,200 lbs, it was a large and cumbersome weapon totally unsuited to guerrilla warfare. Its high rate of fire of 1,000 rounds a minute, with each shell costing $50, coupled with the guerrillas' frequent disregard for any form of fire discipline, would entail considerable quantities of ammunition needing to be provided for each weapon. Moreover, the necessary specialist training of gunners would be a lengthy process. In spite of these and other objections to the weapon, however, the ISI was overruled and up to 50 guns were eventually delivered, the majority being sited near mujahidin bases along Pakistan's border while the remainder were taken into Afghanistan.

Opposition to the supply of Stingers to the mujahidin was eventually overcome following a specific request from General Zia ul-Haq, who had by then agreed that the guerrillas should be equipped with it, and after it was discovered that the Mark 1 model of the missile was about to be withdrawn from service in the US Army and replaced with an enhanced version. Moreover, the manufacturers, General Dynamics, confirmed that they were able to continue production of the Mark 1. On 26 February 1986, the Inter-Agency Sub-Committee gave its approval for the supply to the mujahidin to go ahead. It was not until mid-1987, however, that the Stinger was deployed in Afghanistan in any appreciable quantities, with 250 launchers and 1,000 missiles eventually being delivered via the ISI.

In April 1986, the Soviets mounted an offensive in the eastern border areas of Kunar, Nangarhar and Paktia with the aim of interdicting the supply routes leading into Afghanistan from the mujahidin's forward bases just across the Pakistani border. The main Soviet base in the region was the city of Jalalabad which was garrisoned by the Afghan army's 11th Division and 1st Border Brigade, together with the Soviet 66th Motor Rifle Brigade and a spetsnaz battalion. To the north-east, at Asadabad in the Kunar Valley, was the Afghan 9th Division with another spetsnaz unit based farther up the valley at Asmar. South of Jalalabad was the main town of Khost, occupied by the Afghan 25th Division and 2nd Border Brigade, while other garrisons were located at Ali Khel and Zhawar. Between the two cities, jutting into Afghanistan, was the region known as the Parrot's Beak and its main town of Parachinar through which the ISI routed almost 40 per cent of the arms and equipment it supplied to the mujahidin.

During 1985, guerrilla forces had laid siege to Khost which was surrounded by a number of minefields. In addition, its garrison held the Torgarh, a mountain ridge dominating the south-eastern approaches to the town which would have to be captured before any attacking force could invest Khost itself. The mujahidin had failed to take the ridge or the town and on 20 August the Soviets had launched a major offensive in the eastern area with a force numbering some 20,000, with the aim of evicting the mujahidin from the areas to the west of the Parrot's Beak around Khost, Ali Khel and Azra. Threatened with being caught in a series of major pincer movements, the mujahidin had been forced to lift the siege and withdraw. It had then become evident that the Soviets' ultimate intention was to advance farther south and capture the key guerrilla base at Zhawar which lay south of Khost near the border with Pakistan. The possibility of this base being lost was of major concern to the ISI, but in the event the Soviet offensive had petered out during September and the threat to Zhawar had receded.

Five months later, in March 1986, the threat arose again with preparations by the Soviets for their planned offensive which was due to begin in April. Elements of four Afghan army divisions, the 7th, 8th, 12th and 14th, were concentrated at Khost along with the 37th Commando Brigade and a Soviet air assault brigade. In addition, a number of GRU spetsnaz units known as *okhotniki karavana* (caravan hunters), whose role was to intercept and destroy the mujahidin supply caravans, were also allocated to the operation. As mentioned by Brigadier Mohammad Yousaf in his book, information about these and other indications of the impending operation against Zhawar served to heighten the anxiety of the ISI which attempted to impress upon the mujahidin the urgency of establishing effective defences for the base. Minefields were laid on likely approaches which were also covered by anti-armour weapons and mortars, and headquarters and administrative support elements were installed in deep tunnels; but positions defending the base itself were not dug-in, to the exasperation of Brigadier Yousaf and his officers who continually urged the mujahidin to dig trenches and weapon pits with overhead cover.

The reason for Yousaf's concern was that Zhawar was of major importance to the mujahidin and the ISI. In addition to being a training centre and a base for operations, it also acted as a seat for a local governing body in what was regarded as a liberated area, where courts were conducted and justice administered. The entire base and surrounding area were commanded by Jalaluddin Haqqani, of Mawlawi Younis Khalis's Hizbi-i-Islami, whose forces numbered some 10,000 men deployed to face the Soviet threat in the mountains to the north and in the hills beyond. On their right were mujahidin units belonging to Sayyad Pir Gailani's National Islamic Front and Mawlawi Nabi's Islamic Revolutionary Movement.

The attack on Zhawar began during the first week of April as the Soviet air assault and Afghan commando brigades were deployed first by helicopter, followed by columns of mechanised infantry and armour advancing south from Khost via Tani. To the south of Tani, however, these encountered fierce opposition from mujahidin units and, as they advanced, even stronger resistance from others in the mountains to the north of Zhawar. At the same time, the mujahidin bombarded the airfield at Khost, from which the helicopters and other supporting aircraft were operating, disrupting its operations with salvoes of 107mm rockets.

After a few days the lack of progress was such that the Afghan commander of the operation, Brigadier Abdol Gafur, had to revise his plans. On 11 April, he deployed a battalion of his 37th Commando Brigade in a heliborne operation against Zhawar itself, his intention being to land it behind the mujahidin positions surrounding the base. In the event, the assault went badly wrong when 400 troops were landed by ten helicopters on open ground in broad daylight. They were in full view of guerrillas who opened fire with SA-7 Grail SAMs and heavy machine-guns, hitting three helicopters which crashed. Meanwhile, the troops from the remaining seven aircraft were met by a withering cross-fire and all were either killed or captured.

From 11 to 22 April, Zhawar was subjected to a large number of air strikes in addition to heavy bombardment by artillery. The Stinger had yet to make an appearance at this stage and, with only three 20mm

Oerlikon guns and heavy machine- guns, the mujahidin possessed no effective anti-aircraft defences against attacks by fighter-bombers which bombed the base, scoring several direct hits on the tunnels housing Haqqani's headquarters. A Blowpipe team of ISI personnel was deployed, firing thirteen missiles without effect. Eventually, the mujahidin were forced to retreat and Zhawar fell. During the following 48 hours, Soviet and Afghan troops methodically destroyed the base and everything they found in it before they withdrew. The Kabul regime claimed a major victory, stating that mujahidin losses were 2,000 killed and 4,000 wounded. Brigadier Yousaf, however, gives guerrilla losses as being no more than 300 killed and three truck-loads of arms and ammunition lost, while quantifying Afghan army losses as 1,500 killed or wounded, 100 captured and thirteen helicopters destroyed. Within two days, Zhawar was reoccupied by the mujahidin.

THE MONTH FOLLOWING THE battle at Zhawar saw a change of the Afghan leadership in Kabul. After the appointment of Mikhail Gorbachev as General Secretary of the Communist Party of the Soviet Union on 11 March 1985, the Soviets had reviewed their policy towards Afghanistan. In October, Gorbachev himself held a secret meeting with Karmal at which he attempted unsuccessfully to persuade the Afghan leader to broaden the political base of his regime, by introducing non-communist elements, and come to a compromise with the mujahidin in order to facilitate a Soviet withdrawal. Shortly afterwards, the Soviet Politburo adopted a resolution undertaking to expedite an early withdrawal of Soviet forces from Afghanistan.

In early November, Karmal announced that he would '... enlarge the composition of the state leadership ...' and shortly afterwards appointed non-communists to the posts of Deputy Prime Minister, deputy ministers and ministers of portfolio. This, however, was mere window dressing, as communists continued to hold all positions of power. The Soviets were not convinced of Karmal's willingness to accede to their demands and were further concerned over his refusal to begin discussions on a proposed timetable for a Soviet withdrawal, these having been the subject of negotiations at the UN headquarters in Geneva since June 1982. On 30 March 1986, Karmal flew to Moscow for medical treatment; in poor health, he was suffering from a variety of complaints. During his month-long stay, the KGB increasingly made it plain that he should relinquish power, resigning as General Secretary of the PDPA but remaining as chairman of Afghanistan's Revolutionary Council. On 1 May, Karmal returned to Kabul where he was subjected to continuous pressure by Vladimir Aleksandrovich Kryuchkov, head of the KGB's First Chief Directorate, who finally persuaded him to step down. On 4 May, Karmal announced his resignation, citing the 'Soviet Union's global interests' as the reasons behind it, and was replaced by the head of KHAD, Major General Mohammed Najibullah. Karmal's removal enabled the Soviets to attend the latest round of discussions at the UN in Geneva in a position to begin negotiations for a withdrawal. By November, he had lost all his PDPA and government positions.

The second half of 1986 saw the arrival in Pakistan of the first consignments of Stinger missiles, the CIA by this time having agreed to supply at the rate of 1,200 missiles and 250 launch units per year. In June, the ISI despatched a team of ten Pakistan Army personnel to undergo eight weeks training as instructors while a training facility was established at Camp Ojhri which was equipped with a General Dynamics simulator. Thereafter, three-week courses were conducted for selected mujahidin who had previous experience in using the SA-7 Grail.

Among the first Stingers to appear in Afghanistan was a batch of six taken in by a former member of 22 SAS who later wrote of his experiences under the pseudonym of Gaz Hunter in a book titled *Shooting Gallery*. Prior to going into Afghanistan, he and a team of instructors had been recruited to conduct training in a Middle Eastern country for a group of sixteen Jamiat-i-Islami commanders belonging to Ahmed Shah Massoud. The six-week course covered weapon training, tactics, planning of operations and use of the Stinger for which Hunter and his team were supplied with a simulator. Shortly after returning to Britain, Hunter was approached to take six missiles into Afghanistan, assist one of Massoud's groups with the planning and conduct of its operations and provide further training on the Stinger.

Having infiltrated over the border from Pakistan, Hunter joined the 20-strong group operating in the Panjshir Valley area, participating in an attack on a convoy. He then began training a small number of guerrillas in the use of the Stinger, six of whom eventually proved proficient enough to be selected as the group's air defence team. He also provided instruction on the tactical deployment of the missile, including the use of ambushes close to airbases and sited along approaches or known flight paths, and traps into which aircraft could be lured to present themselves as targets. In addition, he taught the guerrillas to lure aircraft into such traps by using decoy groups or ambushing ground forces who would call for air support. Alternatively, an aircraft could be engaged by a heavy machine-gun, causing it either to take evasive action or head in for an attack, thus exposing itself to a Stinger.

Approximately three weeks later, the group mounted its first Stinger operation against aircraft covering a Soviet supply route in a valley. The mujahidin deployed a decoy group in the hope of luring one of three MiGs observed over the area. These proved difficult prey, however, at one point appearing unexpectedly at low level and attacking the group before the Stinger team could bring its missiles into action.

Having failed in their first attempt to shoot down an aircraft, the guerrillas and Hunter headed for Kabul and on the following day took up another ambush position. Shortly afterwards, however, a detachment of Soviet airborne troops in two BMD airborne infantry vehicles appeared and carried out a search of the area, narrowly failing to find the guerrillas. Evacuating the area just before dawn next day, the guerrilla commander decided that he would have to send a group to carry out an attack on the airfield at Kabul. Hunter was not permitted to participate in the operation but helped plan it in detail. Two members of his Stinger-trained team and eight other guerrillas departed for Kabul. Some two weeks later, on 1 July, a Soviet Antonov An-26 transport, carrying a company of troops, was shot down as it took off from an airfield outside the capital. This is believed to be the first confirmed Stinger 'kill' during the war in Afghanistan.

By all accounts, though, the six missiles taken into the Panjshir Valley by Gaz Hunter may have been the only Stingers received by Massoud's forces. According to US Army Soviet specialist Lieutenant Colonel Scott McMichael in his authoritative book *Stumbling Bear – Soviet Military Performance in Afghanistan*, some two-thirds of the missiles were distributed by the ISI to the mujahidin, with Gulbuddin Hekmatyr's Hizbi-i-Islami and other fundamentalist groups receiving the major share and the remainder going to the traditionalists, with the exception of Massoud, who received none. The latter, according to James G. Shortt, was forced to purchase further Stingers from mujahidin elements in Paktia Province. McMichael alleges that up to a third of the missiles supplied by the CIA were lost: some were siphoned off by the Pakistanis as a 'missile tax', while others were sold by the mujahidin or captured by Soviet or Afghan forces.

The arrival of the Stinger in Afghanistan undoubtedly forced the Soviets to reduce their reliance on air power and compelled pilots to alter their tactics, attacking from higher altitudes and sometimes at night. This in turn allowed the mujahidin to increase the number of caravans bringing supplies into the country and to conduct large-scale operations. Despite claims to the contrary, however, the majority of Soviet and Afghan aircraft losses throughout the nine years of the war were not caused by Stingers. According to Scott McMichael, up to 1986, prior to the Stinger being deployed, Soviet losses totalled approximately 600, caused either by accidents or inflicted primarily by Chinese-supplied 12.7m DShK heavy machine-guns – acknowledged later by the Soviets as the most effective anti-aircraft weapon fielded by the mujahidin.

From late 1986 onward, Soviet and Afghan aircraft losses apparently soared to between 438 and 547 per annum but opinions differ as to how many of these were shot down as opposed to being due to malfunction or pilot error. McMichael points out that 20 per cent of US Army helicopter losses in Vietnam were due to operational attrition and, bearing in mind that flying conditions were considerably harsher in Afghanistan, attributes 75 to 80 per cent of Soviet losses in the first two years of the war to mechanical malfunctions and crashes. Added to these were further losses incurred through sabotage and ground attacks on airbases. With an increased number of anti-aircraft weapons acquired by the mujahidin, the mid-1980s saw a slight increase in Soviet aircraft losses. After late 1986, however, most losses were caused by mujahidin anti-aircraft fire and missiles. McMichael gives a conservative estimate of Soviet losses during the entire conflict as between 1,300 and 1,500 while an Afghan pilot, who defected in 1989, puts Afghan and Soviet losses at 975 and 1,700 respectively.

Similarly, there are differences in opinion as to the effectiveness of the Stinger. One US study after the war found that the missile's hit ratio was at best 50 per cent while another put it at 79 per cent. Some observers, who witnessed the mujahidin in action against aircraft, believed that the lower estimate was more accurate. In fact, whereas the original model of the Stinger, as supplied to the mujahidin, was designed to perform with a hit ratio of over 60 per cent, in practice the US Army expected to achieve only 30 per cent even when the missile was operated by fully trained troops.

In addition to the arrival of the Stinger, 1986 also saw a number of raids carried out by mujahidin groups into Uzbekistan and Tajikistan, two of the three Soviet republics bordering the north of Afghanistan. As described by Brigadier Mohammad Yousaf in his book, this strategy originated with the CIA's Director of Central Intelligence, William Casey. Initial operations had been limited during 1984 to psychological warfare conducted by the ISI, with northern groups of mujahidin crossing the Amu Darya River into Uzbekistan and distributing copies of books, portraying Soviet atrocities in Afghanistan, together with 10,000 copies of the Koran. During 1985, the ISI laid plans for an operation to blow up the 1,000-yard-long 'Friendship Bridge' which spans the Amu Darya approximately seven and a half miles to the west of Termez, providing a major road and rail link between Uzbekistan and Afghanistan, and also carrying an oil pipeline across the river. In late 1985, however, the operation was cancelled on the orders of General Zia ul-Haq himself on the grounds that it might provoke the Soviets into carrying out reprisal attacks on Pakistan.

The next year a number of mujahidin underwent specialist training in Pakistan, much of it devoted to sabotage of railways and rolling stock. A number of attacks were launched across the Amu Darya against the line that followed the northern bank of the river, along which freight trains travelled from Samarkand to Termez. Several of these succeeded but two failed as a result of interception of the raiding parties by the Soviets who, in the opinion of the ISI, had probably been warned beforehand. Other attacks were mounted against traffic along the river with limpet mines, supplied by Britain's SIS, being planted by a specially trained team of mujahidin on boats and barges moored on the northern bank of the Amu Darya.

Other attacks were directed against Soviet border posts, with guerrillas laying mines on roads and tracks in between them while cutting telephone and power lines. Major installations were also targeted and in December 1986 a force of 30 guerrillas crossed the Amu Darya into neighbouring Tajikistan and attacked two hydroelectric power stations. In many instances, targets were attacked with 107mm and 122mm single-barrelled rocket launchers possessing a range of five and a half and seven miles respectively. Among these were an airfield on the northern outskirts of the town of Pyandzh, situated on the northern bank of the Amu Darya, and a fuel storage base spanning the river at Sherkan and Nizhniy Pyandzh on the southern and northern banks respectively.

These attacks continued throughout 1986 into 1987. In early April, an airfield at Shurob East, approximately fifteen and a half miles northwest of Termez but just under from the northern bank of the Amu, was attacked with a heavy bombardment of rockets. At the same time, a second twenty-strong group of mujahidin ambushed a convoy on the road between Termez and the border with Tajikhistan, destroying five vehicles and killing or wounding a number of Soviet troops.

In mid-April, a raid was launched on a factory complex some twelve miles inside Uzbekistan, in an area north of the Amu Darya and the town of Kurgan Tyube which featured a large number of industrial plants, railway installations, power stations and airfields. Having crossed the Amu Darya, the raiding party, equipped with two 107mm rocket launchers and 30 rockets, marched to a lying-up place (LUP) where it remained hidden throughout the next day before continuing their approach march over the mountains during the following night. Arriving at their firing positions, which had been reconnoitred earlier in the month by the group commander and two of his men, the guerrillas set up both launchers and opened fire at the target which lay just under five miles away to the west. They fired a total of twenty high explosive rounds and ten smoke, the latter having an incendiary effect. These caused significant damage by destroying several buildings, and the raiders withdrew before dawn to their LUP. The attack touched off a fierce response from the Soviets, a large number of aircraft and helicopter gunships being dispatched to bomb the area south of the Amu Darya around Imam Sahib, destroying villages and any areas where guerrillas might be concealed.

Next night, the raiders crossed back over the river and headed south towards Imam Sahib. While skirting round the town, however, their commander stepped on an anti-personnel mine and lost a foot. He survived despite the most rudimentary medical treatment applied by members of his group which, during the following six days, was attacked several times by aircraft which wounded four more men. It was several weeks before he and his men reached Pakistan and proper medical attention.

The effect on the Soviets of this operation was to warn Pakistan that any further attacks would result in dire consequences. In Washington and in Islamabad it was apparent that the raids had to cease forthwith and Brigadier Yousaf was ordered to terminate them immediately.

Elsewhere in Afghanistan, the spring and early summer of 1987 witnessed major defeats of government forces. One offensive during May and June in the area of Arghandab, near Kandahar, disintegrated after heavy fighting. Another, in the area of Jaji in Paktia Province, also failed in the face of strong resistance on the part of mujahidin forces from all seven factions. Beginning on 20 May, this was led by Soviet airborne and spetsnaz troops who relieved a besieged garrison at Ali Sher before blocking guerrilla routes into Afghanistan. The known presence of Stingers forced the Soviets to rely on artillery and BM-22 220mm multi-barrelled rocket launchers rather than air support. By this time the Soviets were evidently aware that with a clear sky as background, the Stinger had little problem in locking on to an aircraft, whereas at low level its passive infra-red seeker could be confused by hot rocks and other items emanating heat. On this occasion, as on others, pilots of transport helicopters and gunships adopted the tactic of flying at low-level. This, however, not only made them vulnerable to fire from heavy machine-guns and RPG-7s but also restricted their manœuvrability due to the risk of accidents in the mountainous terrain and steep-sided valleys, so limiting their ability to deploy and support the airborne and spetsnaz troops.

In June 1987, the mujahidin launched a major operation to cut the main highway between Kabul and Jalalabad; and next month, in the north, Ahmed Shah Massoud's Jamiat-i-Islami forces attacked the garrison at Kalafghan in Takhar Province. Several weeks had been devoted to preparations with reconnaissance teams mapping minefields, plotting positions of enemy artillery pieces and mortars, and reconnoitring firing positions for 107mm rocket launchers some 1,000 yards from the objective. Radio nets were established and tested, and commanders of all units were briefed in detail on their individual tasks. On the afternoon of 14 July the five strongpoints forming Kalafghan's defences were subjected to a barrage of rockets which suppressed the garrison's artillery and mortars. At the same time, Massoud's mortars engaged Soviet artillery at a firebase tasked with providing defensive and final protective fire in the event of an attack on Kalafghan, preventing it from opening fire.

Massoud's troops, meantime, were making their way through the reconnoitred gaps in the minefields and shortly afterwards began their assault, overrunning all five strongpoints within an hour. Having sustained very light casualties, they then proceeded to lay waste to the defensive positions, destroying them completely. As dusk fell, they withdrew in trucks called forward immediately after the attack, taking with them their prisoners and large quantities of arms and ammunition. It was not until three days later that a force of Soviet and Afghan troops moved along the road from the firebase to Kalafghan, encountering en route mines and an ambush force left behind by Massoud to prevent any relief force reaching Kalafghan. Finding the garrison base entirely destroyed, the Soviets pulled back to the firebase, being ambushed again as they went.

Late in 1987 the garrison at Khost came under siege again, the mujahidin intercepting all resupply by air with Stingers. Failure at Jadji had led the Soviets to reassert their military dominance and they thus decided to mount a relief operation, concentrating a strong force of 20,000 troops in the area of Gardez. The Soviet element comprised regiments of the 103rd Guards Airborne and 108th Motor Rifle Divisions, a spetsnaz brigade and large numbers of additional supporting arm troops, including artillery and engineers. These were reinforced by the Afghan 7th, 8th and 12th Divisions. In addition to transport helicopters and gunships, air support was provided by two squadrons of Su-25 Frogfoot fighter-bombers flown in from the Soviet Union.

The relief operation, codenamed MISTRAL, began at the end of November with two Afghan divisions and a Soviet airborne brigade advancing along the main road leading from Gardez to Khost via the passes at Sadan Kamvan and Sato Kandau. Strong resistance was encountered almost from the outset, to which the Soviets reacted with heavy use of artillery and BM-22 220mm long-range rockets. These were backed up by the Su-25 Frogfoots although they attacked from high altitude because of the threat of Stingers. Meanwhile, an Afghan brigade carried out a flanking move through the mountains from Urgun in an attempt to cut off the mujahidin forces at the northern ends of both passes; the latter, however, detected this threat and withdrew in time.

The Soviets' next move was to move an airborne brigade forward by helicopter at night and take the town of Mirujan, situated at the southern point of the mountains along the Gardez–Khost road. Another brigade was lifted in under cover of darkness into Khost and then launched a break-out northward along the road towards Gardez. In both instances, the helicopters succeeded in flying very low, below the minimum altitude of the Stinger 'envelope'.

The mujahidin had meanwhile withdrawn from the Gardez–Khost road, having mined it heavily. With airborne troops deployed on the heights on either flank, the armoured and mechanised columns continued their advance south through December, albeit slowed by mines and bombardments of 107mm rockets fired at long range by the mujahidin. Eventually they linked up with the column heading north from Khost and on 30 December the leading elements of the relief force entered the city.

NEGOTIATIONS TO END THE WAR in Afghanistan had been under way since mid-1982, taking the form of indirect talks between the Afghan and Pakistani governments under the supervision of the UN, the process being complicated by the Pakistanis' refusal to recognise the regime in Kabul and thus to engage in direct discourse with its delegation. The UN therefore acted as intermediary between the two sides, being represented by Diego Cordovez, the Special Representative of the Secretary General. Particulars of the negotiations are too protracted and complex to be dealt with here, being described in detail in a book *Out of Afghanistan – The Story of the Soviet Withdrawal* which Cordovez wrote in collaboration with journalist Selig Harrison. During the latter part of 1987 and throughout early 1988, however, the main obstruction to the conclusion of an agreement known as the Geneva Accords, governing a Soviet withdrawal and bringing the war to an end, was disagreement within Pakistan over the nature of the post-war government to be formed in Afghanistan.

The ISI, whose influence had increased dramatically during the years of the conflict under the patronage of General Zia ul-Haq, was determined that a fundamentalist regime should be installed in Kabul, a view fully in accord with that of Zia himself. By this time it was headed by Lieutenant General Hamid Gul who had replaced Lieutenant General Akhtar Abdel Rahman Khan as Director General in March 1987 and whose radical fundamentalist views were well known to the CIA. Pakistan's newly appointed Prime Minister, Muhammed Khan Junejo, and his Foreign Minister, Yaqub Khan, however, favoured the involvement of the exiled king, Zahir Shah, who was acceptable to Moscow and would be supported by nationalist and non-communist elements in playing a central role in any transitory administration. Although Yaqub was permitted by Zia to sound out the Soviets on this idea, he was undermined by the ISI and the President who, in a meeting with Soviet Foreign Minister Anatoliy Kovalyev, emphasised the importance of an Islamic fundamentalist government taking power in Kabul.

During early 1988, the situation was not helped by the fact that Pakistan itself was undergoing a period of political instability with Zia agreeing to parliamentary elections being held in March. A power struggle developed between him and Junejo who had sacked Yaqub in November and assumed the Foreign Affairs portfolio himself, while also increasingly asserting his authority over matters, such as military budgets, which Zia had hitherto considered his own preserve.

Until this juncture, Zia had stood shoulder-to-shoulder with the United States in opposing Soviet demands that any withdrawal should be linked to US and Pakistani agreement to a coalition government being established in Kabul. Now he performed a volte-face, declaring that Pakistan would not sign an agreement unless the Soviets removed Najibullah and agreed to a provisional government elected through a process dominated by the seven mujahidin factions based in Pakistan. He went on to state that the Kabul regime would be permitted indirect minority representation through non-communists acceptable to the PDPA, the proviso being that all these should be 'good Muslims'. He further proposed that a 30-strong ruling council should be established, of which twelve members would be such 'good Muslims'.

The power struggle between Zia and Junejo intensified and came to a head in early March during a conference of the leaders of Pakistan's nineteen political parties. All but the Jamaat-i-Islami and two other fundamentalist groups agreed that Pakistan should sign the Geneva Accords. A similar view was expressed by the Pakistani cabinet which met on the evening of 6 March, all but one minister voting in support of signing.

In the face of such opposition from his own government, as well as from the United States and Moscow, Zia had no option but to climb down and agree to the Geneva Accords which were signed on 14 April. Six weeks later, on 29 May, however, he exacted revenge on Junejo by dismissing him, but in so doing precipitated a political crisis in Pakistan. In the summer, he himself was removed abruptly from the political scene. On 17 August a C-130 Hercules VIP transport of the Pakistan Air Force's No. 6 Squadron crashed while flying from Bahawalpur, in the south-east of the Punjab, to Islamabad. Aboard were Zia, Lieutenant General Akhtar Abdel Rahman Khan, US Ambassador Arnold Raphel and Brigadier General Herbert Wassom, the US Defence Attaché in Islamabad. An investigation by a Pakistani board of inquiry and US experts, including extensive laboratory tests on all parts of the aircraft, concluded that the aircrew had been incapacitated by some form of chemical nerve agent introduced into the cockpit. The culprits were never identified.

The deaths of Zia and Lieutenant General Akhtar Abdel Rahman Khan, while a blow to the mujahidin who had benefited greatly from their support, had no effect on the process of disengagement by the Soviet Union. Withdrawal of Soviet troops had commenced on 15 May when the 66th Motor Rifle Division handed over the base at Jalalabad to Afghan troops and headed via Kabul to Khairkana and Khairatan, crossing the border into the Soviet Union four days later. At the time of withdrawal, Soviet forces comprised 100,300 Soviet troops in eighteen garrisons throughout Afghanistan. During the following months, these were gradually reduced as bases were handed over to Afghan troops who soon found themselves hard-pressed by mujahidin forces. The latter, although not seeking to impede the Soviet withdrawal, nevertheless continued to make their presence felt. In mid-June they cut the highway between Ghazni and Kabul, thus forcing Soviet units to take a longer route, and in August attacked a large ammunition storage depot at Kalgay with 122mm rockets, destroying it completely.

Early in November, the Soviets retaliated by halting the withdrawal temporarily and providing powerful air and missile support for an Afghan army offensive advancing eastward from Jalalabad. Thereafter, the withdrawal resumed and continued until February of the following year when the last Soviet soldier, General Boris Gromov, commander of all Soviet forces in Afghanistan, walked across the Friendship Bridge from Termez into Uzbekistan. The occupation by the Soviet Union of Afghanistan was over; throughout its nine-year duration, 13,310 Soviet troops had been killed, 35,478 wounded and 311 recorded as missing in action. No figures exist for mujahidin casualties, various estimates ranging from 175,000 to a staggering one million.

THE SOVIET WITHDRAWAL DID not result in peace for a country already torn apart by nine years of conflict. The war against Kabul continued despite expectations that the Najibullah regime would collapse. In early March 1989, abandoning their guerrilla tactics, the mujahidin somewhat prematurely resorted to conventional warfare and launched an assault on Jalalabad with the aim of capturing the city and establishing it as the temporary seat of the interim government, formed in Peshawar in December 1988, before moving on Kabul whose fall, they believed, would naturally follow that of Jalalabad. Any notions of a short siege and swift conclusion were soon dispelled. The city was occupied by the Afghan 11th Division, which was fully manned, and its defences, incorporating extensive minefields, were formidable. Moreover, the Afghans made full use, too, of air support, bombing mujahidin positions and subjecting them to salvoes of Scud missiles. By the time the siege ended in September 1989, some 10,000 lives had been lost.

In February of the following year, the United States and the Soviet Union reached agreement on Najibullah remaining in power until UN-supervised elections could be held. In May, the latter announced the introduction of a multi-party political system but the mujahidin resisted all efforts at reconciliation by the Afghan leader.

The two superpowers, meanwhile, were engaged in negotiations over the cessation of military aid to both sides. The Soviet Union was still continuing to supply the Kabul regime on a grand scale; during the first six months of 1989 it had provided $1.5 billion of aid, including 500 Scud missiles. The United States meanwhile had reduced the scale of its support to the mujahidin to a mere trickle. On 13 September, agreement was reached in Moscow by the US Secretary of State, George Baker, and Soviet Foreign Minister, Boris Pankin, and on 1 January 1992 cessation of all arms supplies to both sides by the United States and the Soviet Union became effective.

A postscript to the CIA's secret war in Afghanistan was the disappearance of a large number of the Stinger missiles supplied by the CIA. Following the Soviet withdrawal from Afghanistan, the Agency attempted to purchase missiles back from the mujahidin but with little success; by the mid-1990s they were being sold on the black market for approximately $100,000 each. In Iran, where a consignment of missiles aboard a mujahidin convoy had been captured by Iranian border guards, they were allegedly being purchased from corrupt officials for up to $300,000 each by drug smugglers anxious to acquire them as protection against government helicopters. It was later discovered that during the war members of Gulbuddin Hekmatyr's Hizbi-i-Islami had sold sixteen missiles to Iranian Revolutionary Guards for approximately $1 million. Such was the CIA's anxiety that it obtained $10 million from Congress to finance the repurchase of Stingers but to little avail. By that time, the majority of the missiles were beyond reach, having been distributed far and wide via the international arms black market. There are no figures available with regard to the total numbers of Stingers supplied by the CIA during the war in Afghanistan, the quantities siphoned off as they made their way down the supply pipeline or those which eventually found their way on to the black market. Suffice it to say that the CIA's largesse with this deadly weapon was considerable; in the words of one of its officers, 'We were handing them out like lollipops.'

In April 1992, Najibullah was finally ousted from power after General Abdar Rashid-Dostrum changed sides and used his Uzbek militia to bring him down. Najibullah took refuge in the UN compound in Kabul where he remained a virtual prisoner for the next four years. Shortly afterwards all but one of the leaders of the mujahidin factions signed the Peshawar Accord, consenting to the establishment of a power-sharing interim government which would lead to democratic elections. The missing signatory was Gulbuddin Hekmatyr of the Hizb-i-Islami. Towards the end of June Burhanuddin Rabbani was appointed President of the Islamic State of Afghanistan. In July, inter-factional fighting broke out in Kabul and in December 1992 Rabbani, in disregard of the terms of the Peshawar Accord, was appointed President for a further two years although this was reduced to eighteen months in March of the following year. In June 1993, Gulbuddin Hekmatyr was appointed Prime Minister which resulted in his sworn enemy, Ahmed Shah Massoud of the Jamiat-i-Islami, resigning as Defence Minister. Fighting broke out again in Afghanistan, intensifying in Kabul in January 1994 as General Rashid-Dostrum, who controlled most of northern Afghanistan from his base at Mazar-e-Sharif, formed an alliance with Hekmatyr who abandoned his post and took up arms once again.

IN OCTOBER 1994, A HITHERTO unknown group called the Taliban made its first appearance. Led by Mullah Mohammad Omar, it captured the southern city of Kandahar and surrounding areas. In September of the following year, its forces took Herat and western Afghanistan, thereafter remaining outside Kabul and content to launch rocket attacks on the capital during October. In early September 1996, the Taliban mounted an offensive in eastern Afghanistan, capturing the city of Jalalaba, and on 27 September, took Kabul. Shortly afterwards, Mohammad Najibullah was seized from his lair in the by-then abandoned UN compound and executed.

On 24 May 1997, the Taliban captured Mazar-e-Sharif, General Rashid-Dostrum having fled to Turkey a week earlier after one of his commanders, 'Abd al-Malik Pahlawan, turned against him. Next day Pakistan, Saudi Arabia and the United Arab Emirates recognised it as the government of Afghanistan. On 28 May, however, Pahlawan, changed sides again and in alliance with Hekmatyr's Hizbi-i-Islami forces, drove the Taliban forces out of Mazar-e-Sharif after a fierce battle which saw large numbers of Taliban killed and captured.

In July, an anti-Taliban government was formed with its headquarters in Mazar-e-Sharif and Burhanuddin Rabbani as President. 'Abd ar-Rahim Ghafuzai and Ahmed Shah Massoud were appointed as Prime Minister and Defence Minister respectively, with 'Abd al-Malik Pahlawan assuming the post of Foreign Minister. Shortly afterwards, Pahlawan's and Massoud's forces, reinforced with Hazara Sh'ite militias, drove back the Taliban's forces to within a few miles of Kabul. In September, the Taliban mounted a counter-offensive to recapture Mazar-e-Sharif but this proved unsuccessful. Thus by the end of 1997, Afghanistan was ruled by two de facto governments: the Taliban, ruling the Pushtun-dominated south and east of the country, including Kabul, while the so-called Northern Alliance controlled the Tajik, Uzbek, Turkmen and Hazara areas in the north.

The Taliban had promised to rid the country of the lawlessness and corruption which had continued after the Soviet withdrawal. Its assumption of power was greeted initially with enthusiasm which soon died away as a rigorous Islamic order was instituted; young men were ordered to grow beards, women were forbidden to work, schools were closed and Sharia law was imposed with public floggings, amputations and stonings. Music, books and all forms of entertainment were banned and such was the harsh and retrogressive nature of the Taliban regime that within a few years life in Afghanistan had virtually reverted to that of the Dark Ages.

By this time the CIA's operation in Afghanistan had been over for five years but it had nevertheless left a deadly legacy. After the war ended, large numbers of highly trained and battle-hardened guerrillas of varying nationalities found themselves in refugee camps, no longer needed or indeed wanted by Afghanistan, Pakistan or the United States. Among these were followers of Osama bin Laden, the wealthy Saudi Arabian who had been one of the principal recruiters and fundraisers for the fundamentalist mujahidin. Following the Soviet withdrawal, he formed an organisation called al-Qaeda to provide support for an army of several hundred redundant guerrillas in Pakistan. In 1991, bin Laden returned to his home country where he became prominent among those opposed to the presence of Western non-Muslim troops on Saudi soil. In his absence, however, Pakistan decided that it no longer wished to accommodate the mujahidin who, including bin Laden's own followers, were based in camps in the NWFP. They were now unwelcome guests because of their large numbers and the extremist brand of Islamic fundamentalism they espoused and preached. The Pakistanis turned to the CIA but the latter prevaricated and made little effort to resolve the problem. Eventually losing patience, Pakistan threatened to transport bin Laden's men and those of other factions to the US Embassy in Islamabad and abandon them there unless arrangements were made to remove them from the country.

According to journalist and Middle East specialist Adel Darwish, the CIA turned to Saudi Arabia and other countries in the Persian Gulf, bringing pressure on them to issue passports to the guerrillas who were flown to different locations. Some 900 of them surfaced in Algeria with the extremist Groupe Islamique Armée (GIA) which perpetrated a reign of terror and bloodshed from the early 1990s onward. Others made their way to Egypt where they joined extremist groups seeking to topple the government of President Hjosni Mubarak, or to Bosnia where they joined Muslims fighting Serbian forces. Still more appeared in Lebanon, Azerbaijan and Chechnya, whose capital of Grozny became a transit point for former mujahidin, while members of Abdul Rasul Sayyaf's Ittihad-e-Islami made their way to the Philippines where they joined others of their number who had preceded them some years beforehand.

Many of the guerrillas joined the ranks of Osama bin Laden's al-Qaeda as he set out to wage war against the West, establishing a worldwide terrorist network of Islamic extremists. The United States was his principal target and in 1992 he launched his first attack. On 29 December, in the Yemeni city port of Aden, a bomb exploded in a hotel used by American military personnel in transit to and from Somalia where US troops formed part of the local UN peacekeeping forces. Two Austrian tourists were killed by the blast. Meanwhile, at Aden's airport, a team of terrorists was arrested as it prepared to open fire on a US aircraft.

Months later, terrorists struck a major blow against the United States, this time inside the country itself. On 23 February 1993, a massive bomb, concealed in a rented van, exploded in a car park beneath the twin towers of the World Trade Centre in New York. Six people were killed and over 1,000 injured in the blast which severely damaged the buildings. Four Islamic extremists, Mahmoud Abouhalina, Mohammad Salameh, Ahmad Ajaj and Nidal Ayyad, were subsequently arrested and tried, being convicted on 24 May 1994 for their roles in the bombing and sentenced to life imprisonment. There is reportedly to date no concrete evidence of direct involvement by Osama bin Laden but there are strong suspicions that he provided support for the attack, possibly through the supply of funds and logistical support. Links with him were uncovered by investigators who, having located the safe house used by the bombers, checked telephone records and established that a large number of overseas calls had been made to numbers subsequently identified as belonging to him.

The architect of the bombing, identified as Ramzi Ahmed Yousef, remained at large. Nothing was heard of him until 14 March 1994, when he attempted to mount an attack in the Thai capital of Bangkok. A large bomb was concealed in a hired van and was being driven to its target by one of Yousef's accomplices, later suspected as being either the US or the Israeli Embassy, when it collided with two other vehicles. The terrorist panicked and fled, abandoning the van. It was not until three days later, when the vehicle's owner reclaimed it from the police, that the bomb was discovered in the back of his vehicle along with the body of his driver who had been strangled by one of the terrorist gang. Yousef's fingerprints were found on the bomb but by that time he had fled Thailand and made his way to Pakistan.

Yousef's next mission, allegedly carried out on behalf of bin Laden, took place in mid-1994 when he flew to the Philippines to provide technical assistance and training for the Muslim separatist group called Abu Sayyaf. As mentioned earlier, this comprised several hundred former mujahidin, who had fought in Afghanistan with Abdul Rasul Sayyaf's Ittihad-e-Islami faction which had received support from a number of wealthy Saudis, among them Osama bin Laden. By the mid-1980s a nucleus of the group, led by Abdurajak Abubakar Janjalani, had left Pakistan and made its way to the southern Philippines where it began its campaign for the establishment of a Muslim republic. It carried out a sustained campaign of bomb attacks and kidnappings aimed at preventing peace negotiations between the Filipino government and the Moro National Liberation Front (MNLF), the principal Muslim organisation in the country. By the 1990s, it had established a reputation as the most extreme and violent Islamist group in South East Asia. Osama bin Laden was reportedly continuing to supply funds for Abu Sayyaf and had tasked Yousef with providing it with instruction in the use of explosives and construction of bombs.

Yousef spent several weeks at the Abu Sayyaf base on the island of Basilan where he trained a group in bomb-making. In September 1994, he travelled to the Filipino capital of Manila where he met two members of another Islamic extremist group, Hezbul Dawah Al-Islamiah, which had cells throughout the world including the Philippines. With their assistance, he recruited a group of some twenty Muslims as he prepared for another mission allegedly given to him by Osama bin Laden: the assassination of President Bill Clinton during a forthcoming visit to Manila in mid-November. Yousef devoted much time to planning the operation but ultimately abandoned it because of the extremely high level of security surrounding the President. He then turned his attention to an alternative but equally prominent target, His Holiness Pope John Paul II, who was due to visit Manila in January of the following year.

During the previous weeks, Yousef had designed and developed a highly sophisticated, small but very powerful bomb intended for use in attacks against aircraft. His intention was that numbers of these devices would be planted on aircraft around the world, causing a high death toll when they exploded. On 11 December, he conducted a trial aboard a Philippines Air Lines Boeing 747 carrying 273 passengers and 20 crew from Manila to Tokyo via the city of Cebu, planting the device under his seat before he left the flight there. Two hours after the aircraft had taken off from Cebu for Tokyo, the bomb exploded, killing the passenger in the seat previously occupied by Yousef and blowing a hole in the floor of the aircraft. Despite the severe damage caused to the plane, the pilot managed to reach the island of Okinawa where he landed without any further loss of life.

A few days later, Yousef returned to Manila from Cebu before flying to Islamabad. Then, accompanied by a long-standing friend, Abdul Haki Murad, he returned to the Filipino capital to continue his training of the Abu Sayyaf extremists and to manufacture more bombs. During the first week of January 1995, however, a fire in the apartment where he had set up his bomb-making facility forced him and his accomplices to flee; after the local fire brigade had extinguished the blaze, police entered the apartment and were confronted by an all too obvious bomb factory. A search uncovered a laptop computer, bomb-making manuals, chemicals, electronic timers and a considerable amount of other equipment and documentation. In due course, Abdul Haki Murad was arrested when he returned to the apartment to recover the computer.

Initial examination of its hard disk revealed Yousef's plan to attack airliners flying from South East Asia to destinations elsewhere in the region and to the United States. Further investigation and analysis of the bomb-making equipment and the contents of the computer's memory by the FBI revealed a mass of other information which proved invaluable in revealing details of Yousef's murderous activities and in particular his connection with the bombing of the World Trade Centre.

Yousef fled back to Pakistan but at the end of January travelled with an accomplice to Thailand to mount a bomb attack against a US aircraft flying from Bangkok to the United States. This plan came to naught and both men returned to Islamabad. A few days later, however, Yousef's accomplice contacted the US Embassy and gave details of his where-abouts to members of the Diplomatic Security Service (DSS). On 7 February a small force of FBI and DSS agents, reinforced by a team of ISI officers, arrested Yousef in a guest house later reported as belonging to a member of Osama bin Laden's family.

Yousef's immediate extradition to the United States was followed by reprisals carried out by extremists in Pakistan and elsewhere. On 8 March three members of the US Consulate in Karachi were attacked by gunmen: two of them were killed and the third wounded. Three weeks later, a force of 200 Abu Sayyaf guerrillas attacked Christians in the town of Ipil, in the southern Philippines, killing more than 50 people and wounding hundreds.

Ramzi Ahmed Yousef was brought to trial at the end of May 1996 on charges relating to the bombing of the Philippines Air Lines aircraft and murder of the passenger on 11 December 1994, as well as conspiracy to carry out bomb attacks on aircraft. He was convicted on all counts on 5 September. He stood trial in due course for the bombing of the World Trade Centre and on 12 February 1997 was convicted and was eventually sentenced to 240 years' imprisonment.

Osama bin Laden, meantime, was continuing his war against the United States, Saudi Arabia and other regimes in North Africa whom he regarded as allies of the 'Great Satan'. He was allegedly behind the attempted assassinations of Crown Prince Abdullah of Jordan in June 1993 and President Hosni Mubarak of Egypt during the latter's visit to Ethiopia in June 1995. By that time, however, his activities were causing serious concern in Washington, Riyadh and elsewhere. In April 1994 he had been stripped of his Saudi citizenship and in the following year Sudan, which was by then beginning to enjoy the initial stages of a rap-prochement with the West, came under pressure to ask him to leave.

On the morning of 13 November 1995, in the Saudi capital of Riyadh, a truck bomb exploded outside a Saudi Arabian National Guard com-munications centre. Five Americans and two Indians were killed and more than 60 people, including 34 Americans, were injured in the blast which caused massive damage to the three-storey building. Responsibility was claimed by two organisations, the Islamic Movement for Change and the Tigers of the Gulf, the latter stating, 'If the Americans don't leave the Kingdom as soon as possible, we will continue our actions.' Four Saudi Muslim extremists, Abdul Aziz bin Fahd bin Nasser al-Mothem, Khalid bin Ahmed bin Ibrahim al-Sa'eed, Riyadh bin Suleiman bin Is'haq al-Hajen, and Muslih bin Ayedh al-Shemrani, were subsequently arrested and, following interrogation, were duly beheaded on 30 May 1996. Three of them had been members of the mujahidin in Afghanistan, while the fourth had fought with Muslim forces in Bosnia. Although it has been reported that the Saudis were well aware that Osama bin Laden was behind the attack, any confirmation of this was prevented by the speedy execution of the four men; indeed, it has been suggested that their swift demise was designed to effect just that.

The attack served to infuriate the Saudis who decided to give bin Laden a warning. Shortly after the bombing, his home in Khartoum was subjected to an attack by four gunmen who raked it with automatic fire. Three of them died in a firefight with his guards and the fourth was captured, subsequently being executed by the Sudanese.

In early 1996, an unsuccessful attempt was made on bin Laden's life. This had also been orchestrated by the Saudis who had earlier offered to reinstate his Saudi citizenship and allow him to return to his home country if he abandoned his war. Bin Laden rejected the proposal and therefore the Saudis, together with the United States and Egypt, proceeded to increase the pressure on Sudan which eventually acquiesced and ordered bin Laden to leave. In May of that year, accompanied by his family and some 200 followers, he flew to Afghanistan where he established a new base.

It appears that it was not long, however, before he carried out his next attack. On the night of 25 June, a huge bomb exploded outside a US Air Force housing complex, called Khobar Towers, at the King Abdul Aziz Air Base near Dhahran in Saudi Arabia, killing nineteen US servicemen and injuring 385 others, women and children being among the dead and wounded. The building nearest the blast was completely destroyed and another near by was badly damaged. It later transpired that a 5,000-gallon fuel tanker had been parked just outside the perimeter fence, close to a dormitory building which accommodated US personnel. Two men had been seen leaving the area in a small car three minutes before the explosion took place. Two organisations claimed responsibility: the Legions of the Martyr Abdallah al-Huzayfi and the Hizbollah – the Gulf.

While there was no firm evidence of involvement by Osama bin Laden, who described the bombing as 'heroic', suspicions seemed to be confirmed after telephone intercepts by the US National Security Agency picked up conversations between him and Ayman al-Zawahiri, one of the leaders of an Egyptian group called Harakat al-Jihad al-Islami, during which the latter complimented him on the bombing. In 1983, following the murder of Egyptian president Anwar Sadat two years earlier, al-Zawahiri had been tried on charges of conspiracy to murder and was sentenced to three years' imprisonment, albeit he served only sixteen months. In 1998, he and some of his followers were expelled from Harakat al-Jihad al-Islami due to their increasing links with bin Laden whom al-Zawahiri had first met in 1985. Joining al-Qaeda, he subsequently became bin Laden's deputy and political chief of the organisation.

Eighteen months later, however, came firm evidence of bin Laden's involvement in terrorism. On 7 August 1998, a massive truck bomb exploded outside the US Embassy in the Kenyan capital of Nairobi, killing over 200 people and injuring more than 4,500. Five minutes earlier, another had detonated outside the US Embassy in Dar-es-Salaam, the capital of Tanzania, killing eleven people and injuring 85.

Both attacks had been mounted by suicide bombers belonging to al-Qaeda. Evidence of this was confirmed when Mohamed Saddiq Odeh, the Palestinian leader of the cell which had organised the attack in Nairobi and had flown to Pakistan on the evening before, was arrested and interrogated by the Pakistani authorities and then extradited to the United States. Meanwhile, other members of the al-Qaeda cell were arrested elsewhere, providing further information under interrogation. Among them was Mohamed Rashed Daoud al-Owhali (alias Khalid Salim) who was arrested in Nairobi. He had arrived the previous week from Pakistan and had been aboard the vehicle carrying the bomb, jumping clear and running for his life before his accomplice, the suicide bomber driving the vehicle, detonated it. Injured in the blast, he had been taken to hospital for treatment. Tracked down a few days later, he was also arrested and extradited to the United States. A fourth member of the cell, later identified as Fazul Abdullah Mohammed, succeeded in escaping from Kenya.

One of the men responsible for the Dar-es-Salaam attack was also arrested. Muhammad Sadiq Howaida, another Palestinian, had assembled the bomb and had flown to Pakistan prior to the event, later being arrested as he attempted to enter Afghanistan using a false passport. He was also extradited to the United States where, under questioning, he provided details of the bombing.

On 20 August, the Americans launched a retaliatory strike against bin Laden. Seventy-five RGM-100 Tomahawk cruise missiles were launched by US warships from a carrier group in the Arabian Sea against terrorist bases in Afghanistan. Among those hit was the Al Badr II camp belonging to al-Qaeda and the Amir Muawiya belonging to the Harakat ul-Ansar (HUA), a Kashmiri terrorist group supported by bin Laden in its campaign for independence from India. The Amir Muawiya camp was one of three reportedly operated by Pakistan's ISI which assisted in the training of the Kashmiri guerrillas.

Missiles were also launched by warships in the Red Sea at the El-Shifa pharmaceuticals manufacturing plant situated in Sudan in the industrial area of Bahri, a few miles to the north-east of Khartoum, reducing it to smouldering rubble. Intelligence reports had indicated that it had been dealing with chemicals for use in the production of VX nerve gas but it later transpired that it had been making veterinary goods.

Bin Laden himself had evidently been warned of the attacks beforehand and had taken refuge in northern Afghanistan. The casualties incurred among his followers only served to intensify their hatred of the United States and increase their devotion to their leader, while also promoting his standing among Muslim extremists elsewhere.

His response was not long in coming. On 25 August, a bomb exploded in a Planet Hollywood restaurant in Cape Town, South Africa, killing two people and injuring 27. A telephone caller claiming to be a representative of Muslims Against Global Oppression (MAGO) claimed responsibility, stating that the attack had been in retaliation for the US attack. Cape Town has a large Muslim population and a number of extremist groups were formed during the 1990s, among them MAGO which was reported as having links with an extreme anti-apartheid organisation called Qibla, and another called People Against Gangsterism and Drugs (PAGAD) which originally had been formed as a vigilante group.

After the US attack on his bases, bin Laden apparently established new ones in northern and eastern Afghanistan. Al-Qaeda's main base was moved to Kunduz Province and camps were set up at Tora Bora, Derunta, Melawa and Farm Hadda, near Jalalabad, and at Galrez some 30 miles west of Kabul. Two more were reportedly sited at Khwaja Mastoon Ghundai and Sati Kundao near the border with Pakistan. Bin Laden's network extended into Pakistan itself via Peshawar where a number of safe houses had been established for use as transit centres for members of al-Qaeda travelling to and from Afghanistan.

By the beginning of 1999, the Taliban government of Afghanistan was coming under increasing pressure from the US and British governments to expel Osama bin Laden. The British were becoming increasingly concerned at growing evidence of the involvement of British Muslims with extremist groups after reports of training, allegedly organised by London-based organisations, being conducted at weekends in clandestine camps throughout Britain. Young men attending these camps were apparently being encouraged to seek military training overseas in Yemen and Afghanistan, one report stating that large numbers, of up to 2,000 individuals each year, having done so.

On 24 December 1998, a group of eight British Muslims were arrested in Yemen on charges of conspiring to carry out bomb attacks in Aden, the targets being the British consulate, an Anglican church and two hotels. According to other reports, at least one member of the group had undergone training in Shabwa, a province in eastern Yemen, at a camp run by the Islamic Army of Aden-Abyan which on 28 December kidnapped sixteen Westerners in southern Yemen in an attempt to secure the release of the eight prisoners. Four of the hostages, three Britons and an Australian, died when Yemeni troops carried out a rescue operation on the following day. On 9 August 1999, all eight were convicted; three, however, were released on grounds of time served, while the remainder received prison sentences of between two and seven years.

Six months earlier, Osama bin Laden had been reported to have disappeared. In March 1999, however, Western intelligence services located him in eastern Afghanistan, moving between his network of camps south of Jalalabad. At the same time, there were further reports of his support for a Kashmiri group, the Harakat ul-Ansar (HUA), which was also alleged to be receiving assistance from the ISI. The HUA comprises two groups, both formed during the 1980s to fight in Afghanistan: the Harikat ul-Mujahidin, led by Fazular Rehman Khan, and the even more radical Harakat ul-Jihad. In early 1999, it was revealed that the HUA was recruiting not only from Kashmir but also Afghanistan, Pakistan and Britain.

Evidence of attempts to recruit British Muslims, not only for service in Kashmir but also in Pakistan, Kosovo and Chechnya, was revealed in October 1999 when the *Sunday Telegraph* revealed that Mohammed Sohail, an information technology security adviser working for Railtrack, had allegedly been using the company's computer and e-mail address to recruit volunteers. Working for the Global Jihad Fund, a London-based organisation headed by a Saudi dissident named Mohammed al-Massari, he was also said to have assisted in raising funds for funda-mentalist groups including the HUA. During a conversation with the journalists conducting the investigation, Sohail stated that he worked for al-Massari and Osama bin Laden.

The HUA first came to prominence during the mid-1990s when it kidnapped a number of Westerners in Kashmir. Two Britons were seized during the summer of 1994 but were released unharmed shortly after-wards. In October of that year, three Britons and an American were abducted in the Indian capital of New Delhi and held prisoner in Sharanpur, a small town 150 miles north of the city, while demands were made for the release of ten Kashmiri extremists in exchange for them. Two weeks later, however, all four were rescued by Indian police. In July 1995, Harakat al-Mujahidin, then named al-Faran, kid-napped four Britons, one American and one German, and held them hostage while demanding the release of 21 Kashmiri militants jailed previously in Kashmir and India, including the leader of al-Faran, Malauna Masood Azghar (alias Wali Azam). One of the hostages sub-sequently escaped and another was found beheaded. The remains of one of the Britons, Paul Wells, were reported as having been discov-ered in January 2000, having been identified by DNA tests carried out in India, but further tests in Britain proved that the latter were incorrect. At the time of writing, the fate of the four remaining hostages is still unknown.

In July 1999, the existence of a group even more extreme than al-Qaeda came to light. Called Takfiris, this hitherto unknown organisa-tion had been formed in the 1970s in Egyptian prisons, following the arrests of large numbers of Muslim extremists. Many of its members fought alongside the mujahidin in Afghanistan but when the war ended, the group disappeared from sight. During the first half of 1999, however, it surfaced again amid reports that it was hunting Osama bin Laden, whom it condemned as a 'false prophet', that it had made at least three attempts on his life and that there had been a number of confrontations between members of Takfiris and al-Qaeda.

In October 1999, the Taliban government agreed to close down the terrorist training camps and despatch large numbers of extremists back to Pakistan. This came about after a visit by the ISI chief, Lieutenant General Khawaja Ziauddin, who attended a meeting with the Taliban leader, Mullah Mohammad Omar, on behalf of the Pakistani Prime Minister, Nawaz Sharif. The Taliban, however, refused to hand over Osama bin Laden to the United Nations in order to stand trial in the United States, and on 14 November the latter imposed sanctions on Afghanistan. These included the freezing of the Taliban's bank accounts overseas and the $450 million assets of the Afghan state airline, Ariana, in the United States. This led to riots in Kabul and three bomb and rocket attacks in Islamabad against the US Embassy, the offices of the UN Pakistan Mission and the headquarters of the UN World Food Programme.

Although the Taliban had rejected out of hand the demand to hand over bin Laden, the UN sanctions presented them with a dilemma. On the one hand, they were seeking international recognition and aid while on the other they were harbouring the world's most wanted terrorist suspect with a $3 million price on his head. The precarious nature of his position was apparently not lost on bin Laden himself who was reported to be fearing assassination and to be constantly on the move, accompanied only by members of his family and heavily armed bodyguards. Despite such problems, however, he was evidently still receiving substantial funds from a number of sources; some of these were said to be in Saudi Arabia, including five businessmen allegedly paying him protection money on a regular basis.

The end of 1999 and the eve of the millennium saw a number of countries on a high state of alert for possible attacks by terrorist organisations. In the United States such fears appeared to be well justified when on 14 December an Algerian named Ahmed Ressam was arrested at Port Angeles, in the north-west state of Washington, after arriving on a ferry from the Canadian city of Victoria, British Columbia. A search of his car revealed nitro-glycerine and other bomb-making equipment, including four timers of a type known to have been used previously by al-Qaeda. Ressam, who had fought in Afghanistan with the mujahidin, had been living in Montreal under an alias and was known to have links with the GIA in Algeria. Police subsequently divulged that they believed he intended to attack a millennium celebration in Seattle before escaping to the United Kingdom. When arrested, he was found in possession of air tickets for flights from Seattle to London via New York.

Three days after Ressam's arrest, it was learned that an Algerian accomplice of his, Abdel Dajid Dahoumane, had entered the United States from Montreal. Four days later, a third Algerian, Bouabide Chamchi, was arrested as he arrived from Canada using a false French passport. A search of his vehicle revealed sufficient explosives to manufacture four large bombs. His travelling companion, a Canadian woman, was subsequently reported as being suspected of having links with an Algerian extremist organisation.

Ten months later, Osama bin Laden apparently struck again. On 8 August 2000 the USS *Cole*, a guided missile destroyer, left her home base at Norfolk Naval Station in Virginia and embarked on a five-month deployment. After passing through the Suez Canal, she sailed for Yemen, arriving at the port of Aden on the morning of 12 October to refuel. Having moored some 600 yards offshore, at 10.30 a.m. she began taking on fuel, a process normally expected to take between four and five hours. Forty-seven minutes later, however, a boat packed with explosives was manoeuvred up against the warship's hull and the bomb detonated. Seventeen of the ship's crew died and 39 were wounded in the blast which tore a huge hole in the hull and caused damage worth $240 million. The two suicide bombers manning the boat were also killed.

Investigators later estimated that the size of the bomb was 400–700 lbs. Forensic analysis revealed that the high explosive used in the attack was C4, a military plastic type manufactured in the United States and exported to a number of countries in the Middle East including Saudi Arabia, Kuwait and Iran (during the reign of the Shah). It was also supplied to the mujahidin during the war in Afghanistan. Moreover, some 20 years beforehand, a former member of the CIA, Frank Terpil, was convicted of supplying 21 tons of C4 to Libya, reportedly for the training of terrorists.

Less than 24 hours after the bomb attack on the USS *Cole*, another was carried out at 6.00 a.m. on 13 October on the British Embassy in the Yemeni capital of Sana'a, fortunately causing no casualties. Thrown over a nearby wall, it blew in the windows of the Chancery building and caused considerable internal damage while also destroying a fuel tank connected to an emergency electricity generator.

Three groups subsequently claimed responsibility for the attacks – the Islamic Army of Aden-Abyan and two hitherto unknown organisations: the Army of Mohammed and the Islamic Deterrence Force. As mentioned earlier, the Islamic Army, led by Abu al-Hassan al-Mihdar, had been responsible for the kidnapping of the sixteen Westerners in southern Yemen in December 1998. A splinter group of the Jihad Organisation which had carried out several attacks during the early 1990s, its members included former mujahidin who had fought in Afghanistan as well as extremists from a number of countries. Moreover, it had been linked allegedly with Sheikh Abu Hamza al-Masri, the imam of the Finsbury Park mosque in London, and with the British Muslims imprisoned in Yemen for conspiring to attack US and British targets in Aden.

The Yemeni authorities launched a hunt for the perpetrators of the two attacks and shortly afterwards apprehended 60 individuals for questioning. On 16 October they discovered bomb-making equipment and documents in an apartment in Aden which had been rented for a month by the two suicide bombers, one of them an Arab with a Gulf accent; in a nearby yard, they had parked a fibreglass boat which was found to be missing following the attack. One of them had given forged identification in the name of Abdullah Ahmed Khaled Al-Mousawa to the landlord of the apartment when signing a twelve-month lease. On 23 October, the investigators announced that they had found forged identity cards and other documents in several apartments and vehicles located and searched during their investigations. These had led them to question officials of the civil registration office at Lahij who were arrested after it was revealed that they had not only issued identity cards to the suspected bombers but also had provided them with government cars in which to travel around Aden and Lahij.

The first week of November saw the arrests of four more men. On the 11th, it was reported that some of the suspects had admitted involvement in three further attempts to attack US targets in Yemen. It was later revealed that, a year previously, in November 1999, they had intended to mount an attack on US military personnel on their way to Yemen's National Centre for the Removal of Land Mines; their plan had been foiled by Yemeni troops who found explosives on the route taken daily by the Americans when travelling between the centre and the Royal Hotel in Aden where they were accommodated. A second unsuccessful attempt was targeted on the hotel itself while a third, which took place on 3 January 2000, was aimed at a US destroyer, the USS *Sullivan*, but was aborted after the boat carrying the explosives became unseaworthy.

Further interrogation of the suspects revealed that the mastermind behind the attack on the USS *Cole* was a former mujahid who had also fought in Afghanistan; he was identified as Mohammed Omar al-Harazi (alias Abdul Rahman Hussein Al-Nashari or Al-Nassir), a Yemeni from Haraz, east of Sana'a, who was living in the United Arab Emirates but visited Aden frequently. Subsequently proved by US investigators to have been a cousin of the suicide bomber in the attack on the US Embassy in Nairobi, he had disappeared four days prior to the attack on the USS *Cole*.

The leading suspect being held by the authorities was reported to be Jamal al-Badawi, a Yemeni who had also been a member of the mujahidin in Afghanistan where he had met al-Hazari. In mid-November the Yemeni authorities claimed that they had also identified one of the two suicide bombers, naming him as Saeed Awad Al-Khamri, a Yemeni from the province of Hadramaut situated adjacent to Saudi Arabia where the family of Osama bin Laden has roots.

Eventually, the Yemeni authorities narrowed the number of suspects down to six who were believed to have been accomplices in the two attacks. Others, such as the officials who had provided the bombers with false identification, would be held as witnesses. Meanwhile, US requests for extradition of the six suspects were refused on the grounds that such a measure was not permitted under Yemen's constitution.

On 16 February 2001, two more suspects were arrested as they returned to Yemen from Afghanistan, bringing the total number to eight. They were identified as Mohammed Ahmed al-Ahdal and Ahmed Mohammed Amin, both of whom had also fought in Afghanistan. Following their interrogation of the two men, the Yemeni authorities stated that they believed that Mohammed Omar al-Hazari was in Afghanistan together with another accomplice. Once again, while there was no concrete evidence of the involvement of Osama bin Laden in the two bombings, the Afghan connection led US investigators to believe firmly that he was linked with them.

ELEVEN MONTHS AFTER THE attack on the USS *Cole* came the worst atrocity yet committed by terrorists anywhere in the world. On Tuesday 11 September 2001, at 8.45 a.m. US Eastern Standard Time, a Boeing 767 airliner of American Airlines slammed into the 1,368-feet-tall North Tower of the World Trade Centre in New York. The initial reaction of those who witnessed this horrifying event from the neighbouring South Tower and the streets of Manhattan below was that there had been a dreadful accident. Eleven minutes later at 8.56 a.m., however, any such idea was brutally banished. As millions throughout the United States and overseas watched the scene live on television, another Boeing 767, belonging to United Airlines, flew into the South Tower. As they gazed in horror, the upper storeys of both towers were consumed in flame and black smoke. At 10.07 a.m. the South Tower collapsed, followed by the North Tower 20 minutes later, thousands of people being killed as they did so. Others had already jumped to their deaths rather than face being burned alive.

Meanwhile, in Washington, across the Potomac River from the White House, a third airliner, a Boeing 757 of American Airlines, had crashed into the west wall of the Pentagon at 9.38 a.m., penetrating three of the five concentric rings which make up the huge building and causing part of it to collapse. One hundred and ninety people, including the 58 passengers and six crew, were killed along with the unknown number of terrorists. By this time, the FBI was receiving reports that three aircraft had been hijacked but at 10.30 a.m. came a further report that a fourth aircraft, United Airlines Flight UA 093 en route from Newark to San Francisco, had crashed near Pittsburgh, Pennsylvania 20 minutes earlier.

During the following days and weeks, it transpired that all four aircraft had been hijacked by Arab terrorists and it is believed that it was the gallantry of a group of male passengers aboard United Airlines Flight

UA 093 which prevented a fourth and equally murderous attack. Within a matter of days it became apparent that the attacks were part of a meticulously planned operation by a sophisticated terrorist organisation. Suspicion immediately centred on Osama bin Laden and the intelligence and security services of the Western world were tasked immediately with obtaining the necessary evidence. FBI investigations soon revealed that a terrorist network had established itself within the United States where some of its members had undergone flying training. The nineteen Arab hijackers were named but such was their use of aliases that investigators could not be certain of positive identifications.

During the following weeks, the hunt for evidence against those responsible continued and on 4 October British Prime Minister Tony Blair announced in the House of Commons that incontrovertible evidence had been produced, proving beyond doubt that Osama bin Laden and al-Qaeda were responsible for the attacks on the World Trade Centre and the Pentagon on 11 September, and of the hijacking of United Airlines Flight UA 093. He also revealed that at least three of the nineteen hijackers had been positively identified as known associates of Osama bin Laden with links to al-Qaeda. Fifteen of them were subsequently identified as being Saudi Arabians.

Meanwhile the man held responsible for the worst outrage ever committed in the history of terrorism was lying low in Afghanistan, knowing full well that the United States and its allies were preparing to exact retribution against him and his organisation.

During the latter part of September, US and British naval and military forces deployed in considerable strength to the Arabian Sea and the Persian Gulf, with elements of the 10th US Mountain Division being dispatched to former Soviet bases at Khanabad and Qarshi in Uzbekistan, near the northern border of Afghanistan, where they established two forward operating bases for US and British special forces. On 7 October, US aircraft began strikes against military targets in Afghanistan, these initially being aimed at destroying the Taliban's air defences. In the meantime, US and British special forces were reported as having already infiltrated into Afghanistan, some establishing contact with the forces of the Northern Alliance, the Afghan anti-Taliban coalition.

On 19 October, a raid was carried out in the north-western outskirts of Kandahar by over 100 troops of the 75th Ranger Regiment accompanied by teams of the 1st Special Forces Operational Detachment – Delta (1st SFOD-DELTA), better known as Delta Force. The Rangers were dropped by parachute from MC-130 Combat Talons of a USAF special operations squadron while the Delta Force teams were reportedly inserted by helicopters of the 160th Special Operations Aviation Regiment (SOAR), the 'Night Stalkers', operating from a floating base aboard the aircraft carrier USS Kitty Hawk stationed off the Pakistan coast. The raiding force was dropped and landed in a valley between Baba Sahib and Mian Koh. Supported by AC-130 Spectre gunships, it attacked a complex of buildings containing a Taliban radio communications centre and the residence of the Taliban leader, Mullah Mohammed Omar. According to unconfirmed reports, the raiders met fierce resistance with one US source quoted as stating that some of them had been wounded. They also reportedly struck an airfield, destroying a large cache of weapons, and blew up a bridge before being extracted by 160th SOAR helicopters two hours later.

The raid heralded the beginning of Allied ground operations in Afghanistan and the next phase in the hunt for Osama bin Laden and the destruction of al-Qaeda. As President George W. Bush made clear when he declared war on international terrorism following the outrages of 11 September 2001, it will be a long, hard campaign which will see operations undertaken against al-Qaeda and other organisations not only in Afghanistan but also elsewhere, wherever a terrorist threat is detected.

GLOSSARY

Abu Sayyaf Filipino Muslim extremist guerrilla organisation

Air America Airline owned by a CIA proprietary company - previously called Civil Air Transport

ALN Armée de Libération Nationale (National Liberation Army) - military wing of the FLN in Algeria

Al-Qaeda Muslim extremist terrorist organisation formed in 1989 by Osama bin Laden

ANL Armée National Laotienne (Laotian National Army)

AK Armia Krajowa (Home Army) - WWII Polish resistance movement

Amdowas Tribesmen from the region of Amdo, in eastern Tibet

ARVN Army of the Republic of Vietnam (South Vietnam)

Askars Armed tribesmen in Oman

Assam Rifles Indian para-military border patrol unit

AVIARY FEC-LG airborne operations section, formed in South Korea in August 1950

Bajraktar Albanian clan chieftain in Ghegeria, northern Albania

Baker Section Airborne operations unit formed in 1951 by Attrition Section of Eighth US Army G-3 Miscellaneous Division during Korean War

Baluchis Natives of Baluchistan, the westernmost province of Pakistan

Bangalore Torpedo Explosive charge contained in sectioned pipe – used for blowing gaps in barbed wire defences

BATT British Army Training Team - cover name for 22 SAS during the war in Dhofar

BCRA Bureau Central des Renseignements et d'Action - Free French wartime intelligence service

BEL Bureau des Études et des Liaisons (Studies & Liaison Bureau) - replaced CCI as the overall coordinating body for French intelligence in Algeria in 1960, having absorbed the GRE in 1959

Berbers Ethnic minority group in Algeria, comprising Kabyles, Chaouïas, M'zabites and Tuareg

Bey Albanian landowner in Toskeria, southern Albania

Binh Xuyen Large organisation of gangsters and river pirates operating in and around Saigon

BK Balli Kombëtar (National Front) - Albanian nationalist anti-royalist organisation formed in 1943

BLOSSOM Codename for OPC teams inserted during 1951 by air and sea into the centre and north-east regions of North Korea

BMEO Bataillon de Marche d'Extrême Orient - Franco-Cambodian unit operating in Cochin China and Southern Annam during First Indochina War

Border Scouts Irregular force raised in Sarawak and North Borneo by the British during the Borneo Confrontation

BSLE Bureau de la Statistique de la Légion Etrangère (Foreign Legion Statistical Bureau) - Foreign Legion intelligence service in North Africa

BTLC Bureau Technique de Liaison at de Coordination - a branch of French intelligence in Indochina

Bureau 24 Unit of the SDECE/DGSE Action Service - later known as 24e SA (24th Action Service)

Caid Algerian local official, appointed by the Governor-General during French rule

CAS Combined Area Studies - cover name for CIA activities in South Vietnam

CAT Civil Air Transport - airline owned by CIA proprietary company, later renamed Air America

CCC Command & Control Central-MACV-SOG base at Kontum, in South Vietnam, for operations in South Vietnam, northern Cambodia and Laos

CCE Comité de Coordination et d'Exécution (Coordination & Execution Committee) - Algerian FLN's controlling body in exile in Tunis

CCI Centre de Coordination Interarmées (Inter-Service Coordination Centre) - coordinating body for all French military intelligence in Algeria from July 1957 onwards

CCN Command & Control North - MACV-SOG base at Da Nang, South Vietnam, for operations in North Vietnam and Laos

CCO Clandestine Communist Organisation - organisation in Borneo predominantly based on large Chinese immigrant community in towns of Sarawak during the 1960s

CCRAK Combined Command Reconnaissance Activities Korea - formed in December 1951 to coordinate all UN/US covert operations and related activities during the Korean War

CCS Command & Control South - MACV-SOG base at Ban Me Thuot, South Vietnam, for operations in Cambodia

Centaine Term used by the French for approximately 100-strong irregular or special forces sub-unit

Chushi Gangdrug Tibetan national resistance movement - formed in 1958

CIA Central Intelligence Agency

CIC US Army Counter Intelligence Corps

CIF Centre d'Instruction et de Formation (Training & Formation Centre) - GCMA training centre at Cap St Jacques in southern Vietnam during the First Indochina War

CIG Central Intelligence Group - initial name of CIA

Cinquième Bureau Fifth Bureau - French Army's psychological warfare operations service

CIPS Centre Parachutiste d'Instructions Specialisés (Specialist Parachute Instruction Centre) - one of three specialist training centres replacing 11e RPC in 1995

CLARET Codename for British covert cross-border operations into Kalimantan during Borneo Confrontation

CNEC Centres Nationaux d'Entrainement Commandos (National Commando Training Centres) - four establishments which replaced 11e Choc in 1962

COBBS Combined Operations Beach & Boat Section – Royal Marine unit formed in 1947 from RMBPD and SCOBBS

Company 4000 US Army unit providing cover for Albanian guerrilla group trained by CIA for Operation FIEND

CPA Communist Party of Albania

CPES Centre Parachutiste d'Entrainements Specialisés (Specialist Parachute Training Centre) - one of three training establishments replacing the 11e RPC in 1995

CPEOM Centre Parachutiste aux Opérations Maritime (Maritime Parachute Operations Centre) - one of three training centres replacing the 11e RPC in 1995

Cross-Border Scouts Irregular force raised by 22 SAS for cross-border operations into Kalimantan during the Borneo Confrontation

CRUA Comité Révolutionnaire d'Unité et d'Action - nationalist front formed in Algeria in early 1954, superseded by FLN later that year

CT Communist Terrorist - term used for terrorists of MRLA during the Malayan Emergency

DCI Director of Central Intelligence - head of CIA

DDO Directorate of Operations - current name of CIA's covert operations arm

DDP Directorate of Plans - original name for CIA's covert operations arm, subsequently changed to DDO

Department 13 Department within KGB First Directorate responsible for assassinations

Detachment 2 USAF special operations support unit based at Kadena Air Force Base on Okinawa

Detachment 101 OSS unit which served in South Asia and South East Asia during WWII

Deuxième Bureau French military intelligence service

DGD Direction Générale de Documentation - body responsible for oversight of all French intelligence activities in Indochina during First Indochina War

DGER Direction Générale des Etudes et Recherche (Directorate General of Studies & Research) – first French post-WWII foreign intelligence service, formed in 1944 from DGSS

DGSE French foreign intelligence service, replaced SDECE in 1982

DGSS Direction Générale des Services Spéciaux (Directorate General of Special Services) – Free French intelligence service, replaced BCRA in 1943

DLF Dhofar Liberation Front - dissident movement formed in 1965 in Dhofar, south-western Oman. Subsequently amalgamated with PFLOAG in 1968

DMZ Demilitarised Zone - area of No Man's Land along 17th Parallel between North and South Vietnam

DNI Director of Naval Intelligence, Royal Navy

DOP Détachements Opérationnels de Protections (Operational Protection Detachments) - French military intelligence and interrogation sections in Algeria, operating under CCI

DZ Drop zone

Elint Electronic intelligence gathering

FAC Forward air controller - responsible for directing air support on to ground targets

Firqats Irregular forces raised by 22 SAS during the Dhofar campaign in Oman

FIS French Indochina Section - SLFEO special operations unit based in Ceylon and employed by Force 136 during WWII

FLN Front de la Libération Nationale - Algerian Muslim nationalist organisation formed in October 1954, superseding CRUA

FOE Forsvarsftaben Operativ Enhat - Swedish civilian intelligence service

FOO Forward observation officer - artillery officer attached to infantry company to call for and direct supporting fire

FORAE Codename for MACV-SOG deception operations in North Vietnam

Force 136 SOE unit responsible for operations in Asia and South East Asia

Force K Counter-guerrilla unit formed in Algeria by DST, unknowingly from ALN guerrillas

FTP Francs-Tireurs et Partisans - French communist resistance organisation during WWII

GAUR Codename for French operation in December 1945 to raise guerrilla groups in Laos

GCMA Groupement de Commandos Mixtes Aéroportés (Composite Airborne Commando Group)- cover name for SDECE Action Service unconventional warfare force in Indochina

GLI Groupements Léger d'Intervention (Light Intervention Groups) - cover name for 11e Choc detachments in Algeria

GM Groupement de Marche (Marching Group) - cover name for the 11e Choc in Algeria, later changed to DS 111

GMI Groupe Mixte 'D'Intervention (Composite Intervention Group) - cover name for SDECE Action Service unconventional warfare force in Indochina, replacing name of GCMA in December 1953

GPRA Gouvernement Provisoire de la République Algérienne (Provisional Government of the Republic of Algeria) - FLN government in exile

Goloks Tribesmen from region of Amdo in eastern Tibet

GRE Groupement de Renseignement et d'Exploitation (Intelligence & Exploitation Group) - French military intelligence unit in Algeria, working under CCI

Green Hornets Nickname for 20th Special Operations Squadron – USAF helicopter squadron forming part of MACV-SOG Air Studies Group

HALO High Altitude Low Opening - military free-fall parachuting technique for covert insertion of personnel into a target area

Harkis Irregular troops employed by French against FLN/ALN in Algeria

Hatchet Forces Codename for MACV-SOG strike platoons and companies

Hazaras Shi'ite Muslim tribes from central Afghanistan

Hmong Hill tribes of Laos, also known as Meo

Ho Chi Minh Trail Network of heavily camouflaged roads and trails leading from North Vietnam to southeastern Laos

HUA Harakat ul-Ansar – Kashmiri Muslim separatist group - comprises two elements: Harikat ul-Mujahidin (previously called al-Faran) and Harakat ul-Jihad

Huks Hukbong Magpapalaya ng Bayan (People's Liberation Army) - communist guerrilla organisation in Philippines during late 1940s and 1950s

IBT Indonesian Border Terrorists - Indonesian irregulars during Borneo Confrontation

ISI Inter-Services Intelligence - Pakistani military intelligence service

Jebb Committee Formally known as Cold War Sub-Committee formed by Russia Committee for conduct of political and economic warfare, and to exercise oversight of SIS covert and paramilitary operations against Soviet Union

JEDBURGH Teams Codename for OSS/SOE teams dropped into Normandy in June 1944 in support of French resistance

JPRC Joint Personnel Recovery Centre - cover name for MACV-SOG OPS-80 downed aircrew and PoW rescue unit

JUNGLE Codename for SIS operation in Baltic States in late 1940s and 1950s, landing agents by sea in support of anti-Soviet guerrilla groups

Kempei Tai Japanese secret police during WWII

KGB Soviet intelligence and security service from 1954 until 1991 when replaced by SVR (foreign intelligence service) and FSB (federal security service)

KHAD Afghan intelligence service and secret police during communist regime

KKE Kommunistikon Komma Ellados (Greek Communist Party)

KKO Indonesian marines - during 1960s

KLO Korean Liaison Office - cover name for FECOM intelligence unit in South Korea

KMAG Korean Military Advisory Group - US military assistance unit formed in 1949 to provide assistance for ROK forces

Lao Issara Laotian nationalist movement formed during Japanese occupation in WWII

Legalitei Albanian royalist organisation formed in 1943

LP Landing point

LS Landing strip

LST Landing ship tank

LUP Lying-up position

LZ Landing zone

MAAG Military Assistance Advisory Group - formed in early 1953 to provide military assistance to ARVN

MACV Military Assistance Command Vietnam - formed in February 1962, replacing MAAG

MACV-SOG MACV Studies & Observation Group - joint service organisation formed in January 1964 for conduct of unconventional warfare operations in South Vietnam, Laos and Cambodia

Maghreb North-west area of North Africa formed by Atlas Massif and coastal plain of Morocco, Algeria, Tunisia, and Libya

MAK Mekhtab al-Khidemat al-Mujahidin (Service Office of the Mujahidin) - organisation formed for worldwide recruitment of Muslims to fight in Afghanistan, 1979-1989

Malayan Scouts British Army special forces unit formed during Malayan Emergency - subsequently became 22 SAS in 1952

Maquis Term given by French to indigenous partisan groups during First Indochina War

Mazghen Algerian irregular troops providing intelligence and protection for French SAS officers in Algeria

MCP Malayan Communist Party

MGB Soviet intelligence service - successor in 1946 to NKGB, replaced by KGB in 1954

Min Yuen People's Movement - communist secret organisation in Malaya which provided intelligence and logistical support for MRLA

MI(R) Military Intelligence (Research) - pre-war and early WWII section of British War Office tasked with planning and providing covert support for Eastern European countries overrun by Germany

MNA Mouvement Nationaliste Algérienne (Algerian Nationalist Movement), formerly MTLD

MNLF Moro National Liberation Front - Filipino Muslim separatist organisation

Montagnards Collective term for hill tribes from the central highlands of Vietnam

MPABA Malayan People's Anti-British Army - original title of MRLA

MPAJA Malayan People's Anti-Japanese Army - WWII communist resistance movement

MRLA Malayan Races Liberation Army - post-WWII communist movement

MTLD Mouvement pour le Triomphe des Libertés Démocratiques - the legal cover under which PPA operated in Algeria

Mujahidin 'Soldiers of God' - collective name applied to guerrillas fighting Soviet occupation forces in Afghanistan 1979-1989

MVD Soviet Ministry of Interior

NEFA North East Frontier Agency - north-eastern Indian state now called Arunachal Pradesh

Negd Flat and featureless region to the north beyond Al Qara Mountains in the Dhofar region of south-western Oman

NIFA National Islamic Front of Afghanistan - one of three traditionalist/moderate factions among seven groups of mujahidin fighting Soviet occupation forces in Afghanistan 1979-1989

NKGB Soviet state security/intelligence service - replaced by MGB in 1946

NKPA North Korean People's Army

NKVD Soviet intelligence and security service until 1941 when replaced by MVD (internal security) and NKGB (state security/intelligence) in 1941

Nungs Vietnamese hill tribesmen originally of Chinese origin

NVA North Vietnamese Army

NZSAS New Zealand Special Air Service

NWFP North West Frontier Province

OAS Organisation Armée Secrète (Secret Army Organisation) - terrorist organisation formed by senior French military officers opposed to independence for Algeria

Okhotniki Karavana 'Caravan Hunters' - special GRU spetsnaz unit formed to intercept mujahidin supply caravans during war in Afghanistan

OPLAN 34A Operational Plan 34A - overall plan under which US covert operations were conducted in South Vietnam, Laos and Cambodia from 1964 onwards

OS Organisation Secrète - paramilitary organisation formed in December 1947 by the PPA/MTLD

OSO Office of Special Operations - formed in 1946 as part of CIG (subsequently CIA)

OSS Office of Strategic Services - formed in 1942 as first US intelligence service and unconventional warfare organisation, disbanded in July 1945

Partai Ra'ayat People's Party - political party in Brunei which in early 1960s advocated unification with Sarawak and North Borneo, followed by federation with Malaysia

Pasdaran Iranian Revolutionary Guards

PCA Parti Communiste Algérien (Algerian Communist Party)

PCART Preparatory Committee for the Autonomous Region of Tibet – name of system of communist governing body forced on Tibet by China

PCF Parti Communiste Français (French Communist Party)

PDPA People's Democratic Party of Aghanistan

PDO Parachute dispatch officer

PEO Program Evaluation Office - cover name for early CIA covert operations in Laos

PFF Police Field Force - tactical units of Royal Malay/Malaysian Police

PFLOAG Popular Front for the Liberation of the Occupied Arab Gulf - Soviet and Chinese-backed Marxist revolutionary movement in South Yemen in the 1960s and 1970s

PFLO Popular Front for the Liberation of Oman - formerly PFLOAG

PGT Indonesian air force paratroops - during 1960s

Pieds noirs Name given to European settlers living in Algeria up until early 1960s

PIR Partisan Infantry Regiments

PKI Indonesian Communist Party

PLA People's Liberation Army - armed forces of People's Republic of China

PLOWMAN Codename for MACV-SOG maritime operations

PNI Indonesian National Party

PPA Parti Progressive Algérien (Algerian Progressive Party) - originally called Étoile Nord-Africaine. Established MTLD as legal arm.

Pushtun Pushtu-speaking people of south-eastern Afghanistan and north-western Pakistan who comprise the majority of the population of Afghanistan

Qadi Senior religious leader in Oman

RAF Royal Air Force

RLA Royal Laotian Army

RM Royal Marines

RMBPD Royal Marines Boom Patrol Detachment - cover name for WWII and post-war Royal Marine swimmer-canoeist unit

RNC Republic National Committee - Estonian nationalist movement formed in 1944 during German occupation

RNZAF Royal New Zealand Air Force

ROK Republic of Korea

RR Représentations Régional - GCMA regional headquarters throughout Vietnam and Laos

RRPM Répresentation Régionale Plateaux Montagnards - GCMA regional headquarters in Annamite chain of mountains of central Annam

RRVN Répresentation Régionale Vietnam Nord - GCMA regional headquarters in Tonkin

RRVS Représentation Régionale Vietnam Sud - GCMA headquarters in southern Vietnam

SAC Strategic Air Command (USAF)

SAF Sultan's Armed Forces (Oman)

Sakai Word in Malay meaning 'slave' - used as derogatory term for aborigines

Saladin British six-wheeled armoured car armed with 76mm gun

SAM Surface-to-air missile

Sangar Circular defensive embrasure made from rocks

SAR Search and rescue

SAS Section Administrative Specialisée (Special Administrative Section) - French military administrative organisation covering rural areas throughout Algeria

SAS Special Air Service

SASR Special Air Service Regiment - Australian SAS

SAU 1 Special Activities Unit 1 - USAF intelligence gathering unit formed in South Korea in early 1951, subsequently expanded and redesignated 6004th AISS

SAVAK Iranian intelligence service and secret police during reign of Shah

SBS Special Boat Squadron - Royal Marines special forces unit

SCLL Supreme Committee for the Liberation of Lithuania - nationalist movement formed in 1943 during German occupation

SCOBBS School of Combined Operations Beach & Boat Section – Royal Marine Unit formed in 1946 to retain and develop small boat raiding and combat swimmer skills

SEALs Sea Air Land teams - US Navy special forces

Section D Department of SIS formed in 1940 – responsible for subversion, sabotage and other aspects of unconventional warfare. Subsequently absorbed into SOE

Senoi Pra'ak Fighting Senoi - Royal Malay/Malaysian Police PFF aboriginal reconnaissance unit formed in 1958 during Malayan Emergency

SFF Special Frontier Force - special operations formation, comprising Tibetan personnel, formed by Indian Intelligence Bureau in November 1962

Sigint Signals intelligence gathering

SIS Secret Intelligence Service (MI6)

SLFEO Section de Liaison Française en Extrême Orient (Far East French Liaison Section) - Free French organisation based in India during WWII

SLNA Service de Liaisons Nord-Africaine (North African Liaison Service) - French intelligence organisation in Algeria during 1950s

SMG Special Missions Group - CIA-trained reconnaissance and raiding unit of South Koreans formed in July 1951

SMM Saigon Military Mission - cover name for CIA unit in South Vietnam

SMT Swedish military intelligence service

SOAF Sultan' of Oman's Air Force

SOE Special Operations Executive - British WWII unconventional warfare organisation, disbanded in 1946 with some elements absorbed into SIS

SOG Special Operations Group - special operations unit in Korean War comprising UDT 1 and elements of USMC 1st Marine Reconnaissance Company, formed in Aigust 1951 and disbanded a month later

SON Sultan of Oman's Navy

SOVMAT CIA operation during war in Afghanistan to acquire samples of Soviet weapons, armoured vehicles and aircraft for analysis and testing

Special Branch Branch of Royal Malay/Malaysian Police responsible for provision of intelligence during Malayan Emergency and Borneo Confrontation

Special Operations Branch SIS department formed in 1946 from elements of SOE following its disbandment in 1946

Spetsnaz Soviet special forces

SRO Service de Renseignement Opérationnel (Operational Intelligence Service) - branch of post-WWII French military intelligence

SSPL Sacred Sword of the Patriotic League - MACV-SOG phantom resistance organisation in North Vietnam

Statistical Research Dept. Cover name for Section D, SIS during early part of WWII Research Dept.

ST BARNUM Codename for CIA air operations in support of ST CIRCUS

ST CIRCUS Codename for CIA operation supporting anti-communist resistance in Tibet

Stinger FIM-92A SAM General Dynamics passive infra-red guided, shoulder-fired surface-to-air missile

STORM Codename for 22 SAS operation in Oman

SWITCHBACK Codename for US operation in 1964 to transfer responsibility for covert unconventional warfare operations in South Vietnam from CIA to US Army

SWIVEL CHAIR Codename for covert US operation in which USAF aircraft were supplied with CAT crews to provide support for French forces in Indochina

T'ai Hill tribes of Tonkin comprising different factions denoted by colours (Black, White and Red)

TIMBERWORK Codename for MACV-SOG long-term agent programme

TNKU Tentera Nasional Kalimantan Utara (North Kalimantan National Army) - secret military wing of the Partai Ra'ayat in Brunei in 1960s

TLO Tactical Liaison Office - US Army unit responsible for tactical intelligence-gathering up to 20 miles behind enemy lines during Korean War

Transport Division 111 Sub-unit of USN Task Force 90 comprising four amphibious raiding vessels

UB Urzad Bezpiecznstwa - Polish internal security service

UDRM United Democratic Resistance Movement - Lithuanian movement formed in 1946 to unite all anti-Soviet resistance groups

UDT Underwater Demolitions Teams - US Navy special forces units, predecessors to SEALs

UHVR Ukrainian Supreme Liberation Council – formed by OUNB in 1944 to unite all nationalist factions in Ukraine

UMNO United Malays National Organisation

UN United Nations

UNPFK United Nations Partisan Forces Korea - FEC-LD(K) was redesignated as such from November 1952 onwards

UNPIK United Nations Partisan Infantry Korea -

UPA Ukrainian Insurgent Army - formed from elements of OUNB in early 1943

Viet Cong Popular name for Viet Nam Cong San, guerrilla organisation formed in 1960 as military arm of communist National Liberation Front in South Vietnam

Viet Minh Viet Nam Doc Lap Dong Minh Hoi (League for the Revolution and Independence of Viet Nam) - communist movement formed in Indochina in 1941 under Ho Chi Minh

VNAF Vietnamese Air Force

Wali Local governor of district or province in Oman

WHITE STAR Codename for CIA operation in Laos 1959-1962, providing training for Hmong irregulars

Wilaya An Arabic term applied to numbered FLN/ALN regions of operations during war in Algeria

WiN Wolnosc i Niepodlegtnosc (Freedom and Independence) - Polish post-WWII anti-communist resistance organisation formed in 1946

WOLFPACK Partisan command formed in Korea at the end of 1951 to take over responsibility from LEOPARD for conduct of operations along coast to east and south of Onjin Peninsula

X Codename for operation in which opium was purchased by GCMA from Hmong tribesmen in Laos and sold to Binh Xuyen in Saigon

ZR BLUSH CIA highly classified logistics base, at Kadena Air Force Base on Okinawa, supporting operations throughout the Far East

SELECT BIBLIOGRAPHY

Akehurst, John. *We Won A War – The Campaign in Oman 1965–1975*. Michael Russell, London, 1982.

Amery, Julian. *Approach March*. Hutchinson, London, 1973.

— *Sons of The Eagle – A Study in Guerrilla War*. Macmillan, London, 1948.

Andrugtsang, Gompo Tashi. *Four Rivers, Six Ranges – A True Account of Khampa Resistance to the Chinese in Tibet*. Information & Publicity Office of His Holiness The Dalai Lama, Dharamsala, India, 1973.

Avedon, John F. *In Exile From The Land of Snows*. Alfred A. Knopf, New York, 1984.

Baker, W. D. *Dare To Win – The Story of the New Zealand Special Air Service*. Lothian Publishing, Melbourne, 1987.

Barber, Noel. *The War of The Running Dogs – The Malayan Emergency 1948–1960*. Collins, London, 1971.

Barron, John. *KGB – The Secret Work of Soviet Secret Agents*. Hodder & Stoughton, London, 1974.

Bergot, Erwan. *11e Choc: Bataillon d'Action*. Presses de la Cité, Paris, 1986.

Bethell, Nicholas. *Betrayed*. Times Books, New York, 1984.

Billière, General Sir Peter de la. *Looking For Trouble – SAS to Gulf Command*. Harper-Collins, London, 1994.

Blair, C. N. M. *Guerrilla Warfare*. Ministry of Defence, London, 1957.

Bloch, Jonathan, and Patrick Fitzgerald. *British Intelligence and Covert Action*. Brandon Book Publishers, Dingle, 1983.

Bower, Tom. *The Red Web – MI6 and the KGB Master Coup*. Aurum Press, London, 1989.

Breuer, William B. *Shadow Warriors – The Covert War in Korea*. John Wiley, New York, 1996.

Cave Brown, Anthony. *The Secret Servant – The Life of Sir Stewart Menzies, Churchill's Spymaster*. Michael Joseph, London, 1988.

Cavendish, Anthony. *Inside Intelligence*. Collins, London, 1990.

Chinnery, Philip D. *Any Time, Any Place – A History of USAF Air Commando and Special Operations Forces*. Airlife Publishing, Shrewsbury, 1994.

Cleaver, Frederick W., and George Fitzpatrick, John Ponturo, William Rossiter and C. Darwin Stolzenbach. *UN Partisan Warfare in Korea, 1951–1954*. Operations Research Office, John Hopkins University, Baltimore, 1956.

Conboy, Kenneth, with James Morrison. *Shadow War – The CIA's Secret War in Laos*. Paladin Press, Boulder, Colorado, 1965.

Cookridge, E. H. *Gehlen – Spy of The Century*. Hodder & Stoughton, London, 1991.

Cooley, John K. *Unholy Wars – Afghanistan, America and International Terrorism*. Pluto Press, London, 1999.

Cordovez, Diego, and Selig S. Harrison. *Out of Afghanistan – The Story of the Soviet Withdrawal*. Oxford University Press, New York, 1995.

Cross, J. P. *Jungle Warfare – Experiences and Encounters*. Arms & Armour Press, London, 1989.

— *A Face Like a Chicken's Backside – An Unconventional Soldier in South East Asia 1948–1971*. Greenhill Books, London, 1996.

Currey, Cecil B., *Edward Lansdale – The Unquiet American*. Houghton Mifflin, Boston, 1988.

Davies, 'Trotsky'. *Illyrian Venture – The Story of the British Military Mission to Enemy-Occupied Albania 1943–1944*. Bodley Head, London, 1952.

Dickens, Peter. *SAS – Secret War in South East Asia*. Greenhill Books, London, 1991.

Dorril, Stephen. *MI6 – Fifty Years of Special Operations*. Fourth Estate, London, 2000.

Evanhoe, Ed. *Dark Moon – Eighth Army Special Operations in the Korean War*. Naval Institute Press, Annapolis, 1995.

Faligot, Roger, and Pascal Krop. *La Piscine – The French Secret Service Since 1944*. Basil Blackwell, London, 1989.

Fall, Bernard. *Street Without Joy*. The Stackpole Company, Harrisburg, 1967.

Fielding, Xan. *One Man in His Time – The Life of Lieutenant Colonel N. L. D. ('Billy') McLean DSO*. Macmillan, London, 1990.

Foot, M. R. D. *SOE – The Special Operations Executive 1940–1946*. British Broadcasting Corporation, London, 1984.

Generous, Kevin. *Vietnam – The Secret War*. Bison Books, London, 1985.

Grau, Lester W. (ed). *The Bear Went Over the Mountain – Soviet Combat Tactics in Afghanistan*. National Defense University Press, Washington DC, 1996.

Griffin, Michael. *Reaping the Whirlwind – The Taliban Movement in Afghanistan*. Pluto Press, London, 2001.

Haas, Michael E. *In the Devil's Shadow – UN Special Operations During the Korean War*. Naval Institute Press, Annapolis, 2000.

Harclerode, Peter. *PARA! Fifty Years of The Parachute Regiment*. Arms & Armour Press, London, 1992.

— *Secret Soldiers – Special Forces in The War Against Terrorism*. Cassell, London, 2000.

Hastings, Max. *The Korean War*. Michael Joseph, London, 1987.

Heggoy, Alf Andrew. *Insurgency and Counterinsurgency in Algeria*. Indiana University Press, Bloomington, 1972.

Hoe, Alan, and Eric Morris. *Re-Enter the SAS – The Special Air Service and the Malayan Emergency*. Leo Cooper, London, 1994.

Horne, Alastair. *A Savage War of Peace – Algeria 1954–1962*. Viking Press, New York, 1977.

Horner, D. M. *SAS – Phantoms of the Jungle. A History of the Australian Special Air Service*. Allen & Unwin, Sydney, 1992.

Isby, David. *War in a Distant Country – Afghanistan: Invasion and Resistance*. Arms & Armour, London, 1989.

James, Harold, and Denis Sheil-Small. *The Undeclared War*. New English Library, London, 1973.

Jeapes, Major General Tony. *SAS Secret War*. HarperCollins, London, 1996.

Kelly, Colonel Francis J., *Vietnam Studies – U.S. Army Special Forces 1961–1971*. Department of the Army, Washington DC, 1973.

Kemp, Anthony. *The SAS – Savage Wars of Peace, 1947 to the Present*. John Murray, London, 1994.

Knaus, Kenneth. *Orphans of the Cold War – America and the Tibetan Struggle*. Public Affairs, New York, 1999.

Lansdale, Edward G. *In the Midst of Wars – An American's Mission to South East Asia*. Harper & Row, New York, 1972.

Large, Lofty. *One Man's SAS*. William Kimber, London, 1987.

Malcolm, Col. Ben S., with Ron Martz. *White Tigers – Secret War in Korea*. Brassey's, Washington DC, 1996.

McCarthy, Roger E., *Tears of the Lotus – Accounts of Tibetan Resistance to the Chinese Invasion, 1950–1962*. McFarland & Co., Jefferson, North Carolina, 1997.

McMichael, Scott. *Stumbling Bear – Soviet Military Performance in Afghanistan*. Brassey's (UK), London, 1991.

Miller, Harry. *Jungle War in Malaya – The Campaign Against Communism 1948–60*. Arthur Barker, London, 1972.

Muelle, Commandant Raymond, and Eric Deroo. *Services Spéciaux – GCMA en Indochine 1950–54*. Editions Crépin-Leblond, Paris, 1992.

Noone, Richard, with Dennis Holman. *In Search of the Dream People*. William Morrow, New York, 1972.

Osanka, Franklin Mark. *Modern Guerrilla Warfare*. Free Press of Glencoe, New York, 1964.

Page, Bruce, with David Leitch and Phillip Knightley. *Philby – The Spy Who Betrayed a Generation*. Penguin, London, 1969.

Paret, Peter. *French Revolutionary Warfare from Indochina to Algeria*. Pall Mall Press, London, 1964.

Patterson, George. *Tibet in Revolt*. Faber & Faber, London, 1960.

Peissel, Michel. *Cavaliers of Kham – The Secret War in Tibet*. Heinemann, London, 1972.

Philby, Kim. *My Silent War*. Granada Publishing, London, 1981.

Plaster, John L. *SOG – The Secret Wars of America's Commandos in Vietnam*. Simon & Schuster, New York, 1997.

— *SOG: Photographic History*. Paladin Press, Boulder, Colorado, 2000.

Pocock, Tom. *Fighting General – The Public and Private Campaigns of General Sir Walter Walker*. Collins, London, 1973.

Porch, Douglas. *The French Secret Services – From the Dreyfus Affair to the Gulf War*. Macmillan, London, 1996.

Prados, John. *Presidents' Secret Wars – CIA and Pentagon Covert Operations Since World War II*. William Morrow, New York, 1986.

Reske, Charles F. *MAC-V-SOG Command History – Annexes A, M & N (1964–1966): First Secrets of the Vietnam War*. Alpha Publications, Sharon Center, Ohio, 1992.

— *MAC-V-SOG Command History – Annex B (1971–1972): The Last Secret of the Vietnam War – Volume I*. Alpha Publications, Sharon Center, Ohio, 1990.

— *MAC-V-SOG Command History – Annex B (1971–1972): The Last Secret of the Vietnam War – Volume II*. Alpha Publications, Sharon Center, Ohio, 1990.

Riesen, René. *Jungle Mission*. Hutchinson, London, 1957.

Rositzke, Harry. *The CIA's Secret Operations – Espionage, Counterespionage and Covert Action*. Reader's Digest, New York, 1977.

Schultz, Richard H. *The Secret War Against Hanoi – Kennedy's and Johnson's Use of Spies, Saboteurs, and Covert Warriors in North Vietnam*. Harper Collins, New York, 1999.

Smiley, David. *Albanian Assignment*. Chatto & Windus, London, 1984.

— *Irregular Regular*. Michael Russell, London 1994.

— with Peter Kemp. *Arabian Assignment*. Leo Cooper, London, 1975.

Smith, E. D. *Counter-Insurgency Operations:1 – Malaya and Borneo*. Ian Allan, London, 1985.

Stanton, Shelby. *Green Berets at War – US Army Special Forces in South East Asia 1956–1975*. Arms & Armour Press, London, 1985.

Sudoplatov, Pavel Anatolevich, with Jerrold L. and Leona P. Schechter. *Special Tasks: The Memoirs of an Unwanted Witness – A Soviet Spymaster*. Little, Brown, London, 1994.

Trinquier, Roger. *Modern Warfare – A French View of Counterinsurgency*. Frederick A. Praeger, New York, 1964.

Verrier, Anthony. *Through the Looking Glass – British Foreign Policy in an Age of Illusions*. W. W. Norton, London, 1983.

West, Nigel. *The Friends – Britain's Post-War Secret Intelligence Operations*. Weidenfeld & Nicolson, London, 1988.

Wilkinson, Peter, and Joan Bright Astley. *Gubbins & SOE*. Leo Cooper, London, 1993.

Woodward, Bob. *VEIL: The Secret Wars of the CIA 1981–1987*. Simon & Schuster, London, 1987.

Yousaf, Mohammad, and Mark Adkin. *The Bear Trap – Afghanistan's Untold Story*. Leo Cooper, London, 1992.

INDEX